# Corporate Social Irresponsibility

*Corporate Social Irresponsibility* focuses on ethical failures in order to relate corporate responsibility to business ethics, corporate governance and organization effectiveness. The book advocates a strategic approach to CSR—ethical management cannot, and should not, be divorced from effective management.

Corporate social responsibility has transitioned from oxymoron into a defining challenge of the twenty-first century. Taking the recent financial crisis as a starting point, Alexander examines the underlying ethical and legal crises these events expose in the business world. The problems that have come to light go beyond issues of firm financial performance into the integrity of the manufacturing and marketing processes and relations with consumers. As such, the book presents a model that resolves the apparent conflict between maximizing shareholder value and meeting the interests of other firm stakeholders. Alexander presents a balanced view, contrasting her model with alternative approaches. The book also covers the impact of globalization on management, the ethics of outsourcing and the limits of regulation, as well as poverty alleviation and social entrepreneurship.

Blending a comprehensive theoretical framework with a broad range of cases, this book covers the latest major changes in US legislation, as well as recent corporate scandals, making it a valuable accompaniment to any course in CSR, business ethics, or business, government and society.

**Paula Alexander** is an associate professor at Seton Hall University, US. She also teaches in the MBA program and serves as Curriculum Coordinator for Corporate Social Responsibility. She is an expert in affirmative action and has a background in law and sociology.

# Corporate Social Irresponsibility

Paula Alexander

 Routledge
Taylor & Francis Group

NEW YORK AND LONDON

First published 2015
by Routledge
711 Third Avenue, New York, NY 10017

and by Routledge
2 Park Square, Milton Park, Abingdon, Oxon OX14 4RN

*Routledge is an imprint of the Taylor & Francis Group, an informa business*

*Library of Congress Cataloging-in-Publication Data*
Alexander, Paula Becker.
   Corporate social irresponsibility / Paula Alexander.
      pages cm
   Includes bibliographical references and index.
   1. Social responsibility of business.   2. Business ethics.
3. Organizational effectiveness.   4. Strategic planning.   I. Title.
   HD60.A392 2015
   658.4′08—dc23
   2014029697

ISBN: 978-0-415-72145-5 (hbk)
ISBN: 978-0-415-72146-2 (pbk)
ISBN: 978-1-315-86310-8 (ebk)

Typeset in Minion
by Apex CoVantage, LLC

Printed and bound in the United States of America by
Edwards Brothers Malloy on sustainably sourced paper

To Sienna, Luca and Kaia
Who are our future

# Contents

**UNIT III**

# Foreword

Are the terms corporate social responsibility and business ethics oxymorons? Corporate social responsibility has transitioned from oxymoron to a defining challenge of the twenty-first century. Like the War to End All Wars, which was followed by World War II in less than a generation, so too the Sarbanes Oxley Act, which was thought to prevent future corporate ethical and legal debacles, was followed by a meltdown in financial markets and a failure of financial institutions within six years of its passage! Just as post–World War II diplomacy focused on preventing a third worldwide conflict, perhaps successfully, so it is our hope that ethical debacles will be reduced in the future and corporations will engage in positive strategic corporate responsibility. To this end, MBA programs, encouraged by the Association to Advance Collegiate Schools of Business, focus on ethics education within the business curriculum.

Many of us are concerned that the corporate executives involved in the major scandals, as well the ones that have not attracted the major headlines, have by and large been graduates of leading business schools, MBAs, CPAs or attorneys. We need to examine our consciences collectively about how the business world could come to its current state of affairs. In fact, one might title this book: "Corporate Social Responsibility: What Went Wrong?" The challenge for business educators is to develop managers who will face up to problematic issues, rather than skirt them or sweep them under the rug, so to speak, by fraud or material misstatement.

I have always felt that ethical behavior cannot and should not be divorced from effective management. It is incumbent upon those of us who lead discussions of corporate responsibility to link business ethics, corporate governance and organization effectiveness. Specifically, the role of profits needs to be addressed, and the corporate mantra "the goal of business is to maximize corporate shareholder value" needs to be challenged by the stakeholder model of business. I purport to develop a model that resolves the apparent conflict between maximizing shareholder value and meeting the interests of the other firm stakeholders, which can guide enterprise decision makers in their strategic approach to corporate social responsibility.

It is my hope that the interplay herein between theory, application and case discussion will develop in our students their ability first to recognize and then to manage ethical risk.

Although this book is "sole authored," it, like life itself, has been accomplished in community. Thus, I wish to acknowledge and thank the many people who helped in the development of this project and in bringing it to fruition. Thanks to my commissioning editor, Sharon Golan, Acquisitions Editor, Business, Management and Accounting, Routledge, and to her editorial assistants, Manjula Raman and Jabari LeGendre. Thanks to my colleagues and mentors: John (Jack) Hampton, Elven Riley, Scott Rothbort, Joan Coll, Jason Yin, Richard Smith, Robert Danzig, Richard Hunter, Samuel Estreicher, Stephen Klausner, John O'Connor, Andy Winston, Penina Orenstein, Viswa Viswanathan, Renu Ramnarayanan, Yeomin Yoon, Anthony Loviscek, Kenneth Heaslip, Russ Cavan, Dawn Jaeckel, Julie Burkey, Alan Brill, Lawrence Frizzell, David Bossman, Asher Finkel, Edwin Leung, Shigeru Osuka, Dongdong Chen, Barbara Brown, Fred Stahl, Baocheng Liu, Shengtian Hou, and Stephan Rothlin, Sarah Fahy, Bernard Goldstein and Coralie Farlee. Thanks to Daniela Reed, Tanya Dixon, Maura Grace Harrington, Lindsey Puliti, Alexander Cohn, and to David Alexander, Riad Twal and William Otskey for their administrative and technological support. Their expertise was essential to the success of this project. Thanks to Stillman School of Business Dean Joyce Strawser, Karen Boroff, Dean Emeritus, and Henry Amoroso, Director of the Micah Center for Business Ethics and Economic Justice, for their support. Thanks to Richard Liddy and Terry Liddy for our many years of discussion and engagement at Seton Hall University's Micah Institute for Business and Economics. Thanks to the anonymous reviewers, whose critiques improved this work immensely. Lastly, thanks to my friends and family for their help and support while I labored on this project.

Paula Alexander
June 30, 2014

# Tables and Figures

# Unit I

# 1 Management Effectiveness and Corporate Social Responsibility

## Chapter Outline

Corporate Social Responsibility and Management Effectiveness
Social Responsibilities of Business
    The Debate: What Is the Role of the Corporation?
      The Role of the Corporation is Purely Economic
      An Alternative View: Corporations Have Social Responsibilities
      Corporate Social Responsibility Must Be Integrated with Strategic
      Management
Orientation to Text
Orientation to Cases
End of Chapter Case: Merck Vioxx

## Chapter Introduction

What are the responsibilities of business? Some have argued that the business of business is purely economic and that other agencies and organizations should engage in the creation of social goods. However, many business leaders have moved to an acknowledgement of the social responsibilities of enterprise and some customers value corporate social responsibility. Effective strategic management is fundamental to business enterprise and must be integrated into a model of business ethics and corporate social responsibility.

## Chapter Goal and Learning Objectives

*Chapter Goal:* Describe the role of business in society; introduce the concept of corporate social responsibility.

*Learning Objectives:*

1. Debate the role of the corporation in society: whether the role of the corporation is purely economic or whether the stakeholder model implies that the corporation has social responsibilities.

2.   Relate the concepts of corporate social responsibility, business ethics, corporate governance and their importance to organization effectiveness and strategic management.

## Corporate Social Responsibility and Management Effectiveness

Corporate social responsibility—is the concept of *corporate social responsibility* an oxymoron? Must business ethics and corporate social responsibility be sacrificed on the altar of profit maximization? As we moved into the twenty-first century, we experienced a rash of corporate debacles, involving Enron Corporation, WorldCom, Adelphia Communications, Tyco, and Parmalat, among others. The Sarbanes Oxley Act (SOX) was enacted by the United States Congress within seven months of the Enron bankruptcy and within days of the bankruptcy filed by WorldCom. Yet within six years of the passage of the Sarbanes Oxley Act, the world experienced a meltdown in the global financial markets and institutions not experienced since the Great Depression of the 1930s.

Although recent ethical and legal crises perhaps begin in the mind of the public with the bankruptcy of Enron Corporation, improprieties at Sunbeam, Lucent Technologies and Xerox Corporation all predated the Enron and World-Com frauds. Sunbeam was prosecuted by the Securities and Exchange Commission (SEC) in 2001 for fraud in its financial statements while "Chainsaw" Al Dunlap was CEO in the 1990s.[1] Lucent Technologies' financial restatements for the year 2000 precipitated Lucent's momentous decline in stock price and an inquiry by the SEC into its revenue recognition practices.[2] Xerox Company was investigated by the SEC for restating its 1998 and 1999 financial statements.[3] Each of these cases was related to earning management practices. After the passage of SOX, the chief executives of WorldCom, Adelphia Communications, Tyco International, and Enron were prosecuted and convicted for fraud in the financial statements of their companies, among other charges. Although these prosecutions and convictions were high profile, the problem of ethical and legal violations apparently is much more widespread. After the implementation of SOX, with its imposition of personal liability on CEOs and CFOs for material misstatements in their company's financial statements, many companies filed restatements of their financial statements with the SEC. The filing of financial restatements peaked in 2003, immediately following the implementation of SOX. However, there was a very high filing of financial restatements in 2004; even in 2005, 14% of filers filed material restatements of their financial statements with the SEC.

Recent corporate debacles go beyond issues of firm financial performance and involve the integrity of the manufacturing and marketing processes and relationships with consumers. Merck's Vioxx issues are illustrative of this. Merck was found guilty of deceptive marketing practices in product liability trials in New Jersey, with a $9 million punitive damages award granted by a jury. This outcome is likely to lead to a criminal investigation of Merck, which is headquartered in New Jersey, and where many of the Vioxx product liability trials have been held. In anticipation of such criminal prosecution/ settlement, Merck reserved $950 million dollars in October 2010. Formerly, Merck was considered one of the world's most admired and reputable companies, so the vulnerability of Merck to the Vioxx litigation was nothing less than a corporate tragedy.

The passage and implementation of SOX did not prevent the meltdown of the financial markets and institutions experienced in 2008. The meltdown resulted from the development and use of risk-laden financial instruments, mortgage-backed securities, collateralized debt obligations, and credit derivative swaps. These were high-yield financial instruments that resulted in high levels of executive compensation, likely a driving factor in their development and utilization.

## Social Responsibilities of Business

### The Debate: What Is the Role of the Corporation?

There exists a debate about whether the role of enterprise is purely economic, constrained only by conformity to law and regulation in enforcement of the law, answerable to its stockholders and regulators, or whether the corporation has social responsibilities to its other stakeholders as well, including its employees, its customers, its suppliers and the communities where the firm operates and where its employees live.

Managers must address the issue, in whose interests firms are managed, or, stated differently, what is the goal of a firm? Shareholder capitalism takes the view that the goal of a firm is to maximize shareholder value. In contrast, the stakeholder model of business challenges the corporate mantra that the goal of a firm is to maximize shareholder value.

### The Role of the Corporation Is Purely Economic

Milton Friedman is a leading advocate of the view that the role of the corporation is purely economic. Friedman argues in favor of the shareholder model of capitalism. Friedman advocates the position that "the social responsibility of business is to increase its profits."[4] Friedman considers executives as agents of shareholders and responsible to them, to "accomplish their desires, which generally will be to make as much money as possible while conforming to the basic rules of the society, both those embodied in law and those embodied in ethical custom. . . . [T]he key point is that, in his capacity as a corporate executive, the manager is the agent of the individuals who own the corporation . . . and his primary responsibility is to them."[5]

The context in which Friedman was writing was the 1970s, with its high inflation, oil shortages, and the transformation of the automobile market; the change in the American automobile market involved the increase in sales of foreign imports and the manufacture by United States automakers of small, fuel-efficient cars, the first of which was the Ford Pinto. At this time, General Motors Corporation was considering a proposal to appoint three new directors on its board to represent "the public interest." This proposal was defeated at its annual meeting of shareholders in May 1970, but five directors were appointed to a "public policy committee," and in 1971, Leon Sullivan, a Baptist minister who later articulated the "Sullivan Principles" for engagement of multi-national businesses in apartheid South Africa, was elected to the General Motors' board. However, Friedman viewed the inclusion of other interests or voices in corporate management as "undermining the basis of a free society."

Friedman thus adopts the theory of managerial capitalism articulated by Berle and Means,[6] which views managers as agents of stockholders. It should be noted that Friedman emphasizes ethics and conformity to the "rules of the game," including law and ethical custom. As Chapter 13, "Corporate Responsibility—What Went Wrong? Lessons from the Dark Side," indicates, unfortunately, many of the corporate scandals of the late twentieth and early twenty-first century stemmed from ethical and legal violations; thus these corporations were operating outside of the framework that Milton Friedman specifies. Furthermore Jeff Madrick, in his book *The Age of Greed: the Triumph of Finance and the Decline of America 1970 to Present,*[7] opines that the predominance of the perspective urged by Milton Friedman contributed to the "age of greed" and to the corporate debacles and global financial crisis of 2008 and subsequent years.

*An Alternative View: Corporations Have Social Responsibilities*

Others advocate that the proper role of the corporation involves the creation of social goods as well as economic goods. The creation of social goods by enterprise in the course of conducting its business stems from the stakeholder model of business. Enterprises that manage in view of their multiple stakeholders, creating win-win transactions with their suppliers, their employees, their customers and the communities where they operate and where their employees live, are viewed as going beyond a strictly economic view of enterprise and as fulfilling social responsibilities. The achievement of these multiple goals, with managers juggling priorities, is the essence of March and Simon's behavioral model of the firm.[8] March and Simon suggest that their behavioral model of firms is more realistic than the classical economic model of firms. In fact, Herbert Simon won the Nobel Prize in Economics in 1978 for developing the bounded rationality model of decision-making, from which the Behavioral Theory of the Firm is derived.[9]

Many business leaders themselves acknowledge the social responsibilities of enterprise, and in fact, there was a social movement for corporate social responsibility in the 1990s and the new millennium. For example, Business for Social Responsibility, which was founded in 1992 and which has grown to become a global network of companies, is explicit in its recognition of a stakeholder model for business success and views corporate social responsibility as a competitive advantage, particularly through the integration of corporate social responsibility into all business operations.[10] And the sentencing guidelines provide an incentive to corporations for developing compliance programs such as a code of conduct for their employees.[11]

Corporate social responsibility has become a global concern. For example, the position of Minister for Corporate Responsibility was created in 2000 as a government initiative in the United Kingdom.[12] The European Union also followed suit. The European Commission Directorate for Employment and Social Affairs issued a "green paper" on corporate social responsibility in July 2001 and invited comment from member countries.[13] The World Economic Forum conducted a survey of business leaders in 2003. Corporate social responsibility and good corporate citizenship were considered critical to their firms' relationship to shareholders by the CEOs, CFOs and investor relations officers surveyed by the World Economic Forum's Global Corporate Citizenship Initiative. This phenomenon indicates that (at least some) business executives perceive the responsibility of businesses to accomplish their financial goals in a socially responsible way. Moreover, the International Finance Corporation (IFC), a member of the World Bank Group,[14] has developed standards for private sector funding of global development projects. The IFC funding standards, known as the Equator Principles, incorporate a concern for social as well as environmental impacts and explicitly adopt a stakeholder analysis for considering the impacts of global development projects.

Public opinion indicates that people around the world consider corporate social responsibility an important aspect of business dealings, and consumers consider corporate conduct in their consumer purchases. A poll was conducted by Environics International, at the behest of the Prince of Wales Business Leaders Forum[15] and the Conference Board based in the United States,[16] among 25,000 citizens in 23 countries on six continents about their expectations of companies in the "new millennium." Two-thirds of respondents surveyed in the Millennium Poll, conducted in 1999, held the opinion that business should contribute to social goals in addition to focusing on narrower business goals.[17] There have been consumer boycotts of Nestle Corporation in response to its marketing of infant formula in less economically developed countries and of Nike for operating sweatshops. Corporate social responsibility is thus becoming a global expectation. Consumers as well as business leaders consider the fulfillment of business social responsibilities as fundamental to business strategy and as creating competitive advantage. Students in our business programs perceive the need for increased emphasis on ethics and socially responsible management.[18] The Association to Advance Collegiate Schools of Business, the accrediting body for schools of business, considers business ethics, as well as global perspectives, an essential component of both undergraduate and graduate business curricula.

One wonders, given the surge in concern with corporate social responsibility in the 1990s and change of the millennium, why major corporate debacles occurred immediately on the inauguration of the twenty-first century and within a few years of the "solution" to the accounting and securities fraud illustrated by Enron and WorldCom embodied in the SOX, why a global meltdown in financial markets and institutions happened in 2008.

### Corporate Social Responsibility Must Be Integrated with Strategic Management

The guiding concept of this book is that corporate social responsibility, business ethics, corporate governance and organization effectiveness must be related to each other. Specifically, the role of profits is addressed and the corporate mantra "the goal of business is to maximize shareholder value" is challenged by the stakeholder model of business. There is a sense in which maximizing profits as the goal of a corporation may be true but not in the simplistic sense of the mantra. An alternative to the shareholder model of capitalism has been developed by March and Simon. March and Simon's behavioral theory of the firm takes the approach that firms must achieve multiple, conflicting goals and that managers act as brokers among conflicting interest groups.[19]

Ethical management cannot and should not be divorced from effective strategic management; otherwise, given the orientation of executives and shareholders to "the bottom line," ethics and socially responsibility will most likely lose out. However the corporate debacles of the late twentieth and early twenty-first century have demonstrated the futility, indeed self destructiveness to the corporation and its executives, of managing exclusively for short-term profit maximization. Indeed, the failure of corporate social responsibility has resulted in the withdrawal of support by critical stakeholders. For example, Enron and its investment banks have been the subject of shareholder lawsuits and prosecution by regulators. Lawsuits were also brought by employees who were fraudulently blocked from selling their stock in the fall 2001, while at the same time the executives were dumping their stock, an act of insider trading.[20]

This author's own research comparing the financial performance of ethically managed and "ethically challenged" firms indicates that unethical conduct may be a dysfunctional way of coping with real firm financial duress. For example, Enron had a financial indicator that predicted bankruptcy in 1998.[21] Enron in fact declared bankruptcy in late 2001; the years intervening are the subject of Enron's prosecution for financial fraud and the convictions of Enron's founder and former CEO Kenneth Lay, Jeffrey Skilling, former president and CEO of Enron and Andrew Fastow, Enron's former chief financial officer.[22] In the aftermath of the meltdown of our financial institutions and markets in 2008, the US Congress enacted the Frank-Dodd Wall Street Reform and Consumer Protection Act in 2010 to manage risk and to help prevent future crises in our financial institutions and markets. However, legislation is always backward looking. So one wonders what the next crisis will be and how it can be prevented prospectively. Managers, and the students that are educated in our business schools, need to face up to difficult issues and manage them within ethical and legal constraints. This is an important mandate for contemporary business education.

# Orientation to Text

Organization of the textbook: Chapters 1 and 2 give the basic orientation to corporate social responsibility based on an open system model of enterprise and a stakeholder analysis. We start with a consideration of strategic management, concluding that corporate responsibility and effective management cannot be divorced. Stakeholders and the behavioral theory of the firm are developed in Chapter 2. Chapter 3 considers the ethics of business decision making, focusing on the standards of judgment useful for analyzing and evaluating ethical dilemmas. It develops standards for judging ethical dilemmas without advocating a single dominant approach. Chapter 4 develops a case for corporate social responsibility that goes beyond philanthropy to engagement in the firm's strategic purpose and output/product. Chapters 1 through 4 constitute Unit I. Chapters 5 through 12 are organized around business stakeholders, considering in sequence: the relation of enterprise to its regulators, competitors, supply chain, customers, the environment, employees and investors; these chapters comprise Unit II. Chapters 5 and 6 consider the relationship of an enterprise to its regulators and to its competitors. Chapter 5, titled "Managing the Business-Government Relationship I: Regulation of Business Enterprise and the Relation of the Enterprise to Its Competitors," addresses the justification for regulation of business enterprise and traces the relationship between events, often catastrophes, and subsequent regulation of business enterprise. The role of competitors in provoking the anti-trust prosecution, for example of AT&T and of Microsoft, is discussed and the long-term impact and unintended negative consequences of government regulation, particularly in view of the impact of changing technology, are raised in the case discussions. Chapter 6, "Managing the Business–Government Relationship II: Innovation and Emerging Technologies," asks what is the appropriate role of regulators in emerging fields of endeavor, what is the appropriate role of interest groups in fashioning regulations and how corporations can have voice in a democracy. Chapter 7, "Supply Chain Management," recognizes that control of production is complicated by the fact that suppliers often lay outside the organizational boundaries, in contrast to the vertical integration strategies of the past. Chapter 8, "The Business–Consumer Relationship," raises the relationship between entrepreneurial vision and the creation of value-added product for consumer, addressing in particular negative externalities created by products that harm the consumer, either because they are inherently dangerous products or because they are defectively designed products. Chapter 9, "Sustainable Environmental Management," acknowledges the risks inherent in production technologies, the creation of negative externalities and debates how to manage the risks inherent in the production process. Chapter 10, "Relationship of the Enterprise to its Employees," addresses employees as stakeholders, the new social contract and the growing use of alternative work arrangements. The globalization of labor markets is the topic of Chapter 11, including international labor standards and the issue of abusive labor conditions. Corporate governance is addressed in Chapter 12. It includes discussion of the Sarbanes Oxley Act and the debate about CEO compensation. The book concludes with a consideration of "Corporate Responsibility—What Went Wrong? Lessons from the Dark Side." Chapter 13 identifies the role of high-risk products such as mortgage-backed securities and other collateralized debt obligation and credit derivative swaps in the collapse of financial companies and, ultimately, of investment banks themselves. The final chapter, Chapter 14, addresses the question of the relationship between corporate governance, social responsibility and organizational effectiveness: "Corporate Governance, Social Responsibility and Organizational Effectiveness: The Bottom Line." The final chapters, Chapters 13 and 14 comprise Unit III.

## Orientation to Cases

Specific cases are used to illustrate challenges of particular topics, with cases integrated throughout each chapter; moreover, every chapter concludes with a "contemporary" case, where the long-term consequences may still be developing. For example, the case used in Chapter 1, the Merck Vioxx case, illustrates the risk of succumbing to short-term financial pressures. Merck was in need of a new "blockbuster" drug, in view of the patent expiration in 2007 of several of its important products. Vioxx was that product that Merck expected to be the successor to its expiring patents. It appears that the unintended negative consequences of Vioxx became known prior to its marketing but that the information was swept under the rug so to speak and not properly disclosed to prescribing physicians or their patients. Merck faced civil and criminal product liability litigation. Former Chairman, President and Chief Executive Officer of Merck & Co. Raymond Gilmartin led the organization down a path that put Merck in peril. Merck's management of the unintended negative consequences of Vioxx shows that a firm's risk management strategies must take into account long-term consequences of its conduct. Employees of Merck were angered that Gilmartin benefitted from a "golden parachute" while they were left behind to rebuild the company. The cases associated with Unit I, i.e., Chapters 1 through 4, are intended to establish a framework for the consideration of "big questions" related to CSR.

### Case Guidelines

Teams of students are encouraged to develop, present and lead discussion about the cases illustrating the issues developed in each chapter. The case presentation guidelines below are the basis for the student development of the cases.

1. Identify and summarize key facts.
   (Be sure to include actions that may have given rise to punitive damages.)
2. Dilemma/issue posed to management. What is the root cause of the problem?
3. Identify the alternatives open to management.
4. Identify stakeholders and their stakes.
5. Impact of alternative courses of action on stakeholders.

6. What action management actually took.
7. Cost–benefit analysis of management's actual course of action, as to each stakeholder.
8. Aftermath of incident.
9. Lessons other corporations can learn from this case.
10. Position paper, recommending a specific course of action to CEO and justifying your recommendations. Identify your time frame of reference, which does not need to be current day; could this crisis have been prevented by early intervention? The position paper should be about two pages in length and use an executive memo format.

## Chapter Discussion Questions

1. Describe the responsibilities of business according to Milton Friedman and the economic model of the firm.
2. Describe the responsibilities of business using the stakeholder analysis of business.
3. Is it correct that the predominance of Friedman's orientation laid the groundwork for what Jeff Madrick calls the "age of greed," which resulted in the global failure of financial institutions and markets in 2008?
4. Why didn't the corporate social responsibility movement of the 1990s prevent the corporate ethics debacles of centered around 2001–2002 and 2008?

## Notes

1 Al Dunlap claimed expertise in business turnarounds in *Mean Business: How I Save Bad Companies and Make Good Companies Great* (New York: Crown Publishing Group, 1996).
2 Martha McKay, "SEC Ends Probe of Murray Hill, N.J., Telecom Equipment Maker," *Knight Ridder Tribune Business News* (Washington), Feb. 28, 2003.
3 The SEC issued a complaint against six executives of Xerox Corporation, as well; those executives reached a settlement agreement with the SEC. See James Bandler and Mark Maremont, "SEC Widens Xerox Civil Probe To Ex-Executives and to KPMG," *Wall Street Journal* (Eastern edition), Apr 10, 2002. See also, Andrew Countryman, "Six Former Executives of Xerox Corp. Settle Fraud Case for $22.4 Million," *Knight Ridder Tribune Business News* (Washington), June 6, 2003.
4 *New York Times Magazine*, Sept. 1970. See also, Milton Friedman, *Capitalism and Freedom: Fortieth Anniversary Edition* (Chicago: University of Chicago Press, 2002).
5 *New York Times Magazine*, Sept. 1970.
6 Adolph A. Berle and Gardiner C. Means, *The Modern Corporation and Private Property* (New York: Macmillan, 1932).
7 Jeff Madrick, *The Age of Greed: the Triumph of Finance and the Decline of America 1970 to Present* (New York: Knopf/Doubleday, 2011).
8 James G. March and Herbert A. Simon, *Organizations* (New York: John Wiley and Sons, Inc., 1958); Richard M. Cyert and James G. March, *A Behavioral Theory of the Firm* (Urbana, IL: University of Illinois at Urbana-Champaign's Academy Historical Research Reference in Entrepreneurship, 1963). See also Linda Argote and Heinrich

R. Greve, "A Behavioral Theory of the Firm—40 Years and Counting: Introduction and Impact," *Organization Science* 18, no. 3 (May–June 2007), 337–49.

9   "The Sveriges Riksbank Prize in Economic Sciences in Memory of Alfred Nobel 1978: Herbert A. Simon," *Nobelprize.org*, last modified 2013, http://www.nobelprize.org/nobel_prizes/economics/laureates/1978/.

10  BSR: The Business of a Better World, last modified 2014, http://www.bsr.org.

11  See H. Lowell Brown, "The Corporate Director's Compliance Oversight Responsibility in the Post Caremark Era," *Delaware Journal of Corporate Law* 26, no. 1 (2001): 1–145.

12  Charlotte Villiers, http://www.csrcampaign.org/publications/Excellencereport2002/UK2.

13  European Commission: Directorate General for Employment and Social Affairs, "Promoting a European Framework for Corporate Social Responsibility" (Green Paper), July 2001, http://www.corporatejustice.org/IMG/pdf/greenpaper_en.pdf.

14  See *International Finance Corporation, World Bank Group*, last modified 2014, http://www.ifc.org/.

15  The International Business Leaders Forum was undertaken in Britain as an initiative of the Prince of Wales in 1990. See *International Business Leaders Forum*, last modified 2013, http://www.iblf.org.

16  See *The Conference Board: Trusted Insights for Business Worldwide*, last modified 2014, http://www.conference-board.org.

17  *International Business Leaders Forum*, http://www.iblf.org.

18  Lynnley Browning, "Ethics Lacking in Business School Curriculum, Students Say in Survey," *New York Times*, May 20, 2003: "Ethical conduct in the workplace has become increasingly important to students at leading business school, according to a new survey, but students are worried that their study programs might teach questionable values that may later contribute to mismanagement or corporate fraud."

19  The behavioral theory of the firm is discussed further in Chapter 2.

20  Jeffrey Skilling was found guilty of insider trading for selling his stock on September 17, 2001.

21  Edward Altman developed a statistic, the "Z score," to predict the risk or likelihood of firm bankruptcy. Certain scores predict bankruptcy, and other scores predict that a firm is relatively "safe" from the risk of bankruptcy.

22  Sherron Watkins, Enron's Vice President for Corporate Development, blew the whistle to Kenneth Lay in August, 2001. In an interview after the verdicts were announced in the trials of Kenneth Lay and Jeffrey Skilling, Sherron Watkins, in response to a question of whether she wished she had done anything differently, said that she wished she had blown the whistle as early as 1996. See *Wall Street Journal Report*, May 29, 2006.

## End of Chapter Case: Merck Vioxx

### *"Timeline: The Rise and Fall of Vioxx" by Snigdha Prakash and Vikki Valentine, November 10, 2007, NPR*

Shortly before the FDA approved Vioxx in 1999, drug maker Merck launched a study it hoped would prove that Vioxx was superior to older painkillers because it caused fewer gastrointestinal problems. Instead, the study would eventually show Vioxx could be deadly, causing heart attacks and strokes.

Five years after Vioxx's launch, Merck withdrew the drug from the market. By that time, Merck had sold billions of dollars of the drug worldwide. A timeline of Vioxx's rise and fall:

**November 1998:** Merck asks the Food and Drug Administration (FDA) for approval of Vioxx, having tested the drug on 5,400 subjects in eight studies.

**January 1999:** Merck launches the Vioxx Gastrointestinal Outcomes Research study (VIGOR). With more than 8,000 participants, it is the largest study ever done of the drug. Half take Vioxx and the other half take naproxen. The clinical trial is designed to see whether Vioxx is safer for the digestive system than naproxen, an older painkiller.

**May 1999:** The FDA approves Vioxx, making the drug available by prescription in the United States.

**October 1999:** First meeting of the VIGOR study's data and safety monitoring board (DSMB). Study results as of Oct. 1, 1999, show that Vioxx patients have fewer ulcers and less gastrointestinal bleeding than patients taking naproxen. It looks as if the study will be a success for Merck.

**November 1999:** At the second meeting of the VIGOR safety panel, the discussion focuses on heart problems. As of Nov. 1, 1999, 79 patients out of 4,000 taking Vioxx have had serious heart problems or have died, compared with 41 patients taking naproxen. The minutes of the panel's November meeting note that "while the trends are disconcerting, the numbers of events are small." The panel votes to continue the study and to meet again in a month.

**December 1999:** The safety panel holds its last meeting. It's told that as of Dec. 1, 1999, the risk of serious heart problems and death among Vioxx patients is twice as high as in the naproxen group.

The DSMB votes to continue study, but decides Merck needs to develop a plan to analyze the study's cardiovascular results before the study ends. DSMB Chairman Michael Weinblatt and Merck statistician Deborah Shapiro draft a letter and send it to Merck's Alise Reicin (now vice president of Merck's clinical research).

Later, when defending its decision to continue the study, the safety panel said it couldn't tell if Vioxx was causing the heart problems or if naproxen, acting like low-dose aspirin, protected people from them, making Vioxx just look risky by comparison.

**January 2000:** Merck balks at developing the analysis plan. The company wants to wait and combine the cardiovascular results of VIGOR with results from other Vioxx studies. Weinblatt, the safety panel chair and a rheumatologist with Brigham & Women's Hospital in Boston, pushes for immediate analysis.

**February 2000:** After further discussions, Merck and Weinblatt agree to analyze heart problems reported by Feb. 10, 2000—at least a month before the last patient leaves the study. Events reported later won't be included in the initial analysis.

**Feb. 7, 2000:** Weinblatt fills out a financial disclosure form that says he and his wife own $72,975 of Merck stock.

**Feb. 15, 2000:** Weinblatt agrees to a new consulting contract with Merck. "We are delighted that you have agreed to serve as a member of the VIOXX Multidisciplinary Advisory Board," Merck writes in an invitation to Weinblatt to attend his first advisory board meeting.

Weinblatt signs the new contract on March 6. It involves 12 days of work over two years, at the rate of $5,000 per day.

**March 2000:** Merck gets results of the VIGOR trial.

**May 2000:** Merck submits VIGOR paper to the *New England Journal of Medicine* (NEJM) for publication. The data include only 17 of the 20 heart attacks Vioxx patients have.

**July 5, 2000:** A memo from Merck statistician Deborah Shapiro to Merck scientist Alise Reicin (both are listed as authors of the *NEJM* paper) refers to heart attacks 18, 19 and 20 suffered by patients taking Vioxx during the study.

**July 2000/November 2000:** VIGOR authors submit two sets of corrections to their *NEJM* manuscript. No mention of the three additional heart attacks.

**Oct. 13, 2000:** Merck tells the FDA about heart attacks 18, 19 and 20.

**Nov. 23, 2000:** The VIGOR results are published in *NEJM*, still with no mention of the three additional heart attacks in the Vioxx group. The published results also leave out data on many other kinds of cardiovascular adverse events.

**February 2001:** The FDA holds an advisory meeting on the VIGOR trials. It publishes complete VIGOR data on its Web site, including the additional heart attacks and data on other cardiovascular events.

**Aug. 22, 2001:** Cardiologists Debabrata Mukherjee, Steven Nissen and Eric Topol publish their meta-analysis in the *Journal of the American Medical Association*, based on complete VIGOR data that the FDA has made available.

Their analysis is significant because they take *all* the VIGOR data from the FDA Web site, recrunch them, and cast serious doubt on the hypothesis that naproxen protects the heart.

**January 2002 to August 2004:** Numerous epidemiological studies point to Vioxx's increased risk of cardiovascular problems.

**September 2004:** Merck withdraws Vioxx after a colon-polyp prevention study, called APPROVe, shows that the drug raises the risk of heart attacks after 18 months. By the time Vioxx is withdrawn from market, an estimated 20 million Americans have taken the drug.

Research later published in the medical journal *Lancet* estimates that 88,000 Americans had heart attacks from taking Vioxx, and 38,000 of them died.

**July 14, 2005:** NEJM editor-in-chief Dr. Jeffrey Drazen tells NPR that the journal had been "hoodwinked" by Merck, and that the authors of the VIGOR paper should have told the journal about the additional data.

**August 2005:** A Texas state jury returns a verdict against Merck in the first Vioxx liability case to go to trial. Some 13,000 lawsuits have been filed against the company on behalf of 23,000 plaintiffs who allege the drug caused heart attacks and strokes.

**November 2005:** *NEJM* executive editor Dr. Gregory Curfman is deposed in connection with the Vioxx product-liability cases. At that time, he learns about the July 5, 2000, memo, which shows Merck VIGOR authors knew about heart attacks 18, 19 and 20 well before the paper was published in *NEJM*.

**December 2005:** NEJM issues an "Expression of Concern," writing that "inaccuracies and deletions" in the VIGOR manuscript Merck submitted to the journal "call into question the integrity of the data." The journal asks the study authors to submit a correction to the journal.

**March 2006:** VIGOR study authors respond to *NEJM's* Expression of Concern: "Our evaluation leads us to conclude that our original article followed appropriate clinical trial principles and does not require a correction." The three heart attacks in question, say the authors, occurred after the study's "prespecified cutoff date" for reporting cardiovascular problems.

Journal editors stand by their call for a correction, replying that the cut-off date appeared to be selected shortly before the trial ended, and was a month earlier than VIGOR's cutoff date for gastrointestinal problems. Such a trial design, according to *NEJM*, "skewed" results.

**May 2006:** Outside analysis of data sent to the FDA from the Vioxx APPROVe study show that the cardiovascular risks from Vioxx began shortly after patients started taking the drug. The data also indicate that the risks from Vioxx remain long after patients stop taking the drug.

Merck disagrees with the analysis and maintains that patients aren't at risk unless they had taken the drug for more than 18 months.

This point is worth billions for Merck. Many of those suing the company say they took Vioxx for less than 18 months.

**June 2006:** The seventh trial against Merck begins, with plaintiff Elaine Doherty, 68, alleging the painkiller caused her heart attack and subsequent double heart bypass surgery. The trial, before the New Jersey superior court, is the first since the release of the new Vioxx research results. The data raises questions about how quickly the drug could cause harm and could undermine Merck's credibility.

Out of the six cases that have already gone to trial, Merck has won three and lost three.

Research published in the medical journal *Lancet* estimates that 88,000 Americans had heart attacks from taking Vioxx, and 38,000 of them died.

**November 2007:** Merck announces it will pay $4.85 billion to end thousands of lawsuits over its painkiller Vioxx. The amount, to be paid into a so-called settlement fund, is believed to be the largest drug settlement ever.

The Whitehouse Station, N.J.-based drug maker emphasized that it is not admitting fault.

The settlement lets Merck avoid the personal-injury lawsuits of some 47,000 plaintiffs, and about 265 potential class-action cases filed by people or family members who claimed the drug proved fatal or injured its users.

## Case Discussion Questions

1.  Merck is a research based pharmaceutical company. As such it depends on innovation and patents. The patents for Fosamax expired in 2005 and Zocor expired in 2006. Merck had planned that Vioxx serve as its next big blockbuster drug. What might Merck have done when information came to light that Vioxx may cause cardio-vascular problems?
2.  What were the alternatives open to Merck, to prevent such dependency on a blockbuster? What are the alternatives open to Merck now? Evaluate the impact of each alternative on Merck's stakeholders.
3.  Why have punitive damages been awarded to plaintiffs in the Vioxx cases? What acts of Merck served as the basis for the punitive damages awards?
4.  Was it legally and ethically permissible for Merck to withdraw sponsorship of researchers who take issue with Merck's marketing of Vioxx? Was it "smart" from a marketing point of view?
5.  Compare Merck's actions in influencing reported research results on Vioxx, to the actions of the tobacco companies in the 1950s to "counter" the research that smoking caused cancer, by establishing The Tobacco Industry Research Committee.[1]

## Note

1   See "Smoke in Your Eye," *PBS.org: Frontline*, last modified 1999, http://www.pbs.org/wgbh/pages/frontline/smoke/.

# 2 The Stakeholder Model of Corporate Social Responsibility

## Chapter Outline

## Chapter Introduction

What is the goal or objective of a firm? From a managerial point of view, the goal of a firm is its product or output. Firms are best understood as input-output systems, nested in a set of relationships with suppliers, customers, competitors and regulators.

In whose interests is the firm managed? In the interests of stockholders? In the interest of bondholders? Employees? Suppliers? The community where the firm operates? Stockholders, bondholders, employees, suppliers, the community where the firm operates—all these are stakeholders of the enterprise.

What is the role of a manager? Is it to maximize shareholder wealth? Or is it to broker the competing interests of the firm's multiple stakeholders?

## Chapter Goal and Learning Objectives

*Chapter Goal:* Describe the stakeholder model of corporate social responsibility and explain how it relates to the open systems model of business enterprise. Discuss the goal of the firm according to different perspectives.

*Learning Objectives:*

1.  Understand the role of business in society using an open systems model of business.
2.  Explain the concept of returns to the factors of production and the role and importance of profits.
3.  Understand the stakeholder model of corporate social responsibility; contrast the stakeholder model with the model of shareholder capitalism.
4.  Compare the goal of the firm under the behavioral theory of the firm, contrasted with the classical economic theory of the firm. Explain whether and how these approaches converge.
5.  Understand the role of the manager, according to the behavioral theory of the firm and contrast it with the theory of managerial capitalism.

The premise of the approach developed in this text is that effective strategic management is fundamental to business enterprise and must be integrated into a model of business ethics and corporate social responsibility. We consider, therefore, what enterprise and the management of business enterprise is all about. Managers must address the issue: what is the goal of a firm? From a managerial point of view, managing enterprise for output is fundamental.[1] The manager must understand the value-added created by the enterprise's production system, the utility created for its customers as well as the firm's customer base and its niche relative to its competitors. From this perspective, management is concrete and oriented toward the creation of particular goods. Enterprise is modeled as an input–output system, or an open system, nested in a set of stakeholder relationships.

## Open Systems Model of Business

The *open systems* model of work organizations views enterprise as taking inputs and transforming them into value-added outputs (see Figure 2.1). Under this model, the purpose of enterprise is to produce output or product. Inputs are provided by suppliers and comprise the factors of production: land, labor, capital and raw materials. The production process transforms the inputs into *value-added* outputs, possessing an increase in utility compared to the unassembled inputs. The firm's output becomes the customer's input, in a transaction whereby the firm's product is sold to the customer in exchange for money or other value. The revenues generated from this exchange transaction provide returns to the factors of production and generate profits.

Regulators set the "rules of the game" for enterprise production systems. Competitors provide options for customers; they vie with each other on the utility or value-added that they can create for customers. Competitors may also create a bidding war on inputs from suppliers. Enterprise is thus nested in a set of interdependent relationships with its suppliers, customers, regulators and competitors. These interdependent relationships define the enterprise *task environment.*[2]

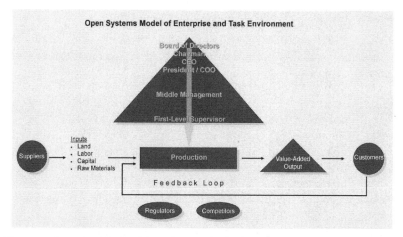

*Figure 2.1* Open Systems Model

### Enterprise Task Environment

The task environment of enterprise consists of a firm's *suppliers*, who provide the inputs required for production, *customers* who receive the firm's output as their input, *regulators* who set the conditions under which a firm can operate and *competitors*.

Ideally, the enterprise pays attention to whether customers actually purchase their output and use a feedback loop to reconfigure its own internal processes if its product is not useful to, or wanted by, customers. Business enterprises that fail to operate as open systems do so at their peril. For example, Chrysler didn't use a feedback loop to revise the production and design of cars. In the 1970s, there was a global energy shortage coupled with high inflation. As a result, US customers switched to smaller, fuel-efficient cars; foreign car imports made inroads into the American automobile market, and the Ford Motor Company designed and produced the Pinto, as the first American compact car.[3] Chrysler continued to spew out large, gas-guzzling New Yorkers. Eventually, Chrysler encountered a financial crunch and so it went to its regulator, the US government, seeking a "bailout" in the form of loan guarantees. Chrysler used the infusion of capital to reconfigure its operations.[4]

Under the economic system of *laissez faire capitalism*,[5] a firm goes out of business if customers don't want its product. But Chrysler looked to the government for survival, rather than suffer the consequences of market supply and demand. In Chrysler's case, the government loan guarantees were forthcoming.[6] Rather than invoking the market discipline of laissez faire capitalism, Chrysler argued that the effects of its failure would lead to unemployment of its workers, with ramifying effects in the communities where its plants are located, as well as negative effects on their suppliers. Chrysler thereby invoked the *stakeholder* model of enterprise. Chrysler's impending failure happened because it didn't use the open systems model feedback loop from customers.

### Return to Factors of Production and Profit Maximization

The classic economic theory of the firm holds that *profit maximization*, or maximizing shareholder value, is the goal of the firm. There is a sense in which maximizing profits is a true vision of firm purpose and a sense in which it may be too limited a vision of firm purpose. From the point of view of the open systems model of enterprise, each of the *factors of production* requires an appropriate return. The return to raw materials is cost of goods sold , the return to land is rent, the return to labor is wages, the return to capital is interest if the source of capital is debt, the suppliers being bondholders or banks, and profits if the source of capital is equity provided by shareholders. See Table 2.1, Return to Factors of Production.

Without a return to each of the factors of production, a firm cannot remain a going concern. Thus the sense in which maximizing profits is a correct statement of firm purpose, is that capital as a factor of production must have an appropriate return. The returns to providers of equity capital is at risk; firms pay the costs of their raw materials, rent, wages and interest to providers of debt capital first; what remains is profits, available for return to providers of equity capital. Since all factors of production other than equity capital are paid first, in order to have appropriate returns to shareholders,[7] the firm must engage in a strategy of "maximizing profits." Since the returns to the providers of equity capital, i.e., stockholders, are most at risk, the strategy of "maximizing share-holder value" ensures returns to all the factors of production, including a return to the providers of equity capital. The "profits" returned to the suppliers of equity capital are returned as dividends or stock price increases.[8]

But it is too limited a vision of firm purpose if "maximizing shareholder value" is interpreted or implemented as managing exclusively in the interest of the providers of equity capital. A firm cannot remain a going concern if it cannot generate sufficient revenues from the sale of its products to customers to provide returns to all the factors of production.[9] Without returns to each factor sufficient to offset the *opportunity costs* of using each factor, a firm cannot remain a *going concern*. For example, the financial exigency necessitating the Chrysler bailout stemmed from the fact that Chrysler did not pay enough attention to the changing tastes and desires of its customers to remain a going concern. Chrysler did not generate enough revenues to survive because its products did not match the tastes and preferences of its customers. However,

*Table 2.1* Return to Factors of Production

| Factor of Production: | Return to Factor: |
| --- | --- |
| Factor: Land | Return: Rent |
| Factor: Labor | Return: Wages |
| Factor: Raw Materials | Return: Cost of Goods Sold |
| Factor: Capital | Return: Interest or Profits |

the polity may have a public interest in the survival of a firm that cannot remain a going concern through the sale of its products. For example, Congress determined that there was a public interest in the survival of Chrysler.[10] If Chrysler went under, its employees would be laid off and in the worst case, the employees themselves might face bankruptcy. Firm suppliers may face bankruptcy in a domino effect created by Chrysler's failure to remain a going concern. And the communities where Chrysler plants are located and where its employees live would face an erosion of their tax bases; the enterprises that benefit from the spending of Chrysler's employees would also suffer declining revenues, were Chrysler's employees to be laid off. Communities have an interest or stake in their maintenance of their tax bases and in spending by employees, both of which would be eroded if employees were to be laid off because Chrysler ceased to be a going concern. These arguments and concerns were resurrected in the bailout of the U.S. auto industry by Congress in the fall 2008 after the crash of the financial markets.

A great benefit of the government's loan guarantees to Chrysler was that Chrysler reinvented itself. Chrysler designed the minivan and in so doing, transformed the traditional auto market. Most vehicles sold as cars are minivans and sport utility vehicles. The traditional car is a minority product on the current car market.[11]

Moreover, the polity may have a public interest in continued access to the products of a firm that cannot remain a going concern from the sale of its products to its customers.[12] The federal government provides subsidies to maintain the services for which there is a public interest and that would not be provided by a profit-driven firm; this is particularly important in with respect to mass transit. Indeed, as a condition of its license, Amtrak must serve destinations and markets that it might otherwise discontinue from a profit-and-loss consideration. Similar conditions have been imposed on the airline industry: the license to fly is contingent on serving certain routes that the airline might cut from a profit-and-loss point of view. And in the spring 2011, the US Senate passed a bill that would provide funds to the US Postal Service but a condition of those funds was that small, rural post offices scheduled to be closed would remain open.[13]

## Competing Theories of the Firm

The theory of the firm has competing answers to the question: in whose interest is the firm managed? Under classic economic theory, a firm is managed in the interests of shareholders. However Berle and Means, who articulated the *theory of managerial capitalism*, recognized a distinction of interests between owner shareholders and managers.[14] Managers have an interest in holding onto their jobs; corporate survival and growth are, therefore, in the interests of managers.[15] The interests of managers can be distinguished from the interests of shareholders who want to maximize profits. Stock options to executives represent an effort to more closely align the interests of managers and shareholders.[16]

Cyert, March and Simon's *behavioral theory of the firm*[17] gives an alternative and competing answer to the question: in whose interest is the firm managed? According to the behavioral theory of the firm, the goal of a firm is to optimize multiple, conflicting goals. Competing goals include market share and quarterly profits, for example. Moreover, corporations experience conflict between the various functions that coordinate to produce the firm's output: manufacturing or production departments, marketing, research and development and quality control departments.[18] Such conflict can benefit the organization as a whole. Manufacturing performs the line function of the organization, producing the firm output. However, there is a risk that manufacturing will emphasize production quantity at the cost of production quality or standards. Unless quality control has sufficient organizational power, manufacturing quality may deteriorate. This, for example, was a problem at NASA, where it was ultimately determined that responsibility for safety should be separated out organizationally so that safety concerns would not be subordinated or sacrificed to concerns of the more powerful program managers.[19] A similar re-structuring was done at BP after the well blowout in the Gulf of Mexico in April 2010.[20]

## Role of the Manager

The role of the manager is approached differently by shareholder capitalism and by the behavioral theory of the firm. Under *shareholder capitalism,* a manager acts as a fiduciary of the interests of shareholders, although the theory of managerial capitalism distinguishes between the interests of shareholders and managers.[21] A competing approach is provided by the behavioral theory of the firm. The manager acts as a broker among competing interest groups according to the behavioral theory of the firm.[22] The Chrysler bailout was based on a stakeholder view of corporate enterprise, with managers brokering the interests of the multiple stakeholders of an enterprise.[23]

### Managers as Decision Makers

Classic economic theory's identification of the goal of a firm as maximizing profits rests on certain assumptions underlying the rational model of decision making, sometimes called rational choice theory.[24] The rational model of decision making assumes: 1) complete information with no transaction costs; 2) a known preference hierarchy; and 3) means-end rationality. Complete information means that all information relevant to a decision is known at no cost; moreover, there are no transaction costs related to decision choices. A firm may have multiple, even conflicting, goals, but known preference hierarchy means that these goals are prioritized or sequenced in priority order for their achievement. Means-end rationality means that decision makers always pick that means that is most efficient and effective in attaining the goal.

The assumptions of the rational model of decision making don't hold in the real world. Herbert Simon developed the *bounded rationality model of decision making*, for which he won the Nobel Prize in 1978.[25] Herbert Simon took the position that the classical model articulates a set of assumptions that are false: this is not way the world is. Simon preferred to develop a theory of decision making that rests on true assumptions: 1) incomplete information; 2) multiple, conflicting goals; and 3) bounded rationality. Incomplete information means that gathering information costs resources and that actors face *transaction costs*. (See Box 2.1 for an example of the difference between complete and incomplete information.) Multiple, conflicting goals mean that decision makers facing multiple, conflicting goals can't resolve the conflicts by a strict prioritization among them. Instead managers adopt a "both . . . and" approach.[26] The balanced scorecard approach to decision making and performance is an example of managing for multiple, conflicting goals. The business simulations used in business policy courses often measure the performance of the simulated enterprise using balanced scorecard criteria. Moreover, decision makers in the real world don't act with means end rationality but rather they experience bounded rationality. Real universe decision makers have limits in their ability to behavior calculate. This leads to satisficing behavior; rather than choosing the maximizing alternative, the satisficing decision maker picks the first satisfactory or good enough alternative.

---

### Box 2.1  Bridge vs. Chess

**Bridge vs. Chess**

The difference between *complete information* and *incomplete information* is illustrated by the difference in the game of chess and the game of bridge. In the game of chess, there is complete information. Each player knows all possible alternatives and the consequences of each alternative, in theory at least. In fact, players differ in their skill level, whether the player sees the range of option open to him or her and understands the impact of making a particular play. Computer programs play chess; the different skill levels programmed in computer chess games are differentiated by the decision maker's ability to foresee the consequences his or her choices and to foresee the strategy the opponent will make in response to player's moves.

The game of bridge is a game of incomplete information. Bridge is played in two partnerships, with four players total. Each player knows with certainty 13 of the 52 cards in a deck. The bidding process is a procedure whereby information is shared among the players. The difference in skill level among players lies in the inferences that players can draw from the bidding process. When a partnership wins the bid, one hand is laid down as the "dummy" hand. Every player knows what is in the dummy hand, and they can make inferences about what is in the remaining hands. Differences in skill levels among bridge players lay in the ability of the player to remember which cards were played and which cards remain and to make inferences about where the cards lay.

Even though the satisficing model of decision making is a more realistic model of actual managerial behavior, managers may be too quick to reach a "satisficing" decision. For example, the NASA managers failed to seriously consider the full range of consequences of the damage to the Columbia Shuttle by the falling debris on liftoff.[27] This premature narrowing of the range of possible alternative consequences of the damage to the Columbia Shuttle was directly related to the failure to take action that may have saved the shuttle and its crew from burning up upon re-entry.

### Output/Product as Super-Ordinate Goal

Although under the classic economic theory of a firm, the firm's single, maximizing goal can be over-simplified as maximizing profits, the approach is correct if the firm's *super-ordinate goal* is understood as the creation of firm output. The strategic purpose of a firm is the creation of value-added output. The output or firm product serves as the firm's organizing concept or super-ordinate goal. Firm output becomes the integrating or organizing principle for the enterprise. The firm's division of labor is organized to achieve the firm's strategic purpose. Profits derive from the production and sale of the firm's product or output and, as noted previously, represent a return to the factor of production of equity capital. Classical decision-making theory is useful in identifying the firm output as the super-ordinate goal. The classical decision theory approach can be usefully applied in terms of the firm product serving as the enterprise's super-ordinate goal.

### Decision Theory and Stakeholder Analysis

The behavior theory of the firm views satisficing managers as optimizing multiple, conflicting goals. The behavioral theory of the firm recognizes that firms are composed of competing interest groups, each of which advocate a particular goal or outcome. The behavioral theory of the firm is highly consistent with the stakeholder model. It recognizes the interests of many players in the firm remaining a going concern. Suppliers, customers, employees and the general community are stakeholders that have an interest in the firm remaining a going concern, rather than it going out of business. In contrast, the shareholder model of capitalism gives priority to the interests of one stakeholder, namely the providers of equity capital. However, when the classic economic theory of decision making views firm output as a "super-ordinate" goal, managing for product becomes the organizing principle for the enterprise. Managing for product leads naturally to a concern for customers. Thus when the classic economic theory of the firm understands firm product as the super-ordinate goal, it converges with a stakeholder approach.

## Managing Stakeholder Relationships

Corporations benefit from proactively managing their relationships with their stakeholders. For example, when General Motors faced Campaign G.M. in 1975, the corporation accommodated some demands by electing Leon Sullivan, who later developed the Sullivan Principles for engagement in South Africa, to the GM Board of Directors. GM's responsiveness to the demands of its stakeholders contrasts with the response of Nestle Corporation to its consumer boycott. Nestle faced a consumer boycott in 1977 and after when the association between feeding with infant formula and infant mortality in less developed countries came to light. It took a long time for Nestle to accommodate to the consumer boycott; finally in 1982, Nestle employed Senator Edmund Muskie to lead its accommodation to consumer sentiment and to support the United Nations standards on marketing infant formula. As the GM and Nestle examples show, corporations must identify those issues important to their stakeholders, which will generate goodwill and support the company's brand management.

The public relations function, invested with the responsibility of a company's brand management, can help manage the corporation's stakeholder relations by monitoring the corporation's environment. Environmental scanning is important to corporate issues management. In undertaking an environmental scan to identify issues critical to a corporation's successful management of its relations with stakeholders, the executives responsible a corporation's issues management might engage in a strengths, weaknesses, opportunities and threats (SWOT) analysis (see Table 2.2). A SWOT analysis identifies opportunities and threats and may bring particular issues to light that need managing relative to the corporation's publics. SWOT analysis assists a firm in assessing its competitive advantage. SWOT analysis identifies a firm's strengths, weakness, opportunities and threats. Strengths and weakness are internal to a firm, while opportunities and threats relate to a firm's environment. The alignment of external opportunities with firm strengths and core competencies creates strategic purpose for a firm.[28]

Firms appropriately take a defensive position with respect to their weaknesses and external threats. Alternatively, firms can create a strategic alliance to compensate for their weaknesses and to cope with threats posed by

*Table 2.2* SWOT Analysis: Strengths, Weaknesses, Opportunities and Threats

| Orientation: | Strategic Purpose | Defend/ Compensate Strategic Alliance |
| --- | --- | --- |
| Internal | Strengths (Core Competencies) | Weaknesses |
| External | Opportunities | Threats |

environmental factors. A firm's ability to engage in effective environmental scanning and in the critical self analysis needed for a SWOT analysis requires reality-based examination of internal and external factors, free from group think.[29] When issues management is tied to a SWOT analysis, issues management and stakeholder relations become strategic for the enterprise and create competitive advantage.[30]

## Theoretical Orientation to Text

An open systems model of enterprise serves as an underlying perspective of this textbook. The open systems model of enterprise gives rise to the stakeholder model of organization, as well as raising the question: what is the goal

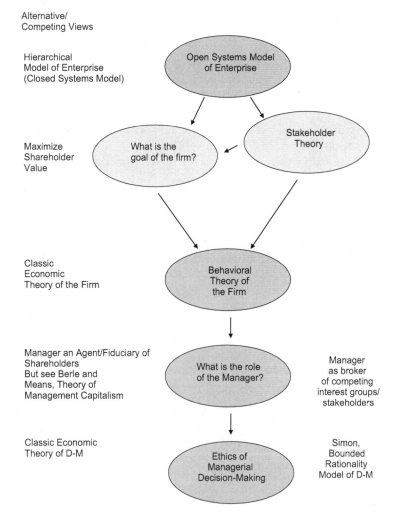

*Figure 2.2* Overview of Alexander's Theoretical Model

of the firm? The behavioral model of the firm can be derived from the stakeholder model of enterprise. The behavioral model of the firm in turn raises the issue: what is the role of the manager? The role of the manager raises issues of ethics of managerial decision making. At each step of the way, there are competing models or theories. For example, a closed systems model of organization serves as an alternative to the open systems model. Maximizing shareholder value is one possible answer to the question: what is the goal of the firm? The classic economic theory of the firm serves as an alternative or competing model to the behavioral theory of the firm. Managers as agents or fiduciaries of shareholders contrasts with the perspective that managers are brokers among competing interest groups, implied by the behavioral theory of the firm. The classic economic model of managerial decision making contrasts with Herbert Simon's bounded rationality model of decision making. The ethics of managerial decision making is placed in this framework. The driving perspective as well as the competing or alternative approaches are discussed at relevant points in the textbook chapters. An overview of my theoretical model is given in Figure 2.2.

## Chapter Discussion Questions

1. Explain the main components of the open systems model of business enterprise. Explain how the stakeholders of a firm derive from a firm's task environment.
2. Explain the return to each factor of production and explain the role and importance of profits
3. Compare and contrast the goal of the firm under the classic economic theory of the firm with the goal of the firm under the behavioral theory of the firm. Explain the pros and cons of the classic economic theory of the firm. Explain the pros and cons of the behavioral theory of the firm.
4. Define the role of the manager, according to the behavioral theory of the firm. Contrast it with the role and obligations of the manager under the theory of managerial capitalism.
5. Explain how a firm's strategic purpose can be derived from a SWOT analysis.

## Notes

1 Excellent companies focus on product and customers. See, for example, Thomas J. Peters and Robert H. Waterman, *In Search of Excellence: Lessons from America's Best-Run Companies* (New York: HarperCollins, 2006), as well as Jerry I. Porras and James C. Collins, *Built to Last: Successful Habits of Visionary Companies* (New York: HarperCollins, 2002).
2 James D. Thompson, *Organizations in Action: Social Science Bases of Administrative Theory*, (1967, Reprint, New Brunswick, NJ: Transaction Publishers, 2003).
3 In its rush to market, Ford designed and produced the Pinto in twenty-four months, whereas designing and producing a new model automobile typically required sixty months.

4  See Robert B. Reich and John D. Donahue, *New Deals: The Chrysler Revival and the American System* (New York: Times Books, 1985).

5  Adam Smith's, *The Wealth of Nations*, published in 1776, launched the economic era of *laissez faire* capitalism.

6  Chrysler's bailout was in the form of guaranteed government loans, the Chrysler Loan Guarantee Act of 1979.

7  The returns to the providers of equity capital must be sufficient to offset the opportunity cost for the use of the capital.

8  The pressure for meeting quarterly earnings targets is related to stock price: meeting or exceeding quarterly earnings targets supports stock price but missing quarterly earning targets leads to a decrease in stock price. See Harris Collingwood, "The Earnings Game: Everyone Plays, Nobody Wins," *Harvard Business Review*, June 2001. Earnings management practices are discussed further in Chapter 12.

9  Who owns the factors of production is irrelevant to the issue that each factor requires a return. It is a matter of indifference whether the inputs are owned or leased; each factor of production requires a return. For example, land requires a return, rent. It is a matter of indifference whether the land is owned or leased. Oliver Williamson, in his book, *Markets and Hierarchies* (New York: Free Press, 1975), considers whether corporations transact based on markets or as a matter of vertical integration or hierarchy. Accountants consider it a matter of indifference whether items necessary for production are leased or purchased.

10  Congress passed the Chrysler Loan Guarantee Act in 1979.

11  Nora Naughton, "Big Sedans Are Losing Ground," *Automotive News*, June 9, 2014, http://www.autonews.com/article/20140609/RETAIL01/306099980/big-sedans-are-losing-ground.

12  Public choice theory is an area of economics dealing with government regulation. See "Public Choice," *Wikipedia*, last modified June 19, 2014, http://en.wikipedia.org/wiki/Public_choice_theory. See also this article about James Buchanan, who won the Nobel Prize in Economics in 1986 for his development of public choice theory: "The Sveriges Riksbank Prize in Economic Sciences in Memory of Alfred Nobel 1986: James M. Buchanan, Jr.," *Nobelprize.org*, last modified 2013, http://www.nobelprize.org/nobel_prizes/economics/laureates/1986/.

13  Devin Henry, "Franken, Other Lawmakers Scramble to Keep Post Offices Open," *MinnPost*, April 27, 2012, http://www.minnpost.com/dc-dispatches/2012/04/franken-other-lawmakers-scramble-keep-post-offices-open.

14  Adolf Berle and Gardiner Means, *The Modern Corporation and Private Property* (New York: Macmillan, 1932).

15  Deborah Solomon and John S. Lublin, "Democracy Looks for an Opening in the Boardroom: SEC Plan to Boost the Role Of Investors in Elections Draws Ire of Companies," *Wall Street Journal*, March 22, 2004.

16  The unintended negative consequences of executive stock options are discussed below in Chapter 12, "Corporate Governance" and in Chapter 13, "Corporate Responsibility—What Went Wrong? Lessons from the Dark Side."

17  Richard Cyert and James March, *A Behavioral Theory of the Firm* (Englewood Cliffs, NJ: Prentice-Hall, 1963).

18  Daniel Katz and Robert L. Kahn state that managers' roles affect their perspectives on and definition of problems, and that problem definition may conflict according

to the roles held by managers within the firm. Daniel Katz and Robert L. Kahn, *The Social Psychology of Organizations* (New York: John Wiley, 1966).

19 Jim Wilson, "Space Shuttle Columbia and Her Crew," *National Aeronautics and Space Administration*, last modified Aug. 23, 2006, http://www.nasa.gov/columbia/home/index.html.

20 BP carved out a new, independent safety and operation risk unit in the aftermath of the April 2010 well blow out in the Gulf of Mexico. See "BP CEO To Restructure Safety Practices," *CBC News*, last modified September 29, 2010, http://www.cbc.ca/news/business/story/2010/09/29/bp-fires-executive.html.

21 Berle and Means.

22 "The political philosopher Charles Blattberg has criticized stakeholder theory for assuming that the interests of the various stakeholders can be, at best, compromised or balanced against each other. Blattberg argues that this is a product of its emphasis on negotiation as the chief mode of dialogue for dealing with conflicts between stakeholder interests. He recommends conversation instead and this leads him to defend what he calls a 'patriotic' conception of the corporation as an alternative to that associated with stakeholder theory." "Stakeholder Theory," *Wikipedia*, last modified May 21, 2014, http://en.wikipedia.org/wiki/Stakeholder_theory. See also Chapter 6 of Charles C. Blattberg, *From Pluralist to Patriotic Politics: Putting Practice First* (New York: Oxford University Press, 2000).

Blattberg's distinction between negotiation and "conversation" confuses the realities of negotiation. The behavioral theory of the firm places the manager in the role as broker among competing stakeholder interests.

However to the extent that Blattberg uses "patriotism" as a super-ordinate value, then competing interests are resolved, not by negotiation, but by using a single value, the super-ordinate goal, to resolve conflict.

23 Robert Reich and John D. Donahue, "Lessons from the Chrysler Bailout," *California Management Review* 27, no. 4 (1985): 157–83.

24 Gary Becker received the Nobel Prize in Economics in 1992 for his work on the development of rational choice theory. See Assar Lindbeck, "Award Ceremony Speech (December 10, 1992)," *Nobelprize.org*, last modified 2013, http://www.nobelprize.org/nobel_prizes/economics/laureates/1992/presentation-speech.html.

25 See "Studies of Decision-Making Lead to Prize in Economics (16 October 1978)," *Nobelprize.org*, last modified 2013, http://www.nobelprize.org/nobel_prizes/economic-sciences/laureates/1978/press.html.

26 Collins and Porras found that built to last firms used a "both . . . and" approach to their goals and performance. See Collins and Porras, *Built to Last*.

27 Wilson, "Space Shuttle Columbia and Her Crew."

28 See Michael E. Porter, *Competitive Strategy: Techniques for Analyzing Industries and Competitors* (New York: Free Press, 1980).

29 In his sequel to *Built to Last*, Jim Collins identified factors that characterized companies that transitioned from good to great. The ability to "confront the brutal facts" is a key ability of the good to great companies. See Jim Collins, *Good to Great: Why Some Companies Make the Leap . . . And Others Don't* (New York: HarperCollins, 2001).

30 See Michael Porter, *Competitive Advantage: Creating and Sustaining Superior Performance* (New York: Free Press, 1985). See also W. Chan Kim and Renee Mauborgne, *Blue Ocean Strategy: How to Create Uncontested Market Space and Make Competition Irrelevant* (Harvard Business School Press, 2005).

## End of Chapter Case: BP Oil Well Blowout in the Gulf of Mexico

### BP and the Deepwater Horizon Disaster of 2010[*]

*Christina Ingersoll, Richard M. Locke, Cate Reavis*

When he woke up on Tuesday, April 20, 2010, Mike Williams already knew the standard procedure for jumping from a 33,000 ton oil rig: "Reach your hand around your life jacket, grab your ear, take one step off, look straight ahead, and fall."[1] This would prove to be important knowledge later that night when an emergency announcement was issued over the rig's PA system.

Williams was the chief electronics technician for Transocean, a U.S.-owned, Switzerland-based oil industry support company that specialized in deep water drilling equipment. The company's $560 million Deepwater Horizon rig was in the Gulf of Mexico working on the Macondo well. British Petroleum (BP) held the rights to explore the well and had leased the rig, along with its crew, from Transocean. Of the 126 people aboard the Deepwater Horizon, 79 were from Transocean, seven were from BP, and the rest were from other firms including Anadarko, Halliburton, and M-1 Swaco, a subsidiary of Schlumberger.

Managing electronics on the Deepwater Horizon had inured Williams to emergency alarms. Gas levels had been running high enough to prohibit any "hot" work such as welding or wiring that could cause sparks. Normally, the alarm system would have gone off with gas levels as high as they were. However, the alarms had been disabled in order to prevent false alarms from waking people in the middle of the night. But the emergency announcement that came over the PA system on the night of April 20 was clearly no false alarm.

Moments after the announcement, Williams was jolted by a nearby thud and a hissing sound, followed by the revving of one of the rig's engines. Before he knew it, there were two explosions forcing him and other crew members to abandon ship by jumping into the partially flaming ocean.[2] Of the 126 workers on board the Deepwater Horizon, 17 were injured, including Williams, and 11 were killed. The rig burned for 36 hours, combusting the 700,000 gallons of oil that were on board, leaving a trail of smoke over 30 miles long. The Deepwater Horizon sank on April 22, taking with it the top pipe of the well and parts of the system that were supposed to prevent blowouts from occuring.[3]

As of 2010, the Deepwater Horizon disaster was the largest marine oil spill ever to occur in U.S. waters. By the time the well was capped on July 15, 2010, nearly five million barrels of oil (205.8 million gallons) had spilled into the

Gulf of Mexico. Federal science and engineering teams revised their estimates on the rate of oil flow several times, and in August they concluded that between April 20 and July 15, 53,000–62,000 barrels per day spilled into the Gulf,[4] an amount that was equivalent to a spill the size of the 1989 Exxon Valdez every four to five days.[5] Before the Deepwater Horizon disaster, the Exxon Valdez held the record for the largest spill in U.S. waters.

It was surprising to many analysts how such a disaster could happen, particularly involving a company like BP, which publicly prided itself on its commitment to safety. It did seem clear that, in an effort to close up the Macondo well, several key decisions were made, each involving multiple stakeholders and trade-offs of time, money, safety, and risk mitigation. The public debate began immediately on whether the result of these decisions indicated operational or management problems on the rig, and whether these problems were endemic to the oil industry, or resided within BP itself. To help answer these questions, several task forces were formed to investigate the root causes of the disaster and who among the various players involved with the Macondo well bore responsibility for the disaster and for its resolution.

## British Petroleum

The company that would become BP was founded in 1909 as the Anglo-Persian Oil Company (APOC) shortly after Englishman William Knox D'Arcy struck oil in Iran after an eight-year search. In its early years, profitability proved elusive for APOC and, in 1914, Winston Churchill, who was head of the British Navy and believed Britain needed a dedicated oil supply, convinced the British government to buy a 51% stake in the nearly bankrupt company.

The British government's majority ownership of BP lasted until the late 1970s when the government, under Prime Margaret Thatcher, a proponent of privatization, began selling off its shares in an attempt to increase productivity in the company. When the government sold its final 31% share in 1987, BP's performance was floundering. The company's performance continued to decline as a newly private company; in 1992, BP posted a loss of $811 million. Nearing bankruptcy, the company was forced to take dramatic cost cutting measures.

Things started to improve measurably in the mid-1990s. With a streamlined workforce and portfolio of activities, BP's new CEO began implementing an aggressive growth strategy, highlighted by mergers with rivals Amoco in 1998, and ARCO (the former Atlantic Richfield) in 2000.

Along with focusing on growth, BP began repositioning itself. In 2001, the company launched the new tagline "Beyond Petroleum" and officially changed its name to "BP." The associated green branding campaign indicated that BP wanted to be known as an environmentally-friendly oil company. Over the next decade, the company launched an Alternative Energy division and was, for a time, the world's largest manufacturer of solar cells and Britain's largest producer of wind energy. BP invested $4 billion in alternative energy between 2005 and 2009.[6] BP's total company investment over the same time period was $982 billion.[7]

In May 2007, Tony Hayward, who had been chief executive of Exploration and Production (BPX), replaced John Browne as CEO. Hayward marked his appointment with a speech pledging to "focus like a laser on safety issues, put the brakes on growth and slash production targets."[8] Hayward was able to improve corporate performance, in part, by dramatically shrinking the Alternative Energy division and further reducing headcount at both managerial and lower staff levels.[9] Between 2006 and 2009, BP's workforce fell from 97,000 to 80,300.[10]

In addition to cutting four levels of management, Hayward also spoke publicly about his desire to transform BP's culture to one that was less risk averse. He believed that too many people were making too many decisions leading to extreme cautiousness. "Assurance is killing us," he told U.S. staff in September of 2007.[11]

Despite Hayward's concern about the company's risk averse culture, in a relatively short period of time, BP had transitioned from a small, state-sponsored company to one of the six largest non-stateowned oil companies in the world and, in the month before the Deepwater Horizon disaster, the largest company listed on the London Stock Exchange. The transition required numerous mergers and acquisitions, and strict cost cutting measures. Along the way, BP's organizational structure was also dramatically transformed.

## Organizational Strategy

BP in the late 1980s comprised several layers of management in a matrix structure that made it difficult for anyone to make decisions quickly. In some cases, simple proposal changes required 15 signatures. At the same time, the company was overleveraged and its overall performance was suffering.[12] Robert Horton, who was appointed CEO in 1989, started a radical turnaround program in an effort to cut $750 million from BP's annual expenses. He removed several layers of management and slashed the headcount at headquarters by 80. Horton also intended to increase the speed of managerial decision-making and, thereby, the pace of business in general. Horton transformed hierarchically structured departments into smaller, more flexible teams charged with maintaining open lines of communication.[13]

Horton transferred decision-making authority away from the corporate center to the upstream and downstream business divisions. While deep cuts were made to capital budgets and the workforce, employees at all levels were encouraged to take responsibility and exercise decision-making initiative. In 1992 David Simon was appointed CEO replacing Robert Horton. Simon continued Horton's policy of cost cutting, especially in staffing.

The biggest changes during this period occurred in BPX, which was led by John Browne. Building upon his predecessors' efforts, Browne, who envisioned creating a spirit of entrepreneurship among his staff, extended decision-making responsibilities to employees at more levels in the organization. Under the new strategy, decision-making authority and responsibility for meeting performance targets was no longer held by BP's regional operating companies, but by onsite asset managers.[14] Asset managers contracted with BP to meet certain performance targets and extended this practice among all employees working on a given site. Employee compensation was tied to asset performance and the overall performance of the site. The model, which was known as an "asset federation," was later applied across the company after Browne took over as CEO in 1995.

One tradeoff with the asset federation model was that because each site manager managed their "asset" autonomously and was compensated for its performance, there was little incentive to share best practices on risk management among the various BP exploration sites.[15] There were also downsides to a system in which a centralized body had little oversight over the setting of performance targets, particularly in an industry where risk management and safety were essential to the long-term success of an oil company. And BP had had its shares of safety breaches.

## Safety Issues at BP

In the mid-2000s, disaster struck BP twice within a 12-month period. The first happened on March 23, 2005 when an explosion at BP's Texas City Refinery killed 15 people and injured another 180, and resulted in financial losses exceeding $1.5 billion. BP commissioned James Baker, a former U.S. secretary of state and oil industry lawyer, to write an investigative report on the Texas City tragedy. One of the key findings highlighted in the *Baker Report* was that the company had cut back on maintenance and safety measures at the plant in order to curtail costs, and that responsibility for the explosion ultimately rested with company senior executives.[16]

Another concern outlined in the report was that while BP had emphasized personal safety and achieved significant improvements, the company "has mistakenly interpreted improving personal injury rates as an indication of acceptable process safety, creating a false sense of confidence."[17] The report goes on to state the following:

> The Panel's refinery-level interviews, the process safety culture survey, and some BP documents suggest that significant portions of the U.S. refinery workforce do not believe that process safety is a core value at BP. As many of the refinery interviewees pointed out, and as some BP documents and the process safety culture survey seem to confirm, one of the reasons for this belief is that BP's executive and corporate refining management have not communicated a consistent and meaningful message about the importance of process safety and a firm conviction that process accidents are not acceptable. The inability of many in the workforce to perceive a consistent and meaningful corporate message about process safety is easy to understand given the number of "values" that BP articulates:
>
> • BP's 18 "Group values," only one of which encompasses health and safety—the company's broad, aspirational goal of "no accidents, no harm to people, and no harm to the environment."

- Four "Brand values," which BP claims, "underpin everything we do": being performance driven, innovative, progressive, and green.

None of these relates to safety.

These messages to the BP workforce on so many values and priorities contribute to a dilution of the effectiveness of any management message on process safety. This is consistent with a recent observation from the organizational expert that BP retained under the 2005 OSHA settlement relating to Texas City: There appears to be no one, over-arching, clearly-stated worksite policy at Texas City, regardless of respondents' answers. The BP stated policy on health and safety, "no accidents, no harm to people and no damage to the environment" is not widely known at Texas City and points to a weak connection between BP Texas City and BP as a corporation. Safety communication is viewed more as a function of particular individuals in Texas City versus a BPwide commitment.

Until BP's management, from the Group Chief Executive down through the refinery superintendents, consistently articulates a clear message on process safety, it will be difficult to persuade the refining workforce that BP is truly committed on a long-term basis to process safety excellence.[18]

In March 2006, as *The Baker Report* was being written, a second disaster struck BP, this time in Alaska's Prudhoe Bay, where more than 200,000 gallons of oil poured into the bay from a corroded hole in the pipeline, making it the largest oil spill in Alaska.[19] Inspectors found that several miles of the steel pipe had corroded to dangerously thin levels. Alaskan state regulators had been warning BP since 2001 that its management procedures were out of alignment with state regulations, and that critical equipment needed to be better maintained.

BP took several actions in response to *The Baker Report* and other reports, including one that was overseen by John Mogford, a senior group vice president of safety for BPX, on its safety. According to Appendix F, a supplement to *The Baker Report*, these actions included:

- **Leadership visibility.** John Browne, BP's group chief executive, met with the company's top 200 leaders to stress BP's commitment to safety and communicate his expectations regarding safety. Members of the new Safety and Operations organization visited BP's U.S. refineries and gave presentations regarding the importance of process safety and the importance of the Mogford Report recommendations. Additionally, BP senior managers have attended town hall meetings with employees to discuss safety issues. The chief executive, Refining and Marketing, conducted meetings for all U.S. refining employees, and the president of BP America conducted meetings and sent written communications to BP America employees regarding safety issues.

- **Review of employee concerns.** BP appointed retired United States District Judge Stanley Sporkin to hear and review BP employee concerns.
- **Auditing.** The Safety and Operations organization is creating an enhanced audit function, including additional audit personnel and a number of external hires. BP has listed auditfinding closure as one element of a six-point plan for sustained development. The new audit group is developing enhanced audit protocols to better assess actual operations against applicable standards.
- **Resources for plant, equipment, and systems.** BP has announced that it has earmarked $7 billion over the next four years to upgrade all aspects of safety at its U.S. refineries and to repair and replace infield pipelines in Alaska. The company has also announced $300 million in funding and significant external input for process safety management renewal in refining.

Though some of these changes were company-wide, many were specific either to Texas City or the refinery operations within BP.[20] Still, BP executives clearly realized that when it came to safety, there was room for improvement.[21] Between June 2007 and February 2010, 97% (829 of 851) of the willful safety violations by an oil refinery handed down by the Occupational Safety and Health Administration went to two BP-owned refineries in Texas and Ohio.[22]

## The Macondo Well Project

The Macondo Prospect was located 52 miles south of the port of Venice, Louisiana in the Gulf of Mexico. At nearly 5,000 feet below sea level, the well demonstrated great potential for extracting oil, but was also somewhat hazardous. Natural gas levels were high in the reservoirs, which made drilling challenging.[23]

Drilling in deep water and ultra-deep water[24] started to become economically profitable and technically feasible on a large scale in the mid-2000s, due to higher world prices for crude oil and improvements in drilling technology. The number of deep water rigs in the Gulf of Mexico increased from just three in 1992 to 36 in 2008.[25] Because of the complexities of deep water operations, creating a productive deep water oil field was extremely expensive compared to shallow water oil drilling. But the potential payoff was enticing. A well producing in shallow water might yield a few thousand barrels of oil a day. By contrast, deep water wells could yield more than 10,000 barrels per day.[26]

BP acquired the rights to the Macondo Prospect from the U.S. Minerals Management Service in March of 2009.[27] As the oil industry regulator, the MMS issued permits to oil companies wanting to drill on U.S. land or in U.S. waters. In exchange, it received royalty revenue from oil companies. BP was the principal developer and operator of the prospect and held a 65% financial share in the project.[28] While BP maintained operational decision-making authority, Transocean employees, who performed the majority of the work on the rig, had some decision-making authority over operations and maintenance. BP started drilling the Macondo well in October of 2009. Drilling, however, was interrupted in the aftermath of Hurricane Ida. BP commenced drilling on February 3, 2010 leasing Transocean's Deepwater Horizon rig.[29]

Transocean charged BP approximately $500,000 per day to lease the rig, plus roughly the same amount in contractor fees.[30] BP originally estimated that drilling the Macondo well would take 51 days and cost approximately $96 million. By April 20, 2010 the rig was already on its 80th day on location and had far exceeded its original budget.[31]

## The Deepwater Horizon Rig

The Deepwater Horizon rig came with a long list of maintenance issues. In September 2009, BP conducted a safety audit on the rig, which was in use at another BP drilling site at the time. The audit identified 390 repairs that needed immediate attention and would require more than 3,500 hours of labor to fix.[32] It was later learned that the Deepwater Horizon had not gone to dry-dock for nine years previous to the disaster and never stopped working at any point between the September 2009 audit and April 20, 2010.[33]

As Transocean's Chief Electronics Technician Mike Williams experienced, the crew had to be adept at developing workarounds in order to maintain the function of the rig. Williams was responsible for maintaining the Drilling Chairs—the three oversight computers that controlled the drilling technology. These computers, operating on a mid-1990s era Windows NT operating system, would frequently freeze. If Chair A went down the driller would have to go to Chair B in order to maintain control of the well. If somehow all three chairs went down at once, the drill would be completely out of control.[34] Williams frequently reported the software problems and the need to have them fixed.[35]

Despite the hazards of the Macondo well site, the known maintenance issues on the rig, and the setbacks that had caused the project to be over budget, BP felt confident that it had found oil.

However, since the Deepwater Horizon was an exploratory vessel, the crew was under orders to close the well temporarily[36] and return later with another rig to extract the oil.

## Anatomy of a Disaster

While the process of closing a well is always complex, closing the Macondo well proved particularly so due to competing interests of cost, time and safety, as well as the number of people and organizations involved in the decision-making process. (See **Exhibit 1.**) As one example, 11 companies[37] played a role in the construction of the casing[38] for the Macondo well, all with different responsibilities for various aspects of setting the well. Halliburton, for instance, was responsible for cement-related decisions, although many of these decisions were contingent on decisions made by BP managers on well design.

*Exhibit 1* Companies Involved with Deepwater Horizon Rig

| | |
|---|---|
| BP | World's third largest oil company, headquartered in London; project operator with a working interest in the well; hired Transocean's rig to drill the well. |
| Transocean | World's largest offshore drilling operator, based in Switzerland and Houston; owned an operated the rig. |
| Cameron | Houston-based manufacturer of oil and gas industry equipment; provided the rig with a blowout preventer—a devise designed to stop uncontrolled flow of oil or gas—but the part apparently failed to operate. |
| Halliburton | Oilfield services company based in Houston and Dubai; provided several services to the rig, including cementing on the well to stabilize its walls. |
| Hyundai | South Korean company is the world's largest shipbuilder; built the Deepwater Horizon, completed in 2001. |
| Anadarko | Anadarko, a large, independent, Texas-based petroleum company; has nonoperating interest in the well |

Source: Reuters, Hoovers, the companies as published in Daniel Chang and Jennifer Lebovich's "Gulf Oil Spill Overview," McClatchy Newspapers, May 15, 2010.

| Name | Title | Days/Months in Position |
|---|---|---|
| Patrick O'Bryan | VP, Drilling and Completions, Gulf of Mexico | 3 months |
| David Rich | Wells Manager | 6 months |
| David Sims | Drilling Operations Manager | 18 days |
| Robert Kaluza | Well Site Leader | 4 days |
| Greg Walz | Drilling Engineering Team Leader | 18 days (took David Sims's previous position) |

*Figure 1* Deepwater Horizon Chain of Command

Note: **Exhibit 2** is a corrected version based on court testimonies that includes full names and titles.

Source: BP as presented at the hearings of the US Coast Guard and the Interior Department's Bureau of Ocean Management, Regulation and Enforcement, August 26, 2010.

Adding to the complexities of decision making on the Deepwater Horizon was the fact that many of BP's decision makers for the Macondo well had only been in their positions for a short time before disaster struck. See **Figure 1**.

As the Deepwater Horizon Disaster was dissected in various public forums, questions arose as to whether, in concert with the chaotic mix of decision makers, three key decisions on closing the Macondo well played a role in the downing of the 33,000 ton oil rig. (U.S. Congressional Representatives Henry Waxman and Bart Stupak called out these decisions in a letter dated June 14, 2010 to BP CEO Tony Hayward just days before his testimony before the Subcommittee on Oversight and Investigations. See **Exhibit 3**.)

*Exhibit 2*

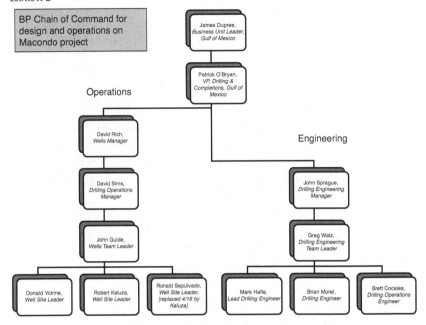

Operations

Engineering

BP Chain of Command for design and operations on Macondo project

James Dupree,
*Business Unit Leader, Gulf of Mexico*

Patrick O'Bryan,
*VP, Drilling & Completions, Gulf of Mexico*

David Rich,
*Wells Manager*

David Sims,
*Drilling Operations Manager*

John Guide,
*Wells Team Leader*

John Sprague,
*Drilling Engineering Manager*

Greg Walz,
*Drilling Engineering Team Leader*

Donald Vidrine,
*Well Site Leader*

Robert Kaluza,
*Well Site Leader*

Ronald Sepulvado,
*Well Site Leader, [replaced 4/16 by Kaluza]*

Mark Hafle,
*Lead Drilling Engineer*

Brian Morel,
*Drilling Engineer*

Brett Cocales,
*Drilling Operations Engineer*

*Exhibit 3*  Excerpt of Letter to BP CEO Tony Hayward

On June 14, 2010 Chairmen Henry A. Waxman and Bart Stupak sent a letter to Tony Hayward, Chief Executive Officer of BP, prior to his testifying before the Committee, detailing the questions the investigation has raised about BP decisions in the days and hours before the Deepwater Horizon explosion.

Mr. Tony Hayward
Chief Executive Officer
BPPLC
I St. James's Square
London SWI Y 4PD
United Kingdom
June 14, 2010

Dear Mr. Hayward:

We are looking forward to your testimony before the Subcommittee on Oversight and Investigations on Thursday, June 17, 2010, about the causes of the blowout of the Macondo well and the ongoing oil spill disaster in the Gulf of Mexico. As you prepare for this testimony, we want to share with you some of the results of the Committee's investigation and advise you of issues you should be prepared to address.

The Committee's investigation is raising serious questions about the decisions made by BP in the days and hours before the explosion on the Deepwater

Horizon. On April 15, five days before the explosion, BP's drilling engineer called Macondo a "nightmare well." In spite of the well's difficulties, BP appears to have made multiple decisions for economic reasons that increased the danger of a catastrophic well failure. In several instances, these decisions appear to violate industry guidelines and were made despite warnings from BP's own personnel and its contractors. In effect, it appears that BP repeatedly chose risky procedures in order to reduce costs and save time and made minimal efforts to contain the added risk.

At the time of the blowout, the Macondo well was significantly behind schedule. This appears to have created pressure to take shortcuts to speed finishing the well. In particular, the Committee is focusing on five crucial decisions made by BP: (I) the decision to use a well design with few barriers to gas flow; (2) the failure to use a sufficient number of "centralizers" to prevent channeling during the cement process; (3) the failure to run a cement bond log to evaluate the effectiveness of the cement job; (4) the failure to circulate potentially gasbearing drilling muds out of the well; and (5) the failure to secure the wellhead with a lockdown sleeve before allowing pressure on the seal from below. The common feature of these five decisions is that they posed a tradeoff between cost and well safety.

Well Design. On April 19, one day before the blowout, BP installed the final section of steel tubing in the well. BP had a choice of two primary options: it could lower a full string of "casing" from the top of the wellhead to the bottom of the well, or it could hang a "liner" from the lower end of the casing already in the well and install a "tieback" on top of the liner. The liner-tieback option would have taken extra time and was more expensive, but it would have been safer because it provided more barriers to the flow of gas up the annular space surrounding these steel tubes. A BP plan review prepared in mid-April recommended against the full string of casing because it would create "an open annulus to the wellhead" and make the seal assembly at the wellhead the "only barrier" to gas flow if the cement job failed. Despite this and other warnings, BP chose the more risky casing option, apparently because the liner option would have cost $7 to $10 million more and taken longer.

Centralizers. When the final string of casing was installed, one key challenge was making sure the casing ran down the center of the well bore. As the American Petroleum Institute's recommended practices explain, if the casing is not centered, "it is difficult, if not impossible, to displace mud effectively from the narrow side of the annulus," resulting in a failed cement job. Halliburton, the contractor hired by BP to cement the well, warned BP that the well could have a "SEVERE gas flow problem" if BP lowered the final string of casing with only six centralizers instead of the 21 recommended by Halliburton. BP rejected Halliburton's advice to use additional centralizers. In an e-mail on April 16, a BP official involved in the decision explained: "it will take 10 hours to install them. . . . I do not like this." Later that day, another official recognized the risks of proceeding with insufficient centralizers but commented: "who cares, it's done, end of story, will probably be fine."

Cement Bond Log. BP's mid-April plan review predicted cement failure, stating "Cement simulations indicate it is unlikely to be a successful cement job due to formation breakdown." Despite this warning and Halliburton's prediction of severe gas flow problems, BP did not run a 9- to 12-hour procedure called a cement bond log to assess the integrity of the cement seal. BP had a crew from Schlumberger on the rig on the morning of April 20 for the purpose of running a cement bond log, but they departed after BP told them their services were not needed. An independent expert consulted by the Committee called this decision "horribly negligent."

Mud Circulation. In exploratory operations like the Macondo well, wells are generally filled with weighted mud during the drilling process. The American Petroleum Institute (API) recommends that oil companies fully circulate the drilling mud in the well from the bottom to the top before commencing the cementing process. Circulating the mud in the Macondo well could have taken as long as 12 hours, but it would have allowed workers on the rig to test the mud for gas influxes, to safely remove any pockets of gas, and to eliminate debris and condition the mud so as to prevent contamination of the cement. BP decided to forego this safety step and conduct only a partial circulation of the drilling mud before the cement job.

Lockdown Sleeve. Because BP elected to use just a single string of casing, the Macondo well had just two barriers to gas flow up the annular space around the final string of casing: the cement at the bottom of the well and the seal at the wellhead on the sea floor. The decision to use insufficient centralizers created a significant risk that the cement job would channel and fail, while the decision not to run a cement bond log denied BP the opportunity to assess the status of the cement job. These decisions would appear to make it crucial to ensure the integrity of the seal assembly that was the remaining barrier against an influx of hydrocarbons. Yet, BP did not deploy the casing hanger lockdown sleeve that would have prevented the seal from being blown out from below.

These five questionable decisions by BP are described in more detail below. We ask that you come prepared on Thursday to address the concerns that these decisions raise about BP's actions.

The Committee's investigation into the causes of the blowout and explosion on the Deepwater Horizon rig is continuing. As our investigation proceeds, our understanding of what happened and the mistakes that were made will undoubtedly evolve and change. At this point in the investigation, however, the evidence before the Committee calls into question multiple decisions made by BP. Time after time, it appears that BP made decisions that increased the risk of a blowout to save the company time or expense. If this is what happened, BP's carelessness and complacency have inflicted a heavy toll on the Gulf, its inhabitants, and the workers on the rig.

During your testimony before the Committee, you will be asked about the issues raised in this letter. This will provide you an opportunity to respond to these concerns and clarify the record. We appreciate your willingness to appear and your cooperation in the Committee's investigation.

Sincerely,

Henry A. Waxman, Chairman, Committee on Energy and Commerce
Bart Stupak, Chairman, Subcommittee on Oversight and Investigations

## Well Casing

Deep water wells are drilled in sections. The process of deep water drilling involves drilling through rock at the bottom of the ocean, installing and cementing casing to secure the well hole, then drilling deeper and repeating the process. On April 9, 2010, the crew of the Deepwater Horizon finished drilling the last section of the well, which extended 18,360 feet below sea level and 1,192 feet below the casing that had previously been inserted into the well.[39]

During the week of April 12, BP project managers had to decide how best to secure the well's final 1,192-foot section. One option involved hanging a steel tube called a liner from a liner hanger on the bottom of the casing already in the well and then inserting another steel liner tube called a "tieback" on top of the liner hanger. The liner/tieback casing option provided four barriers of protection against gas and oil leaks getting into the well accidentally. These barriers included the cement at the bottom of the well, the hanger seal that attaches the liner to the existing casing in the well, the cement that secures the tieback on top of the liner, and the seal at the wellhead.[40]

The other casing option, known as "long string casing," involved running a single string of steel casing from the seafloor all the way to the bottom of the well. (Both options are depicted in **Figure 2**.) Long string casing provided two barriers to the flow of gas up the annular space that surrounded the casing: the cement at the bottom of the well and the seal at the wellhead. Compared to the liner tie-back option, the long string casing option took fewer days to install.

The decision about which casing design to use changed several times during the month of April. A BP *Forward Plan Review* from mid-April 2010 recommended against using long string casing because of the inherent risks of having fewer gas barriers. But internal communications within BP indicated the company was actually leaning towards using the long string casing

Note: A liner completion incorporates a short casing string, hung off from a predetermined point in the intermediate casing string. This provides several benefits, including reduced material cost and greater flexibility in the selection of completion components in the upper wellbore area.

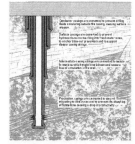

Note: Pipe is run into the wellbore and cemented in place to protect aquifers, to provide pressure integrity and to ensure isolation of producing formations.

*Figure 2* Diagram of a Liner and Diagram of a Casing String

Source: Schlumberger.

option. On March 25, 2010, Brian Morel, a BP drilling engineer, emailed Allison Crane, a materials management coordinator for BP, that choosing long string casing "saves a lot of time . . . at least 3 days . . ." On March 30, he emailed Sarah Dobbs, the BP completions engineer, and Mark Hafle, another BP drilling engineer, that "not running the tieback . . . saves a good deal of time/money."[41] On April 15, BP estimated that using a liner instead of the long string casing "will add an additional $7—$10 million to the completion cost."[42]

A few days after BP completed the first version of its *Forward Plan Review*, the company released a revised version which referred to the long string casing option as "the primary option" and the liner as "the contingency option."[43] Like the earlier version of the *Forward Plan Review*, this version acknowledged the risks of long string casing, but considered it the "best economic case and well integrity case for future completion operations."[44]

## Centralizers

In closing up the well, BP was responsible for cementing in place the steel pipe that ran into the oil reservoir. The cement would fill the space between the outside of the pipe and surrounding rock, allowing a more uniform cement sheath to form around the pipe, while preventing any gas from flowing up the sides. Centralizers are special brackets that are used to help keep the pipe centered.

To help inform decision-making on the well pipe centralization, BP hired Halliburton, the cementing contractor, to run technical model simulations and cement lab tests. Jesse Marc Gagliano was the Halliburton account representative for BP. He worked in BP's Houston office and was on the same floor as the BP Macondo well management team of John Guide, who was part of the operations unit, and Brett Cocales, Brian Morel, and Mark Hafle who were part of the engineering unit.[45] Gagliano also worked with the Halliburton crew members on the rig to advise them on logistics and ordering products.

One of Gagliano's chief responsibilities was running the OptiCem model, a multi-factor simulation designed to help predict potential gas flow that might interfere with getting a good cement job on a well site. The OptiCem model, considered highly reliable, took data inputs from BP engineers and evaluated the likely effectiveness of various well designs. As he explained in his testimony before The Joint United States Coast Guard/Bureau of Ocean Energy Management, Regulation and Enforcement hearing, "It is a model. It is as good as the information you put into it. So the more accurate information you have, the more accurate the output will be."[46] After running the model, Gagliano discovered that if BP used only six centralizers, as was planned, the risk for gas flow problems was quite significant. He found that at least 21 centralizers would be needed to significantly lower the risk.[47]

Though nothing was written down, court testimony revealed that on April 15, Gagliano had discussed the modeling results with Morel, Hafle, Cocales, and Greg Walz, BP's drilling engineering team leader, in their Houston office. During their discussion, Gagliano expressed concern that the Opti-Cem results indicated a very high risk that the cement job would encounter "channeling."[48] BP's Morel, however, questioned the reliability of the results because some of the earlier outputs related to compression factors in the well were different than what the crew engineers measured onsite.[49] According to Gagliano, the group spent much of the morning trying to figure out the best way to use the centralizers they did have. After their meeting, a series of emails were exchanged, leading off with one from Morel at 4:00pm on Thursday, April 15.

**From:** Morel, Brian P
**Sent:** Thursday. April 15, 2010 4:00 PM
**To:** Jesse Gagliano; Hafle, Mark E; Cocales, Brett W; Walz, Gregory S
**Subject:** RE: OptiCem Report
**Attachments:** image002.jpg; image003.jpg

We have 6 centralizers, we can run them in a row, spread out, or any combinations of the two. It's a vertical hole so hopefully the pipe stays centralized due to gravity. As far as changes, it's too late to get any more product to the rig, our only options is to rearrange placement of these centralizers. Please see attached diagram for my recommendation.

A few hours after Morel sent his email, Walz wrote a lengthy email to Guide, the Macondo well operations manager, expressing his concern about using just six centralizers.

**From:** Walz, Gregory S
**To:** Guide, John
**Sent:** Fri Apr 16 00:50:27 2010
**Subject:** Additional Centralizers

John,

Halliburton came back to us this afternoon with additional modeling after they loaded the final directional surveys, caliper log information, and the planned 6 centralizers. What it showed, is that the ECD at the base of sand jumped up to 15.06 ppg. This is being driven by channeling of the cement higher than the planned TOC.

We have located 15 Weatherford centralizers with stop collars (Thunder Horse design) in Houston and worked things out with the rig to be able to fly them out in the morning. My understanding is that there is no incremental cost with the flight because they are combining the planned flights they already had. The maximum they could fly is 15.

The model runs for 20 centralizers (6 on hand + 14 new ones) reduce the ECD to 14.65 ppg, which is back below the 14.7+ ECD we had when we lost circulation earlier.

There has been a lot of discussion about this and there are differing opinions on the model accuracy. However, the issue, is that we need to honor the modeling to be consistent with our previous decisions to go with the long string. Brell and I tried to reach you twice to discuss things. David was still here in the office and I discussed this with him and he agreed that we needed to be consistent with honoring the model.

To be able to have this option we needed to kick things off at 6:00 pm tonight, so I went ahead and gave Brett the go ahead. We also lined up a Weatherford hand for installing them to go out on the same flight. I wanted to make sure that we did not have a repeat of the last Atlantis job with questionable centralizers going into the hole.

John, I do not like or want to disrupt your operations and I am a full believer that the rig needs only one Team Leader. I know the planning has been lagging behind the operations and I have to turn that around. I apologize if I have over step my bounds.

I would like to discuss how we want to handle these types of issues in the future. Please call me tonight if you want to discuss this in more detail.

Gregg
Drilling Engineering Team Leader
GoM Drilling & Completions
Office:
Cell:
E-mail:

Guide responded to Walz's email early in the afternoon on Friday, April 16, expressing concern about the decision made by his supervisor, David Sims, to order additional centralizers.

**From:** Guide, John
**To:** Walz, Gregory S
**Sent:** Fri Apr 16 12:48:11 2010
**Subject:** Re: Additional Centralizers

I just found out the slop collars are not part of the centralizer as you stated. Also it will take 10 hrs to install them. We are adding 45 pieces that can come off as a last minute addition. I do not like this and as David approved in my absence I did not question but now I very concerned about using them

**From:** Walz, Gregory S
**Sent:** Friday, April 16, 2010 12:53 PM
**To:** Guide, John
**Subject:** Re: Additional Centralizers
I agree. This is not what I was envisioning. I will call you directly.
Gregg Walz
Sent From my BlackBerry

When asked in court why he would ever question the OptiCem model's results, Guide responded, "There were several reasons, first of all, it's a model, it's a simulation, it's not . . . the real thing. From past experiences sometimes it's right and sometimes it's wrong. And I also know in this particular case . . . they made reference to having to tinker with it to try to get some of the results that were reasonable."[50]

Meanwhile, Morel had gotten 3D profile information on the well hole, which indicated that it was actually very straight: 6/10ths of a degree off of vertical. In an email to Cocales, Morel questioned Gagliano's recommendation to use more centralizers. He believed doing so could slow down the process of sealing and cementing the well.[51]

> **From:** Morel, Brian P
> **Sent:** Friday, April 16, 2010 4:04 PM
> **To:** Cocales, Brett W
> **Subject:** FW: Macondo STK geodetic
>
> This is why I don't understand Jesse's centralizer requirements. You can see from the plot we aren't moving much in terms of footage over long intervals.
>
> Brian

Based on the information about the straightness of the well hole, Cocales believed that despite the OptiCem model's results, additional centralizers would only add a small additional measure of safety.[52] In his reply to Morel, Cocales indicated he was in agreement with Guide.

> **From:** Cocales, Brett W
> **Sent:** Friday, April 16, 2010 4:15 PM
> **To:** Morel, Brian P
> **Subject:** RE: Macondo STK geodetic
>
> Even if the hole is perfectly straight, a straight piece of pipe even in tension will not seek the perfect center of the hole unless it has something to centralize it.
>     But, who cares, it's done, end of story, will probably be fine and we'll get a good cement job. I would rather have to squeeze than get stuck above the WH. So Guide is right on the risk/reward equation.
>     Best Regards,
>     Brett

As it turned out, the additional centralizers that Sims gave the green light to order were a "slip-on" variety that took more time to install on a pipe, and were considered risky because of fears they might come off during installation and get stuck in the casing above the well-head.[53] As a result, Guide and Walz decided not to use any additional centralizers. Gagliano later learned of their decision from another Halliburton employee who was on board the Deepwater

Horizon.[54] In his witness testimony to The Joint United States Coast Guard/ Bureau of Ocean Energy Management, Regulation and Enforcement hearing in July 2010, Guide revealed that no one had considered postponing or putting a stop work order on the cement job until centralizers of the right kind were located.[55]

On April 18, two days after Guide and Walz decided not to use the additional centralizers, Gagliano sent the formal report of the OptiCem results as an email attachment to the Macondo well management team. Page 18 of the report included the following observation: "Gas Flow Potential, 10.29 at Reservoir Zone Measured Depth, 18200.0. Based on the well analysis of the above outlined well conditions, this well is considered to have a SEVERE gas flow problem. Wells in this category fall into Flow Category 3."[56] However, the text of the email that Gagliano sent to the BP managers on April 18 did not say anything about the hazards of the Macondo well. Cocales and Guide later testified that neither had read page 18—both had merely skimmed the report for the information they were most interested in.[57]

## Circulating Mud and the Cement Bond Log

The whole process of cementing an oil well is notoriously tricky. A 2007 study by the MMS found that cementing was the single most significant factor in 18 of 39 well blowouts in the Gulf of Mexico over a 14-year period.[58]

Before cementing a well, it is common industry practice to circulate the drilling mud through the well, bringing the mud at the bottom all the way up to the drilling rig. This procedure, known as "bottoms up," allows workers to check the mud to see if it is absorbing gas leaking in. If so, the gas has to be separated out before the mud can be re-submerged into the well. According to the American Petroleum Institute, it is cementing best practice to circulate the mud at least once.[59] In the case of the Macondo well, BP estimated that circulating all the mud at 18,360 feet would take anywhere from six to 12 hours. According to the drilling logs from Monday, April 19, mud circulation was completed in just 30 minutes.[60]

In concert with the decision to do a partial circulation, BP managers chose not to run a test called a "cement bond log" to check the integrity of the cement job after it was pumped into the well, despite Gagliano's warnings of potential channeling. Workers from Schlumberger had been hired to perform a cement bond log if needed,[61] but on the morning of Tuesday, April 20, about 12 hours before the blowout, BP told the Schlumberger workers their services would not be needed.[62] According to Schlumberger's contract, BP would pay a cancellation fee equal to 7% of the cost of having the cement bond log and mechanical plug services completed. See **Figure 3**.

BP and the engineers on site had used a decision tree, a system of diagnostic questions to define future actions, to determine whether they would need to perform a cement bond log. (See **Exhibit 4**.) BP ultimately followed their own decision tree accurately, but when reviewed in court, it was pointed out

| Equipment and Labor | Estimated Cost if Performed | Actual Cost upon Cancellation |
|---|---|---|
| Cement bond log | $128,258.77 | $10,165.43 |
| Mechanical plug | $53,075.06 | $1,870.01 |

*Figure 3* Costs and Cancellation Costs for Schlumberger's Services

Source: http://energycommerce.house.gov/documents/20100614/Schlumberger-Cost.of.Completing.
Cement.Bond.Log.v.Canceled.Contingency.pdf

*Exhibit 4* BP's Cement Bond Log Decision Tree

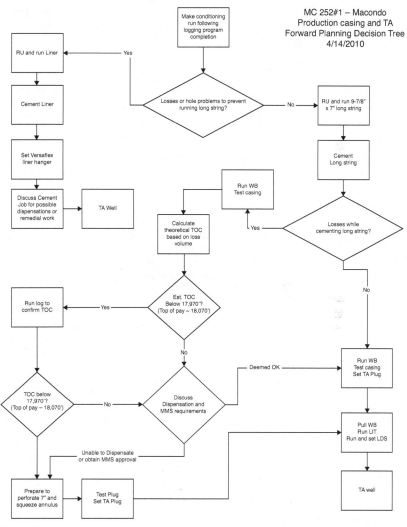

Source: Casewriter.

that there could have been channeling in the well pipe during the cement job. Channeling was considered highly likely given that far fewer centralizers were used than what the OptiCem model had recommended. Such mud-cement channeling would not have been picked up in the diagnostic tests listed in BP's decision tree.[63] In fact, the only way to accurately diagnose a bond failure due to channeling was with a cement bond log.[64] However, when asked in court about the decision not to run a cement bond log despite seeing a loss return of 3,000 barrels of drilling mud,[65] Mark Hafle, one of BP's drilling engineers, responded that the model he had from Halliburton indicated that the cement job should be fine.[66] He also went on to explain that a cement bond log would be done *at some point* on this well, but that it was usually done pre-production:

> So, that cement bond log is an evaluation tool that is not always 100% right. There's many factors that can affect its quality. It's not a quantitative tool. It does not tell you the exact percentage of cement at any given point. . . . It's a tool in the engineering tool box that has to be used with a bit of caution. But if it shows there's no cement two or three years from now when we come to do the completion we will do a remedial cement job on that casing.[67]

## Fallout from the Disaster

The impact of the Deepwater Horizon explosion and the subsequent Macondo well oil leak was devastating on a number of fronts, the most obvious being the death of 11 crew members and the injuries sustained by another 17.

The environmental damage from the oil spill was extensive, with 25 national wildlife refuges in its path.[68] Oil was found on the shores of all five Gulf States,[69] and was responsible for the death of many birds, fish, and reptiles. The total amount of impacted shoreline in Louisiana alone grew from 287 miles in July to 320 miles in late November 2010.[70] Unlike conditions with the Alaskan Exxon-Valdez oil spill, the contaminated Gulf shoreline was not rock but wetland. Grasses and loose soil, a perfect sponge for holding oil, dominated wetland ecosystems. The spill also occurred during breeding season for pelicans, shrimp, and alligators, and most other Gulf coast species. Ecologists anticipated that entire generations of these animals could be lost if they were contaminated with oil.[71]

In terms of direct economic damages, the sinking of the Deepwater Horizon rig represented a $560 million loss for Transocean and Lloyds of London, the insurance company which had unwritten the rig.[72] The unprecedented loss of an entire semi-submersible rig was predicted to change underwriting policies for all oil rigs. As one underwriter noted, "It's never happened that a semi could burn into the sea and completely sink. Now underwriters have to include that as a risk. That's probably $10,000 to $15,000 more *per day* in rig insurance. They'll make it up by charging more on a per-rig basis."[73]

BP's price tag for the lost oil—five million barrels at the average market crude oil price (for April 20, 2010 through July 15, 2010) of $74.81 per barrel[74]—was $374 million. In addition, if a federal court ruled that the company was grossly negligent, BP could face up to $3.5 billion in fines, or $4,300 per spilled barrel.[75] Of course the company's losses didn't end there. On April 15, five days before the disaster, BP's stock was trading on the NYSE at $60.57 and on June 25, it hit a 14-year low of $27.02.[76] In addition to the frustration felt by shareholders and the public at large that the company had failed at several attempts to stop the leak, they were also unimpressed with BP's PR strategy, citing skepticism over the company's offer to pay fishermen if they signed a waiver promising not to sue the company.[77]

Alongside those companies directly involved with the Macondo well project, the Deepwater Horizon disaster affected the oil industry as a whole. On May 28, 2010, Secretary of the Interior Ken Salazar issued a moratorium on all deep water oil drilling in U.S. waters.[78] The purpose of the moratorium was to allow time to assess the safety standards that should be required for drilling, and to create strategies for dealing with wild wells[79] in deep water. Government analysts estimated that about 2,000 rig worker jobs were lost during the moratorium and that total spending by drilling operators fell by $1.8 billion. The reduction in spending led to a decline in employment—estimates indicated a temporary loss of 8,000 to 12,000 jobs in the Gulf Coast[80]—and income for the companies and individuals that supplied the drilling industry. The moratorium also reduced U.S. oil production by about 31,000 barrels per day in the fourth quarter of 2010 and by roughly 82,000 barrels per day in 2011. This loss, however, was not large relative to total world production, and was not expected to have a discernable effect on the price of oil.[81] The moratorium, originally intended to last until the end of November, was lifted in mid-October 2010.[82]

The economic losses also extended to the thousands of coastal small business owners including fishermen, shrimpers, oystermen, and those whose livelihood depended in whole or in part on fishing or tourism. The tourism industries in Alabama, Louisiana, and Florida were particularly hard hit. Ironically, analysts had previously predicted that tourism in the Gulf region, which was devastated by Hurricane Katrina in 2005, would return to pre-Katrina levels in 2010.[83] Between the energy, fishing, shrimping, and tourism industries, the Gulf region lost an estimated 250,000 jobs in 2010.[84]

In anticipation of the economic aftershocks that would be felt from the oil spill, BP pledged to compensate those individuals whose livelihoods would be affected. On June 16, 2010, in agreement with the U.S. government, the company established the Gulf Coast Claims Facility (GCCF), an escrow fund of $20 billion to pay for the various costs arising from the oil spill. GCCF staff evaluated the claims of companies and individuals who suffered demonstrable damages from the oil spill. The fund was also intended to pay municipalities, counties, and state organizations for lost tax revenue or additional clean-up costs.[85] Kenneth Feinberg, who led the September 11 Victim Compensation Fund, was appointed to oversee the GCCF.

By February 28, 2011, the GCFF had received over 500,000 claims, and 170,000 people and businesses had been paid over $3.6 billion. Some people accused the facility of not acting quickly enough to process claims and make payments. In response, the GCCF increased transparency of the system and hired staff in the Gulf to answer questions from applicants in person.[86] The GCCF was scheduled to remain in place until August 2013.[87]

## Conclusion

As of early 2011, investigations into the actual causes of the Deepwater Horizon disaster were ongoing, and the various parties involved in the Macondo well project were engaged in a highly publicized finger pointing exercise. The three major decisions on closing the Macondo well involving the well casing, the number of centralizers used, and the decision not to perform a cement bond log *may* have contributed to the conditions that caused the well to blow out.

Regardless of what the ultimate causes are found to be, the conditions on the Deepwater Horizon, and the culture and organizational architecture of BP and its relationships with its contractors is worth examining. Each of the three decisions discussed above, as well as decisions on how to convey dangerous model results and earlier decisions about how best to structure incentive systems, may have played a role in the outcome. Throughout the decision making process, we see some actors who were advocates of caution over cost, for fixing problems even when inconvenient. Yet court testimony indicates that the three key decisions, and perhaps others as well, came down on the side of cost-reduction and expediency, over caution.

## Appendices

*Appendix 1* Petroleum Value Chain

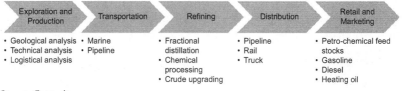

Source: Casewriter.

*Appendix 2* Macondo Well Design Diagram with Predicted Problem Sites

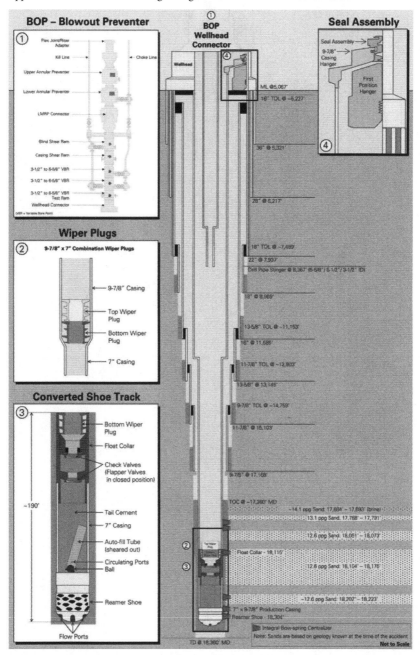

Source: BP. Deepwater Horizon Accident Investigation Report Appendix C. September 8, 2010.

*Appendix 3*

# SIX STEPS THAT DOOMED THE RIG

The blowout of BP's Macondo oil well on April 20 was the result of a string of five human errors and one final, colossal mechanical failure, when the blowout preventer failed to close off the exploding well. The choices were made in the final hours before the exploratory well was to be completed and the Deepwater Horizon removed. BP engineers knew they had an especially tough well, but repeatedly made quicker, cheaper and ultimately more dangerous choices. They seemed to consider each danger in a vacuum, never thinking they could all add up to 11 dead rig workers, a sunken rig and millions of barrels of crude fouling the Gulf.

## 1 FEWER BARRIERS TO GAS FLOW

BP had two choices of how to line the well with metal tubes and cement seals. Its engineers considered using a typical industry practice of a short liner at the bottom, with additional seals. But they ultimately chose a method that saved the company up to $10 million.

**THE BP METHOD:**
BP used a single, long string of casing in the middle of the hole, one designed for later use in extracting oil. That created an open space along the sides and fewer plugs in the middle.

A series of metal casings line the well.

At the bottom of each casing, cement is pushed between it and the bedrock.

Usually the space between casings, called the annulus, is closed off with an O-ring called a liner hanger.

A liner hanger was not placed between the two lowest casings. This is one possible route the natural gas that ignited the rig took to the surface.

Additionally, only a single plug was cemented in the bottom of the well. If this plug failed, this is the other route that would have allowed the natural gas a clear path to the rig.

**A BETTER WAY:**
Common industry practice is to use a shorter tube called a "liner" at the bottom of the hole, then a separate tool called a tie-back. These would have created an additional barrier, as well as the addition of a second plug in the middle of the well, but it would have cost millions of dollars more and BP chose not to do it.

Squeeze additional cement between metal casings

Tieback casing seal is added between joints of liner casing

Liner hanger seal used between inner and outer casings

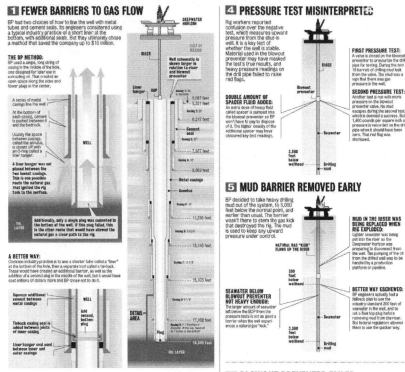

## 2 FEWER CENTRALIZERS TO KEEP CEMENT EVEN

BP chose to use six of the devices for keeping tubes centered, ignoring Halliburton models calling for 21. It's important to have the telescoping tubes centered in the hole because that's where cement is poured. If a tube is sitting to one side, the cement slurry will follow the path of least resistance and set unevenly, leaving weak points where gas could seep in.

**THE RIGHT WAY:**
Cement is pumped down the metal casings and is then forced up into the spaces between the outer casing and the sediment wall of the hole.

If the casing is centered in the hole, the cement can harden around it completely and seal it to the surrounding earth.

SIDE VIEW / TOP VIEW / Centered casing

Centered casing
Cement flows evenly
Cement

**THE WRONG WAY:**
Problems arise during the cementing process if the casing has moved closer to one side of the well hole.

An uncentered casing prevents the cement from fully surrounding it. These gaps are potential pathways for oil and gas.

Casing that has shifted
Cement flows to one side
Casing shifted to the side
Poorly cemented area where gas can leak through

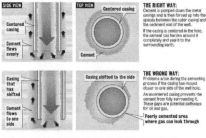

## 3 NO BOND LOG TO TEST CEMENT INTEGRITY

BP had hired contractor Schlumberger to run tests on the newly cemented well. But BP sent Schlumberger's crew home on a helicopter without having it run the test, called a cement bond log. It would have cost $100,000 more, taken time and required a month of remedial work if it found problems, at a likely additional cost of $30 million.

## 4 PRESSURE TEST MISINTERPRETED

Rig workers reported confusion over the negative test, which measures upward pressure from the shut-in well. It is a key test of whether the well is stable. Material used in the blowout preventer may have masked the test's true results, and heavy pressure readings on the drill pipe failed to raise red flags.

**DOUBLE AMOUNT OF SPACER FLUID ADDED:**
An extra dose of heavy fluid called spacer is pumped into the blowout preventer so BP won't have to pay to dispose of it. The higher density of the additional spacer may have obscured key test readings.

**FIRST PRESSURE TEST:**
A valve is closed on the blowout preventer to pressurize the drill pipe for testing. During the test 15 barrels of drilling mud leak from the valve. The mud was a sign that there was gas pressure in the well.

**SECOND PRESSURE TEST:**
Another test is run with more pressure on the blowout preventer valve. No mud escapes during the second test, which is deemed a success. But 1,400 pounds per square inch of pressure is recorded on the drill pipe when it should have been zero. That red flag was dismissed.

## 5 MUD BARRIER REMOVED EARLY

BP decided to take heavy drilling mud out of the system, to 3,000 feet below the normal point, and earlier than usual. The barrier wasn't there to stem the gas kick that destroyed the well. The mud is used to keep any upward pressure under control.

**SEAWATER BELOW BLOWOUT PREVENTER NOT HEAVY ENOUGH:**
The larger amount of seawater left below the BOP from the pressure tests is not as good a barrier when the well experiences a natural gas "kick."

**MUD IN THE RISER WAS BEING REPLACED WHEN RIG EXPLODED:**
Lighter seawater was being put into the riser as the Deepwater Horizon was preparing to disconnect from the well. The pumping of the oil from the drilled well was to be handled by a production platform or pipeline.

**BETTER WAY ESCHEWED:**
BP engineers actually had a fallback plan to use the industry-standard 300 feet of seawater in the well, and to set a final top plug before removing mud from the riser. But federal regulators allowed them to use the quicker way.

## 6 BLOWOUT PREVENTER FAILED

It's unclear exactly why, but the last line of defense to close in the well never worked. A hydraulic could have been the culprit, or a plumbing issue, or debris could have fouled it up, or there may have been more pipes running through it than it was designed to cut.

**Two annular valves:** Closes in and seals on the drill pipe. Or if the drill pipe is not in use, it closes the open hole. The valves' rubber may have been damaged weeks earlier.

**The BOP STACK is a 450-ton series of valves developed to prevent a gusher if the mud control is overwhelmed.**

**Yellow control pod:** Recieves messages from rig to control blowout preventer valves and arms. Had a hydraulic leak and was placed in neutral to prevent fluid from leaking.

**Lower marine riser package disconnect:** Should have disconnected the rig from the blowout preventer after the accident, but it didn't work.

**Shear rams:** The final fail-safe, it is designed to close the well by cutting through and sealing the drill pipe. But they are not designed to cut two drill pipes or through joints where two pipe sections connect. The shear rams were unsuccessful.

Riser adapter
Flex joint
Blue control pod
Blind rams
Drill pipe
Test ram
Wellhead connector

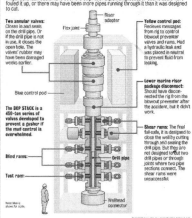

EMMETT MAYER III / THE TIMES-PICAYUNE

*Appendix 4*  BP Organizational Chart 2007

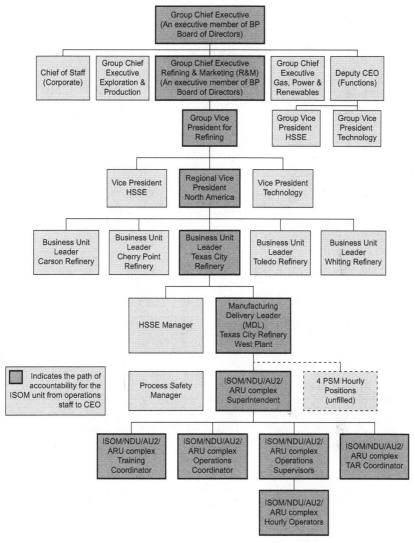

*Source*: Prepared for the Chemical Safety Board Final Investigation Report for the Texas City Disaster, March 20, 2007.

## Notes

*  This work is licensed under the Creative Commons Attribution-Noncommercial-No Derivative Works 3.0 Unported License. To view a copy of this license visit http://creative commons.org/licenses/by-nc-nd/3.0/ or send a letter to Creative Commons, 171 Second Street, Suite 300, San Francisco, California, 94105, USA.

1  Testimony from Michael Williams, The Joint United States Coast Guard/The Bureau of Ocean Energy Management, "FUSCG/BOEM Marine Board of Investigation into

the marine casualty, explosion, fire, pollution, and sinking of mobile offshore drilling unit deepwater horizon, with loss of life in the Gulf of Mexico 21–22 April 2010," Transcript, July 23, 2010, pp. 24–25.

2 The Joint United States Coast Guard/The Bureau of Ocean Energy Management, "FUSCG/BOEM Marine Board of Investigation into the marine casualty, explosion, fire, pollution, and sinking of mobile offshore drilling unit deepwater horizon, with loss of life in the Gulf of Mexico 21–22 April 2010," Transcript, July 23, 2010, pp. 10–14.

3 U.S. House of Representatives Committee on Energy and Commerce, "Chronology of Deepwater Horizon Events," June 15, 2010.

4 Campbell Robertson and Clifford Kraus, "Gulf Spill is Largest of Its Kind, Scientists Say," *The New York Times*, August 3, 2010.

5 Calculation based on a spill size of 10.8 million gallons for the *Exxon Valdez*. Justin Gillis and Henry Fountain, "New Estimates Double Rate of Oil Flowing Into Gulf," *The New York Times*, June 10, 2010.

6 "BP Sustainability Reporting 2009: Alternative Energy," *BP Publication*, April 15, 2010.

7 BP annual financial statements: 2007 and 2009.

8 Tony Hayward, "BP 2008 Strategy Presentation," *BP Publication*, February 27, 2008.

9 Ibid.

10 BP.com archive information on employment, for 2006 data; "BP at a Glance" from BP.com, accessed October 10, 2010 for 2009 data.

11 Graeme Wearden, "BP to Take Axe to Management," *The Guardian*, September 25, 2007.

12 John Roberts, "Organizing for Performance: How BP Did It," *Stanford Business*, February 2005.

13 "BP After Horton," *The Economist*, July 4, 1992.

14 Each physical well site was called an asset and the site managers were "asset managers."

15 David Apgar, "Time to Break BP Up," *The Globalist*, June 22, 2010.

16 James Baker et al., "The Report of the BP U.S. Refineries Independent Safety Review Panel," January 2007. pp. 82–85.

17 Ibid, p. 72.

18 Ibid, p. 61.

19 Abraham Lustgarten and Ryan Knutson, "Reports at BP over Years Find History of Problems," *Washington Post*, June 8, 2010.

20 Baker Report Appendix F—BP post Texas City Measures. p. F-1.

21 The BP U.S. Refineries Independent Safety Review Panel, 2007.

22 Pierre Thomas, Lisa A. Jones, Jack Cloherty, and Jason Ryan, "BP's Dismal Safety Record," *ABC World News*, May 27, 2010.

23 http://www.deepwaterinvestigation.com/external/content/document/3043/856 507/1/7–23–10.pdf p. 70.

24 "Ultra-deep water" is considered water 5000 or more feet below sea level.

25 Lesley D. Nixon et al., "Deepwater Gulf of Mexico 2009: Interim Report of 2008 Highlights," *OCS Report* (New Orleans: U.S. Department of the Interior Minerals Management Service Gulf of Mexico OCS Region), May 2009.

26 Fred H. Bartlit, Jr., Chief Counsel, National Commission on the BP Deepwater Horizon Oil Spill and Offshore Drilling. Macondo Gulf Oil Disaster Chief Counsel's Report 2011, February 17, 2011.

27 "Macondo," SUBSEAIQ, (http://www.subseaiq.com/Data/Project.aspx?project_Id=562) accessed October 10, 2010.

28 BP's financial partners for Macondo were Texas-based Anadarko Petroleum Corporation which owned a 25% share, and MOEX Offshore 2007, a unit of Japan-based Mitsui, which owned a 10% share.

29 "Macondo," SUBSEAIQ, (http://www.subseaiq.com/Data/Project.aspx?project_Id=562) accessed October 10, 2010.

30 Ben Casselman and Russell Gold, "BP Decisions Set Stage for Disaster," *Wall Street Journal*, May 27, 2010.

31 BP, *GOM Exploration Wells Me 252 #1—Macondo Prospect Well information* (Sept 2009) (BP-HZN-CEC008714) (http://energycommerce.house.gov/documents/20100614).

32 Robbie Brown, "After Another Close Call, Transocean Changed the Rules," *The New York Times*, August 16, 2010.

33 Ibid; Testimony from Michael Williams, The Joint United States Coast Guard/The Bureau of Ocean Energy Management, "FUSCG/BOEM Marine Board of Investigation into the marine casualty, explosion, fire, pollution, and sinking of mobile offshore drilling unit deepwater horizon, with loss of life in the Gulf of Mexico 21–22 April 2010," Transcript, July 23, 2010, p. 153.

34 Ibid, pp. 42–44.

35 Ibid, pp. 98–102.

36 "Temporary abandonment" is the industry term for temporarily closing but not plugging a well.

37 BP, Weatherford, Hydril, Allamon, Blackhawk, Halliburton, Schlumberger, Sperry, M-I SWACO, Nexen, and K&B.

38 Casing is the lining of the drilled well hole. Ensuring a sound casing is essential to preventing any oil or gas leakage and maintaining the well as a resource for future oil production.

39 BP, PowerPoint Presentation, *Washington Briefing, Deepwater Horizon Interim Incident Investigation*, May 24, 2010.

40 Briefing by Tommy Roth, Vice President of Cementing, Halliburton, to House Committee on Energy and Commerce Staff (June 3, 2010); Halliburton, PowerPoint Presentation, *Energy and Commerce Committee Staff Briefing* (June 3, 2010).

41 http://energycommerce.house.gov/documents/20100614/BP-March30.Email-string.costs.less.than.tieback.pdf.

42 BP, *Drilling & Completion MOC Initiate* (Apr. 15, 2010) (BP-HZN-CEC021656).

43 http://energycommerce.house.gov/documents/20100614/BP-Production.Casing.TA.Options-String.Again.Best.Option.pdf.

44 Ibid.

45 http://www.deepwaterinvestigation.com/external/content/document/3043/903579/1/USCGHEARING%2024_Aug_10.pdf Ibid; Testimony from Jesse Marc Gagliano, The Joint United States Coast Guard/The Bureau of Ocean Energy Management, "FUSCG/BOEM Marine Board of Investigation into the marine casualty, explosion, fire, pollution, and sinking of mobile offshore drilling unit deepwater horizon, with loss of life in the Gulf of Mexico 21–22 April 2010," Transcript, August 24, 2010, p. 242.

46 Ibid. p. 273.

47 Ibid, p. 296.

48 Channeling occurs when you do not get a full circulation of cement to displace the drilling mud. Some of the mud will be left behind. In any place where there is mud left in place, it will prevent a proper cement bond. This problem would appear in a

cement bond log. To solve the problem, a tool is sent down the well pipe to puncture the pipe and insert additional cement.

49  http://www.deepwaterinvestigation.com/external/content/document/3043/903 579/1/USCGHEARING%2024_Aug_10.pdf; Testimony from Jesse Marc Gagliano, The Joint United States Coast Guard/The Bureau of Ocean Energy Management, "FUSCG/BOEM Marine Board of Investigation into the marine casualty, explosion, fire, pollution, and sinking of mobile offshore drilling unit deepwater horizon, with loss of life in the Gulf of Mexico 21–22 April 2010," Transcript, August 24, 2010 p. 296.

50  http://www.deepwaterinvestigation.com/external/content/document/3043/856503/ 1/7–22–10.pdf, p. 69.

51  http://www.deepwaterinvestigation.com/external/content/document/3043/903 599/1/USCGHEARING%2027_Aug_10.pdf, p. 27.

52  Ibid, pp. 27, 249–250.

53  Ibid, p. 191.

54  http://www.deepwaterinvestigation.com/external/content/document/3043/903 579/1/USCGHEARING%2024_Aug_10.pdf, p. 333.

55  http://www.deepwaterinvestigation.com/external/content/document/3043/856 503/1/7–22–10.pdf, p. 363.

56  http://www.deepwaterinvestigation.com/external/content/document/3043/903 599/1/USCGHEARING%2027_Aug_10.pdf, p. 23.

57  Ibid; http://www.deepwaterinvestigation.com/external/content/document/3043/856503/ 1/7–22–10.pdf, p. 271.

58  Chris Morrison, "Gulf Oil Spill: Who's to Blame? BP, Halliburton and the Feds are All Implicated," *CBS Interactive Business Network,* May 3, 2010.

59  Ben Casselman and Russell Gold, "BP Decisions Set Stage for Disaster," *Wall Street Journal,* May 27, 2010.

60  http://energycommerce.house.gov/documents/20100614/BP-Daily.Operations. Report.4.18.10.pdf.

61  http://energycommerce.house.gov/documents/20100614/Schlumberger.MC.252. Timeline.pdf.

62  Ibid.

63  http://www.deepwaterinvestigation.com/external/content/document/3043/903579/ 1/USCGHEARING%2024_Aug_10.pdf, p. 270.

64  Ibid, p. 271.

65  A "loss return" happens when the amount of spacer fluid (drilling mud in this case) expected to be displaced by the well cement is not returned to the rig, indicating a leak somewhere in the well hole system.

66  Mark Hafle's testimony before the Coast Guard Joint Commission, May 28, 2010, p. 46.

67  Ibid, p. 96.

68  Standard and Poor's Industry Surveys: Oil & Gas, Production and Marketing. August, 2010.

69  Juan A. Lozano, "Tar Balls in Texas Mean Oil Hits All 5 Gulf States," *The Associated Press,* July 6, 2010.

70  Bowermaster, Jon, "Measuring the extent of oil spillage," Gadling, November 29, 2010.

71  David A. Fahrenthold and Juliet Eilperin, "Scientists Watch for Environmental Effects of Gulf of Mexico Oil Spill," *Washington Post,* May 1, 2010.

72  "Chilean Earthquake and Deepwater Horizon," *Lloyds Press Release,* May 26, 2010.

73  Ford Gunter, "An Explosive Situation," *Porfolio.com,* April 28, 2010.

74  Calculated based on data from U.S. Energy Information Administration, "Petroleum Navigator," (http://www.eia.doe.gov/dnav/pet/) accessed October 10, 2010.

75 Joshua Schneyer, "Special Report: Civil Fine in Gulf Spill could be $4,300 barrel," *Reuters,* May 26, 2010.

76 Joshua Schneyer, "Special Report: Civil Fine in Gulf Spill could be $4,300 barrel," *Reuters,* May 26, 2010.

77 Anne C. Mulkern, "BP's PR Blunders Mirror Exxon's, Appear Destined for Record Book," *New York Times,* June 2010.

78 Jonathan Tilove, "Deepwater Drilling Moratorium Report Delivered to Interior Secretary," *Nola.com,* October 1, 2010.

79 A wild well was a well that had blown out of control and was leaking gas, water or oil.

80 "Estimating the Economic Effects of the Deepwater Drilling Moratorium on the Gulf Coast Economy," *Economics and Statistics Administration of the United States Department of Commerce,* September 16, 2010.

81 Ibid.

82 Mark Guarino, "Deep-water Drilling Moratorium Lifted: why neither side is happy," *Christian Science Monitor,* October 12, 2010.

83 Charisse Jones and Rick Jervis, "Oil Spill Takes Toll on Tourism on Gulf Coast," *USA Today,* June 25, 2010.

84 Standard and Poor's Industry Surveys: Oil & Gas, Production and Marketing, August, 2010.

85 Rig workers who lost their jobs as a result of the government moratorium on deep water drilling were not covered by the $20 billion fund. These workers were compensated by a separate $100 million fund.

86 Kenneth Feinberg, "Update on the BP claims compensation process resulting from the Gulf of Mexico oil spill," *Foreign Press Center, Washington, D.C.,* February 28, 2011.

87 Ibid.

88 "Transocean Oil Rig Suffered Start of Blow-Out in North Sea," *The Guardian,* December 7, 2010, http://www.guardian.co.uk/environment/2010/dec/07/transocean-oil-rig-north-sea-deepwater-horizon.

## Case Discussion Questions

1. Explain the management issues involved in the BP oil leak. Did BP meet its corporate social responsibilities? Justify your answer.

2. What role did the culture of BP in the oil leak of April 2009?

3. Explain the management issues on the part of Transocean in the BP oil leak. Did Transocean meet is corporate social responsibilities? Justify your answer.

4. Explain the management issues on the part of Halliburton in the BP oil leak. Did Halliburton meet is corporate social responsibilities? Justify your answer.

5. Explain the role and responsibilities of Mineral Mining Service (MMS) with respect to deep water drilling. Was it reasonable for President Obama to halt all deep water drilling for six months after the BP oil spill?

6. The BP oil well blowout in the Gulf of Mexico, although a rare event, was not unique. See for example, a blowout on a rig that was owned by Transocean was averted in the North Sea.[88] Develop strategies to manage the risks of this technology.

# 3 Ethics of Business Decision Making

## Chapter Outline

## Chapter Introduction

What standards of judgment should be invoked to evaluate ethical challenges managers face in the workplace? There are multiple competing theories of ethical behavior, including ethical standards based on rights, ethical standards based on justice, virtue ethics, and the ethics of care. A manager must chose among competing ethical standards to decide specific ethical challenges he or she faces in the workplace. The personal integrity of the manager is also involved, particularly the manager's ability to recognize and resolve conflicts of interest. Management decisions about ethical challenges create a corporate culture.

## Chapter Goal and Learning Objectives

*Chapter Goal:* To identify standards of judgment to evaluate ethical challenges in the workplace.

*Learning Objectives:*

1. Compare and contrast a rights-based approach with a justice-based approach to business ethics.
2. Explain Kant's categorical imperative as a model of ethical conduct.
3. Explain the concept of materiality in ethical dilemmas and the application of the disclosure rule to ethical decision making.
4. Discuss the role of personal integrity, including the manager's ability to identify and deal with conflicts of interest in ethical decision making and how decisions made by organizational leaders give rise to an organizational culture.

## What Standards of Judgment Should Be Invoked to Evaluate Ethical Challenges in the Workplace?

What standards of judgment should be invoked to evaluate ethical challenges in the workplace? Major parameters for judging ethical challenges are based on either a *rights* standard or a *justice* standard. Even when addressing rights, there are alternative approaches to rights: property rights and rights of contract, new property rights, human rights, and rights of minorities.

### Rights Standards

*Property Rights and Rights of Contract*

Property rights are fundamental to a capitalist, market-driven system of enterprise. *Property rights* are grounded in the philosophy of John Locke. Locke recognized that with the gift of life, we have the right to the stuff needed to sustain our lives and that conveys the right to individual property. An implication of Locke's approach to individual property rights is that when our life ceases, the stuff we've used to sustain our lives returns to the common pool of humanity. Property rights in the United States are guaranteed by the Fifth and Fourteenth Amendments. The right to property is also viewed as a fundamental human right by the United Nations Declaration of Human Rights.[1]

*Rights of contract* are recognized as rights of competent adult persons. The right to contract is also fundamental to a capitalist, market-driven system of business. Contracts are the basis of transactions among the linked enterprises that comprise specific markets and the global economy as a whole. The law of contract, including insurance contracts protecting property rights, must be developed in the former Soviet Union and the contemporary Communist regime of the Peoples' Republic of China as a condition of these nations participating in the global web of economic transactions. Moreover equal rights of contract are fundamental to the principle of non-discrimination. In the United States, equal rights of contract for Blacks are affirmatively protected by 42 USC 1981, a civil rights statute passed after the abolition of slavery in the United States.[2]

Conflict between property rights and rights of contract. A recurring challenge for decision makers is how to balance conflicting rights of property owners as well as parties to a contract. Historically, property and rights of contract are considered a conservative approach to rights. For example, the United States Supreme Court has invoked employer property rights and rights of contract to overturn the expansion of legislated rights of employees, such as the right of workers to unionize and bargain collectively.[3] For example, yellow dog contracts, which limited workers' right to unionize,[4] were prohibited by the Erdman Act of 1898, but this law was struck down by the Supreme Court in 1908 on the grounds that it interfered with the parties' freedom of contract and the employer's property rights.[5] Thereafter, the Supreme Court applied antitrust laws to unions, undermining the expanding right of workers to unionize and bargain collectively. While the Supreme Court developed a "rule of reason" standard in applying the Sherman Anti-Trust Act (SATA) to business combinations,[6] it applied the SATA to the organizing activities of labor unions as control over supply of goods in inter-state commerce.[7] Casting the organizing activities of labor unions as control over the supply and price of labor effectively undermined the ability of workers to unionize.[8] The National Labor Relations Act was passed in 1935; it affirmatively protected the right of workers to unionize. The constitutionality of the National Labor Relations Act was challenged, but the law was ultimately affirmed by the United States Supreme Court in the teeth of a threat by President Franklin Delano Roosevelt to "pack the court."

Moreover, certain contracts may be illegal, so that parties are prohibited from agreeing on their terms. For example, the Taft-Hartley Act of 1947, amending the Wagner Act, prohibited the closed shop and permitted the union shop but allowed states by referendum to prohibit even the union shop.[9] Courts may also determine the enforceability of contracts. For example, in New Jersey, the Supreme Court decided that surrogate parent contracts are unenforceable; thus, although surrogate parent contracts are not made illegal, if the surrogate mother refuses to convey the custody of her birth child, the courts will not enforce the terms of the contract.[10]

### New Property Rights and Human Rights

New property rights and human rights are evolving. Most of us sustain our lives not by living from the returns generated by our ownership of capital or our ownership of land but by the fruit of our labor. We own our hands and our bodies and live from the fruit of our labor, which includes knowledge work.[11]

Jobs and education become the basis for people's income earning capacity. A person's job and education are fundamental to their economic well-being. However, the right to an education and the right to a job are not established rights, like property rights and rights of contract. Moreover, our right to Social Security, which provides income in the event of disability and in retirement, and to Medicare, which provides medical care during retirement are evolving as *new property rights*.

These newly recognized new property rights sometime conflict with traditional individual property rights. For example, the Supreme Court of New Jersey has interpreted the New Jersey Constitution's equal protection clause to require equal access to education. The New Jersey Supreme Court stated that funding education on the basis of property taxes is unconstitutional; richer towns had better education systems when schools were funded by municipal property taxes, while poorer towns were disadvantaged. The New Jersey Supreme Court required a statewide tax as the basis to fund the New Jersey public schools. The solution adopted was the New Jersey income tax to fund the New Jersey public schools.[12] However, there is no federally recognized right to an equal education.[13]

In addition, there is no "guarantee" of employment in the United States, and the Congress struggles with employment policy. For example, the predominant employment relationship is "at will" in the US, and unemployment is predominantly a problem of the individual person who is unemployed. However, there are significant differences across countries about the right to work. For example, in spring 2006, France was gripped by strikes because legislation was passed that adversely affected younger workers' rights to their jobs: workers under age 26 years who had worked for their company less than two years could be laid off without cause, in contrast to the usual procedures for layoffs under French law.[14] The law was eventually revoked after the widespread social movements that occurred in France.

Some rights have been recognized as fundamental human rights. Thus, for example, the United Nations identified basic human rights and is pressing for a global recognition of these rights, irrespective of the form of government or its governing documents. The right to own property is considered a fundamental human right in the UN Declaration of Human Rights.

Employers are faced with the challenge of respecting and implementing fundamental human rights of their employees and perhaps other stakeholders. For example, Unocal was charged with responsibility for the human rights violations by the Myanmar (Burmese) government in the construction of the natural gas pipeline across Burma. Although the responsibility of Unocal for the human rights violations was never fully litigated, Unocal decided to settle the case after the Ninth Circuit Court of Appeals permitted the litigation to go forward. A fuller consideration of the dilemma faced by Unocal is given in the end of chapter case. Challenges of respecting worker rights is considered in Chapters 10 and 11 on labor markets.

### Justice Standards

A *justice standard* is an alternative to a rights standard for deciding ethical dilemmas. Justice standards are based on two perspectives: procedural due process and distributive justice. *Procedural due process* addresses whether a fairness standard is met by the actions taken in a controversy or disputed situation. Procedural due process addresses the fairness of the dispute resolution process itself, such as the impartiality of the decision maker in the controversy. The United States Constitution in its Fifth, Fourteenth and Sixth Amendments, guarantees procedural due process.[15] The Fourteen Amendment guarantees US citizens that they may not be deprived of life, liberty or property without due process of law; however, with due process, one can be deprived of life, liberty and property. The Fourteenth Amendment also promises the equal protection of the laws to United States citizens, establishing a principle of non-discrimination in the application of law. The Fifth Amendment promises procedural due process in federal proceedings while the Sixth Amendment establishes the right to trial by a jury of one's peers in criminal proceedings.

The concept of equal protection is expansive and undergoing evolution in its application. For example, in June 2003, the United States Supreme Court struck down a Texas law prohibiting homosexual relations.[16] The Texas law was struck down as violating the Due Process Clause of the Fourteenth Amendment. In the aftermath of the *Lawrence v. Texas* decision, Wal-Mart, the largest private employer in the United States, announced that it would not discriminate against its workers based on their sexual orientation.[17] Although Title VII law constrains employers against gender discrimination, discrimination based on sexual orientation is not prohibited by federal law, so that companies must make choices about their policies affecting their gay and lesbian employees. Certain states, such as New Jersey, prohibit discrimination based on sexual orientation. Moreover, the Massachusetts Supreme Court interpreted the equal protection clause of the Massachusetts Constitution as requiring gay marriage; homosexual individuals must have the same protections of the laws as heterosexual individuals.[18] Massachusetts was the first state to do so.

*Distributive justice* is oriented to who gets what and how much. Conflicts among stakeholders arise about what is an appropriate distribution of the goods and rewards of society or, conversely, the bads of society. John Rawls developed a provocative theory on the just distribution of social goods and bads.

**John Rawls, *A Theory of Justice*.** John Rawls, in his book, *A Theory of Justice*,[19] proposes an innovative approach to distributive justice. Many philosophers as well as politicians have addressed the question of what constitutes a fair or just society. For example, Karl Marx protested the social dysfunctions and social inequalities associated with the rise of capitalism in the early stages of the industrial revolution. In the twentieth century, Russia and China developed communist systems to attempt to construct a fair or just society, attempting to minimize differentials in wealth, power, privilege and status.

Rawls addresses the question: must differentials in wealth, power, privilege and status be minimized in order to have a just society? Do we have to seek the lowest common denominator? Russia and Communist China have been unsuccessful in creating a classless society, in part because leadership requires differentials in power and access to resources; with these differentials, differences in status also become magnified.[20] Also, differences in natural abilities and talents are inherent in human populations. The demise of the USSR and the transition of the People's Republic of China to a market-driven economy reveal that the socialist or communist systems did not succeed in establishing classless societies, wherein differentials in wealth, power, privilege and status are abolished.

Rawls asks the question: under what conditions would the privileged or top dogs as well as underdogs buy into the social arrangements? Typically, top dogs have a vested interest in status quo, while underdogs foment change. Rawls proposes to construct a society in everyone would "buy into" the social arrangements, irrespective of whether they were born as top dogs or underdogs.[21]

Rawls' solution is that a just society is one in which the differentials accruing to the top dogs work to the advantage of the underdogs, so that the less privileged benefit by the greater wealth, power, privilege and status of the top dogs. However, this principle is a limiting factor on permissible differentials in the distribution of goods. Any differentials in wealth, power, privilege or status that do not work to the benefit of the underdogs would be taxed away under a distributive justice principle.[22] Rawls' solution does not require the minimization of differentials in social goods.

**Utilitarianism.** *Utilitarianism* evaluates a solution as just as that choice that creates the greatest good to the greatest number of individuals. A utilitarian standard might lead to conclusion, in the Johns Manville case for example, that it would be ethical to continue production of asbestos products. The executives of the Johns Manville Company might have invoked a utilitarian standard in addressing the issue whether asbestos should be used for industrial products requiring fire-retardant properties, even after they knew that asbestos can harm workers who mined and produced asbestos products. Moreover, the bankruptcy settlement of Johns Manville arguably created a just solution under a utilitarian analysis: were the fund established by the bankruptcy settlement not have been created, early claimants would have exhausted the resources of the firm; the bankruptcy permitted latter claimants to be compensated too.

However, application of a utilitarian standard can trammel the rights of minorities, since minorities are by definition not members of the majority served by the utilitarian solution.

### Minority Rights

A majoritarian or utilitarian standard may trammel *rights of minorities*. The UN Declaration on Human Right speaks to the rights of minorities. The US Bill of Rights, the first ten amendments to the Constitution of 1789, guarantees rights of minorities. Moreover, under a constitutionally based system of checks and balances, the role of the judiciary is to protect minorities from having their rights trammeled by a majoritarian standard. In addition, an important role of a leader to is to protect voices of minorities. Small group studies show that groups in which the correct solution was held by a minority voice within the group adopt correct solutions more frequently if they have an effective leader compared to groups without an effective leader. A rights perspective on the asbestos problem at Johns Manville would require that the safety of workers who mined and manufactured asbestos products would be protected and the workers give informed consent to work under the hazardous condition, even if the public benefits from the use of asbestos in public buildings as a fire retardant.

### Other Standards by which to Judge Ethical Dilemmas

#### The Disclosure Rule

The Disclosure Rule is a test whether some action withstands the light of day. The *Disclosure Rule* goes to materiality of information; information is material if a prudent decision maker or investor would want to have this information to make the decision or investment. Beech-Nut apple juice fraudulently advertised its baby juice as 100% natural.[23] Beech-Nut executives, in the face of an order to submit juice samples to the New York Department of Agriculture, moved the subpoenaed product under cover of darkness to New Jersey, thus creating a barrier to the New York Department of Agriculture's jurisdiction to test the product. The act of transferring the apple juice under cover of night across state lines might have created feedback to the Beech-Nut executives that something was awry; that they cannot in good faith argue that the apple juice is not adulterated.

Likewise the disclosure rule would have been useful to Philip Morris Tobacco when it undertook a country-specific study of Eastern European markets, promoting the advantages to the Czech Republic of having low barriers to the importation of cigarettes because the polity saves $1,200 by each smoker's early death.[24] The American Legacy Foundation ran an ad carried by all major newspapers, except the *Wall Street Journal*, which disclosed the study and its marketing pitch. Philip Morris apologized in a press release to the *Wall Street Journal* and immediately to put an end to future studies.[25] The disclosure rule would have prevented Philip Morris' commissioning the study and saved it the great embarrassment caused by the disclosure of its marketing plan.

#### The Categorical Imperative

The *categorical imperative* or the principle of universalizability of Immanuel Kant addresses the ethics of behavior which, when generalized, might harm the social fabric and whether an individual would make exception for himself or herself given special circumstances. The test is whether the exception could be generalized to others similarly situated. The rule of *universalizability* extends a similar right of act to others similarly situated and serves as a test as to whether behavior is ethical. For example, stealing in general is wrong or immoral, but stealing to prevent yourself or others from starvation is ethically permissible. The principle of universalizability was illustrated in *Doctor Zhivago*, when Zhivago is stealing wood to burn to keep his family warm during the Moscow winter; his brother, an officer of the Red army, sees him, but lets him go, reflecting that one man stealing wood is pathetic, but all men stealing wood is dangerous.

Also, the ethics of polluting and dumping are subject to the test of universalizability. For example, many homeowners dump leftover gasoline for lawn mowers at the end of the mowing season, rather than take the gasoline to the recycling/disposal center, which also charges the homeowner for the costs of disposal. The problem with simply dumping the gasoline, even in one's own yard, is that the gasoline can seep down to the water table and pollute the groundwater. Although the damage caused by a single instance of dumping gasoline might be tolerated by the environment, if all homeowners disposed of their gasoline in this manner, a major problem of groundwater contamination would likely develop. Therefore, dumping does not pass the universalizability test.

## Reciprocity or Test of Reversibility

Reciprocity or *test of reversibility* embodies the rule, "Do unto Others as You Would Have Them Do unto You"—or your family and loved ones. The test of reciprocity, or reflexivity, is another aspect of Kant's categorical imperative. The Ford Pinto case is an example of failure of *test of reciprocity*. The Ford executives who decided to market Ford Pinto knowing that it was subject to fire upon low speed rear-end collision would not make the decision to manufacture the car with this defect, then pay damages, were they themselves, their wives or children to be burned then be paid damages. The test of reciprocity or reversibility would clarify the ethics of the cost–benefit approach Ford used with the Pinto.[26]

## Feelings about a Choice

The *gut test* tests the ethics of a decision based on the decision maker's emotional response to his or her choice. The *red face test* is a heuristic rule this author learned from her mentor at NYU Law School; I have found the red face test gives particularly useful guidance for making innovative arguments in my legal practice. Attorneys push the envelope; the red face test queries whether the attorney can make an innovative argument without blushing. The *gag test* is somewhat similar to the red face test. The gag test queries whether the attorney can make an innovative argument without choking on his or her words.

The "*smell test*" can be useful in addressing questions of conflicts of interest and the appearance of impropriety. For example, does the award of a contract by the board of a company to a board member pass the "smell test"?

Each of the feeling-based tests, the gut test, the red face test, the gag test, and the smell test, is based on an emotional response to an ethical decision and uses self-based feedback to the decision maker. The feeling-based tests tie to the managerial skill, emotional intelligence. The emergence of emotional intelligence as a key managerial skill lends authenticity and supports the use of feelings-based tests of the ethics of a decision.[27]

## Personal Integrity

### Lawrence Kohlberg's Stages of Moral Reasoning

Lawrence Kohlberg has articulated a developmental theory of moral decision making.[28] Kohlberg has identified stages of moral reasoning related to an individual's development: a pre-conventional stage, a conventional stage and a post-conventional or principled stage.[29] These stages parallel the stages of cognitive development identified by Jean Piaget.[30]

At the pre-conventional level, children identify as moral those rules established by their parents as right or wrong.[31] That is good that satisfies the child's needs. In the second stage of pre-conventional moral reasoning, the individual engages in social exchange and follows rules in his or her self-interest. The pre-conventional level is a stage which lasts up to age nine years, when the individual is focused on himself or herself. The conventional level of moral reasoning occurs between ages nine years and adolescence. At the conventional level, children start to understand the point of view of the other; they understand expectations of their reference group; morality is seen as conforming to the obligations and expectations of their reference group, including parents, teachers and their peers. The post-conventional level of moral reasoning can be achieved by adolescents and adults and corresponds to Piaget's cognitive stage of formal reasoning. In the post-conventional level of moral reasoning, individuals understand that different groups have different standards of rules and laws; morality is seen as upholding the social contract of one's group. Utilitarianism, achieving the greatest good for the greatest number, is characteristic of Kohlberg's first stage of post-conventional moral reasoning. In the second stage of post-conventional moral reasoning, the individual makes decisions based on universal ethical principles, involving individual rights and justice principles.

### Ethics of Care

The *ethics of care*[32] approach, developed from the criticism that Kohlberg's stages of moral reasoning, with its emphasis on rights and obligations, is gender biased.[33] Carol Gilligan, a professor of education at Harvard University who had an interest in the psycho-social development of adolescent girls, conducted extensive interviews with young women. Gilligan developed her approach from these interviews, as *In a Different Voice*.[34] Later Gilligan interviewed women considering abortion after *Roe v. Wade*, the United States Supreme Court decision that decided that women have a legal right to abortion.[35] The *Roe v. Wade* decision grounded its approach in a privacy right inferred in the United States Constitution and a woman's right to autonomy over her own body.[36]

However, Gilligan found that the women considering whether to have an abortion after the legalization of abortion by the *Roe v. Wade* decision were not basing their decision on their rights but on their relationships. "I was listening at the time to women who were pregnant and thinking about abortion in the immediate aftermath of the *Roe v. Wade* decision. Women's concerns were often driven by experiences of disconnection which rendered relationships difficult to maintain, but their voices carried a sense of connection, of living and acting in a web of relationships which went against the grain of the prevailing discourse of individual rights and freedom."[37]

**Duty of Care.** A duty of care is owed by a parent to a child, by spouses to each other, by a teacher to a student, by a manufacturer to its customers. A duty of care is recognized in the law of torts. A tort is an injury to another that is actionable at law. A tort is committed when: 1) a duty of care is owed to another; 2) that duty of care is breached; and 3) an injury is incurred that is proximately caused by the breach of the duty of care owed to the other person. There is no duty of rescue among strangers, if the person in peril was not put in peril by the act of the other stranger; however, if a stranger acts as a Good Samaritan, the rescuer owes a duty not to further injury the imperiled person by the rescuer's negligence. The concept of duty of care ties the ethics of care to concepts of rights and justice. Moreover, care is a virtue fundamental to good human development.[38] Care ethics would urge the view that caring and caring relationships are essential to human flourishing, a concept central to virtue ethics.

### Virtue Ethics

*Virtue ethics* focuses on the character of the individual actor or decision maker. Virtue ethics is based on Plato and Aristotle's examination of the basis for well-being in the republic or state.[39] The goal is human flourishing. Human flourishing is achieved by citizens of virtue or good character who exercise practical wisdom.

There are different perspectives on virtues, defined as mind sets, habits or dispositions to act by a human agent. Thomas Aquinas, for example, identifies "cardinal virtues," including prudence, temperance, justice and courage or fortitude. Vices are also identified; the Christian tradition identifies seven "capital" or "deadly" sins, including greed, lust, anger, envy, sloth, gluttony and pride. Other traditions identify important or fundamental virtues differently. For example, Robert Thurman, a professor at Columbia University and a noted Buddhist scholar, in his recent book, *Infinite Life: Seven Virtues for Living Well*, identifies the Buddhist approach to virtues as: generosity, morality, tolerance, creativity, contemplation, wisdom and art (of living).[40]

### Personal Vision

Personal vision, a habit of "highly effective people,"[41] is a component of managerial decision making. Personal vision and values underlie the individual manager's values and decision framework. A cognitive-based approach to decision making, Image Theory, considers values and personal principles the basis for choice and decision making.[42] Decisions are adopted, according to Image

Theory, only if a particular choice is compatible with the individual's values, goals and strategies. Individual managers might very productively engage in a process of values clarification, surfacing their decision framework and the personal values they would use to decide ethical dilemmas.

### *Conflicts of Interest*

A touchstone of personal integrity is the ability and willingness of an individual to recognize and to resolve conflicts of interest. The tests of ethical decision making that use an individual's emotional response to a decision, the red face test, the gag test and the gut test, require an informed or sensitive conscience.[43] The Freudian defense mechanisms, denial, rationalization and reaction formation, can interfere with an individual's recognition and coping with conflict of interest issues. As discussed in Chapter 13, Corporate Responsibility—What Went Wrong? Lessons from the Dark Side, many of the corporate scandals were related to fraudulent earnings management practices, which justified stock price increases and that were tied to executive compensation, a policy that creates a conflict of interest between the personal interests of the manager and the interests of the enterprise in transparency and fair dealing in the market. Conflicts of interest were an important factor in the Enron failure; for example, the Board of Directors suspended the Enron code of conduct about conflicts of interest.

Moreover, it is possible that the conflicts of interest between patients and shareholders in for-profit medical enterprise is so fundamental that the best interests of patients cannot be served by a for-profit organizational structure.[44] The drive to cut costs in order to maximize profits, serving the interests of providers of equity capital, may so directly conflict with the best interests of patients that the for-profit medical services organizations may not be an appropriate form or organization for the delivery of health care services. It may be that the conflicts of interest between patients, stockholders and managers are such that the interests of patients become sacrificed to the interests of stockholders and managers of the for-profit medical services organizations. This dilemma and conflict of interest has been recognized in the public health literature, where studies show a higher mortality rate and other adverse indicants of patient care for patients in for-profit hospitals.[45]

## Deciding Ethical Dilemmas

In deciding specific ethical dilemmas, an individual must decide which standard of judgment is appropriate for specific cases or in specific situations. The decision maker can test the standards of judgment and undertake an ethical evaluation of each standard using stakeholder analysis. Using a decision matrix, managers can evaluate whether the proposed act is ethical under a given standard. The decision matrix should list the alternative standards of decision making as well as the stakeholders and determine whether or not the proposed action is ethical as to each stakeholder. See Table 3.1 for a method to test choices about ethical dilemmas.

Table 3.1 Which Standards of Judgment for Deciding Ethical Dilemmas?

| | Stakeholder | | | | | | | | | | |
|---|---|---|---|---|---|---|---|---|---|---|---|
| | Customer | Employees | Shareholders | Executive Management | Suppliers of debt capital | Suppliers of raw materials | Competitors | Community where the firm operates | Environment | Regulators | Others Impacted by Management Actions (specify) |
| Standard of Judgment | Ethical? What acts are required by this standard? | Ethical? What acts are required by this standard? | Ethical? What acts are required by this standard? | Ethical? What acts are required by this standard? | Ethical? What acts are required by this standard? | Ethical? What acts are required by this standard? | Ethical? What acts are required by this standard? | Ethical? What acts are required by this standard? | Ethical? What acts are required by this standard? | Ethical? What acts are required by this standard? | Ethical? What acts are required by this standard? |
| Property rights | | | | | | | | | | | |
| Rights of contract | | | | | | | | | | | |
| Human Rights | | | | | | | | | | | |
| Procedural Justice | | | | | | | | | | | |
| Distributive Justice | | | | | | | | | | | |
| Utilitarianism | | | | | | | | | | | |
| Disclosure Rule | | | | | | | | | | | |
| Universalizability | | | | | | | | | | | |
| Reversibility | | | | | | | | | | | |
| Red face test/ Gag test/ Smell test | | | | | | | | | | | |
| Gut test | | | | | | | | | | | |
| Ethics of Care | | | | | | | | | | | |
| Virtue Ethics | | | | | | | | | | | |

**View:** High Noon

## Chapter Discussion Questions

1.  Identify a specific dilemma or controversy and discuss whether an analysis using a rights-based approach yields a different outcome than a justice-based approach.
2.  Why didn't Kant's categorical imperative constrain the Ford executives in their decisions about the defective design of the Ford Pinto?
3.  Why did Phillip Morris executives apologize for their pitch to the Czech Republic after the publication of the market analysis? Why didn't they anticipate the response of the public?
4.  Identify and analyze conflicts of interest that you face in your work.
5.  Develop proposals to remediate the organizational culture of a specific firm that has engaged in significant wrong-doing.

## Notes

1  Article 17: (1) everyone has the right to own property alone or in association with others. (2) No one shall be arbitrarily deprived of his property. "The Universal Declaration of Human Rights," *The United Nations*, last modified 2014, http://www.un.org/en/documents/udhr/index.shtml.

2  In the United States, the Thirteenth, Fourteenth, and Fifteenth Amendments, together known as the reconstruction amendments, abolished the institution of slavery in the United States. These amendments were passed after the conclusion of the Civil War. Slavery had been abolished by the Emancipation Proclamation, an executive order of President Lincoln under his emergency war powers. See the movie *Lincoln*, directed by Stephen Spielberg (Touchstone Pictures, 2012) for a dramatization of the passage of the Thirteenth Amendment abolishing involuntary servitude (slavery) in the United States.

   42 USC § 1981. Equal rights under the law

   (a) Statement of equal rights. All persons within the jurisdiction of the United States shall have the same right in every State and Territory to make and enforce contracts, to sue, be parties, give evidence, and to the full and equal benefit of all laws and proceedings for the security of persons and property as is enjoyed by white citizens, and shall be subject to like punishment, pains, penalties, taxes, licenses, and exactions of every kind, and to no other.

   (b) "Make and enforce contracts" defined. For purposes of this section, the term "make and enforce contracts" includes the making, performance, modification, and termination of contracts, and the enjoyment of all benefits, privileges, terms, and conditions of the contractual relationship.

   (c) Protection against impairment. The rights protected by this section are protected against impairment by nongovernmental discrimination and impairment under color of State law.

   Act May 31, 1870, ch 114, § 16, 16 Stat. 144.

3  The National Labor Relations Act, also called the Wagner Act, was passed in 1935. The Wagner Act affirmatively protected the right of workers to unionize. The

constitutionality of the National Labor Relations Act was affirmed by the United States Supreme Court in the teeth of a threat by President Franklin Delano Roosevelt to "pack the court," i.e., to pass an amendment to the US Constitution increasing the number of justices on the Supreme Court.

4  Yellow dog contracts were promises made by employees, as a condition of employment, that the employee was not a member of a union or, if the employee was already a member of a union, that he would quit the union.

5  *Adair v. U.S.*, 208 U.S. 161 (1908) struck down section of the Erdman Act of 1898, prohibiting employers from using yellow dog contract in the railroad industry.

6  For example, American Sugar Refining Company controlled 98% of the sugar refining market; Standard Oil Company controlled 85–90% of US refining capacity, and American Tobacco controlled 97% of the production of domestic cigarettes. See, *Standard Oil Company of New Jersey v. United States*, 221 U.S. 1 (1911); *United States v. American Tobacco Company*, 221 U.S. 106 (1911). See also, *United States v. E.C. Knight Company*, 156 U.S. 1 (1895), *United States v. United Shoe Machinery Co.*, 227 U.S. 32 (1913) and *United States v. United States Steel Corporation*, 251 U.S. 417 (1920). Benjamin J. Taylor and Fred Witney, *U.S. Labor-Relations Law: Historical Development* (Englewood Cliffs, NJ: Prentice Hall, 1992), 48–50.

7  *Loewe v. Lawlor*, 208 U.S. 274 (1908).

8  The Clayton Anti-Trust Act, billed as labor's Magna Carta, was passed in 1914, specifically to prevent the application of the SATA to the activities of labor unions. However the Clayton Anti-Trust Act itself was narrowly construed to protect only the activities of workers in a direct employer-employee relationship by *Duplex Printing Press Co. v. Deering*, 254 U.S. 443 (1921), whereas the interests of unionized workers lay in extending union contracts to employers in the same industry that were not organized by the unions. The force of the Clayton Anti-Trust Act was thus undermined by extending its protections only to workers only in a direct employer-employee relationship and not to those workers with an interest in the working conditions at the target employer. The Norris La Guardia Act of 1932 was drafted specifically to overcome the narrow interpretation of the Clayton Anti-Trust Act. The Norris La Guardia Act outlawed the yellow dog contract and prohibited federal courts from issuing injunctions in labor disputes in situations where workers had an interest in the labor dispute. It was succeeded by the National Labor Relations Act, which granted workers an affirmative right to organize and bargain collectively. The National Labor Relations Act was passed during the 1930s depression to promote industrial peace and interstate commerce. Although there was some question initially whether the Supreme Court would uphold the constitutionality of the Wagner Act, then President Franklin Delano Roosevelt threatened to "pack the court" by passing an amendment to the US Constitution increasing the number of justice on the Supreme Court. The Supreme Court in fact upheld the constitutionality of the Wagner Act.

9  The difference between a union shop and a closed shop relates to when the employees join the union. A closed shop requires that employees be members of the union prior to their hire, in effect requiring the employer to hire out of the union hall. The union shop requires employees to join the union as a condition of employment but permits employees to join the union after they are hired by the company. Right to work states are those states, all in the South, which have prohibited the union shop. See, Taft Harley Act, Section 14b.

10  This was known as the "Baby M" case, Supreme Court of New Jersey, 109 N.J. 396, 1988.

11  Karl Marx protested the status of workers who owned only their hands, i.e., the labor factor of production, at the time when capital was becoming a key resource in the production process. The exploitation of labor during the Industrial Revolution was the subject of Karl Marx's *Das Kapital*.

12  In addition, the New Jersey Supreme Court has required richer towns to have "affordable housing."

13  *San Antonio Independent School District v. Rodriguez*, 411 U.S. 1 (1973).

14  Elaine Sciolino, "French Protests Over Youth Labor Law Spread to 150 Cities and Towns," *New York Times*, March 19, 2006, http://www.nytimes.com/2006/03/19/international/europe/19paris.html?_r=0.

15  The Fourteenth Amendment is one of the reconstruction amendments. The Thirteenth, Fourteenth and Fifteenth Amendments to the United States Constitution, together known as the reconstruction amendments, abolish slavery and promise due process and the equal protection of the laws to the former slaves who became newly recognized U.S. citizens.

16  *Lawrence v. Texas*, 539 U.S. 558, '123 S. Ct. 2472 (2003). *Lawrence v. Texas* over-ruled a prior Supreme Court decision upholding the constitutionality of a Georgia sodomy statute, *Bowers v. Hardwick*, 478 U.S. 186 (1986).

17  Joshua Partlow, "Wal-Mart Forbids Bias Against Gays: New Policy, Hailed by Rights Groups, Follows Corporate Trend" *Washington Post*, Thursday, July 3, 2003.

18  Supreme Judicial Court of Massachusetts.
Opinions of The Justices to the Senate.
Feb. 3, 2004.
Background: Senate requested opinion on constitutionality of bill which prohibits same-sex couples from entering into marriage, but allows them to form civil unions with all benefits, protections, rights, and responsibilities of marriage. Holding: The Supreme Judicial Court held as a matter of first impression that the bill violates the equal protection and due process requirements of the state constitution.
Question answered.

19  John Rawls, *A Theory of Justice* (Cambridge, MA: Belknap, Harvard University Press, 1971).

20  Reinhard Bendix and Seymour Martin Lipset, ed., *Class, Status and Power: A Reader in Social Stratification* (New York: Free Press, 1963).

21  Rawls invokes a "veil of ignorance," whereby people do not know their position in the social hierarchy.

22  For example, the tax proposals of Jeremy Rifkin in his book, *The End of Work: The Decline of the Global Labor Force and the Dawn of the Post-Market Era* (New York: Putnam, 1995) and of Robert Reich in his book, *The Work of Nations: Preparing Ourselves for 21st Century Capitalism* (New York: Vintage, 1992), although not central to their major theses, address distributive justice issues and recommend tax-based solutions.

23  Leonard Buder, "Beech-Nut Is Fined $2 Million for Sale of Fake Apple Juice," *New York Times*, Nov. 14, 1987.

24  Lee Dembart, "Tobacco Giant's Analysis Says Premature Deaths Cut Costs in Pensions and Health Care: Critics Assail Philip Morris Report on Smoking," *New York Times*, July 18, 2001.

25  Gordon Fairclough, "Philip Morris Apologizes for Report Touting Benefits of Smokers' Deaths," *Wall Street Journal*, July 26, 2001.

26  Mark Dowie, "Pinto Madness," *Mother Jones*, Sept./Oct. 1977.

27  James Goleman, *Emotional Intelligence: Why It Can Matter More Than IQ* (New York: Bantam, 1995).

28  Lawrence Kohlberg, "Moral Stages and Moralization: The Cognitive-Developmental Approach," in *Moral Development and Behavior: Theory, Research, and Social Issues*, ed. Thomas Lickona, consulting eds. Gilbert Geis and Lawrence Kohlberg (New York: Holt, Rinehart and Winston, 1976). Lawrence Kohlberg, *The Philosophy of Moral Development* (New York: Harper & Row, 1981). Carol Gilligan, *In a Different Voice: Psychological Theory and Women's Development* (Cambridge: Harvard University Press, 1982). Jeanne M. Logsdon and Kristi Yuthas, "Corporate Social Performance, Stakeholder Orientation and Organizational Moral Development," *Journal of Business Ethics* 16 (1997): 11–36.

29  Kohlberg, "Moral Stages and Moralization." See also Kohlberg, *The Philosophy of Moral Development.*

30  Piaget, in his *Theory of Cognitive Development*, has identified specific stages in the cognitive development of children. Kohlberg has identified specific stages in the moral development of children. Individuals' cognitive development and their ability to engage in moral reasoning and decision making are interdependent.

31  The super-ego or conscience develops in the child in interaction with the parent. The voice of the parent becomes internalized as the super-ego or conscience. In transactional analysis, the super-ego is called the parent. See Thomas Anthony Harris, *I'm OK, You're OK* (New York: Harper & Row, 1969).

32  Carol Gilligan, *In a Different Voice.*

33  "When I began the work that led to In a Different Voice (1982), the framework was invisible. To study psychology at that time was like seeing a picture without seeing the frame, and the picture of the human world had become so large and all-encompassing that it looked like reality or a mirror of reality, rather than a representation. It was startling then to discover that women for the most part were not included in research on psychological development, or when included were marginalized or interpreted within a theoretical bias where the child and the adult were assumed to be male and the male was taken as the norm. . . . Bringing women's voices into psychology posed an interpretive challenge: how to listen to women in women's terms, rather than assimilating women's voices to the existing theoretical framework. And this led to a paradigm shift."

Gilligan, "Hearing the Difference: Theorizing the Connection," *Hypatia* 10, no. 2 (Spring 1995): 120.

34  Gilligan, *In a Different Voice.*

35  Gilligan, "Hearing the Difference," 120.

36  410 U.S. 113 (1973).

37  Gilligan, "Hearing the Difference," 120.

38  Raja Halwani, "Care Ethics and Virtue Ethics," *Hypatia* 18, no. 3 (Summer 2003): 161.

39  Plato, *The Republic.*

40  Robert Thurman, *Infinite Life: Seven Virtues for Living Well* (New York: Riverhead Books, 2004). Generosity, morality, tolerance, creativity, contemplation, wisdom and art (of living).

41  Stephen Covey, *Seven Habits of Highly Effective People* (New York: Free Press, 1989). See also Peter Senge, *The Fifth Discipline: The Art and Practice of the Learning Organization* (New York: Doubleday/Currency, 1990).

42  Kevin Morrell, "Decision Making and Business Ethics: The Implication of Using Image Theory in Preference to Rational Choice," *Journal of Business Ethics* 50, no. 3 (March 2004): 239–52.

43  The conscience is the super-ego, in terms of Freudian theory of personality.

44   Vince Galloro, "Regulators Scrutinize Oklahoma Nursing Home Company," *Modern Healthcare* 31, no. 16 (April 16, 2001): 17.
45   Charlene Harrington, Steffie Woolhandler, Joseph Multan, Helen Carrillo, and David Himmelstein, "Does Investor Ownership of Nursing Homes Compromise the Quality of Care?," *American Journal of Public Health* 91, no. 9 (September 2001): 1452–55. See also Steffie Woolhandler and David Himmelstein "Payments for Care at Private For-Profit and Private Not-for-Profit Hospitals: A Systematic Review and Meta-analysis," *Canadian Medical Association Journal,* 170 no. 12 (June 2004): 1817–24.

## End of Chapter Case: Unocal in Myanmar and Human Rights Violations

The *Myanmar v. Unocal* case raises the issue of global corporate citizenship. Unocal was part of an international joint venture to mine oil and gas and to construct a pipeline across Myanmar (formerly Burma) to Thailand. Citizens of Myanmar complained that they were forced to work on an oil and gas pipeline project managed by Unocal. The military government provided security for the project. The security forces allegedly coerced villagers in Myanmar to work on the pipeline project, including helicopter pads for the Unocal executives. Some of the workers forced to work on the project sued Unocal in the United States under the Alien Tort Act. It raised the question whether a company is liable for the human rights violations committed by the security forces of a less developed country when the company knew of these violations or whether a company can "pass the buck" and deny culpability for human rights violations against its workforce done by others who were engaged to protect the project being done by the company. A United States Court of Appeals ruled that Unocal may be liable for the human rights violations that occurred on the project. The case then settled.

JOHN DOE I, individually & as Administrator of the Estate of his deceased child Baby Doe I, & on behalf of all others similarly situated, et. al. v. UNOCAL CORPORATION, a California Corporation; TOTAL S.A., a Foreign Corporation; JOHN IMLE, an individual; ROGER C. BEACH, an individual, Defendants-Appellees.

UNITED STATES COURT OF APPEALS FOR THE NINTH CIRCUIT
395 F.3d 932

December 3, 2001, Argued and Submitted, Pasadena, California September 18, 2002, Filed

**Prior History:** Appeal from the United States District Court for the Central District of California. D.C. No. CV-96–06959-RSWL. D.C. No. CV-96–06112-RSWL. Richard A. Paez and Ronald S.W. Lew, District Judges, Presiding

**Subsequent History:** Vacated by, Rehearing, en banc, granted by Doe v. Unocal Corp., 395 F.3d 978 (9th Cir., 2003)

**Related case:** 403 F.3d 708 (9th Cir. 2005)

Order: The district court opinion in Doe v. Unocal Corp., 110 F. Supp. 2d 1294 (C.D. Cal. 2000), [granting defendant Unocal Corp. motion for summary judgment] is VACATED.

**OPINION:** PREGERSON, Circuit Judge:

This case involves human rights violations that allegedly occurred in Myanmar, formerly known as Burma. Villagers from the Tenasserim region in Myanmar allege that the Defendants directly or indirectly subjected the villagers to forced labor, murder, rape, and torture when the Defendants constructed a gas pipeline through the Tenasserim region. The villagers base their claims on the Alien Tort Claims Act, 28 U.S.C. § 1350 . . . as well as state law.

The District Court, through dismissal and summary judgment, resolved all of Plaintiffs' federal claims in favor of the Defendants. For the following reasons, we reverse in part and affirm in part the District Court's rulings.

## I. Factual and Procedural Background

A.   Unocal's Investment in a Natural Gas Project in Myanmar.

Burma has been ruled by a military government since 1958. In 1988, a new military government, State Law and Order Restoration Council ("the Myanmar Military"), took control and renamed the country Myanmar. The Myanmar Military established a state owned company, Myanmar Oil and Gas Enterprise ("Myanmar Oil"), to produce and sell the nation's oil and gas resources.

In 1992, Myanmar Oil licensed the French oil company Total S.A. ("Total") to produce, transport, and sell natural gas from deposits in the Yadana Field off the coast of Myanmar ("the Project"). Total set up a subsidiary, Total Myanmar Exploration and Production ("Total Myanmar"), for this purpose. The Project consisted of a Gas Production Joint Venture, which would extract the natural gas out of the Yadana Field, and a Gas Transportation Company, which would construct and operate a pipeline to transport the natural gas from the coast of Myanmar through the interior of the country to Thailand.

Also in 1992, Unocal Corporation and its wholly owned subsidiary Defendant-Appellant Union Oil Company of California, collectively referred to below as "Unocal," acquired a 28% interest in the Project from Total. Unocal set up a wholly owned subsidiary, the Unocal Myanmar Offshore Company ("the Unocal Offshore Co."), to hold Unocal's 28% interest in the Gas Production Joint Venture half of the Project. Similarly, Unocal set up another wholly owned subsidiary, the Unocal International Pipeline Corporation ("the Unocal Pipeline Corp."), to hold Unocal's 28% interest in the Gas Transportation Company half of the Project. Myanmar Oil and a Thai government entity, the Petroleum Authority of Thailand Exploration and Production, also acquired interests in the Project. Total Myanmar was appointed Operator of the Gas Production Joint Venture and the Gas Transportation Company. As the Operator, Total Myanmar was responsible, inter alia, for "determining . . . the selection of . . .

employees [and] the hours of work and the compensation to be paid to all . . . employees" in connection with the Project.

B.   Unocal's Knowledge that the Myanmar Military Was Providing Security and Other Services for the Project.

It is undisputed that the Myanmar Military provided security and other services for the Project, and that Unocal knew about this. The pipeline was to run through Myanmar's rural Tenasserim region. The Myanmar Military increased its presence in the pipeline region to provide security and other services for the Project. A Unocal memorandum documenting Unocal's meetings with Total on March 1 and 2, 1995 reflects Unocal's understanding that "four battalions of 600 men each will protect the [pipeline] corridor" and "fifty soldiers will be assigned to guard each survey team." A former soldier in one of these battalions testified at his deposition that his battalion had been formed in 1996 specifically for this purpose. In addition, the Military built helipads and cleared roads along the proposed pipeline route for the benefit of the Project.

There is also evidence sufficient to raise a genuine issue of material fact whether the Project hired the Myanmar Military, through Myanmar Oil, to provide these services, and whether Unocal knew about this. A Production Sharing Contract, entered into by Total Myanmar and Myanmar Oil before Unocal acquired an interest in the Project, provided that "[Myanmar Oil] shall . . . supply[]or make available . . . security protection . . . as may be requested by [Total Myanmar and its assigns]," such as Unocal. Unocal was aware of this agreement. Thus, a May 10, 1995 Unocal "briefing document" states that "according to our contract, the government of Myanmar is responsible for protecting the pipeline." Similarly, in May 1995, a cable from the U.S. Embassy in Rangoon, Myanmar, reported that Unocal On-Site Representative Joel Robinson "stated forthrightly that the companies have hired the Burmese military to provide security for the project."

Unocal disputes that the Project hired the Myanmar Military or, at the least, that Unocal knew about this. For example, Unocal points out that the Production Sharing Contract quoted in the previous paragraph covered only the off-shore Gas Production Joint Venture but not the Gas Transportation Company and the construction of the pipeline which gave rise to the alleged human rights violations. Moreover, Unocal President John Imle stated at his deposition that he knew of "no . . . contractual obligation" requiring the Myanmar Military to provide security for the pipeline construction. Likewise, Unocal CEO Roger Beach stated at his deposition that he also did not know "whether or not Myanmar had a contractual obligation to provide . . . security." Beach further stated that he was not aware of "any support whatsoever of the military[,] . . . either physical or monetary." These assertions by Unocal President Imle and Unocal CEO Beach are called into question by a briefing book which Total prepared for them on the occasion of their April 1996 visit to the Project. The briefing book lists the "numbers of villagers" working as "local helpers hired by battalions," the monthly "amount paid in Kyats" (the currency of Myanmar) to "Project

Helpers," and the "amount in Kyats" expended by the Project on "food rations (Army +Villages)."[1]

Furthermore, there is evidence sufficient to raise a genuine issue of material fact whether the Project directed the Myanmar Military in these activities, at least to a degree, and whether Unocal was involved in this. In May 1995, a cable from the U.S. Embassy in Rangoon reported: [Unocal Representative] Robinson indicated . . . Total/Unocal uses [aerial photos, precision surveys, and topography maps] to show the [Myanmar] military where they need helipads built and facilities secured. . . . Total's security officials meet with military counterparts to inform them of the next day's activities so that soldiers can ensure the area is secure and guard the work perimeter while the survey team goes about its business.

A November 8, 1995 document apparently authored by Total Myanmar stated that "each working group has a security officer . . . to control the army positions." A January 1996 meeting document lists "daily security coordination with the army" as a "working procedure." Similarly, the briefing book that Total prepared for Unocal President Imle and Unocal CEO Beach on the occasion of their April 1996 visit to the Project mentions that "daily meetings" were "held with the tactical commander" of the army. Moreover, on or about August 29, 1996, Unocal (Singapore) Director of Information Carol Scott discussed with Unocal Media Contact and Spokesperson David Garcia via e-mail how Unocal should publicly address the issue of the alleged movement of villages by the Myanmar Military in connection with the pipeline. Scott cautioned Garcia that "by saying we influenced the army not to move a village, you introduce the concept that they would do such a thing; whereas, by saying that no villages have been moved, you skirt the issue of whether it could happen or not." This e-mail is some evidence that Unocal could influence the army not to commit human rights violations, that the army might otherwise commit such violations, and that Unocal knew this.

C.   Unocal's Knowledge that the Myanmar Military Was Allegedly Committing Human Rights Violations in Connection with the Project.

Plaintiffs are villagers from Myanmar's Tenasserim region, the rural area through which the Project built the pipeline. Plaintiffs allege that the Myanmar Military forced them, under threat of violence, to work on and serve as porters for the Project. For instance, John Doe IX testified that he was forced to build a helipad near the pipeline site in 1994 that was then used by Unocal and Total officials who visited the pipeline during its planning stages. John Doe VII and John Doe X, described the construction of helipads at Eindayaza and Po Pah Pta, both of which were near the pipeline site, were used to ferry Total/Unocal executives and materials to the construction site, and were constructed using the forced labor of local villagers, including Plaintiffs. John Does VIII and IX, as well as John Does I, VIII and IX testified that they were forced to work on building roads leading to the pipeline construction area. Finally, John Does V and IX, testified that they were required to serve as "pipeline porters"—workers who performed menial tasks such as such as hauling materials and cleaning the army camps for the soldiers guarding the pipeline construction.

Plaintiffs also allege in furtherance of the forced labor program just described, the Myanmar Military subjected them to acts of murder, rape, and torture. For instance, Jane Doe I testified that after her husband, John Doe I, attempted to escape the forced labor program, he was shot at by soldiers, and in retaliation for his attempted escape, that she and her baby were thrown into a fire, resulting in injuries to her and the death of the child. Other witnesses described the summary execution of villagers who refused to participate in the forced labor program, or who grew too weak to work effectively. Several Plaintiffs testified that rapes occurred as part of the forced labor program. For instance, both Jane Does II and III testified that while conscripted to work on pipeline-related construction projects, they were raped at knife-point by Myanmar soldiers who were members of a battalion that was supervising the work. Plaintiffs finally allege that Unocal's conduct gives rise to liability for these abuses.

The successive military governments of first Burma and now Myanmar have a long and well-known history of imposing forced labor on their citizens. See, e.g., Forced labour in Myanmar (Burma): Report of the Commission of Inquiry appointed under article 26 of the Constitution of the International Labour Organization to examine the observance by Myanmar of the Forced Labour Convention, 1930 (No. 29) Parts III. 8, V. 14(3) (1998) (describing several inquiries into forced labor in Myanmar conducted between 1960 and 1992 by the International Labor Organization, and finding "abundant evidence . . . showing the pervasive use of forced labour imposed on the civilian population throughout Myanmar by the authorities and the military"), http://www.ilo.org/public/english/standards/relm/gb/docs/gb273/myanmar.htm. As detailed below, even before Unocal invested in the Project, Unocal was made aware—by its own consultants and by its partners in the Project—of this record and that the Myanmar Military might also employ forced labor and commit other human rights violations in connection with the Project. And after Unocal invested in the Project, Unocal was made aware—by its own consultants and employees, its partners in the Project, and human rights organizations—of allegations that the Myanmar Military was actually committing such violations in connection with the Project.

Before Unocal acquired an interest in the Project, it hired a consulting company, Control Risk Group, to assess the risks involved in the investment. In May 1992, Control Risk Group informed Unocal that "throughout Burma the government habitually makes use of forced labour to construct roads."[2] Control Risk Group concluded that "in such circumstances UNOCAL and its partners will have little freedom of manoeuvre." Unocal's awareness of the risk at that time is also reflected in the deposition testimony of Unocal Vice President of International Affairs Stephen Lipman:

"In our discussions between Unocal and Total [preceding Unocal's acquisition of an interest in the Project], we said that the option of having the [Myanmar] Military provide protection[3] for the pipeline construction and operation of it would be that they might proceed in the manner that would be out of our control and not be in a manner that we would like to see them proceed, I mean, going to excess."

On January 4, 1995, approximately three years after Unocal acquired an interest in the Project, Unocal President Imle met with human rights organizations at Unocal's headquarters in Los Angeles and acknowledged to them that the Myanmar Military might be using forced labor in connection with the Project. At that meeting, Imle said that "people are threatening physical damage to the pipeline," that "if you threaten the pipeline there's gonna be more military," and that "if forced labor goes hand and glove with the military yes there will be more forced labor."

Two months later, on March 16, 1995, Unocal Representative Robinson confirmed to Unocal President Imle that the Myanmar Military might be committing human rights violations in connection with the Project. Thus, Robinson wrote to Imle that he had received publications from human rights organizations "which depicted in more detail than I have seen before the increased encroachment of [the Myanmar Military's] activities into the villages of the pipeline area." Robinson concluded on the basis of these publications that "our assertion that [the Myanmar Military] has not expanded and amplified its usual methods around the pipeline on our behalf may not withstand much scrutiny."[4]

Shortly thereafter, on May 10, 1995, Unocal Representative Robinson wrote to Total's Herve Madeo: From Unocal's standpoint, probably the most sensitive issue is "what is forced labor" and "how can you identify it." I am sure that you will be thinking about the demarcation between work done by the project and work done "on behalf of" the project. Where the responsibility of the project ends is very important. This statement is some evidence that Unocal knew that the Myanmar Military might use forced labor in connection with the Project.

In June 1995, Amnesty International also alerted Unocal to the possibility that the Myanmar Military might use forced labor in connection with the Project. Amnesty International informed Unocal that comments from a Myanmar Department of Industry official "could mean that the government plans to use 'voluntary' labor in conjunction with the pipeline." Amnesty International went on to explain that "what they call 'voluntary' labor is called forced labor in other parts of the world."[5]

Later that year, on December 11, 1995, Unocal Consultant John Haseman, a former military attaché at the U.S. Embassy in Rangoon, reported to Unocal that the Myanmar Military was, in fact, using forced labor and committing other human rights violations in connection with the Project. Haseman told Unocal that "Unocal was particularly discredited when a corporate spokesman was quoted as saying that Unocal was satisfied with ... assurances [by the Myanmar Military] that no human rights abuses were occurring in the area of pipeline construction." Haseman went on to say: Based on my three years of service in Burma, my continuous contacts in the region since then, and my knowledge of the situation there, my conclusion is that *egregious human rights violations have occurred, and are occurring now, in southern Burma. The most common are forced relocation without compensation of families from land near/along the pipeline route; forced labor to work on infrastructure projects supporting the pipeline . . . ; and imprisonment and/or execution by the army of those opposing such actions. . . . Unocal, by seeming to have accepted [the Myanmar Military]'s version of events, appears at best naive and at worst a willing partner in the situation.*[6]

Communications between Unocal and Total also reflect the companies' shared knowledge that the Myanmar Military was using forced labor in connection with the Project. On February 1, 1996, Total's Herve Chagnoux wrote to Unocal and explained his answers to questions by the press as follows: By stating that I could not guarantee that the army is not using forced labour, I certainly imply that they might, (and they might) but I am saying that we do not have to monitor army's behavior: we have our responsibilities; they have their responsibilities; and we refuse to be pushed into assuming more than what we can really guarantee. About forced labour used by the troops assigned to provide security on our pipeline project, let us admit between Unocal and Total that we might be in a grey zone.

And on September 17, 1996, Total reported to Unocal about a meeting with a European Union civil servant in charge of an investigation of forced labor in Myanmar: "We were told that even if Total is not using forced labor directly, the troops assigned to the protection of our operations use forced labour to build their camps and to carry their equipments." In reply, Total acknowledged that forced labor did indeed occur in connection with the pipeline: "We had to mention that when we had knowledge of such occurrences, the workers have been compensated." Unocal President Imle testified at his deposition that in Unocal's discussions with Total, "surrounding the question of porters for the military and their payment was the issue of whether they were conscripted or volunteer workers." Imle further testified that "the consensus was that it was mixed," i.e., "some porters were conscripted, and some were volunteer." On March 4, 1997, Unocal nevertheless submitted a statement to the City Counsel of New York, in response to a proposed New York City select purchasing law imposed on firms that do business in Myanmar, in which Unocal stated that "no [human rights] violations have taken place" in the vicinity of the pipeline route.

## II. Analysis

### A. Liability Under the Alien Tort Claims Act.

Forced Labor

a.  Forced labor is a modern variant of slavery to which the law of nations attributes individual liability such that state action is not required.
b.  Unocal may be liable under the ATCA for aiding and abetting the Myanmar Military in subjecting Plaintiffs to forced labor.

**Murder, Rape, and Torture**

a.  Because Plaintiffs testified that the alleged acts of murder, rape, and torture occurred in furtherance of forced labor, state action is not required to give rise to liability under the ATCA.

b.  Unocal may be liable under the ATCA for aiding and abetting the Myanmar Military in subjecting Plaintiffs to murder and rape, but Unocal is not similarly liable for torture.

## III.  Conclusion

For the foregoing reasons, we REVERSE the District Court's grant of summary judgment in favor of Unocal on Plaintiffs' ATCA claims for forced labor, murder, and rape . . . We REMAND the case to the District Court for further proceedings consistent with this opinion.

**View:** Total Denial

## Notes

1   Moreover, in March 1996, a cable from the U.S. Embassy in Rangoon reflects the Embassy's understanding that "the consortium building the pipeline pays the Burmese military a hard-currency fee for providing security."

2   In the same year, the U.S. Department of State similarly reported that "the military Government [in Myanmar] routinely employs corvee labor on its myriad building projects" and that "the Burmese army has for decades conscripted civilian males to serve as porters." U.S. Department of State, Country Reports on Human Rights Practices for 1991 796–97 (1992).

3   As noted above, the Production Sharing Contract between Total Myanmar and Myanmar Oil provided that "[Myanmar Oil] shall . . . supply[] or make available . . . security protection . . . as may be requested by [Total Myanmar and its assigns]," such as Unocal.

4   Similarly, the briefing book that Total prepared for Unocal President Imle and Unocal CEO Beach on the occasion of their April 1996 visit to the Project listed the following "area[]of concern": "army = additional burden on the local population."

5   Also in 1995, Human Rights Watch informed Unocal that forced labor was so pervasive in Myanmar that Human Rights Watch could not condone any investment that would enrich the country's current regime. That same year, the General Assembly of the United Nations "strongly urged the Government of Myanmar . . . to put an end to . . . the practices of torture, abuse of women, forced labour . . . , and . . . disappearances and summary executions. . . . " Situation of Human Rights in Myanmar, U.N. General Assembly, 50th Sess., Agenda Item 112(c), U.N. Doc. A/RES/50/194 (1995), http:www.un.org/documents/ga/res/50/ares50-194.htm.

6   Similarly, on May 20, 1996, a State Department cable stated: "Forced labor is currently being channeled, according to [non-governmental organization] reports, to service roads for the pipeline to Thailand. . . . There are plans for a helicopter pad and airstrip in the area . . . in part for use by oil company executives." Emphasis added.

## Case Discussion Questions

1. Why was it necessary to force the villagers in the district of Tenasserim, Myanmar (Burma) to work on the pipeline project? In other words, individuals in less developed countries are often pleased to work for multinational countries; for example, the Union Carbide plant in Bhopal, India attracted villagers from other areas; they constructed the shanty towns surrounding the plant.

2. Do you think that it is fair to hold Unocal liable for the forced labor of the residents of Myanmar? Why or why not? Cite specific reasons.

3. Does it matter that the executive of Unocal knew that the workers on their pipeline project were being forced to work on the project and were even being intimidated?

4. If the Unocal case was going to trial in California, would you recommend to Unocal that they settle the case or that the case be tried? What is the basis for your recommendations?

5. What do you predict would be the outcome of the trial? Would Unocal be found guilty for the forced labor of the villagers?

6. If Unocal were found guilty for the forced labor of the villagers on their pipeline project, what are the lessons for other companies having projects in less developed countries, particularly ones without a democratic tradition?

# 4  Strategic Social Responsibility

## Chapter Outline

What Are the Social Responsibilities of Business?
    The Doctrine of Caveat Emptor
    Managing Negative Externalities
    Creating Positive Externalities: Public Goods
        Corporate Philanthropy
        Benefit Corporations
Corporate Social and Environmental Reporting
    The Global Reporting Initiative
    Corporate Codes of Conduct
Global Corporate Citizenship
Corporate Culture and Organizational Vision
The Common Good
End of Chapter Case: Texaco Oil Co. Drilling Oil in Ecuador

## Chapter Introduction

How do the social responsibilities of business relate to firm goals and objectives? Fundamentally, enterprise output is the basis by which we sustain our lives; we obtain food, housing, clothing, transportation not by creating them ourselves by and large but through market transactions. Enterprise, if it does not externalize its costs of production, contributes to the common good by the creation and distribution of value-added products.

What are the social responsibilities of business? While some argue that the business of business is purely economic and that other agencies and organizations should engage in the creation of social goods, many business leaders have moved to an acknowledgement of the social responsibilities of enterprise: that in its production, enterprise has an affirmative obligation to avoid the creation of harms, including negative externalities and unintended negative consequences. Moreover, some companies strategically create positive externalities and many successful entrepreneurs and business leaders engage in corporate philanthropy. Corporations affirmatively manage their stakeholder relationships, articulating corporate codes of conduct, undertaking corporate social audits and managing for the triple bottom line, reporting financial, environmental and social performance.

## Chapter Goal and Learning Objectives

*Chapter Goal:* Explain how corporate social responsibility is fundamental to enterprise strategic management.

*Learning Objectives:*

1. Discuss whether, and if so how, corporate social responsibility relates to strategic management.
2. Explain the concepts of reasonably foreseeable consequences, negative externalities and unintended negative consequences, as well as positive externalities.
3. Explain managing for the triple bottom line.
4. Debate the role of corporate philanthropy.
5. Discuss the role of business in creating the common good in society.

## What Are the Social Responsibilities of Business?

Enterprise output is the basis by which we sustain our lives; we obtain food, housing, clothing, transportation not by creating them ourselves by and large but through market transactions. Enterprise thereby contributes to the common good by the creation and distribution of value- added products. But what about the negative aspects of business? What are the social responsibilities of business? New notions of appropriate corporate behavior and corporate social responsibility are evolving. Historically, businesses have acted according to a *caveat emptor* standard in the management of their relations with customers. The question arises: have corporations transitioned from a *caveat emptor* framework for doing business, even with customers, to a basis for action that mandates the rule, "first do no harm"?

### *The Doctrine of Caveat Emptor*

Business organizations in the eighteenth century acted under a doctrine of *caveat emptor* or let the buyer beware. The doctrine of *caveat emptor* regulated the sale of goods. The doctrine as applied by the courts allowed fraud in the sale of goods. For example, in *Barnard v. Kellogg*, the seller of wool skins misrepresented the quality of wools skins shipped from South America; the good skins were laid on top of a ship's hold, while the skins underneath were rotten; the buyer was invited to inspect the entire shipment but declined to do so in the expectation that the skins on top represented the quality of the entire shipment. The United States Supreme Court declined to compensate the purchaser on the basis of *caveat emptor*.[1]

However, the doctrine of *caveat emptor* was eroded by the development of the common law on fraud as well as by statute. In particular, the Securities and Exchange Acts of 1933 and 1934 prohibit fraud in the sale of securities and require disclosure of information material to an investment decision.[2] The Uniform Commercial Code abandoned the doctrine of *caveat emptor* with respect to the sale of goods; contracts for the sale of goods carry an implied guarantee of merchantability.[3]

Although the doctrine of *caveat emptor* persisted in the sale of real property, the doctrine is even being eroded in the realm of real estate transactions.[4] Many states have passed legislation imposing an affirmative duty on sellers to disclose known defects.[5] And, with the emergence of e-commerce, some experts called for specific regulation of e-commerce transactions to correct the problem of fraud in e-commerce transactions.[6] For example, the PayPal system was developed specifically for e-commerce transactions to prevent the theft or misuse of credit information of purchasers by sellers on the Internet. Thus the modern concept of acceptable business behavior has moved away from "let the buyer beware" approach; the doctrine of *caveat emptor* has been abandoned at law and in practice.

Having abandoned the practice of *caveat emptor*, the question arises: have businesses moved to the norm, "first, do no harm"?[7] Extended from the medical to the business context, the doctrine of "first do no harm" would serve as an affirmative approach whereby corporations would be obligated to minimize the negative consequences of their actions with respect to their customers and other stakeholders. For example, with the emergence of the Internet and the consequent interdependence of both individuals and business enterprise, viruses infecting and spreading throughout the Internet obstruct individual and business communications and transactions. Experts, therefore, called for the application of the doctrine of "first do no harm" to the Internet.[8]

### Managing Negative Externalities

The doctrine of "first do no harm" can be extended to the creation of negative externalities by business enterprise. *Negative externalities* are costs generated by enterprise that are levied on the consumer, such as defective products, or on the general public, such as pollution. Negative externalities result from the failure of a company to internalize its costs of production and amount to the creation of public bads.[9] The principle of *primum non nocere* (first do no harm) would require that companies avoid creation of negative externalities. For example, Union Carbide India created tremendous negative externalities by its industrial accident. The surrounding community, many of whom were individuals who had located close to the plant to work, was burned by the MIC leak. Current estimates of injuries are that 15,000 people died and more than 500,000 were compensated for injuries by the Bhopal victims' compensation fund.[10]

Extending the principle, first do no harm, the issue arises: do companies have an affirmative, ethical obligation to avoid harm that is known to them or that is reasonably foreseeable? For example, the Nestle case is about harms suffered by the consumers of infant formula from the improper use or misuse of the product. Nestle infant formula is not a product that is harmful in itself but which became harmful as used by consumers. When the association between feeding with infant formula and higher infant mortality in less developed countries became known, did Nestle have an obligation to act to minimize the harms that arose from the use of its product by consumers? Patagonia is a company which includes in its mission, "cause no unnecessary harm." See Box 4.1 below.

---

### Box 4.1  Patagonia's Mission: "Cause No Unnecessary Harm"

In the spring of 1988, Patagonia opened a store in Boston on Newbury Street. Within days, the people who worked in the store were sick: mainly headaches. We hired an engineer who told us the problem was the ventilation system: it was recycling the same tired air. But what was in the air? Probably formaldehyde, she told us. From the finish on the cotton clothes stored in the basement. Formaldehyde? This led us to commission a study of conventional cotton, and the discovery that cotton grown with pesticides is one of the most destructive crops in the agricultural world.

Knowing that, we could not in good conscience continue to use conventional cotton for our sportswear. So we went organic in 1996. It was expensive, time-consuming and scary (so few farmers grew organic cotton that we were constantly checking the weather in California's Central Valley).

#### That was just the beginning

Over the next 18 years, we began moving to what happens in Patagonia's name in every step of the supply chain, from crop to fabric to finished garment. We measured the environmental impacts of selected articles of clothing and published them on The Footprint Chronicles®. We worked with outside auditors and hired a team of in-house corporate responsibility specialists to track (and improve) the working conditions and pay for every person who sews a Patagonia garment. We learned how to make fleece jackets from soda bottles and then how to make fleece jackets from worn out fleece jackets. We partnered with bluesign® to employ methods and materials in the manufacture of many of our fabrics to conserve resources and minimize impacts on people and the environment.

We gave one percent of sales to grassroots activists. In 2014, for example, we supported Trout Unlimited's efforts to protect Bristol Bay in Alaska—one of the last great salmon fisheries on the planet. And Save Our Wild Salmon to bring down deadbeat dams. This one percent commitment isn't typical philanthropy. Rather, it's part of the cost of doing business, part of our effort to balance (however imperfectly) the impact we have on natural systems—and to protect the world on which our business, employees, and customers rely.

We took more steps, influenced by our environmental campaign The Responsible Economy. We began working with Fair Trade USA to get factory workers closer to a living wage. We continued our work with sheep ranchers in Argentina who raise sustainably grazed merino wool that's helping to restore damaged grasslands. Our down clothing is now insulated with Traceable Down—no force-fed geese, no live plucking. We are also using reclaimed fabrics and, as of spring 2015, all sportswear will exemplify our commitment to the environment.

Once you start down on this road, you can't stop. "Living the examined life," said our founder, Yvon Chouinard, "is a big pain."

In the end, Patagonia may never be completely responsible. We have a long way to go and we don't have a map—but we do have a way to read the terrain and to take the next step, and then the next.

By Nora Gallagher, Environmental Editor,
Patagonia Environmental and Social Initiatives 2014
http://www.patagonia.com/pdf/en_US/ENV14-Printed_r2.pdf

Sometimes even well-intended actions have *unintended negative consequences.* Unintended negative consequences are harmful impacts created by well-intended actions. For example, the donation of used clothing and its export to Africa has the unintended negative consequence of driving local clothing merchants, both manufacturers and distributors, out of business. Local craft work thus also is declining. The intentions of the clothing donors and the actions themselves were good but nevertheless had unintended negative consequences on other stakeholders in Africa.[11]

### Creating Positive Externalities: Public Goods

In addition to avoiding the generation of negative externalities and minimizing unintended negative consequences, some companies deliberately generate positive externalities. *Positive externalities* are created by companies as public goods. For example, the location of a plant on a large piece of property, well landscaped, that generates tax revenues more than those minimally necessary for the production facility would be an example of the creation of positive externalities by a company. The Johnson & Johnson company engages in such a strategy of creating positive externalities for the communities in which their plants are located, as can be seen by traveling along the roads where their facilities are built. Other examples of positive externalities intentionally created by companies include volunteerism by employees within the communities where the company facilities operate and where the employees live; some companies encourage and facilitate the volunteer efforts of their employees with community-based organizations, such as Habitat for Humanity.

### Corporate Philanthropy

Corporate philanthropy is a kind of positive externality whereby corporations, or the foundations they establish, give gifts to the community. Corporate philanthropy is based on the recognition that corporations have multiple stakeholders. In permitting corporate gift giving, the courts have effectually supported a stakeholder model of corporate enterprise. In 1956, the courts decided that it was not a breach of an executive's fiduciary duties to shareholders to engage in corporate philanthropy. Some shareholders had opposed charitable giving as an inappropriate transfer of assets of the corporation to the recipients of the charitable giving. However, the courts endorsed the view that firm interests can encompass charitable giving.[12]

Corporate philanthropy can also have a strategic purpose for the donor enterprise.[13] It provides visibility and positive press, which augments the company's products and services. It provides leadership opportunities and the ability to hone leadership skill development for its executives. Corporate philanthropy continues the American practice of individualism in the creation of social goods and welfare, rather than depending on the state for the creation of social goods. Corporate philanthropy directs giving to those social goods that the corporation deems important, rather than relying only on government to further the corporate mission, and the donor organization is able to take advantage of the tax deduction permitted for charitable giving. Additionally, corporate giving enhances the community in which the corporation has facilities. It creates a positive bond of goodwill with the communities and the reciprocation of friendship with the recipients of the charitable giving.

*Strategic corporate philanthropy* aligns a firm's philanthropic giving with the corporate purpose.[14] Strategic philanthropy aligns corporate charitable activities with corporate core competencies.[15] For example, Merck & Co., a major pharmaceutical company, donated drugs to cure river blindness to countries in equatorial Africa.[16] The countries affected by the high incidence of river blindness could not afford the cost of the drugs, so Merck donated the drugs. Merck engaged in charitable activities using its core competencies. Merck's philanthropy generated good will and enhanced its reputation. Merck's strategic corporate philanthropy was a social investment, which rebounded to the company's long-term financial and market interests by enhanced reputation.[17] Current opportunities for strategic philanthropy by pharmaceutical companies pertain to AIDS in sub-Saharan Africa, where 25% of the adult population is infected with HIV.[18]

Other opportunities for strategic philanthropy relate to the distribution and use of information technologies. Individuals without access to information and communication technologies (ICT) are disadvantaged relative to individuals with access to ICT, according to the United States Department of Commerce.[19] The differential in access to information and communication technologies is called "the digital divide." Those companies whose core competencies are in the area of information technologies have the opportunity to bridge the digital divide. The Gates Foundation, created by Bill Gates from his wealth generated by Microsoft Corporation, is attempting through its philanthropic activities to address the digital divide. The Gates Foundation targets public libraries in the United States, as well as in Canada and Chile, to assist the libraries to provide public access to information and communication technologies, free of charge.[20] These efforts represent strategic philanthropy by the Gates Foundation, which is making community investments aligned with Bill Gates and Microsoft's core competencies. Such investment by the Gates Foundation also represents corporate social investment.

*Benefit Corporations*

Benefit corporations are a new form of corporate organization that focuses the performance of the enterprise on the creation of social goods, such as employment.[21] The Community Interest Corporation (CIC) is a form available in the United Kingdom. In the United States, some states such as Vermont, as well as New York, California, New Jersey, Virginia and Maryland, have implemented legislation enabling the benefit corporation or similar forms of organization. A significant advantage of the benefit corporation is that bonds can be used for financing CICs.[22] For example, in the United Kingdom, "Bristol Together" a social enterprise to train ex-offenders, was financed by bonds.[23] Benefit corporations are a form that facilitates the establishment of enterprise by social entrepreneurs. Venture capitalists fund some innovative start-up corporations, but ventures formed by social entrepreneurs may not attract traditional forms of capital for financing the enterprise, so B-bonds are an innovative source of funding for social enterprise.

## Corporate Social and Environmental Reporting

Some corporations, taking into account their generation of negative and positive externalities and the multiplicity of their stakeholders, broaden their reporting from economic and financial reporting to include social and environmental reporting. This trend may have been spurred, historically, by social protests about apartheid in South Africa. Shareholder concern over apartheid in South Africa led some universities and other institutional investors to sell off their investments in companies doing business in South Africa. The debate over whether companies should remain in South Africa or withdraw from the patently unjust institutional system embodied by apartheid led to the development by the Reverend Leon Sullivan of principles for doing business in South Africa. These became known as the Sullivan Principles.[24] The Sullivan Principles provide a standard for reporting corporate actions with respect to areas of concern to its stakeholders, including its socially concerned investors. Social and environmental reporting in addition to financial reporting is responsive to an enterprise's multiple stakeholders, including shareholders, as well as its employees, customers and the communities affected by the company's operations.

Managing social and environmental issues, in addition to financial and economic issues, is managing for the *triple bottom line*. The triple bottom line, assessing a company's financial, environmental and social performance, is a way for enterprise to evaluate and monitor its performance as a corporate citizen. Managing for the triple bottom line can enhance a company's reputation and brand, creating competitive advantage.

Many companies now issue reports on corporate social responsibility. Issuance of *corporate social audits* reflects a changed corporate climate. For example, Ford Motor Company issued its first Corporate Citizenship Report in 2002. In its corporate citizenship reports, Ford emphasized its environmental initiatives.[25] Even while it issued its environmental reports, Ford was embroiled in the controversy of its Explorer roll-over problem and allegations of defective design of its Explorer. Some critics suggest that Ford's environmental reporting creates obfuscation clouding real problems, such as product design defects. *Corporate social audits* may be reported externally to shareholders in a corporation's annual report, published as a corporate citizenship report, as did Ford Motor Company, or published as an internal document, for example as was done when Ernst and Young audited Nike's sub-contractor manufacturing facilities.[26]

### The Global Reporting Initiative

The *Global Reporting Initiative* (GRI) proposes standards for the reporting a corporation's citizenship behaviors. The GRI was developed by the Coalition for Environmentally Responsible Economies, which extended the Valdez Principles, developed in the aftermath of the Exxon Valdez oil spill.[27] The standards of the GRI are premised on managing for the triple bottom line.[28]

The Ford Motor Company used the GRI standards for its Corporate Citizenship Report, 2003–2004. It reported its actions concerning the following categories: vision and strategy; company profile; governance structure; economic performance, including indicators affecting customers, suppliers, employees, providers of capital, and the public sector; indirect economic impacts; environmental impacts, including impacts on materials, energy, water, biodiversity, emission, effluents and waste; social impacts with respect to labor practices and "decent work," including employment, labor/management relations, health and safety, training and education, diversity and opportunity; social impacts with respect to human rights including non-discrimination, freedom of association and collective bargaining, child labor, forced and compulsory labor; social impacts on the general society, including bribery and corruption, and political contributions; product responsibility, including customer health and safety and respect for privacy.[29] This is consistent with the GRI of other corporations. See for example, Wal-Mart's social responsibility report.[30]

### Corporate Codes of Conduct

Some corporations have articulated their corporate citizenship aspirations in the form of a corporate code of conduct. The United States Sentencing Guidelines for Organizations, enacted in 1991, provide an incentive for corporations to develop a corporate *code of conduct*.[31] A corporate code of conduct can be used as a shield against punitive damages if the corporation through its employees and agents engages in wrong doing. The sentencing guidelines allow for mitigating circumstances; if a company has enacted a corporate code of conduct, disseminated it, engaged in training about its code of conduct, and designated a high-level manager to ensure compliance, the company can defend itself against punitive damages and plead for the reduction of fines and other penalties by defending on the basis that its employees and agents should have known better and that the corporation should be liable only for compensatory damages to those injured by the wrongdoing of its employees or agents.

There is a global trend toward the adoption of corporate codes of conduct and other standards for ethical business conduct by transnational corporations. For example, the Caux Roundtable is an association of business leaders from Europe, the United States and Japan, founded in 1986 by the president of Phillips Electronics and the vice chairman of INSEAD and with the leadership of the CEO of Canon Inc. The Caux Roundtable established Principles for Business that are based on a stakeholder model of global enterprise and that urge global corporate responsibility and the responsibility of global businesses to contribute to the economic and social development of the nations in which they operate.[32]

However, the enactment of even an excellent code of conduct does not guarantee good corporate conduct. The case of Enron should serve as a cautionary tale. Enron Corporation had a comprehensive, excellent code of conduct.[33] However, the Enron board suspended its code of conduct as to conflicts of interest to permit the establishment of its special purpose entities, which were used to accomplish the fraud in its financial statements; the partnerships were controlled by Enron CFO Andrew Fastow.[34]

The Sarbanes-Oxley Act, passed by the United States Congress in the summer 2002 in response to the Enron Corporation fraud and bankruptcy and other corporate debacles of 2001, particularly the bankruptcy of WorldCom, provides that companies should develop a code of conduct for officers and directors. Although the code of conduct for officers and directors is not compulsory, a company must explain why a code of conduct for its officers and directors is not necessary. The Sarbanes Oxley Act is discussed further in Chapter 12, Corporate Governance.

## Global Corporate Citizenship

Participation of businesses as citizens in a global context is a consequence of the globalization of business enterprise.[35] With globalization, multinational enterprises face a multi-regulatory environment. Although multinational enterprises do business globally, they do not face even a consistent regulatory environment, much less a uniform regulatory environment. This is problematic for multi-national corporations. Although the production processes may be uniform in a global environment, the regulation of the production process and a corporation's externalities are not uniform.[36]

For example, the disposal of the by-products of the oil refining process is regulated differently in the United States and in Ecuador. Citizens of Ecuador brought suit against Texaco Oil Company for the disposal oil by-products, which are toxic, in violation of prevailing industry standards. Texaco defended itself based on the fact that that they were conforming to Ecuador's regulations.[37] The suit was initially brought in the United States court under the Alien Tort Act of 1789; the trial court and the appellate court, however, denied jurisdiction over the suit, so the case was tried in Ecuador. This case raises a question of an international double standard. If there is a prevailing industry production standard, can a company in good faith produce under conditions that do not conform to the prevailing industry standard, rationalizing its actions on a less stringent regulatory environment? The case against Texaco in Ecuador raises the issue whether in the future companies will be obligated to follow industry best practices even if the practice is not compelled by local law. The question of an international double standard is also raised by the international marketing of tobacco products, for example by Philip Morris's marketing campaign targeting the Czech Republic.

Logsdon and Wood offer a framework for implementing global business citizenship to assist companies in resolving the question of what policies a corporation should implement in specific circumstances.[38] They develop a typology relating cultural and ethical norms to strategic choice. Companies choose between a multi-domestic strategy or a globally integrated strategy. A globally integrated strategy would be implemented by adopting a credo or code of conduct. When specific policies are adopted based on local practice, a multi-domestic strategy is adopted. Texaco adopted a multi-domestic strategic approach in its operations in Ecuador case; the complaining citizens of Ecuador argue in effect that Texaco should adopt a globally integrated best practices strategy and that "do not pollute" is a hyper norm, cutting across cultures.

The focus on corporate social responsibility and corporate philanthropy, managing for the triple bottom line, should not, however, divert attention from the problem of corruption and bribery. Bribery and corruption is a global problem. Bribery was outlawed in the United States in 1977, with the passage of the *Foreign Corrupt Practices Act*. The Foreign Corrupt Practices Act represents a policy imposed on multinational corporations by the United States Congress, which requires a globally integrated strategy based on a "hyper norm" of honesty and fair dealing. The Foreign Corrupt Practices Act was passed in response to the revelation of bribery by US multinational companies of foreign officials.[39] The systems effects of bribery can be devastating on the social fabric of a nation. See for example, Transparency International's survey, Corruption Perceptions Index (CPI).[40] The negative consequences of bribery are illustrated by Nigeria, which consistently scores at the bottom of Transparency International's CPI survey, being replaced, however, in 2003 as the country with the highest level of perceived corruption by Bangladesh. Bangladesh has improved its standing in the CPI survey, so that in 2010, Somalia, Afghanistan, and Myanmar were at the bottom of the CPI index.[41] By 2014, the least transparent countries are in the Middle East, likely reflecting the wars and political turmoil in the larger area.[42]

For many years, the Foreign Corrupt Practices Act was viewed as creating a competitive disadvantage to United States-based multinational companies, which were restrained from bribing foreign officials, whereas multinational corporations based in other countries were not subject to a similar constraint.[43] But in 1997, Organisation for Economic Co-operation and Development member countries and five non-member countries, Argentina, Brazil, Bulgaria, Chile and the Slovak Republic, adopted a Convention on Combating Bribery of Foreign Public Officials in International Business Transactions.[44] The convention outlaws bribery of foreign officials, money laundering and fraudulent accounting.[45]

In addition, the United Nations adopted a Convention Combating Bribery of Foreign Public Officials in International Business Transactions on November 21, 1997.[46] The Foreign Corrupt Practices Act was amended to bring it into conformity with the convention.[47] Although the Convention on Combating Bribery was signed on December 17, 1997, by the United States and 32 other nations, and adopted by the General Assembly of the United Nations in 2003, bribery nevertheless remains an ongoing occurrence in international business transactions. For example, in 2004, Lucent Technologies was under investigation for alleged bribery and undue influence in Saudi Arabia's allocation of communication technologies contracts.[48] Halliburton has been under ongoing investigation for alleged bribery in Nigeria and other places.[49] In this situation and others like it, there is a gap between the regulatory framework that companies profess to adhere to and their actions to gain a competitive edge. Given the now universal policy ban on bribery, corporations need to move from a mere endorsement of transparency and a policy prohibiting bribery to effective implementation. A company's freedom of action is thereby constrained and executives may be loath to lose either an equal footing with their competitors, if they view bribery as a normal business practice, or an advantage relative to their competitors.

The issue is complicated by the practice or expectation of bribery by public officials in countries that are target markets for multinational companies. The expectation of bribery, payoffs or kickbacks appears to be at issue in Lucent Technologies' payoffs to an official in Saudi Arabia who was vested with the authority to award the contracts to install the communications systems there. In order to comply with an anti-bribery policy, companies must be willing to forego business on such terms, as well as raise a red flag about such illegal practices when they are proposed. This course of action might be evaluated as "bad business" if companies think that by rejecting bribery as an option they will be losing business. The loss of business from refusing to engage in bribery is a short-run result, whereas in the long run the losses from engaging in bribery may be even greater. For example, Lucent Technologies faced a charge of extortion from a supplier company related to the Saudi Arabia contracts.[50] If, however, a company views the costs of bribery and its attendant losses, for example damages for extortion and reduction in future business contracts, as a "cost of doing business," an enterprise may conclude that the benefits exceed the overall costs of bribery. In such cases, the regulators need to step in to change the cost–benefit ratio if the polity is serious about avoiding bribery as a way of doing business.

Wal-Mart allegedly engaged in payoffs and bribes to zoning officials in Mexico to enable the construction of new Wal-Mart stores. Wal-Mart is now the largest merchandiser in Mexico, and 20% of its stores are located in Mexico.[51] Bribery as a cost of doing business in this case was justified by the growth of Wal-Mart internationally, which is very problematic from both an ethical and a legal point of view. Wal-Mart's CEO and President Mike Duke was replaced as a result of the Mexican bribery.[52] This case illustrates also the issues of dealing with corrupt regimes, which was also at play in the cases of Unocal in Myanmar, Texaco in Ecuador and Royal Dutch Petroleum in Nigeria.[53]

## Corporate Culture and Organizational Vision

Just as personal vision and values underlie the individual manager's values and decision framework, organizational vision and corporate culture provide the framework within which specific decisions are made and ethical dilemmas are resolved within the organization. As discussed above, organizational vision is sometimes articulated in a corporate code of conduct or other internal document, as for example, Johnson & Johnson's credo. However, as the Enron debacle illustrates, an excellent code of conduct in itself does not ensure ethical behavior.[54]

*Corporate Culture.* Ethical ways of doing business must be incorporated into corporate culture, so that people who are called upon to make a decision during a corporate crisis or when faced with an ethical dilemma are guided by the standard, "the way we do things around here" is "ethically."[55] Doing business ethically must be operationalized in concrete terms. At this point the firm's answer to the question: "in whose interests is the firm managed?" becomes relevant. If the firm is managed primarily in the interests of shareholders, under the shareholder capitalism model the ethical dilemma or corporate crisis would be resolved in view of the interests of shareholders. If the stakeholder approach serves as the management model, the ethical dilemma would be resolved taking into account the interests of consumers, employees, suppliers, and the community where the firm operates, as well as the interests of shareholders. Decision making under both the shareholder model and the stakeholder model is made under the constraints imposed by regulators.

For example, culture appears to be at work in Ford's continuing issues of defective car design. David Halberstam, in his book *The Reckoning*[56] about the history of Ford Motor Co. notes an ongoing conflict between finance and engineering that rises to the level of an issue of corporate culture. Ford has had an ongoing problem with defective car design—the Ford Pinto, Ford Explorer,

Ford Crown Victoria all had defective designs—that derives from the conflict between engineering and the marketing and finance departments. Internal documents at Ford, Johns Manville, Enron and other companies that have undergone major ethics meltdowns indicate that at least some insiders to the company were aware of the ethical problem that the company faced and raised red flags over the specific issues that were problematic. A challenge for enterprise leaders is how to develop mechanisms within the organization to encourage, rather than suppress, the identification of important ethical quandaries that the organization faces and to correct problems at early stages, rather than let the problem develop to the point where the survival of the organization is put at risk, such as happened with Johns Manville, Enron, and accounting firm Arthur Andersen.

## The Common Good

The issue of corporate citizenship or corporate social responsibility ultimately comes down to a question about the effect enterprise creates on the social fabric of a society. Is the society better off or worse off from the operation of the enterprise? Firms create the goods by which we sustain our lives through market transactions. Enterprise thus contributes to the common good. The contribution of business to the common good is acknowledged, for example, by the Caux Roundtable Principles.[57] However, the manner is which the firm operates must be addressed to assess its effect on the social fabric of a society. Does the firm's production process cause injury to consumers, to the environment, to its workers? Does the firm deal fairly with competitors and honestly and transparently with regulators? Or, is the firm managed in the interests of shareholders to the exclusion and detriment of other stakeholders? Does the firm culture reflect an "any thing goes to make a profit" mentality, harkening back to the *caveat emptor* tradition of business dealings? Leading business strategist Michael Porter proposes the corporate strategy of creating shared value as one that "can give rise to the next major transformation of business thinking. . . . Companies must take the lead in bringing business and society back together . . . The solution lies in the principle of shared value, which involves creating economic value in a way that also creates value for society by addressing its needs and challenges. Businesses must reconnect company success with social progress."[58]

The *common good*, therefore, can be defined as: *the systems effect created by socially responsible enterprise.* Johnson & Johnson in its management of the Tylenol poisoning crisis provides an excellent example of managing for the common good. Johnson & Johnson's credo was the guiding force behind CEO Burke's management of the Tylenol crisis. The credo identifies the interest of patients as preeminent.[59] J & J managed the Tylenol crisis in a manner consistent with its credo. In doing so, J & J's CEO Burke saved the brand and overcame the initial downturn in stock price and market share associated with the Tylenol poisonings. The J & J shareholders thereby benefited in the long run. However, at the time, Burke put the company at risk in his management of the Tylenol crisis: he didn't know that the brand would be rehabilitated, or that the company could overcome the financial losses associated with the recall of Tylenol.

The definition of the common good as the systems effect created by socially responsible enterprise implies the "common bad," which can be defined as the systems effect created by socially irresponsible enterprise. For example, Dr. Seuss's *The Lorax* portrays the systems effects created by socially irresponsible enterprise.[60] Managers and directors of an enterprise should determine whether and in what respects the firm's corporate social responsibility performance supports the strategic purpose of the firm.

## Chapter Discussion Questions

1. Define and give examples of negative externalities, unintended negative consequences and positive externalities.
2. Debate whether corporate philanthropy can offset damage to the environment or injuries to consumers from defectively designed products.
3. How is managing for the triple bottom line different from managing for firm financial performance?
4. Look up the corporate social responsibility reports of Wal-Mart and Ford Motor Company. Discuss whether their reports are consistent with an independent auditor's view of their CSR.

## Notes

1 *Barnard v. Kellogg*, Supreme Court of the United States , 77 U.S. 383; 19 L. Ed. 987; 1870 U.S. LEXIS 1130; 10 Wall. 383, January 23, 1871, Decided; December, 1870, Term. See also Walton H. Hamilton, "The Ancient Maxim of Caveat Emptor," *Yale Law Journal* 40, no. 8 (1931): 1133–87.

2 *Securities and Exchange Commission v. Capital Gains Research Bureau, Inc., et al.*, Supreme Court of the United States, 375 U.S. 180; 84 S. Ct. 275; 11 L. Ed. 2d 237; 1963 U.S. LEXIS 2446, October 21, 1963, Argued, December 9, 1963, Decided.

3 Uniform Commercial Code Section 2–314 provides in full: "(1) Unless excluded or modified (sections 2–316), a warranty that the goods shall be merchantable is implied in a contract for their sale if the seller is a merchant with respect to goods of that kind. Under this section the serving for value of food or drink to be consumed either on the premises or elsewhere is a sale. (2) Goods to be merchantable must be at least such as (a) pass without objection in the trade under the contract description; and (b) in the case of fungible goods, are of fair average quality within the description; and (c) are fit for the ordinary purposes for which such goods are used; and (d) run, within the variations permitted by the agreement, of even kind, quality and quantity within each unit and among all units involved; and (e) are adequately contained, packaged, and labeled as the agreement may require; and (f) conform to the promises or affirmations of fact made on the container or label if any. (3) Unless excluded or modified (section 2–316) other implied warranties may arise from course of dealing or usage of trade."

4 Leo Bearman, Jr., "*Caveat Emptor* in Sales of Realty—Recent Assaults Upon the Rule," *Vanderbilt Law Review* 14 (1960–61): 541+. See also Florrie Young Roberts, "Disclosure Duties in Real Estate Sales and Attempts to Reallocate the Risk," *Connecticut Law Review* 34, no. 1 (2001): 1.

"An example of **caveat emptor** in practice can be seen in a 1941 Massachusetts case where the court found in favor of a seller who, at the time of the sale of his house, knew it was infested with termites but failed to disclose this to the purchaser. No false statement or representation was alleged. Rather, 'the charge [was] concealment and nothing more.'"

5 Roberts, "Disclosure Duties in Real Estate Sales."

6 Miriam R. Albert, "E-Buyer Beware: Why Online Auction Fraud Should Be Regulated," *American Business Law Journal* 39, no. 4 (2002): 575–644.

7 "primum non nocere." The doctrine of *primum non nocere* (first do no harm) developed initially in the practice of medicine.

8 See Susan P. Crawford, "First Do No Harm: The Problem of Spyware," *Berkeley Technology Law Journal* 20 (2005): 1433–75.

9 Negative externalities will be discussed further in Chapter 9 on the environment and with respect to the externalization of labor costs in Chapter 11 on global labor markets.

10 See Edward Broughton, "The Bhopal Disaster and Its Aftermath: A Review," *Environmental Health, US National Library of Medicine: National Institutes of Health*, last modified May 10, 2005, http://www.ncbi.nlm.nih.gov/pmc/articles/PMC1142333/.

11 Carter Dougherty, "Trade Theory vs. Used Clothes in Africa," *New York Times*, June 3, 2004.

12 *A. P. Smith Manufacturing Company v. Barlow, et al.*, 13 N.J. 145 (1953).

13 Interview with Elizabeth Stone Becker (Director of Finance and Development, National Board, YWCA [retired] and co-founder, Women in Development), interview by the author, Apr. 28, 2009.

14 "Through their philanthropy, corporations aspire to achieve a lasting and positive impact on society. Companies' resources extend well beyond money and include corporate leadership and reputation, processes and disciplines and employee time and talent." Council on Foundations, *Stewardship Principles for Corporate Grantmakers*, Aug. 2, 2004.

15 Management core competencies are identified by SWOT analysis.

16 "River Blindness Campaign Ends; West Africans Return to Fertile Farmlands," News Releases, *World Health Organization*, last modified 2014, http://www.who.int/mediacentre/news/releases.

17 Merck has been ranked as one of Fortune's "most admired companies" more than any other Fortune 500 company. See Charles J. Fombrun, "Indices of Corporate Reputation: An Analysis of Ranking and Ratings by Social Monitors," *Corporate Reputation Review* 1, no. 4 (1998): 327–340.

18 See *UN AIDS*, last modified 2014, http://www.unaids.org.

19 National Telecommunications & Information Administration, United States Department of Commerce (1995, 1998, 1999, 2000 & 2002).

20 "What We Do: Global Libraries Strategy Overview," *Bill & Melinda Gates Foundation*, last modified 2014, http://www.gatesfoundation.org/What-We-Do/Global-Development/Global-Libraries.

21 Dana Brakman Reiser, "Benefit Corporations—A Sustainable Form of Organization?," *Wake Forest Law Review* 46 (2011), http://wakeforestlawreview.com/benefit-corporations%E2%80%94a-sustainable-form-of-organization.

22  See *Office of the Regulator of Community Interest Companies*, last modified 2014, http://www.bis.gov.uk/cicregulator/. See also Tom Pratt, "Q & A: Setting Up a Community Interest Company," *The Guardian*, Dec. 1, 2009, http://www.guardian.co.uk/society/2009/dec/01/setting-up-community-interest-company.

23  See David Ainsworth, "Community Interest Company Plans £1.6m Bond Scheme to Help Ex-Offenders," *Third Sector Online*, November 2, 2011, http://www.thirdsector.co.uk/news/1101937/.

24  "When Leon Sullivan joined the Board of Directors at General Motors in 1971, he used his corporate foothold to oppose apartheid, the government policy of segregation in South Africa. Since the passage of a Declaration of Grand Apartheid in 1948, a number of reformers, including Nelson Mandela, had tried unsuccessfully to end apartheid. . . . General Motors was the largest employer of blacks in South Africa at that time, and Sullivan decided to use his position on the Board of Directors to apply economic pressure to end the unjust system. The result was the Sullivan Principles, which became the blueprint for ending apartheid."
    Source: "Rev. Leon Sullivan: A Principled Man," *Marshall University*, http://www.revleonsullivan.org.

25  "Sustainability," *Ford Motor Company*, last modified 2014, http://corporate.ford.com/our-company/sustainability.

26  See Nike, discussed below in Chapters 7 and 11 of this textbook.

27  The development of the Valdez Principles, and the CERES Principles derived from them, are unintended, positive consequences of the Exxon Valdez oil spill.

28  *Global Reporting Initiative*, last modified 2014, http://www.globalreporting.org/. See also *United Nations Global Compact*, last modified 2014, http://www.unglobalcompact.org.

29  "Sustainability," *Ford Motor Company*, http://corporate.ford.com/our-company/sustainability.

30  *Walmart: 2013 Global Responsibility Report*, last modified 2013, http://cdn.corporate.walmart.com/39/97/81c4b26546b3913979b260ea0a74/updated-2013-global-responsibility-report_130113953638624649.pdf.

31  Henry Amoroso, "The Federal Sentencing Guidelines Endorsement of Corporate-Level Restitution: Furtherance of Public Policy or Discrimination on the Basis of Entity Capitalization?," *Campbell Law Review* 18, no. 2 (1996): 225–39. See also the ILO's discussion of the Sentencing Guidelines: "Corporate Codes of Conduct," *International Labour Organization*, last modified 2004, http://www.itcilo.it/actrav/actrav-english/telearn/global/ilo/code/main.htm.

32  See "Principles for Business," *Caux Round Table: Moral Capitalism at Work*," last modified 2014, http://www.cauxroundtable.org/index.cfm?menuid=8.

33  "Enron Code of Ethics, July 2000," *The Smoking Gun*, www.thesmokinggun.com.

34  "Former Enron Chief Financial Officer Andrew Fastow Pleads Guilty to Conspiracy to Commit Securities and Wire Fraud, Agrees to Cooperate with Enron Investigation," January 14, 2004, National Press Releases of the Federal Bureau of Investigation, last modified 2014, http://www.fbi.gov/news/pressrel/press-releases/former-enron-chief-financial-officer-andrew-fastow-pleads-guilty-to-conspiracy-to-commit-securities-and-wire-fraud.

35  Robert Reich, in his book *The Work of Nations* (New York: Alfred A. Knopf, 1991), identifies the "global web" of business enterprise.

36  John R. Boatright, "Business Ethics and The Theory of the Firm," *American Business Law Journal* 34, no. 2 (Winter 1996): 217–38. Boatright views a limitation of shareholder capitalism that firms "are free to externalize costs whenever possible."

37 Denis Arnold, "Texaco in the Ecuadorian Amazon," in *Case Studies in Business Ethics*, 5th ed., ed. Al Gini (Upper Saddle River, NJ: Prentice Hall, 2005).

38 Jeanne M. Logsdon and Donna J. Wood, "Business Citizenship: From Domestic to Global Level of Analysis," *Business Ethics Quarterly* 12, no. 2 (2002): 155–87.

39 Unlawful Corporate Payments Act of 1977, 95th Cong., 1st sess., 1977 HR Rep. 95–640, http://www.justice.gov/criminal/fraud/fcpa/history/1977/houseprt-95-640.pdf.

40 "Corruption Perceptions Index," *Transparency International: The Global Coalition Against Corruption*, last modified 2013, http://www.transparency.org/policy_ research/surveys_indices/cpi/2010/in_detail. See also "Press Releases," *Transparency International: The Global Coalition Against Corruption*, http://www.transparency.org/ news/pressreleases. The Transparency International Corruption Perceptions Index 2003 charts levels of corruption in 133 countries. Seven out of ten countries score less than 5 out of a clean score of 10, while five out of ten developing countries score less than 3 out of 10.

41 See also United Nations, *Global Corruption Report* 82 (2001).

42 "Corruption Perceptions Index, 2013," *Transparency International: The Global Coalition Against Corruption*, last modified 2013, http://cpi.transparency.org/cpi2013/results/.

43 Jack G. Kaikati, George M Sullivan, John M Virgo, T R Carr, and Katherine S Virgo, "The Price of International Business Morality: Twenty Years Under the Foreign Corrupt Practices Act," *Journal of Business Ethics* 26, no. 3. (Aug 2000): Part 1.

44 *OECD: Better Policies for Better Lives*, last modified 2014, http://www.oecd.org.

45 "OECD Convention on Combating Bribery of Foreign Public Officials in International Business Transactions," *OECD: Better Policies for Better Lives*, last modified 2011, http:// www.oecd.org/document/21/0,2340,en_2649_34859_2017813_1_1_1_1,00.html.

46 "United Nations Convention Against Corruption," *United Nations Office on Drugs and Crime*, last modified 2014, http://www.unodc.org/unodc/en/treaties/CAC/.

47 The FCPA was amended by the International Anti-Bribery and Fair Competition Act of 1998.

48 Christopher Rhoads, "Lucent Faces Bribery Allegations In Giant Saudi Telecom Project: Lawsuit Says U.S. Supplier Arranged Funds to Support Minister's Lavish Lifestyle," *The Wall Street Journal*, Nov. 16, 2004.

49 Ryan Dezember and Tess Styne, "Halliburton to Pay Nigeria $35 Million to Settle Bribery Case," *Wall Street Journal*, Dec. 22, 2010.

50 Christopher Rhoads, "Lucent Faces Bribery Allegations in Giant Saudi Telecom Project: Lawsuit Says U.S. Supplier Arranged Funds to Support Minister's Lavish Lifestyle," *The Wall Street Journal*, Nov. 16, 2004.

51 David Barstow, "Vast Mexico Bribery Case Hushed Up by Wal-Mart After Top-Level Struggle," *New York Times*, April 22, 2012.

52 David Voreacos and Renee Dudley, "Wal-Mart Says Bribe Probe Cost $439 Million in Two Years," *Bloomberg*, Mar. 26, 2014. See Alistair Barr and Kevin McCoy, "Wal-Mart replaces its CEO with company insider," *USA TODAY*, Nov. 25, 2013. See also, Phil Wahba, "At Wal-Mart annual meeting, dissenting shareholders strike out," *Fortune*, June 6, 2014, http://fortune.com/retail/walmart-annual-meeting/.

53 Royal Dutch Petroleum is being sued under the Alien Tort Statute of 1789 in the case of *Kiobel v. Royal Dutch Shell et al.*, decided by the U.S. Supreme Court in 2013. See Paula Alexander Becker, "Alien Tort Statute of 1789 and International Human Rights Violations: Kiobel v. Royal Dutch Petroleum Co.," *New England Journal of Entrepreneurship*, ed. Khawaja Mamun, special issue (May 2014).

54 The pervasiveness of Enron's culture of corporate arrogance is illustrated by the audio tapes of conversations between energy traders released May 2004. See Richard

A. Oppel, Jr. and Jeff Gerth, "Enron Forced Up California Prices, Documents Show," *New York Times*, May 7, 2002; and Alex Berenson, "Mystery of Enron and California's Power Crisis," *New York Times*, May 9, 2002. See also the documentary *Enron: The Smartest Guys in the Room*, directed by Alex Gibney (Magnolia Pictures, 2005).

55   Terry Deal and Allan Kennedy define culture as "the way we do things around here is . . . " Terry Deal and Allan Kennedy, *Corporate Cultures: The Rites and Rituals of Corporate Life* (Boulder, CO: Perseus Press, 1982).

56   David Halberstam, *The Reckoning* (New York: Avon Books, 1986).

57   [The Caux] principles are rooted in two basic ethical ideals: kyosei and human dignity. The Japanese concept of kyosei means living and working together for the common good, enabling cooperation and mutual prosperity to coexist with healthy and fair competition. "Human dignity" refers to the sacredness or value of each person as an end, not simply as a means to the fulfillment of others' purposes or even majority prescription. *Caux Round Table: Moral Capitalism at Work*, last modified 2014, http://www.cauxroundtable.org.

58   Michael Porter and Mark R. Kramer, "Creating Shared Value," *Harvard Business Review,* January 2011.

59   "Our credo: We believe our first responsibility is to the doctors, nurses and patients, to mothers and fathers and all others who use our products and services." *Johnson & Johnson*, last modified 2014, http://www.jnj.com/our_company/our_credo.

60   Dr. Seuss, *The Lorax* (New York: Random House, 1971). *The Lorax* purports to be a children's book, but like Mark Twain's *Huckleberry Finn*, *The Lorax* contains profound social criticism of its day. *The Lorax* also questions the social value of firm output (the "thneed"). Dr. Seuss challenged the creation of socially useless product.

## End of Chapter Case: Texaco Oil Co. Drilling Oil in Ecuador

*The Human Rights Situation of the Inhabitants of the Interior of Ecuador Affected by Development Activities Report, Organization of American States, Commission on Human Rights, April 24, 1997*

### Introduction

The interior of Ecuador, known as the Oriente, is home to approximately 500,000 inhabitants. It has been the home of indigenous peoples, including the Quichua, Shuar, Huaorani, Secoya, Siona, Shiwiar, Cofan and Achuar for hundreds of years. Over the last several decades, pursuant to the discovery of commercially viable oil deposits and the opening of roads, the area has become home to settlers who have relocated from the highlands and the coast.

The attention of the IACHR was first drawn to this region of Ecuador by the filing of a petition on behalf of the indigenous Huaorani people in 1990. The petitioners alleged that the most basic human rights of the Huaorani were threatened by oil development activities about to commence within their traditional lands, and sought that the Government be required to halt development activities in the concession area known as "Block 16." The complaint alleged that these activities threatened the physical and cultural survival of the Huaorani as an indigenous people. The fundamental harm alleged was that oil exploitation activities would contaminate the water, soil and air which form the physical environment of these communities, to the detriment of the health and lives of the inhabitants.

In studying the petition, and in reviewing information submitted by and gathered from other sources concerning the human rights conditions in the Oriente, the Commission determined that the situation as a whole merited further attention.[1] With respect to the Huaorani, in addition to Block 16, other concession areas within or adjacent to their traditional lands were slated for development, including Blocks 8, 9–13, 14, 17 and 22. Other sectors of the Oriente and other indigenous peoples, particularly the Cofan, Siona-Secoya and Quichua peoples, have been subjected to the full impact of oil development and production for up to several decades. Settlers who have come to the region more recently have also been affected by oil exploitation.

It was in this context that a delegation travelled to the Oriente during the Commission's on site visit to Ecuador. In Lago Agrio, the delegation met with representatives of the Shuar, Siona and Secoya peoples, as well as representatives of campesino organizations, the Carmelite Mission, and the Frente por la Defensa de la Amazonia. The delegation spoke with individuals as it travelled east to Dureño, and returned to Lago Agrio to head south to Shushufindi. Near Shushufindi, they met with members of the organization La Delicia and with representatives and residents of the settlement of La Primavera. From there they travelled to Coca, and held a series of meetings, principally with representatives of the Huaorani and Quichua peoples, as well as with representatives of the Capuchin Mission, the Rainforest Information Center and the Sierra Club Legal Defense Fund. Additionally, the Commission met in Quito with a range of Government officials whose responsibilities bear on questions relevant to the interior, including the Minister of Mines and Energy and the Subsecretary for Indigenous and Afro-Ecuadorean Affairs, and with indigenous leaders and representatives of human rights and environmental groups.

This chapter details the present situation in the Oriente, reviews the applicable legal regime, and sets forth the Commission's conclusions and recommendations.[2] The focus of this discussion is on the ability of the Oriente's inhabitants to realize their rights to life and physical security in an environment that has been subjected to severe environmental pollution. The information received and analyzed by the Commission, as well as the data and insights gathered during its on site observation, have largely substantiated the concerns voiced by the affected population, thereby prompting the recommendations which conclude this chapter.

## The Situation in the Oriente

Ecuadorean law provides that all subsurface minerals are the property of the State. Consequently, the State exploits oil and mineral deposits, either directly through the state-owned oil company PetroEcuador, or indirectly, through concessions and service contracts with foreign oil companies.

The exploitation of oil resources in the Oriente since the 1960's, when commercially viable deposits were first discovered, has had a profound impact on the region and its people.[3] The north Oriente, comprising the provinces of Napo and Sucumbios, has been most affected, as development activities were initially centralized there. However, the area available for oil and mineral development has gradually been expanded. New concessions have been established, and additional bidding rounds have been opened by the Government over the last several years.[4] Current Oriente operations involve, inter alia, over 300 producing wells, regional oil refineries, secondary pipelines, transfer lines and gas lines, and the network of roads that serves the industry.

The individuals and groups from whom the Commission has received information, both during and after its on site visit, represent both settler and indigenous communities. These inhabitants of oil development sectors have been unanimous in claiming that the operations generally, and the improper handling and disposal of toxic wastes in particular, have jeopardized their lives and health. They claim that oil exploitation activities taking place in or near their communities have contaminated the water they use for drinking, cooking and bathing, the soil they cultivate to produce their food, and the air they breathe. Residents of affected sectors indicated that their rivers, streams and groundwater were contaminated with crude oil and toxic production wastes released into the environment due to improper treatment and disposal of toxic wastes, collapsed or leaching waste pits, and oil spills. These are, in most cases, the only water sources available for drinking, cooking and bathing, as well as for the watering of livestock, domestic animals and wildlife. Residents of a number of communities complained that the air they breathe is contaminated when waste oil and gas are burned off without any kind of emission controls. Numerous people live and walk along roads which have been sprayed with waste crude, and complain that they are constantly exposed to this oil and oil-coated dust particles in the air.

The Commission was advised by representatives of communities near oil development sites that, as a result of exposure to contaminated water, soil and air, some of their members suffered from skin diseases, rashes, chronic infections and fevers, gastrointestinal problems, and that the children particularly suffered frequent bouts of diarrhea. CONFENIAE and the Unión de Promotores Populares de Salud de la Amazonia Ecuatoriana provided specific data comparing the health situation of communities adjacent to oil development sites with those further away.[5]

In addition, a number of people told the delegation that contamination of the physical environment was hindering their ability to feed their families. The Commission has received reports that the pollution of local rivers, streams and lakes has contaminated the fish residents depend on as a dietary staple, and that development activities and contamination have driven away the wildlife they hunt as an important source of protein. In a number of instances, separation stations, exploratory or production wells, and waste pits are located immediately adjacent to or even within local communities. Many facilities, including those the Commission observed, are not fenced in or otherwise secured. Settlers reported that animals they raise to eat and to sell had become sick from drinking contaminated water, or had died after drinking from or becoming trapped in local waste pits. In several cases, the Commission received reports from settlers who had lost animals, fields or crops due to oil spills which had spread onto their land.[6]

The inhabitants allege that the Government has failed to regulate and supervise the activities of both the state-owned oil company and of its licensee companies. They further allege that the companies take few if any measures to protect the affected population, and refuse to implement environmental controls or to utilize existing technologies employed in other countries. Those who spoke before the delegation indicated that the Government had failed to ensure that oil exploitation activities were conducted in compliance with existing legal and policy requirements. Throughout its travels in the Oriente, the delegation received claims that the Government of Ecuador has violated and continues to violate the constitutionally protected rights of the inhabitants of the region to life and to live in an environment free from contamination.

Oil development and exploitation do, in fact, alter the physical environment and generate a substantial quantity of toxic byproducts and waste. Oil development activities include the cutting of trails through the jungle and seismic blasting. Substantial tracts of land must be deforested in order to construct roads and build landing facilities to bring in workers and equipment. Installations are built, and exploratory and production wells drilled. Oil exploitation then generates byproducts and toxic wastes through each stage of operations: exploratory drilling, production, transportation and refining.

Reports have only recently begun to document how these toxic byproducts have been dealt with. Waste products generated by exploratory drilling[7] have reportedly been disposed of in open pits, which may overflow and spill into rivers, streams and groundwater. Other wastes have reportedly been disposed of in buried pits, which, without proper lining or capping may leach into the environment.[8] Waste oil from the testing process has, in some cases, reportedly been burned off without temperature or environmental controls.[9]

In the production phase, oil extracted from wells is pumped to separation stations.[10] Drilling and produced water wastes have generally been collected in waste pits at well sites and separation stations, although some operations have recently begun efforts to reinject a percentage of such wastes. Waste pits have reportedly often been unlined, susceptible to collapse and to being washed out by heavy rains, and constructed so that when the contents reach a certain level they drain to lower-lying areas away from the pit. The contents of the waste pits, reportedly often left untreated, may eventually leach into adjacent soil and ground water. The Ministry of Energy and Mines reportedly estimated that some 19 billion gallons of these produced water wastes had "been dumped without treatment into the waters and soils of the Oriente" since 1972.[11] Drilling wastes vary from site to site, but typically may contain such toxins as arsenic, lead, mercury, benzene, napthalene and other hydrocarbons.[12] Some companies have sprayed waste crude oil over local roads, ostensibly to keep down the dust. The run off from the roads drains into adjacent fields, groundwater and streams.

Crude oil has also been released into the environment through spills in the production and transportation phases of operation, particularly through spills from the Trans-Ecuadorean Pipeline.[13] The Ecuadorean Government reported that, as of 1989, 30 different spills from the Trans-Ecuadorean pipeline had involved the release of a total of 16.8 million gallons of crude.[14] There have been a number of substantial spills in the interim, and ruptures in secondary pipelines have resulted in substantial additional discharge into the environment. An additional 1,000 to 2,000 gallons of oil reportedly spill from the flowlines connecting the wells to the stations every two weeks.[15] It has been estimated that since 1972, over "30 billion gallons of toxic wastes and crude oil have been discharged into the land and waterways of the Oriente."[16]

The Commission delegation which travelled from Lago Agrio to Coca visited five different oil production sites: Dureño One, Atacapi, Shushufindi North, a site adjacent to the Population Center of Primavera, and finally a site known as Pozo Nueve de Agua Rico. Some of the roads the delegation travelled over had been sprayed with crude oil. The productions sites observed appeared to vary in terms of functionality. In at least two of the sites, visibly impure production water was being discharged into adjacent tributaries on the day of the visit. At each of the sites it could be seen that the waste pits are constructed with pipes which allow for drainoff to lower lying areas when the contents reach a certain level. That these lower lying areas tend to lead to streams or rivers was clearly evidenced in the cases of the Shushufindi North and Pozo Nueve de Agua Rico sites.

At the site near Primavera, equipment was in place to evacuate crude and other heavy deposits from a portion of a large unlined waste pit. The Pozo Nueve de Agua Rico site consisted of one lined and a larger unlined waste pit. The Commission was met there by a company representative who explained that this site had already been subjected to an intensive clean up, and a certificate was produced attesting that the pool had been tested and the water found to be within acceptable contamination limits. Visual inspection indicated that the surface of both pits was covered with a film of oil. At the back of the larger unlined pit the delegation saw that a narrow channel had recently been dug. The channel was still separated from the pit by a strip of earth, but once that had been removed, the channel would have the effect of draining the pit into an area leading directly to a river.

At the Dureño One site, natural gas and other byproducts were being burned off by a flare some 20 feet off of the ground. At Shushufindi North, byproducts were being burned off from a pipe located at ground level directly over the first waste pit. At the Primavera and Pozo Nueve de Agua Rico sites, refuse soaked with crude was being incinerated in small open fires on the ground.

## Government Action on the Issue of Oil Development

In recent years, the Government has taken certain legislative and policy measures to address the effects of oil development on the people and the environment of the Oriente. The September 1993 establishment of the Environmental

Advisory Commission of the Presidency to coordinate action in this sphere led to the June 1994 issuance of Executive Decree 1802, entitled "Basic Environmental Policies of Ecuador,"[17] outlining national priorities in this area. During a meeting with the Commission, the Minister of Mines and Energy informed its members that, for almost a decade, companies interested in exploiting petroleum had been required to submit environmental impact and other plans.[18] Decree 1802 specifies that companies are required to prepare an Environmental Impact Study and a Program of Environmental Mitigation, as well as to seek the corresponding authorization prior to the initiation of activities which could degrade or contaminate the environment. The Development Plan adopted during the Durán-Ballén Administration calls for foreign companies to apply the highest standards and requirements of their home country in their operations in Ecuador, without prejudice to compliance with Ecuadorean law. As noted by the Government in its observations of March 19, 1997, the Environmental Advisory Commission was transformed into the Ministry of the Environment in August of 1996.[19]

Ecuadorean law provides certain protections against environmental pollution, including the Law for the Protection and Control of Environmental Contamination, concerning the protection of air, soil and water resources. Contamination which is harmful to human life, health and well-being, harmful to the flora and fauna, or which degrades air, water or soil quality is prohibited.[20] The 1981 Law of Forestry and Conservation of Natural Areas and Wildlife provides for the protection of designated national parks or natural reserves. Additional legislation speaks to oil exploitation operations, contractual requirements, and other aspects of environmental protection.[21]Notwithstanding the existence of an emerging corpus of environmental regulation, little implementation or enforcement action has been taken.[22]

Responsibility for action in this sphere has to date been decentralized. While the Ministry of Mines and Energy, through the DINAMA, bears principal responsibility for environmental matters, questions concerning health, water and water quality come within the jurisdiction of the Ministry of Health. The Instituto Ecuatoriano Forestal de Areas Naturales y Vida Silvestre is in charge of environmental protection zones and national parks. Processes to inform local communities about the effects of development would fall within the responsibility of the Public Relations Ministry. It seems likely that the recent establishment of the Ministry of the Environment will enhance coordination in this sphere.

One of the Government's most visible activities with respect to the effects of oil development has been its effort to ensure that Texaco finance and implement a plan to clean up areas that were contaminated during the company's twenty-plus years of operation in the Oriente. In the spring of 1992, after Texaco withdrew from its exploitation operations in Ecuador, the Government contracted for an environmental audit to assess the situation resulting from the company's operations. Based on the results of that process, the Government and Texaco signed a series of agreements in late 1994 and 1995 obliging the company to undertake certain activities to remedy the environmental consequences of its operations in the Oriente. These reportedly include clean up activities, revegetation efforts, and the establishment of a one million dollar fund to be used for projects developed by a particular indigenous federation and approved by Texaco and the Ministry of Mines and Energy.

The response of the affected communities has evidently been mixed. A number of communities have indicated their rejection of the audit and the agreements signed to date on the stated basis that: they were excluded from direct participation in the process, the agreement did not adequately repair the damages suffered, and the process failed to provide for any independent review or evaluation of the results.[23] The Confederation of Indigenous Nationalities of the Ecuadorean Amazon [CONFENIAE] communicated its rejection of the accords to the Minister of Mines and Energy at the end of 1995, indicating that the agreements failed to take into account "20 years of oil spills, deforestation [and] water contamination," failed to provide guarantees, and failed to address causes of ongoing contamination.[24] Some leaders indicated that they lacked sufficient information to take a position, while other communities welcomed the planned clean up activities as a positive step.

## The Applicable Legal Framework

### 1. Relevant Domestic Law

The domestic law of Ecuador recognizes the relationship between the rights to life, physical security and integrity and the physical environment in which the individual lives. The first protection accorded under Article 19 of the Constitution of Ecuador, the section which establishes the rights of persons, is of the right to life and personal integrity. The second protection establishes "the right to live in an environment free from contamination." Accordingly, the Constitution invests the State with responsibility for ensuring the enjoyment of this right, and for establishing by law such restrictions on other rights and freedoms as are necessary to protect the environment. Thus, the Constitution establishes a hierarchy according to which protections which safeguard the right to a safe environment may have priority over other entitlements.

The amendments to the Constitution adopted in 1996 complement the foregoing protections. The new provisions set forth that the State will protect the right of the population to a safe environment and guarantee sustainable development. The Constitution now provides that the following shall be regulated by law: the preservation of the environment, ecosystems and biodiversity; the prevention of environmental contamination; the sustainable development of natural resources; the requirements that public and private activities affecting the environment must meet; and the establishment of a system of natural protected areas. These recent amendments also set forth the legal framework of state and individual responsibility for violations of norms to protect the environment.

Ecuador is Party to or has supported a number of instruments which recognize the critical connection between the sustenance of human life and the environment, including: the Additional Protocol to the American Convention in the Area of Economic, Social and Cultural Rights,[25] the ICCPR and the ICESCR, the Stockholm Declaration, the Treaty for Amazonian Cooperation,[26] the Amazon Declaration,[27] the World Charter for Nature,[28] the Convention on Nature Protection and Wildlife Preservation in the Western Hemisphere,[29] the Rio Declaration on Environment and Development[30] and the Convention on Biological Diversity.[31]

## 2. *Relevant Inter-American Law*

The realization of the right to life, and to physical security and integrity is necessarily related to and in some ways dependent upon one's physical environment. Accordingly, where environmental contamination and degradation pose a persistent threat to human life and health, the foregoing rights are implicated.

The American Declaration of the Rights and Duties of Man, which continues to serve as a source of international obligation for all member states, recognizes the right to life, liberty and personal security in Article I, and reflects the interrelationship between the rights to life and health in Article XI, which provides for the preservation of the health and well being of the individual.[32] This priority concern for the life and physical preservation of the individual is reflected in the American Convention in Article 4, which guarantees the right to life, and Article 5, which guarantees the right to physical, mental and moral integrity.

The right to life recognized in Article 4 of the American Convention is, as noted in Chapter IV of this report, fundamental in the sense that it is nonderogable and constitutes the basis for the realization of all other rights. Article 4 protects an individual's right to have his or her life respected: "This right shall be protected by law. . . . [n]o one shall be arbitrarily deprived of his life." The right to have one's life respected is not, however, limited to protection against arbitrary killing. States Parties are required to take certain positive measures to safeguard life and physical integrity. Severe environmental pollution may pose a threat to human life and health, and in the appropriate case give rise to an obligation on the part of a state to take reasonable measures to prevent such risk, or the necessary measures to respond when persons have suffered injury.

## *Analysis*

The Commission recognizes that the right to development implies that each state has the freedom to exploit its natural resources, including through the granting of concessions and acceptance of international investment. However, the Commission considers that the absence of regulation, inappropriate regulation, or a lack of supervision in the application of extant norms may create serious problems with respect to the environment which translate into violations of human rights protected by the American Convention.

The Government stated in its observations on the present report that the environment had been damaged by deforestation, erosion, the over-exploitation of resources, and high levels of contamination from oil exploitation and mining.

As has been recognized by the Government of Ecuador and numerous international observers, it is clear that the activities of the state-run oil company and the acts and omissions of licensee companies have resulted in severe environmental pollution. The Ministry of Mines and Energy has reported this in various figures and assessments it compiled (some of which are cited in this report), and the Government has acknowledged it as a factual matter, as, for example, in the series of remediation agreements signed with Texaco. The Executive policy directive of June, 1994 acknowledged that some entities performing oil exploitation activities have used sub-standard technology to the detriment of society and the environment. In July of 1994, a Commission of the National Congress, responding to and supporting the suit that had been filed by several indigenous groups against Texaco abroad, noted by resolution the serious injury to health and life sustained by the inhabitants of the affected sectors.[33]

Human exposure to oil and oil-related chemicals, through the skin or ingested in food or water, or through fumes absorbed via the respiratory system, has been widely documented to cause adverse effects to human health and life. In the instant case, emerging data indicates the considerable risk posed to human life and health by oil exploitation activities in the Oriente. The Unión de Promotores Populares de Salud de la Amazonia Ecuatoriana [UPPSAE] carried out a study in 1993 to gather specific data on the effects of oil exploitation on the health of settler communities.[34] The study examined 1,465 people in ten communities established by settlers around Dureno and Pacayacu in Sucumbios Province. 1,077 of the study subjects lived in oil-contaminated areas, and 388 in non-contaminated areas. There are five petroleum camps in the area. The results of the study indicated significantly higher rates of spontaneous abortion,[35] headache, nausea, anemia, dermatitis and fungal infection in the population exposed to oil.[36]

A representative of CONAIE reported that the organization had surveyed 21 communities along the Napo and Quinchiyacu Rivers affected by oil development activities, and had found that roughly three fourths of the community members complained of gastro-intestinal problems; half, of frequent headaches; a third of skin problems; and just under a third of other body aches and fevers. It was also noted that various studies done on the effects of oil contamination indicated that affected populations are at a greatly increased risk of cancer and other grave illnesses. The Director of the Coca Hospital has been cited as indicating an increase in infant mortality due to water contamination and accidents related to petroleum, and local health workers have reported a rise in birth defects, juvenile illnesses and skin infections.[37]

The Center for Economic and Social Rights, an NGO based in New York, conducted a project to collect and analyze water samples from development-affected sectors of the Oriente. The samples were taken from water used for drinking, bathing and fishing, and from produced water (from oil processing), and analyzed for levels of polycyclic aromatic hydrocarbons (linked to health effects ranging from skin irritation to cancer) and volatile organic compounds (which commonly include benzene and benzene derivatives linked to skin, nervous system and blood disorders, leukemia, and which may harm fetal development).[38] The study concluded that Oriente residents are exposed to levels of oil-related contaminants far in excess of internationally recognized guidelines, and that human ingestion of water or fish from the waters sampled poses a significantly increased risk of serious health effects including cancer, neurological and reproductive problems.[39]

Oil development activities have also been linked, directly and indirectly, with problems in food supply and malnutrition.[40] The sectors of Orellana, Shushu-findi and Sacha, which are centers of petroleum development activity, register the highest indicators of malnutrition in Ecuador.[41] As stated in the preamble of the World Charter for Nature, adopted by the UN General Assembly in 1982: "Mankind is a part of nature and life depends on the uninterrupted function-ing of natural systems which ensure the supply of energy and nutrients."

According to the Government's own figures, billions of gallons of untreated toxic wastes and oil have been discharged directly into the forests, fields and waterways of the Oriente.[42] The resulting consequences for the inhabitants of the affected areas have been and remain grave. The right to life and the pro-tection of the physical integrity of the individual are norms of an imperative nature. Article 2 of the American Convention requires that where these rights are not adequately ensured through legislative and other means, the State must take the necessary corrective measures. Where the right to life, to health and to live in a healthy environment is already protected by law, the Convention requires that the law be effectively applied and enforced.

The information analyzed above on the impact of oil exploitation activities on the health and lives of the affected residents raises serious concern, and prompts the Commission to encourage the State of Ecuador to take the measures nec-essary to ensure that the acts of its agents, through the State-owned oil com-pany, conform to its domestic and inter-American legal obligations. Moreover, the Commission encourages the State to take steps to prevent harm to affected individuals through the conduct of its licensees and private actors. The State of Ecuador must ensure that measures are in place to prevent and protect against the occurrence of environmental contamination which threatens the lives of the inhabitants of development sectors.[43] Where the right to life of Oriente residents has been infringed upon by environmental contamination, the Government is obliged to respond with appropriate measures of investigation and redress.[44]

## Conclusions

The American Convention on Human Rights is premised on the principle that rights inhere in the individual simply by virtue of being human. Respect for the inherent dignity of the person is the principle which underlies the fun-damental protections of the right to life and to preservation of physical well-being. Conditions of severe environmental pollution, which may cause serious physical illness, impairment and suffering on the part of the local populace, are inconsistent with the right to be respected as a human being. In the context of the situation under study, protection of the right to life and physical integrity may best be advanced through measures to support and enhance the ability of individuals to safeguard and vindicate those rights. The quest to guard against environmental conditions which threaten human health requires that individuals have access to: information, participation in relevant decision-making processes, and judicial recourse.

Access to information is a prerequisite for public participation in decision-making and for individuals to be able to monitor and respond to public and private sector action. Individuals have a right to seek, receive and impart information and ideas of all kinds pursuant to Article 13 of the American Convention. Domestic law requires that parties seeking authorization for projects which may affect the environment provide environmental impact assessments and other specific information as a precondition. However, individuals in affected sectors have indicated that they lack even basic information about exploitation activities taking place locally, and about potential risks to their health. The Government should ensure that such information as the law in fact requires be submitted is readily accessible to potentially affected individuals.

Public participation in decision-making allows those whose interests are at stake to have a say in the processes which affect them. Public participation is linked to Article 23 of the American Convention, which provides that every citizen shall enjoy the right "to take part in the conduct of public affairs, directly or through freely chosen representatives," as well as to the right to receive and impart information. As acknowledged in Decree 1802, while environmental action requires the participation of all social sectors, some, such as women, young people, minorities and indigenous peoples, have not been able to directly participate in such processes for diverse historical reasons. Affected individuals should be able to be informed about and have input into the decisions which affect them.

The right to access judicial remedies is the fundamental guarantor of rights at the national level. Article 25 of the American Convention provides that "[e]veryone has the right to simple and prompt recourse, or any other effective recourse, to a competent court or tribunal for protection against acts that violate his fundamental rights recognized by the constitution or laws of the state concerned or by this Convention. . . . " This means that individuals must have access to judicial recourse to vindicate the rights to life, physical integrity and to live in a safe environment, all of which are expressly protected in the Constitution. Individuals and NGO's have indicated to the Commission that, for various reasons, judicial remedies have not proven an available or effective means for individuals threatened by environmental pollution to obtain redress.

The norms of the inter-American human rights system neither prevent nor discourage development; rather, they require that development take place under conditions that respect and ensure the human rights of the individuals affected. As set forth in the Declaration of Principles of the Summit of the

Americas: "Social progress and economic prosperity can be sustained only if our people live in a healthy environment and our ecosystems and natural resources are managed carefully and responsibly."

As the Commission observed at the conclusion of its observation in loco: "Decontamination is needed to correct mistakes that ought never to have happened." Both the State and the companies conducting oil exploitation activities are responsible for such anomalies, and both should be responsible for correcting them. It is the duty of the State to ensure that they are corrected.

## Recommendations

Given that it is the obligation of the State to respect and ensure the rights of the inhabitants of the Oriente, and the responsibility of the Government to implement the measures necessary to remedy the current situation and prevent future oil and oil-related contamination which would threaten the lives and health of these people, and having noted the concern expressed by some government officials over the seriousness and scope of this problem, the Commission recommends and encourages the State to adopt the measures necessary to translate this concern into preventive and remedial action.

The Commission recommends that the State continue and enhance its efforts to address the risks identified by the Ministry of Mines and Energy with respect to other development activities, such as gold mining being carried out in the Oriente, which poses a serious risk of contamination and danger to human health, due to the use by small-scale operators of unsophisticated methods involving mercury and cyanide.

The Commission recommends that the State implement the measures to ensure that all persons have the right to participate, individually and jointly, in the formulation of decisions which directly concern their environment. The Commission encourages the State to enhance its efforts to promote the inclusion of all social sectors in the decision-making processes which effect them.

Given that the American Convention requires that all individuals of the Oriente have access to effective judicial recourse to lodge claims alleging the violation of their rights under the Constitution and the American Convention, including claims concerning the right to life and to live in an environment free from contamination, the Commission recommends that the State take measures to ensure that access to justice is more fully afforded to the people of the interior.

Finally, as the right to participate in decision-making and the right to effective judicial recourse each require adequate access to information, the Commission recommends that the State take measures to improve systems to disseminate information about the issues which affect them, and to enhance the transparency of and opportunities for public input into processes affecting the inhabitants of development sectors.

See also: HBO documentary *Crude*[45] and "Jungle Law," *Vanity Fair*, May 2007.[46]

## Notes

1  The initial processing of the communications led the Commission to conclude that a number of the claims raised by the petitioners appeared to be prospective in nature. With this in mind, and given the already apparent indications that the situation complained of was not isolated to the Huaorani people, but appeared to have important bearing on the situation of many inhabitants of the region, the Commission determined that the situation should be treated within the framework of a general evaluation of the human rights situation in the area.

2  The situation in the Oriente with respect to oil exploitation has special implications for the indigenous peoples for whom the Amazon Basin has been home for ages beyond memory. These issues, which center around the right of indigenous peoples to special protection and preservation of their cultures, are dealt with in Chapter IX.

3  A consortium led by Texaco and Gulf first discovered commercially viable quantities of petroleum in the traditional lands of the Cofan people in 1967.

4  Pursuant to the seventh round of bidding for oil and gas production licensing, opened during the first half of 1994, foreign companies were awarded contracts to develop six additional blocks in the Oriente of 200,000 hectares each. See, Latin American Weekly Report, 10 February 1994, at 52; 23 June 1994, at 268. Three other blocks were opened for development along the Pacific coast, and additional blocks extending further south have been designated for an eighth round. Id. at 268.

5  This data is discussed, infra, in the section entitled "analysis."

6  Residents from the Canton of Shushufindi, members of the local Precooperativa, provided a list of the animals they had each lost over time for such reasons: "21 head of livestock;" "15 head of livestock;" "18 head of cattle;" "8 pigs, two horses, seven cows;" "15 pigs, two horses;" and "8 head of cattle, 11 pigs and hens." One resident living adjacent to the North Station presented the certificate of a veterinarian attesting to his eight dead cattle. Another community testified to similar losses in a meeting with the Commission.

7  It has been estimated that each exploratory well drilled "produces an average of 4,165 cubic meters of drilling wastes containing a mixture of drilling muds (used as lubricants and sealants), petroleum, natural gas, and formation water from deep below the earth's surface (containing hydrocarbons, heavy metals and high concentrations of salt)." Center for Economic and Social Rights [CESR], "Rights Violations on the Ecuadorean Amazon," 1 HEALTH & HUMAN RTS. 83, 84–85 (Fall, 1994), citing J. Kimerling, Amazon Crude (1991), which attributes the per well estimate to Drilling Department of Ecuador's National Directive of Hydrocarbons. Kimerling, at p. 59 n. 24.

8  J. Kimerling, supra at 61.

9  Id. at 59 (citing 1989 estimate by DINAMA that each exploratory well produces approximately 42,000 gallons of waste oil).

10  The oil is then separated from wastes comprised of formation water, oil remnants, gas and toxic chemicals. The vast majority of the natural gas which is separated from the petroleum is burned off as waste, without temperature or emission controls. Id. at 63 (noting that DINAMA was studying the advisability of reinjecting the gas for later reclamation); CESR, supra at 85.

11  J. Kimerling, supra, at 65. The produced water wastes also contain petroleum. It is estimated that "roughly 2,100 to 4,200 gallons of oil are discharged every day" as part

of these wastes. Id. (citing Ministry of Mines and Energy, 1989). One Government study involving 187 wells found that crude oil was systematically dumped into the forest, farmlands and various bodies of water. See, Fundación Natura, "Desarollo y Conservación en la Amazonia Ecuatoriana," at 13 (citing DIGAMA study of 1987). Another Government study which tested samples of water taken from streams and rivers near production sites found elevated levels of oil and grease in every sample, and concluded that oil development was linked to deterioration of both land and aquatic ecosystems. Kimerling, at 67,citing CEPE, "Analisis de la Contaminación Ambiental en los Campos Petroleros Libertador y Bermejo," 1987.

12 See, Kimerling, supra, at 59 (listing additional toxins).

13 The Texaco-Gulf consortium (see n. 3, supra) constructed the Trans-Ecuadorean Pipeline, completed in 1972. The pipeline, or Sistema del Oleoducto Trans-Ecuatoriano (SOTE) runs for just under 500 kilometers from Lago Agrio to Esmeraldas on the Pacific Coast.

14 Kimerling, supra at 69. The comparison often cited is to the 10.8 million gallon spill from the Exxon Valdez.

15 CESR, supra, at 85, citing sources including interviews with Minister of Energy and Mines and DINAMA personnel. See, Kimerling, supra, at 63 (citing DINAMA as source for data on spills from flowlines).

16 CESR, supra.

17 The documents entitled "Basic Principles for Environmental Action in Ecuador" and "Basic Environmental Policies of Ecuador" were approved in December 1993 and June of 1994, respectively. An "Ecuadorean Environmental Plan" was reportedly in development at the time of the Commission's visit.

18 The Minister further indicated that, since approximately 1988, development contracts with the Government had included clauses concerning the defense of the environment, and that agreements arising out of the seventh round would contain strong measures in this regard.

19 Until mid-1996, the Ministry of Energy and Mines had been tasked with environmental oversight through its Subsecretariat of the Environment and the Dirección Nacional de Medio Ambiente (DINAMA).

20 Law for the Prevention and Control of Environmental Contamination, Ch. I, para. 1, R.O. No. 97, May 31, 1976. Implementing regulations were passed concerning water in 1989, and for air in 1991. See e.g., Law of Waters, art. 22, R.O., No. 69, May 30, 1972; General Regulations for the Application of the Law of Waters, arts. 89–90, R.O., No. 233, Ja. 26, 1973.

21 See generally, Ministry of Energy & Mines and PetroEcuador, Environmental Legislation: Compilation of Laws, Regulations and Norms Related to the Environment and the Conservation of Nature, for the Hydrocarbon and Mining Sector, Sept. 1993.

22 In fact, Decree 1802 acknowledged that, while Ecuadorean law provided a sufficient theoretical framework for environmental action, compliance with extant regulations had been partial. The policy directive accordingly called for action to reinforce the effective and efficient application of the existing regulations.

Community and NGO representatives indicated that existing remedies have proven ineffectual in providing protection in this sphere, and referred to the filing of a claim before the Tribunal of Constitutional Guarantees in 1989 seeking to prevent the Government from authorizing oil exploitation in the Yasuni National Park. The Corporación de Investigaciones Juridico-Ecologicas y de Defensa de Vida (CORDAVI) had argued that the planned exploitation would violate the Constitutional right of the Park's inhabitants to live in a safe environment, and violate the Forestry Law's prohibition of exploitation in protected areas. The Tribunal's ruling of October 2, 1990 held that the right to live in a safe environment mandated that no further exploitation be permitted in protected areas. However, on October 31, 1990, the Tribunal issued a second opinion allowing the concessions, without having received filings from the parties and absent any explanation for the reversal.

23  It should be noted that members of the Cofan, Quichua and Secoya communities and settlers affected by Texaco's oil exploitation activities filed a class action suit against the company in federal district court in New York (the site of Texaco's headquarters), on November 3, 1993. This was closely followed by a second filing on behalf of a class of Peruvian plaintiffs seeking damages to remedy what they allege to be the downstream contamination caused by Texaco's operations in Ecuador. See, Aguinda v. Texaco, Complaint dated Nov. 3, 1993, No. 93 CIV. (S.D.N.Y.); Jota et al. v. Texaco, CIV., S.D.N.Y.

24  El Comercio, 27 de dic. de 1995, at C2.

25  Ecuador deposited its instrument of ratification on March 25, 1993. The Additional Protocol will enter into force upon the deposit of the eleventh ratification.

26  17 I.L.M. 1045 (1978).

27  28 I.L.M. 1303 (1989).

28  G.A. Res. 37/7, U.N. Doc. A/37/51 (1982).

29  161 U.N.T.S. 229 (1940).

30  31 I.L.M. 874 (1992).

31  31 I.L.M. 818 (1992).

32  See, Article 29, American Convention, which specifies that "no provision of this Convention shall be interpreted as: . . . d. excluding or limiting the effect that the American Declaration of the Rights and Duties of Man and other international acts of the same nature may have." See also, Advisory Opinion OC-10/89 of July 14, 1989 "Interpretation of the American Declaration of the Rights and Duties of Man within the Framework of Article 64 of the American Convention on Human Rights," Ser. A No. 10, para. 46.

33  Resolution of the National Congress "La Comisión de Fiscalización Frente a la Demanda de los Cofanes en Contra de la Texaco," de 4 de julio de 1994. The resolution affirmed the clear mandate of the Constitution to protect the right to live in an environment free from contamination, and recognized that this right had been subject to grave violation. The resolution cautioned that human life and health, as well as the Amazonian ecosystem had been endangered.

34  UPPSAE, Culturas Bañadas en Petroleo: Diagnóstico de salud realizado por promotores, 1993.

35  The study showed that women residing within 200 meters of oil contaminated sites experienced lower live birth rates than the same women had experienced when living in other areas of the country, and that women living within 200 meters of such sites had a higher rate of spontaneous abortion than women living more than 200 meters away from the sites. UPPSAE study, p. 56, fig. 22, 23.

36  Rates of anemia, tuberculosis and malnutrition were reported to be twice as high in areas designated as oil-contaminated. Skin infections were four times more likely in such areas. UPPSAE study, p. 61.

37  Hoy: Blanco y Negro, "La Calamidad Amazonica," No. 26, Domingo 23 de octubre de 1994, p. 2.

38  CESR, at 12–20. "Fingerprinting" analysis was used to link contamination in samples to specific sources. For example, "[f]ingerprinting analysis of hydrocarbon distribution indicated that the contamination source of drinking water samples from the San Pablo spring . . . and Shushufindi well . . . matches the PAH distribution found in produced water from the Shushufindi North Station." Id. at 18, app. VI(a).

39  Id. at 19–20.

40  See, UPPSAE study, at 53.

41  See, E. Martínez, "Indicadores sociales y culturales de los impactos producidos por la actividad petrolera," in, Acción Ecologica, Amazonia por La Vida 41, 43–44 (1994) (citing, M. Chiriboga, R. Landín and J. Borja, Los Cimientos de una Nueva Sociedad (IICA 1989); CEPAR, 1993).

42  It may also be noted that, in 1992, pursuant to the claim of the non-governmental organization CORDAVI, the International Water Tribunal [an independent forum funded by European environmental organizations of a non-governmental and governmental character] held a juried hearing on claims that Petroecuador, Texaco and City Investing were responsible for having contaminated water sources in the Oriente. The Tribunal (which exercises no legal jurisdiction in Ecuador) found that the companies had failed to take adequate precautionary measures in their exploitation processes; had discharged large amounts of hazardous wastes into the waters and soils of the Oriente; and should therefore compensate the victims. International Water Tribunal, CORDAVI v. Petroecuador, Texaco Petroleum and City Investing, Amsterdam, February 20, 1992.

43  See, "Yanomami Case," Res. No. 12/85 Case 7615, in Annual Report of the IACHR 1985–86, OEA/Ser.L/V/II.66, Doc. 10 rev. 1 (1985) (finding violation of Article XI of Declaration where Government failed to implement measures of "prior and adequate protection for the safety and health of the Yanomami Indians" against invasion of groups of *garimpeiros*).

44  While the Commission has analyzed the human rights situation in the Oriente through the example of oil exploitation activities, it must be noted that other types of development activities raise similar factual and legal concerns. One pertinent example concerns the effects of gold mining in the interior. The processes employed involve various types of chemicals, including cyanide and mercury, which may be emitted into streams and rivers. The toxicity of these substances to humans has been thoroughly documented.

45  *Crude*, directed by Joe Berlinger (Entendre Films, 2009). See also Aubrey Anne Parker, "'Crude' Director Joe Berlinger Fights Against Chevron's Subpoena," *Circle of Blue*, June 27, 2010, http://www.circleofblue.org/waternews/2010/world/crude-director-joe-berlinger-fights-against-chevrons-subpoena/.

46  William Langenwiesche, "Jungle Law," *Vanity Fair*, May 2007, http://www.vanityfair.com/politics/features/2007/05/texaco200705.

## Case Discussion Questions

1.  Is it acceptable for a global company to produce its product under different standards, depending on local regulation? Or does doing so amount to an international double standard?

    Debate this question, using pro and con arguments.

2.  Do you agree with the conclusion of the Report of the AOS that the environmental damages rise to a human rights violation of the indigenous people of Ecuador? Why or why not?
3.  Is there such a thing as gasoline whose price is too low? Note that the May 2007 *Vanity Fair* article states that Texaco's drilling practices in Ecuador resulted in low gasoline prices in California.

    Debate this question from the point of view of the producing company and from the point of view of the consumer.

# Unit II

Chapters 5 through 12 are organized around the systems model of enterprise, considering in sequence: the relation of enterprise to its regulators, competitors, suppliers, customers, the environment, employees and shareholders (corporate governance).

# 5 Managing the Business–Government Relationship I

## Regulation of Business Enterprise and the Relation of the Enterprise to Its Competitors

### Chapter Outline

### Chapter Introduction

What are the justifications for government regulation in a market-driven, capitalist economy? *Laissez faire* capitalism favors only that regulation necessary to correct deficiencies to a competitive market. However, new regulation sometimes derives from changing social values and is often tied to historical events and accidents. Moreover, the complaints of competitors sometimes lead to enforcement actions of the regulator against the aggressive market tactics and strategies of an enterprise. Competitors played a key, and perhaps, decisive role in causing the United States Department of Justice to prosecute both AT&T and Microsoft under the United States anti-trust laws.

## Chapter Goal and Learning Objectives

*Chapter Goal:* Describe the justifications for regulation of business enterprise by government in the context of a market-driven economy.

*Learning Objectives:*

1.   Discuss the evolution of *laissez faire* capitalism.
2.   Discuss the market-failure justification for regulation of business enterprise, as well as other justifications for business regulation.
3.   Debate monopoly power as an ethical issue; understand the development of anti-trust regulation.
4.   Discuss the role of competitors vis-à-vis each other and in the enforcement of anti-trust and other law.
5.   Discuss unintended negative consequences of regulation and the alternatives to regulation.

## *Laissez Faire* Capitalism

We live in the age of the *"market-driven" economies.* Market-driven economies rely on the *law of supply and demand.* Adam Smith, in his classic work, *An Inquiry into the Nature and Causes of the Wealth of Nations,*[1] argued that the market should not be constrained by government regulation, characteristic of *mercantilism.* Mercantilism was the period of economic history during the Age of Exploration and European colonialism that regulated business by licenses issued by the monarch.[2] Adam Smith's book, written in 1776, ushered in a period of economic history called *laissez faire capitalism.* According to *laissez faire* capitalism, the market should be guided by the "invisible hand" of supply-and-demand and enterprises should compete with one another in that market. Even the *centrally planned economies* of the former Soviet Union and of the People's Republic of China, which relied on the government as planner and consumer of enterprise production, have transitioned to market-driven economies.

### *The Industrial Revolution and the Rise of the Market-Driven Economy*

*Laissez faire* capitalism coincided with the rise of manufacturing and the Industrial Revolution. The *Industrial Revolution*[3] represented a transition from agriculture and handicraft production of goods to mass production of goods.

The rise of manufacturing, followed by the conversion of manufacturing technology from cottage industry to capital-intensive, mass production of goods, was based on a series of inventions, including the cotton gin, improvements in weaving that supported the growth of the textile industry in England and the steam engine, for example.[4]

Alvin Toffler, in his book *The Third Wave*,[5] identified the factors underlying and facilitating the Industrial Revolution. He called these factors "the code of the second wave." According to Toffler, the Industrial Revolution is based on the following "code": 1) standardization (of parts), 2) specialization (of labor), 3) synchronization (of tasks), 4) concentration (of capital), 5) centralization (of decision making), and 6) maximization (of profits). Two other factors, the discovery and harnessing of electricity enabling the mass production or high volume production of goods using capital equipment,[6] and the development of railroads, enabled the distribution of the mass produced goods to remote markets, far away from the site of production.[7]

***The Rise of Corporations.*** Corporations were chartered during the period of mercantilism as entities licensed by the monarch to claim the lands discovered by expeditions and to exploit the natural resources of the newly discovered and claimed lands. Modern corporations derived from the British trading companies. One of these trading companies, the British East India Trading Company, played a significant role in both the Indian sub-continent and American history. The Boston Tea Party, which was a factor leading to the American war of rebellion against Britain, was instigated by the tea tax levied by the British East India Trading Company.

Prior to 1844, corporations were chartered by the crown or by special act of Parliament.[8] The passage in England in 1844 of the Joint Stock Companies Act of 1844 and then The Limited Liability Act of 1855 facilitated the development of the modern business corporation, organized specifically for economic purposes. The Joint Stock Companies Act of 1844 provided a mechanism for the establishment of a corporation (a joint stock company) without a charter from the crown or special enactment by Parliament. The Limited Liability Act of 1855 provided that the financial exposure or liability of members of a joint stock company would be limited to their investment, thus managing and limiting the risk of undertaking new ventures. Corporations became the vehicle for the emergence of new ventures, including steamship lines, railroads, and other enterprises that furthered economic development during the Industrial Revolution.

The Civil War further spurred the growth of industrial enterprise. In the post-Civil War United States, corporations were recognized as legal persons. In the decision *Santa Clara County v. Southern Pacific Railroad Company*, the United States Supreme Court case decided in 1886, corporations came to be recognized as legal persons.[9] The taxes levied by Santa Clara County on the fences along the railroad tracks were at issue in the Southern Pacific Railroad case. The Southern Pacific Railroad was part of the complex of railroad networks that created the transcontinental railroad. At the time, railroads threw sparks along the tracks, which sometimes caused fires. It was the practice to construct fences along the railroad's right of way to protect the adjacent lands. The railroad argued that the fences were not taxable and that the taxes levied by the county violated the rights of the railroad to equal protection of the laws, guaranteed to persons under the Fourteenth Amendment.[10] The implication that corporations are legal persons is that the rights extended to persons by the Fourteenth Amendment of the United States Constitution, including equal protection and due process, are granted to corporations.

The application of the Fourteenth Amendment to corporations was an unanticipated legal development of the law. All the rights and privileges extended by the United States Constitution to persons were thereby applied to corporations. For example, one of the basic rights of persons under the Constitution of the United States is the right of free speech. The right of Nike Corporation to free speech was at issue in the *Nike v. Kasky* case, discussed in Chapter 7. Nike asserted that it did not operate sweatshops and Kasky argued that Nike must be held to a "truth in advertising" standard. Nike countered that it was engaged in political speech, where opinions are permitted, rather than commercial speech, where a "truth in advertising" standard is applied. The participation of corporations in the political process, also guaranteed to persons under the First Amendment, is discussed in Chapter 6.

## Justifications for Government Regulation of Business Corporations According to *Laissez Faire* Capitalism

*Laissez faire* capitalism prefers that markets be regulated by the laws of supply-and-demand, rather than legislation. *Laissez faire* in fact means "leave to act," a rough translation from the French. Therefore, regulation under *laissez faire* capitalism must be justified by special circumstances. Market "failure" is a justification for regulation under *laissez faire* capitalism.

### *Correcting Market "Failure"*

The justification for government regulation of corporations under *laissez faire* capitalism is to correct situations where the laws of supply and demand fail to operate in a given market. In *The Wealth of Nations*, Smith promoted the benefits of the "invisible hand," the operation of the laws of supply and demand as the best way to promote economic development and prosperity, rather than the customary government regulation of enterprises of his day, including trading companies, under the mercantilist approach.

"Market failure" happens when the assumptions underlying a free market do not operate in reality. A free or rational market rests on the assumption of many firms competing among each other. Such firms absorb all costs of production, without externalizing their costs. The decision-making processes of such firms are based on complete information, and they act to maximize profits.[11] The profit-maximizing choices are based on means-ends rationality, whereby those

*Table 5.1* Assumptions of a "Free" or Rational Market Economy

---

The assumptions of a "free" or rational market economy include:

(1) no monopoly power;

(2) no external costs;

(3) complete information;

(4) profit maximization;

(5) means-ends rationality;

(6) labor force mobility;

(7) no transaction costs.

---

means are always chosen that are best adapted to attaining desired goals. The free market rests on an assumption of labor force mobility, whereby workers are free to move to those firms that offer the best terms of employment, even if geographic relocation is involved. The assumption of a free market also assumes that there are no transaction costs to choices; for example, that workers who move to those firms that maximize their wages assume no costs in doing so. The assumptions of a "free" or rational market economy are given in Table 5.1.

The problem with the assumptions underlying the free market is that they do not operate in the real world. Herbert Simon won the Nobel Prize in Economics in 1978 for developing a theory of decision making and of firm behavior that rests on more realistic assumptions.[12] Simon takes issue with each of the assumptions of a rational market, noting that these are not realistic, i.e. not the way the world really works. Instead, Simon notes that decision makers work in situations with: 1) incomplete information; 2) multiple, conflicting goals; and 3) bounded rationality.[13] More realistic views of actual markets acknowledge that in some markets firms exert monopoly power, so that actual competition does not exist in the market. Some firms generate external costs, failing to internalize their full costs of production. There may also be limited labor force mobility, because of worker's taste, including preferences for remaining near their own families. Finally, firms and workers actually incur transaction costs associated with their choices. To the extent that the assumptions of a free or rational market do not exist in fact, or when market forces fail to generate actual competition, government regulation is justified.

For example, the Sarbanes Oxley Act of 2002 was passed as a result of the Enron Corporation corporate debacle and bankruptcy. Enron, by its corporate accounting and securities fraud, created a fraud on the market, depriving investors of a sound basis for making their decision to invest or not to invest in Enron. Securities laws had been passed in the 1930s, after the stock market crash of 1929, and the ensuing depression, requiring disclosure to the SEC so as to create corporate transparency. But these securities laws were insufficient to prevent the Enron and other corporate frauds. Congress, therefore, saw fit to amend the securities laws.[14]

The advantage of regulation to correct market failure is that the playing field among competitors is leveled, equalizing the cost structure among all players within an industry. For example, the goal of the Sarbanes Oxley Act is to provide transparency about a corporation that is a prospective investment target for investors. The effect of much regulation is to prohibit negative externalities, forcing companies to internalize their costs of production and protecting the interests of consumers. Examples of such regulation include the Environmental Protection Act or the Occupational Safety and Health Act.

### Redistribution of Goods

Market regulation can also be used to redistribute good within the population and among citizens. John Rawls, in his book *A Theory of Justice*,[15] espoused the position that in a just society, all differentials in wealth, power, and privilege must work to the benefit of the underdog. In constructing his just society, Rawls invokes the "veil of ignorance." Rawls posits that no members of society know ahead of time what social status they will hold. Social rules must constructed for the society, so that all members must be willing to buy into, without knowing their location in that society, whether they will be privileged or at the bottom of the social ladder. Rawls argues that if all differentials in social goods work to the benefit of the underdog, all members of society working under the veil of ignorance would be willing to buy into it. To the extent, therefore, that such differentials in wealth, power and privilege do not work to the benefit of the underdog, they would be disallowed, presumptively taxed away and re-distributed to the underdogs in the society.[16]

Legislation reflecting changed values occurred with the global depression of the 1930s, after the United States stock market crash of 1929: the rise of the welfare state.[17] Germany and Britain both implemented social welfare programs under their national leadership.[18] President Roosevelt, who was elected in 1932 and who assumed office in 1933, initiated a program called the New Deal. The New Deal represented the rise of the "welfare state" in the United States. Legislation enacted as part of the New Deal included: the Tennessee Valley Authority Act; the Unemployment Relief Act, creating the Civilian Conservation Corps; the Works Progress Administration and the Wagner-Peyser Act of 1933 establishing the US Employment Service; the Social Security Act; the Fair Labor Standards Act; and the National Labor Relations Act.[19] Aid to Families with Dependent Children was also established as part of the New Deal legislation. The programs enacted by Roosevelt's New Deal initiative involved redistribution of wealth to the less privileged of the society. New Deal programs are given in Table 5.2.

### Evolving/New Social Norms

Legislation derives from and reflects the values of the citizenry. After the New Deal, civil rights and other legislation reflecting new social norms was passed.

*Table 5.2* Legislation Affecting Redistribution of Goods

| Legislation | Year Enacted |
| --- | --- |
| Social Security Act | 1935 |
| Aid to Families with Dependent Children | 1935 |
| Fair Labor Standards Act | 1938 |
| National Labor Relations Act | 1935 |
| Reverse Income Tax | 1975 |
| Welfare Reform | 1996 |

In the aftermath of World War II, the civil rights movement emerged. Initially the civil rights movement was concerned with racial integration in the military. The participation of African-Americans in the segregated United States armed services led to pressure for desegregation of the armed services after World War II. A. Philip Randolph[20] emerged as the leader of Committee Against Jim Crow in Military Service and Training. He also founded the League for Non-Violent Civil Disobedience Against Military Segregation, a social movement by which African-American youth would resist recruitment into a reinstated draft unless the military services were racially integrated. President Harry Truman ended segregation in the United States armed services on July 26, 1948, by issuing Executive Order 9981. Executive Order 9981 established the President's Committee on Equality of Treatment and Opportunity in the Armed Services and provided: "there shall be equality of treatment and opportunity for all persons in the armed services without regard to race, color, religion or national origin."[21]

After racial integration in the military was achieved in the 1950s during the Korean War, the movement for racial equality focused on desegregation in the schools. In 1954, a landmark U.S. Supreme Court decision, *Brown v. Board of Education of Topeka, Kansas*, reversed an earlier decision that had upheld the principle of "separate but equal" as constitutional under the Fourteen Amendment.[22] *Brown v. Board of Education* declared that segregated school systems are "inherently unequal."[23]

The civil rights movement gained momentum when an African-American woman, Rosa Parks, refused to follow the law and give up her seat on a bus in Montgomery, Alabama, to a white rider.[24] Rosa Parks was arrested for her civil disobedience. The boycott of the Montgomery buses that ensued was a direct factor leading to the passage of the Civil Rights Act of 1964. It reflected evolving and new social norms. The Civil Rights Act of 1964 was followed by a series of new laws protecting the rights of minorities, including racial, ethnic and religious minorities, women, older workers and disabled workers. (See Table 5.3) Worker rights were also protected by the Occupational Safety and Health Act, passed in 1970.

The consumer movement was also launched during the 1960s with the publication of Ralph Nader's book *Unsafe at Any Speed*, criticizing the Chevrolet

*Table 5.3* Legislation Reflecting Changing Social Norms

| Legislation | Year Enacted |
| --- | --- |
| Equal Pay Act | 1963 |
| Civil Rights Act | 1964 |
| Environmental Protection Act | 1970 |
| OSHA | 1970 |
| Equal Employment Opportunity Act | 1972 |
| Pregnancy Discrimination Act | 1978 |
| Age Discrimination in Employment Act | 1990 |
| Americans with Disabilities Act | 1990 |
| Family Medical Leave Act | 1993 |

Corvair, manufactured by General Motors.[25] The consumer movement gave rise to many laws protecting consumers. Product liability law protecting consumers changed fundamentally in the 1960s. Manufacturers of defectively designed products put into the stream of commerce were held to a standard of strict liability.[26] The Johns Manville Company was held strictly liable for the injuries caused by asbestos.[27] The asbestos trials later resulted in punitive damages.[28] The doctrine of *caveat emptor* was rejected by the courts[29] and in the Uniform Commercial Code.[30]

The environmental movement also emerged in the 1960s. Rachel Carson published a book, *Silent Spring*, criticizing the use of pesticide, and warning of their impact on the environment.[31] In 1969, the National Environmental Policy Act established the Environmental Protection Agency.[32] A national environmental day was established in 1970, as the celebration of "Earth Day" on April 22 of each year.[33] See Table 5.3.

### Evolving/New Social Norms and Redistribution of Goods

After the assassination of United States President John F. Kennedy and the assumption of the presidency by Lyndon Johnson, the 1964 Civil Rights Act was passed as part of JFK's legacy. President Johnson then undertook initiatives he called the "Great Society." A legislative initiative of the Great Society included a 1965 amendment of the Social Security Act to provide for medical care for the elderly, known as Medicare.[34] President Johnson declared a "War on Poverty," a program enacted by Congress as the Economic Opportunity Act. The War on Poverty included Head Start, focusing on early childhood education, VISTA (Volunteers in Service to America) and the Job Corps, programs administered by the Office of Economic Opportunity.

There has been a national backlash against redistribution programs enacted during the New Deal and the Great Society. The backlash to redistribution was institutionalized in the United States as welfare reform. Welfare reform, an initiative of President Bill Clinton, enacted by Congress in 1996, changed fundamentals of the Aid to Families with Dependent Children, a program put in place during the New Deal. The Clinton welfare reform represented a change in redistribution programs, which limited individual and family eligibility for welfare and required adult recipients to work. To some extent, the change in welfare reform reflected recognition of the unintended negative consequences of some programs of the Great Society. The public policy concerns driving the change in welfare legislation included concern for the weak incentives, or even disincentives, to work provided by the welfare system prior to the welfare reform of 1996. Welfare reform required many welfare recipients to work. To overcome the disincentives to work for low-income workers, the United States Congress enacted a program of Earned Income Tax Credit in 1996. The Earned Income Tax Credit refunds dollars to poor working families to offset the loss of benefits experienced by the working poor.

Johnson's Great Society initiative involved redistribution of wealth to the poor of society, while the welfare reform enacted under the leadership of Clinton represented change in some earlier welfare-state initiatives, including some programs of the New Deal. Overall, the legislation implemented during the 1960s and 1970s, during President Johnson's Great Society initiative and later, represents the implementation of new social norms, particularly about race and gender equality, and about consumer rights as well as environmental issues.

Although many of the law embodying new social norms were legislated in the 1960s and 1970s, new legislation reflecting evolving social norms continues to be enacted. Work–life balance has emerged as an important workplace issue. Currently, 70% of women with children under 18 participate in the work force.[35] The Family Medical Leave Act (FMLA) was passed in 1993 to address issues of work–life balance. The FMLA granted both female and male workers the right to unpaid leave for taking care of family members, either at the birth or adoption or a child but also including care of a spouse or parent or the illness of the worker him or herself.[36] The FMLA addresses work–life balance associated with the dual-career family. We can expect that as new issues come to the forefront of the public interest, new legislation addressing these emergent issues will be enacted. Some present day emergent issues relate to the development of communication and information technology and to biotechnology. The regulation of communication and information technology is discussed in the following and the regulation of biotechnology is discussed in Chapter 6.

## Government Authority to Regulate

The government's authority to make laws and enact implementing regulation is based on the Commerce Clause. The Commerce Clause provides: "The Congress shall have power to regulate Commerce with foreign Nations, and among the several States, and with the Indian Tribes." The United States constitution also empowers Congress to levy taxes to "provide for the general welfare." Most

*Table 5.4* Accidents and Other Crises Leading to New Legislation

| Accident | Year | Legislative Response | Regulatory Rule Change |
|---|---|---|---|
| Love Canal | 1978, 1980 | EPA Superfund | |
| Water contamination, Woburn, Mass | 1979, 1991 | | EPA largest superfund clean up |
| Ford Pinto | 1971–1978 | | Federal Motor Vehicle Safety Standard 301 |
| Union Carbide, Bhopal, India | 1984 | | Industry groups implement Community Awareness & Emergency Response (CAER); Canadian Responsible Care program |
| Exxon Valdez oil spill | 1989 | Oil Pollution Act of 1990 Double hulled vessels required by 2015 | Valdez Principles CERES Principles |
| September 11, 2001 | 2001 | The Patriot Act | Department of Homeland Security |

statutes are based either on the Commerce Clause or on Congress's power to tax.[37] The Reconstruction amendments also endow Congress with specific power to enact implementing legislation.

Legislation and regulation is reactive and based on political compromise among competing interest groups. Rather than proactively anticipating problems and crises, Congress responds reactively, after accidents or crises. The mobilization of public opinion following a disaster creates the political will and energy as well as the motivation to reach compromise among competing interest groups necessary to pass new legislation. See Table 5.4, relating crises and their subsequent regulation.

Congress did not pass new environmental legislation in response to the BP oil well blowout in 2010. Regulatory enforcement has relied on prior environmental legislation, except that Congress passed the Restore Act, which specifically allocates 80% of BP's civil damages to the region affected by the spill, rather than the funds going to the Oil Spill Liability Trust Fund.[38]

### Regulatory Agencies

The growth of regulation discussed previously, whether the regulation is related to overcoming market failure, redistribution of wealth or the emergence of new social norms, has been accompanied by the development of regulatory agencies to implement and enforce the enacted legislation. The role and obligations of regulatory agencies are to enforce the statute that they are entrusted to administer. Major regulatory agencies associated with their statutory responsibilities are given in Table 5.5.

The role and obligations of the regulator, the FDA, is raised the Vioxx case. The question raised in the Vioxx case, going to sufficiency of information is

*Table 5.5* Regulatory Agencies

| Regulatory Body | Year Created | Statutory Responsibility |
| --- | --- | --- |
| Food and Drug Administration | 1906 | Food and Drug Act |
| Federal Reserve Board | 1913 Created by Owen-Glass Act; | Regulate banks; implement monetary policy. |
| Federal Trade Commission | 1914 | Anti-Trust Laws |
| Federal Deposit Insurance Corporation | 1933 Created by Glass-Steagall Act | Separation of commercial from investment banking; insurer of commercial bank deposit accounts. |
| Securities and Exchange Commission | 1934 | Security and Exchange Act of 1934 |
| Federal Communications Commission | 1934 | Federal Communications Act |
| National Labor Relations Board | 1935 | National Labor Relations Act |
| Equal Employment Opportunity Commission | 1964 | 1964 Civil Rights Act as amended |
| Environmental Protection Agency | 1970 | Environmental Protection laws |
| National Highway Transportation Safety Administration and National Highway Transportation Safety Board | 1970 Created by Transportation Safety Act of 1974 | Investigate transportation accidents and determine their probable cause; make safety recommendations |
| Occupational Safety and Health Administration | 1971 | Occupational Safety and Health Act |
| Consumer Product Safety Commission | 1972 | Consumer Product Safety Act; Child Safety Protection Act; recall unsafe products |
| Public Accounting Oversight Board | Sarbanes Oxley 2002 | Oversee audits and auditing process for publicly traded companies. |
| Financial Stability Oversight Council | Dodd-Frank 2010 | Identify threats to financial stability;promote market discipline;respond to emerging risks. |

posed: When did the FDA know, or when should the FDA reasonably have known, that the products were harmful? Also, transparency and appropriate disclosure by the enterprise to the regulator are raised in the Vioxx case. Moreover, the withdrawal of Vioxx from the market in the fall of 2004 also poses issues of adequate regulatory action by the FDA.[39]

## Anti-Trust Law: The Regulation of Competitor Relations

The legislative motivation for the Sherman Anti-Trust Act of 1890 lies in the competitive tactics of the industrialists of the 1880s such as John D. Rockefeller, Andrew Carnegie, Jay Gould, Cornelius Vanderbilt, and J. P. Morgan. These industrialists are known as "captains of industry" because they founded enterprises basic to the industrial revolution, such as oil, steel and transportation, including steamships and railroads, as well as banking and finance.[40] They are also known, more pejoratively, as "robber barons."[41] Trusts or holding companies were established within industries, among oil companies, steel manufacturers, and sugar manufacturers and railroads. Journalists, known as the "Muckrakers," published critiques of the industrialists of the Gilded Age, for example of the Standard Oil trusts, in *McClure's Magazine*.[42]

### Sherman Anti-Trust Act of 1890

The Sherman Anti-Trust Act was passed in 1890. It prohibits monopolies and restraint of trade or commerce (see Box 5.1).

---

### Box 5.1  The Sherman Anti-Trust Act

Section 1: "Every contract, combination in the form of trust or otherwise, or conspiracy in restraint of trade of commerce . . . is hereby declared to be illegal
  Section 2: "Every person who shall monopolize, or attempt to monopolize . . . trade or commerce . . . shall be deemed guilty."

---

The Department of Justice was entrusted with its enforcement; illegal activities could be enjoined. If a company was convicted of a monopoly or restraint of trade, triple damages could be incurred.

President Theodore Roosevelt prosecuted the Northern Securities Trust in 1902, a holding company for the railroads. The Standard Oil Trust, which had been the subject of the Muckraker's critique in *McClure's* by Ida M. Tarbell, was prosecuted in 1911. The American Tobacco Company was also prosecuted in 1911 and broken up as a result. However, the Sherman Anti-Trust Act was also used to thwart efforts of workers to unionize. In 1908, the Sherman Anti-Trust Act was applied to the organizing efforts of unions.[43] Secondary labor boycotts were considered combinations in restraint of trade; the threat of the triple damages provision seriously threatened the financial resources of the unions, and the use of the labor injunction hampered union organizing efforts.[44]

## Amendments to the Sherman Anti-Trust Act

### Clayton Anti-Trust Act (1914)

The Clayton Anti-Trust Act was passed in 1914 and added to the provisions of the Sherman Anti-Trust Act that private parties could seek injunctions for violations of anti-trust law.[45] The Clayton Anti-Trust Act also addressed the application of the Sherman Anti-Trust Act to unions. The Clayton Anti-Trust Act was hailed as "labor's magna carter" because it declared "labor is not a commodity or article of commerce" (see Box 5.2).

---

**Box 5.2  Clayton Anti-Trust Act (1914)**

"Sec. 6. That the labor of a human being is not a commodity or article of commerce. Nothing contained in the antitrust laws shall be construed to forbid the existence and operation of labor, agricultural, or horticultural organizations, instituted for the purposes of mutual help, and not having capital stock or conducted for profit, or to forbid or restrain individual members of such organizations from lawfully carrying out the legitimate objects thereof; nor shall such organizations, or the members thereof, be held or construed to be illegal combinations or conspiracies in restraint of trade, under the antitrust laws."

"Sec. 20. That no restraining order or injunction shall be granted by any court of the United States . . . in any case between an employer and employees . . . involving, or growing out of, a dispute concerning terms or conditions of employment, unless necessary to prevent irreparable injury to property, or to a property right, of the party making the application, for which injury there is no adequate remedy at law."

---

The language appeared to exempt unions from anti-trust prosecution. However, the United States Supreme Court, in a 1921 decision, narrowly interpreted the language of the Clayton Anti-Trust Act to apply its provisions only to employees in a direct employer–employee relationship;[46] whereas the interests of unionized workers lay in extending union recognition to non-union establishments, thereby protecting the gains the unions had won for their workers. The wage gains achieved by unions would be threatened by the lower wage and benefits costs of non-union establishments, which, therefore, can sell their product at a lower price. Because of the narrow construction of the Clayton Anti-Trust Act language, secondary labor boycotts continued to be enjoined. The Norris-La Guardia Act of 1932 was specifically drafted to overcome the limitations of the Clayton Anti-Trust Act, as interpreted and applied by the United States Supreme Court in the *Duplex Printing Press Co. v. Deering* case.

*Federal Trade Commission Act (1914)*

The Federal Trade Commission (FTC) was established by Congress in 1914 to prevent unfair competition and deceptive practices. The FTC was endowed with the responsibility, along with the Department of Justice, to enforce enacted anti-trust law. The FTC has the power to prohibit unfair competition and deceptive practices.[47]

*Robinson-Patman Price Discrimination Act (1936)*

The Robinson-Patman Act of 1936, amending Sections 13a, 13b, and 21a of the Clayton Act, makes it unlawful for any seller engaged in commerce to discriminate in the sale price charged on commodities of comparable grade and quality where the effect might injure, destroy or prevent competition.

*The Hart-Scott-Rodino Antitrust Improvement Act (1976)*

The Hart-Scott-Rodino Antitrust Improvement Act of 1976 requires notification by companies that are proposing to merge if the merger meets certain standards in terms of the valuation of the proposed merger. The FTC and the Department of Justice evaluate the effect of proposed mergers on the market. The FTC and the Department of Justice together have developed guidelines to evaluate the effect of proposed *horizontal mergers*, i.e., mergers between competitors within the same industry, on competitiveness, and whether a proposed merger comports with U.S. anti-trust law.[48] There is a particular concern about horizontal mergers, as distinct from *vertical mergers*, which are mergers within the chain of production, because horizontal mergers reduce the number of firms within the industry. Examples of mergers that were approved include Time Warner and Turner Broadcasting and AOL, whereas a proposed merger between Staples and Office Depot was not approved because of the projected anti-competitive effect of increasing concentration within the office supply industry. An example of mergers that require approval includes the proposed merger of Comcast with Time Warner Cable Co.[49]

The Hart-Scott-Rodino Act also permits state attorneys general to bring *parens patriae suits* on behalf of those injured by violations of the Sherman Antitrust Act.

Other Amendments to the Sherman Anti-Trust Act include the Antitrust Criminal Penalty Enhancement and Reform Act of 2004, which increased the maximum Sherman Act corporate fine to $100 million but "de-trebles" the damages provisions of the Sherman Anti-Trust Act. The de-trebeling provision is intended to increase the incentive for corporations to self-report illegal conduct and to cooperate with the Department of Justice in the enforcement of anti-trust law. It was enacted at the time that the U.S. Department of Justice and private parties such as Sun Microsystems were engaged with Microsoft for its anti-trust violations.

The Standards Development Organizations Act of 2004 amends the National Cooperative Research and Production Act of 1933[50] to increase the protections for organizations that develop standards for products that can interface across manufacturers within an industry, such as standards for the wireless industry or standards for the manufacture of video recording equipment.[51] The Standards Development Organizations Act of 2004 changed the standard for violation of anti-trust law from a *"per se" rule* to the *"rule of reason."*

### The Role of Competitors

Complaints of competitors sometimes lead to enforcement actions of the regulator against the aggressive market tactics and strategies of an enterprise. Competitors played a key, and perhaps decisive, role in causing the United States Department of Justice to prosecute Microsoft, and before that AT&T,[52] under United States anti-trust laws.

Microsoft Corporation began when Bill Gates and Paul Allen developed an operating system for the IBM personal computer. IBM permitted Microsoft to license its operating system. Microsoft then developed a series of personal computers, and in 1987 Microsoft installed a graphic user interface on its personal computer. Steven Jobs, who had founded Apple Computer Company, complained that Microsoft had stolen Apple's intellectual property in the form of the graphic user interface and brought suit against Microsoft in 1988. Other competitors of Microsoft also complained about Microsoft's competitive tactics. Netscape Company developed a "browser" to access the World Wide Web, which was available for general use by 1994. Microsoft developed its own browser and "bundled" it with the operating system in 1995. Sun Microsystems developed a platform-free language, JAVA, for accessing the World Wide Web, making applications independent of Microsoft's operating system. Sun complained that Microsoft modified its platform-free language, thus injuring Sun's interests. The competitors of Microsoft formed an alliance, a professional lobbying organization, the Council for a Competitive Electronic Marketplace.[53] Finally, in the Department of Justice brought anti-trust suits against Microsoft. Microsoft settled the initial complaint by the Department of Justice with a consent decree in 1994. But the Department of Justice brought another complaint in 1998, alleging Microsoft's failure to abide by the terms of the consent decree. The 1998 lawsuit was litigated and then settled by Microsoft.[54]

*Corporate Culture.* Corporate culture played a perhaps not insignificant role in Microsoft Company's dealings with its competitors. Indeed, even the trial judge in the Microsoft anti-trust litigation found Microsoft Corporation to be arrogant.[55] Market dominance in itself is not actionable under the United States anti-trust law. For example, consumer choice resulting in market dominance occurred with Intel Company's microprocessor, but Intel avoided anti-trust prosecution at that time.[56] IBM permitted Microsoft to license its operating system to other original equipment manufacturers at the time when the personal computer market was developing. It is possible that in doing so, IBM wished to avoid possible anti-trust litigation by the Department of Justice, similar to that had been brought against AT&T. IBM was dominant in the mainframe computer market and possibly wished to avoid dominance in the emergent personal computer market also.

Microsoft settled damages claims in the US with its competitors, Apple Computer Company, Netscape and Sun Microsystems. In Europe, Microsoft was prosecuted for anti-competitive behavior. Microsoft will face new competitive challenges as technology changes and new products and applications are developed. For example, Microsoft and Apple are competing on multimedia applications. Apple controlled 70% of the global music download market by 2005. Microsoft developed a search engine that competes with the more dominant Google search engine.[57] Microsoft engaged in a joint venture with Barnes and Noble on their e-reader, the Nook, to compete with Google's Kindle and Apple's iPad.[58]

### Unintended Consequences of Regulatory Enforcement

Regulatory enforcement may have unintended negative consequences. For example, a consequence of the AT&T breakup, with AT&T retaining the long-distance market, Bell Labs, and Western Electric, was the decline of Bell Labs as a major research and development center that constitutes a national asset.[59] Bell Labs and Western Electric were later combined in 1989 as a division of AT&T, Lucent Technologies. Lucent Technologies was spun off by AT&T in 1996. Arguably, the transformation of Bell Labs from a basic research unit into an operating business unit, which was expected to be a profit center, was an inappropriate strategy. By 2001, Lucent Technologies was investigated by the SEC for channel stuffing and other financial misstatements; Lucent Technologies stock price declined radically and has never recovered. Ultimately, Lucent was sold to Alcatel.

It may have been caution about the unintended negative consequences of regulatory enforcement that led the anti-trust regulators, the Department of Justice and the courts not to seek the break up of Microsoft as the remedy for its violation of the anti-trust laws.

### The Impact of Changing Technology

Technological change had a major impact undermining the assumptions underlying the AT&T break-up: the terms of the breakup distinguished telecommunications from information services. The terms of the consent agreement reached between the United States Department of Justice and AT&T provided that: 1) AT&T would engage in long-distance telecommunications services, retain Bell Labs and Western Electric, and be free to enter the information technology market; while 2) the local regional operating companies, commonly known as "baby Bells," would provide local telecommunications services and be prohibited from providing information services. Subsequent to the break-up of AT&T, NYNEX, a baby Bell company, was criminally prosecuted for contempt of court for violating the terms of the modified final judgment.

On appeal, the D.C. Court of Appeals found that the clear distinction between telecommunications services and information services could no longer be maintained. The erosion of the distinction between information services and telecommunication required a change in the terms of the modified final judgment. This became embodied in a subsequent change in the law: the Federal Communications Act of 1996.

The Federal Communications Act of 1996 was passed because of the impact of changing technology. Wireless communications was not even envisioned at the time that the AT&T break-up transformed telecommunications. The Federal Communications Act of 1996 permitted the regional operating companies to enter the long-distance market and allowed competition within local markets.[60] The impact of emerging technologies will be discussed in Chapter 6.

## Chapter Discussion Questions

1. Discuss the evolution of *laissez fair* capitalism.
2. Discuss the market failure justification for regulation of business enterprise, as well as other justifications for business regulation.
3. Debate monopoly power as an ethical issue; understand the development of anti-trust regulation.
4. Discuss the role of competitors vis-à-vis each other and in the enforcement of anti-trust and other law.
5. Discuss unintended negative consequences of regulation and the alternatives to regulation.

## Notes

1 Adam Smith, *An Inquiry into the Nature and Causes of the Wealth of Nations* (1776).
2 See J. W. Horrocks, *A Short History of Mercantilism* (New York: Bretano's, 1925).
3 Arnold Toynbee coined the term "Industrial Revolution" to describe England's economic development from 1760 to 1840.
4 "They Made America," *pbs.org*, last modified June 30, 2004, http://www.pbs.org/wgbh/theymadeamerica/whomade/.
5 Alvin Toffler, *The Third Wave* (New York: William Morrow, 1980). See Chapter 2, "The Code of the Second Wave." Toffler refers to the post-Industrial Revolution, sometimes called the Information Age, as the "Third Wave." He refers to the Industrial Revolution as the "second wave."
6 Michael Faraday discovered how to generate electricity; he built the first electrical motor, the first electrical generator. However, it was only in 1873 that enough electricity could be generated to support factory production. See "Michael Faraday: 1791–1867," *BBC History*, last modified 2014, http://www.bbc.co.uk/history/historic_figures/faraday_michael.shtml.
7 The invention of railroads and their expansion supported the Industrial Revolution. Raw materials could be transported from the locale where they were mined to the factories where they were used and the mass produced goods could be distributed from the site of manufacture to regional or national markets. See "Transcontinental

Railroad," *History.com*, last modified 2014, Http://www.history.com/topics/inventions/transcontinental-railroad .

8  See Robert Sobel, *The Age of Giant Corporations: A Microeconomic History of American Business, 1914–1970*. (Westport, CT: Greenwood Press, 1972).

9  118 U.S. 394.

10  "Under the constitution and laws of California, relating to taxation, fences erected upon the line between the roadway of a railroad and the land of coterminous proprietors are not part of 'the roadway,' to be included by the State Board in its valuation of the property of the corporation, but are "improvements" assessable by the local authorities of the proper county." 118 U.S. 394.

11  The assumptions of a free market are similar to the assumptions of classical model of decision making, discussed in Chapter 2.

12  The approach that Herbert Simon founded is called "institutional economics." See, for example: Ronald Coase, "The Nature of The Firm," *Economica*, November 1937, 386–495. Reprinted in George J. Stigler and Kenneth E. Boulding, eds, *Readings in Price Theory* (Chicago: Richard D. Irwin, 1952), 331–51. See also R. H. Coase, *The Firm, the Market and the Law* (Chicago: The University of Chicago Press, 1988), 33–55; and O. Williamson and S. Winter, eds., *The Nature of the Firm: Origins, Evolution and Development* (New York: Oxford University Press, 1991).

13  Herbert A. Simon, *Administrative Behavior: A Study of Decision-Making Processes in Administrative Organization*, (New York: Macmillan, 1947).

14  See Corporate and Auditing Accountability, Responsibility, and Transparency Act of 2002, 107th Cong., 2d sess, 2002, HR Rep 107–414 - Background and Need For Legislation,  http://www.gpo.gov/fdsys/pkg/CRPT-107hrpt414/pdf/CRPT-107hrpt414.pdf.

15  John Rawls, *A Theory of Justice* (Cambridge, MA: Belknap Press, 1971).

16  The current tax system in the United States permits unlimited differentials in wealth, so long as the wealthiest individuals and corporations meet their obligations under the enacted tax system.

17  The welfare state is defined in terms of government regulation "overriding" market forces:

"Welfare state, in which government overrides market forces to protect individuals against specified contingencies and to guarantee people a minimum standard of living."

See Paul A. Samuelson and William D. Nordhaus, *Economics*, 18th ed. (Boston: Irwin/McGraw-Hill, 1998), 392.

18  Samuelson and Nordhaus, *Economics*, 392.

19  The National Labor Relations Act of 1935 was modeled after Section 7 of the National Industrial Recovery Act, which was declared unconstitutional by the United States Supreme Court, in the case, *A.L.A. Schechter Poultry Corp. v. United States*, 295 U.S. 495 (1935).

20  A. Philip Randolph founded the Brotherhood of Sleeping Car Porters in 1925, a union affiliated with the AFL-CIO. See: *A. Philip Randolph Institute: The Senior Constituency Group of the American Federation of Labor and Congress of Industrial Organizations*, last modified 2014, http://apri.org/.

21  See: "This Day in Truman History July 26, 1948: President Truman issues Executive Order No. 9981 Desegregating the Military," *Harry S. Truman Library and Museum*, last modified 2014, http://www.trumanlibrary.org/anniversaries/desegblurb.htm.

22  *Plessy v. Ferguson*, 163 US 537 (1896).

23  *Brown v. Board of Education*, 347 US 483 (1954).

24  See *Medaloffreedom.com*, http://www.medaloffreedom.com/RosaParks.htm.

25  Ralph Nader, *Unsafe at Any Speed: The Designed-In Dangers of the American Automobile* (New York: Grossman Publishers, 1965).

26  *Greenman v. Yuba Power Products, Inc.* (27 Cal. Reptr. 697) 2d. 897 (1962).

27  *Beshada v. Johns Manville Products Co.*, 90 N.J. 191 (1982), striking the "state of the art" defense and imposing strict liability on Johns Manville for injuries caused by its products.

28  *James Fischer v. Johns Manville Co.*, 103 N.J. 643 (1984).

29  See *Securities and Exchange Commission v. Capital Gains Research Bureau, Inc.*, 375 US 180 (1963).

30  Uniform Commercial Code Section 2–314 provides in full: "(1) Unless excluded or modified (sections 2–316), a warranty that the goods shall be merchantable is implied in a contract for their sale if the seller is a merchant with respect to goods of that kind. Under this section the serving for value of food or drink to be consumed either on the premises or elsewhere is a sale. (2) Goods to be merchantable must be at least such as (a) pass without objection in the trade under the contract description; and (b) in the case of fungible goods, are of fair average quality within the description; and (c) are fit for the ordinary purposes for which such goods are used; and (d) run, within the variations permitted by the agreement, of even kind, quality and quantity within each unit and among all units involved; and (e) are adequately contained, packaged, and labeled as the agreement may require; and (f) conform to the promises or affirmations of fact made on the container or label if any. (3) Unless excluded or modified (section 2–316) other implied warranties may arise from course of dealing or usage of trade."

31  Rachel Carson, *Silent Spring* (Boston: Houghton Mifflin, 1962).

32  42 U.S.C. 4321–4347. See "Laws & Regulations," *United States Environmental Protection Agency*, last modified June 3, 2014, http://www.epa.gov/epahome/laws.htm.

33  "The Congress, recognizing the profound impact of man's activity on the interrelations of all components of the natural environment, particularly the profound influences of population growth, high-density urbanization, industrial expansion, resource exploitation, and new and expanding technological advances and recognizing further the critical importance of restoring and maintaining environmental quality to the overall welfare and development of man, declares that it is the continuing policy of the Federal Government, in cooperation with State and local governments, and other concerned public and private organizations, to use all practicable means and measures, including financial and technical assistance, in a manner calculated to foster and promote the general welfare, to create and maintain conditions under which man and nature can exist in productive harmony, and fulfill the social, economic, and other requirements of present and future generations of Americans." Sec. 101 [42 USC § 4331]. Congressional Declaration of National Environmental Policy, Title I.

34  See "Social Security History," *Social Security Administration*, last modified 2014, http://www.ssa.gov/history/ssa/lbjmedicare1.html.

35  "Employment Characteristics of Families Summary," *Bureau of Labor Statistics, United States Department of Labor*, last modified April 25, 2014, http://www.bls.gov/news.release/famee.nr0.htm.

36  "Wage and Hour Division: Family Medical Leave Act," *United States Department of Labor*, last modified 2014, http://www.dol.gov/whd/fmla/.

37  U.S. Const., Section 8.
    "The Congress shall have Power To lay and collect Taxes, Duties, Imposts and Excises, to pay the Debts and provide for the common Defense and general Welfare of the United States; but all Duties, Imposts and Excises shall be uniform throughout the United States;

    To borrow Money on the credit of the United States;

    To regulate Commerce with foreign Nations, and among the several States, and with the Indian Tribes . . ."

38  See http://gulfoilspill.audubon.org/citizens-guide-restore-act.

39  Gardiner Harris, "F.D.A.'s Drug Safety System Will Get Outside Review," *New York Times*, Nov. 6, 2004.

40  See: Peter Collier and David Horowitz, *The Rockefellers: An American Dynasty* (New York: Holt, Rinehart and Winston, 1977); Harold C. Livesay, *Andrew Carnegie and the Rise of Big Business* (Boston: Little, Brown and Company, 1975); Maury Klein, *The Life and Legend of Jay Gould* (Baltimore: John Hopkins University Press, 1988); Frederick Lewis Allen, *The Great Pierpont Morgan* (New York: Harper & Row, 1949); Ron Chernow, *The House of Morgan: An American Banking Dynasty and the Rise of Modern Finance* (New York: Atlantic Monthly Press, 1990); Wheaton J. Lane, *Commodore Vanderbilt: An Epic of the Steam Age* (New York: Alfred A. Knopf, 1942); Robert L. Frey, ed., *Railroads in the Nineteenth Century* (New York: Facts on File, 1988); Alfred D. Chandler, Jr., *The Railroads: The Nation's First Big Business* (New York: Harcourt, Brace & World, 1965); George Rogers Taylor, *The Transportation Revolution, 1815–1860* (New York: Rinehart, 1962).

41  See Matthew Josephson, *The Robber Barons: The Great American Capitalists* (New York: Harcourt, Brace and Co., 1934).

42  See Arthur Weinberg and Lila Weinberg, *The Muckrakers* (Champaign, IL: University of Illinois Press, 1961). See also Upton Sinclair, *The Jungle* (New York: Grosset and Dunlap, 1906).

43  *Loewe v. Lawlor* (1908), commonly called the Danbury Hatters case.

44  Secondary labor boycotts were a union organizing technique, outlawed by the Taft Hartley Act of 1947, whereby unionized workers refuse to do business with or perform services for a company that is doing business with another company that is involved in a labor dispute. It was a technique for pressuring non-union employers to recognize the union.

45  §4 Clayton Act, 15 U.S.C. §15 provides: "any person who shall be injured in his business or property by reason of anything forbidden in the antitrust laws may sue therefore in any district court of the United States in the district in which the defendant resides or is found or has an agent, without respect to the amount in controversy, and shall recover threefold the damages by him sustained, and the cost of suit, including a reasonable attorney's fee."

46  *Duplex Printing Press Co. v. Deering*, 254 U.S. 443 (1921).

47  Section 45. Unfair methods of competition unlawful; prevention by Commission. See Joshua D. Wright, "Section 5 Recast: Defining the Federal Trade Commission's Unfair Methods of Competition Authority," *Federal Trade Commission*, last modified June 19, 2013, http://www.ftc.gov/sites/default/files/documents/public_statements/section-5-recast-defining-federal-trade-commissions-unfair-methods-competition-authority/130619section5recast.pdf.

48  See the Horizontal Merger Guidelines http://www.ftc.gov/bc/docs/horizmer.htm.

49  "FCC Should Approve the Comcast-Time Warner Cable Merger but Keep a Watchful Eye," *Washington Post*, April 14, 2014.

50  The National Cooperative Research and Production Act of 1933 Congress created a statutory "safe harbor" to encourage some types of innovative research and production activities, such as research consortia.

51  When VCRs were first developed, there were two alternatives, VHS and Betamax. Eventually the VHS VCR won out as the industry standard.

52  AT&T was a licensed monopoly under the Kingsbury Commitment of 1913, under which AT&T agreed to provide universal telephone service, using an integrated system. AT&T developed a manufacturing organization, Western Electric, and a research and development organization, Bell Laboratories. In 1949, the Department of Justice initiated an anti-trust action against AT&T, which was resolved in 1956 by a consent decree; under that agreement AT&T agreed to limit its business to telecommunications and government contract work. That is, AT&T would not enter the newly emergent computer and information technology market, even though Bell Labs was a leader in developing computer technology. Moreover, AT&T's exclusive use of Western Electric as an equipment supplier was challenged by competitors. In 1968, the FCC issued the Carterfone Decision, which required AT&T to permit non-AT&T manufactured equipment to be used on their network. The Carterfone decision was spurred by the manufacture of mobile equipment to be used in the oil drilling industry; Carterfone was a competitor to Western Electric. Subsequent to the Carterfone decision, MCI developed a private line service for corporate customers for long-distance telecommunications. However MCI needed to link into the AT&T network in St. Louis and Chicago, the two cities where the first private line service was licensed by the FCC. MCI was not satisfied with the terms of its arrangements and brought suit against AT&T in 1973. The United States Department of Justice brought an anti-trust suit against AT&T in 1974 based in large measure on the MCI complaints.

53  Steve Hamm, with Susan B. Garland and Owen Ullmann, "Going After Gates: Janet Reno isn't the only one getting tough with Microsoft," *Business Week*, Nov. 3, 1997.

54  "The Case Against Microsoft," *CBSNews.com*, last modified 2008, http://www.cbsnews.com/htdocs/microsoft/framesource_timeline2.html.

55  See Ken Auletta, *World War 3.0: Microsoft and Its Enemies* (New York: Random House, 2001). Judge Jackson was subsequently disqualified from the remedies component of the Microsoft trial.

56  See Harris Collingwood, "The Earnings Game: Everyone Plays, Nobody Wins," *Harvard Business Review* 79, no. 6 (June 2001).

57  Google made an initial public offering in April 2004.

58  "Barnes & Noble, Microsoft Form Strategic Partnership to Advance World-Class Digital Reading Experiences for Consumers," *Microsoft News Center*, April 30, 2012, http://www.microsoft.com/en-us/news/press/2012/apr12/04–30corpnews.aspx.

59  See Jeremy Bernstein, *Three Degrees Above Zero: Bell Labs in the Information Age* (New York: C. Scribner's, 1984).

60  Telecommunications Act of 1996:

> "The Telecommunications Act of 1996 is the first major overhaul of telecommunications law in almost 62 years. The goal of this new law is to let anyone enter any communications business—to let any communications business compete in any market against any other.

The Telecommunications Act of 1996 has the potential to change the way we work, live and learn. It will affect telephone service—local and long distance, cable programming and other video services, broadcast services and services provided to schools."

"Telecommunications Act of 1996," Federal Communications Commission, last modified May 31, 2011, http://www.fcc.gov/telecom.html.

## End of Chapter Case 5.1: Microsoft Corporation and Anti-Trust Litigation: USA and EU

IP/04/382
Brussels, 24 March 2004

### Commission Concludes on Microsoft Investigation, Imposes Conduct Remedies and a Fine

*The European Commission has concluded, after a five-year investigation, that Microsoft Corporation broke European Union competition law by leveraging its near monopoly in the market for PC operating systems (OS) onto the markets for work group server operating systems[1] and for media players.[2] Because the illegal behaviour is still ongoing, the Commission has ordered Microsoft to disclose to competitors, within 120 days, the interfaces[3] required for their products to be able to 'talk' with the ubiquitous Windows OS. Microsoft is also required, within 90 days, to offer a version of its Windows OS without Windows Media Player to PC manufacturers (or when selling directly to end users). In addition, Microsoft is fined € 497 million for abusing its market power in the EU.*

"Dominant companies have a special responsibility to ensure that the way they do business doesn't prevent competition on the merits and does not harm consumers and innovation" said European Competition Commissioner Mario Monti. "Today's decision restores the conditions for fair competition in the markets concerned and establish clear principles for the future conduct of a company with such a strong dominant position," he added.

After an exhaustive and extensive investigation of more than five years and three statements of objections,[4] the Commission has today taken a decision finding that US software company Microsoft Corporation has violated the EU Treaty's competition rules by abusing its near monopoly[5] (Article 82) in the PC operating system.

Microsoft abused its market power by deliberately restricting interoperability between Windows PCs and non-Microsoft work group servers, and by tying its Windows Media Player (WMP), a product where it faced competition, with its ubiquitous Windows operating system.

This illegal conduct has enabled Microsoft to acquire a dominant position in the market for work group server operating systems, which are at the heart of corporate IT networks, and risks eliminating competition altogether in that market. In addition, Microsoft's conduct has significantly weakened competition on the media player market.

The ongoing abuses act as a brake on innovation and harm the competitive process and consumers, who ultimately end up with less choice and facing higher prices.

For these very serious abuses, which have been ongoing for five and a half years, the Commission has imposed a fine of € 497.2 million.

## Remedies

In order to restore the conditions of fair competition, the Commission has imposed the following remedies:

- As regards interoperability, Microsoft is required, within 120 days, to disclose complete and accurate interface documentation which would allow non-Microsoft work group servers to achieve full interoperability with Windows PCs and servers. This will enable rival vendors to develop products that can compete on a level playing field in the work group server operating system market. The disclosed information will have to be updated each time Microsoft brings to the market new versions of its relevant products.

To the extent that any of this interface information might be protected by intellectual property in the European Economic Area,[6] Microsoft would be entitled to reasonable remuneration. The disclosure order concerns the interface documentation only, and not the Windows source code, as this is not necessary to achieve the development of interoperable products.

- As regards tying, Microsoft is required, within 90 days, to offer to PC manufacturers a version of its Windows client PC operating system without WMP. The un-tying remedy does not mean that consumers will obtain PCs and operating systems without media players. Most consumers purchase a PC from a PC manufacturer which has already put together on their behalf a bundle of an operating system and a media player. As a result of the Commission's remedy, the configuration of such bundles will reflect what consumers want, and not what Microsoft imposes.

Microsoft retains the right to offer a version of its Windows client PC operating system product with WMP. However, Microsoft must refrain from using any commercial, technological or contractual terms that would have the effect of rendering the unbundled version of Windows less attractive or performing. In particular, it must not give PC manufacturers a discount conditional on their buying Windows together with WMP.

The Commission believes the remedies will bring the antitrust violations to an end, that they are proportionate, and that they establish clear principles for the future conduct of the company.

To ensure effective and timely compliance with this decision, the Commission will appoint a Monitoring Trustee, which will, inter alia, oversee that

Microsoft's interface disclosures are complete and accurate, and that the two versions of Windows are equivalent in terms of performance.

***

Brussels, 27 June 2012

## Antitrust: Commission Welcomes General Court Judgment in Microsoft Compliance Case

The European Commission welcomes today's judgment by the General Court in case T-167/08 *Microsoft v Commission*—see statement by Vice President Joaquin Almunia (MEMO/12/498). The judgment essentially upholds a 2008 Commission decision imposing a penalty payment on Microsoft for not complying with the Commission's 2004 Microsoft Decision (see IP/04/382), which was upheld by the Court in 2007 (see MEM0/07/359). The judgment is the first in which the General Court has ruled on a penalty payment imposed on a company for non-compliance with an antitrust prohibition decision. The Court's ruling vindicates the Commission's efforts to ensure full compliance with its antitrust decisions, in particular the 2004 decision. As a result of the Commission's enforcement action, a range of innovative products have come to market that would otherwise not have seen the light of day.

The 2004 Microsoft Decision found that Microsoft had abused its dominant position in PC operating systems by withholding critical interoperability information from its competitors. This meant that providers of rival work group server operating systems were unable to compete effectively even though they were rated more highly by users than Microsoft's products on a range of parameters such as reliability, security and speed.

The Commission ordered Microsoft to disclose certain specified "interoperability information" on reasonable and non-discriminatory terms to vendors of work group servers, so that they could develop and distribute interoperable products.

The 2008 penalty payment decision (see IP/08/318), on which the General Court ruled today, was adopted under Article 24(2) of Regulation 1/2003 and found that, prior to 22 October 2007, Microsoft had charged unreasonable prices for access to interoperability documentation for work group servers and therefore did not comply with its obligations under the 2004 Microsoft Decision.

## The General Court Judgment

The General Court essentially upheld the Commission's main findings that Microsoft's pricing of interoperability information was not compliant with the 2004 Microsoft Decision, whilst reducing the penalty payment marginally from €899 million to €860 million. In particular, the General Court confirmed that in the absence of convincing evidence as to the innovative character of

Microsoft's non-patented interoperability information, Microsoft's remuneration schemes prior to 22 October 2007 were unreasonable under the 2004 Microsoft Decision. In this regard, the General Court confirmed that allowing Microsoft to charge for merely interoperating with its dominant PC and work group server operating system—the very essence of the original abuse—would in effect allow it to transform the benefits of the abuse into remuneration.

The General Court reduced the penalty payment marginally to take account of the fact that although Microsoft was obliged to make interoperability information available to third parties, the Commission had allowed Microsoft to await the General Court's judgment on the Commission's 2004 Decision before allowing the actual distribution of interoperable products by open source developers.

This judgment confirms that non-compliance with an antitrust decision constitutes serious misconduct which the Commission is entitled to sanction in order to compel compliance.

Following the 2008 penalty payment decision Microsoft has posted the interoperability information subject to the decision free of charge on its web site.

## The Investigation

In December 1998, Sun Microsystems, another US company, complained that Microsoft had refused to provide interface information necessary for Sun to be able to develop products that would "talk" properly with the ubiquitous Windows PCs, and hence be able to compete on an equal footing in the market for work group server operating systems.

The Commission's investigation revealed that Sun was not the only company that had been refused this information, and that these non-disclosures by Microsoft were part of a broader strategy designed to shut competitors out of the market.

This relegated to a secondary position competition in terms of reliability, security and speed, among other factors, and ensured Microsoft's success on the market. As a result, an overwhelming majority of customers informed the Commission that Microsoft's non-disclosure of interface information artificially altered their choice in favour of Microsoft's server products. Survey responses submitted by Microsoft itself confirmed the link between the interoperability advantage that Microsoft reserved for itself and its growing market shares.

In 2000, the Commission enlarged its investigation, on its own initiative, to study the effects of the tying of Microsoft's Windows Media Player with the company's Windows 2000 PC operating system.

This part of the investigation concluded that the ubiquity which was immediately afforded to WMP as a result of it being tied with the Windows PC OS artificially reduces the incentives of music, film and other media companies, as well software developers and content providers to develop their offerings to competing media players.

As a result, Microsoft's tying of its media player product has the effect of foreclosing the market to competitors, and hence ultimately reducing consumer choice, since competing products are set at a disadvantage which is not related to their price or quality.

Available data already show a clear trend in favour of WMP and Windows Media technology. Absent intervention from the Commission, the tying of WMP with Windows is likely to make the market "tip" definitively in Microsoft's favour. This would allow Microsoft to control related markets in the digital media sector, such as encoding technology, software for broadcasting of music over the Internet and digital rights management etc.

More generally, the Commission is concerned that Microsoft's tying of WMP is an example of a more general business model which, given Microsoft's virtual monopoly in PC operating systems, deters innovation and reduces consumer choice in any technologies which Microsoft could conceivably take interest in and tie with Windows in the future.

## Note

The European Commission enforces EU competition rules on restrictive business practices and abuses of monopoly power for the whole of the European Union when cross-border trade and competition are affected.

The Commission has the power to force changes in company behaviour and to impose financial penalties for antitrust violations of up to 10% of their annual turnover worldwide.

Commission decisions can be appealed to the European Court of First Instance in Luxembourg.

For comparison, the Findings of Fact in the U.S.A. v. Microsoft case are found at: http://www.iustice.gov/atr/cases/f3800/msiudge.pdf.

## Notes

1 These are operating systems running on central network computers that provide services to office workers around the world in their day-to-day work such as file and printer sharing, security and user identity management.
2 A media player is a software product that is able to 'play back' music and video content over the Internet.
3 The interfaces do not concern the Windows source code as this is not necessary to achieve the development of interoperable products. The interfaces are the hooks at the edge of the source code which allow one product to talk to another.
4 A Statement of Objections marks the opening of a formal investigation as the Commission states its charges or objections to the company(ies) concerned.
5 Microsoft's operating systems equip more than 95% of the world's personal computers.
6 The European Union plus Norway, Iceland and Liechtenstein.

## Case 5.1  Discussion Questions

1. What was the role and importance of complaints on the part of Microsoft's competitors in the Department of Justice's prosecution of Microsoft for violations of the Sherman Anti-Trust Act?

2. What lessons can be learned for the possible breaking-up of Microsoft by the breaking-up of AT&T in settlement of the Department of Justice's anti-trust prosecution?

3. The general public may not support the anti-trust prosecution of Microsoft. The general public may even be against the anti-trust prosecution, on account of the negative effect of the prosecution on Microsoft's stock price. Does public sentiment make a difference?

4. Have consumers benefited or been harmed by Microsoft's dominance of the operating system market and its tactics in the Internet browser market?

5. Apple Computer, Sun Micro Systems and Netscape argue that Microsoft's anti-trust violations stymied innovation. How could the stifling of innovation be ascertained? If this is true, have consumers been harmed, as well as Microsoft's competitors?

6. Explain why Microsoft continued its anti-trust actions in the EU, after being convicted in the US.

## End of Chapter Case 5.2: Corporate Personhood*

### Corporate Personhood, Business Leadership, and the U.S. Presidential Election of 2012

*Leigh Hafrey, Cate Reavis*

> Lead the people by laws and regulate them by penalties, and the people will try to keep out of jail, but will have no sense of shame. Lead the people by virtue and restrain them by the rules of decorum, and the people will have a sense of shame, and moreover will become good.
>
> —Confucius, *The Analects* (II:3)[1]

The corporation's status as a legal person might seem an arcane matter, relative to the dire individual and organizational circumstances that set in following the subprime mortgage crisis of 2007. That crisis had evolved into the "Great Recession," which still weighed on many real, flesh-and-blood human beings in the U.S. and global economies in 2012. Yet by 2012, corporate personhood had become an issue in no less an event than the election of a U.S. president. Former Massachusetts Governor, Republican presidential candidate, and former Bain Capital CEO Mitt Romney commented to an interlocutor at the Iowa State Fair, in August 2011: "Corporations are people, my friend. . . . Everything corporations earn ultimately goes to people. Where do you think it goes?"[2] Incumbent President and Democratic candidate for re-election Barack Obama responded with equal certainty the following spring, telling an audience at a campaign stop in Ohio in May: "I don't care how many ways you explain it, corporations are not people. People are people."[3] If the debate over corporate personhood mattered to the American electorate as much as the candidates appeared to believe it should, how might businesspeople and the business community at large assess a core structural element of global business practice: the corporation?

## The Great Recession and Corporate Free Speech

In early 2012, after five years of economic turmoil, glimmers of light indicated that the United States was emerging from the long dark tunnel that it had entered five years earlier.[4] The stock market was nearing 13,000, unemployment had inched its way down to 8.3%–after hitting a high of 10% in October 2009–[5] and the home foreclosure rate for the year (at 1.9 million homes, according to Realty Trac) was the lowest since 2007. Banks were showing signs of renewed confidence. Commercial and industrial lending was up 10% in the third quarter of 2011, compared to a 1.7% decline the previous four years.[6] However, the country's debt-to-GDP ratio remained a matter of deep concern: it had started a steep upward climb right at the time the U.S. Government began bailing out financial institutions, with a ratio of 40% in 2008, and over 70% at the end of 2011.

As the economy appeared to improve, public attention focused on who should be held responsible for a crisis that had nearly brought down not only the U.S., but the entire global financial system. Heightened by a number of best selling books, including *The Big Short, Too Big To Fail,* and *13 Bankers: The Wall Street Takeover and the Next Financial Meltdown;* investigative pieces broadcast on the television news program *60 Minutes;* feature films including *Inside Job* and *Margin Call;* and the Occupy Wall Street protest movement, the public's interest turned to the role that financial corporations had played in the crisis. While many firms faced civil charges,[7] no firm had been criminally charged for its involvement, no executives prosecuted.[8] Beyond the possibility of criminal action lay the question of ethical responsibility: what curbs might corporations, or the boards and executives who ran them, have placed upon their operations during the run-up to the crisis? Could they themselves, as well as the society in which they operated, expect them to exercise such care, and if so, by what mechanism?

Under U.S. law, corporations had rights and responsibilities, like natural persons. In the *Santa Clara County vs. Southern Pacific Railroad Company* ruling in 1886, the chief justice of the U.S. Supreme Court, Morrison Waite, is reported to have begun oral arguments by stating, "The court does not wish to hear argument on the question whether the provision in the Fourteenth Amendment to the Constitution, which forbids a State to deny to any person within its jurisdiction the equal protection of the laws, applies to these corporations. We are all of the opinion that it does."[9] Though the legal standing of Justice Waite's statement has been questioned,[10] the opinion has been widely taken to confirm corporate personhood in U.S. law. In 2010, the concept of the corporation as a fictitious person gained new complexity when the U.S. Supreme Court, in *Citizens United v. Federal Election Commission,* prohibited the government from banning corporate and union expenditures related to political campaigns; in the Court's opinion, the ban violated the First Amendment right to free speech. As Gov. Romney and President Obama's opposing views suggested, public opinion was sharply divided—often along political party lines—on whether corporations were indeed people, and if they were, what values they might choose to voice by exercising their right to free speech.

## The Accountability Question

Ultimately, the question of personhood underlay the leadership role that both individuals at the top of the corporation and the corporations themselves had played or failed to play in the downturn. Those who believed that financial firms should be held accountable for their actions, including liability for harms committed by their agents,[11] argued that, like people, corporations were granted rights, but also held to responsibilities that extended beyond the law to moral or ethical commitments to certain values. People who fell into this group believed that financial institutions needed to be held legally accountable for their actions leading up to the financial crisis. Others, who also blamed the financial firms, were wary of holding entire firms responsible for their actions at a time when the economy was still recovering. They remembered what had happened to Arthur Andersen during the Enron scandal[12]: the thought of punishing, and ultimately destroying, an entire firm for the bad behavior of a minority didn't sit well.

At the same time, many observers and industry players saw the banks and other financial services providers as victims or innocent bystanders rather than culprits. Some felt that the public sector had precipitated the crisis when it deliberately eased banking regulations starting in the late 1990's, with the goal of making homeownership a reality for more Americans. In essence, they thought that government hadn't done its job, and it wasn't fair or right to blame financial institutions. Still others believed that responsibility for the crisis should be placed on the society as a whole. Financial firms, Congress, regulators, credit agencies, accounting firms, and consumers—all had played a role in the downturn; in other words, we were all to blame.

## 1. Corporations

Among those who believed that financial firms should be held responsible for the financial crisis was William K. Black, a professor of economics and law at the University of Missouri and a senior regulator for the Federal Home Loan Board during the savings and loan banking crisis of the 1980' s. "I think this crisis was driven by fraud and I believe it was systemic," he stated. Furthermore, he believed, the fraud had begun in CEOs' offices and boardrooms.[13]

According to Black, certain firms had participated in accounting-control fraud, a term Black himself had coined. A control fraud occurs when a person in a position of responsibility in a company or state subverts the organization and engages in extensive fraud for personal gain. The savings and loan crisis and Enron were examples of control frauds as was, in Black's opinion, the sub-prime mortgage Crisis.

Black believed that compensation was a key factor in creating what he called the criminogenic environment at many Wall Street banks and even the government-sponsored entities Fannie Mae and Freddie Mac. The latter were responsible for purchasing and securitizing mortgages, thereby ensuring that funds were consistently available to the institutions that lent money to home buyers. In his view, compensation schemes in these firms created perverse incentives not only at the executive, but also at the lower levels of the company hierarchy. For example, loan officers at Washington Mutual and the brokers they hired were put on volume commissions. Black commented:

> Now that's insane. We know it will produce intense adverse selection. And we know that it will produce a negative expected value. Even the brokers were tempted with commissions of $20,000 for every loan that was approved, which perpetuated false reporting of income and assets on millions of loan applications. Now the broker doesn't believe they are doing anything wrong. They're helping the client get a loan and be able to become a homeowner. They know the lender is in on it and they're not cheating the lender, or at least the lender's management.

Black believed the control fraud, motivated by perverse compensation systems, extended to major investment firms like Goldman Sachs. "The investment banks all knew that the asset values of the CDOs were massively overstated, because the incredible problems in asset quality were deliberately being covered up," Black explained. As Black noted, the industry was warned several times that mortgage fraud was "epidemic" and would likely cause an economic crisis. The FBI issued its first warnings in September 2004, in open testimony to the House of Representatives, and the industry's anti-fraud experts released a warning in early 2006 that liar's loans[14] had a fraud incidence rate of 90%. The banks, however, continued to issue these loans. Credit Suisse reported that 49% of new originations in 2006 (more than 1 million) were liar's loans.[15]

Jeff Shames, former CEO and chairman of MFS Investment Management and a senior lecturer in finance at the MIT Sloan School of Management, believed the large Wall Street banks bore a good deal of responsibility. As he put it, "Nothing would have happened without the CDO vehicle in place that Wall Street firms and financial engineers created. CDOs allowed banks to make instant profits on risky securities by converting them into riskless securities.'[16]

Unlike Black, however, Shames didn't accuse the banks of fraud. "No corporation sets out to lie. Everything starts out legitimate. And some risky type of business gets created that some people have qualms about but the quantitative models show that it's risky, but within the bounds. And if the firm diversifies enough, it will work. So nobody in these firms believes they are doing anything fraudulent or unethical. They think 'This is the industry norm right now. It's working fine.'"

Like Black, Shames placed blame on the industry's compensation system, which rewarded people for short-term gains, not long-term growth:

> Wall Street's broken in the sense that the compensation system doesn't work for what's good for society. Financial corporations should have a bigger obligation to society. You could drive the Internet off a cliff, and nothing happens to society. You can't drive the financial industry off a cliff. As a result, a financial company can't be treated like an Internet company or a manufacturing company. Financial firms have to be held to higher standards because of their effect on the financial system and on society. Do we want finance people to be the highest paid people in society? Definitely not. The compensation structure has got to be restructured in a dramatic way or else we need to make the business less profitable by forcing banks to keep a lot more of their capital.

Many believed that expecting financial firms to act with high moral standards was unrealistic. As Leo Strine, Chancellor of the Delaware Court of Chancery,[17] remarked:

> Instead of recognizing that for-profit corporations will seek profit for their stockholders using all legal means available, we imbue these corporations with a personality and assume they are moral beings capable of being 'better' in some way in the long-run than the lowest common denominator. We act as if entities in which only capital has a vote will, when a choice has to be made between profit for those who control the board's re-election prospects and employees and communities who don't, somehow be able to deny the stockholders their desires.[18]

Robert Reich, former labor secretary under President Clinton, believed that endowing corporations with moral compasses was misguided:

> Corporate executives are not authorized by anyone—least of all by their investors—to balance profits against the public good. Nor do they have any expertise in making such moral calculations. Democracy is supposed to

represent the public in drawing such lines. And the message that companies are moral beings with social responsibilities diverts public attention from the task of establishing such laws and rules in the first place. . . . By pretending that the economic success corporations enjoy saddles them with particular social duties only serves to distract the public from democracy's responsibility to set the rules of the game and thereby protect the common good.[19]

Milton Friedman, the Nobel Laureate in economics, had argued precisely Reich's points in an article he published in the *New York Times Magazine* on September 13, 1970: "The Social Responsibility of Business Is to Increase Its Profits." Enormously influential in the U.S. and abroad during the last decades of the 20th century, Friedman saw government as the umpire to the games businesses play. Hadn't the corporation changed during that time, though? What to make of the retort to Friedman implicit in management guru Charles Handy's 21st century comment that "It used to be said that the business of business was business, but that was before those businesses became larger than countries"?[20] One might argue that the burden of responsibility on the business community had moved it beyond the freedom to play games with other people's money, let alone their lives: the analogy of controls on big finance, like the ones that the Federal Drug Administration applied to pharmaceutical companies, had begun to proliferate.

### 2. Government

The size and reach of 21st-century corporations notwithstanding, many believed that government was largely responsible for the financial crisis. David Schmittlein, John C Head Dean of the MIT Sloan School of Management, commented:

> I think a lot of people would like to make it about a few big banks that got together and did something naughty. And it isn't fair, and it's barely even true. The banks were not the root cause of the problem, They did not inflate housing prices. The housing bubble was first and foremost the result of an expansive monetary policy by the federal government, under multiple presidential administrations, and secondly the result of federal government policies and institutions aimed at expanding home ownership.

Many argued that financial institutions, under extreme pressure to deliver short term results, were merely pushing boundaries that government had set too loose. As Leo Strine noted:

> It is well known that businesses aggressively seeking profit will tend to push right up against, and too often blow right through, the rules of the game as established by positive law. The more pressure business leaders are under to deliver high returns, the greater the danger that they will violate the law and shift costs to society generally, in the form of externalities. In that

circumstance, if the rules of the game themselves are too loosely drawn to protect society adequately, businesses are free to engage in behavior that is socially costly without violating any legal obligations.[21]

Nouriel Roubini, an economist at New York University, was more assertive in blaming the government decision to loosen regulations. He believed the financial crisis represented a massive failure of public policy:

> There was an ideology for the last decade in Washington that was critical to this financial crisis. [It] was an ideology of laissez-faire, Wild West unregulated capitalists. The base of this ideology was the idea that banks and financial institutions will self-regulate. And as we know, self-regulation means no regulation. It was the ideology of relying on market discipline, and we know when there is irrational exuberance, there is zero market discipline. . . .
>
> The job of the Fed is to take away the punchbowl when the party gets going but unfortunately not only did the Fed not take away the punchbowl, it added vodka, whiskey, gin and every toxic stuff to it. Greenspan was the biggest cheerleader of this kind of financial innovation: zero down payment, no verification of income, assets and jobs, interest-only mortgages, negative amortization, teaser rates, all this toxic stuff.[22]

Why didn't Alan Greenspan, then head of the Federal Reserve, "take away the punchbowl"? Simon Johnson, the former IMF chief economist and a professor at the MIT Sloan School of Management, believed that the government had fallen victim to regulatory capture. In essence, the government had allowed a few big financial institutions to use their size and power to reshape the political and regulatory landscape to their advantage. As a result, they had become too big to fail:

> The political influence of Wall Street helped create the laissez-faire environment in which the big banks became bigger and riskier until by 2008 the threat of their failure could hold the rest of the economy hostage. That political influence also meant that when the government did rescue the financial system, it did so on terms that were favorable to the banks. What 'we're all in this together' really meant was that the major banks were already entrenched at the heart of the political system, and the government had decided it needed the banks as much as the banks needed government. So long as the political establishment remained captive to the idea that America needs big, sophisticated, risk-seeking, highly profitable banks, they had the upper hand in any negotiation. Politicians may come and go, but Goldman Sachs remains.[23]

## 3. Society

Andrew Lo, a professor of finance at the MIT Sloan School of Management and the director of MIT's Laboratory of Financial Engineering, believed that responsibility for the crisis could not be placed on one group or even shared among financial corporations and the government:

> When you have society-wide disregard for certain practices, then effectively what's happening is that the rules are being rewritten. I think this is about a broader set of issues that interact between ethics and sociology and economic behavior.
>
> This is not just about one group that fell asleep at the wheel. It was systemic. And the reason it was systemic is pretty simple. When things go well—politicians are getting reelected, regulators are getting kudos for how stable the markets are, shareholders are making money, mortgage brokers are making money, homeowners are making money—nobody wants to leave the party early. It takes an enormous amount of courage to stand up to that. And people did and they were crushed. The whistle-blowers at Citi and Countrywide were fired.[24] We have to think much more expansively then simply saying corporations were irresponsible. There are plenty of people that were irresponsible in addition to corporations.

Americans' cozy relationship with consumption and, therefore, debt, also bore a share of the blame. As David Beim, a finance professor at Columbia Business School, argued in early 2009:

> The ongoing recent global economic collapse is so monstrous, so broad and so deep that it requires a big-picture explanation. This isn't just about some stupid moves by mortgage brokers in California—how could that have such a vast impact on the global economy? It isn't just about Wall Street greed—hasn't Wall Street been greedy forever?
>
> For the past 25 years we have been over-consuming and over-borrowing . . . The problem is debt itself. All that borrowing by individuals had a powerful stimulatory effect on the economy. Business sales grew, and production increased to meet improved demand. But debt was growing faster than income, so the aggregate 'credit ratio' of household debt to median household income steadily deteriorated. People maxed out their credit cards and pulled the equity out of their houses. And most people stopped worrying about ever paying the debt back, since the abundant liquidity in our system made it seem that debt could always be rolled over and refinanced. More of our prosperity than we have been willing to admit has been driven by debt.[25]

### A Business Solution?

If "we" were the cause, if all of us were to blame, what was the proper response to the crisis? Was it a matter of, in Beim's words, ending our addiction to overindulgence?[26] What clinic would or could coordinate such a collective detoxification? Andrew Lo believed that significant societal change might be in order:

> I think we have come to the conclusion that we cannot conduct business as usual any longer because our society has gotten so complex and it just doesn't work anymore. It's fine for the financial sector to do what it did when there were 1.5 billion people on this planet back in 1900. But we are now 7 billion people. And we may be at a point in our evolution where our technological advances have gotten a bit ahead of our ability to manage them responsibly. We may have to reinvent not just the corporation, but the way that we deal with regulatory issues, the way we handle social and political interactions.

But again, who were "we"? What role might corporations—and more specifically, financial institutions—play in the voluntary and many-faceted change that Lo envisioned? Could or should corporations step up to the complex role that their "personhood" implied, and that the sector leadership roles of AIG, J.P. Morgan Chase, Goldman Sachs and others brought with them?

The absence of swift and significant corporate punishment resulting from the financial crisis, together with the high-profile Supreme Court decision on Citizens United, suggested that corporate rights were being given precedence over responsibilities, and not just by the corporations. Yet Leo Strine argued that, whatever the implications of the Fourteenth Amendment for corporate freedoms, corporations likely could not claim First Amendment-free speech-rights:

> The standing, bipartisan statement of the federal judiciary had been that corporations are creatures of the state and have only such authority as is entrusted to them. The problem with Citizens United is that it ignores this. No one ever believed that the corporation was a human being for first amendment purposes. I don't think we should be treating corporations as if they're human beings. And I think it's incredibly important that we don't, precisely because the whole reason that you have for-profit corporations is to fuel economic growth. And there are great dangers in that, and that's why they have to be regulated.

It was hard to imagine where one might draw a line on the kind of adjustment Strine invoked, given the hostility towards corporations expressed by some citizens on the political spectrum, and the politicians who represented them. The repeal of corporate personhood was supported by a number of national and local lawmakers,[27,28,29] as well as Move to Amend, a social and economic justice coalition made up of hundreds of organizations.[30] One could conceivably reverse the legal precedents establishing corporate personhood, and eliminate the protections that firms had gradually acquired through them to enhance their operating freedom. Doing so might undo the structural benefits, such as lower transaction costs, that Ronald Coase had identified, in his influential 1937 essay "The Theory of the Firm," as a motivation for forming business entities: groups of people doing together what no individual or group of unaffiliated individuals could hope to achieve alone. It would likely entail a massive redefinition of the corporate entity and rethinking of the incorporation process, with a return to state chartering of corporations in a narrowly defined public interest; with that would come, at least in principle, much tighter state monitoring of corporate activity. As Robert Reich argued, "If the purpose of capitalism is to allow corporations to play the market as aggressively as possible, the challenge for citizens is to stop these economic entities from being the authors of the rules by which we live."[31]

The most obvious alternative had its own strong advocates and detractors. One might keep to the concept of "corporate personhood" and, recognizing that corporations had too often, sometimes inadvertently, sometimes for the best of motives, turned privilege into presumption, put in place a more structured system of responsibilities that were enforced as vigorously as corporate rights were protected. This approach underlay the renewed interest, as the 21st century began, in seeing business as a profession, with the commitment to service and expertise idealized in occupations like the law and medicine.[32] To translate individual into organizational responsibility, the business community would need to develop the commitment to a code, and a willingness among business people to monitor themselves through an organization of their own devising. This would allow corporations to maintain their current legal status, with the understanding that, as H.D. Thoreau had put it in *Civil Disobedience* over a century and-a-half before, "It is truly enough said that a corporation has no conscience; but a corporation of conscientious men is a corporation with a conscience.[33] With that shift in emphasis, corporate ethics would become a necessity, rather than the luxury for which it was too often mistaken, in both the corporation and society at large. The shift might also force a redefinition of corporate leadership, one that aligned with the general social perception that leaders should demonstrate a higher-order self-discipline in their dealings, even as they took higher-order risks to insure the well-being of those they led.

Behind both choices, of course, lay the possibility of a systemic status quo: by 2012, the financial services community had become more powerful than it was before the downturn began,[34] with all of the attendant benefits and risks of its operations magnified. The election of 2012 would take place regardless of action on the part of the business community-some would say, *because* of that community's actions. Yet, as of mid-2012, the Great Recession continued not to yield the real gains in employment, overall economic growth, and social stability that constituents were seeking: other responsible parties to these events aside, who in the business community might step up to offer what an effective majority considered a sustainable path forward, and on what terms?

## Notes

1 Simon Leys, *The Analects of Confucius* (New York: W.W. Norton & Company, Inc., 1997).
2 Philip Rucker, "Mitt Romney Says 'Corporations Arc People' at Iowa State Fair." *The Washington Post*, August 11, 2011.
3 http://www.youtube.com/watch?v=mt1E6CMRzpM (accessed May 23, 2012).
4 "The Global Financial Crisis of 2008–2009; The Role of Fear, Greed and Oligarchs," provides a more detailed description of the financial crisis. The note can be accessed at https://mitsloan.mil.edu/MSTIR/world.economy/Crisis-2008–2009/Pages/default.aspx.
5 U.S. Bureau of Lahar Statistics, http://www.bls.gov/cps/tables.htm#empstat.
6 Steve Matthews and llano Kolct, "Bank Credit Highest Since Before Lehman as U.S. Growth Continues," Bloomberg, December 11, 2011.
7 A number of firms had paid fines for misleading investors without denying or admitting guilt. In 2011. Goldman Sachs settled a lawsuit with the Securities and Exchange Commission (SEC) agreeing to pay $550 million (4.1% of its 2010 net income) and JP Morgan agreed to pay the SEC $153.6 million (.9% of its 2010 net income). That same year, Citigroup agreed to pay $285 million (2.7% of its 2010 net income), to settle civil charges that it had defrauded customers during the housing bubble. As part of the settlement, the company made a pledge to the SEC that it would never again violate one of the main antifraud provisions of the nation's securities laws, The company had made the same pledge in July 2010, May 2006, March 2005, and April 2000. In September 2011 the Federal Housing Finance Agency, Fannie Mac and Freddie Mac's conservator since 2005, filed a lawsuit against 17 financial institutions: Ally Financial, Inc., Bank of America, Barclays Bank, Citigroup, Inc.; Countrywide Financial Corporation; Credit Suisse Holdings, Inc.; Deutsche Bank. AG; First Horizon National Corporation; Goldman Sachs & Co.; HSBC North America Holdings, Inc.; JPMorgan Chase & Co.; Merrill Lynch & Co./First Franklin Financial Corp.; Morgan Stanley; Nomura Holding America Inc.; The Royal Bank of Scotland PLC; Societe Generale—alleging violations of securities laws and common law in the sale of mortgage-backed securities. Seeking damages of $200 billion the FHFA alleged that "the loans had different and more risky characteristics than the descriptions contained in the marketing and sales materials provided to the Enterprises for those securities."
8 Jean Eagle sham, "Financial Crimes Bedevil Prosecutors," *The Wall Street Journal*, December 6, 2011.

9   Santa Clara County v. Southern Pacific RR Co. 118 U.S. 394 (1886), hnp://supremc.
   justia.com/cascslfcderal/us/I18/394/case.html (accessed June 4, 2012).

10  Jack Beatty, *Age of Betrayal* (New York: Alfred A. Knopf. 2007). p. 110.

11  Susan Farbstein and Tyler Giannini, "Liability for Harms," *The New York Times*, February 28, 2012.

12  In June 2002, a federal jury convicted the accounting firm Arthur Andersen of
   obstruction of justice for destroying documents pertaining to its accounting work
   with Enron. In addition to being fined $500,000 and sentenced to five years proba-
   tion, the firm agreed to stop auditing public companies, which led to the demise of
   the business. In the United States alone, 28,000 people lost their jobs. In 2005, the
   United Slates Supreme Court overturned the conviction finding fatal flaws in the jury
   instructions on which the conviction was based. For more on this see Elizabeth K.
   Ainslie, "Indicting Corporations Revisited: Lessons of the Arthur Andersen Prosecution," *American Criminal Law Review*, Vol. 43: 107, 2006.

13  Interview with Bill Moyers on Bill Moyers Journal, April 3, 2009, http://www.pbs.org/
   moyer/joumaI/04032009/transcript4.htm.

14  A liar loan described a category of mortgages that required little if any documentation verifying the borrower's income and assets. These loans helped encourage
   unethical behavior by both borrowers and lenders. For more on this see William K.
   Black. "When 'Liar's Loans' Flourish," *The New York Times*, January 30, 2011.

15  William K. Black, "When 'Liar's Loans' Flourish," *The New York Times*, January 30,
   2011.

16  For a more detailed description of the CDO market see Michael Lewis, *The Big Short:
   Inside the Doomsday Machine* (W.W. Norton & Company, 2010).

17  The Delaware Court of Chancery is a non-jury trial court that serves as Delaware's court
   of original and exclusive equity jurisdiction, and adjudicates a wide variety of cases
   involving trusts, real property, guardianships, civil rights, and commercial litigation.

18  Leo E. Strine, Jr., "Bailed Out Bankers, Oil Spills, Online Classifieds, Dairy Milk, and
   Potash: Our Continuing Struggle with the Idea that For-Profit Firms Seek Profit,"
   The University of Western Ontario, The Beattie Family Lecture in Business Law,
   March 5, 2011.

19  Robert Reich, "How Capitalism Is Killing Democracy," *Foreign Policy*, September/
   October, 2007.

20  Charles Handy, "Tocqueville Revisited: the Meaning of American Prosperity," *Harvard Business Review* (Reprint # ROIOIC), January 1, 2001, p. 10.

21  Leo E. Strine, Jr., "Why Excessive Risk-Taking is Not Unexpected," *The New York
   Times*, October 5, 2009.

22  "Blame Washington More Than Wall Street for the Financial Crisis," Intelligence
   Squared US, March 17, 2009.

23  Simon Johnson and James Kwak, *13 Bankers: The Wall Street Takeover and the Next
   Financial Meltdown* (New York: Pantheon, 2010). p. 6.

24  For more on this see: "Prosecuting Wall Street," 60 Minutes, December 4, 2011, http://
   www.cbsnews.com/8301-18560_162-57336042/prosecuting-wall street/?tag=content
   Main;cbsCarousel.

25  David. O. Beim, "It's All About Debt," *Forbes*, March 19, 2009.

26  Karen Ingraham, "Anatomy of a Meltdown: Table Talk with David O. Beim, '58," *The
   Exeter Bulletin,* Spring 2009, p. 10.

27  Supreme Court Justice Sonia Sotomayor hinted at her support for a repeal when she
   said, during a campaign finance case, that the court should reconsider the 19th century

rulings that first afforded corporations the some rights flesh-and-blood people have (Jess Bravin, "Sotomayor Issues Challenge t0 a Century of Corporate Law," *The Wall Street Journal*, September 17, 2009).

28 Senator Bernie Sanders of Vermont and Representative Jim McGovern of Massachusetts had both introduced constitutional amendments in their respective legislative bodies calling for the repeal of corporate personhood (Steven Rosenfeld, "The Hard Truth About Citizens United," Salon.com, January 21, 2012).

29 The cities of New York, Los Angeles. Albany. Boulder, and Oakland had all passed resolutions urging Congress to overturn corporate personhood ("New York City Council Passes Resolution Opposing Corporate Personhood," The Huffington Post, January 5, 2012).

30 http://movetoamend.org/mta.coalition.

31 Robert Reich, "How Capitalism Is Killing Democracy," *Foreign Policy*, September/October, 2007.

32 Rakesh Khurana and Nitin Nohria, "It's Time to Make Management a True Profession," *Harvard Business Review*, October 2008.

33 Henry David Thoreau. "Civil Disobedience," Part 1. Paragraph 4. This essay was originally published in 1849 as "Resistance to Civil Government." (http://thoreau.eserver. orglcivill.html, accessed March 13. 2012).

34 David Lynch, "Banks Seen Dangerous Defying Obama's Too-Big-to-Fail Move," Bloomberg, April 16, 2012.

## Case 5.2  Discussion Questions

1. The United States Supreme Court overruled congressional legislation regulating campaign contributions passed in the aftermath of the Nixon Watergate scandal, which led to President Nixon's resignation. Do you agree or disagree that this amounts to "judicial activism"? Justify your position.

2. The adage "money talks" arguably has been embodied in the *Citizens United* decision, overruling certain limits on campaign contributions as an unconstitutional infringement of free speech. What are the implications of this decision for political participation and voice?

# 6 Managing the Business–Government Relationship II

## Innovation and Emerging Technologies

### Chapter Outline

Production Innovation
    Companies Reinvent Themselves
    Innovation and Supplier Relations
    Product Innovation and Competitor Relations
Emergent Technologies and Regulation
    Unintended Negative Consequences of New Technologies
Role of Interest Groups in Fashioning Regulations and Proposing Public
    Policy
Corporate Voice in a Democracy: Lobbying, Political Action Committees
    and Campaign Financing
    Campaign Finance Reform
    Political Action Committees
    Lobbying
        Access to the Corridors of Power
What Is the Optimum Amount and Type of Regulation?
    Unintended Consequences of Deregulation
    Innovation in a Global Context and Global Competitiveness
End of Chapter Case: Genetically Engineered Salmon

### Chapter Introduction

What is the appropriate role and obligation of government regulators in emerging fields of endeavor? What is the appropriate role of interest groups in fashioning regulations? What is the appropriate corporate voice in a democracy? What are the unintended negative consequences of regulation or deregulation?

### Chapter Goal and Learning Objectives

*Chapter Goal:* Consider the appropriate amount and nature of regulation of innovation and emerging technologies.

*Learning Objectives:*

1. Understand the importance of innovation and new technologies in maintaining enterprise competitiveness.
2. Debate the role of interest groups, including corporate lobbying, in fashioning regulation.
3. Debate the appropriate role of regulators and the appropriate amount and nature of regulation in emerging fields of endeavor.
4. Discuss regulatory failure and unintended negative consequences of deregulation.
5. Develop alternatives to regulation.

## Production Innovation

Product innovation is the lifeblood of a going concern. Competitive advantage relative to other enterprise within the industry is gained by such factors as time to market and lower cost or higher quality and more product features embedded in the product. A cautionary note, however, is that several cases included herein giving rise to ethical and legal debacles involve the race to market, such as the Ford Pinto, which was the first American compact car.[1]

Products have a life cycle. In order for a company, or a division, to avoid decline as its product enters the decline phase of its life cycle, a company must innovate and bring new products to market. Charles Handy calls this the "S" curve.[2] As one product peaks, the enterprise should be bringing out another product, so that its growth phase offsets the decline phase of another product. Figure 6.1 shows how continuous innovation overcomes the limits of product/technology life cycles.

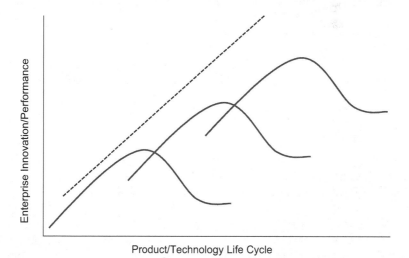

*Figure 6.1* The "S" Curve of Continuous Product Innovation

The problem of continuous innovation is particularly acute for firms that depend on patents, such as research-based pharmaceutical companies, because patents expire in 20 years, from the first date of filing for the patent,[3] and because pharmaceutical companies face a particularly competitive environment relative to their competitors within the industry. Ethical and legal challenges can arise as companies deal with the issue of patents and patent rights in the pharmaceutical industry. For example, Sam Waksal, the founder and CEO of ImClone Systems, Inc., sold his stock when he learned in December 2001 that FDA would not review ImClone's application to bring a colon cancer-fighting drug, Erbitux, to market. Martha Stewart also became involved in this situation: she sold ImClone stock on the day before ImClone received its rejection letter from the FDA. Although Martha Stewart was not tried for insider trading, she was prosecuted for, then convicted of, obstruction of justice and lying to prosecutors; as a result, she spent five months in jail and five months under house arrest. Waksal was sentenced to seven years in prison for insider trading. ImClone's Erbitux was later approved by the FDA for marketing.[4] These are tragedies in the personal lives of the corporate leaders and shareholders of ImClone but also dramatically illustrate the ethical and legal risks of a highly competitive corporate environment that requires product innovation.

An issue with continuous innovation is that there is no "formula" for innovation. Innovation is by its very nature a non-routine task, with high uncertainty and with risks of failure attendant. However, some companies are good at bringing multiple innovative products to market, not just single inventions. For example, Lockheed Martin developed a division oriented to invention and innovation: their "Skunk Works." At the time when the Skunk Works division was founded, the Lockheed client, the United States Department of Defense and the United States' allies in World War II, faced a significant threat, namely the possibility of superior German air power. Innovation was a necessity, given the exigencies of World War II, as was rapid production and time to market.[5] The innovative culture and practice at Lockheed Martin Skunk Works was related to de-bureaucratization of the organization and the development of small, cross-functional teams. Lockheed formalized these characteristics as 14 "rules" that related to organizational success in innovation.[6]

### Companies Reinvent Themselves

To sustain long-term competitive advantage, companies must reinvent themselves. Technology changes over time,[7] creating threats or opportunities for companies within a market. For example, United Parcel Company, which was founded in 1907 as a messenger company, has grown into the largest package delivery company and has defined itself as a global logistics company involved in supply chain management services.[8] UPS uses information technology to create competitive advantage in scheduling and monitoring global operations, which it has named the COMPASS system.[9]

Moreover, the CEO of General Electric, Jack Welch, is credited with reinventing General Electric and transforming it from an appliance manufacturing firm to a global firm, oriented also to services.[10] Welch served as CEO between 1980 and 2001; during this time GE acquired NBC and GE Capital Services division, which was restructured in 1982, with the result that it contributes 40% of earnings. Each of these companies has transformed itself over time.

### Innovation and Supplier Relations

Relationships with suppliers have been a source of innovation and competitive advantage for some companies. For example, Hammer and Champy, in their book, *Re-engineering the Corporation*,[11] identified a linkage between Procter & Gamble and its distributors, whereby distributors that tracked their own inventory of Pampers brand disposable diapers were permitted to reorder Pampers directly from Procter & Gamble's warehouses. Wal-Mart is also an innovator in supply chain relationships. By the mid- and late 1980s, Wal-Mart had started setting up direct linkages with its vendors through Electronic Data Interchange, as well as experimenting with Quick Response Inventory Systems.[12] More recently, Wal-Mart suppliers are using wireless inventory tracking tags employing radio frequency identification (RFID).[13] The successor to bar codes, RFID can track goods as they move from the supplier via distribution channels to the distributor's warehouse to the retail outlet; cartons as well as individual items can be tracked.[14] Wal-Mart launched its own six-channel satellite communication network in 1987. The system, which allows two-way data communication, sends data from all stores to headquarters, providing real-time inventory data.[15] In each of these cases, the enterprise is sharing control of its inventory or other management system with its suppliers to create competitive advantage.

In addition to *tight coupling*[16] with suppliers on inventory management, increasingly companies are subcontracting or "outsourcing" their research and development functions, in addition to outsourcing their manufacturing operations.[17] Some companies, such as IBM, are in fact becoming networks of relationships with suppliers and customers. Oliver Williamson, in his book *Markets and Hierarchies*,[18] suggests the either keeping functions in-house (hierarchy) or subcontracting (market) are rational options for management, depending on transaction costs and the enterprise need for control. However, as *Business Week* notes, outsourcing innovation can produce the unintended negative effect of developing competitors who are better at innovation that the company originally contracting out the research and development services. In addition, shareholders might raise questions about whether they should transfer their capital investment into the more productive or innovative R&D suppliers.

### Product Innovation and Competitor Relations

Clayton Christensen, in two provocative books, *The Innovator's Dilemma*[19] and *The Innovator's Solution*,[20] identifies *"disruptive" technologies* as a kind of innovation that can drive a successful business out of business. Disruptive technologies are innovations that fundamentally change the nature of the product delivered to the market and the relationship with the customer. Disruptive technologies take away markets from established firms. Disruptive technologies are distinguished from *"sustaining" technologies* or incremental change. An example of a "disruptive" technology is the invention by 3M Company of the Post-it note. An example of "incremental" technologies is the permutations that 3M has made with the Post-it note, including color, size, and even form, such as sticker arrows to serve as markers. Perhaps a more significant example is the role that Nucor Steel, with its cold milling process using steel scrap, played as a disruptive technology relative to U.S. Steel Co. and other "integrated" steel mills.

The genetic decoding methodology developed by Craig Venter of Celera Genomics disrupted the Human Genome Project.[21] Celera Genomics identified individual genes, rather than mapping out the genes on chromosomes, the procedure followed by the Department of Energy and the National Institutes of Health (NIH).[22] Collaboration was subsequently developed between Celera Genomics and NIH, with the result that the Human Genome Project, decoding the human genome, was completed early. The task remained, however, of sequencing the genes on chromosomes.[23] Disruptive technologies and the firms that invent and market them upend the established market and often lead to business failure of the firms engaged in "sustaining" technologies in that market.

## Emergent Technologies and Regulation

What is the appropriate role and obligation of government regulators in emerging fields of endeavor? What the appropriate regulations should be in emerging fields of endeavor is uncertain and controverted. The regulator has the obligation to protect the public interest. But what happens when information is incomplete and uncertain? Uncertainty about appropriate regulatory action is particularly acute with emergent technologies, when the long-term consequences of a new technology may not be known. This problem is particularly acute with new drug therapies. Negative reactions of patients may become known only after long-term therapy; moreover, the negative reactions may be statistically rare, thus raising the question of cause and effect. The unintended negative consequences of new technologies can be rare, so that they take a while to become known. For example, in the 1960s, a medication to control morning sickness during pregnancy, thalidomide, was found to cause birth defects in the growing fetus.[24] The effect of thalidomide was not discovered until after the births of the deformed babies.[25] The problem of possible but unknown injurious side effects is particularly acute with new drugs and therapies. This was an issue, for example, with Vioxx, where the risk of heart attack and stroke appears to increase with long-term use, even though the damage to the digestive tract is reduced with the attendant risks of hemorrhage. The problem of emergent knowledge of long-term, rare consequences was an issue as well with antidepressant therapy among adolescents, where it appears that the use of antidepressants may increase the risk of suicide.

Genetic engineering as an emergent technology is particularly controversial with respect to the question: what is "appropriate" regulation? The FDA initially permitted companies to label and market their products as not genetically modified (GM); for example, Polaner Company labeled their fruit spread products as "non-GM." However, the FDA changed its position and does not permit companies to advertise "non-GM" in cases where the genetically modified product is *substantially equivalent* to the non-genetically modified product.

Monsanto and other agricultural companies such as American Cyanamid develop seed with genetically modified characteristics. Ecologists are concerned about the unintended negative consequences of plant genetic engineering, especially ecological system effects. Ecologists are particularly concerned with presently unknown unintended negative consequences of genetically modified plants. For example, it is presently known that Bt corn kills the larvae of the monarch butterfly when the pollen from the Bt corn blows on milkweed plants on which the larvae feed.[26] Ecologists are also concerned about the long-term system effects of Roundup Ready corn and soybeans. Roundup Ready agricultural seed are not killed by the herbicide Roundup when applied to weeds surrounding the corn or soybeans. Ecologists fear that certain weeds will develop resistance to Roundup, very much like the process by which humans develop resistance to antibiotics. If weeds were to develop resistance to Roundup products, then "super-weeds" not susceptible to currently marketed herbicides might infest crops.[27] Recently in response to consumer concerns about genetically modified goods, McDonald's Corporation reversed its corporate sourcing practices and has ceased purchasing genetically modified potatoes.[28] Previously McDonald's was one of the largest consumers of genetically modified potatoes.[29]

### Unintended Negative Consequences of New Technologies

New technologies may have unintended negative consequences. Therapeutic applications deriving from the Human Genome Project and from stem cell research are currently being developed. The scientific basis for the therapeutic applications is very recent: human stem cells were isolated in 1998, a working draft of the human genome was decoded in 2001, with chromosome mapping being completed in 2003. Many applications are still in the scientific development stages, as discussed in the following, but some therapeutic applications are being delivered as experimental treatments. The risks of even the experimental therapies are emergent. For example, a clinical trial participant at the University of Pennsylvania died after being treated with a genetically modified cold virus.[30] Similar to the conflicts of interest riddling the development and marketing of the Dalkon Shield IUD at Johns Hopkins University, the principal investigators for the University of Pennsylvania gene therapy trials had an undisclosed financial interest in the therapies being developed. There is the potential that similar conflicts of interest with respect to newly developed gene therapies and stem cell research applications will riddle the scientific community now and in the foreseeable future as breakthrough applications are invented.

## Role of Interest Groups in Fashioning Regulations and Proposing Public Policy

Corporations take an active role in fashioning regulations and proposing public policy. *Regulatory agencies*, such as the FDA, the National Highway Traffic Safety Administration (NHTSA), and the Federal Communications Commission propose *regulations* to enforce the laws, the administration for which they are responsible. Notice of proposed regulations is given in the *Federal Register* as a *notice of proposed rulemaking*. Rules enacted after hearings are published in the *Code of Federal Regulations* and such rules have the force of law. In addition, congressional committees and Congress itself as a body holds public and private hearings. Corporate leaders respond to proposed regulations and testify before Congress in both private and public hearings. For example, CEO of General Motors testified to Congress about GM's failure to recall its defective ignition switch.[31]

Enterprise affected by regulation play an active role in the regulatory process. For example, the NHTSA proposed Regulation 301, Fuel System Integrity, which would require automobiles to withstand rear-end direct impacts of 30 mph. At the time Regulation 301 was proposed, Ford Motor Company was designing and manufacturing the Ford Pinto, a subcompact car designed for fuel economy and to compete with foreign imports; Ford planned to bring the Pinto to market in 1971. Ford engineers knew that the Pinto, as designed, would not conform to the proposed Regulation 301. Ford Motor Company opposed Regulation 301 in the rule-making process, which finally came into force in 1977. In the meantime, Ford manufactured and sold the Pinto automobile, which was recalled as defectively designed in 1978. Corporations, such as Ford, and industry lobbies, such as the Motor Vehicle Manufacturers Association, take an active role vis-à-vis the regulator in proposing[32] and responding to proposed regulations.

The pharmaceutical industry and the scientific and medical communities lobby Congress and the president about regulations affecting cloning technology and stem cell research. The Jones Institute for Reproductive Medicine in Virginia spearheaded in vitro fertilization techniques for infertile couples in the United States. The first "test tube" baby was born in 1978 in Britain, while the first "test tube" baby was born in the United States in 1981. The process of in vitro fertilization creates extra embryos, which are frozen until they are wanted for possible subsequent pregnancies, after which they are discarded. When procedures to isolate human stem cells from embryos were invented in 1998, scientists searched for sources of stem cells, including stem cells from aborted fetuses and from the extra embryos available from fertility clinics.[33] In August 2000, the NIH promulgated regulations permitting NIH funding of stem cell research only if the stem cells were derived from embryos created for fertility treatment and which were no longer needed and only if the cells were extracted from the embryos without using federal funds. In August 2001, President George W. Bush issued an announcement that federal funds would be available for stem cell research using 64 stem cell lines derived prior to his August 9, 2001, announcement. Certain conditions were set on the federal funding; the embryonic stem cells must be obtained: 1) with the informed consent of the donors; 2) from excess embryos created solely for reproductive purposes; and 3) without any financial inducements to the donors.[34] Some scientists viewed the Bush guidelines for federal funding of stem cell research as unduly restrictive. Stem cell research policies became a political campaign issue in the United States presidential election of November 2004. The son of former Republican President Ronald Reagan became a Democrat and addressed the Democratic National Convention in the summer of 2004, advocating less restrictive public policies on stem cell research, which has the potential to cure Alzheimer's disease, the disease from which Reagan suffered, as well as other medical conditions such as Parkinson's disease and diabetes. New stem cell legislation was passed by the United States House of Representative in May 2005 but vetoed by President Bush.[35] However, President Bush signed a different bill passed by Congress, the Stem Cell Therapeutic and Research Act of 2005; it established umbilical blood cord banks.[36] President Obama used an executive order to lift the restrictions on NIH stem cell research imposed by President Bush's executive orders.[37]

## Corporate Voice in a Democracy: Lobbying, Political Action Committees and Campaign Financing

Corporate political participation is constitutionally based, deriving from the recognition by the United States Supreme Court that corporations are legal persons[38] endowed with constitutional rights, including free speech and the right of association. Free speech includes the right to both political and commercial speech.

### Campaign Finance Reform

A fundamental tension with corporate political participation and monetary contributions arises because of the possibility that corruption and bribery influences the outcome of elections. There is a troubling relationship between campaign financing and actually winning elections. The United States Supreme Court recognizes the fundamental values involved in political participation— freedom of speech and freedom of association. However, the court has recognized that the interests that underlie legislated limits on political contributions are interests in preventing: 1) the actual corruption threatened by large financial contributions; and 2) the eroding of public confidence in the electoral process through the appearance of corruption. "To the extent that large contributions are given to secure a political *quid pro quo* from current and potential office holders, the integrity of our system of representative democracy is undermined."[39]

The Federal Election Campaign Act of 1971 (FECA) was passed in the aftermath of the election of President Richard Nixon to a second term and the disclosure of the Watergate scandal.[40] FECA was amended after the Enron Corporation debacle and the disclosure of that Enron had made large campaign contributions. Senator John McCain sponsored campaign financing reform, passed in 2002 as the McCain-Feingold Act, which imposed spending limits on political action committees (PACs) and on political organizations. The McCain-Feingold Act is otherwise known as the Bipartisan Campaign Reform Act of 2002. The McCain-Feingold Act prohibits national political parties or political committees from raising and spending "soft money," for which there is no limit for contributions,[41] and limits "electioneering ads," which advocate a particular position at issue in an election during 30 days prior to a primary or general election.

The constitutionality of the McCain-Feingold Act was immediately tested in the courts. The United States Supreme Court fundamentally upheld the law, in the case *McConnell v. FEC*, decided in 2003.[42] Some expenditure limits were upheld, while others were struck down as unconstitutional infringements on the right of free speech. Title II of the Bipartisan Campaign Reform Act of 2002, as originally passed, required political parties to choose between expenditures coordinated with a political candidate and independent expenditures during the post- nomination pre-election period; this section was declared unconstitutional as violating the federal Constitution's First Amendment by impermissibly burdening the parties' right to make unlimited independent expenditures.[43]

However a "loophole" in the McCain-Feingold Act was discovered and exploited during the 2004 presidential election: 527 organizations are not subject to the campaign donations or spending limits of the McCain-Feingold Act. During the 2004 presidential campaign, both presidential candidates used 527 organizations effectively; these organizations are not subject to the limits of the Federal Election Campaign Act. For example, George Soros contributed "*soft money*" to 527 organizations, such as America Coming Together, a voter registration and "get out the vote" effort and organization. Donations to 527 organizations by and large get around the soft money restrictions imposed in the Federal Election Campaign Act, as amended.

*Citizens United v. FEC* determined that monetary contributions to political organizations are a form of free speech and that to restrict independent monetary contributions to PACs unconstitutionally infringes on First Amendment free speech rights.[44] Moreover McCain- Feingold's restrictions on "electioneering ads" 30 days prior to a primary or 60 days prior to a general election were struck down. Since corporations are legal persons, they cannot be restricted in their First Amendment exercise of free speech; political speech is the most carefully protected of free speech rights, while commercial speech is more restricted; see for *example Nike v. Kasky* and "truth in advertising" law. *Citizens United* partially overruled *McConnell v. FEC* (2003), which had held that the McCain-Feingold Act was constitutional.

In the wake of Citizens United, 501(c)(4) organizations were organized. These 501(c)(4) organizations are distinguished from 527 organizations; 527 organizations are political organizations that may collect unlimited amounts of soft money, but they must disclose donors. However, 501(c) organizations are charitable organizations that are not required to report their donors. "Just as with 501(c)(4) groups, political groups organized under Section 527 are tax-exempt, but unlike 501(c)(4) nonprofits, these groups have significant transparency and disclosure requirements. The *Citizens United* decision engendered a land rush for these groups seeking nonprofit status as 501(c)(4) organizations, with the sole purpose of avoiding the congressionally mandated donor-disclosure requirements of Section 527."[45] This distinction is at the heart of the IRS scrutiny of "Tea Party" 501(c)(4)s applying for tax-exempt status. The IRS was scrutinizing whether they were engaging in political activity. If so, they are required to report their donors, as 527 organizations; 501(c)(4)s are not required to disclose their contributors.[46]

### Political Action Committees

The political participation of corporations and interests groups can be channeled via *political action committees*. PACs are vehicles under United States election law whereby corporations, trade unions and other interest groups can make donations to candidates for federal office or to groups advocating a particular position, pro or con, on a topic such as immigration reform.[47] The Federal Election Campaign Act of 1971, which was passed in the post-Watergate era, established spending limits by PACs.[48] But in 2014, the United States Supreme Court struck down the aggregate limits on contributions to PACs, federal political candidates and political parties.[49] The individual limits are still in place: "Currently, individuals may contribute up to $2,600 per election to a federal candidate, $10,000 per calendar year to a state party committee, $32,400 per calendar year to a national party committee and $5,000 per calendar year to a PAC." Although the limits on individual contributions are currently in place, an individual can donate the maximum permissible contributions to an unlimited number of federal candidates, PACs or political parties.

### Lobbying

Lobbying is a practice of advocacy of public policy by interest groups or other self-interested parties. Lobbyists often represent industry or professional groups, including the Motor Vehicle Manufacturers Association, the Chamber of Commerce, the National Association of Manufacturers, the National

Education Association, which represents school teachers, the American Medical Association and the American Association of Retired Persons. The American Insurance Association, representing the insurance industry, has lobbied vigorously with Congress about asbestos liability and has proposed legislation, "Fairness in Asbestos Injury Resolution Act," which was passed by the Senate in 2005. Medical malpractice liability is considered by the U.S. Congress as tort reform. Insurance companies also lobby for "tort reform," advocating limitations on jury payouts to injured parties. The Association of Trial Lawyers often counters the advocacy of other lobby organizations. Some business advocacy groups, such as the Business Roundtable, influence public policy in the role of presenting expert opinion, by issuing reports and position papers.[50] The range of advocacy of the Business Roundtable is wide ranging and directly involves federal legislation, including for example immigration reform.[51]

The constitutionally based rights of freedom of speech and freedom of association give business organizations and interest groups broad rights to engage in political campaigns and political advocacy, including donating and spending money for political campaigns. Concerns arise about undue financial influence and the possibility of corruption. Among these concerns are issues of access.

*Access to the Corridors of Power*

A troubling aspect of political donations is the question of whether financial donations purchase political access and influence. Concern over special access by large political contributors was addressed by Congress in its investigation and report on the 1996 elections, by the McCain-Feingold Act and by the Supreme Court in its *McConnell v. FEC* decision, which upheld the constitutionality of the McCain-Feingold Act.[52] Even the *McCutcheon v. FEC* decision of 2014 leaves in place the prohibition of *Buckley v. Valeo* of "quid pro quo" donations, which are recognized as corrupting.[53]

For example, concerns about access to the corridors of power and concerns about the effect of political donations on public policy formation arose about the access of Enron to Vice President Dick Cheney. Enron CEO Kenneth Lay met with Vice President Cheney six times in 2001 for discussion of energy policy. The General Accounting Office sued Vice President Cheney to disclose the membership on his Energy Task Force. The vice president and president invoked "executive privilege." Other groups, including the Sierra Club, have also sued about the disclosure of information on the Energy Task Force.[54] The White House claimed executive privilege in refusing to reveal the composition of the Energy Task Force.[55]

Moreover, there is a phenomenon that C. Wright Mills identified as "the circulation of elites," whereby leadership rotates among industrial, military and political institutions.[56] For example, General Colin Powell served as the chairman of the Joint Chiefs of Staff during the Desert Storm operation in the early 1991 during the Kuwait-Iraq conflict. He then became Secretary of State during the George W. Bush administration from 2001–2005. Colin Powell also served on the board of AOL and has founded a not-for-profit group, America's Promise. The circulation of elites rotates leadership among the military, industrial, and governmental institutions, creating a network of relationships among these leadership elites. Some critics would charge that circulation of elites can raise conflict of interest concerns. See for example, Michael Moore's "Fahrenheit 9/11" documentary[57] and his concerns about possible conflicts of interest in the Carlyle Group.[58] The ethical and regulatory concerns about corporate voice and participation in a democracy focus on the possibility of improper influence and corruption on the political process.

## What Is the Optimum Amount and Type of Regulation?

The question arises: what is the optimum amount and type of regulation? Either of the regulation of enterprise with respect to their relationships with competitors, i.e., anti-trust regulation, or the regulation of innovation and emerging technologies. *Laissez faire* capitalism urges a minimum of regulation, only those regulations necessary to overcome the limits of an "imperfect" market. However, we have discussed that regulation also reflects concerns about fairness and equity, as well changing social values. As capitalism becomes the dominant model globally, with the demise of centrally planned economies,[59] and with the industrialization of predominantly agrarian societies in the Third World, the question of appropriate regulation is a globally pressing issue. A significant benefit of regulation is to level the playing field among competitors and to protect the interests of stakeholders, particularly consumers from unsafe products, communities and the environment from pollution and employees from unsafe or exploitive working conditions, by requiring producing enterprise to internalize their full costs of production. Regulation that requires the internalization of production costs is especially salient to newly industrializing countries, since their regulatory frameworks are less developed than the regulatory frameworks of nations with already developed economies.

### Unintended Consequences of Deregulation

United States public policy over the past several decades, and in some respects, the public policy of Britain, has been to deregulate certain industries. Experience with deregulation has shown that deregulation can have unintended negative consequences. Some unintended negative consequences of industry deregulation include enterprise failure leading to enterprise or even industry-wide bailouts in cases where the industry goods and services are deemed essential to the public welfare, with resultant levying of costs on the general taxpaying public. The British railroad system deteriorated after privatization and has been partially renationalized.[60] After the deregulation of the American airline industry, there was significant financial distress, bankruptcies, and consolidation of air carriers, as well as the emergence of regional, niche- specific carriers such as Jet Blue. However, major air carriers, including United Airlines,[61] Continental,[62]

TWA,[63] Pan Am,[64] Eastern Airlines, Braniff,[65] US Airways,[66] underwent repeated bankruptcies after the passage in the United States of the Airline Deregulation Act of 1978, while American Airlines and Delta engaged in bankruptcy avoidance strategies.[67] Continental Airlines, which underwent bankruptcy restructuring and emerged competitively, proposed a $5 per one-way trip increase in ticket price to cover the increased costs of jet fuel. Under competitive pressures, Continental rescinded the ticket price increase. Duress was also experienced in the banking industry after the deregulation of banking.[68] The energy crisis in California, including the manipulation of supply and price of energy by Enron, arguably represents a failure of deregulation.[69]

A new model may be emerging whereby special funds are established to pay for the costs of firm or industry failure or costs of negative externalities. This model was established during the New Deal with respect to unemployment insurance but more recently has been extended to other situations. For example, the Superfund, established as part of the Environmental Protection Act, requires enterprise polluters within an industry to share cleanup costs. For example, the Environmental Protection Agency required the joint polluters to share the costs of cleanup in Woburn, Massachusetts. Also, the Pension Benefit Guarantee Corporation (PBGC)[70] was established by statute as an insurer of pensions to which enterprises contribute funds.[71] United Airlines was permitted in the spring of 2005 by the bankruptcy court to transfer its pension obligations to the PBGC as it emerged from bankruptcy. An asbestos compensation fund was established by the Johns Manville bankruptcy.

### Innovation in a Global Context and Global Competitiveness

These days, globalization not only involves global sourcing of raw materials, or global sourcing or "outsourcing" of labor, but globalization of innovation also is happening. Now, there is global competition for innovation. No single country has a "lock" on innovation. Regulatory frameworks can place a country at a competitive disadvantage. For example, when the Foreign Corrupt Practices Act, prohibiting bribery in the solicitation of contracts, passed, some United States firms felt at a competitive disadvantage because bribes remained tax-deductible expenses in other countries; indeed, Europe has only recently outlawed bribery in the solicitation of international business contracts. Some scientists and leaders of the pharmaceutical industry in the United States feared that the US regulation of stem cell and cloning research under the Bush administration put the American scientific and medical communities and the pharmaceutical industry at a competitive disadvantage, compared to the regulation of stem cell research in other countries. The scientific and medical communities and pharmaceutical industry fear that there is a risk that the United States will be less competitiveness in terms of global biotechnology. International competition has developed in the biotechnology industry. In Britain, the regulatory framework provides both public funding and public-private ventures in the field of stem cell research and cloning. This is in contrast to the United

States regulatory framework, where there were limitations on public funding for stem cell research but few constraints on private funded ventures.

Innovation now is, or can be, accomplished in a global context. Do we face a future of international collaboration or competition? Will we capture the benefits of international cooperation? Will transnational or global ethical standards develop for innovative technologies?

Evidence that the future tends toward the development of transnational or global standards for innovative technology is lent by the United Nations Resolution on Cloning.[72] A UN resolution was endorsed by the United States to establish international standards for stem cell research and cloning. Britain voted against the UN declaration because the reference to "human life" might be interpreted as possibly calling for a ban on therapeutic cloning. France, Japan, the Republic of Korea and China also voted against the resolution. The high number of abstentions as well as opposing votes indicates a failure of international consensus, focusing more particularly on the support of therapeutic cloning. An alternative to the regulation of human cloning by international agencies, in the form of a convention or declaration, is the development of standards by the scientific community, or interest group associations, such as the global pharmaceutical industry. No matter what the specific form the international regulation takes, international standards for biotechnology, as well as other issues such as intellectual property, are being developed. Globalization is moving in the direction of the development of consensus about international standards for innovation.

## End of Chapter Discussion Questions

1. What are/could be the unintended negative consequences of genetically engineered plants, such as Round-up Ready soybeans?
2. Is fetal farming (to harvest the stem cells) for pharmaceutical applications ethical? Is there an ethical difference between using "extra" embryos from infertility clinics and developing embryos specifically by in vitro fertilization or by cloning?
3. Debate the merits of internal development of innovation compared to the strategy of "purchasing" innovation.
4. Discuss examples of regulatory failure and unintended negative consequences of deregulation. What are the lessons learned for the future?
5. Propose alternatives to regulation in areas of developing technologies, such as new energy generation.

## Notes

1 Lee Iacocca's requirement for the Pinto design and production team was to get the car to market in 24 months, whereas the usual time for a newly designed model was 60 months.
2 Charles Handy, *The Age of Unreason* (Cambridge, MA: Harvard Business School Press, 1990).

3 "Patents issued by the Patent Trademark Office (PTO) grant patent holders the right to exclude others from making, using, or selling an invention. The granting of this exclusive right is designed to encourage innovation. The patent holder is likely to reap greater profits if protected from direct competition. These profits are intended to serve as incentives for creating innovative products that benefit the public.

The Uruguay Rounds Agreements Act (Public Law 103-465), which became effective on June 8, 1995, changed the patent term in the United States. Before June 8, 1995, patents typically had 17 years of patent life from the date the patent was issued. Patents granted after the June 8, 1995 date now have a 20-year patent life from the date of the first filing of the patent application. However, the effective patent term is frequently less than 20 years because patents are often obtained before products are actually marketed. Many factors influence the length of the effective patent term, including the requirements in the Federal Food, Drug, and Cosmetic Act and the Public Health Service Act that certain products receive FDA approval before marketing. New human drug products generally must undergo extensive testing in animals and humans to show that the drugs are both safe and effective before FDA will approve the product for marketing. Consequently, in order to stimulate product development and innovation, Congress in 1984 enacted Title II of the Drug Price Competition and Patent Term Restoration Act (Public Law 98-417) to extend patent life to compensate patent holders for marketing time lost while developing the product and awaiting government approval. Title II of the Act created a program whereby patent holders whose patents claim a human drug product, medical device, food additive or color additive could recoup some of the lost patent time. In 1988, Congress enacted the Generic Animal Drug and Patent Term Restoration Act (Public Law 100-670) which contained provisions for patent restoration to animal drug products. The regulations governing the Patent Term Restoration program are located in the Code of Federal Regulations, 21 CFR Part 60."

"Small Business Assistance: Frequently Asked Questions on the Patent Term Restoration Program," *U.S. Food and Drug Administration*, last modified Mar. 31, 2009, http://www.fda.gov/drugs/developmentapprovalprocess/smallbusinessassistance/ucm069959.htm.

4 Erbitux was approved for marketing in February 2004.
FDA News
FOR IMMEDIATE RELEASE
P04–20
February 12, 2004
Media Inquiries: 301-827-6242
Consumer Inquiries: 888-INFO-FDA
FDA Approves Erbitux for Colorectal Cancer

FDA today approved Erbitux (cetuximab) to treat patients with advanced colorectal cancer that has spread to other parts of the body. Erbitux is the first monoclonal antibody approved to treat this type of cancer and is indicated as a combination treatment to be given intravenously with irinotecan, another drug approved to fight colorectal cancer, or alone if patients cannot tolerate irinotecan.

Erbitux was approved under FDA's accelerated approval program, which allows FDA to approve products for cancer and other serious or life-threatening diseases based on early evidence of a product's effectiveness. Although treatment with Erbitux has not been shown to extend patients' lives, it was shown to shrink tumors in some patients and delay tumor growth, especially when used as a combination treatment.

Erbitux is a genetically engineered version of a mouse antibody that contains both human and mouse components. (Antibodies in the body are substances produced by the immune system to fight foreign substances.) It can be produced in large quantities in the laboratory. This new monoclonal antibody is believed to work by targeting a natural protein called "epidermal growth factor receptor" (EGFR) on the surface of cancer cells, interfering with their growth.

For patients with tumors that express EGFR and who no longer responded to treatment with irinotecan alone or in combination with other chemotherapy drugs, the combination treatment of Erbitux and irinotecan shrank tumors in 22.9% of patients and delayed tumor growth by approximately 4.1 months. For patients who received Erbitux alone, the tumor response rate was 10.8% and tumor growth was delayed by 1.5 months.

Colorectal cancer—cancer of the colon or rectum—is the third most common cancer affecting men and women in the U.S. and, according to the Centers for Disease Control and Prevention (CDC), and is the second leading cause of cancer-related death. Colorectal cancer is also one of the most commonly diagnosed cancers in the U.S.; approximately 147,500 new cases were diagnosed in 2003.

The manufacturer of Erbitux, ImClone Systems Incorporated, Branchburg, N.J., submitted their original request for approval in several sections between June 28 and October 31, 2001. Subsequent to ImClone's original submissions, FDA determined that their application could not be reviewed because approximately half of the patients (94) studied had not failed the approved treatments for colon cancer; and important information about the safety and effectiveness of Erbitux in a portion of the remaining patients (102) was missing. In their new request for approval on August 14, 2003, Imclone submitted the results of a large, well-run trial that included 329 patients as well as the results of the earlier two studies. For the studies submitted in their original 2001 request for approval, ImClone successfully collected substantial amounts of missing information from hospital records and other sources.

"FDA Approves Erbitux for Colorectal Cancer," *U.S. Food and Drug Administration*, Feb. 12, 2004, last modified Mar. 29, 2013, http://www.fda.gov/newsevents/newsroom/pressannouncements/2004/ucm108244.htm.

5  Skunk works at Lockheed Martin, http://www.lockheedmartin.com.

6  Kelly's 14 Rules, Lockheed Martin, last modified 2014, http://www.lockheedmartin.com. Among the rules was: "Push more basic inspection responsibility back to subcontractors and vendors. Don't duplicate so much inspection." This principle is recognized as key in supply chain management. Another principle, "There must be mutual trust between the military project organization and the contractor with very close cooperation and liaison on a day-to-day basis [which] cuts down misunderstanding and correspondence to an absolute minimum," emphasizes decentralization and lateral communications.

7  Jeremy Rifkin, *The End of Work: The Decline of the Global Labor Force and the Dawn of the Post-Market Era* (New York: Putnam Publishing Group, 1994).

8  "About UPS," *UPS*, last modified 2014, http://www.ups.com/about/about.html. See also Thomas L. Friedman's discussion of UPS in *The World Is Flat: A Brief History of the Twenty-First Century* (New York: Farrar, Straus and Giroux, 2005).

9  COMPASS is an acronym for Computerized Operations Monitoring, Planning and Scheduling System. "1981–1990," *UPS*, last modified 2014, http://www.ups.com/content/us/en/about/history/1990.html.

10  "GE's Jack Welch Named Manager of the Century," *Fortune*, Nov. 1, 1999.

In "The Ultimate Manager," *Fortune* Editorial Director Geoffrey Colvin describes how the genius in Manager of the Century Jack Welch's thinking is that he returned power to the little people: the worker and the shareholder. Welch transformed GE and multiplied its value beyond anyone's expectations: from a market capitalization of $14 billion to more than $400 billion today—making GE the second-most-valuable company on Earth.

Welch took the reins at GE at a time when the old, manufacturing-based world started giving way to the new one. According to Colvin, Welch leads the annals of management history not for anticipating the new world's changes ahead but for acting on them.

Geoffrey Colvin, "The Ultimate Manager in a Time of Hidebound, Formulaic Thinking, General Electric's Jack Welch Gave Power to the Worker and the Shareholder. He Built One Hell of a Company in the Process," *Fortune*, Nov. 22, 1999, http://archive.fortune.com/magazines/fortune/fortune_archive/1999/11/22/269126/index.htm.

11  Michael Hammer and James Champy, *Re-Engineering the Corporation* (New York: HarperCollins, 1993).

12  Matt Waller, M. Eric Johnson, and Tom Davis, "Vendor-managed Inventory in the Retail Supply Chain," *Journal of Business Logistics* 20 (1999): 183–204, http://www.datalliance.com/vmi_retail_sc.pdf.

13  See Thomas Wailgum, "45 Years of Wal-Mart History: A Technology Time Line: For Nearly Half a Century Wal-Mart Has Led the Information Technology Charge to Cope with Growth and Fuel Its Global Expansion," *CIO*, Oct. 17, 2007, http://www.cio.com/article/2437873/infrastructure/45-years-of-wal-mart-history—a-technology-time-line.html. See also Miguel Bustillo, "Wal-Mart Radio Tags to Track Clothing," *Wall Street Journal*, July 23, 2010, http://online.wsj.com/news/articles/SB10001424052748704421304575383213061198090.

14  See Wailgum, "45 Years of Wal-Mart." See also Bustillo, "Wal-Mart Radio Tags."

15  Waller, Johnson, and Davis, "Vendor-managed Inventory."

16  James D. Thompson, author of *Organizations in Action: Social Science Bases of Administrative Theory* (1967; repr., New Brunswick, NJ: Transaction Publishers, 2003) describes the relationship between an enterprise and its task environment in terms of tight or loose coupling.

17  Pete Engardio and Bruce Einhorn, with Manjeet Krialani, et al., "Outsourcing Innovation," *Business Week*, March 21, 2005.

18  Oliver Williamson, *Market and Hierarchies: Analysis and Anti-trust Implications* (New York: Basic Books, 1975).

19  Clayton M. Christensen, *The Innovator's Dilemma: Why New Technologies Cause Great Firms to Fail* (Boston, MA: Harvard Business School Press, 1997).

20  Clayton M. Christensen and Michael E. Raynor, *The Innovator's Solution: Creating and Sustaining Successful Growth* (Boston, MA: Harvard Business School Press, 2003).

21  *Celera*, last modified 2014, http://www.celera.com/. See Prepared Statement of J. Craig Venter, Ph.D. President and Chief Scientific Officer Celera Genomics, A PE Corporation Business Before the Subcommittee on Energy and Environment U.S. House of Representatives Committee On Science, Apr. 6, 2000, http://clinton4.nara.gov/WH/EOP/OSTP/html/00626_4.html. See also Frederic Gloden and Michael D. Lemonick, "The Race Is Over; The great genome quest is officially a tie, thanks to a

round of pizza diplomacy. Yet lead researcher Craig Venter still draws few cheers from his colleagues," *Time*, July 3, 2000.

22 See "Major Events in the Human Genome Project and Other Related Projects," *Human Genome Project Information Archive* 1990–2003, last modified March 6, 2014, http://www.ornl.gov/sci/techresources/Human_Genome/project/timeline.shtml.

23 Bert Thompson, "Cracking the Code—The Human Genome Project in Perspective [Part II]," *Reason & Revelation: A Monthly Journal of Christian Evidences* 20, no. 9 (Sept. 2000): 65–71, http://www.apologeticspress.org/apPubPage.aspx?pub=1&issue=509.

24 "50th Anniversary of the Kefauver-Harris Drug Amendments of 1962—Interview with FDA Historian John Swann," *U.S. Food and Drug Administration*, last modified Sept. 26, 2012, http://www.fda.gov/drugs/newsevents/ucm320927.htm.

25 Celgene Corporation, "Proposed Changes to Approved Thalomid Package Insert," *U.S. Food and Drug Administration*, http://www.accessdata.fda.gov/drugsatfda_docs/label/2006/021430lbl.pdf.

26 A 1999 study by Cornell University School of Agriculture conducted a controlled experiment, using true experimental design. This conclusion was also confirmed by a study at Iowa State University. See Marlin Rice, "Monarchs and BT Corn: Questions and Answers," *Integrated Crop Management*, June 14, 1994, 93–95, http://www.ipm.iastate.edu/ipm/icm/1999/6–14–1999/monarchbt.html. This result is controverted, however, by a field study published by the Agricultural Research Service (ARS), U.S. Department of Agriculture. See "Q&A: BT Corn and Monarch Butterflies," *United States Department of Agriculture, Agricultural Research Service*, last modified Mar. 29, 2004, http://www.ars.usda.gov/is/br/btcorn/index.html#bt1.

27 See, e.g., "GE Oilseed Rape—Out of Control in Canada, Genetic Engineering Briefing Pack," April 2002, *Greenpeace*, http://archive.greenpeace.org/~geneng/reports/gmo/canada.pdf.

28 See Marc Gunther, "McDonald's GMO dilemma: Why Fries Are Causing Such a Fuss," *The Guardian*, Dec. 4, 2013, and "Harvest of Fear: Exploring the Growing Fight Over Genetically Modified Food," *Nova/Frontline*, *PBS*, last modified April 2001, http://www.pbs.org/wgbh/harvest/.

29 Michael Pollan, *The Botany of Desire: A Plant's Eye View of the World* (New York: Random House, 2001).

30 Susan FitzGerald and Virginia A. Smith, "Settlement with Research Scientists: Penn to Pay $517,000 in Gene Therapy Death," Feb. 10, 2005, http://articles.philly.com/2005–02–10/news/25444587_1_paul-gelsinger-gene-therapy-jesse-gelsinger.

31 Jeff Bennett and Siobhan Hughes, "GM Officials Ignored Alert on Car Stalling: Switch Engineer, Others Were Sent 2005 Warning Over Bump Disabling Engine," *Wall Street Journal*, June 18, 2014.

32 For example, Johnson & Johnson Co. played a proactive role in proposing tamper-resistant standards for the pharmaceutical industry after the Tylenol poisonings in 1982.

33 "Stem Cell Basics," *National Institutes of Health*, last modified Apr. 28, 2009, http://stemcells.nih.gov/info/basics/Pages/Default.aspx.

34 "President's Embryonic Stem Cell Research Policy," Fact Sheet, White House, Office of the Press Secretary, Aug. 9, 2001, http://www.whitehouse.gov/news/releases/2001.

35 Sheryl Gay Stolberg, "House Approves a Stem Cell Research Bill Opposed by Bush," *New York Times*, May 25, 2005; see also "Bush Vetoes Embryonic Stem-Cell Bill," Sept. 25, 2006, http://www.cnn.com/2006/POLITICS/07/19/stemcells.veto/.

36 Office of Legislative Policy and Analysis: Stem Cell Therapeutic and Research Act of 2005 P.L. 109–129 (H.R. 2520, S. 1317), http://olpa.od.nih.gov/legislation/109/publiclaws/stemthera.asp.

37 Fact Sheet on Presidential Executive Order Removing Barriers to Responsible Scientific Research Involving Human Stem Cells, March 2009, http://www.whitehouse.gov/the_press_office/Fact-Sheet-on-Presidential-Executive-Order.

38 *Santa Clara County v. Southern Pacific Railroad Company*, 118 U.S. 394 (1886). See discussion in Chapter 5.

39 *Buckley v. Valeo*, 424 U.S. at 26–27 (1976).

40 The Federal Elections Campaign Act is 2 USCS §§ 431 et seq. Subtitle H of the Internal Revenue Code of 1954 (26 USCS 9001 et seq.) also provides for public financing of Presidential election campaigns.

41 McCain-Feingold permitted $10,000 of soft money contributions to state political parties.

42 540 U.S. 93 (2003).

43 Section 315(d)(4) of the Federal Election Campaign Act (2 USCS § 441a(d)(4)). Independent financial expenditures are expenditures by a political committee that are not coordinated with the candidate for political office.

"Under § 315(d)(4), a party that wished to spend more than $5,000 in coordination with its nominee (a) forfeited the right to make independent expenditures for express advocacy of a candidate's election or defeat, and (b) was thus forced to forgo the category of independent expenditures that made use of 'magic words,' such as 'Elect John Smith' or 'Vote Against Jane Doe.'" 540 U.S. 93 (2003).

44 *Citizens United v. Federal Election Commission* Appeal from the United States District Court for the District of Columbia, Jan. 21, 2010, 558 U.S. 310, http://www.supremecourt.gov/opinions/09pdf/08–205.pdf.

45 "Former NPR CEO Ken Stern: The IRS Had the Right Idea," *NPR*, May 25, 2013, http://www.thedailybeast.com/articles/2013/05/25/former-npr-ceo-ken-stern-the-irs-had-the-right-idea.html.

46 Brian Naylor, One Reason To Apply For Tax-Exempt Status: Anonymity, NPR, May 15, 2013,
One Reason To Apply For Tax-Exempt Status: Anonymity
http://npr/12vbo7U
http://www.npr.org/2013/05/15/184223558/one-reason-to-apply-for-tax-exempt-status-anonymity

47 Summer Lollie, Immigration Debate Sparks Record Spending by Numerous Special Interest Groups, July 3, 2010, https://www.opensecrets.org/news/2010/07/the-immigration-debate-sparks-passi/.

48 In *Buckley v. Valeo*, 424 U.S. 1 (1976) and in *Republican National Committee v. FEC* 445 U.S. 955 (1980), the court voided limitations on campaign spending by PACs. The McCain-Feingold Law, formally known as Bipartisan Campaign Reform Act of 2002, permits unlimited expenditures by individuals and PACs if the campaign spending is not coordinated with the political candidate.

49 "Because aggregate limits restricting how much money a donor may contribute to candidates for federal office, political parties, and political action committees do not further the government's interest in preventing quid pro quo corruption or the appearance of such corruption, while at the same time seriously restricting

participation in the democratic process, they are invalid under the First Amendment." *McCutcheon v. FEC*, 572 U.S. ___ (2014).

50  http://www.businessroundtable.org/.

51  The Business Roundtable's task forces frequently develop reports on issues of importance within the public policy realm. The Roundtable issues white papers, policy statements and reports from the perspective of our chief executive officers to help advance our goals of economic growth and job creation within the U.S. marketplace.
Source: *Business Roundtable*, last modified 2014, http://www.businessroundtable.org/.

52  540 U.S. 93 (2003). However, *Federal Election Commission v. Wisconsin Right to Life, Inc.*, 551 U.S. 449 (2007) held that "issue ads" may be run during the "electioneering" black-out period, and thereby overruled that portion of McConnell that upheld "electioneering prohibitions" on issues before the electorate within 30 days of an election.

53  Robert Barnes, "Supreme Court Strikes Down Limits on Federal Campaign Donations," *Washington Post*, Apr. 2, 2014; *McCutcheon v. FEC*, 572 U.S. ___ (2014).

54  *Sierra Club v. Cheney*, 967 F.2d 590 (1992). An interesting side note to the *Sierra Club v. Cheney* case is that Justice Scalia refused to recuse himself.

55  John W. Dean, "GAO v- Cheney Is Big-Time Stalling: The Vice President Can Win Only If We Have Another Bush v. Gore-like Ruling," *FindLaw*, Feb. 01, 2002, http://writ.news.findlaw.com/dean/20020201.html.

56  C. Wright Mills, *Power Elite* (New York: Oxford University Press, 1956).

57  See "Factual Back-Up for [Michael Moore's] *Fahrenheit 9/11*," Section Four, *Third World Traveler*, http://www.thirdworldtraveler.com/Michael_Moore/Factual_BackUp_F911.html.

58  See The Carlyle Group: Global Alternative Asset Management, last modified 2014, http://www.carlyle.com/.

59  Even the People's Republic of China has moved, at least in part, to a market-driven economy, even while retaining a Communist political system.

60  Privatization of the British railroad industry was accomplished between 1994 and 1997 under the Thatcher administration but has been partially renationalized as Network Rail. The World Bank reports: "Governments worldwide should look to the British experience for examples of how not to engage in railroad reform, the World Bank said in its first comprehensive report on the British experiment in privatization, which was released this week. Lou Thompson, the primary author of the report and the World Bank's most experienced rail specialist, said the Bank has no money in the British rail system. He wrote the report, he said, because the topic comes up in every conversation with the Bank's many rail borrowers around the world. Thompson also said the Bank wanted to give the best available analysis of British Rail's privatization experience to developing countries. Over time, the British Rail system has retreated from the concept of full private ownership to the point that the public and the private role is now about a 50–50 split. That is closer to a viable solution, the World Bank says, than a fully privatized system, which exists nowhere in the world." The World Bank, last modified 2014, http://www.worldbank.org. See also William Pfaff, "The Privatization of Public Utilities Can Be a Disaster," *International Herald Tribune*, Feb. 22, 2001.

61  United Airlines declared bankruptcy in 2002 but experienced financial duress in 2005 as it emerged from bankruptcy. United Airlines was granted permission by a US bankruptcy court to shift its pension obligations.

62  Barbara Kiviat, "Can Bankruptcy Work? Will Bankruptcy Help Save GM or Chrysler? A Look at Three Major Bankruptcies—Continental Airlines, Kmart and Fruit of the Loom—Shows that Outcomes Can Vary Widely: Bankruptcy Survivors: Continental Airlines," *Time*, Apr. 2, 2009. See also Amy Stromberg, "Continental Case Fueled Stiffer Laws on Bankruptcy," *Sun Sentinel*, Mar., 9, 1989, and Agis Salupkas, "Continental Files for Bankruptcy," *New York Times*, Dec. 4, 1990.

63  Elaine X. Grant, "TWA—Death of a Legend," *Saint Louis Magazine*, July 28, 2006, http://www.stlmag.com/TWA-Death-Of-A-Legend/. See also James Brumley, "The Carl Icahn 'Accountability' Statement Rings Hollow: Icahn's Actions speak Louder Than His Words," *Investor Place*, May 12, 2014, http://investorplace.com/2014/05/carl-icahn-accountability/#.U7Jh3rdOUlY.

64  Pan Am declared bankruptcy in 1991 and its successor Pan American World Airways declared bankruptcy in 1998. See Robert E. Dallos and Denise Gellene, "Pan Am, a 50-Year Leader in Aviation, Goes Bankrupt: Economy: Carrier Cites Fuel Costs, Downturn and Flight 103 Bombing. It Says Travelers Will Not Be Affected.," *Los Angeles Times*, Jan. 9, 1991, http://articles.latimes.com/1991–01–09/news/mn-7223_1_fuel-costs. See also "American Joins Long List of Airline Bankruptcies," *The Associated Press*, Nov. 29, 2011, http://www.boston.com/business/articles/2011/11/29/american_joins_long_list_of_airline_bankruptcies/#sthash.1TOjrWun.dpuf and Barnaby Conrad III, *Pan Am: An Aviation Legend* (Emeryville, CA: Woodford Press, 1999).

65  Braniff International declared bankruptcy twice, in 1982 and 1989.

66  US Airways declared bankruptcy twice, in 2002 and 2004; its predecessor, New York Air, declared Chapter 11 bankruptcy in 1979.

67  American Airlines' efforts to avoid bankruptcy are discussed in Chapter 9, with respect to the new employment contract. The CEO of AMR, the American Airlines parent, was forced to resign when his own compensation package came to light, after he requested bankruptcy avoiding concessions from the unions.

68  The deregulation of the banking industry was accomplished by series of statutes, including the Depository Institutions Deregulation and Monetary Control Act of 1980, the Financial Institutions Recovery, Reform and Enforcement Act of 1989, and the Graham-Leach Act 1999, which rescinded the Glass-Steagall Act of 1933.

69  See James E. Post, Anne T. Lawrence, and James Weber, "California's Energy Crisis: A Deregulation Failure," Exhibit 7-B in *Business and Society: Corporate Strategy, Public Policy, Ethics*, 10th ed. (Boston: McGraw-Hill/Irwin, 2002), 176. See also Pfaff, "The Privatization of Public Utilities."

70  The Pension Benefit Guaranty Corporation was created as part of the Employee Retirement Income Security Act of 1974.

71  "PBGC is not funded by general tax revenues. PBGC collects insurance premiums from employers that sponsor insured pension plans, earns money from investments and receives funds from pension plans it takes over. PBGC pays monthly retirement benefits, up to a guaranteed maximum, to about 518,000 retirees in 3,479 pension plans that ended. Including those who have not yet retired and participants in multiemployer plans receiving financial assistance, PBGC is responsible for the current and future pensions of about 1,061,000 people." *Pension Benefit Guaranty Corporation: A U.S. Government Agency*, last modified 2014, http://www.pbgc.gov/.

72  See "Ad Hoc Committee on an International Convention Against the Reproductive Cloning of Human Beings," United Nations, last modified 2005, http://www.un.org/law/cloning/.

## End of Chapter Case: Genetically Engineered Salmon

*"Debating Genetically Modified Salmon"*
Talk of the Nation, *December 9, 2011, NPR*

JOE PALCA, HOST

This is SCIENCE FRIDAY. I'm Joe Palca. Ira Flatow is away this week. The biotech company AquaBounty Technologies of Waltham, Massachusetts, has developed a genetically modified Atlantic salmon that grows twice as fast as regular salmon. How has it done this? By tinkering with the salmon's genome, adding a growth hormone gene from one fish plus an antifreeze gene from another.

The result: fish that grow to market size rapidly. AquaBounty's application to market these bioengineered fish has been under FDA review for 15 years. Last fall, the Food and Drug Administration held a public hearing and convened a panel of experts to review the food safety and environmental risks posed by these salmon. Their conclusion: AquaBounty salmon was safe, as safe as food from conventional Atlantic salmon.

But some scientists and environmental groups have said there are questions about the safety of genetically modified fish remain unanswered. This hour: the science and safety of bioengineered fish. And joining us for this discussion is Dr. Alison Van Eenennaam. She's an extension specialist in animal genomics and biotechnology at University of California, Davis. She was on the FDA's panel of experts that evaluated AquaBounty's proposal last year. She co-authored a piece in Nature Biotechnology about the company's regulatory battle. She joins us from Eugene, Oregon. Welcome, Dr. Van Eenennaam.

ALISON VAN EENENNAAM: Good Afternoon, Joe.

PALCA: Good afternoon. And also with us is Dr. Anne Kapuscinski. She's a professor of sustainability science and chair of the Environmental Studies Program at Dartmouth College. She has been a scientific advisor to the federal government on several issues relating to genetically modified organisms, and she joins us from Hannover, New Hampshire. Welcome to the program, Dr. Kapuscinski.

ANNE KAPUSCINSKI: Good afternoon, Joe.

PALCA: Good afternoon. And if you want to weigh in on the science and the safety of genetically modified salmon, give us a call. Our number is 1-800-989-8255. That's 1-800-989-TALK. If you're on Twitter, you can tweet us your question by writing the @ sign followed by scifri, and there's also more information on the website, www.sciencefriday.com, where you'll find links to our topic.

So Dr. Van Eenennaam, let's start with you. You were on this committee that was evaluating. How long did you have to evaluate the company's data saying this food is—this fish is safe to eat and safe to grow and release into the marketplace?

EENENNAAM: So the veterinary medicine advisory committee that looked at all that data had about two weeks prior to the meeting, which was held last

September. It was actually released to the committee the same day it was made publicly available on the FDA's website.

PALCA: And what sorts of material were available to you?

EENENNAAM: It was about 172-page briefing package, which included information on the safety of the fish from a food consumption standpoint and also information about how the construct was created, whether or not the fish grew faster or not and information also included there on the environmental assessment that the company had done to look at the environmental concerns associated with the fish.

I guess one thing, just I know environmental concerns are always something that people are concerned about, this fish actually getting out into wild populations, and the way that the product was being regulated through the FDA, it was proposed, and it is proposed, that this particular fish is going to be raised in land-based tanks, so on land in tanks, and it would also be triploid female product, which means that all of the fish would be female so they couldn't interbreed with each other, and also triploid, and triploidy would result in those animals being sterile.

And so the company tried to have some risk mitigation in place to prevent any possibility of those fish interbreeding with wild populations.

PALCA: Right, and just finally on this meeting, and this meeting took place last September, 2010, the conclusion of the meeting was that this group said to the FDA we think that this is a product that you could approve for marketing.

EENENNAAM: Basically the idea of the veterinary medicine advisory committee was to look at all of the data that the FDA had looked at. The FDA's conclusion was there was a reasonable certainty of no harm from a food safety perspective, and also they looked at the environmental assessment. And basically, the committee was there to look and see if there was anything that they had overlooked.

And I think the conclusion of the committee was that they agreed with the FDA that there was a reasonable certainty of no harm from food safety perspective and also from the environmental assessment perspective.

PALCA: And that reasonable certainty of no harm is one of those terms of art that means, we don't think it's a problem.

EENENNAAM: Well, yeah.

PALCA: That's basically. I just wanted to make sure people understood that. OK, so you said things looked OK, but Dr. Kapuscinski, I mean obviously you and other scientists think either—well, tell me what you think. Did they not look at the data correctly, or did they not realize that more data was needed or were needed?

KAPUSCINSKI: Well, I think my main concern was that the kind of data presented had gaps, and the quality of the analysis of the data, especially the statistical analysis, was really quite a low bar. So my main concern is that this application is really setting a precedent, and it's actually an application for a fairly small grow-out facility to raise some of these salmon in an undisclosed location in Panama.

So this one facility doesn't really represent what's coming down the road. It's really more, you can think of it as sort of putting the camel's nose under the tent. But because it's going to set a precedent, it's really important that the quality of the science be as high as scientific standards would normally expect and that the risk assessment is complete.

So, I was concerned that there were some problems with small sample sizes, some problems with statistical analysis, and I was even more concerned that there were key parts missing from the risk assessment. It seemed like the approach taken, the risk assessment, wasn't really up to speed with the state of the art risk assessment.

So there were really three things that I thought were missing. One was the lack of what we would call a failure mode analysis, basically lack of a quantitative analysis of what would—what could go wrong in the multiple confinement system that the company proposed.

As Alison just explained, they have some biological confinement methods, which I think is a very good thing that they have that, and then they had also a number of physical confinement methods combined with that. The problem is, with confinement systems, there are always possibilities of things going wrong, and their interactions can be complex.

And it's now a pretty standard practice, when you're assessing a technology, that you do a failure analysis. So that was missing. The other part that was missing is, if some of the fish did escape, they didn't really go the next step of answering the question, well, what could happen if they did escape. And one might argue that there would be a very low number of fish escaping, but it doesn't obviate the need to still do that second step of the risk assessment.

And then finally, and in a way the most important, is the risk assessment lacked a formal uncertainty analysis. And this is really important, especially in environmental risk assessment, because there are always going to be scientific uncertainties.

Living organisms and ecosystems where these fish might end up, are very complex. There's a lot of variability. There are always things that the scientists don't fully understand. That doesn't need to paralyze, though, the risk-assessment process. Instead, the state of the art in risk assessment nowadays is that you carry out a formal uncertainty analysis throughout the risk assessment. And you gather the results of that at the end, and you make that part of the conclusions that you had to the decision-makers, so that the decision-makers are much better informed about, really, what are they accepting, and what assumptions are they making if they give an approval or if they give a denial.

So I think really in a sense I was worried that if this application is approved with these low standards of science and these missing parts of a risk assessment, and it sets the message, the precedent that this is what the U.S. government will expect.

And also, many other countries are actually watching to see what the U.S. government will do because there are other groups around the world developing transgenic fish. That would just be a really unfortunately way too low bar.

PALCA: I'm just curious, though, Alison Van Eenennaam said that the expectation was that these fish would all be—the ones that were released or the ones that would leave the breeding facility—were all female and were triploid, meaning they were sterile. Doesn't that mean that they—I mean, if they got out, nothing would happen, they'd live their lives, and then they'd die, and that would be the end of it?

KAPUSCINSKI: Well, it's—unfortunately, it's not quite that simple. There are two things that we still have to think about. The first one is that there is some low percentage of fish in which the triploid induction which makes them sterile doesn't always succeed. And again because of this one application being fairly small, that low number, you know, it might be anything as low as .1 percent to one percent of the fish not being totally sterile, that low percentage might not be a problem for this particular case.

But there should have been an actual failure analysis of that, if this is again going to set the model for what you do in the future. So that's the first problem because in future applications you might have much larger numbers of fish, total numbers escaping, especially if this approval ends up triggering a proliferation of genetically engineered salmon being taken up by the salmon farming industry, which is a global industry, a global commodity, then small percentages can add up when you're starting to have operations that raise anything from 500,000 to a million fish in a particular fish farm.

But then the second issue is if fish escape, and they're sterile, they don't die out immediately. They still live in the ecosystem and interact with other organisms. So again the question of scale becomes important. For this particular application, we were given really no information about the organisms living in the undisclosed—in the river in the undisclosed place in Panama. So it's really hard to know are there other fish in that ecosystem that any escapes could interact with? If there are, are they fish that are endangered? We know that freshwater fish species throughout the world are in decline or in a lot of trouble because of other human impacts. So we need to have those kinds of questions at least addressed.

PALCA: This is SCIENCE FRIDAY. I'm Joe Palca. We're talking this hour about how a proposal to market genetically modified salmon is raising concerns. My guests are Dr. Alison Van Eenennaam, an extension specialist in animal genomics and biotechnology at the University of California, Davis; and Dr. Anne Kapuscinski, professor of sustainability science and chair of the Environmental Studies Program at Dartmouth College.

And I think I'd like to ask Dr. Van Eenennaam: You heard some of the concerns about missing data or inadequate date or safety data that she would like to see. How does all that strike you?

EENENNAAM: Well, a couple of points, I think. The FDA made it very clear that this particular approval was for the particular location in Panama that the company was proposing to grow these fish in, which again is an inland tank location.

And that's an FDA-inspected site, and the FDA has been there and seen that there's multiple levels of physical containment, things like nets and cages and things to stop any fish from escaping there, and also the physical location of where the actual site is has a number of geographical attributes that would prevent those fish from if fish did actually escape from that location from ever reaching the sea.

There's a number of thermal lethal rivers that the fish would have to get through if they ever were to escape. And so I guess we have to think about risk assessment in terms of there is a potential hazard, that is that the fish escaped, but there's a number of risk mitigation approaches that the company's put into place. And these are numerous and multiple and redundant.

So let's just talk about the triploid, which I agree is not 100 percent effective. So let's just say we've got .1 percent of the fish that are actually fertile, but then you've got all of these multiple physical and biological containment measures in place to try to reduce the risk of any fish ever escaping down to zero.

And I think you'll never say zero, but there's a number of multiple factors in place to try to minimize that risk as a result of all of these risk mitigation measures.

PALCA: All right, fair enough, but I want—now I want to include our listeners to this conversation because they, I'm sure, will have questions. So let's go first to Luke(ph) in Kansas City, Missouri. Luke, you're on SCIENCE FRIDAY, welcome.

LUKE: Hi, my question is that: Why is there so much attention surrounding the genetically modified salmon when we've been consuming, like, modified vegetables and other foods injected with who knows what for years now?

PALCA: Interesting question. Maybe Dr. Kapuscinski, you'd like to try that.

KAPUSCINSKI: Sure. I think that there's that much attention for two reasons. One is this will be the first genetically modified animal approved for widespread commercial production and human food. But secondly, this kind of animal, a fish especially, is not that removed from its wild relatives, and are—have much closer interactions with ecosystem than some of the vegetables that we grow.

Also, we're dealing with a species—Atlantic salmon—that many of the places where it's farmed are also the native range of wild Atlantic salmon, and those are—unfortunately, those wild Atlantic salmon populations are in deep trouble around the world.

So that's not directly the case for this particular application, as Alison pointed out, but I want to come back to my earlier point that we have to keep thinking about the broader context here. This application is setting the precedent for what would be expected of an applicant to show environmental safety to a reasonable degree in the future.

And if this application is approved, and if the salmon farming industry decides that this is a good product for their business, then it's going to be adopted and farmed in places where there may not be as good confinement and where if the fish escape in some of those places—like eastern Canada, the state of Maine, parts of Europe—where they can escape, interact with wild Atlantic salmon.

PALCA: Right.

KAPUSCINSKI: So, you know, vegetables don't move around as easily.

PALCA: Right, but there is also the case, at least as Dr. Van Eenennaam said, about they'll need their own applications, and someone will have to decide if their control measures are adequate. But let's go now to Roger(ph) in Commerce, Michigan. Roger, welcome to SCIENCE FRIDAY.

ROGER: Hey there.

PALCA: Hey.

ROGER: Yeah, my main concern was, when I hear about genetically modified foods, in general, I hear from a lot of people the complaint about not being safe to eat, which always drive me crazy. It's perfectly safe to eat. My only concern is like what people were talking about earlier, from the genetic diversity and getting involved with wild species.

But couldn't it be perfectly safe if it was just in a controlled environment, unlike the certain Asian carp where it wasn't in a proper place? If they were raise some place, you know, flood plains, or totally landlocked, away from the ocean. Give an extreme example like Nevada. We have no problem growing it over there and even encouraging it. And I'll take my comments off the air.

PALCA: Okay, thanks. So the question is, you know, absent the ecological questions, is this fish safe to eat? And are you satisfied, Dr. Kapuscinski, that that question has been answered?

KAPUSCINSKI: Well, the food safety area is not as much my area of expertise, but I did—I did attend the VMAC . . .

PALCA: That's that meeting, the veterinary . . .

KAPUSCINSKI: Yes, and I heard some of the other comments and read some of them and also actually read the report from the committee. And, you know, some of the concerns that were made that sort of resonated for me based on my having skimmed the food safety section of it was again concerns about small sample sizes and some problems with the statistical analysis.

So for example, one of the legitimate things to ask about is whether the engineering of these salmon has increased their allergenicity, and the data that was used to conclude the conclusions about that involved only six fish. And even the statistician on the veterinary medicine advisory committee commented that, you know, there could be some ways to improve the statistical analysis.

And there was a paragraph about that in the final report from the chair of that committee. So my concern there is also really about the quality of the science.

PALCA: Okay, Dr. Van Eenennaam, what about you at this point? Are you more or less satisfied that this is safe to eat, or do you think there's still more to find out?

EENENNAAM: I'm comfortable that it's safe to eat. I guess I will touch on the allergenicity question because that's always an issue with genetically engineered foods. And the concern is that the protein that's being introduced through the genetic engineering would create allergens.

For example, if you brought, I don't know, a peanut protein into a fish, it might result in an allergen. And that is not the case in the case of the growth hormone that's in the salmon. And so the allergenicity question got down to the question of whether or not people who were allergic to fish would be more likely to be allergic to this particular fish.

KAPUSCINSKI: And there's really no consensus in the scientific or medical communities regarding the magnitude of an increase in kind of the endogenous allergens, the fish allergens, if you will, That would pose an additional risk to public health. And I think in the absence of knowing what level you're looking for, it's difficult to know what would be the appropriate work to do.

EENENNAAM: We don't even know, really, the levels of allergens that are in naturally occurring salmon, and so in the absence of that information, it's difficult to know what levels would trigger a concern. And we didn't see—in that absence of that information, it's difficult to make a determination.

PALCA: Okay, let's take another call now and this time go to—let's see, how about Jerry(ph) in—no, Brian(ph) in Portland, Oregon. Brian, welcome to the program.

BRIAN: Yeah, I had a question about the failure analysis. I read an article about either this fish or a very similar fish, and the article I read is about 10 years ago, and it stated that if some of these fish that grow extra fast were to escape into the wild, within 50 years or something, it would supplant the wild fish because it grows so much faster. And then they would destroy themselves because they would eat so much of the food so quickly, there would be a population collapse. And this is a catastrophic failure, and this is a computer analysis I heard about, again about 10 years ago. I wanted to know if your panel has heard (unintelligible).

PALCA: Fair enough, thanks, Brian. What about that, Dr. Kapuscinski, maybe you've heard of this?

KAPUSCINSKI: I suspect that the caller is referring to a study that described a theoretical Trojan gene effect. And in this case, I anticipate that Allison and I probably agree.

PALCA: Wait, excuse me, can you explain what a Trojan gene effect is?

KAPUSCINSKI: Sure, the idea is that this engineered gene would give a mating advantage to the fish, for example because larger salmon are maybe more successful at competing for a mate. So it would give them a mating advantage that would drive the engineered into a wild population.

But then there's some other aspect of the gene that causes reduced viability in the offspring, and so over generations, that drives the population to extinction. Now, the problem was that the original model that was used to come up with the theoretical prediction was really very simplistic.

And some geneticists questioned it at that time. Now, we actually have some additional studies that have tried to add some of the things that were left out of that model—for example, the possibility of a evolutionary process; the fact that environmental factors can actually influence the actual traits of a fish, the way the gene gets expressed in the final—things like the final size. So we now have pretty good evidence that all points in the same direction, that the Trojan gene effect is not very likely. However, I don't think that that means then that there's absolutely nothing to worry about. There still are other important ecological effects questions.

PALCA: OK. Dr. Van Eenennaam, do you have anything you'd like to add to that?

EENENNAAM: You know, I mean, I think there's some data that has come out that in this particular fish's case shows that there actually would have reduced reproductive performance, at least the males would, relative to controlled. That's the study that came out this year. But I guess my question is the relevance of that given the proposed containment that's associated with this particular application, and that these fish are not going to be interacting with the environment. The proposal is to have them on—in land-based facilities.

PALCA: OK. Fair enough. Let's now go to Jerry in Ehrhardt, South Carolina. Jerry, welcome to SCIENCE FRIDAY. You're on the air.

JERRY: Hi, good afternoon. If you would ask your guest to comment on the origin of the extreme resistance of genetic modification because it does seems to me that for a millennia we've been practicing husbandry with animals. We've been breeding them. We've been grafting plants. And the only objection to me seems to be the speed involved rather than the quality of the product because, ironically, the, excuse me, the European resistance is on the quality and is it safe, where for the layman standpoint it seems like the speed involved is the main thing and not the quality of the result because we've been doing this for generations, for millennia.

PALCA: Well, thank you for that, Jerry. So the question, basically, is genetic modification is the same as, I mean, the engineering it in the lab is just the faster way of doing the same thing that people have always done in terms of breeding crops that they want or fish that they want or anything that they want. Dr. Van Eenennaam, what about that?

EENENNAAM: Yeah, it's a very interesting question, the level of resistance to this. And I guess one of the things that I think is really important when we're talking about risks is having a look at what the current methods of producing food, in this case salmon, are. And we're comparing, I mean, all of the Atlantic salmon that's farmed is effectively imported into the U.S. And it's raised in net pens in countries like Scotland. And net-pen aquaculture of salmon has its own ecological concerns. There's some pollution concerns. There's some disease concerns. There's actually escapes from most net pens are of those diploid, fertile growth—animals that have been selected for growth just sort of natural breeding ways that are getting out into the wild.

And there's certainly some risks associated with that particular approach to aquaculture. And so I think when we're looking at the risks associated with genetic engineering, it's always important to have a look at the risks associated with the current approaches to raising fish. And this particular application, I might argue, is actually a more sustainable approach to raising salmon for aquaculture because you're taking the whole product on land and removing any risks associated with net-pen aquaculture and producing a more efficient, sustainable product for human consumption.

PALCA: We're talking about the science and safety of bioengineered fish. I'm Joe Palca. And this is SCIENCE FRIDAY from NPR. So, Dr. Kapuscinski, what about that? I mean, is there something special about genetically modified organisms that needs a higher level of scrutiny?

KAPUSCINSKI: Well, the actual—the reason why people are interested in doing genetic engineering is because it has new powers, and it allows you to actually introduce genes that are either were never in that animal or that are expressed at times that have never been expressed. So it really does have the potential to fundamentally change the biology of the whole organism. It doesn't mean it'll do that all the time, but that potential is there. And I think that's why there's interest in greater scrutiny. So an example with salmon is there's one study with genetically engineered Coho salmon that also had a growth hormone gene added to them that showed that their tolerance of warmer temperatures change, so that they actually grew faster at a warmer temperature than they would have at a colder temperature that's usually the optimal temperature for salmon.

And with selective breeding, traditional breeding, we hadn't yet seen that with salmon. So that's an example of something new that you can do. In a way, the dilemma is that the very power of genetic engineering that makes it exciting and potentially a very useful tool for some applications also raises some new questions about unexpected effects, which is I think why we're gaining more scrutiny.

PALCA: So—well, I'm just curious, Dr. Kapuscinski, I mean, in the end of the day, can you imagine a time when you will have enough information to feel comfortable about saying, this particular salmon or any genetically modified animal is safe to bring in to the marketplace?

KAPUSCINSKI: I think if the things that I was saying were missing were addressed, if there was a quantitative failure analysis, if some of the fairly important questions about ecological effects—if fish did escape—were answered, and if you did a good uncertainty analysis so that the overall quality of the signs and the completeness of the risk assessment were there, I would be much more comfortable with it. And the reason I keep pushing on this is I don't think it actually really makes sense to focus only on this one application, because it is such a small scale application. And we know that if it gets approved, it's then going open the door to much larger-scale use of this fish and many other fish farms. So if we, for example, come back to Dr. Van Eenennaam's idea that if you were to shift the farming of salmon from cages to inland facilities, that that would be more sustainable, what we have to ask is, first of all, I don't know if the salmon farming industry would really be willing to do that, but let's say they did. When you shift it to inland, although you are now reducing, greatly reducing the escapes compared to cages, you are going to have much higher energy use.

PALCA: It's one of those topics that's got people very interested and excited, but thank you, Dr. Kapuscinski, for joining us today. She's a professor of sustainable—sustainability science and chair of the Environmental Studies Program at Dartmouth. And thank you also to Dr. Alison Van Eenennaam, extension specialist in animal genomics and biotechnology at the University of California, Davis.

## Case Discussion Questions

1.  Evaluate the arguments of the position in support of the FDA approval for the marketing of the genetically engineered AquAdvantage Salmon.
2.  Evaluate the arguments of the position against the FDA approval for the marketing of the genetically engineered AquAdvantage Salmon.
3.  Evaluate the FDA's risk management analysis for determining whether genetically engineered products may be marketed to the general public.
4.  Currently the FDA does not permit the labeling of foods as "non-GMO." Do you agree or disagree with the FDA's standard? Justify your position.
5.  Europeans are, in general, less disposed to genetically modified foods than we in the United States. Are they more sensitive to possible unintended negative consequences than we?

# 7 Supply Chain Management

## Chapter Outline

## Chapter Introduction

As companies strategically outsource production, managing the supply chain becomes critical to the socially responsible conduct of the enterprise. Managing the supply chain is complicated by the fact that suppliers may lay outside the organizational boundaries, in contrast to the vertical integration strategies of the past. The development and enforcement of supplier codes of conduct becomes critical to ethical supply chain management.

## Chapter Goal and Learning Objectives

*Chapter Goal:* To identify the ethical challenges of managing an enterprise's supply chain and decide how to manage its supply chain.

*Learning Objectives:*

1. Contrast vertical integration with outsourcing of production operations.
2. Debate the responsibility of the outsourcing company for misconduct of the supplier company and their sub-contracted companies.
3. Develop strategies for managing risk in the supply chain.
4. Explain Nike's supplier code of conduct as it has evolved over time. Critique Nike's inspection and enforcement procedure for its supplier code of conduct.
5. Debate whether Toyota lost its way in its cost-cutting programs.

## Supply Chain Management and Global Sourcing

Early outsourcing occurred in in the textile industry. So called 807 sourcing, whereby cut (fabricated) materials were sent to the Caribbean and Mexico, assembled there, and then reshipped back to the United States reduced costs in the United States apparel industry.[1] As a result, 807 and 807a sourcing worked to make the United States apparel manufacturers more competitive in view of the growth of developing countries, particularly in Asia, in the apparel industry.[2] Apparel manufacturing and the production of footwear is a major source of production in less developed economies and the trend has increased from the 1970s until the present time.[3]

Nike is a company that from its inception strategically used global sourcing. Phil Knight, Nike's co-founder, developed a business plan while he was at Stanford Graduate School of Management for the company he ultimately founded as Nike with his running coach from the University of Oregon, Bill Bowerman. The strategic plan called for sourcing the manufacturing process to Asia, which is both geographically accessible by container shipping and a place where the costs of labor-intensive manufacturing are lower than in the United States, Canada or Europe, where Germany was the leading manufacturer of running shoes.[4] Nike has since become the world's leading footwear company.

Global sourcing is made possible by the "flattening" of the world, identified by Thomas L. Friedman, in his book *The World is Flat*.[5] Friedman thinks that information technologies and communication systems have driven the "flattening" of the world, whereas some others think that containerization and low cost shipping have enabled the economic interdependencies embodied by global sourcing and global trade.[6] Innovations in inventory management have also supported complex production systems. Wal-Mart innovated in supply chain management by the application of RFIDs.[7] The use of RFIDs was made possible by the convergence of multiple technologies, including materials development, information technologies and global positioning satellites.[8]

Global sourcing and managing a chain of suppliers of independent enterprises is different from strategies of the past, whereby many corporations used a strategy of vertical integration. Vertical integration involves controlling the production process from the acquisition of raw materials to the marketing and delivery of the finished product.[9] However Oliver E. Williamson suggested a different approach in his book *Markets and Hierarchies*.[10] Williamson suggested that firms face a choice whether to engage in a vertical integration strategy (hierarchy) or an outsourcing (market) strategy.

There are certain risks in a "market" strategy for an enterprise production process, since enterprise partners are outside the organization boundaries, posing problems of organizational control. Moreover, additional risks are associated with high-volume, low- cost production strategy.

## Risks Associated with High-Volume, Low-Cost Production Strategy

Mattel is the world's largest toy producer, and about 65% of Mattel toys are produced in China, much of it as outsourced production. Mattel experienced a problem with materials substitution by subcontractors of a supplier/contractor in China. Lead paint was substituted for non-lead-based paint on its die cast toy cars, such as Hot Wheels, as well as dolls, such as Dora the Explorer. When the lead paint was discovered, the Mattel toys were recalled in a series of recalls over the summer 2007.[11] Other toy manufacturers such as RC2, the maker of Thomas & Friends trains, also were affected by the lead paint and recalled their products.[12] There were also other raw material substitutions discovered in products outsourced to China, including: diethylene glycol, often used in antifreeze for a substitute for glycerin in toothpaste and melamine in dog and cat food.[13] Also, in a problem confined to China itself, melamine was added to infant formula to increase the tested nitrogen content by suppliers to China's largest dairy producer, Sanlu Group.[14] Each of these raw material substitutions was harmful to the product's user. The materials substitutions by subcontractors were not errors but deliberate substitutions of a lower cost ingredient for a higher cost raw material. Control processes should be improved to avert harms to the consumers from raw materials substitutions in the supply chain. Procedures for managing a producer's supply chain are given in Box 7.1.

---

### Box 7.1  Managing the Supply Chain for Low-Cost Production Operations

1. Manufacturing standards. Include clauses in contracts that require that manufacturing must be done in conformity to the production standards of the recipient customer, rather than the standards of the sourced factories. Also include choice of law clauses that specify that contract enforcement and litigation be done under the law of the recipient customer.
2. Supplier subcontractors. Suppliers should develop contracts and inspection systems for their subcontractors that reflect and implement the contract specifications between the supplier and its customer.
3. Approval of second- or third-tier supplier subcontractors. Include in contracts specifications for suppliers and supplier subcontractors, that is, second- and third-tier suppliers. Supplier subcontracting must be approved by the customer.
4. Develop warrantees and insurance. Suppliers should warrantee against fraud, so that materials not to specifications would be at the cost of the supplier, not borne by the purchaser.
5. Right of inspection. Right of inspection, subject to rejection by the corporate customer/recipient of manufactured goods; the costs of goods produced

that are not in conformity with specifications will be borne by the supplier, including the out of spec production by subcontractors arranged by the supplier.

6. Testing and documentation. It is recommended that control procedures be instituted that include testing and documentation at all levels of the supply chain and documentation of all ingredients in the supply chain. Documentation and testing results accompany the products at all stages in the supply chain. The documentation should be bilingual or multilingual, in the language of the inspector and of the purchaser; in cases where a subcontractor is producing products for a contractor, the documentation should be in the language of the merchandiser for which the products are being made.

7. Punish the individual wrongdoers in situations of fraud, such as the substitution of lead paint on Mattel children's toys. Holding the executives of companies responsible for the injuries that their product cause is a good start and certainly sends a message to other executives. However, the root causes of the problems must be corrected.

8. Punitive damages. Punitive damages and criminal prosecution for knowingly using materials that harm the consumer, or recklessly using such materials, or knowingly or recklessly designing products that will harm the consumer, should be enforceable against all participants in the supply chain.

9. State regulatory codes. It is recommended that state regulatory codes be developed, including the right of testing and inspection, with the right to close manufacturing operations, right to fine or jail and right to recall unsafe or contaminated products.

10. International protocols. It is recommended that international protocols on the production of children's toys and food products marketed internationally.[i] Such conventions might prohibit the use of lead paint and known toxic materials, and require documentation at all levels of the supply chain. Such conventions were developed, for example, for the marketing of infant formula and cigarettes, under the auspices of the World Health Organization (WHO).[ii]

Adapted from:

"The Ethical Challenges for Enterprise And Risks To Consumers Of Large Market Share Through Low-Cost Supplier Strategy" by Paula Alexander Becker, *Journal of International Business Ethics,* Vol. 1, No. 1, 2008. With Permission.

i A United States-Sino Product Safety Summit was held in September 2007 after the Mattel lead paint crisis; it was agreed at the summit that lead paint on children's toys would be prohibited. See: "The Testimony of the Honorable Nancy A. Nord," U.S. Consumer Product Safety Commission, September 12, 2007, http://www.cpsc.gov//PageFiles/129065/nord091207.pdf.

ii See the description of the WHO's Tobacco Convention at http://www.who.int/features/2003/08/en/index.html. The Global Compact is a vehicle for the protection of human rights in less developed countries. See "Third World Way," *The Economist,* July 20, 2007, http://www.economist.com/business/globalexecutive/displaystory.cfm?story_id=9531002

## Supplier Code of Conduct and Compliance Systems

Nike's supplier code of conduct and compliance systems have evolved from a situation in 2000 when the University of Oregon joined the Worker's Rights Consortium and Phil Knight refused to donate to the University of Oregon, his alma mater,[15] to a point where Nike now serves as an industry leader in supply chain management. Allegations were leveled against Nike for operating sweatshops in Vietnam and other less economically developed nations.[16] Knight denied that Nike operated sweatshops. Then an environmentalist in California brought a "truth in advertising suit" against Nike: *Kasksy v. Nike*. Nike defended on the basis that its defense that it does not operate sweatshops was political speech and, therefore, the truth of the statement need not be demonstrated. The California Supreme Court agreed with Kasky that Nike's promises that it does not operate sweatshops constitutes commercial speech.[17] The United States Supreme Court granted certiorari, but when the writ of certiorari was dismissed by the United States Supreme Court as "improvidently granted," Nike settled the case.[18]

Nike became one of the founding members of the Fair Labor Association (FLA), funding it as part of the settlement of the Kasky case.[19, 20]

Since Nike posted its first code of conduct in 1991, the company developed increasingly detailed supplier codes of conduct and inspection systems. Now Nike has changed its orientation from a compliance orientation to a "partnership" with its suppliers. Nike's supplier code of conduct is given in Box 7.2.

---

### Box 7.2  From Monitoring Factories to Empowering Workers

Our greatest responsibility as a global company is to play a role in bringing about positive, systemic change for workers within our supply chain and in the industry. When we look at our overall impact on the world, the needs of workers in Nike's contract supply chain overshadows any other group. We also know the size and scale of the combined manufacturing operations has a considerable environmental impact.

We've run the course—from establishing Codes of Conduct that cover worker protections as well as environmental impacts—to pulling together an internal team to enforce it, to releasing our contract factory Audit Tools and working with external bodies to monitor factories and engaging with stakeholders. What we've learned, after nearly a decade, is that monitoring alone hasn't solved the problems. And many of the problems are recurring in the industry.

Our focus now is on getting to the root of the problems, evaluating our supplier and manufacturing relationships, and finding new ways to define and share responsibility. We believe that placing the worker at the heart of the workplace and having a factory management that respects and invests in its workforce will result in lasting positive results for workers, the factory and Nike.

---

## Active Factories

In 2005, we were the first company in our industry to disclose our factory list, providing a complete list of contracted factories for NIKE Brand. We've now furthered our commitment to transparency by disclosing the factories world-wide that manufacture all NIKE, Inc. (NIKE Brand, Converse, Hurley, Jordan Brand and Nike Golf) products. We remain committed to supply chain transparency and continue to update our publicly available list to encourage and support transparency and collaboration around issues affecting our suppliers.

Our supplier list, which can be filtered for collegiate factories, is available for export on our Interactive Global Manufacturing Map.

Source: Nike website: Manufacturing
http://nikeinc.com/pages/manufacturing Retrieved June 6, 2014.

The recommendations made previously assume that there is an established relationship between supplier and customer. However, the practice of using purchasing agents obscures the transparency of the supplier-customer relationship, particularly in the global garment supply chain. This use of "indirect sourcing" creates even higher risk in managing enterprise supply chains.[21]

Challenges in supply chain management exist even in companies employing high-end technologies. Toyota developed lean management and the "Toyota way" became a model globally for just-in-time inventory control and continuous improvement.[22] However, Toyota decided to cut supplier costs by 30% beginning in 2000, first as part of its Construction of Cost Competitiveness in the 21st Century (CCC21) program and then in 2005 as its Value Innovation (VI) program.[23] When the economy crashed in 2008, Congress enacted stimulus programs, including "cash for clunkers." Toyota was the largest beneficiary of the "cash for clunkers" program and Toyota became the world's largest automaker, beating out General Motors.[24] Then in 2009, drivers experienced runaway Toyotas. A series of recalls ensured, and in March 2014, Toyota agreed to a $1.2 billion settlement, the largest criminal settlement for an auto manufacturer in the United States, because of defective parts causing runaway vehicles.[25]

Toyota cut costs to a point where product quality was undercut. Toyota reached the limit of low-cost production. An enterprise, or its suppliers, whose strategy is high-volume, low-cost production may nevertheless still seek to lower costs beyond the limit for a given technology.[26]

A graphic portrayal of the concept of limit is shown in Figure 7.1.

If lower costs are to be achieved once the limit for a given production technology is achieved (more correctly, "approached"), then a new production technology must be utilized.[27] This is sometimes achieved by materials substitution. A switch in production technology/function also carries risks, as experienced by Boeing in its design of the 787 Dreamliner. Boeing's entire Dreamliner 787 fleet was grounded in early 2013 because some of the lithium-ion batteries

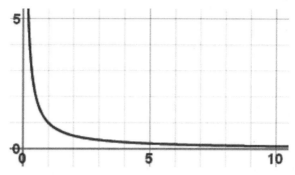

*Figure 7.1* Graphic Portrayal of a Mathematical Limit in Calculus

caught on fire.[28] Lithium-ion batteries were substituted for nickel cadmium batteries because lithium-ion batteries are lighter and more efficient, although the risk of "thermal runaway," causing batteries to catch on fire, is higher for lithium-ion batteries.

Flexible manufacturing systems also work to reduce costs. Agile and flexible manufacturing systems are both effective and highly desirable, if difficult to achieve.[29] For example, between December 2011 and January 2012, there was a 9% increase in the ownership of tablets and e-readers, such as Amazon's Kindle and Apple's iPad and iPad mini.[30] Investigations of working conditions at Fox-Conn and other Apple suppliers were widely publicized and led to changes in Apple's supply management, including Apple's membership in the FLA as the first technology company to join the FLA.[31] The ethical risk in developing a flexible manufacturing system is that an enterprise may engage in the practices alleged, and denied, by Apple Co. in requiring workers to work double shifts under circumstances where workers are already working 60 hours a week or more.[32]

A related challenge is faced by Mattel, the world's largest toy merchandiser. Mattel experienced unexpected high demand for Frozen dolls in 2014 after a song from the movie *Frozen*, "Let It Go," won the Academy Award for best original song and the movie itself won the Golden Globe Award and the Oscar for the best animated feature film. It was Disney's first best animated feature film Academy Award.[33] Mattel noted the risk of "underproduction" of popular toys in its 2013 annual report issued April 2014.[34] Mattel apparently has not developed a flexible manufacturing system to meet unexpected higher demand levels, particularly outside the traditional winter holiday peak demand period. The inability to meet higher than expected or forecast demand for enterprise product represents foregone opportunity for the enterprise. The challenge for enterprise is to meet unexpectedly high demand without unreasonable over-time. It is one reason that enterprises use outsourcing as well as contingent workers, discussed in the following.

## Exploiting Information Asymmetries in the Production Process

By their nature, companies have more information about their internal workings, including production, as well as financial and other transactions, than customers or regulators. Reliance is placed by customers, regulators and even auditors for honesty in reporting. Information asymmetries pose a significant ethical challenge for enterprise. Because of information asymmetries, the opportunity for enterprise exists to dissemble. Exploitation of information asymmetries were at work in Ford Motor Company's production and release to the market of the Pinto, in the General Motors ignition problem with the Chevy Cobalt, and with the Toyota production of vehicles with a "runaway" problem. As outlined in its settlement with the United Sates Department of Justice, Toyota had knowledge of design and product defects but Toyota failed to warn consumers about them or to disclose them, as required, to its regulators.[35] Instead of dealing with the problem in a transparent way, Toyota acted against the interests of its customers and misrepresented the situation both to its customers and to its regulators. The norm of "transparency" serves to counter the exploitation of information asymmetries. And when discovered, fraud in reporting is punished by regulators and by the market as loss of reputation and brand value.

Whether enterprise uses a vertical integration strategy or the "market" strategy of outsourcing, an enterprise cannot sidestep the issue of managing risks, information, coordination and communication, whether the communication occurs within organizational boundaries or across the organizational boundaries. In managing the ignition defect in the GM Chevy Cobalt, GM failed to define the issue as a critical safety issue and to act on the problem, once identified, as documented the Valukas report to the General Motors Board of Directors issued June 5, 2014. The recommendations in the Valukas report run the gamut from organizational structure to recordkeeping.[36] Problem identification and diagnosis and cross-functional communication are required for effective and ethical management whether organizations choose either a market or hierarchy solution to supply chain management.

## Chapter Discussion Questions

1. All companies have internal information and knowledge that are unknown to consumers and to regulators. What are the costs and benefits of enterprises relying on such information asymmetries to hide damaging information?

2. Is the norm of "transparency" effective in limiting a company's propensity to cover-up damaging information? Why or why not?

3. How can a company ethically gear-up to meet unexpectedly high demand for its product, such as that experienced by Apple in late 2011 and early 2012, and by Mattel in 2014?

4.  When a company and its suppliers approach the limits of low-cost production, what can they do to continue to lower costs in an ethical way? Are there mechanisms for innovation to change the production function so as to sidestep the ethical dilemma?

5.  Is the answer to low-cost supplier strategy tighter and more specific controls? Defend your answer.

6.  Is cost control an ethical issue? List the pros and cons on this question.

## Notes

1   Lauren Murray, "Unraveling Employment Trends in Textiles and Apparel," *Monthly Labor Review*, Aug. 1995. See Footnotes 19 and 20 in particular. The *Monthly Labor Review* is published by the Bureau of Labor Statistics.

2   807a sourcing provides exemption from import duties of the time if the assembling operations used US-made textiles, in addition to using material that had been cut in the United States.

3   "World Development Indicators (WDI) 2010 released," *World Bank*, last modified Apr. 22, 2010, http://data.worldbank.org/news/world-development-indicators-2010-released.

4   "History & Heritage," *Nike*, last modified 2014, http://nikeinc.com/pages/history-heritage.

5   Thomas L. Friedman, *The World Is Flat* (New York: Farrar, Straus and Giroux, 2005).

6   Friedman, *The World Is Flat*.

7   Lutz Miller, "Is it Time for RFID? Wal-Mart's Lead Signals Widespread Adoption," *Toy Directory*, March 2008, http://www.toydirectory.com/monthly/article.asp?id=3105.

8   Ron Weinstein, "RFID: a Technical Overview and Its Application to the Enterprise," *IT Professional* 7, no. 3 (2005): 27–33.

9   See, for example, Ben Worthen, Cari Tuna and Justin Scheck, "Companies More Prone to Go 'Vertical,'" *Wall Street Journal*, last modified Nov. 30, 2009, http://online.wsj.com/news/articles/SB125954262100968855.

10  Oliver Williamson received the Nobel Prize in Economics in 2009. See Oliver Williamson, *Markets and Hierarchies: Analysis and Antitrust Implications* (New York: Free Press, 1975). See his interview in the *Journal of Institutional Economics* 3, no. 3 (2007): 373–386, available at http://www.millennium-economics.com/user/image/20073williamsoninterview.pdf. See also his lecture on the receipt of the Nobel Prize, *Nobelprize.org*, last modified 2013, http://www.nobelprize.org/mediaplayer/index.php?id=1225.

11  Louise Story, "Lead Paint Prompts Mattel to Recall 967,000 Toys," *New York Times*, Aug. 2, 2007, http://www.nytimes.com/2007/08/02/business/02toy.html. See also Louise Story and David Barboza "Mattel Recalls 19 Million Toys Sent from China," *New York Times*, Aug. 15, 2007, http://www.nytimes.com/2007/08/15/business/worldbusiness/15imports.html?pagewanted=all&_r=0&gwt=regi and David Barboza, "Why Lead in Toy Paint? It's Cheaper," *New York Times*, Sept. 11, 2007, http://www.nytimes.com/2007/09/11/business/worldbusiness/11lead.html?pagewanted=all.

12  Louise Story, "Toy-Train Maker Discusses Lead Paint Problem," *New York Times*, July 26, 2007, http://www.nytimes.com/2007/07/26/business/26thomas.html.

13  Jake Hooker and Walt Bogdanich, "China Says 2 of Its Companies Played a Role in Poisonings," *New York Times,* June 1, 2007, http://www.nytimes.com/2007/06/01/world/asia/01panama.html. See also David Barboza and Alexei Barrionuevo, "Filler in Animal Feed Is Open Secret in China," *New York Times,* April 30, 2007, http://www.nytimes.com/2007/04/30/business/worldbusiness/30food.html?pagewanted=all.

14  Jim Yardley, "Chinese Baby Formula Scandal Widens as 2nd Death Is Announced," *New York Times,* Sept. 15, 2008, http://www.nytimes.com/2008/09/16/world/asia/16milk.html?ref=asia.

15  Steven Greenhouse. "Nike's Chief Cancels a Gift over Monitor of Sweatshops," *New York Times,* April 25, 2000, http://www.nytimes.com/2000/04/25/us/nike-s-chief-cancels-a-gift-over-monitor-of-sweatshops.html.

16  "Empowerment Case Studies: Nike in Vietnam—The Tae Kwang Vina Factory," *World Bank,* http://siteresources.worldbank.org/INTEMPOWERMENT/Resources/14826_Nike-web.pdf.

17  *Kasky v. Nike, Inc.*, 27 Cal. 4th 939 (2002).

18  539 U.S. 654 (2003).

19  "History," *Fair Labor Association,* last modified 2012, http://www.fairlabor.org/about-us/history.

20  The Fair Labor Association was founded during the Clinton administration, at a time when Levi Strauss withdrew its operations from China and while China was being granted Most Favored Nation status by the United States, then was later admitted to the World Trade Organization (WTO). James Areddy, "Levi's Faced Earlier Challenge in China: Jeans Company Walked Out 17 Years Ago, but Today Has 501 Stores," *Wall Street Journal,* last modified Jan. 14, 2010, http://online.wsj.com/news/articles/SB10001424052748704675104575000831581315788. See also, Mark Landler, "Reversing Course, Levi Strauss Will Expand Its Output in China," *New York Times,* Apr. 9, 1998, http://www.nytimes.com/1998/04/09/business/international-business-reversing-course-levi-strauss-will-expand-its-output.html.

21  Sarah Labowitz and Dorothee Baumann-Pauly, "Business as Usual Is Not an Option: Supply Chains and Sourcing after Rana Plaza," April 2014, http://www.stern.nyu.edu/cons/groups/content/documents/webasset/con_047408.pdf.

22  Jeffrey Liker, *The Toyota Way* (New York: McGraw Hill, 2004) and Taiichi Ohno, *Toyota Production System: Beyond Large Scale Production* (Portland, OR: Productivity Press, 1988).

23  See "Putting CCC21 into Action," *Toyota,* last modified 2012, http://www.toyota-global.com/company/history_of_toyota/75years/text/leaping_forward_as_a_global_corporation/chapter4/section7/item2.html. See also Chang-Ran Kim, "Toyota Sees Cost Savings over $2.7 Billion Annually," Reuters, Dec. 11, 2007, http://www.baselinemag.com/project-management/Toyota-Sees-Cost-Savings-over-27-Billion-Annually/.

24  Kendra Marr, "Toyota Passes GM as World's Largest Automaker," *Washington Post,* Jan. 22, 2009, http://archive.today/ek4IM#selection-3861.11–3861.27.

25  "Justice Department Announces Criminal Charge Against Toyota Motor Corporation and Deferred Prosecution Agreement with $1.2 Billion Financial Penalty," *United States Department of Justice,* last modified March 19, 2014, http://www.justice.gov/opa/pr/2014/March/14-ag-286.html.

26  "Limit" is a fundamental concept in the mathematics of calculus: for every function, there is a limit. It is represented by the "flattening" of a curve, so that it continues at that level indefinitely, approaching infinity.

27  In mathematics/calculus this is described as a new "function."

28  Christopher Drew, Jad Mouawad and Matthew L. Wald, "FAA Grounds US-Operated Boeing 787s," *New York Times*, Jan. 16, 2013, http://www.nytimes.com/2013/01/17/business/faa-orders-grounding-of-us-operated-boeing-787s.html?pagewanted=all&gwt=regi.

29  See for example, Steve Blank, *The Four Steps to the Epiphany: Successful Strategies for Products That Win*, 5th ed. (Pescadero, CA: K&S Ranch Press, 2013) and Eric Reis, *The Lean Startup* (New York: Crown Business, 2011).

30  Demetrius Crasto, "Pew: Tablet and Reader Doubled in the USAmongst Adults This Holiday Season," *TechShout*, last modified 2013, http://www.techshout.com/gadgets/2012/24/pew-tablet-and-ereader-doubled-in-the-us-amongst-adults-this-holiday-season/.

31  "Apple," *Fair Labor Association*, last modified 2012, http://www.fairlabor.org/affiliate/apple.

32  Charles Duhigg and David Barboza, "In China, Human Costs Are Built into an iPad," *Part 2: A Punishing System, New York Times*, Jan. 25, 2012, http://www.nytimes.com/2012/01/26/business/ieconomy-apples-ipad-and-the-human-costs-for-workers-in-china.html?pagewanted=all.

33  "Disney's FROZEN is Officially Highest Grossing Animated Film Internationally," *Broadwayworld.com*, Apr. 20, 2014, http://www.broadwayworld.com/bwwmovies/article/Disneys-FROZEN-is-Officially-Highest-Grossing-Animated-Film-Internationally-20140420#.U1VvoLdOUlY.

34  "2013 Annual Report of Mattel Inc.," *Mattel,* http://corporate.mattel.com/PDFs/2013_AR_Report_Mattel%20Inc.pdf.

35  The WARN Act, passed in the United States by Congress after the Ford Explorer rollovers, required auto manufacturers to notify the NHTSA of defects that had been discovered in other countries. Toyota had identified and remedied the sticky pedal problem in Europe, but Toyota failed to notify the NHTSA of this problem.

36  Anton R. Valukas, "G.M. Internal Investigation Report," *New York Times*, last modified June 5, 2014, http://www.nytimes.com/interactive/2014/06/05/business/06gm-report-doc.html.

## End of Chapter Case: Toyota Recall and Settlement with US Department of Justice

> Justice Department Announces Criminal Charge against Toyota Motor Corporation and Deferred Prosecution Agreement with $1.2 Billion Financial Penalty
>
> March 19, 2014

In the fall of 2009, Toyota deceived consumers and its U.S. regulator, the National Highway Traffic Safety Administration ("NHTSA"), by claiming that it had "addressed" the "root cause" of unintended acceleration in its vehicles through a limited safety recall of eight models for floor-mat entrapment, a dangerous condition in which an improperly secured or incompatible all-weather floor mat can "trap" a depressed gas pedal causing the car to accelerate to a high speed. Such public assurances deceived customers and NHTSA in two ways: First, at the time the statements were made, Toyota knew that it had *not* recalled some cars with design features that made them just as susceptible to floor-mat entrapment as some of the recalled cars. Second, only weeks before these statements were made, Toyota had taken steps to hide from NHTSA another type of unintended acceleration in its vehicles, separate and apart from floor-mat entrapment: a problem with accelerators getting stuck at partially depressed levels, known as "sticky pedal."

## Floor-Mat Entrapment: A Fatal Problem

Toyota issued its misleading statements, and undertook its acts of conceal-ment, against the backdrop of intense public concern and scrutiny over the safety of its vehicles following a widely publicized Aug. 28, 2009 accident in San Diego, Calif., that killed a family of four. A Lexus dealer had improperly installed an incompatible all-weather floor mat into the Lexus ES350 in which the family was traveling, and that mat entrapped the accelerator at full throt-tle. A 911 emergency call made from the out-of-control vehicle, which was speeding at over 100 miles per hour, reported, "We're in a Lexus . . . and we're going north on 125 and our accelerator is stuck . . . there's no brakes . . . we're approaching the intersection . . . Hold on . . . hold on and pray . . . pray." The call ended with the sound of the crash that killed everyone in the vehicle.

The San Diego accident was not the first time that Toyota had faced a prob-lem with floor-mat entrapment. In 2007, following a series of reports alleging unintended acceleration in Toyota and Lexus vehicles, NHTSA opened a defect investigation into the Lexus ES350 model (the vehicle involved in the 2009 San Diego accident), and identified several other Toyota and Lexus models it believed might likewise be defective. Toyota, while denying to NHTSA the need to recall any of its vehicles, conducted an internal investigation in 2007 which revealed that certain Toyota and Lexus models, including most of the ones that NHTSA had identified as potentially problematic, had design features render-ing entrapment of the gas pedal by an all-weather floor mat more likely. Toyota did not share these results with NHTSA. In the end, the Company negotiated a limited recall of 55,000 mats (no vehicles)—a result that Toyota employees touted internally as a major victory: "had the agency . . . pushed for recall of the throttle pedal assembly (for instance), we would be looking at upwards of $100 million + in unnecessary costs."

Shortly after Toyota announced its 2007 mat recall, company engineers revised internal design guidelines to provide for, among other things, a minimum clearance of 10 millimeters between a fully depressed gas pedal and the floor. But Toyota decided those revised guidelines would only apply where a model was receiving a "full model redesign"—something each Toy-ota and Lexus model underwent only about once every three to five years. As a result, even after the revised guidelines had been adopted internally, many new vehicles produced and sold by Toyota—including the Lexus ES350 involved in the 2009 San Diego accident—did not comply with Toyota's 2007 guidelines.

After the fatal and highly publicized San Diego accident, Toyota agreed to recall eight of its models, including the ES350, for floor-mat entrapment susceptibility. Thereafter, as part of an effort to defend its brand image, Toyota began issuing public statements assuring customers that this limited recall had "addressed the root cause of unintended acceleration" in its U.S.-sold vehicles.

As Toyota knew from internal testing it had completed by the time these statements were made, the eight-model recall had not in fact "addressed the root cause" of even the floor-mat entrapment problem. Models *not* recalled—and therefore still on the road—bore design features rendering them just as susceptible to floor-mat entrapment as those within the recall population. One engineer working at a Toyota facility in California had concluded that the Corolla, a top-selling car that had not been recalled, was among the three "worse" vehicles for floor-mat entrapment. In October 2009, Toyota engineers in Japan circulated a chart showing that the Corolla had the lowest rating for floor-mat entrapment under their analysis. None of these findings or this data were shared with NHTSA at the time.

## The Sticky Pedal Problem

What is more misleading, at the same time it was assuring the public that the "root cause" of unintended acceleration had been "addressed" by the 2009 eight-model floor-mat entrapment recall, Toyota was hiding from NHTSA a second cause of unintended acceleration in its vehicles: the sticky pedal. Sticky pedal, a phenomenon affecting pedals manufactured by a U.S. company ("A-Pedal Company") and installed in many Toyota brand vehicles in North America as well as Europe, resulted from the use of a plastic material inside the pedals that could cause the accelerator pedal to become mechanically stuck in a partially depressed position. The pedals incorporating this plastic were installed in, among other models, the Camry, the Matrix, the Corolla, and the Avalon sold in the United States.

The sticky pedal problem surfaced in Europe in 2008. There, reports reflected instances of "uncontrolled acceleration" and unintended acceleration to "maximum RPM," and customer concern that the condition was "extremely dangerous."

In early 2009, Toyota circulated to European Toyota distributors information about the sticky pedal problem and instructions for addressing the problem if it presented itself in a customer's vehicle. These instructions identified the issue as "Sudden RPM increase/vehicle acceleration due to accelerator pedal sticking," and stated that should a customer complain of pedal sticking, the pedal should be replaced with pedals manufactured by a company other than A-Pedal Company. Contemporaneous internal Toyota documents described the sticky pedal problem as a "defect" that was "[i]mportant in terms of safety because of the possibility of accidents."

Toyota did not then inform its U.S. regulators of the sticky pedal problem or conduct a recall. Instead, beginning in the spring of 2009, Toyota quietly directed A-Pedal Company to change the pedals in new productions of affected models in Europe, and to plan for the same design changes to be rolled out in the United States (where the same problematic pedals were being used) beginning in the fall of 2009. The design change was to substitute the plastic used in the affected pedal models with another material and to change the length of the friction lever in the pedal.

Meanwhile, the sticky pedal problem was manifesting itself in U.S. vehicles. On or about the same day the San Diego floor-mat entrapment accident occurred, staff at a U.S. Toyota subsidiary in California sent a memorandum to staff at Toyota in Japan identifying as "critical" an "unintended acceleration" issue separate and apart from floor-mat entrapment that had been identified in an accelerator pedal of a Toyota Matrix vehicle in Arizona. The problem identified, and then reproduced during testing of the pedal on Sept. 17, 2009, was the sticky pedal problem. Also in August, the sticky pedal problem cropped up in a U.S. Camry.

On Sept. 9, 2009, an employee of a U.S. Toyota subsidiary who was concerned about the sticky pedal problem in the United States and believed that Toyota should address the problem prepared a "Market Impact Summary" listing (in addition to the August 2009 Matrix and Camry) 39 warranty cases that he believed involved potential manifestations of the sticky pedal problem. This document, which was circulated to Toyota engineers and, later, to staff in charge of recall decisions in Japan, designated the sticky pedal problem as priority level "A," the highest level.

By no later than September 2009, Toyota recognized internally that the sticky pedal problem posed a risk of a type of unintended acceleration—or "overrun," as Toyota sometimes called it—in many of its U.S. vehicles. A September 2009 presentation made by a manager at a U.S. Toyota subsidiary to Toyota executives gave a "current summary of O/R [overrun] types in NA [North American] market" that listed the three confirmed types as: "mat interference" (*i.e.*, floor-mat entrapment), "material issue" (described as "pedal stuck and . . . pedal slow return/deformed") and "simultaneous pedal press" by the consumer. The presentation further listed the models affected by the "material issue" as including "Camry, Corolla, Matrix, Avalon."

## Hiding Sticky Pedal from NHTSA and the Public

As noted, Toyota had by this time developed internal plans to implement design changes for all A-Pedal-Company-manufactured pedals in U.S. Toyota models to address, on a going- forward basis, the still-undisclosed sticky pedal problem that had already been resolved for new vehicles in Europe. On Oct. 5, 2009, Toyota engineers issued to A-Pedal Company the first of the design change instructions intended to prevent sticky pedal in the U.S. market. This was described internally as an "urgent" measure to be implemented on an "express" basis, as a "major" change—meaning that the part number of the subject pedal was to change, and that all inventory units with the old pedal number should be scrapped.

On Oct. 21, 2009, however, in the wake of the San Diego floor-mat entrapment accident, and in the midst of Toyota's discussions with NHTSA about its eight-model entrapment recall, engineers at Toyota and the leadership of Toyota's recall decision group decided to cancel the design change instruction that had already been issued and to suspend all remaining design changes planned for A-Pedal Company pedals in U.S. models. U.S. Toyota subsidiary employees who had been preparing for implementation of the changes were instructed, orally, to alert the manufacturing plants of the cancellation. They were also instructed not to put anything about the cancellation in writing. A-Pedal Company itself would receive no written cancellation at this time; instead, contrary to Toyota's own standard procedures, the cancellation was to be effected without a paper trail.

Toyota decided to suspend the pedal design changes in the United States, and to avoid memorializing that suspension, in order to prevent NHTSA from learning about the sticky pedal problem.

On Nov. 17, 2009, before Toyota had negotiated with NHTSA a final set of remedies for the eight models encompassed by the floor-mat entrapment recall, Toyota informed NHTSA of the three Corolla reports and several other reports of unintended acceleration in Toyota model vehicles equipped with pedals manufactured by A-Pedal Company. In Toyota's disclosure to NHTSA, Toyota did not reveal its understanding of the sticky pedal problem as a type of unintended acceleration, nor did it reveal the problem's manifestation and the subsequent design changes in Europe, the planned, cancelled, and suspended design changes in the United States, the August 2009 Camry and Matrix vehicles that had suffered sticky pedal, or the September 2009 Market Impact Summary.

## Toyota's Misleading Statements

After the August 2009 fatal floor-mat entrapment accident in San Diego, several articles critical of Toyota appeared in U.S. newspapers. The articles reported instances of Toyota customers allegedly experiencing unintended acceleration and the authors accused Toyota of, among other things, hiding defects related to unintended acceleration.

On Nov. 25, 2009, Toyota, through a U.S. subsidiary, announced its floor-mat entrapment resolution with NHTSA. In a press release that had been approved by Toyota, the U.S. subsidiary assured customers: "The safety of our owners and the public is our utmost concern and Toyota has and will continue to thoroughly investigate and take appropriate measures to address any defect trends that are identified." A spokesperson for the subsidiary stated during a press conference the same day, "We're very, very confident that we have addressed this issue."

In truth, the issue of unintended acceleration had not been "addressed" by the remedies announced. A-Pedal Company pedals which could experience stickiness were still on the road and still, in fact, being installed in newly-produced vehicles. And the best-selling Corolla, the Highlander, and the Venza—which had design features similar to models that had been included in the earlier floormat entrapment recall—were not being "addressed" at all.

> Again, on Dec. 23, 2009, Toyota responded to media accusations that it was continuing to hide defects in its vehicles by authorizing a U.S. Toyota subsidiary to publish the following misleading statements on the subsidiary's website: "Toyota has absolutely not minimized public awareness of any defect or issue with respect to its vehicles. Any suggestion to the contrary is wrong and borders on irresponsibility. We are confident that the measures we are taking address the root cause and will reduce the risk of pedal entrapment." In fact, Toyota had "minimized public awareness of" both sticky pedal and floor-mat entrapment. Further, the measures Toyota had taken did not "address the root cause" of unintended acceleration, because Toyota had not yet issued a sticky pedal recall and had not yet recalled the Corolla, the Venza, or the Highlander for floor-mat entrapment.

## Toyota's False Timeline

When, in early 2010, Toyota finally conducted safety recalls to address the unintended acceleration issues it had concealed throughout the fall of 2009, Toyota provided to the American public, NHTSA and the United States Congress an inaccurate timeline of events that made it appear as if Toyota had learned of the sticky pedal in the United States in "October 2009," and then acted promptly to remedy the problem within 90 days of discovering it. In fact, Toyota had begun its investigation of sticky pedal in the United States no later than August 2009, had already reproduced the problem in a U.S. pedal by no later than September 2009, and had taken active steps in the months following that testing to hide the problem from NHTSA and the public.

Source: http://www.justice.gov/opa/pr/2014/March/14-ag-286.html.

Update: Toyota issued two additional recalls in early 2014: the hybrid Prius was recalled in February for a defect in its software causing the vehicle to stop and 6.4 million vehicles were recalled on April 9, 2014 for previously unannounced defects.

## Case Discussion Questions

1. Debate whether Toyota's cost control initiatives CCC21 and VI were the root cause of its defective vehicles.
2. What actions could Toyota have taken with A-Pedal Company, the supplier of defective parts related to the sticky pedal sudden acceleration? What did Toyota actually do?

3.  Did the actions of Toyota in hiding defects, failing to recall vehicles for all known problems and delaying the re-design of cars to correct the defects put Toyota ahead financially?

4.  Debate whether the recalls issued in February and April 2014, unrelated to the criminal settlement announced in March 2014 for the sudden, unintended acceleration of vehicles in 2009 and 2010, were in fact tied to the deferred prosecution agreement included in the settlement with the US Department of Justice. Did Toyota have exposure were the problems to come to light after its settlement with the Department of Justice?

5.  What recommendations would you make to get Toyota "back on track" to the Toyota way?

# 8 The Business–Consumer Relationship

## Chapter Outline

## Chapter Introduction

The consumer–enterprise nexus is at the heart of corporate purpose. Entrepreneurial vision creates value-added product for the consumer. The creation of goods and services by private enterprise in a capitalist or market-driven production system contributes to the standard of living for the society. However, some products harm consumers, either because they are inherently dangerous or because the product is defectively designed or produced. The creation of such negative externalities can be prevented or remedied by the internalization of production costs but the price of products will be increased to consumers as a result. Corporate responsibility requires the manufacture of products without externalizing costs on consumers or workers.

## Chapter Goal and Learning Objectives

*Chapter Goal:* Consider the relationship of enterprise to its consumers.

*Learning Objectives:*

1. To understand the consumer–enterprise nexus and the ethical obligations on the part of the corporation that arise from this relationship.
2. To understand the role of advertising, including direct-to-consumer advertising, and ethical constraints on corporate advertisements.
3. Explain the liability of enterprise for harms to consumers and the assumption of risk by consumers.
4. Distinguish products that harm consumers because the products are inherently dangerous from products that are defectively designed.
5. To develop policies to investigate whistleblower complaints.

## The Business–Consumer Relationship Is the Crux of Enterprise

The business–consumer relationship is the crux of enterprise. The purpose of enterprise is to create value-added output, which becomes customer input in an exchange transaction. Entrepreneurial vision involves conceptualizing and creating value-added product for consumers. The output of enterprise raises the standard of living in a society, which benefits from the availability of consumer goods and services. Enterprise output thus contributes to the creation of the common good or the commonweal.

Enterprise competitive edge can be created by innovation. Innovation is entrepreneurial and large enterprise or economically developed countries do not have a monopoly on entrepreneurial innovation. Clayton Christiansen takes the position that successful large companies can easily get stuck in their success and fail to innovate. They thereby become vulnerable to "disruptive technologies." The creation of breakthrough technologies disrupts the production systems and competitiveness of previously established or sustaining technologies and companies.[1] In fact, according to Thomas L. Friedman, the playing field is being leveled globally by information and communications technologies. Small enterprise can now compete with large companies and less developed countries can successfully compete with developed countries.[2] The information and communications technologies act as "levelers," which make it possible for small enterprise and entrepreneurs in less developed countries to compete in the global marketplace.[3]

### Market Niche and Consumer Advertising

Firm strategic purpose occurs at the junction of firm strengths and core competencies with environmental opportunities. Enterprise strategic purpose defines the relationship of enterprise to its customers and identifies *market niche*. Advertising informs consumers, who constitute the *target market* of the firm, about the product, the utility the product creates for the consumer and by its imaging suggests who the appropriate consumer of this product is.

#### Advertising and Free Speech Rights of Corporations

Advertising by corporations promotes product sales and is constitutionally protected as free speech.[4] Corporate free speech rights include both political and commercial speech. *Commercial speech* promotes the self-interest of enterprise in the marketplace. The promotion of enterprise self-interest through commercial speech is done through advertising, a long-time phenomenon; however, the recognition that advertising even of prices is a constitutionally protected form of commercial speech is relatively recent.[5] Commercial speech, when is it not fraudulent, false or misleading, works to the benefit of consumers, because consumers benefit from truthful advertising that informs them of product availability and price competition.

#### Direct-to-Consumer Advertising

Corporations have undertaken advertising to consumers for goods that are not directly available for purchase. For example, prescription drugs are not available for purchase directly on the market by consumers, but *direct-to-consumer advertising* encourages consumers to request prescriptions for a particular medication of physicians. Examples of direct advertising of prescription drugs to consumers includes anti-inflammatory arthritis drugs such as Celebrex and Vioxx and erectile dysfunction (ED) drugs such as Viagra, Levitra and Cialis.[6]

A General Accounting Office analysis shows that direct-to-consumer advertising has increased dramatically over time. Moreover, those prescription drugs most heavily advertised have sometimes been misleading and have been the subject of FDA or other intervention. See for example, the FDA notification regarding the television advertising of Levitra. The FDA regulates direct to-consumer advertising, requiring a statement of the indications for the drug's use, the contra-indications for the drug's use and its major side effects. The Division of Drug Marketing, Advertising, and Communications of the FDA issued regulatory warnings to the manufacturer and marketers of Levitra for misleading advertising and failure to disclose indications, contra-indications and failure to label according to FDA regulations.[7]

Manufacturer failure to disclose risks has been a problem for several direct-to-consumer drugs, in addition to ED drugs, including Vioxx, as well as antidepressants such as Paxil and Zoloft. The FDA issued a public health advisory on the increased risk of suicide among children and adolescents on antidepressants and requires a "boxed warning" of these risks.[8] Notwithstanding the FDA labeling requirements of boxed warnings for antidepressant medications and the FDA's public health advisory, a consumer watchdog group complained in a two-page ad run in the *New York Times* in October 2004 that Pfizer failed to include the FDA-required warnings.[9]

Transparency is a major issue in direct-to-consumer advertising by pharmaceutical manufacturers. Industry guidelines were put into place in the year following the recall of Vioxx by Merck, when an internal "Dodge" marketing memo came to light, and when Pfizer, responding to the FDA, revised its labeling and added a black box warning of cardiovascular as well as gastrointestinal risks to its anti-arthritis drug Celebrex.[10, 11]

### False Advertising and the Federal Trade Commission

In addition to the FDA regulation of direct-to-consumer and other advertising, the Federal Trade Commission (FTC) also regulates advertising. Corporations must be able to prove the verity of their claims and may not engage in deceptive or unfair advertising.[12] Additionally, the FTC warned that web site designers and other advertisers who collaborate in the development of marketing materials for enterprises doing e-business may be liable for the deceptive advertising if they knew or reasonably should have known that the claims were deceptive or unfair.[13]

Moreover, when Nike Corporation became embroiled in its "sweatshop" controversy, it defended its corporate reputation by asserting that it did not operate sweatshops and that any adverse conditions among the subcontractors in its supply chain had been corrected. A consumer activist in California brought suit against Nike for "false and deceptive" advertising.[14] Kasky argued that Nike was engaged in commercial speech and that Nike's claims must be verifiable. Nike defended the charges against it on the basis that it was engaged in political speech, for which there is wide latitude in opinion giving. Although the ACLU defended Nike's position that it was engaged in political speech, marketers generally conclude that Nike was using its statements that it did not operate sweatshops to induce consumers to purchase its products and, therefore, Nike's statements constitute commercial speech. However, the case settled, without the issue in controversy being determined: whether Nike was engaged in political or commercial speech and whether corporations would be held to a "truth in advertising" standard when they assert to their customers that they do not operate sweatshops.[15]

### Relationship Marketing

Some firms are revisiting their approach to marketing, switching from a single transaction approach to a relationship marketing approach. In *relationship marketing*, sometimes called *customer relationship marketing* or *customer relationship management,* firms promote consumer loyalty and repeat purchasing behavior, i.e., product or brand loyalty. In economic terms, the goal of relationship marketing is recurring transactions between the firm and consumers who purchase the firm's products. The recurring transactions model contrasts with the classic model of decision making or game theory, which focuses on maximizing value in a single transaction. A relationship marketing or recurring transactions approach envisions a long-term relationship between a firm and its customers and promotes a cooperative or win-win approach to customer service and customer satisfaction. Even if a single transaction with a customer is not cost-effective from the firm point of view, as for example, when the firm permits a return of a product that while not defective, does not meet customer expectations, the trust and confidence that is engendered in the customer promotes repeat business and long-run revenues and profits.

For example, Amazon's goal is articulated as "to be the Earth's most customer-centric company." It actively works to satisfy customer complaints.[16]

Relationship marketing extends the focus of the firm also to its relationships with suppliers. For example, consumers who are seeking to purchase a book from the Amazon.com website also may be offered the opportunity to purchase the desired product from suppliers other than Amazon.com. Amazon monitors customer satisfaction with the vendors available on its site, even though Amazon is not directly responsible for the delivery of product to the book purchaser. Moreover, the end of the doctrine and practice of *caveat emptor,* discussed in Chapter 4, promotes relationship marketing by building trust between consumers and producing firms.

## Rise of the Consumer Movement

*Consumerism* was identified by Thorstein Veblen in his work The *Theory of the Leisure Class,* first published in 1899.[17] Veblen observed that as society becomes industrialized and urbanized, individuals signal their social reputation by *"conspicuous consumption."* Conspicuous consumption is unnecessary in a society where everyone knows everyone else but when people move to cities and areas where neighbors are strangers to each other, conspicuous consumption becomes the means of signaling one's social standing.[18]

The *consumer movement* has its historical roots in the writings of the Muckrakers. For example, Upton Sinclair wrote *The Jungle,* an expose of the Chicago meat-packing industry.[19] *The Jungle* gave political impetus for the Food and Drug Administration, which was created by the Pure Food and Drug Act of 1906, the same year that Sinclair published *The Jungle.* Veblen and Sinclair, as well as other Muckrakers, wrote during the Progressive Era, a time period that included the presidency of Theodore Roosevelt from 1901–1909. The Progressive Era was a time when the unintended negative consequences of industrialization and the Industrial Revolution were addressed through social criticism and legislative reform. The consumer movement was further developed by the work of Stuart Chase and F.J. Schlink, who published *Your Money's Worth,* which promoted consumer literacy.[20] Chase and Schlink founded Consumer Research, a consumer advocacy group as well. Chase also proposed industrial policy during the Great Depression of the 1930s. In fact, President Franklin Roosevelt's initiative, the New Deal, articulated in the speech in which he accepted the Democratic Presidential Nomination, was named after Chase's 1933 book, *The New Deal*. The New Deal policies enhanced worker purchasing power and thereby promoted consumerism, as well as combatting the Great Depression.[21] See the discussion of changing values and regulation in Chapter 5.

The consumer movement became a significant force in the 1960s and after. John F. Kennedy, who was the Democratic nominee against Republican nominee Richard Nixon in the 1959 elections for US president, ran on platform of creating a "New Frontier" to combat the Cold War[22] and to engage in domestic reforms. Kennedy promoted consumer protection, including consumers' right to safe products, the right to be informed, the right to choose, and the right to be heard in his speech to Congress on March 15, 1962 (see Box 8.1).

---

### Box 8.1 Special Message on Protecting the Consumer Interest

Statement read by President John F. Kennedy
Thursday, March 15, 1962

I have sent to the Congress today a Special Message on protecting the consumers interests. All of us are consumers. All of us have the right to be protected against fraudulent or misleading advertisement and labels—the right to be protected against unsafe or worthless drugs and other products—the right to choose from a variety of products at competitive prices.

But modern living is so complex that the present laws on the statute book are inadequate to secure these rights. Thousands of common household items contain potentially harmful substances. Every year new chemicals are being added to our food or sprayed on crops. Ninety percent of the prescriptions written today are for drugs which were unknown twenty years ago. Unless the housewife is an expert dietician, mathematician, chemist and mechanic, she cannot properly and economically run her house and shop for her family.

This administration has already taken steps to increase Federal inspection of food, drugs, meat and poultry, to increase safety on the highways and in the airways, to cut back deceptive trade practices, false advertising, monopolies, and high utility bills, to improve the consumers' opportunity to purchase a less expensive home and enjoy great recreational opportunities.

But much more needs to be done, and I have asked the Congress first of all for strengthened regulatory authority over food, drugs and cosmetics. Since 1913 an Act of Congress has protected hogs, sheep and cattle against the marketing of worthless drugs. It is time we [give] men, women and children the same protection.

New drugs are being placed on the market every day, without any requirement of advance proof that they will be effective in treating the conditions for which they are recommended. Over twenty percent of the new drugs available since

1956 were found to be incapable of bearing out one or more of their sponsors' claims on which their effect would be.

This means that people not only are wasting their money but are also suffering needlessly. Similarly, two billion dollars of cosmetics are sold every year without any requirement that they be tested for safely—and as a result, thousands of women have suffered burns and other injuries to the eyes, skin and hair.

A fifth of all the meat we eat is not inspected by the Department of Agriculture, and extensive underground traffic exists in habit-forming barbiturates and stimulants. Drugs which could also be sold by a simple common name are too often sold by complex scientific names which confuse the purchaser—and raise the price.

All of these problems are covered by my recommendations to the Congress today. Other recommendations call for a law to require consumers to know how much they are being charged in interest and at what rate, when they purchase goods on credit or on the installment plan.

A law to require new televisions sets to be capable of receiving seventy ultra high frequency channels as well as the twelve VHF channels.

And laws to tighten up our safeguards against monopoly and mergers, which injure the consumers' interests.

None of these recommendations is very costly. But I believe that they can be immensely important to the well-being of every American family.

The consumer rights movement in the United States was spurred and shaped by the efforts of Ralph Nader. Nader, with the publication of his book *Unsafe at Any Speed* in 1965 became a national leader of the consumer movement in the United States. He founded a public interest watchdog group, Public Citizen, and inspired the founding in the 1970s of the Public Interest Research Group, a set of state-based consumer watchdog groups linked together as a national association that lobbies on behalf of consumers, as well as identifying and exposing "unsafe products and unfair business practices." The emergence of the consumer rights movement in the United States, marked by President Kennedy's speech to Congress and his legislative initiatives, as well as Nader's initiatives for consumer rights, occurred in the context of an emergent world consumer rights movement. For example, Consumer's International, an association of consumer unions, was founded in 1960. Kennedy's initiatives gave further impetus to the global consumer rights movement. In 1983, the United Nations declared March 15 as World Consumer Rights Day, and on April 9, 1985, the UN General Assembly adopted the UN Guidelines of Consumer Protection.[23] Consumer International promotes the international consumer movement by organizing World Consumer Rights Day, celebrated globally on March 15 of every year.

The consumer rights movement has also spurred the establishment of regulatory agencies to protect consumers.

### Consumer Protection Agencies

#### Consumer Product Safety Commission

The Consumer Product Safety Commission (CPSC) was established by Congress in 1972.[24] Congress passed the legislation establishing the CPSC because too many products posed "an unreasonable risk of injury" to consumers and because consumers were often unable to identify and minimize the risks associated with the use of consumer products. The purposes of the CPSC are: 1) to protect consumers against "unreasonable risks of injury"; 2) to assist consumers in evaluating the comparative safety of consumer products; 3) to develop uniform safety standards for consumer products; and 4) to promote research and investigation into the causes and prevention of product-related deaths, illnesses, and injuries.[25] The CPSC regulates all consumer products, except those under the purview and authority of other regulatory agencies, such as the FDA or the NHTSA. The CPSC works with industry groups to develop voluntary standards to minimize the risk of injury to consumers on such products as children's toys and equipment, including cribs, bunk beds and children's pajamas, as well as household items such as garage door openers, chainsaws, and all terrain vehicles. Each of these products poses a risk of injury to the consumer.

#### National Highway Traffic Safety Administration

The NHTSA was created by act of Congress in 1970 to administer the safety programs mandated by the National Traffic and Motor Vehicle Safety Act of 1966 and the Highway Safety Act of 1966. The NHTSA is part of the Department of Transportation. The NHTSA is responsible for reducing deaths and injuries from motor vehicle accidents, to set and enforce safety standards, to investigate safety defects in motor vehicles and to conduct research about and promote public policies that improve traffic safety.[26]

The NHTSA was reauthorized by Congress in 1991 and again in 1998. The National Highway Traffic Safety Administration Authorization Act of 1991 mandated the NHTSA to engage in rule-making in the areas of child restraints, air bags, drunk driving, and to develop standards to minimize the occurrence of head injuries from side impact collisions as well as to develop anti-lock brake standards.[27]

The effectiveness of the NHTSA was raised in the Ford Explorer and Firestone Tire case.[28] In response to the Ford Explorer-Firestone tire recall, Congress passed the Transportation Recall Enhancement, Accountability, and Documentation Act (TREAD). TREAD requires automobile manufacturers to report to the Secretary of Transportation defects and safety programs undertaken by the manufacturer in a foreign country and recalls or safety programs imposed on the manufacturer by a foreign government in cases where vehicles are identical or "substantially similar" to vehicles sold in the United States. These requirements were imposed because Ford knew of the roll-over problem with the Ford

Explorer and the problem of tire blowout in foreign countries such as Venezuela and Saudi Arabia, but Ford failed to notify the NHTSA of these safety defects. A further provision requires an automobile manufacturer that knowingly installs defective or non-complaint tires on a vehicle to notify the Secretary of Transportation. TREAD also required the Secretary of Transportation to determine the feasibility of collecting accident data from private automobile insurers. This provision was enacted because the NHTSA was alerted to the Ford Explorer-Firestone tire problem by notification from a State Farm Insurance Company researcher. The NHTSA was criticized for not acting quickly to recall the Firestone tires installed on Ford Explorers. The enactment of TREAD reinforces the point made in Chapter 4 on regulation—that regulation is typically reactive, rather than proactive or preventative.

## Negative Externalities

*Negative externalities* occur when the full costs of production are not internalized by the producing company, with the consequence that costs are levied on, or involuntarily paid by, the consumer in the form of injuries or other harms.[29] Economist Ronald Coase predicted that regulation or negotiation between private parties can lead to efficient outcomes, balancing the marginal costs with the marginal benefits of reducing negative externalities. Coase defines the efficient outcome as that set of choices that minimizes total social costs, identified as the intersection of the curves plotting marginal social benefits with marginal social costs.[30] His approach is called the *Coase Theorem*. The Coase Theorem predicts that companies, irrespective of government regulation, will limit their creation of negative externalities to the point of minimizing total social costs, including the costs of injuries and the costs of care.

The Coase Theorem is based on several assumptions, however, that may undermine the attainment of efficient outcomes through negotiations between private parties. These assumptions are: 1) that property rights of the parties are well defined; 2) that there are no transaction costs; 3) that there are a limited number of parties to the negotiations; and 4) that there is complete information between the parties.[31] The Coase Theorem may be challenged by the case of Ford Motor Co. Ford determined, based on a cost–benefit analysis comparing the costs of recall and repair of the defectively designed Ford Pinto to the costs of injuries to the victims of accidents, to market the defectively designed vehicle and pay the costs of damages. However, Ford committed a key error in underestimating the costs of injuries.[32] Ford had projected a cost per burn victim or death based on the NHTSA allocation of costs for deaths and injuries. However, when juries learned of Ford's approach to consumer safety, punitive damages were awarded to victims based on Ford's "outrageous conduct." For example, $125 million was awarded by the jury in a single case, *Grimshaw v. Ford Motor Company*, although the punitive damages were remitted by the trial court to $3.5 million.[33] The Coase Theorem also is based on an assumption of indifference about social costs, whereas social values and some ethical standards, for example a minority rights analysis, might reject a willingness to absorb certain social costs, such as the knowing but indifferent infliction of injuries or death by manufacturers of defectively designed products.

*Asymmetric information* is an additional barrier to private parties negotiating an efficient outcome, one that minimizes total social costs.[34] Asymmetric information means that one party to negotiations has a fuller knowledge of the problem and the risks than the other party to negotiations or to a transaction.[35] For example, in general, manufacturers know more information about product safety and design defects than consumer/purchasers. To overcome the imbalance of information, regulators may require manufacturers to give notice to about product safety issues or risks to consumers by warnings on the labels of the products. For example, the FDA required Bayer and GlaxoSmithKline to revise their advertising of Levitra. In addition in 2005, the FDA also required all manufacturers of ED drugs to include a warning of possible sudden vision loss as a rare side effect of ED drugs. These regulations were put into place to compensate for asymmetrical information on the part of the manufacturer.

## Product Liability

Products can cause injuries to consumers either because the products are defectively designed or because the products are inherently dangerous. The Coase Theorem predicts that manufacturers will act to reduce injuries and other negative externalities through a negotiated process with those affected by the externalities, even without government regulation requiring them to do so. However, not all the assumptions underlying the Coase Theorem hold up and there is also the problem of asymmetric information. Social values may require minimizing negative externalities, whereas the Coase Theorem only reduces negative externalities to a socially efficient solution. All these factors justify regulation.

### Defective Design

Products that are *defectively designed* injure users in their ordinary and foreseeable use. For example, the Ford Pinto and the Ford Explorer, prior to its redesign in 2002, were defectively designed. The Ford Pinto, which was introduced to the market in 1971, was recalled in 1978. The NHTSA did not find that the Ford Explorer was defectively designed,[36] although juries did conclude that the Ford Explorer was defectively designed.[37] As noted above, the Ford Explorer was redesigned in 2002 to overcome the design deficiencies related to its propensity to roll over.

### Inherently Dangerous Products

Some products are *inherently dangerous*. Examples of inherently dangerous products include tobacco products, alcohol products, chainsaws, automobiles and construction machinery. Consumers who knowingly use inherently dangerous products assume the risk of being injured by their use of such products. This is called *assumption of risk* by the consumer.

Furthermore, consumers can be negligent in their use of inherently dangerous products. If consumer negligence has been a factor in the consumer sustaining injuries, this phenomenon is called *contributory negligence*.[38] Ford Motor Co. defended against lawsuits involving its defectively designed vehicles based on driver fault or contributory negligence. In fact, the drivers of the Ford Pinto who were the subject of the *Indiana v. Ford Motor Co.* wrongful death lawsuit were negligent in their driving, as was the driver of the van that rear-ended them.

A problem with an assumption of risk defense by a manufacturer of an inherently dangerous product is asymmetrical information: the manufacturer knows more about the risks than the consumer/purchaser has information about product safety and design. Warnings can be posted on product labels of inherently dangerous products. Warnings don't eliminate risks, but they can warn of hidden risks and inform consumers of inherently dangerous products and of procedures to minimize risk.

Industry standards can also be developed to minimize risks of inherently dangerous products to consumers. For example, the Chainsaw Manufacturer's Association developed voluntary industry standards for the manufacture of chainsaws.[39] The American National Standards Institute (ANSI) is a private not-for-profit organization that develops voluntary industry standards. The ANSI serves as the United States representative to the International Organization for Standardization. Regulatory bodies such as the NHTSA, FDA, or the Consumer Product Safety Commission can require standards to minimize or eliminate risks or they can negotiate "voluntary standards" with industry associations. Sometimes the occasion for the negotiation of "voluntary standards" is proposed regulation by a government agency such as the NHTSA or FDA. Regulatory agencies post advance notice of proposed rulemaking and solicit responses from manufacturers, industry associations and consumers. For example, the NHTSA posted an notice regarding TREAD on the topic of the standards to be developed for reporting defective vehicles overseas.[40]

### Product Liability Law

The present status of the law of product liability in the United States is to hold manufacturers who put defectively designed or inherently dangerous products into the *stream of commerce* liable for injuries deriving from defectively designed or inherently dangerous products that are deemed "unreasonably dangerous." But the law has evolved over time. Initially, the doctrine of *caveat emptor* ("let the buyer beware") was the prevailing law. However the doctrine of *caveat emptor* has been eroded by the evolution of product liability law.

Product liability law is grounded in the law of torts. A *tort* is a wrong committed against another person or his or her property in a situation where the wrongdoer owes a *duty of care* to the injured person; for a tort to be committed, that duty of care must have been breached, and the breach of the duty of care must be the immediate or proximate cause of the injury sustained. Torts can be negligently or intentionally inflicted. Ordinarily the individual who has been tortiously injured receives *compensatory damages*. But the intentional infliction of injuries may lead to an assessment of *punitive damages*. Punitive damages are intended to punish the wrongdoer and to prevent the wrongdoer from engaging in future similar acts.

### Manufacturer Negligence

Manufacturer liability for injuries to a consumer through manufacturer negligence arose in the case of *MacPherson v. Buick Motor Co.*[41] In *MacPherson,* the New York court overcame the prior rule in negligence cases, namely, that recovery could only be had against the immediate link in a supply chain; the previous rule required *privity*, or a direct contract with the party against whom the injured party is seeking redress. In order words, under the rule of privity, the dealer would have an action against Buick Motor Co. for its defective product but not the consumer who purchased the car from the dealer. What happened in the *MacPherson* case is this. A wheel collapsed on the Buick car which MacPherson was driving, and MacPherson was thrown from the automobile and was injured. The wheel was made of wood and one of the spokes broke, causing the wheel to collapse. Buick had purchased the wooden wheels from a supplier and had installed them on their cars without inspecting the wheels. Judge Cardozo writing for the MacPherson court held, "If the nature of a thing is such that it is reasonably certain to place life and limb in peril when negligently made, it is then a thing of danger. Its nature gives warning of the consequences to be expected. If to the element of danger there is added knowledge that the thing will be used by persons other than the purchaser, and used without new tests, then, irrespective of contract, the manufacturer of this thing of danger is under a duty to make it carefully." The MacPherson court ruled that Buick owed a duty of care to the ultimate purchaser of the automobile, not just the dealer in the supply chain, breaking with the prior rule that a relationship of privity or contract must exist between the manufacturer held liable in negligence and the injured party. The court held that Buick was negligent for not inspecting the wheels and, therefore, was liable for the injuries that MacPherson suffered when the defective wheel collapsed.

The duty of care required of automobile manufacturers was extended to foreseeable injuries, so that automobile manufacturers are obligated to design cars to minimize risk of injury in view of the foreseeability of car accidents. In *Larsen v. General Motors*,[42] the driver of a Chevrolet Corvair[43] was injured when he was involved in a head-on collision with another car. (Remember that the Chevrolet Corvair was the subject of criticism by Ralph Nader in his book *Unsafe at Any Speed*.) There was no defect in the Corvair that caused the car accident. However, the car was designed so that Larsen's injuries were greater than might have occurred if the car had been designed differently.

The problem with the Corvair was that the steering column was a single shaft extending from the front tires to the steering wheel in the driver's compartment. Its construction caused the steering shaft to move toward the driver in a left-of-center head- on collision. In Larsen's case, the steering wheel hit his head, being displaced from the head on accident, so that Larsen sustained severe head injuries. Larsen contended that either he would not have sustained the injuries that he did or that they would not have been as severe if General Motors had designed the steering shaft so that it would not be displaced toward the driver in a head-on collision. The Eighth Circuit Court of Appeals held that General Motors' design of the Corvair breached its duty to Larsen because accidents, including head-on accidents are foreseeable, and that the design of the Corvair created an extra hazard that was a hidden defect that GM failed to disclose. *Larsen v. General Motors* is a provocative case in light of the Ford Motor Co.'s Pinto defective car design. The theory of the *Larsen v. GM* decision could be used to require Ford to design the Ford Pinto gas tank in such a manner that even if it met federal standards applicable at the time, Ford would be required to minimize injuries to drivers and passengers since rear-end collisions are reasonably foreseeable. In fact, Ford was held civilly, but not criminally liable,[44] for injuries to drivers and passengers of Ford Pinto automobiles who were burned in collisions.[45] The Grimshaw court found that Ford Motor Co., in designing the Pinto with its defective gas tank, had acted with "malice," so as to justify punitive damages, by "conduct evincing a conscious disregard of the probability that the actor's conduct will result in injury to others."[46]

The rule of liability of a merchant for foreseeable injuries has been extended beyond defectively manufactured products to other circumstances where risks to a consumer are foreseeable. For example, in *Helen Butler v. Acme Markets, Inc.*, a woman was assaulted in a grocery store parking lot, where she was loading groceries into the car.[47] There had been a number of assaults at that grocery store, and the grocery store had hired private security guards, to protect the premises as well as to prevent shoplifting. On the night that the plaintiff, Helen Butler, was assaulted in the grocery store parking lot, there were no security guards outside to protect the premises, although there was a guard inside to prevent shoplifting, and the grocery store had posted no warning of the risk of assault in the parking lot. The court held in *Butler* that the proprietor of the grocery market had invited the public to do business on its premises, that the proprietor owes a duty of care to protect the patrons whom it has invited to do business on its premises and that a reasonable person would take steps to prevent what was a foreseeable harm. Acme Markets, therefore, was liable for Helen Butler's injuries from her assault. This ruling recognizes a duty of care owed by proprietors and other merchants to their customers to protect customers from harms that are foreseeable and to undertake measures that a reasonable person would undertake to prevent the foreseeable harms.

## Breach of Warranty

*Express warranty.* *Express warranty* is contained in a contract of sale, and it explicitly guarantees specific aspects of the product. Express warranties are limited to the description of the goods in the contract of sale; a sample or model is a warrantee that the entire batch conforms to the model or sample. Express warranties are described in the Uniform Commercial Code.[48] Express warranties are used by manufacturers to limit liability to the express or explicit guarantee. However, attempts by manufacturers to limit their liability to express warranties have been eroded by the doctrine of "implied warranty."

*Implied warranty.* *Implied warranty* means that the reasonable expectations of consumers or purchasers of a product that it is "reasonably suited for ordinary use" must be met and that the manufacturer is liable to the buyer for damages if their product as manufactured is not "reasonably suited for ordinary use."[49]

The Uniform Commercial Code embodies the norm and expectation in contracts of sale of implied warranty of fitness for use. Case law developments also embody the rule of law that products introduced into the stream of commerce by manufacturers will be "reasonably suited for ordinary use." This constitutes an "implied warranty of merchantability."

In *Henningsen v. Bloomfield Motors, Inc.,*[50] Claus Henningsen had signed a contract of sale for a car with Bloomfield Motors that included a warranty clause as follows:

> It is expressly agreed that there are no warranties, express or implied, made by either the dealer or the manufacturer on the motor vehicle, chassis, or parts furnished hereunder except as follows: The manufacturer warrants each new motor vehicle (including original equipment placed thereon by the manufacturer except tires), chassis or parts manufactured by it to be free from defects in material or workmanship under normal use and service. Its obligation under this warranty being limited to making good at its factory any part or parts thereof which shall, within ninety (90) days after delivery of such vehicle *to the original purchaser* or before such vehicle has been driven 4,000 miles, whichever event shall first occur, be returned to it with transportation charges prepaid and which its examination shall disclose to its satisfaction to have been thus defective; *this warranty being expressly in lieu of all other warranties expressed or implied, and all other obligations or liabilities on its part,* and it neither assumes nor authorizes any other person to assume for it any other liability in connection with the sale of its vehicles.
>
> (Emphasis added)[51]

Mrs. Henningsen was driving her car, a Plymouth, within 10 days of its purchase when the steering mechanism failed and she crashed into a wall. The insurance adjuster calculated the damage to the car as a total loss and offered the opinion that the accident had been caused by a defect in the steering column that extended from the front wheels to the driver's compartment. The car was so damaged that the Henningsen's were unable to send the defective part to Chrysler, which was the manufacturer. Chrysler then denied liability for the damage because the Henningsen's did not meet the conditions of the warranty. The court determined that the express warranty could not overcome an implied warranty of merchantability and fitness for ordinary use: "under modern marketing conditions, when a manufacturer puts a new automobile in the stream of trade and promotes its purchase by the public, an implied warranty that it is reasonably suitable for use as such accompanies it into the hands of the ultimate purchaser."[52]

The doctrine of *good faith and fair dealing* is also relevant to implied warranties. For example, the New Jersey Supreme Court, as well as courts in other states, has held that implied in every contract is a "covenant of good faith and fair dealing." The case that decided that a covenant of good faith and fair dealing is implied in every contract was *Palisades Properties, Inc. v. Brunetti.*[53] It involved a dispute between a property developer in Fort Lee, New Jersey, south of the George Washington Bridge, about the development of land and the height of buildings that would be permitted. John D. Rockefeller, Jr., had donated land and established a charitable organization, the Sealantic Fund, for the purpose of preserving the scenic beauty of the Palisades. Between 1952 and 1956, a series of property transactions and contracts were consummated between Sealantic and Fort Lee that had the effect of allowing property development, while satisfying the Sealantic Fund's purposes of preserving the scenic beauty of the Palisades. Height restrictions were included in the contracts of sale. In 1962, Marriott Motor Hotels, the parent of Palisades Properties, proposed to build a tower higher than the height restrictions in the 1956 contract between Fort Lee and the Sealantic Fund on lots that had been acquired from private owners. Sealantic charged that if the tower would be built, it would deprive Sealantic of the "fruits" of the 1956 contract it had bargained for with Fort Lee. In deciding that Fort Lee had a duty to observe the restrictive covenants regarding building heights embodied in its 1956 contract with Sealantic, the New Jersey Supreme Court held: "In every contract there is an implied covenant that 'neither party shall do anything which will have the effect of destroying or injuring the right of the other party to receive the fruits of the contract; in other words, in every contract there exists an implied covenant of good faith and fair dealing.'" The covenant of good faith and fair dealing require contracts to be interpreted so that the contracting parties enjoy the fruits of their bargain.

### Strict Liability

*Strict liability* holds a manufacturer or other parties in the supply chain liable for injuries sustained by consumers during ordinary and foreseeable use of the product, without requiring a showing of negligence on the part of the manufacturer. The public policy benefits of strict liability were advocated in 1944 by

Judge Traynor in *Escola v. Coca Cola Bottling Co.*[54] but implemented by *Greenman v. Yuba Power Products, Inc.* in 1963.[55] William Greenman was injured when he was using a combination power tool that could be used as a saw, a drill and a wood lathe. While he was lathing a block of wood, it flew out of the machine and hit William Greenman in the head, causing him serious injuries. A jury ruled in favor of Greenman, awarding his compensatory damages, and Yuba appealed the verdict. The appellate court sustained the jury verdict, holding: "A manufacturer is strictly liable in tort when an article he places on the market, knowing that it is to be used without inspection for defects, proves to have a defect that causes injury to a human being."[56] The demonstration that a product is defective appears in the proof: that the consumer was in fact injured. The doctrine of strict liability is grounded in public policy: "the purpose of [strict] liability is to insure that the costs of injuries resulting from defective products are borne by the manufacturers that put such products on the market rather than by the injured persons who are powerless to protect themselves. . . . Sales warranties [i.e. express warrantees] serve this purpose fitfully at best."[57]

The evolution of product liability law shifts the risks and costs of injuries to manufacturers and distributors who put products into the stream of commerce and who profit there from. It is based on a public policy judgment about who is in the best position to bear the costs of defects and injuries.[58] For example, in the Tylenol poisonings, who was better situated to pay the costs of the poisonings, Johnson & Johnson or the families of the poisoned victims? The families of the victims sued J&J for the deaths, even though J&J did not directly cause the poisonings, on the basis that product tampering was reasonably foreseeable and that J&J had not taken precautions to prevent product tampering that in fact harmed the consumers. J&J settled the cases before trial. J&J clearly was better situated to bear the costs of the poisonings than victims of the poisonings and their families. Product liability law involves social policy, values and judgments about the allocation of risks and the costs of injuries. Thereafter the FDA implemented tamper-proof packaging requirements.

## Corporate Efforts to Cure or Prevent Defective Products

### *Product Recalls*

When a company recognizes that its product is defectively designed or manufactured, the company may withdraw the product from the market or recall it. Regulatory agencies can either force a recall or negotiate a recall or a voluntary withdrawal of a product from the market. Numerous defective products have been withdrawn from the market, including A. H. Robins' Dalkon Shield, Dow Corning's silicone breast implants, and Merck's Vioxx. The Ford Pinto was recalled in 1978, in the aftermath of the *Grimshaw v. Ford Motor Co.* trial and the jury's punitive damages award of $125 million.[59] Ford replaced the Wilderness ATX tires, manufactured by Firestone and that had been installed on the Ford Explorer, and Firestone later issue a "voluntary recall" under pressure from the NHTSA because the tires were defective.[60] Johnson & Johnson issued a broad recall of Tylenol during the Tylenol poisonings incident in 1982. But after the second round of Tylenol poisonings in 1986, which happened after the product was manufactured with "tamper proof" packaging, Johnson & Johnson stopped manufacturing Tylenol in capsule form, which was more subject to tampering than pills in solid form. Most recently, Toyota settled a criminal penalty with the US Department of Justice for failing to give notice of defects and to recall defective vehicles in a timely way. And GM also failed to timely recall vehicles with a defective ignition switch. The Toyota recall was the subject of the end of chapter case for Chapter 7. The GM ignition switch defect and recall is the end of chapter case for this chapter.

Manufacturers and regulatory agencies must balance the early release to the market of products that may later be found to have defects or to cause rare but injurious side effects with the benefit to society and to the particular consumers of the products. If injuries occur, even rarely, the manufacture will be liable for compensatory damages under the principles of product liability discussed above. Punitive damages, which are only imposed in situations of egregious, "hard hearted" and outrageous conduct, are more problematic for the company. Ethical management comes into play in the avoidance of actions that give rise to punitive damages.

### Whistleblowers

Whistleblowers can benefit an enterprise that has created a defective product or engaged in accounting fraud[61] or other mistaken behavior. Organizational insiders are in the position to identify problematic behavior and events within the enterprise. Engineers at Ford, and it turns out also at GM, identified the defective design of the Pinto and of the Chevy Cobalt ignition switch, respectively. But a problem with whistleblowers is that they carry bad news, which managers may prefer not to hear. Organizational culture, expressed as "the way we do things around here," may work to suppress or obstruct the upward flow of bad news. For example, David Halberstam in his book *The Reckoning* takes the position that the culture of Ford Motor Co. involves at its core a conflict between engineering and marketing and finance and that in a crunch, marketing and finance win out. This conflict played out in the design and marketing of the Pinto, to the detriment of Ford customers, and to the ultimate detriment of Ford Motor Co. itself. A similar cultural issue appears to have been at work in how GM dealt with its ignition defects. An analysis of GM corporate culture is given in Box 8.2.

---

#### Box 8.2   General Motors Vehicle Recalls

In June 2014, *Business Week* reported in detail about the events leading up to massive vehicle recalls. The articles are based partly upon a 325-page assessment of GM's ignition switch problems by a former US Attorney. The report condemned GM's behavior. Mary Barra, the relatively new CEO, said the report was "extremely thorough, brutally tough, and deeply troubling." She was right on all three counts.

## Personal Reference Point

As a young Army captain, I reported a fire in the company kitchen. The result was an excruciating investigation as to the cause of the minor damage. When I complained to my fellow commanders, I learned that two of them also had fires but did not report them and nothing else happened. Since then, I have often warned my bosses and colleagues, "Do not report fires in the company mess hall." Thus, we come to understand the culture at General Motors.

## Kelley's Actions

Courtland Kelley never got the message. With a father and grandfather who worked at GM previously, he joined the company in 1983. He held a series of positions to find and report defects in GM automobiles. As the years passed and he rose in the ranks, he found increasingly common and serious defects that affected safety of vehicle occupants. He aggressively reported his findings and found rare responses to make essential corrections. As a result of his behavior, he was identified as a troublemaker.

The situation began moving toward a crisis in 2001 when he discovered a defective fuel line connection that could cause a crash where someone was injured or killed. After pressing unsuccessfully for a recall, a senior executive helped him and GM recalled 60,000 vehicles to fix the defect. Subsequently, he learned the recall did not cover all defective vehicle models. After many more battles, he forced a larger recall.

## What Was Kelley's Job?

Shortly after this second effort, GM transferred Kelley to a "special assignment." He had no real responsibilities. He said he was told to "come up with charts, predict warranty for the vehicle, but not find every problem that GM might have." His colleagues sympathized with his position but encouraged him to leave the company on the basis that "nobody goes against GM and survives."

In 2003 he filed a "whistleblower lawsuit" against GM. Such laws have been around forever, even as they rarely protect anyone who reports wrongdoing. They did not protect Courtland. Since he still had a job and was receiving the same salary and benefits, he would have difficulty proving damage.

The lawsuit did tip off the arrogance of GM and its legal team. A conversation during one deposition went something like the following:

GM attorney. "Was it part of your description to raise concerns about trucks?"
Kelley. "I felt morally responsible . . ."
GM attorney. "That's not what I asked you."
Kelley. " . . . to fix a problem that I found in a vehicle."
GM attorney. "Was it part of your job description?"
Kelley: "No."

### Aftermath

After the lawsuit failed, Kelley stayed at GM in a variety of jobs. GM continued to manufacture the faulty ignition switches. Over an 11-year period, a number of people were killed or injured by accidents caused by the defective part. GM showed no urgency to fix the situation until 2014, when the GM problems became front page news and GM recalled more than 20 million cars.

### *Cultural Problem at GM?*

By any assessment, the recall fiasco at GM stems from a corporate culture that would not tolerate any dissent from the company line or deviation from management directive. The behavior was institutionalized, as illustrated by two overt behaviors:

- **GM Nod.** At a meeting participants would shake their heads up and down to indicate concurrence with an action even though they had no intention to follow through to achieve it.
- **GM Salute.** At a meeting attendees would lock their arms across the front of their chests as an indication that a problem being discussed was not their responsibility.

### Word to the Wise

Don't report fires in the mess hall unless you are ready to deal with the consequence.

**Footnote:** Things seem to have changed under the leadership of Mary Barra. In June 2014, GM issued a statement, "We are going to reexamine Mr. Kelley's employment claims as well as the safety concerns that he has (raised) . . . ."

John J. Hampton, Ph.d.
Blog, June 24, 2014
Available at: http://jacksblog9.homestead.com/

A challenge for managers within an enterprise is to create a culture where individuals who identify a problem feel free, and indeed are encouraged, to come forward with the problem.

### *Total Quality Control*

Total quality control (TQC), called in the United States *total quality management* (TQM) is a program to manage quality and minimize product defects. It reflects a program of continuous improvement. TQC was developed and used in Japan and then spread to the United States. TQC methodologies include Deming statistical quality control and the Deming Prize, six sigma production and the Baldrige Prize, and ISO 9000 standards.

***The Deming Method.*** US Professor Deming introduced statistical quality control methods in Japan after World War II, when the Japanese industrial infrastructure and Japanese industry were being rebuilt. These statistical quality control methods are known as the *Deming method*. United States manufacturing firms became interested in the Deming method somewhat later. There is an accreditation or award process for companies that implement the Deming quality control process, namely the Deming Prize.[62]

***Six Sigma.*** The reduction of defect rates and continuous improvement is the goal of the *Six Sigma production* system. Six Sigma refers to the reduction of variation to six standard deviations from the mean and translates to defect rate of .0000034, that is, 3.4 defects in one million units.[63] Six Sigma production systems use a stakeholder model, assessing the company processes from the perspective of customers, suppliers and employees. Six Sigma Production and TQM involve a reversal of the principle of "separation of planning from doing" that was a fundamental principle of Frederick Taylor's scientific management.[64] The *Malcolm Baldrige National Quality Award* was established Congress in 1987 and is administered by the National Institute of Standards and Technology.[65] The Motorola Company, which implemented a Six Sigma program to turn around the company from a deteriorating market position relative to foreign competitors, received the Malcolm Baldrige National Quality Award in 1988.[66] Allied Signal, Honeywell[67] and General Electric Company have also implemented Six Sigma programs.[68] Six Sigma programs are thought to produce significant cost savings for a company implementing them.

***ISO 9000.*** *ISO 9000* is a set of standards developed by the International Organization for Standardization (ISO) to manage quality in organizations.[69] The ISO uses stakeholder analysis in developing and implementing standards to manage quality in organizations. ISO standards are also concerned with continuous improvement. ISO 9000 standards are known as "generic management system standards," not specific to a particular material, product or production process. For example, implementation of ISO standard 9001:2000 assures that enterprise product meets customer specifications and regulatory requirements. ISO standard 9004:2000 is designed to satisfy all other stakeholders of an enterprise, including owners, employees, suppliers and society/the community.

---

### Box 8.3  ISO Quality Management Principles

This document introduces the eight quality management principles on which the quality management system standards of the revised ISO 9000:2000 series are based. These principles can be used by senior management as a framework to guide their organizations toward improved performance. The principles are derived from the collective experience and knowledge of the international experts who participate in ISO Technical Committee.

- Principle 1: Customer focus
- Principle 2: Leadership

- Principle 3: Involvement of people
- Principle 4: Process approach
- Principle 5: System approach to management
- Principle 6: Continual improvement
- Principle 7: Factual approach to decision making
- Principle 8: Mutually beneficial supplier relationships

Source: http://www.iso.org/iso/en/iso9000–14000/

Enterprise efforts to manage quality, to warn of product risks and to recall or remove dangerous products from the market build trust with customers, embodied as "good will." Such efforts also build corporate and brand reputation. This is the lesson of the Tylenol crisis. Although Johnson & Johnson management did not know whether their course of action in voluntarily recalling Tylenol in 1982 would be cost-effective from a financial point of view, in fact Tylenol recovered its market prior to the poisoning within a year.[20]

Corporate responsibility requires the manufacture of product without externalizing costs on consumers, the environment or workers; such production increases the global standard of living and contributes to the common good.

## Chapter Discussion Questions

1. How can large, successful companies avoid being trapped in their success as sustaining technologies?
2. Does continuous innovation require "skunk works," or is it possible to incorporate a process of continuous innovation throughout an enterprise? If the latter, how can continuous innovation be incorporated into the organization as a whole?
3. Develop an advertising policy for products that are inherently dangerous but which also create benefits for some consumers.

   For example, certain products previously withdrawn from the market have been re-introduced, such as thalidomide and silicone breast implants.
4. What can be done to encourage a deeper look at consumer complaints, for example, about the Chevy cobalt ignition switch, so that possible design or product defects are recognized?
5. Develop policies to investigate whistleblower complaints. Be specific. See for example, the complaints to the SEC flagging Bernard Madoff's securities as a possible pyramid scheme, in Chapter 12.

## Notes

1  Clayton Christensen, *The Innovator's Dilemma: When New Technologies Cause Great Firms to Fail* (Cambridge, MA: Harvard Business Review Press, 1997). See also

Clayton Christensen and Michael Raynor, *The Innovator's Solution: Creating and Sustaining Successful Growth* (Cambridge, MA: Harvard Business School Press, 2003).

2　Friedman, *The World Is Flat*.

3　Examples of the information and communication technologies that are among the forces that have flattened the world, according to Friedman, include: the development of personal computers and the Windows operating system, the development of Internet and the conversion "from a PC-based computing platform to an Internet-based platform," and the development of standardized software, leading to software that can be used across the globe, such as PayPal used for paying for internet purchase transactions.

4　Corporations are legal persons, and as such are granted the constitutional guarantees of free speech.

5　*Virginia State Board of Pharmacy et al. v. Virginia Citizens Consumer Council, Inc., et al.*, 425 U.S. 748 (1975).

6　"Prescription Drugs: FDA Oversight of Direct-to-Consumer Advertising Has Limitations," GAO, last modified October 28, 2002, http://www.gao.gov/new.items/d03177.pdf.

7　"Warning Letters and Notice of Violations Letters to Pharmaceutical Companies," U.S. Food and Drug Administration, last modified January 15, 2009, http://www.fda.gov/Drugs/GuidanceComplianceRegulatoryInformation/EnforcementActivitiesbyFDA/WarningLettersandNoticeofViolationLetterstoPharmaceuticalCompanies/ucm055666.htm.

8　"Suicidality in Children and Adolescents Being Treated with Antidepressant Medications," U.S. Food and Drug Administration, last modified October 15, 2004, http://www.fda.gov/cder/drug/antidepressants/default.htm. See also "Antidepressant Use in Children, Adolescents, and Adults," *U.S. Food and Drug Administration*, last modified May 2, 2007, http://www.fda.gov/cder/drug/antidepressants/.

9　Complaint to FDA: Pfizer Failed to Disclose Zoloft Suicide Risk in NYT Advertisement
　　Letter dated November 1, 2004
　　To Thomas W. Abrams
　　Director
　　Office of Medical Policy Division of Drug Marketing,
　　　Advertising, and Communications
　　Food and Drug Administration
　　From: Vera Hassner Sharav
　　THE ALLIANCE FOR HUMAN RESEARCH PROTECTION
　　veracare@ahrp.org
　　Available online at http://www.ahrp.org/infomail/04/11/01.php.

10　"Pfizer Adds Cardio-Risk Warning to Celebrex Label," *The Star Ledger*, Aug. 2, 2005.

11　See "FDA to Review Drug Marketing to Consumers," *Wall Street Journal*, August 2, 2005.

12　For the regulation of comparison ads, see, for example, Federal Trade Commission Commercial Practice Rule 16 CFR §14.15. See also Laura Stampler, "That Awesome Banned SodaStream Commercial Is Going to Be a Super Bowl Ad," *Business Insider*, Dec.4,2012,http://www.businessinsider.com/banned-sodastream-ad-to-air-during-super-bowl-2012–12#ixzz35zhg0h4b.

13　See "Advertising and Marketing on the Internet: Rules of the Road," Federal Trade Commission, last updated 2014, http://www.ftc.gov/bcp/online/pubs/buspubs/ruleroad.htm.

14  *Kasky v. Nike*, 539 U.S. 654 (2003).

15  *Kasky v. Nike* proceeded through the California state trial court, appellate court as well as to the California Supreme Court. The verdict of the California Supreme Court was appealed to the US Supreme Court, which granted certiorari in the case. The US Supreme Court determined that Kasky had standing under California law to bring the suit on behalf of consumers, but that the writ of certiorari had been improvidently granted, with the result that the United States Supreme Court would not decide the issues in the case. The case then settled.

16  See Brad Stone, *The Everything Store: Jeff Bezos and the Age of Amazon* (New York: Little, Brown: 2013). *The Everything Store* was the Financial Times/Goldman Sachs best business book of the year 2013.

17  Thorstein Veblen, *The Theory of the Leisure Class* (New York: Macmillan, 1899).

18  Thorstein Veblen's portrayal of conspicuous consumption occasioned by the rise of urban, industrialized society resonates in Ferdinand Tonnies' distinction between Gemeinschaft (community, including family and neighborhood) and gesellschaft (society, including the city and state). Tonnies wrote his book, *Gemeinschaft und Gesellschaft* in 1877, during the rise of the industrial revolution; it was translated into English in 1957 as *Community and Society* by Charles P. Loomis (East Lansing, MI: Michigan State University Press, 1957).

19  Upton Sinclair, *The Jungle* (New York: Grosset and Dunlap, 1906).

20  Stuart Chase and F.J. Schlink, *Your Money's Worth: A Study in the Waste of the Consumer's Dollar* (New York: Macmillan, 1927).

21  Stuart Chase, *A New Deal* (New York: Macmillan, 1933).

22  The launching of Sputnik, the first satellite to orbit the earth, by the Russians on October 4, 1957, inaugurated the "space race."

23  "United Nations Guidelines for Consumer Protection (as expanded in 1999)," *United Nations Conference on Trade and Development*, last modified 2013, http://unctad.org/ en/docs/poditcclpm21.en.pdf.

24  An umbrella agency, the Consumer Protection Agency, was proposed but defeated during the administration of President Jimmy Carter in 1976.

25  United States Code, TITLE 15—COMMERCE AND TRADE
CHAPTER 47—CONSUMER PRODUCT SAFETY
Section 2051. Congressional findings and declaration of purpose.

26  See *National Highway Traffic Safety Administration*, last modified 2014, http://www. nhtsa.gov/.

27  Pub. L No. 102–240 (1991).
See also National Highway Traffic Safety Administration Reauthorization Act Of 1998 (Title Vii Subtitle A Sec. 7101–7107 At 112 Stat. 465).

28  The Ford Explorer had higher than normal roll-over rates, but there was also an interaction with the Firestone tires; the Firestone tires produced at a particular plant, where the regular workers were on strike, and where the company used strikebreakers for producing the tires, had a higher than average defect rate. See John Chartier, "Firestone, Ford under fire: Companies try to pin blame on each other, but others say both are at fault," *CNN Money*, Sept. 6, 2000.

29  The costs of negative externalities may also be paid by third parties, i.e., the "general public" in the case of negative externalities outputted to the environment. Negative externalities levied on the general public in the form of environmental pollution are discussed in Chapter 9.

30  The Coase Theorem is based on several assumptions, however, which may undermine the attainment of efficient outcomes through negotiations between private

parties. These assumptions are: 1) that property rights of the parties are well defined; 2) that there are no transaction costs; 3) that there are a limited number of parties to the negotiations; and 4) that there is complete information between the parties.

31 See Donald H. Regan, "The Problem of Social Cost Re-visited," *Journal of Law and Economics* 15 (1972): 427–37. The Coase Theorem has been stated by Regan as: "in a world of perfect competition, perfect information and zero transaction costs, the allocation of resources in the economy will be efficient and will be unaffected by legal rules regarding the initial impact of costs resulting from externalities" (427). The assumptions underlying the Coast Theorem, and the fact that they may not hold up in real life, at least in some circumstances, resonates in the challenge of Herbert Simon to the classical/rational model of decision making; Simon formulated a model of decision making, the satisficing or bounded rationality model of decision making, based on more realistic assumptions. Simon won the Nobel Prize in Economics for his reformulated model.

32 Ford had estimated the costs of injuries at $49.5 million and the costs of recall and repair at $137 million.

33 174 Cal. Rptr. 348 (1981). The initial jury award of $125 million dollars in the *Grimshaw v. Ford Motor Co.* litigation represented the jury's estimate for Ford's profits from manufacturing and selling the Ford Pinto.

34 Asymmetric information runs contrary to the assumption of complete information between the parties to a transaction. Asymmetric information constitutes a market imperfection of incomplete information. These assumptions were discussed in Chapter 2.

35 Economists James Mirrlees and William Vickrey shared the Nobel Prize in Economics in 1996 for their work on asymmetric information. Tore Frängsmyr, ed., *Les Prix Nobel (The Nobel Prizes 1996)*, (Stockholm: Nobel Foundation, 1997).

36 Joseph B. White and Stephen Power, " NHTSA Rejects Firestone Request For Investigation of Ford Explorer," *Wall Street Journal*, Feb. 13, 2002.

37 *Agop and Catherin Gozukara v. Ford Motor Company.* Although the jury found that the Ford Explorer was defectively designed and manufactured, it found that the Ford Explorer design was not the proximate cause of Catherin or Agop's injuries.

38 Previously under American tort law, if a consumer was guilty of contributory negligence, any recovery for his or her injuries was barred; now, however, the compensatory damages award is reduced proportionately by the degree of consumer negligence.

39 U.S. Consumer Product Safety Commission
Office of Information and Public Affairs Washington, DC 20207
June 20, 1980 Release # 80–023
Commission Approves Mandatory Approach Toward Reducing Chain Saw Injuries From "Kickback." In response to the CPSC advance notice of proposed rule-making, the CSMA proposed a voluntary industry standard. Later the ANSI implemented standards for chain saws, and the ISO also has standards for chainsaws.

40 *Federal Register* 66, no. 197, October 11, 2001, http://www.nhtsa.dot.gov/cars/rules/rulings/tread/MileStones/66FRpg51907.htm.
[Proposed Rules]
[Page 51907–51918]
From the Federal Register Online via GPO Access [wais.access.gpo.gov]
[DOCID:fr11oc01–28]
DEPARTMENT OF TRANSPORTATION
National Highway Traffic Safety Administration
49 CFR Part 579

[Docket No. NHTSA 2001–10773; Notice 1]

RIN 2127-AI26

Reporting of Information About Foreign Safety Recalls
And Campaigns Related to Potential Defects

AGENCY: National Highway Traffic Safety Administration (NHTSA), DOT.

ACTION: Notice of proposed rulemaking (NPRM).

SUMMARY: This document requests comments on a proposal to implement the foreign safety recall and safety campaign reporting requirements of the Transportation Recall Enhancement, Accountability, and Documentation (TREAD) Act. Section 3(a) of the TREAD Act requires a manufacturer of motor vehicles or motor vehicle equipment to report to the National Highway Traffic Safety Administration (NHTSA) whenever it has decided to conduct a safety recall or other safety campaign in a foreign country covering vehicles or equipment that are identical or substantially similar to vehicles or equipment offered for sale in the United States. The manufacturer must also report whenever it has been notified by a foreign government that a safety recall or safety campaign must be conducted covering such vehicles or equipment.

41  217 N.Y. 382 (1916).

42  *Larsen v. General Motors*, 391 F. 2d 495 (8th Cir. 1968).

43  It may be remembered that the Chevrolet Corvair was the subject of criticism by Ralph Nader in his book *Unsafe at Any Speed: The Designed-In Dangers of the American Automobile* (New York: Grossman Publishers, 1965).

44  *Indiana v. Ford Motor Co.*

45  *Grimshaw v. Ford Motor Co.*, 119 Cal. App. 3d 757 (1981).

46  *Grimshaw v. Ford Motor Co.*, 119 Ca. App. 3d at 808.

47  *Helen Butler v. Acme Markets, Inc.*, Superior Court of New Jersey, Appellate Division 177 N.J. Super. 279 (1981).

48  The Uniform Commercial Code provides:

"§ 2–313. Express Warranties by Affirmation, Promise, Description, Sample

(1) Express warranties by the seller are created as follows:

(a) Any affirmation of fact or promise made by the seller to the buyer which relates to the goods and becomes part of the basis of the bargain creates an express warranty that the goods shall conform to the affirmation or promise.

(b) Any description of the goods which is made part of the basis of the bargain creates an express warranty that the goods shall conform to the description.

(c) Any sample or model which is made part of the basis of the bargain creates an express warranty that the whole of the goods shall conform to the sample or model.

(2) It is not necessary to the creation of an express warranty that the seller use formal words such as 'warrant' or 'guarantee' or that he have a specific intention to make a warranty, but an affirmation merely of the value of the goods or a statement purporting to be merely the seller's opinion or commendation of the goods does not create a warranty."

49  The relevant sections of The Uniform Commercial Code include: § 2–314. Implied Warranty: Merchantability; Usage of Trade and § 2–315. Implied Warranty: Fitness for Particular Purpose.

50  32 N.J. 358 (1960).

51  32 N.J. at 367.

52  32 N.J. at 384.

53  44 N.J. 117 (1965).

54   24 Cal. 2d 453 (1944).

55   59 Cal. 2d 57 (1963)

56   59 Cal. 2d at 61.

57   59 Cal. 2d at 63.

58   *Escola v. Coca Cola Bottling Co.*, 24 Ca. 2d 453, 462.

"[T]he manufacturer's negligence should no longer be singled out as the basis of a plaintiff's right to recover in cases like the present one. In my opinion [Traynor, J, concurring in the judgment] it should now be recognized that a manufacturer incurs an absolute liability when an article that he has placed on the market, knowing that it is to be used without inspection, proves to have a defect that causes injury to human beings. McPherson v. Buick Motor Co. . . .established the principle, recognized by this court, that irrespective of privity of contract, the manufacturer is responsible for an injury caused by such an article to any person who comes in lawful contact with it . . . In these cases [citations omitted] the source of the manufacturer's liability was his negligence in the manufacturing process or in the inspection of component parts supplied by others. Even if there is no negligence, however, public policy demands that responsibility be fixed wherever it will most effectively reduce the hazards to life and health inherent in defective products that reach the market. It is evident that the manufacturer can anticipate some hazards and guard against the recurrence of others, as the public cannot. Those who suffer injury from defective products are unprepared to meet its consequences. The cost of an injury and the loss of time or health may be an overwhelming misfortune to the person injured, and a needless one, for the risk of injury can be insured by the manufacturer and distributed among the public as a cost of doing business. It is to the public interest to discourage the marketing of products having defects that are a menace to the public. If such products nevertheless find their way into the market it is to the public interest to place the responsibility for whatever injury they may cause upon the manufacturer, who, even if he is not negligent in the manufacture of the product, is responsible for its reaching the market. However intermittently such injuries may occur and however haphazardly they may strike, the risk of their occurrence is a constant risk and a general one. Against such a risk there should be general and constant protection and the manufacturer is best situated to afford such protection."

59   The punitive damages in Grimshaw were later remitted to $3.5 million.

60   See "Proposed New Pneumatic Tires for Light Vehicles," *National Highway Traffic Safety Administration*, last modified October 2001, http://www.nhtsa.dot.gov/cars/rules/rulings/UpgradeTire/Econ/TireUpgradeI.htm.

61   Sherron Watkins blew the whistle on Enron's accounting fraud.

62   See *The W. Edwards Deming Institute*, last modified 2014, http://www.deming.org/demingprize/demingprize.html.

63   "What Is Six Sigma?," *I Six Sigma*, last modified 2014, http://www.isixsigma.com/sixsigma/six_sigma.asp.

64   See, for example, "Historical Perspective on Productivity Improvement," *ACCEL Team Development*, last modified 2014, http://www.accel-team.com/scientific/scientific_02.html.

65   See "Baldrige Performance Excellence Program," *National Institute of Standards and Technology*, last modified June 24, 2014, http://www.quality.nist.gov/.

66   "The Baldrige Award is given by the President of the United States to businesses—manufacturing and service, small and large—and to education and health care organizations that apply and are judged to be outstanding in seven areas: **leadership;**

strategic planning; customer and market focus; measurement, analysis, and knowledge management; human resource focus; process management; and results" (emphasis added).

Congress established the award program in 1987 to recognize U.S. organizations for their achievements in quality and performance and to raise awareness about the importance of quality and performance excellence as a competitive edge. "Baldrige Performance Excellence Program," http://www.quality.nist.gov/.

See also *Quality America Inc.*, last modified 2014, http://www.qualityamerica.com/knowledgecente/articles/PYZDEKSixSigRev.ht.

67  Allied Signal and Honeywell Corporation merged in 1999.

68  See "Six Sigma Costs and Savings," *I Six Sigma*, last modified 2012, http://www.isixsigma.com/library/content/c020729a.asp., showing savings attributed to six sigma programs. Regarding GE's six sigma program, see "What Is Six Sigma?," *General Electric Company*, last modified 2014, http://www.ge.com/sixsigma/.

69  *International Organization for Standardization*, last modified 2014, http://www.iso.org/iso.

70  Tylenol had regained 70% of its previous market share within five months of the 1982 poisoning. See Lawrence G. Foster, "The Johnson & Johnson Credo and the Tylenol Crisis," *The New Jersey Bell Journal*, 6, no. 1. (1983). See also Tamar Lewin, "Tylenol Maker Finding New Crisis Less Severe," *The New York Times*, Feb. 12, 1986. See also Richard W. Stevenson, "Johnson & Johnson's Recovery," *New York Times*, July 5, 1986.

## End of Chapter Case: GM Ignition Switch: Anton Valukas' Written Testimony to Congress

Written Testimony of
   Anton R. Valukas
   Jenner & Block LLP
   353 N. Clark Street
   Chicago, IL 60654
   Before the Committee on Energy and Commerce
   Subcommittee on Oversight and Investigations
   United States House of Representatives
   "The GM Ignition Switch Recall: Investigation Update"
   June 18, 2014
   Chairmen Murphy and Upton, Ranking Members DeGette and Waxman, and members of the Committee:

Thank you for having me here to testify about my report on the Cobalt ignition switch.

In March of this year GM asked me to determine why it took so long to recall the Cobalt and other vehicles that contained the faulty ignition switch. I approached this task in much the same way that I did in conducting my review of the Lehman Brothers matter, albeit on a much more expedited timetable. My job was to find the facts as to how and why this occurred and set forth those facts in a report.

Jenner & Block was given unfettered access to GM witnesses and documents and was asked for an unvarnished account. We interviewed more than 230 witnesses and collected more than 41 million documents. We obtained and reviewed forensically imaged hard drives, including those belonging to top executives. We searched server-based e-mails and shared drives, electronic databases, and hundreds of boxes of hard-copy documents, all in an effort to identify any documents that would bear on our assignment to find out why the Cobalt recall was delayed for so many years. If we discover any new information that materially affects our report, we will supplement our findings to the Board.

In our report, we did not simply repeat what any individual GM employee told us. We tested those assertions against the extensive documentary record we gathered and against the statements of other witnesses.

I will not summarize the report in any detail—it speaks for itself. I will, however, highlight a few broad conclusions that tie directly to our recommendations.

- GM personnel approved the use of an ignition switch in the Cobalt and other cars that was far below GM's own specification. This was done by a single engineer and was not known by those who were investigating the Cobalt from the time of the approval until 2013.

- From the time it first went into production, the Cobalt (and the Ion before it) had problems because the ignition switch could too easily be turned to Accessory, resulting in a moving stall including the loss of power steering and power brakes. GM engineers were fully aware of this problem but did not consider it a safety issue. That conclusion was the wrong one—amazingly, the engineers investigating the Cobalt in 2004 and 2005 did not understand that, when the key turned to Accessory, the airbags would fail to deploy.

  - Because GM personnel failed to understand the potential hazard caused by the ignition switch, GM engineers debated through various committees whether any of the potential fixes were cost-effective. This focus on cost was driven by the failure to understand that a safety defect was at issue and the consequences of that defect.

  - In 2006, the engineer who authorized the below-specification switch in the first place increased the torque in the ignition switch by authorizing a change to the switch. He approved a change to the switch, but did not change the part number, thereby concealing the change and leading to years of confusion among investigators about why, if the ignition switch was mechanically the same in all model years, accident data was so markedly different before and after Model Year 2008.

  - GM personnel began recognizing the problem of non-deployment of airbags in the Cobalt as fax back as 2007, but failed to take advantage of all the resources at their disposal—including information in GM's own databases—to understand that the non-deployment was related to the known problem of the ignition switch. Others—outside GM—made this connection as early as 2007. But, as fatalities and injuries mounted in cases in which airbags did not deploy in Cobalts, GM personnel displayed no sense of urgency in determining the cause.

- By 2011, GM personnel knew that there was a pattern of non-deployments in Cobalts and that the ignition switch might be to blame. GM's outside counsel warned GM that it might be liable for punitive damages for failing to deal with the problem for so many years.
- But, once again, GM personnel failed to display any sense of urgency. The non-deployment investigation languished, even as it became more and more clear that the ignition switch was the problem.
- And the investigation was further delayed when the engineer who originally approved the faulty switch told GM safety engineers that he had never changed the switch, when, in truth, he had.
- By 2013, the investigation had not progressed, and it was only when an outside expert hired by a plaintiff's lawyer took the switches apart and compared them that GM personnel finally understood that the switch had been changed. Even then, however, GM took another ten months to recall the Cobalt.

The story of the Cobalt is one of a series of individual and organizational failures that led to devastating consequences. Throughout the decade that it took GM to recall the Cobalt, there was a lack of accountability, a lack of urgency, and a failure of company personnel charged with ensuring the safety of the company's vehicles to understand how GM's own cars were designed. We found failures throughout the company—including individual errors, poor management, byzantine committee structures, lack of training, and inadequate policies.

In our report, we review these failures, including cultural issues that may have contributed to this problem, and we provide recommendations to ensure that it never occurs again.

I understand that while this report answers many questions, it leaves open others:

- Government officials (and perhaps judges and juries) will assess the credibility of witnesses and whether there was civil or criminal culpability;
- GM will have to make decisions about how to ensure that this never happens again;
- Others, whether courts or Mr. Feinberg, will make decisions about which specific accidents were caused by the Cobalt's faulty ignition switch.

Our role was to find the facts as to why this recall took far too long. I believe we have done so.

## Case Discussion Questions

1. Advise GM CEO Mary Barra how to deal with whistleblower Courtland Kelley.
2. What can be done to change the culture at GM, so that the "GM nod" and the "GM salute" are no longer the way things are done at GM? Make specific recommendations.
3. Do you agree with Anton Valukas' conclusion exonerating top management in the GM ignition switch defect and delayed recall? Defend your conclusion.

# 9 Sustainable Environmental Management

## Chapter Outline

Risks Inherent in the Technology of Production
    Assessment of Risk: Probability-Impact Matrix
    Unintended Negative Consequences
    Free Goods
    Negative Externalities
    Sustainable Production
Sustainability
    Sustainable Development
        The Kyoto Protocol and Global Warming
        Cap and Trade
    Managing for the Triple Bottom Line: Environmental Reporting
        The Global Reporting Initiative
        ISO 1400
    Issues in Sustainability: Supply Chain/Product Sourcing
    Sustainability Drives Technological Innovation
    Sustainability and Product Pricing: The Bottom Line
    End of Chapter Case: Fukushima Nuclear Power Plant Meltdown

## Chapter Introduction

Risks are inherent in the process of production. Corporate responsibility and ethical management practice mandate that executives proactively manage such risks and act to minimize negative externalities. The principle "first do no harm" takes on particular meaning for environmental management. Leading corporation citizens are managing for the triple bottom line—for economically, socially and environmentally sustainable enterprise. Sustainable production and consumption are global concerns, addressed by partnerships between corporations, governments, non-governmental organizations, and coordinated in important ways by the United Nations.

## Chapter Goal and Learning Objectives

*Chapter Goal:* To identify ways in which enterprise can engage in sustainable environmental management.

*Learning Objectives:*

1.  Identify the risks inherent in production and alternative risk management strategies.
2.  Discuss managing for the triple bottom line and corporate initiatives to "go green."
3.  Relate sustainable production to sustainable consumption and global initiatives for sustainability.
4.  Discuss the conflict of interest among roles of individuals: as consumers seeking low price, as workers desiring job security and as citizens desiring quality of life.

## Risks Inherent in the Technology of Production

Risks are inherent in the production process. *Risk management* thus becomes a key responsibility of ethical and socially responsible management. Different risks are associated with different production technologies. For example, the risk of explosion is inherent in process production technologies, such as nuclear power generation and oil refining. Oil spills and well blowouts are a risk of drilling for oil and of oil transport.[1] The Exxon Valdez accident in 1989 was not the largest oil spill, but it caused the most environmental damage because it occurred in an enclosed area, Prince William Sound, Alaska, rather than in the open seas.[2] Although oil spills are a risk inherent in oil drilling and transport, human factors, including alcohol abuse by the captain of the tanker, caused and aggravated the Exxon Valdez spill. Human factors were also a factor in the BP oil spill of 2010 in the Gulf of Mexico, which was the largest oil well blowout and the largest unintended oil spill.[3]

A comparison of the Chernobyl accident with the nuclear power plant accident at Three Mile Island, Pennsylvania, and the Fukushima nuclear power plant meltdown in Japan illustrates not only the risks inherent in technology but also demonstrates social choices about the allocation of risks. The technology used to generate nuclear energy, and the structure of the Chernobyl nuclear power plant, externalized more risk on the general public than did the Three Mile Island nuclear power plant.[4] The Chernobyl plant used graphite rods and did not use a cement containment structure. The construction of the Chernobyl nuclear power plant thereby externalized risk on the surrounding community by its construction, whereas the nuclear power plant at Three Mile Island was constructed so as to reduce the risks on the surrounding community.[5] Social choices were at work in the choices about the construction and management of both the Chernobyl and the Three Mile Island nuclear power plants.

In addition, TEPCO, the manager of the Fukoshima nuclear power plant that melted down after an earthquake and tsunami in March 2011, externalized risks and costs on the surrounding community in the construction and management of the meltdown in 2011. TEPCO recognized the option of flooding the Daiichi reactor with seawater but did not do so because the seawater would corrode the equipment.[6] The report of the Carnegie Foundation for Peace also concluded that social and cultural factors figured in TEPCO's failure to manage the risks of external events, such as the tsunami that flooded the Fukushima plant.[7]

Safety measures are often considered overhead costs that can be deferred in tight budget situations, rather than costs integral to the production process. This was illustrated in the operation by Union Carbide and its subsidiaries of the Bhopal plant in India (see Box 9.1).

---

**Box 9.1  The Good, the Bad or the Ugly: The Bhopal Accident**

The Bhopal accident occurred as a result of an explosion in a process production technology of producing the pesticide Sevin. An intermediate product of the production process methyl isocyanate (MIC) is unstable when mixed with water. Water was added to the MIC storage tank at the Union Carbide plant in Bhopal, India. The environmental and human injuries from the explosion of the Union Carbide plant in Bhopal resulted in large measure from the failure to manage the risks involved in the production process.[8] These included: the failure to have the storage tanks cooled with a refrigeration system; the failure to have spare storage tanks available; the failure to have functional vent gas scrubbers; and the failure to have functional flare towers to burn off released gases.

Questions for discussion:

1. Is there an ethical obligation to shut-down operations, rather than to continue low-cost/shoe string operations, if continuing production is unsafe?

2. Is compliance with local law enough with respect to safety of operations and pollution? What about the international double standard? Manufacturers in the United States are subject to OSHA and EPA regulation and requirements. Note that there is a similar manufacturing facility in West Virginia.

3. In view of the risks of manufacturing MIC, could/should Union Carbide have negotiated with the government of India regarding the latter's requirement that even intermediate products be manufactured in India, if they are to be sold there? Should Union Carbide have stopped producing Sevin, and withdrawn from the Indian market, if the government of India continued to require the manufacture of MIC there?

Social choices, including choices about who bears the downside risk, are reflected in the regulatory requirements for the construction and operation of nuclear power plants and other production operations.

### Assessment of Risk: Probability-Impact Matrix

A *probability-impact matrix* manifests the probability and the risk of an environmental or other disaster. A probability-impact matrix rates the probability of event as high or low and the impact of an event as high or low, yielding four possible outcomes: a high-probability/high-impact event, a low-probability/high-impact event, a high-probability/low-impact event and a low-probability/low-impact event.

The management of high-probability, high-impact risks must be given priority, as well as insured. For example, the risk assessment done by the Federal Emergency Management Agency in 2001 projected the environmental and other risks to New Orleans of a force five hurricane, such as Hurricane Katrina that actually devastated New Orleans in August 2005.[9] The New Orleans *Times-Picayune*, as well as PBS, attempted to arouse public concern over the risks to the Gulf Coast of a large-scale hurricane. In that respect, the devastation wrought in New Orleans in 2005 was predicted as a high-probability, high-impact event. The failure to manage the high-probability/high-impact event was a strategic management and governmental failure.

*High-probability, low-impact* events must also be managed via control processes and standard operating procedures and methods. Although any single event may be "low impact," because the risk of the occurrence is high, resources will be frittered away unless high-probability/low-impact events are managed, thereby reducing risks and lowering the impacts. Management of *low-probability/high-impact* events was previously neglected or relegated to a contingency plan. The Exxon Valdez spill was a low-probability/high-impact event. The probability of an oil spill such as occurred with the Exxon Valdez was assessed at one in 240 years. However, the risks were mis-conceptualized because the oil spill would not necessarily occur in the 240th year; although the risk of a spill of the magnitude that occurred in the Exxon Valdez spill was only one time in 240 years, the event could occur randomly over the entire period. Moreover, the agencies responsible for managing the contingency plan for a spill in Alaska, including Alyeska, had been lulled into complacency and were unprepared for the emergency oil spill from the Exxon Valdez. The

*Table 9.1* Probability-Impact Matrix

| Impact | Probability | |
|---|---|---|
| | *High* | *Low* |
| **High** | High-Probability/High-Impact Event | Low-Probability/High-Impact Event |
| **Low** | High-Probability/Low-Impact Event | Low-Probability/Low-Impact Event |

unpreparedness for the Exxon Valdez spill was similar to the unpreparedness of Union Carbide India for the Bhopal accident. In both cases, the mechanisms required for managing an actual accident were out of commission. Moreover, the probability of the oil well blowout that occurred in the Gulf of Mexico in April 2010 was considered so remote that the United States Mineral Mining Service did not require a risk analysis.[10]

Risk management strategies for managing *low-probability, high-impact* events have gained legitimacy from an understanding of the most currently accepted theory accounting for the extinction of the dinosaurs.[11] The currently accepted explanation for the sudden extinction of the dinosaurs is that a comet hit the earth, falling into a fault in the ocean. The hit spewed up so much volcanic ash that the sunlight was blocked; plants, which are dependent for photosynthesis on sunlight, died; as a result, the plant-eating dinosaurs died, followed by the carnivorous dinosaurs. Since the consequences of a low-probability, high-impact event can be devastating, risk management strategies should incorporate contingency planning as well as insure for such events. *Low-probability, low-impact* events are appropriately self-insured. Since risks are inherent in the production process, risk management is an essential aspect of effective and ethical, socially responsible management.

### Unintended Negative Consequences

Unintended negative consequences may result from production processes or even consumption patterns.[12] Rachel Carson, with the publication in 1962 of her book *Silent Spring*,[13] explained the unintended negative consequences of the pesticide DDT. The publication of *Silent Spring* launched the environmental movement in the United States and perhaps globally. Ecologists are concerned about long-term system consequences to ecological systems, particularly unintended negative consequences of production processes, the probability of which increase with interdependence within a system. The devastating effects of Hurricane Katrina experienced by the United States Gulf Coast, and particularly the city of New Orleans in Louisiana, were an unintended negative consequence of the flood management program for the Mississippi River. The ecological systems effects of barricading the Mississippi River by constructing levies for flood prevention caused the erosion of the wetlands that serve as a barrier to storm systems from Gulf of Mexico flooding.[14] The Army Corps of Engineers is now trying to reverse the damage to the ecological systems created by the leveeing of the Mississippi River. New levies are being built that can open to permit flooding and re-silting of the Mississippi Delta. However, the allocations of monies needed to remedy the environmental degradation of the Mississippi Delta and to correct identified risks was considered a political issue by Congress, rather than a matter of national security.[15]

Part of the problem of managing unintended negative consequences of production processes or consumption patterns is that the unintended negative consequences occur over the long term and the causal links may be complex and even uncertain. Moreover, some natural resources used in production have been conceptualized as "free goods."

### Free Goods

The air and water used in enterprise production processes have been considered *free goods*.[16] Economists have reconceptualized land, traditionally considered a factor of production (see Table 2.1), as *natural capital*.[17] Natural capital is defined as "natural resources and the ecological systems that provide vital life-support services."[18] Ecological concerns about sustainability of enterprise production systems often involve natural capital, including air and water. Ethical concerns are also raised about who pays the costs when companies pollute natural resources that have been used as free goods and when land itself becomes contaminated.

### Negative Externalities

Negative externalities occur when the full costs of production are not internalized by the producing company. For example, if clean air, obtained as a free good, is inputted as a component of the production process, but that air is reintroduced back to the atmosphere in a polluted form, then a negative externality has been created. The same may happen with water, which is often obtained as a free good. For example, production plants are often located along a river; the river water is used for cooling purposes or to rotate a turbine engine. If the water used in the production process is reintroduced to the environment in a degraded or polluted form, then a negative externality has been created. This happened for example, when California Public Gas and Electric added hexavalent chromium to the water used in its cooling towers and then stored the wastewater on their property in unlined collection ponds.[19] An additional example is given by the pollution of the waterbed in Woburn, Massachusetts. The disposal of waste products deriving from the production processes by a number of businesses in Woburn, Massachusetts, caused the land to be degraded and the waterbed to become polluted in the town of Woburn.[20] Even raised water temperatures can cause changes to the ecological system when re-introduced to a river. Although companies may "own" the land that becomes contaminated, issues of *intergenerational fairness* are raised if the land or the underlying waterbeds become polluted.

The costs of negative externalities such as polluted air, polluted water, and contaminated soil are often paid by third parties, such as the community where a firm operates. For example, the communities in Woburn, Massachusetts, suffered higher rates of leukemia as a result of the dumping of the toxic wastes on the land and the resultant contamination of the wells in Woburn. The residents of Hinkley and Kettleman, California, also experienced higher rates of cancer as a result of California Public Gas and Electric's utilization of chromium six in its compressors. Union Carbide also externalized its costs of production onto the community where it operated in Bhopal, India. By failing to manage the risks inherent in the production process, and by failing to properly maintain required safety systems, Union Carbide suffered an industrial accident that caused damage to the environment and especially to the people living near the plant. More recently, China's Songhua River became polluted by an explosion at the China National Petroleum plant, a benzene manufacturing plant in Jilin. Benzene flowed into the river; since benzene is carcinogenic, water supplies to Harbin, a city along the river, were cut off in November 2005 so to prevent harm to the households from the polluted water.[21] The impact of the toxic pollution of the Songhua River crossed national boundaries, affecting Russia by the downstream pollution.[22]

Strip mining is another example of production process that externalizes damage to the environment on the surrounding community. Where the mining companies do not remediate the land that they have mined for natural resources, externalized costs are borne by the community in the form of ugliness and degradation of the land, as well as ill health effects from the air and water pollution caused by the mountaintop removal strip mining.[23] Congress has enacted legislation, the effect of which is to prevent or remediate the negative externalities of strip mining. The Surface Mining Control and Reclamation Act, passed by Congress in 1977, requires coal mining companies to meet certain environmental standards and to restore the land to its original condition, unless the mining company shows that the flattened land will be used for commercial development. The Clean Water Act, also passed by Congress in 1977,[24] prohibits coal companies from dumping mining waste into streams. Companies were prohibited in 1999 by a federal court in West Virginia from burying streams with the mountaintop soil and rocks.[25] However in 2002, the Bush administration changed the rule to permit the burial of streams by mountaintop removal strip mining.[26] This change in regulation met with opposition from environmental groups, including the Sierra Club.[27] The Army Corps of Engineers subsequently suspended the licenses of four mining companies for mountaintop removal coal mining.[28] Mountaintop removal represents a conflict among stakeholders about the utilization of a particular production technology and the impact of that technology on the environment and surrounding community.

### Sustainable Production

The creation of negative externalities results in the underpricing of the goods produced, since the essence of a negative externality is that enterprise fails to incorporate the full costs of production into the product price. Products would be priced higher if the product price incorporates the costs of cleaning the air or the water used in the production process. Consumers must be willing to pay the increased priced of products if corporations are to effectively eliminate the externalization of production costs and the creation of negative externalities.

The costs of production in less economically developed countries (LEDCs) may be lower due to a less stringent regulatory environment. As a consequence, enterprises in some LEDCs may be permitted to externalize costs to the environment or to workers in the form of unsafe working conditions. When the North American Free Trade Agreement (NAFTA) was being negotiated between the United States, Canada, and Mexico, there was a concern that products manufactured in Mexico would have a competitive advantage because Mexico has a less stringent regulatory environment than Canada or the United States. Therefore, the North American Commission for Environment Cooperation was established in addition to the creation of NAFTA's environmental standards.[29] The North American Commission for Environmental Cooperation addresses transnational, continental environmental concerns and was intended to create synergistic effects by cooperation among the nations participating in NAFTA.

In managing enterprise relationships with the environment, ending negative externalities is a first step. Remediating environmental degradation is a second step, by such means as the Land Reclamation Act discussed previously. But in the long run, companies and countries must engage in sustainable production. For example, the soccer ball industry, whose production is concentrated in LEDCs, has been criticized for exposing workers to toxic fumes and for using child labor. The World Federation of the Sporting Goods Industry participated in a global form for sports and environment in conjunction with the United Nations Environmental Programme. The third global forum for the World Federation of the Sporting Goods Industry developed the Global Sports Alliance Principles for socially responsible production of sporting goods, committing the sporting goods industry to principles of sustainable production and to the reduction of environmental harms, including toxic and chemical wastes generated in the production process. These principles were embodied as The Lahore/Sialkot Declaration on Corporate Responsibility.[30]

## Sustainability

*Sustainability* addresses the long-term consequences of an enterprise's production system and questions whether the long-term consequences can be sustained or whether those consequences lead to the long-term degradation of the system. *Ecological systems theory* is used to evaluate enterprise sustainability. Ecological systems theory views *ecological systems* as *closed systems*. Viewing the ecological system as a closed system forces producers and consumers to assess the consequences of their production and consumption patterns. Under a closed system approach, negative consequences cannot be ignored; they must be taken into account. Ecological systems theory focuses particularly on unintended negative consequences of production systems. *The Lorax* by Dr. Seuss, nominally a children's book, uses an allegory to explain the interdependencies within an ecological system and illustrates the unintended negative consequences of that production system.[31]

Americans, with the history and experience of frontier, can easily fall prey to an "open system" approach, whereby the negative by-products of a production system can be externalized to the frontier. For example, testing of nuclear weapons was done in the deserts of Nevada[32] and high-level nuclear waste products originally were stored in Hanford, Washington. The assumptions underlying these actions were that no living beings would experience the negative consequences of nuclear testing or disposal of nuclear by-products. However, the storage containers deteriorated at Hanford, requiring re-containment.[33] In 1982, Congress provided that high-level nuclear waste requiring long-term storage be stored at the Nevada nuclear test site in Yucca Mountain, which was formed from a volcano.[34] Now some ecologists are concerned that the fissures in the mountain will allow the escape of radiation from the stored nuclear waste products.[35]

### Sustainable Development

Sustainable economic development emphasizes sustainable consumption patterns and the role of women and households who are primarily responsible for consumption patterns and the generation of waste products. Developed, high-income countries presently are engaged in non-sustainable patterns of consumption, including energy consumption, and generate waste products that are injurious to the environment. The non-sustainability of the industrialized world's consumption patterns is evident by the principle of universalizability: if the less developed countries and their populations engaged in the consumption patterns and production patterns of the developed world, those patterns of consumption and production would be injurious to the environment and would exhaust natural resources. Sustainability efforts, therefore, focus on the use of renewable resources and methods of production and consumption that are less wasteful and that generate fewer waste products.

The United Nations has exerted significant leadership in raising awareness about sustainable development and in developing principles for sustainable development.[36] The United Nations Environmental Programme (UNEP) was established in 1972 after the Stockholm conference on the human environment. UNEP then established the Intergovernmental Panel on Climate Change in 1988. The Intergovernmental Panel on Climate Change convenes an international group of scientists that support the United Nations Framework Convention on Climate Change. The United National Framework Convention on Climate Change was negotiated as the outcome of the first Earth Summit held in Rio de Janeiro, Brazil in 1992. The Earth Summit also issued the Rio Declaration on Environment and Development. The Rio Declaration provides principles for sustainable development.[37] The principles for sustainable development articulated in the Rio Declaration, while recognizing national sovereignty, include a concern for environmental needs across generations, i.e., future generations as well as present generations, and the goal of eradicating poverty on a global basis, as well as a concern that nations do not externalize their environmental problems onto the surrounding nations.[38, 39]

The United Nations Commission on Sustainable Development was also created in 1992. It oversees the implementation of the Rio Declaration, as well as Agenda 21, an environmental program deriving from the Earth Summit held in 1992.[40] These principles were reaffirmed by the World Summit on Sustainable Development held in Johannesburg, South Africa, September 2002. Sustainable consumption and production and energy for sustainable development are the recent foci of the Commission on Sustainable Development.[41] Energy utilization and the impact of energy utilization on the environment, including air pollution and global warming are of great concern to the UNEP and other agencies concerned with long-term effects of our production and consumption patterns on the environment.

### The Kyoto Protocol and Global Warming

The Kyoto Protocol was developed as a means of addressing climate change resulting from human activities.[42] The Kyoto Protocol was negotiated in 1997 and amends the United Nations Framework Convention on Climate Change, which was concluded at the Earth Summit in Rio de Janeiro in 1992. The Kyoto Protocol has the goal of reducing greenhouse gas emissions and mitigating global warming and consequent global climate change. *Global warming* is the phenomenon that the earth's atmosphere and oceans are increasing their average temperature.[43] These temperature changes are thought to result from human activities and their impact on the natural environment, particularly *greenhouse gas emissions*. Greenhouse gas emissions include the release of carbon dioxide, methane gas, nitrous oxide, ozone, hydrofluorocarbons, perfluorocarbons and sulfur hexafluoride. Greenhouse gas emissions result from, among other processes, the mining and combustion of fossil fuels. Reforestation reduces greenhouse gas emissions, because plants use carbon dioxide as a component of photosynthesis, and environmental strategies for climate control include reforestation programs. The impact of global warming is to reduce ice masses at the Artic and Antarctic, thus raising the sea level and increasing storm systems and flooding. Also as ocean temperatures rise, life forms in the sea can be affected.

The signatories to the Kyoto Protocol agreed that the industrialized nations will reduce greenhouse gas emissions to below 1990 levels by the year 2012.[44] The United States did not ratify the Kyoto Protocol, which came into force in February 2005. The Bush administration withdrew support for the Kyoto protocol in early 2001. President Bush criticized the Kyoto Protocol for failing to require LEDCs to curb greenhouse gas emissions. There may be some merit to this concern: for example, Russia ratified the Kyoto Protocol in November 2004, thereby creating the conditions for the Kyoto Protocol to come into force, as it did in February 2005. However, because of the collapse of the economies of many states of the former Soviet Union, Russia does not have to reduce its emissions and in fact may sell credits to other nations that are obligated under

the Kyoto Protocol to reduce their emissions.[45] Efforts for sustainable production methods become more urgent as the LEDCs undergo economic development and industrialization.

The Intergovernment Panel on Climate Change won the Noble Peace Prize
in 2007, shared with Vice President Al Gore.[46] The Intergovernment Panel on
Climate Change issues reports on climate change that "created an ever-broader
informed consensus about the connection between human activities and global
warming. Thousands of scientists and officials from over one hundred countries have collaborated to achieve greater certainty as to the scale of the warming." Al Gore wrote and promoted a book, *An Inconvenient Truth*, as well as an
earlier bestseller, *Earth in the Balance*; he was honored as a politician who raised
awareness and created social action to correct global warming.

*Cap and Trade*

Cap and trade is a system for managing enterprise and even a nation's carbon
footprint. Proposals for cap and trade were brought before the US Congress but
never passed. Instead, the EPA implemented regulations limiting greenhouse
gas emissions through its New Source Performance Standards; these standards
included rules for cross-state air pollution.[47] And in 2013, President Barack
Obama issued an executive order to create a task force of governors and mayors
to consider ways to deal with the impacts of climate change, such as extreme
weather, including 2012's Superstorm Sandy.[48] And in 2014, the United States
Supreme Court upheld the authority of the EPA to issues CO2 standards but
limited regulation to "stationary sources" that are already subject to EPA standards, and upheld its rules on cross-state air pollution.[49]

### Managing for the Triple Bottom Line: Environmental Reporting

An unintended, positive consequence of the Exxon Valdez spill was the development of the Valdez Principles for environmental management. The Valdez
Principles were later transformed into the CERES Principles (see Box 9.2).

---

**Box 9.2  The Ceres Principles**

Ceres was formed in 1989 as a groundbreaking partnership between leading
environmental groups and institutional investors. Ceres emerged just as the
Exxon Valdez oil spill in Alaska motivated the environmental and investor communities to push for higher standards of corporate environmental performance
and disclosure. In the fall of 1989, Ceres announced the creation of the Valdez
Principles (later renamed the Ceres Principles), a ten-point code of corporate
environmental conduct to be publicly endorsed by companies as an environmental mission statement or ethic.

Source: http://www.ceres.org/ceres/ (2004 website)

---

The Ceres Principles include: 1) protection of the biosphere; 2) sustainable use of resources; 3) reduction of waste; 4) energy conservation; 5) risk management and risk reduction; 6) production of products and services injuries, either to the environment or to people; 7) restoration of the environment; 8) notification to the public of environmental hazards and a policy of non-retaliation for employees who report unsafe conditions.[50] CERES developed the Global Reporting Initiative.[51]

## The Global Reporting Initiative

The Global Reporting Initiative (GRI) provides guidelines for companies to report on their triple bottom line, including economic, social and environmental indicators. Companies that subscribe to the CERES Principles engage in sustainability reporting. The CERES organization, in collaboration with the Association of Chartered Certified Accountants, an international accounting organization, recognize firms that have made an outstanding effort in sustainability reporting. This has since been developed into the Global Initiative for Sustainability Ratings, in partnership with the Tellus Institute.[52] The financial component of the triple bottom line has morphed into a governance standard.[53] Popularly, the triple bottom line is referred to as the 3 Ps: people, planet and profits.[54] The GRI thus explicitly uses a stakeholder approach.

## ISO 14000

The ISO has also developed standards for environmental management: ISO standard 14000.[55] Concern for and development of standards for environmental sustainability reporting have developed into a more general concern for corporate social responsibility and the development of transnational standards for corporate social responsibility. ISO, in cooperation with Global Reporting Initiative, has undertaken the development of Guidelines for Social Responsibility, ISO standard 26000.[56]

## Issues in Sustainability: Supply Chain/Product Sourcing

Concern with the negative impacts of production technologies on the environment have transformed into an affirmative concern for product sourcing. "Going green" is a corporate trend. For example, in 2004 The Conference Board sponsored a Conference on Business and Sustainability. Participants included DuPont, General Motors Corporation, Celanese Americas Company, Abbott Laboratories, Citigroup Inc., Starbucks Corporation, IBM, SwissRe, Mattel, Inc., BASF Corporation and 3M Company. General Electric launched a marketing campaign, "Eco-Imagination," promoting its environmental "green" initiatives.[57] Starbucks developed a program regarding product sourcing and pricing of its coffee. See Box 9.3.

## Box 9.3   Starbucks, Fair Trade and Coffee Social Responsibility

• **Starbucks and the Fair Trade movement share a common goal: to help ensure that farmers receive an equitable price for their coffee and strengthen their farms for the future.**

Purchasing Fair Trade Certified™ coffee is one of a number of ways Starbucks cultivates stable relationships with farmers. Additional steps include paying substantial premiums for all coffee purchases, long-term contracts and affordable credit for farmers, direct purchasing, investing in social projects in coffee communities, and C.A.F.E. Practices buying guidelines.

• **Starbucks is North America's largest purchaser of Fair Trade Certified™ coffee.**

In fiscal 2005, Starbucks purchased 11.5 million pounds of Fair Trade Certified™ coffee, compared to 4.8 million pounds in fiscal 2004. This represents approximately 10 per cent of global Fair Trade Certified™ coffee imports. In fiscal 2006, Starbucks plans to increase sales of our newly introduced Fair Trade product offerings and purchase 12 million pounds of Fair Trade Certified™ coffee.

• **Starbucks sells Fair Trade Certified coffee around the world.**

Starbucks is the only company licensed to sell Fair Trade Certified™ coffee in 23 countries, including Austria, Australia, Canada, China, France, Germany, Greece, Indonesia, Japan, Korea, Malaysia, New Zealand, Philippines, Singapore, Spain, Switzerland, Taiwan, Thailand, United Kingdom and the United States.

• **Starbucks is committed to paying equitable prices for *all* of our coffee. We do that to ensure that farmers make a profit and to encourage future production of high quality coffee.**

Starbucks pays premium prices that are substantially over and above the prevailing commodity-grade coffee prices. In fiscal 2003, when prices for commercial-grade *arabica* coffee ranged from $0.55-$0.70 per pound, Starbucks paid an average of $1.20 per pound for all of our coffee. In fiscal 2005, Starbucks paid an average price of $1.28 per pound, which was 23 percent higher than the average New York "C" market price during the same time frame.

- **Fair Trade Certified coffee is one part of a larger effort by Starbucks to be socially responsible in our relationships with coffee farmers and communities.**

Starbucks is committed to purchasing our coffee in an ethical and sustainable manner, regardless of labels and certifications. The Fair Trade system only certifies cooperatives of small-holder. family-owned farms, a system that currently produces about two percent of the world's coffee supply. The majority of the high-quality coffee Starbucks purchases is grown by farmers outside this system, many of whom are small-holders Fair Trade Certified™ coffee is one source of supply for our global coffee purchases.

- **Starbucks works with several organizations to make credit available to coffee growers, which enables them to postpone selling their crops until the price is favorable.**

In fiscal 2004. Starbucks committed $1 million to Calvert Foundation, $2.5 million to Verde Ventures, managed by Conservation International, and $2.5 million to EcoLogic Finance for loans to coffee farmers. And additional $2.5 million was provided to EcoLogic Finance in fiscal 2005, not only to extend loans to coffee farmers but also to cocoa farmers.

- **Starbucks is helping build schools, health clinics, coffee mills and other projects that benefit coffee communities.**

For many years, Starbucks and a number of farms have collaborated to help improve the quality of life for farming families and their communities. Starbucks provides funding for projects by adding a "social development premium" over and above the price of coffee purchased from participating farms. The farm often matches Starbucks contribution with its own investment to support the project. In fiscal 2005, Starbucks invested $1.5 million in 40 social projects that ranged from education programs in Nicaragua to a hospital renovation in Papua New Guinea.

*For more information about Starbucks sustainability practices, please review our Corporate Social Responsibility Annual Report at www.starbucks.com/ csrannualreport.*

Updated 3/07/06

Starbuck acts as a leading corporate citizen for responsible environmental management and stakeholder relations.

### *Sustainability Drives Technological Innovation*

The environmental impacts created by the utilization of fossil fuels, global warming, the political implications of dependency on oil imports, as well as cost pressures from oil prices, are providing the impetus for technological innovation and the development of new kinds and new sources for fuel. For example, the market for ethanol fuel is increasing. Technologies for the manufacture of ethanol already exist and new technologies for the manufacture of ethanol are being developed. Ethanol can be extracted from plant waste so that the food-providing parts of the plants are not destroyed in the ethanol manufacture process.[58] Other technologies are being developed for the extraction of ethanol from waste products collected from households and business.[59] Disposal of collected garbage, rather than being a cost to municipalities and companies such as Waste Management, may become an income-producing process.

Solar and wind power are being developed as green technologies, predominantly for electrical power generation. The efficiency of solar and wind generation of electricity is increasing and the costs are declining.[60]

Responsible environmental management can thus give rise to innovation, as well as opportunities for enterprise growth and new sources of revenue.

### *Sustainability and Product Pricing: The Bottom Line*

The issues of product sourcing, negative externalities and underpricing of goods and concern for sustainable consumption carry implications for consumers. Sustainability is concerned with the future; consistent with John Locke's recognition of the human right to private property, sustainability is grounded in an understanding that we are "stewards" of the earth and return our private property to the common pool of humanity on our deaths. There can be a conflict of interest among roles played by individuals: consumers value low price, workers want job security and citizens value quality of life and ecology. The ethical standard of universalizability challenges the developed, industrialized countries and their corporations to convert their non-sustainable methods of production and consumption to sustainable methods of production and consumption.

## Chapter Discussion Questions

1. Was the failure to manage Hurricane Katrina as a high-probability/high-impact event an ethical breach to some stakeholders? If so, which stakeholders? Justify your answer.
2. Did BP violate the Clean Water Act? If so, what actions of BP violated the Clean Water Act?
3. If property is owned by a person, either an individual or a corporation, why shouldn't they be permitted to do whatever they want to that property? What are the limits to property rights?
4. What is global warming? How is global warming caused? Debate whether human activities, particularly related to economic development, cause global warming?

5.  What is meant by "carbon footprint"? What is meant by carbon trading? Debate the merits of carbon trading.
6.  Debate whether it is fair to require LEDCs to conform to current standards in sustainability, whereas the economically developed world was not subject to these standards during its period of economic development.

## Notes

1   See Jonathan L. Ramseur, *Oil Spills in U.S. Coastal Waters: Background and Governance*, Congressional Research Office, January 11, 2012, http://www.fas.org/sgp/crs/misc/RL33705.pdf.

2   National Response Team, *The Exxon Valdez Oil Spill: A Report to the President: Executive Summary*, Environmental Protection Agency, May 1989, http://www2.epa.gov/aboutepa/exxon-valdez-oil-spill-report-president-executive-summary. Also, view *Dead Ahead: The Exxon Valdez Disaster*, directed by Paul Seed (HBO Films, 1992), http://www.youtube.com/watch?v=bXtsB4Go0hg.

3   The story of the BP Oil Well blowout was the subject of the end of chapter case for Chapter 2 on stakeholder management. See also, "Oil Spill Fast Facts," *CNN Library*, last modified April 8, 2014, http://www.cnn.com/2013/07/13/world/oil-spills-fast-facts/index.html. The greatest oil spill was the deliberate dumping of oil into the Persian Gulf by Iraqi armed forces during the 1991 Gulf War.

4   "The Chernobyl reactors are of the RBMK type. These are high-power, pressure-tube reactors, moderated with graphite and cooled with water."

"To stop the fire and prevent a criticality accident as well as further substantial release of fission products, boron and sand were dumped on the reactor from the air. In addition, the damaged unit was entombed in a concrete 'sarcophagus,' to limit further release of radioactive material."

"U.S. reactors have different plant designs, broader shutdown margins, robust containment structures, and operational controls to protect them against the combination of lapses that led to the accident at Chernobyl."

"Backgrounder on Chernobyl Nuclear Power Plant Accident," *United States Nuclear Regulatory Commission*, last modified Apr. 25, 2014, http://www.nrc.gov/reading-rm/doc-collections/fact-sheets/chernobyl-bg.html.

5   "The accident at the Three Mile Island Unit 2 (TMI-2) nuclear power plant near Middletown, Pennsylvania, on March 28, 1979, was the most serious in U.S. commercial nuclear power plant operating history, even though it led to no deaths or injuries to plant workers or members of the nearby community. But it brought about sweeping changes involving emergency response planning, reactor operator training, human factors engineering, radiation protection, and many other areas of nuclear power plant operations. It also caused the U.S. Nuclear Regulatory Commission to tighten and heighten its regulatory oversight. "Three Mile Island Accident," *United States Nuclear Regulatory Commission*, last modified 2014, http://www.nrc.gov/reading-rm/doc-collections/fact-sheets/3mile-isle.pdf.

6   Fumiya Tanabe, "Analysis of Core Melt Accident in Fukushima Daiichi-Unit 1 Nuclear Reactor," *Journal of Nuclear Science and Technology* 18, no. 8 (2011): 1135–39.

7  James M. Acton and Mark Hibbs, Why Fukushima Was Preventable, (Washington, DC: Carnegie Foundation for Peace, March 6, 2012), http://carnegieendowment.org/files/fukushima.pdf. This report serves as the end of chapter case for this chapter.

8  See Dan Kurzman, *A Killing Wind: Inside Union Carbide and the Bhopal Catastrophe* (New York: McGraw-Hill, 1987).

9  "In 2001, the Federal Emergency Management Agency ranked a major hurricane strike on New Orleans as 'among the three likeliest, most catastrophic disasters facing this country,' directly behind a terrorist strike on New York City." See "How Not to Prepare for a Hurricane," *The Progress Report*, Aug. 30, 2005, http://www.alternet.org/story/24799.

10  The National Environment Policy Act (NEPA) and a Review of MMS NEPA Documents Prepared for the National Commission on BP Deepwater Horizon Oil Spill and Offshore Drilling, October 19, 2010, report developed by Meg Caldwell, Executive Director of the Center for Ocean Solutions, Debbie Sivas, Luke W. Cole Professor of Environmental Law and Director of the Stanford Environmental Law Clinic, and Kimiko Narita (Stanford J.D./M.S. '11), research assistant at the Center for Ocean Solutions, http://energyseminar.stanford.edu/sites/all/files/eventpdf/The%20National%20Environmental%20Policy%20Act%20(NEPA)%20and%20a%20Review%20of%20MMS%20NEPA%20Documents.pdf.

11  "Dinosaur Extinction," *National Geographic*, last modified 2014, http://science.nationalgeographic.com/science/prehistoric-world/dinosaur-extinction/.

12  The unintended ecological effects of consumption patterns is a reason why the United Nations Environmental Programme and other related agencies emphasize sustainable consumption, as well as sustainable production.

13  Rachel Carson, *Silent Spring* (Boston: Houghton Mifflin Company, The Riverside Press: 1962).

14  *Disappearing Delta Overview*:
"Three years ago this month, NOW presented a two-part story on the disappearance of the Mississippi River delta. 'Losing Ground,' uncovered how one of the biggest civil engineering projects in U.S. history—the leveeing of the Mississippi River—had brought Louisiana and the nation to the brink of what could be the most costly environmental disaster in history. In 'The City in a Bowl,' NOW examined another ominous effect of this crisis—the risk that a massive hurricane could drown New Orleans. Hurricane Katrina has now made these predictions a reality."
See Transcript, "City in a Bowl," *NOW with Bill Moyers*, PBS.org, Sept. 20, 2002, http://www.pbs.org/now/transcript/transcript_neworleans.html. See also Transcript, "Losing Ground," *NOW with Bill Moyers*, PBS.org, Sept. 26, 2002, http://www.pbs.org/now/transcript/transcript_delta.html and "New Orleans and the Delta," *NOW with Bill Moyers*, PBS.org, Sept. 2, 2005, http://www.pbs.org/now/science/neworleans.html.

15  Eric Berger, "Keeping Its Head above Water: New Orleans Faces Doomsday Scenario," *Houston Chronicle*, Dec. 1, 2001. See also Eric Lincoln, "Old Plans Revived for Category 5 Hurricane Protection," *United States Army Corps of Engineers*, Sept.–Oct. 2004. A category five hurricane was considered a 1 in 500-year-event.

16  Free goods are defined by Samuelson and Nordhaus as: "Those goods that are not economic goods. Like air or seawater, they exist in such large quantities that they need not be rationed out among those wishing to use them. Thus, their market price is zero." Economic goods are defined as: "A good that is scarce relative to the total

amount of it that is desired. It must therefore be rationed, usually by charging a positive price." Paul A. Samuelson and William D. Nordhaus, *Economics*, 18th ed. (Boston: Irwin/McGraw-Hill, 1998).

17  Paul Hawken, *Growing a Business* (New York: Simon and Schuster, 1987); Paul Hawken, *The Ecology of Commerce* (New York: HarperCollins, 1993); and Paul Hawken, Amory Lovins, and L. Hunter Lovins, *The Ecology of Commerce, Natural Capitalism: Creating the Next Industrial Revolution* (New York: Little, Brown and Company, 1999). See also *Paul Hawken*, last modified 2010, http://www.paulhawken.com.

18  This definition of natural capitalism is given by Paul Hawken, Amory Lovins and L. Hunter Lovins at their website, *Natural Capitalism*, last modified 2014, http://www.natcap.org/. See also Hawken, Lovins, and Lovins, *Natural Capitalism*.

19  See Annual Report filed by PG&E Corporation for fiscal year 2005, filed with SEC on Feb. 17, 2006, at http://pcg.client.shareholder.com/investors/financial_reports/EdgarDetail.cfm?CompanyID=PCG&CIK=75488&FID=1004980–06–67&SID=06–00&filings=UTILITY&formchoose=insider#FORM10K_HTM_COMPRESSORSTATIONCHROMIUMLITIGATION. See also Marc Lifsher, "PG&E's Toxic Plume Creeps Toward L.A. Water Supply," *LA Times*, Mar. 6, 2004. The toxic contamination in Hinkley, California, is dramatized in the movie *Erin Brockovich*, directed by Steven Soderbergh (Universal Pictures, 2000).

20  See the EPA description of the Woburn, Massachusetts, Superfund site cleanup, at "Waste Site Cleanup and Reuse in New England," *United States Environmental Protection Agency*, last modified Sept. 23, 2013, http://yosemite.epa.gov/r1/npl_pad.nsf/f52fa5c31fa8f5c885256adc0050b631/1E8F7D6FFCD9B61B85256A0F00067136?OpenDocument. The toxic contamination in Woburn, Massachusetts was dramatized in the movie *A Civil Action*, directed by Steven Zaillian (Touchstone Pictures, 1998).

21  "A Chinese city of 3.8 million people closed schools and was trucking in drinking water Wednesday after shutting down its water system following a chemical plant explosion that officials said polluted a nearby river with toxic benzene.

   An explosion on Nov. 13 at a chemical plant in the nearby city of Jilin left the Songhua River, Harbin's main water source, polluted with benzene, a toxic, flammable liquid, the government said.

   Russian television reports said Wednesday that concern was growing over the pollution threat in the border city of Khabarovsk, about 700 kilometers down river from Harbin on the Songhua.

   "Chinese City Shuts off Water after Toxic Spill," *The Moscow Times*, Nov. 24, 2005, http://www.moscowtimes.ru/stories/2005/11/24/251.html.

22  "Russia plans to cut off drinking water supplies from River Amur to its far eastern city of Khabarovsk, which is threatened by a toxic benzene spill in China.

   Oleg Mitvol with the Russian environmental agency told the BBC heating would not be affected but tap water would be cut for a few days. He said fish from the Amur also would be contaminated.

   Chinese officials say they expect the spill to take two weeks to reach the Amur River. China's Songhua River flows into the Amur River separating China and Russia."

   "Russia braces for Chinese water pollution," United Press International, Nov. 24, 2005, http://www.sciencedaily.com/upi/?feed=TopNews&article=UPI-1–20051124–10464000-bc-russia-chinapollution-1stld.xml.

23  "Mountaintop mining is a form of surface coal mining in which explosives are used to access coal seams, generating large volumes of waste that bury adjacent

streams. The resulting waste that then fills valleys and streams can significantly compromise water quality, often causing permanent damage to ecosystems and rendering streams unfit for drinking, fishing, and swimming. It is estimated that almost 2,000 miles of Appalachian headwater streams have been buried by mountaintop coal mining." "2011 News Releases: EPA Issues Final Guidance to Protect Water Quality in Appalachian Communities from Impacts of Mountaintop Mining/Agency to provide flexibility while protecting environment and public health," *United States Environmental Protection Agency*, July 21, 2011, available at http://yosemite.epa.gov/opa/admpress.nsf/1e5ab1124055f3b28525781f0042ed40/1dabfc17944974d4852578d400561a13!OpenDocument. See also John McQuaid, "Mining the Mountains," *Smithsonian Magazine*, Jan. 2009, http://www.smithsonianmag.com/ecocenter-energy/mining-the-mountains-130454620/?no-ist. and "Beyond Coal: Destroying Mountains," *Sierra Club*, http://content.sierraclub.org/coal/mining-destroying-mountains.

24 The Clean Water Act amended the Federal Water Pollution Control Act of 1972.

25 However, in 2001, the Fourth Circuit Court of Appeals overturned the federal court ruling prohibiting coverage of streams; the fourth circuit ruled that the trial court did not have jurisdiction. The ruling left open the possibility that the practice could be appealed in state court. See James Dao, "Rule Change May Alter Strip-Mine Fight," *New York Times*, Jan. 26, 2004, http://www.nytimes.com/2004/01/26/national/26COAL.html. See also "Bush Administration Told by Congress and Court: Changing Environmental Rules to Allow Waste Dumps in Waters Violates the Clean Water Act," *EarthJustice*, May 8, 2002, http://www.earthjustice.org/news/display.html?ID=367.

26 Joby Warrick, "Appalachia Is Paying Price for White House Rule Change," *Washington Post*, Aug. 17, 2004, http://www.washingtonpost.com/wp-dyn/articles/A6462–2004Aug16.html. See also Dao, "Rule Change May Alter."

27 See for example, "Burying Valleys, Poisoning Streams," *New York Times*, Editorial of May 4, 2002, http://www.nytimes.com/2002/05/04/opinion/burying-valleys-poisoning-streams.html.

28 "Army Corps of Engineers Suspends Mountaintop Removal Mining Permits," *EarthJustice*, last modified June 8, 2006, http://www.earthjustice.org/news/press/2006/army-corps-of-engineers-suspends-mountaintop-removal-mining-permits.html. See also "Judge Rules Against Mountaintop Mining," *Associated Press/NBC News*, last modified June 14, 2007, http://www.nbcnews.com/id/19231612/#.U7CZqeLD_X4 and "Supreme Court Rejects Coal Industry Lawsuit, Defends EPA Veto of Mountaintop Removal Mine," *EarthJustice*, Mar. 24, 2014, http://www.democraticunderground.com/1014763706.

29 "Looking to the Future: Strategic Plan of the Commission for Environmental Cooperation 2005–2010," *Commission for Environmental Cooperation of North America*, last modified June 17, 2005, http://www.cec.org/pubs_docs/documents/index.cfm?varlan=english&ID=1761.

30 "The Lahore/Sialkot Declaration on Corporate Responsibility," *United Nations Environment Programme*, last modified Nov. 26, 2004, http://www.unep.org/Documents.Multilingual/Default.asp?DocumentID=412&ArticleID=4673&l=en.

31 Dr. Seuss, *The Lorax* (New York: Random House, 1971).

32 For information on Frenchman Flat, Nevada, the site of the first nuclear atmospheric test that took place in 1951, see Phil Garlington, "Nevada—Blasts From The Past:

Touring A-Bomb Test Site," *The Seattle Times*, Jan. 25, 1998 and "Photo Library: Nevada National Security Site," *United States Department of Energy*, last modified Feb. 20, 2014, http://www.nv.doe.gov/library/photos/nts.aspx.

33 "Backgrounder on Radioactive Waste," *United States Nuclear Regulatory Commission*, last modified June 27, 2014, http://www.nrc.gov/reading-rm/doc-collections/fact-sheets/radwaste.html. See also "Hanford Nuclear Waste Cleanup Plant May Be Too Dangerous; Safety Issues Make Plans to Clean up a Mess Left Over from the Construction of the U.S. Nuclear Arsenal Uncertain," *Scientific American*, May 9, 2013.

34 "Topic: Yucca Mountain," *Las Vegas Sun*, last modified June 29, 2014, http://www.lasvegassun.com/news/topics/yucca-mountain/.

35 Ken Silverstein, "Nuclear Waste Will Never Be Laid to Rest at Yucca Mountain," *Forbes*, Aug. 24, 2013.

36 A global social movement on the environment occurred at this time, as discussed above earlier in this chapter, as well as in Chapters 5 and 7.

37 "Agenda 21," *United Nations Environment Programme*, last modified 2014, http://www.unep.org/Documents.Multilingual/Default.asp?DocumentID=52.

38 This happened, as discussed above by the environmental spill in China, which affected Russia down river.

39 The Chernobyl explosion spread a nuclear cloud over Europe, and in fact, the Russians failed to disclose the Chernobyl nuclear accident. Its occurrence was discovered by an air monitoring station in Scandinavia. "Soviet Minds Sheltered From Catastrophes," *New York Times*, Editorial of May 15, 1986.

40 "AGENDA 21 United Nations Conference on Environment & Development," Rio de Janeiro, Brazil, June 3–14, 1992, United Nations Sustainable Development Knowledge Platform, http://sustainabledevelopment.un.org/content/documents/Agenda21.pdf.

41 "Trends in Sustainable Development," 2006, United Nations Sustainable Development Knowledge Platform, http://sustainabledevelopment.un.org/content/documents/trends_rpt2006.pdf.

42 Its full title is the Kyoto Protocol to the United Nations Framework Convention on Climate Change.

43 "Global Warming," Wikipedia, last modified June 27, 2014, http://en.wikipedia.org/wiki/Global_warming.

44 "Kyoto Protocol to the United Nations Framework Convention on Climate Change," United Nations Framework Convention on Climate Change, last modified 2014, http://unfccc.int/resource/docs/convkp/kpeng.html.

45 "Kyoto Protocol," United Nations Framework Convention on Climate Change, last modified 2014, http://unfccc.int/kyoto_protocol/items/2830.php.

46 O. Edenhofer et al., eds., "IPCC, 2014: Summary for Policymakers," Climate Change 2014, Mitigation of Climate Change. Contribution of Working Group III to the Fifth Assessment Report of the Intergovernmental Panel on Climate Change (New York: Cambridge University Press, 2014).

47 Brad Plumer, "Is U.S. Climate Policy Better Off Without Cap-and-Trade?," *Washington Post*, Oct. 25, 2012.

48 Federal Leadership in Environmental, Energy and Economic Performance—Exec. Order No. 13,514 (Oct. 25, 2009), http://www.whitehouse.gov/administration/eop/ceq/sustainability.

49  *Utility Air Regulatory Group v. Environmental Protection Agency,* _ U.S. _ (2014). See
    Adam Liptak, "Justices Uphold Emission Limits on Big Industry," *New York Times,*
    June 23, 2014.
50  Ceres.org, last modified 2014, http://www.ceres.org/ceres/.
51  Global Reporting Initiative, last modified 2014, https://www.globalreporting.org/
    Pages/default.aspx.
52  "Global Initiative for Sustainability Ratings: Harnessing Sustainability Ratings to
    Move Markets," Ceres.org, last modified 2014, http://www.ceres.org/about-us/
    the-global-initiative-for-sustainability-ratings.
53  "About GISR: Vision and Mission," Global Initiative for Sustainability Ratings, last
    modified 2014, http://ratesustainability.org/about/.
54  See for example, the Net Impact national conference in San Jose, CA, Oct. 2013,
    https://netimpact.org/netimpactconference.
55  "ISO 14000—Environmental Management," International Organization for Standard-
    ization, last modified 2014, http://www.iso.org/iso/home/standards/management-
    standards/iso14000.htm. See also "Management System Standards," International
    Organization for Standardization, last modified 2014, http://www.iso.org/iso/home/
    standards/management-standards.htm.
56  See International Organization for Standardization, last modified 2014, http://www.
    iso.org/iso/en/info/Conferences/SRConference/home.htm. ISO standard 26000 is a
    guidance standard only, and not certified by third-party audits.
57  "GE Goes Green," *Forbes,* Aug. 15, 2005. See also "Ecomagination," General Electric,
    last modified 2014, http://ge.ecomagination.com/@v=06012006_1843@/index.html.
58  Source: David Evans, "High Oil Propels Biofuels into Global Mainstream," Reuters,
    June 9, 2006, http://today.reuters.com/news/newsArticle.aspx?type=reutersEdge&st
    oryID=2006-06-09T082528Z_01_L08103403_RTRUKOC_0_US-FOOD-BIOFU-
    ELS-WORLD.xml&pageNumber=4&imageid=&cap=&sz=13&WTModLoc=News
    Art-C1-ArticlePage4.
59  "Co-Production of Ethanol and Electricity from Waste," Green Car Congress: Energy,
    Technologies, Issues and Policies for Sustainable Mobility, last modified June 9, 2005,
    http://www.greencarcongress.com/2005/06/coproduction_of.html.
60  Steven B. Smiley, "Wind and Solar Energy Beats Fracking," Cleveland.com, Feb. 8,
    2014, http://www.cleveland.com/opinion/index.ssf/2014/02/wind_an_solar_energy_
    beats_fra.html. See also Joel Hruska, "New Solar Power Plant Is the First to
    Go 'Supercritical', but Solar's Long-Term Cost and Efficiency Still Questioned,"
    *Extreme Tech,* June 17, 2014, http://www.extremetech.com/extreme/184501-new-
    solar-power-plant-is-the-first-to-go-supercritical-but-solars-long-term-cost-and-
    efficiency-still-questioned.

## End of Chapter Case

### The Carnegie Papers

#### *Why Fukushima Was Preventable*

*James M. Acton and Mark Hibbs*

NUCLEAR POLICY MARCH 2012

## Carnegie Endowment

*For International Peace*

WASHINGTON DC • MOSCOW • BEIJING • BEIRUT • BRUSSELS

## Introduction

The accident at Fukushima Daiichi Nuclear Power Station on March 11, 2011, has put safety concerns front and center of the ever-contentious debate about nuclear energy. With large quantities of radioactivity released into the environment, over three hundred thousand residents evacuated from the vicinity of the plants,[1] and a cleanup operation that will take decades and cost tens, if not hundreds of billions of dollars, critics have argued that nuclear power is too dangerous to be acceptable. But are they right? Can nuclear power be made significantly safer? The answer depends in no small part on whether nuclear power plants are inherently susceptible to uncommon but extreme external events or whether it is possible to predict such hazards and defend against them.

To date, there have been three severe accidents at civilian nuclear power plants. Two of these led to significant releases of radiation, which averages out to about one major release every seven thousand five hundred years of reactor operation. The International Atomic Energy Agency's (IAEA's) International Nuclear Safety Group believes that if best practices are implemented, major releases of radiation from existing nuclear power plants should occur about fifteen times less frequently.[2] Indeed, improvement on this scale is probably necessary for nuclear power to gain widespread social and political acceptance.

It is clear that the two major nuclear accidents before Fukushima— Chernobyl in 1986 and Three Mile Island in 1979 (which involved extensive damage to nuclear fuel but a relatively small release of radiation)—were preventable. In each case the cause was inadequate operator training and flaws in reactor design, exacerbated by inadequate understanding of potential risks. Better training and better design (areas in which the global nuclear industry has made significant strides) should prevent a recurrence of similar events.

By contrast, the Fukushima accident—superficially at least—appears to be very different. The plant was hit by a massive earthquake and then a tsunami, triggering a chain of events that led to fuel melting and a significant off-site release of radiation. The accident has reinforced public sentiment worldwide— from Japan to Switzerland, and Germany to India—that nuclear power is unacceptably risky.

One year after the Fukushima accident, however, a picture is emerging that suggests that the calamity was not simply an "act of god" that could not be defended against. There is a growing body of evidence that suggests the accident was the result of failures in regulation and nuclear plant design and that both were lagging behind international best practices and standards. Had these been heeded and applied, the risks to the Fukushima Daiichi Nuclear Power Station would likely have been recognized and effective steps to prevent a major accident could have been taken. In this sense, we believe the Fukushima accident—like its predecessors—was preventable.

## The Accident Sequence

On March II, 2011, at 2:46 pm local time, Japan was struck by a magnitude 9.0 earthquake, centered in the Pacific Ocean about 80 kilometers east of the city of Sendai, that set a powerful tsunami in motion.[3] This was the largest earthquake ever recorded in Japan and, according to the United States Geological Survey, the fourth largest recorded worldwide since 1900.[4]

Three of the six reactor units at Fukushima Daiichi Nuclear Power Station (units 1, 2, and 3) were operating at the time and are shown schematically in Figure 9.1.

When the earthquake hit, these units automatically "scrammed," that is, control rods were inserted into the reactor cores to suppress nuclear fission. Nonetheless, the reactors still required cooling—as all reactors do immediately after shutdown, since the highly radioactive material accumulated during operation continues to decay and produce heat.

With the reactor shut down and the plant no longer generating electricity, the post-shutdown cooling systems at the Fukushima Daiichi reactors, like at all currently operating power reactors, required an alternative electricity supply (although there was one system in each reactor that did have limited functionality in the absence of a power supply).[5] Because all six external power lines from Japan's grid to the plant were destroyed by the earthquake,

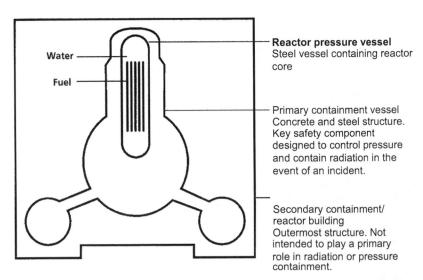

*Figure 9.1* Highly simplified schematic diagram of a boiling water reactor defining key terms used in this report. Many important components, including those for converting steam to electricity, are not shown. Not drawn to scale.

the on-site emergency diesel generators began operating. With electricity still available, cooling appeared to proceed normally in units 2 and 3 before the tsunami arrived. In unit 1, for reasons that are not yet known, the temperature and pressure of the core dropped unexpectedly quickly. In order to avoid damage to the reactor vessel and in keeping with the plant's operating procedure, operators turned the emergency cooling system on and off repeatedly to slow the rate of cooling. The system happened to be disabled at the time all electrical power to the plant was lost following the tsunami.[6] Had it been operating, the subsequent accident sequence may have unfolded more slowly at unit 1.[7]

About forty-five minutes after the earthquake, the station was inundated by a series of tsunami waves that caused serious damage. Eleven of the twelve emergency diesel generators in service at the time failed (one connected to unit 6 worked) as they required water cooling, which was no longer possible because the tsunami had destroyed the sea water pumps. This resulted in the complete loss of AC power from both internal and external sources for units 1–5, a situation that is known as a station blackout. The plants were equipped with DC batteries to compensate for the station blackout; however, the batteries in units 1 and 2 were flooded and rendered inoperable.

> Regulatory deficiencies in Japan were ultimately rooted in the lack of accountability in Japan's "nuclear culture" and in low tolerance in Japanese society for challenging authority.

The batteries in unit 3 continued to function for about thirty hours—far beyond their eight-hour design life. In addition, the power distribution buses that would have allowed an external power source to be connected to the plant were also swamped and extensively damaged.[8] The seawater pumps and their motors, which were responsible for transferring heat extracted from the reactor cores to the ocean (the so-called "ultimate heat sink") and also for cooling most of the emergency diesel generators, were built at a lower elevation than the reactor buildings. They were flooded and completely destroyed. Thus, even if electricity had been available to drive the emergency cooling systems, there would have been no way of dissipating the heat.

Over the next three days, one by one, the three reactors that had been operating when the earthquake struck lost core cooling capability, resulting in a loss of coolant accident: without cooling, the water in the reactor pressure vessels boiled, uncovering the fuel, which subsequently melted. In this situation, there was a risk that the "corium" (the molten mix of fuel and reactor components) could burn through the steel reactor pressure vessel and the concrete and steel primary containment vessel into the earth below, thus increasing the likely quantity of radiation released into the environment. Simulations by the plant's owner, Tokyo Electric Power Company (TEPCO), performed with extremely conservative assumptions, suggest that even in the absolute worst case where corium burned through the reactor pressure vessels in all three of the damaged units at Fukushima Daiichi, it would not have completely penetrated the containment (although in unit 1 it could have come within 37 centimeters, or 15 inches, of the outer steel lining).[9] Other simulations suggest that although fuel may have melted and collected at the base of the pressure vessel, it did not burn through.[10] It bears emphasizing, however, that the exact extent of the damage will only be known when the pressure vessels and primary containments can be observed directly, several years from now.

A large quantity of radioactivity from the damaged fuel escaped into the environment. As cooling water evaporated and turned into steam, pressure inside the primary containment grew, creating leaks that allowed radiation to escape. More radiation was deliberately released when, after some delays, workers "vented" the containments to try to reduce the internal pressure. Yet more radiation was released by a series of explosions that occurred in the reactor buildings of units 1, 3, and 4 in the four days following the tsunami. As the reactors overheated and the fuel melted, highly flammable hydrogen was generated (mostly by a reaction between steam and zirconium "cladding" that surrounds the fuel). It built up in the reactor buildings of units 1 and 3 before eventually exploding. Hydrogen may also have caused an explosion in unit 4 after it migrated there from unit 3 along their common venting system.[11]

In its June 2011 report to the IAEA explaining the accident, the Japanese government estimated that the quantity of radiation released into the atmosphere by the accident was about 15 percent of the radiation released from Chernobyl. That accident resulted in the permanent evacuation of over 200,000 people and is ultimately likely to result in thousands of "excess" cancer cases.[12] For many days, Soviet authorities were unable to prevent the uninterrupted release of large amounts of radiation after a severe explosion inside the reactor core directly exposed its burning fuel to the environment. By contrast, at Fukushima considerably more of the fuel inventory in the cores was contained, and Japanese authorities were able to far more quickly and effectively limit the accident's impact to human health. In any case, the quantity of radiation released by the Fukushima accident has proved controversial and estimates may change as more information becomes available. A much smaller quantity of radiation was released into the Pacific Ocean, most of it in the form of overflow of contaminated water that had been used to cool the reactors.

On December 16, 2011, Japanese officials announced that the plant had been brought into a state of "cold shutdown." This declaration attracted criticism from some reactor safety experts on the grounds that it gives the false impression that the damaged Fukushima Daiichi units now pose no more risk than any undamaged reactor after shutdown. While there is certainly some truth to this criticism, the declaration is reasonable if it is understood to be a judgment call on the part of the plant's owner and officials that the remains of the plant cores are now being stably cooled, that radioactive emissions have been brought down to near acceptable levels, and that, barring an unforeseen accident, the status quo can be maintained indefinitely.

With appropriate foresight by Japan's authorities and industry, it appears that the accident could have been avoided or prevented.

Nonetheless, complete remediation of the site is likely to take three or four decades, and the biggest challenge will probably be removing all the melted fuel. The road to complete recovery will be an extremely long and expensive one.

## Summary

Public sentiment in many states has turned against nuclear energy following the March 2011 accident at Japan's Fukushima Daiichi Nuclear Power Station. The large quantity of radioactive material released has caused significant human suffering and rendered large stretches of land uninhabitable. The cleanup operation will take decades and may cost hundreds of billions of dollars.

The Fukushima accident was, however, preventable. Had the plant's owner, Tokyo Electric Power Company (TEPCO), and Japan's regulator, the Nuclear and Industrial Safety Agency (NISA), followed international best practices and standards, it is conceivable that they would have predicted the possibility of the plant being struck by a massive tsunami. The plant would have withstood the tsunami had its design previously been upgraded in accordance with state-of-the-art safety approaches.

The methods used by TEPCO and NISA to assess the risk from tsunamis lagged behind international standards in at least three important respects:

- Insufficient attention was paid to evidence of large tsunamis inundating the region surrounding the plant about once every thousand years.
- Computer modeling of the tsunami threat was inadequate. Most importantly, preliminary simulations conducted in 2008 that suggested the tsunami risk to the plant had been seriously underestimated were not followed up and were only reported to NISA on March 7, 2011.
- NISA failed to review simulations conducted by TEPCO and to foster the development of appropriate computer modeling tools.

At the time of the accident, critical safety systems in nuclear power plants in some countries, especially in European states, were—as a matter of course—much better protected than in Japan. Following a flooding incident at Blayais Nuclear Power Plant in France in 1999, European countries significantly enhanced their plants' defenses against extreme external events. Japanese operators were aware of this experience, and TEPCO could and should have upgraded Fukushima Daiichi.

Steps that could have prevented a major accident in the event that the plant was inundated by a massive tsunami, such as the one that struck the plant in March 2011, include:

- Protecting emergency power supplies, including diesel generators and batteries, by moving them to higher ground or by placing them in watertight bunkers;
- Establishing watertight connections between emergency power supplies and key safety systems; and

- Enhancing the protection of seawater pumps (which were used to transfer heat from the plant to the ocean and to cool diesel generators) and/**or** constructing a backup means to dissipate heat.

Though there is no single reason for TEPCO and NISNs failure to follow international best practices and standards, a number of potential underlying causes can be identified. NISA lacked independence from both the government agencies responsible for promoting nuclear power and also from industry. In the Japanese nuclear industry, there has been a focus on seismic safety to the exclusion of other possible risks. Bureaucratic and professional stovepiping made nuclear officials unwilling to take advice from experts outside of the field. Those nuclear professionals also may have failed to effectively utilize local knowledge. And, perhaps most importantly, many believed that a severe accident was simply impossible.

In the final analysis, the Fukushima accident does not reveal a previously unknown fatal flaw associated with nuclear power. Rather, it underscores the importance of periodically reevaluating plant safety in light of dynamic external threats and of evolving best practices, as well as the need for an effective regulator to oversee this process.

## Notes

1 Reconstruction Unit Secretariat, "Report on the Number of Evacuees Across the Country, Prefectural and Other Refugees," February 1, 2012, www.reconstruction. go.jp/topics/20120201zenkoku-hinansyasu.pdf.

2 International Nuclear Safety Advisory Group, "Basic Safety Principles for Nuclear Power Plants," 75-INSAG-3 Rev. 1, 1999, www-pub.iaea.org/MTCD/publications/ PDF/P082_scr.pdf, para 27.

3 The description of the accident presented in this section is largely drawn from the IAEA report on Fukushima, except where otherwise stated. IAEA, "IAEA International Fact Finding Expert Mission of the Fukushima Daiichi NPP Accident Following the Great East Japan Earthquake and Tsunami," June 16, 2011, www-pub. iaea.org/MTCD/meetings/PDFplus/2011/cn200/documentation/cn200_Final-Fukushima-Mission_Report.pdf.

4 U.S. Geological Survey, "Largest Earthquakes in the World Since 1900," http:// earthquake.usgs.gov/earthquakes/world/10_largest_world.php.

5 The systems with limited functionality in the absence of power were an isolation condenser (in unit 1) and a reactor core isolation cooling (RCIC) system (in units 2 and 3). An isolation condenser takes steam from the reactor core, passes it through a tank of water to cool and condense it, and then feeds it back as water into the reactor pressure vessel. The flow is gravity driven (i.e., no pumps are needed). The system in unit 1 had a thermal capacity of about eight hours. RCICs use steam from the core to drive a turbine and pump that replenishes the water in the pressure vessel. Although electricity is not required to drive pumps in either an isolation condenser or an RCIC, it is needed for instrumentation and to open and close the valves used for control. Moreover, RCICs will only function if the steam is above a certain pressure. In addition to an IC or RCIC, all units at Fukushima Daiichi contained various cooling systems that did require electricity. One of these, the HPCI (high-pressure

coolant injection) system was activated in unit 3 (where some battery power was available) after the RCIC in that unit had failed.

6   Institute of Nuclear Power Operators (INPO), "Special Report on the Nuclear Accident at the Fukushima Daiichi Nuclear Power Station," INPO 11-005, revision 0, November 2011, www.nei.org/filefolder/11_005_Special_Report_on_Fukushima_Daiichi_MASTER_11_08_11_1.pdf, 14.

7   According to one experienced nuclear power regulator, the fail-safe position for the relevant valves was closed, i.e., the isolation condenser was designed to be disabled in the event that control of the valves was lost. In this case, the state of the valves just prior to station blackout may have been immaterial. Personal communication, February 2012.

8   TEPCO, "Fukushima Daiichi Nuclear Power Station: Response After Earthquake," June 18, 2011, www.tepco.co.jp/en/press/corp-com/release/betu11_e/images/1106 18e15.pdf, 4.

9   Justin McCurry, "Fukushima Fuel Rods May Have Completely Melted," Guardian, December 2, 2011, www.guardian.co.uk/world/2011/dec/02/fukushima-fuel-rodscompletely-melted.

10  INPO, "Special Report on the Nuclear Accident at the Fukushima Daiichi Nuclear Power Station," 9–10.

11  TEPCO, "Fukushima Nuclear Accident Analysis Report," summary of interim report, December 2, 2011, www.tepco.co.jp/en/press/corp-com/release/betu11_e/images/111202e13.pdf, 10.

12  This includes $1.6 \times 10^{17}$ Bq of I-131 and $1.5 \times 10^{16}$ Bq of Cs-137 leading to a total emission of $7.6 \times 10^{17}$ Bq I-131 equivalent. By comparison, the total emission from Chernobyl was $5.2 \times 10^{18}$ Bq I-131 equivalent. Nuclear Emergency Response Headquarters, Government of Japan, "Report of the Japanese Government to the IAEA Ministerial Conference on Nuclear Safety: The Accident at TEPCO's Fukushima Nuclear Power Stations," June 2011, available from www.iaea.org/newscenter/focus/fukushima/japan-report, VI–1.

## Case Discussion Questions

1.   Identify the cultural factors related to the failure of TEPCO to manage the risks of a nuclear plant meltdown.

2.   Do you agree that the Fukushima plant meltdown was preventable? Support your conclusion with evidence.

3.   What changes need to be made to nuclear power plants to prevent disasters such as Fukushima, Chernobyl and Three Mile Island?

4.   What are the lessons learned for the management of other natural disasters, such as Superstorm Sandy?

# 10 Relationship of the Enterprise to Its Employees

## Chapter Outline

## Chapter Introduction

Employees are a key stakeholder of business enterprise. It is the work of production employees and the chain of managerial command that creates enterprise output. Employees seek voice in the employer–employee relationship. Although labor markets are highly regulated in industrialized economies, a new social contract between employees and their employing company is evolving. Moreover the utilization of alternative work arrangements has emerged as a common business practice. Knowledge workers are key employees in the increasingly service-based economies of industrialized nations. Ethical management of employees requires that employers do not discriminate against their employees and meet other legal requirements affecting their relationship with employees.

## Chapter Goal and Learning Objectives

*Chapter Goal:* To understand the role of employees as enterprise stakeholders.

*Learning Objectives:*

1. Discuss employees as the labor factor of production.
2. Understand the evolution of labor market regulation in terms of labor history and the major laws regulating labor markets.
3. Explain the principle of non-discrimination in employment, and debate the role of affirmative action in employment.
4. Explain the role of the knowledge workers and debate the role of contingent workers in the new world of work.
5. Compare and contrast the new social contract to the old social contract.

## Employees as Stakeholders

Employees represent the labor factor of production of a firm. Employees are responsible for the production of enterprise output. Employees are, therefore, key stakeholders of enterprise. As stakeholders, employees seek a voice and influence in the employer–employee relationship. A component of ethical management requires managers to attend to the design of their work systems and how those work systems affect employees. The management of production employees is the responsibility of line management. The assumptions that managers make about the nature and character of their employees, such as McGregor's Theory X and Theory Y, affect how managers deal with employees.[1] For example, Chris Argyris has criticized the task-oriented management style and highly specialized design of jobs often used in mass production systems. Argyris' critique is that close supervision style and narrow, repetitive job design are incompatible with the needs of a mature personality.[2] New models of job design have been developed that better meet the needs of production workers for achievement.[3] Moreover, Peter Senge advocates management systems that promote "learning organizations."[4] Such management systems not only better meet the needs of employees but also promote enterprise competitiveness.

### From High-Volume to High-Value Work Systems

The Industrial Revolution was based on the creation of high-volume work systems. Alvin Toffler, in his book *The Third Wave*,[5] offers an explanation of the infrastructure underlying the Industrial Revolution. He titled his understanding, "The Code of the Second Wave."[6] Toffler refers to the Industrial Revolution as "the Second Wave." The rise of manufacturing began in about 1800 in Europe and the United States. At first, goods were manufactured by handicraft production by skilled artisans. The Industrial Revolution occurred in Europe and the United Sates about 1850. The Industrial Revolution represents a transition to capital-intensive, mass production of goods. According to Toffler, the schema of the Industrial Revolution includes production based on: 1) standardization, 2) specialization, 3) synchronization, 4) concentration, 5) maximization, and 6) centralization. *Standardization of parts* is the basis of mass production. Mass production involves high-volume production of goods based on standardized, interchangeable parts. Instead of craft-workers making a whole good, mass production is based on *specialization of labor*: workers engage in narrow, repetitive jobs. Specialization of labor increases productivity, as noted and advocated by Adam Smith in *The Wealth of Nations*. *Synchronization of tasks* involves the coordination of work among specialized workers. For example, the moving assembly line invented by Henry Ford is a means of synchronizing the work of many specialized workers, each engaged in narrow, repetitive jobs. The coordination of the each worker's specialized task makes possible the production of a whole good. *Concentration of capital*: with the Industrial Revolution, capital became concentrated, and cities arose as centers of capital. The "captains of industry" consolidated their industries, often driving their competitors out of business using very aggressive tactics.[7] Maximization refers primarily to *maximization of profits*, but the maximization of enterprise size is also included in the second wave's schema "maximization." Centralization refers to *centralization of decision making*. The bureaucracies developed for the mass production of goods centralized decision making at the top of the organization.

The factors identified by Toffler as constituting the infrastructure underlying the Industrial Revolution worked together to de-skill work. The result was that production workers acted as machine tenders. The machine-tending workers of the Industrial Revolution banded together to increase their bargaining power relative to enterprise owners and managers by forming unions. Unions represent a coalition of workers to increase their bargaining power and effective voice with respect to enterprise management.

## History of the Labor Movement

The early history of unionization in the United States is predominantly a history of management opposition to unions. A legal precedent was established in the United States in 1806 imported from previously established English case law.[8] The Philadelphia cordwainers decision held that unions constituted criminal conspiracies, thereby establishing the *criminal conspiracy doctrine*.[9] Efforts of workers to unionize could be, and were, prosecuted as illegal criminal conduct. However, by the 1850s, the criminal conspiracy doctrine was supplanted by the *illegal purpose doctrine*.[10] The illegal purpose doctrine held that unions were not illegal in themselves; rather the legality of the efforts of workers to unionize were judged based on the purpose of their collective efforts. Strikes often were judged to have an illegal purpose.

Two major umbrella organizations for unions were established in the 1870s and 1880s, the Knights of Labor and the American Federation of Labor (AFL).

The Knights of Labor was short-lived, declining after Haymarket Square in 1886,[11] but the AFL has survived to the present day.

As the strength of the union movement increased, employers developed tactics to oppose the efforts of workers for *recognition* and for *collective bargaining*. Two of the most effective weapons were the *labor injunction* and the *yellow dog contract*. The blanket labor injunction was a court order to cease and desist all activities whatsoever against all parties whomsoever. An example of exactly how broad the blanket labor injunction could be is the violation of a blanket labor injunction by a barber who posted a sign in the shop window "scabs not welcome here."[12]

In the 1890s, legislatures started to affirmatively protect the right of workers to unionize. The earliest efforts prohibited the use of the yellow dog contract in the railroad industry. The *yellow dog contract* was a promise by a worker that he was not a member of a union; this promise was a condition of employment. Thus a worker who had been a member of a union was required to quit the union. However, the law prohibiting the yellow dog contract in the railroad industry, the Erdman Act, was declared unconstitutional by the United States Supreme Court, in the *Adair* decision (see Box 10.1).

---

### Box 10.1  *Adair v. United States*

### Supreme Court of The United States

#### 208 U.S. 161 (1908)

The first inquiry is whether the part of the tenth section of the act of 1898 [The Erdman Act][i] upon which the first count of the indictment was based is repugnant to the Fifth Amendment of the Constitution declaring that no person shall be deprived of liberty or property without due process of law. In our opinion that section, in the particular mentioned, is an invasion of the personal liberty, as well as of the right of property, guaranteed by that Amendment. Such liberty and right embraces the right to make contracts for the purchase of the labor of others and equally the right to make contracts for the sale of one's own labor; each right, however, being subject to the fundamental condition that no contract, whatever its subject matter, can be sustained which the law, upon reasonable grounds, forbids as inconsistent with the public interests or as hurtful to the public order or as detrimental to the common good. This court has said that "in every well-ordered society, charged with the duty of conserving the safety of its members, the rights of the individual in respect of his liberty may, at times, under the pressure of great dangers, be subjected to such restraint, to be enforced by reasonable regulations, as the safety of the general public may demand." . . . Without stopping to consider what would have been the rights of the railroad company under the Fifth Amendment, had it been indicted under the act of Congress, it is sufficient in this case to say that as agent of the railroad company and as such responsible for the conduct of the business of one of its departments, it was the defendant Adair's right—and that right inhered in his personal liberty, and was also a right of property—to serve his employer as best he could, so long as he did nothing that was reasonably forbidden by law as injurious to the public interests. It was the right of the defendant to prescribe the terms upon which the services of Coppage would be accepted, and it was the right of Coppage to become or not, as he chose, an employee of the railroad company upon the terms offered to him. Mr. Cooley, in his treatise on Torts, p. 278, well says: "It is a part of every man's civil rights that he be left at liberty to refuse business relations with any person whomsoever, whether the refusal rests upon reason, or is the result of whim, caprice, prejudice or malice. With his reasons neither the public nor third persons have any legal concern. It is also his right to have business relations with any one with whom he can make contracts, and if he is wrongfully deprived of this right by others, he is entitled to redress."

In *Lochner v. New York*, 198 U.S. 45 (1906),[ii] which involved the validity of a state enactment prescribing certain maximum hours for labor in bakeries, and which made it a misdemeanor for an employer to require or permit an employee in such an establishment to work in excess of a given number of hours each day, the court said: "The general right to make a contract in relation to his business is part of the liberty of the individual protected by the Fourteenth Amendment of the Federal Constitution.... Under that provision no State can deprive any person of life, liberty or property without due process of law. The right to purchase or to sell labor is part of the liberty protected by this amendment, unless there are circumstances which exclude the right." [The U.S. Supreme Court struck down the law which limited hours of bakers to 10 hours a day, and 60 hours a week as an unjustified exercise of state police powers.]

. . . The right of a person to sell his labor upon such terms as he deems proper is, in its essence, the same as the right of the purchaser of labor to prescribe the conditions upon which he will accept such labor from the person offering to sell it. So the right of the employee to quit the service of the employer, for whatever reason, is the same as the right of the employer, for whatever reason, to dispense with the services of such employee.[iii] It was the legal right of the defendant Adair—however unwise such a course might have been—to discharge Coppage because of his being a member of a labor organization, as it was the legal right of Coppage, if he saw fit to do so—however unwise such a course on his part might have been—to quit the service in which he was engaged, because the defendant employed some persons who were not members of a labor organization. In all such particulars the employer and the employee have equality of right, and any legislation that disturbs that equality is an arbitrary interference with the liberty of contract which no government can legally justify in a free land.

Mr. Justice Holmes, dissenting.

. . . As we all know, there are special labor unions of men engaged in the service of carriers. These unions exercise a direct influence upon the employment of labor in that business, upon the terms of such employment and upon the business itself. Their very existence is directed specifically to the business, and their connection with it is at least as intimate and important as that of safety couplers, and, I should think, as the liability of master to servant, matters which, it is admitted, Congress might regulate, so far as they concern commerce among the States. . . .

The ground on which this particular law is held bad . . . that it interferes with the paramount individual rights, secured by the Fifth Amendment. The section is, in substance, a very limited interference with freedom of contract, no more. It does not require the carriers to employ any one. It does not forbid them to refuse to employ any one, for any reason they deem good. . . . The section simply prohibits the more powerful party to exact certain undertakings, or to threaten dismissal or unjustly discriminate on certain grounds against those already employed. . . . It cannot be doubted that to prevent strikes, and, so far as possible, to foster its scheme of arbitration, might be deemed by Congress an important point of policy, and I think it impossible to say that Congress might not reasonably think that the provision in question would help a good deal to carry its policy along. But suppose the only effect really were to tend to bring about the complete unionizing of such railroad laborers as Congress can deal with, I think that object alone would justify the act. I quite agree that the question what and how much good labor unions do, is one on which intelligent people may differ,—I think that laboring men sometimes attribute to them advantages, as many attribute to combinations of capital disadvantages, that really are due to economic conditions of a far wider and deeper kind—but I could not pronounce it unwarranted if Congress should decide that to foster a strong union was for the best interest, not only of the men, but of the railroads and the country at large.

[i] The Erdman Act prohibits yellow dog contracts:

"That any employer subject to the provisions of this act and any officer, agent, or receiver of such employer, who shall require any employee, or any person seeking employment, as a condition of such employment, to enter into an agreement, either written or verbal, not to become or remain a member of any labor corporation, association, or organization; or shall threaten any employee with loss of employment, or shall unjustly discriminate against any employee because of his membership in such a labor corporation, association, or organization; or who shall require any employee or any person seeking employment, as [***15] a condition of such employment, to enter into a contract whereby such employee or applicant for employment shall agree to contribute to any fund for charitable, social, or beneficial purposes; to release such employer from legal liability for any personal injury by reason of any benefit received from [*169] such fund beyond the proportion of the benefit arising from the employer's contribution to such fund; or who shall, after having discharged an employee, attempt or conspire to prevent such employee from obtaining employment, or who shall, after the quitting of an employee, attempt or conspire to prevent such employee from obtaining employment, is hereby declared to be guilty of a misdemeanor, and, upon conviction thereof in any court of the United States of competent jurisdiction in the district in which such offense was committed, shall be punished for each offense by a fine of not less than one hundred dollars and not more than one thousand dollars."

[ii] "There is no reasonable ground, on the score of health, for interfering with the liberty of the person or the right of free contract, by determining the hours of labor, in the occupation of a baker. Nor can a law limiting such hours be justified a health law to safeguard the public health, or the health of the individuals following that occupation.

[iii] This articulates the "at will employment relationship." The court however does not recognize the difference in economic bargaining power between the employer and his employees.

At the same time, the United States Congress was concerned about the aggressive consolidation of new industries, including the oil industry, the railroad industry, and the sugar industry. In response, Congress passed the Sherman Anti-Trust Act. The Sherman Anti-Trust Act was passed in 1890 to promote freedom of competition among business enterprise and to limit monopolies and restraint of trade in interstate commerce. However, in the early enforcement of the Sherman Anti-Trust Act (SATA), the United States Supreme Court applied the SATA using the "rule of reason" standard to business combinations.[13] The application of the "rule of reason" standard permitted the growth of trusts and combinations dominating particular industries.

In contrast to the narrow interpretation of the SATA as it applied to the activities of corporate enterprise, the Supreme Court used an expansive interpretation of the SATA to apply it to the activities of labor unions. The SATA considered the organizing activities of unions to control the supply and price of labor. Actually, this is quite correct. Thereafter, the Supreme Court applied anti-trust laws to unions, undermining the right of workers to unionize and bargain collectively, which had been protected by congressional legislation. Thus, while the United States Supreme Court invoked the "rule of reason" in applying the SATA to business competition, it applied the SATA to the organizing activities of labor unions as control over supply of goods in interstate commerce.[14] The application of the SATA to the organizing efforts of unions was unanticipated and did not fall within the congressional intent in passing the SATA. Congress, therefore, amended the SATA by the passage of the Clayton Anti-Trust Act. The Clayton Anti-Trust Act, billed as labor's "Magna Carta," was passed in 1914 specifically to prevent the application of the SATA to the activities of labor unions. However the Clayton Anti-Trust Act was narrowly construed by the Supreme Court to protect only the activities of workers in a direct employer–employee relationship,[15] whereas the interests of unionized workers lay in extending union contracts to employers in the same industry that were not organized by the unions. The force of the Clayton Anti-Trust Act was thus undermined by extending its protections only to workers only in a direct employer– employee relationship and not to those workers with an interest in the working conditions at the target employer.

The Norris La Guardia Act of 1932 was drafted specifically to overcome the narrow interpretation of the Clayton Anti-Trust Act. The Norris La Guardia Act outlawed the yellow dog contract and prohibited federal courts from issuing injunctions in labor disputes in situations where workers had an interest in the labor dispute.[16]

The Norris LaGuardia Act was succeeded by the National Labor Relations Act, which granted workers an affirmative right to organize and bargain collectively. The National Labor Relations Act was passed in 1935 during the 1930s depression to promote industrial peace and interstate commerce (see Box 10.2).[17] Although there was some question initially whether the Supreme Court would uphold the constitutionality of the Wagner Act,[18] then-President Roosevelt threatened to "pack the court"[19] and the Supreme Court in fact upheld the constitutionality of the Wagner Act.[20]

## Box 10.2  The National Labor Relations Act of 1935 [i]

Section 1. The denial by employers of the right of employees to organize and the refusal by employers to accept the procedure of collective bargaining lead to strikes and other forms of industrial strife or unrest, which have the intent or the necessary effect of burdening or obstructing commerce by (a) impairing the efficiency, safety, or operation of the instrumentalities of commerce; (b) occurring in the current of commerce; (c) materially affecting, restraining, or controlling the flow of raw materials or manufactured or processed goods from or into the channels of commerce, or the prices of such materials or goods in commerce; or (d) causing diminution of employment and wages in such volume as substantially to impair or disrupt the market for goods flowing from or into the channels of commerce.

The inequality of bargaining power between employees who do not possess full freedom of association or actual liberty of contract, and employers who are organized in the corporate or other forms of ownership association substantially burdens and affects the flow of commerce, and tends to aggravate recurrent business depressions, by depressing wage rates and the purchasing power of wage earners in industry and by preventing the stabilization of competitive wage rates and working conditions within and between industries.

Experience has proved that protection by law of the right of employees to organize and bargain collectively safeguards commerce from injury, impairment, or interruption, and promotes the flow of commerce by removing certain recognized sources of industrial strife and unrest, by encouraging practices fundamental to the friendly adjustment of industrial disputes arising out of differences as to wages, hours, or other working conditions, and by restoring equality of bargaining power between employers and employees.

It is hereby declared to be the policy of the United States to eliminate the causes of certain substantial obstructions to the free flow of commerce and to mitigate and eliminate these obstructions when they have occurred by encouraging the practice and procedure of collective bargaining and by protecting the exercise by workers of full freedom of association, self-organization, and designation of representatives of their own choosing, for the purpose of negotiating the terms and conditions of their employment or other mutual aid or protection.

Section. 7. Employees shall have the right to self-organization, to form, join, or assist labor organizations, to bargain collectively through representatives of their own choosing, and to engage in concerted activities, for the purpose of collective bargaining or other mutual aid or protection.

[i] Act of July 5, 1935, 49 Stat. 449, 29 U.S.C. 151.

## Labor Market Regulation

### Fair Labor Standards Act

The Fair Labor Standards Act was passed during 1930s depression. During the 1930s, one-third of the workforce was unemployed. The public policies to correct the depression were called the New Deal. New Deal legislation (see Table 5.2) was aimed at reversing the economic downturn of the 1930s by protecting the interests of investors, as well as the interests of workers. For example, the Social Security Act was passed, establishing a retirement system for workers. The Fair Labor Standards Act also was enacted as part of the New Deal legislation. The Fair Labor Standards Act established a minimum wage and established a 40-hour work week, after which workers must be paid overtime. Under the view of economist John Maynard Keynes, it was thought that increased consumer spending was required to cause the end of the depression and that deficit spending would stimulate the economy.[21] The Social Security Act supported minimum income in retirement and encouraged workers to cease their participation in the labor force, thus making way for the employment of other, younger workers. By requiring minimum wage standards and overtime provisions, the Fair Labor Standards Act encouraged employers to spread employment among many workers. It was thought that increasing the spending ability of workers would result in increased demand, stimulating increased business activity to meet the demand, thus ending the depression.

### Employment at Will

The doctrine of employment at will governed the employment relationship between employers and employees during the era of mass production.[22] Under the employment at will doctrine, employees have the right to quit their jobs at any time, for any reason, or for no reason. Correspondingly, the employer can fire the employee at any time for any reason or no reason at all. However, large firms practiced lifetime employment.

The doctrine of at will employment has been eroded. The doctrine of at will employment has been eroded by the doctrine of good faith and fair dealing and recognition that there is a public interest in preventing termination of employment of employees for reasons against the public interest, such as termination for refusing sexual demands of a supervisor or for cheating an employee out of a commission that would come due shortly after the termination of employment.[23]

### Wrongful Termination and the Employer's Obligation of Good Faith and Fair Dealing

Wrongful termination has been recognized under common law as a doctrine that erodes the competing doctrine of employment at will. The covenant of good faith and fair dealing in every contract protects employees from terminations done in bad faith. Moreover, some states have passed statutes that protect workers against wrongful termination, particularly for whistleblowing. Sometimes companies fire employees who have blown the whistle on wrongdoing. The New Jersey Conscientious Employee Protection Act protects employees against termination in retaliation for whistle blowing. The American Law Institute has drafted the Restatement Third on Employment Law.[24]

### Progressive Discipline

Progressive discipline is an aspect of fairness to employees. Most union contracts incorporate progressive discipline into the contract terms. Typically, union contracts incorporate a grievance procedure, which permits employees to complain that the union contract has not been properly enforced. Unionized employees thus have access to several avenues to assure fairness in the employment relationship. The fairness that is addressed by progressive discipline procedures encompasses both procedural and substantive due process. Procedural and substantive due process were discussed in Chapter 3, "Ethics of Business Decision Making," as ethical standards for the evaluation of action.

Nonunion, at-will employees typically have less access to procedures ensuring fairness in the employment relationship. However, increasingly employers are creating internal complaint and investigations procedures and designating managers responsible for such procedures. This may be done not only to ensure fundamental fairness to employees in the teeth of eroding at-will employment doctrines but also to head-off external complaints and investigations by external agencies that enforce non-discrimination law.

### Civil Rights Act of 1964

Title VII of the Civil Rights Act of 1964 prohibits discrimination based on race, color, religion, national origin and gender (see Box 10.3).[25]

---

**Box 10.3  Title VII**

SEC. 703. (a) It shall be an unlawful employment practice for an employer—

1. to fail or refuse to hire or to discharge any individual, or otherwise to discriminate against any individual with respect to his compensation, terms, conditions, or privileges of employment, because of such individual's race, color, religion, sex, or national origin; or
2. to limit, segregate, or classify his employees in any way which would deprive or tend to deprive any individual of employment opportunities or otherwise adversely affect his status as an employee, because of such individual's race, color, religion, sex, or national origin.

---

It was enacted by the U.S. Congress on July 2, 1964.[26] The 1964 Civil Rights Act ended a period of *de facto* and *de jure* segregation in effect since the United States Supreme Court decision *Plessy v. Ferguson*.[27] The *Plessy v. Ferguson* decision held that "separate but equal" facilities comported with the equal protection clause of the Fourteenth Amendment.[28] Title VII also established the Equal Employment Opportunity Commission to enforce the statute.[29]

*Affirmative Action*

*Affirmative action* is a way to overcome the effects of past discrimination. Since overt racial and gender discrimination were common, if not rampant, before the passage of Title VII of the 1964 Civil Rights Act, employees and enterprise were stuck with the past effects of discrimination in the immediate aftermath of the passage of the 1964 Civil Rights Act. Affirmative action considers race, gender or other personal characteristics of the employee in employment decisions, such as hiring and promotion. Title VII explicitly prohibits discrimination based on such personal characteristics, whereas affirmative action explicitly considers such characteristics in employment decisions. Affirmative action is, therefore, a legal defense to the consideration of race, gender or other personal characteristics in employment decisions. Affirmative action programs ordinarily end when the past effects of discrimination have been overcome.[30]

*Diversity*

*Diversity* as a value goes beyond affirmative action. While affirmative action looks to the past to remedy the effects of past discrimination, diversity looks to the present and the future. Diversity is based on First Amendment constitutional interests, including valuing the marketplace of ideas and the expression of different voices. In 2003 the United States Supreme Court in the case *Grutter v. Bollinger* affirmed that the achievement of racial diversity in the student body of a university is constitutionally permissible.[31] The consideration of race in admissions arguably violates the Fourteenth Amendment, equal protection. However, the court viewed the consideration of race in college admission as important to achieving diversity in a college or university student body. The role of universities in training future leaders and the importance of having leadership reflecting the diversity of the citizenry were recognized by the court, whose opinion was written by Justice Sandra Day O'Connor. The principle of non-discrimination is fundamental to ethical management of employees and has been extended to the principle of inclusion.

While the consideration of an individual's personal characteristics in admission to college is permissible, the use of quotas is not. Thus, while the University of Michigan's individualized consideration of applicants to the law school, including consideration of their race, was constitutionally permissible, the procedures used for the admission of minority students to the undergraduate College of Arts and Sciences of the University of Michigan was not. The admission procedure for the College of Arts and Sciences of the University of Michigan required a total of 100 points and allocated 20 points to minority students. This procedure was declared unconstitutional in the *Gratz v. Bollinger* decision.[32]

After the *Grutter* and *Gratz* cases were decided, a ballot initiative to amend the Michigan Constitution was passed by voters in 2006 to prohibit discrimination and preferential treatment based on "race, sex, color, ethnicity, or national origin in college admissions." Since affirmative action is, legally, a defense to the consideration of race, or other ascriptive characteristics of the individual, the Michigan initiative effectively ended the use of affirmative action in college admissions. In April 2014, the United States Supreme Court upheld the constitutionality of Michigan Proposal 2 (Michigan 06–2), also known as the Michigan Civil Rights Initiative.[33] The *Schuette* decision upholds similar propositions passed in other states, including California's Proposition 209. Proposition 209 was a California ballot initiative passed in 1996 prohibiting discrimination, or preferential treatment on account of "race, sex, color, ethnicity, or national origin" in "the operation of public employment, public education, or public contracting."[34,35] *Schuette* does not invalidate or overrule *Grutter* but permits voters to prohibit affirmative action in the admissions to public colleges.

In addition to protecting individuals from discrimination based on their race, gender, religion, national origin and ethnicity, discrimination law has been expanded to include discrimination based on age, disability and family status.

***Age Discrimination in Employment Act.*** The *Age Discrimination in Employment Act* (ADEA) of 1967 protects individuals over age 40 from discrimination based on age.[36] The ADEA prohibits mandatory retirement based on age, except when age is a bona fide occupational qualification, and except for bona fide executives and high-level policymakers, who may be forced to retire at age 65 if they will receive a certain minimum pension.[37]

***Americans with Disabilities Act.*** The *Americans with Disabilities Act* (ADA) was enacted in 1990.[38] The ADA prohibits discrimination against workers with disabilities who are able to perform the "essential functions of the job."[39] The ADA uses a *reasonable accommodation* standard of discrimination.[40] The ADA requires a company to make a reasonable accommodation to an otherwise qualified worker with a disability. A reasonable accommodation will help a qualified employee with a disability perform the essential functions of the job. The actual accommodations required of an employer counted as "reasonable" depend on the financial capacity of the employer.

***Family Medical Leave Act.*** The *Family Medical Leave Act* (FMLA) of 1993 guarantees working individuals the right to leave to take care of themselves or family members for a period of 12 weeks over the period of one year.[41] The FMLA does not require paid leave but requires employers to reinstate workers upon their return to an equivalent job without loss of accrued benefits. The FMLA provides for the continuation of group medical health insurance during the period of leave.

Trends in labor market regulation have shifted dramatically over the twentieth century: early labor market regulation protected the right of workers to collective action; then New Deal legislation was oriented to economic minimums, requiring or guaranteeing minimum labor market standards; the 1964 Civil Rights Act was the major piece of legislation of the Great Society; most recently, the emphasis has been on the protection of individual rights, including the ADEA, the ADA and the FMLA. The changing emphasis of labor market regulation mirrors the emergence of a new social contract in employment relations.

## The New Social Contract

A new social contract has emerged with the abandonment of the practice of lifetime employment by large corporations. The *"relational employment contracts"* of the previous era meant that employers and employees made mutual investments in the employment relation. In a relational contract, employers overpay employees relative to their productivity at the beginning of the employment relationship, thus making an initial investment in their employees. During their mid-career years, however, employees are underpaid relative to their productivity. During this time, employers recoup their initial investment in the employees; then the employees themselves make an investment in the employment relationship. In the later stages of the employment relationship, employees expect to recoup their investment; employees do not typically receive pay cuts in their later years of employment, even if their productivity declines. See Figure 10.1.

With the end of the relational contract, the question arises: what is "fair" compensation under circumstances where there is no expectation of long-term employment? Jeremy Rifkin, author of The *End of Work*, acknowledges that technological innovation leads to technological unemployment.[42] Moreover, he predicts that the employment created by newly developed technologies will more than offset the losses that result from technological unemployment. However, the impact on workers may be significant in terms of personal consequences. Often, the individuals employed by new technologies are not the same individuals as those who become unemployed as the result of new technologies. Concern for employment was at the heart of the public demonstrations and general strike occurring in France in March and April 2006 against the change in French law that permits unfettered layoffs of young workers, under age 26 years, who have worked for a company less than one year.[43]

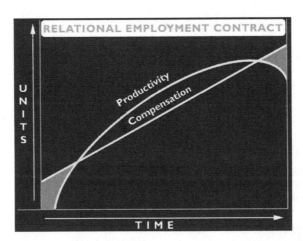

*Figure 10.1* Relational Employment Contract

### Strategic Implications of Labor Costs

The American employment model treats production costs as variable costs. American companies, such as the automobile companies, lay-off workers during periods of downturn. For example, when the production lines are retooled during December, auto manufacturers lay-off the production workers. Another strategy of American companies is to increase the utilization of contingent workers. The utilization of contingent workers increases productivity statistics by reducing headcount.

Some other countries, such as Japan, treat labor production costs as fixed costs.[44] Whether the labor costs for production workers are treated as fixed or variable costs has significant implication for enterprise strategy: treating labor costs as fixed costs pushes the breakeven point farther out, requiring more sales to breakeven, than if labor costs are treated as variable costs. Firms that treat labor costs as fixed, therefore, must engage in strategies that ensure a large volume of sales. Strategies that ensure a large volume of sales include an approach that induces customer loyalty and repeat sales. Customer loyalty and repeat sales can be engendered by product quality and the incorporation of research and development results into product, as well as by marketing.

The American employment model is to consider labor costs as variable and often to externalize labor costs. For example, Wal-Mart has employment policies that externalize labor costs.[45] Wal-Mart employs workers who often qualify for food stamps and Medicaid. Wal-Mart has human resource management policies that assist workers with applying for and receiving tax-based income assistance.[46]

As formerly socialist countries transition to market-driven economies, bankruptcy law are put into place, with attendant layoffs and unemployment. This represents major social change and is one of the issues that such transitioning

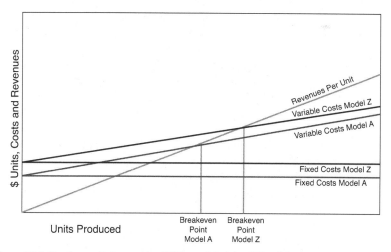

*Figure 10.2* Breakeven Points under Different Models of Fixed Costs

economies must cope with, including the social dislocations of unemployment or underemployment. This is a major issue, for example in Russia, the former Soviet Union. These economies are transitioning from social systems where labor costs were considered fixed costs to systems where labor costs are, at least in some circumstances, variable.

In contrast with the American model, other companies and social systems consider such externalization of labor costs as bad corporate citizenship. See for example, the U.S. general manager of C Ito Trading Company, at the time the largest Japanese trading company in the world, considers layoffs and unemployment to be bad corporate citizenship.[47] This alternative model is articulated by William Ouchi in his influential book as *Theory Z*.[48] In a global context, however, competitive pressures tend toward corporate strategies that seek to reduce labor costs as part of enterprise strategy. Global labor markets are discussed in Chapter 11.

Ethical management of employees requires conformity to labor market regulation at a minimum. The principle of non-discrimination is fundamental to ethical management of employees. Beyond the avoidance of discrimination, employers must remedy the past effects of discrimination; affirmative action is a means to remediate past discrimination. Beyond affirmative action, managing for diversity values differences and seeks to provide role models in leadership positions for the increasingly diverse workforce. Ethical management of employees also requires respecting the voice of employees, as well as fair dealing with employees. Employee voice can be articulated by the collective bargaining relationship or joint labor management committees on subjects important to employee interests. Ethical management of employees also requires fundamental fairness in dealing with employees, including both procedural and substantive due process. The at-will doctrine does not require either procedural or substantive due process and thus can be at odds with the fairness required for the ethical management of employees. The end of lifetime employment and relational contracts requires rethinking of ethical compensation of employees: management must develop a compensation system for employees that pays them fairly based on their present work situation, rather than deferring compensation as a mutual investment based on an expectation of a long-term employment relation.

## Chapter Discussion Questions

1. What is the "code" underlying the Industrial Revolution/era of mass production, according to Alvin Toffler? Has the underlying schema of the "Third Wave"/post-Industrial Revolution changed? If so, how?

2. In the era of mass production, the employment relation existed as an "at will" relationship but many large corporations had a practice of lifetime employment. In the New Economy, the doctrine of "at will" employment has eroded in several respects but there is low employment security in fact and in practice. How has the move from a "relational" contract to an employment relation where there is no expectation of long-term employment affected the workplace?

3. In the United States, corporations seek to make labor costs variable. The move toward the utilization of contingent workers can be viewed as a way of making labor costs variable. Not all systems, for example Europe and Japan, adopt our practice. What are the implications of having higher fixed labor costs?
4. Compare the perspective of the old employer (era of mass production) to the perspective of the employer in an information intensive industry.
5. Compare the perspective of employees in the era of mass production to the perspective of workers in New Economy.

## Notes

1 Douglas McGregor, *The Human Side of the Enterprise.* (New York: McGraw-Hill, Inc.: 1960).
2 Chris Argyris, *Integrating the Individual and the Organization* (New York: Wiley, 1964).
3 See, for example, the Core Job Characteristics Model of Job Design. The Core Job Characteristics Model of Job Design is an out growth of Hertzberg's Dual Factor Theory of Motivation. See J. R. Hackman & G. R. Oldham; "Development of Job Diagnostic Survey," *Journal of Applied Psychology* 60 (1975): 159–70. See also G. R. Oldham & J. R. Hackman, (2010) "Not What It Was and Not What It Will Be: The Future of Job Design Research," *Journal of Organizational Behavior* 31 (2010): 463–79.
4 The five disciplines of the learning organization include: shared vision, systems thinking, mental models, personal mastery and team learning. Peter Senge, *The Fifth Discipline: The Art and Practice of the Learning Organization* (New York: Doubleday/Currency Press, 1990).
5 Alvin Toffler, *The Third Wave* (New York: Bantam Books, 1980).
6 See Chapter 2, "Breaking the Code," in Toffler, *The Third Wave.*
7 It was the aggressive tactics of the robber barons that became the basis for Congress's drafting and passage of the Sherman Anti-Trust Act of 1890.
8 *The King v. Journeymen Tailors of Cambridge* (1721).
9 *Commonwealth v. Pullis, Mayor's Court of Philadelphia* (1806).
10 *Commonwealth v. Hunt,* 45 Mass. 111 (1842). See John R. Commons, *The Economics of Collective Action* (Madison, WI: University of Wisconsin Press, 1970). See also John R. Commons, *A Documentary History of American Industrial Society* (Cleveland, OH: The A.H. Clark Company, 1910).
11 See "Knights of Labor," *History.com,* last modified 2014, http://www.history.com/topics/knights-of-labor.
12 See Commons, *The Economics of Collective Action.*
13 *Standard Oil Company of New Jersey v. United States,* 221 U.S. 1 (1911); *United States v. American Tobacco Company,* 221 U.S. 106 (1911). The "rule of reason" in applying the Sherman Anti-Trust Act permitted American Sugar Refining Company to control 98% of the sugar refining market, the Standard Oil Company, to control 85–90% of US refining capacity and American Tobacco to control 97% of the production of domestic cigarettes. Benjamin Taylor and Fred Witney, *U.S. Labor-Relations Law: Historical Development* (Englewood Cliffs, NJ: Prentice Hall, 1992), 48–50. See also *United States. v. E.C. Knight Company,* 156 U.S. 1 (1895), *United States v. United Shoe Machinery Co,* 227 U.S. 32 (1913) and *United States v. United States Steel Corporation,* 251 U.S. 417 (1920).
14 *Loewe v. Lawlor,* 208 U.S. 274 (1908).

15  *Duplex Printing Press Co. v. Deering*, 254 U.S. 443 (1921).

16  The Norris La Guardia Act was upheld as constitutional by *Milk Wagon Drivers v. Lake Valley Farm Products*, 311 U.S. 91 (1940) and *United States v. Hutcheson*, 321 U.S. 219 (1941).

17  Act of July 5, 1935, 49 Stat. 449, 29 U.S.C. 151.

18  Section 7 of the National Industrial Recovery Act of 1933 granted workers the right to unionize; however, the NIRA itself was declared unconstitutional by *Schecter Poultry Corporation v. United States*, 295 U.S. 495 (1935).

19  The threat to "pack the court" was a threat to propose a constitutional amendment increasing the number of Supreme Court justices from nine to thirteen. If passed, the new constitutional amendment would then allow incumbent president Franklin Delano Roosevelt to appoint four new justices to the Supreme Court.

20  *NLRB v. Jones & Laughlin Steel Co.*, 301 U.S. 1 (1937).

21  Paul Krugman is a present-day Keynesian. Krugman advocated deficit spending to stimulate the economy from the Great Recession of 2008.

22  Horace Gay Wood, *Law of Master and Servant* (Albany, NY: John D. Parsons, 1877) articulated the "employment-at-will" doctrine.

23  Charles J. Muhl, "The Employment-at-will Doctrine: Three Major Exceptions," *Monthly Labor Review*, January 2001.

24  The American Law Institute has drafted The Restatement Third, Employment Law, last modified 2014, http://www.ali.org/index.cfm?fuseaction=publications.ppage&node_id=31.

25  42 USC 2000e et. seq., see http://www.eeoc.gov/laws/statutes/titlevii.cfm.

26  42 U.S.C., Section 2000e et. seq.

27  163 U.S. 537 (1896). See "Plessy v. Ferguson (1896)," *The Rise and Fall of Jim Crow, PBS. org*, last modified 2002, http://www.pbs.org/wnet/jimcrow/stories_events_plessy.html.

28  The Fourteen Amendment is one of three Reconstruction-period amendments. The Thirteenth, Fourteenth and Fifteenth Amendments were passed in sequence, a few years apart after one another. The Emancipation Proclamation was an executive order of President Abraham Lincoln. The Congress passed the Thirteenth Amendment in 1865. The Thirteenth Amendment abolished "involuntary servitude," or slavery. However, the Thirteenth Amendment was insufficient to effectively abolish discrimination against former slaves. The Fourteenth Amendment was passed by Congress in 1868. Even the Fourteenth Amendment did not effectively protect the right of former (male) slaves to exercise political power. Hence the Fifteenth Amendment was passed in 1870. The Fifteenth Amendment provided equal rights to vote for Blacks and former slaves ("The right of citizens of the United States to vote shall not be denied or abridged by the United States or by any State on account of race, color, or previous condition of servitude.").

29  Equal Employment Opportunity Commission SEC. 705. (a) There is hereby created a Commission to be known as the Equal Employment Opportunity Commission, which shall be composed of five members, not more than three of whom shall be members of the same political party, who shall be appointed by the President by and with the advice and consent of the Senate. One of the original members shall be appointed for a term of one year, one for a term of two years, one for a term of three years, one for a term of four years, and one for a term of five years, beginning from the date of enactment of this title, but their successors shall be appointed for terms of five years each, except that any individual chosen to fill a vacancy shall be appointed only for the unexpired term of the member whom he shall succeed. The President shall designate one member to serve as Chairman of the Commission,

and one member to serve as Vice Chairman. The Chairman shall be responsible on behalf of the Commission for the administrative operations of the Commission, and shall appoint, in accordance with the civil service laws, such officers, agents, attorneys, and employees as it deems necessary to assist it in the performance of its functions and to fix their compensation in accordance with the Classification Act of 1949, as amended. The Vice Chairman shall act as Chairman in the absence or disability of the Chairman or in the event of a vacancy in that office.

See "EEOC History," *U.S. Equal Opportunity Employment Commission*, last modified 2014, http://www.eeoc.gov/eeoc/history/index.cfm.

Prevention Of Unlawful Employment Practices

SEC. 706. (a) Whenever it is charged in writing under oath by a person claiming to be aggrieved, or a written charge has been filed by a member of the Commission where he has reasonable cause to believe a violation of this title has occurred (and such charge sets forth the facts upon which it is based) that an employer, employment agency, or labor organization has engaged in an unlawful employment practice, the Commission shall furnish such employer, employment agency, or labor organization (hereinafter referred to as the 'respondent') with a copy of such charge and shall make an investigation of such charge, provided that such charge shall not be made public by the Commission. If the Commission shall determine, after such investigation, that there is reasonable cause to believe that the charge is true, the Commission shall endeavor to eliminate any such alleged unlawful employment practice by informal methods of conference, conciliation, and persuasion. Nothing said or done during and as a part of such endeavors may be made public by the Commission without the written consent of the parties, or used as evidence in a subsequent proceeding. Any officer or employee of the Commission, who shall make public in any manner whatever any information in violation of this subsection shall be deemed guilty of a misdemeanor and upon conviction thereof shall be fined not more than $1,000 or imprisoned not more than one year.

30  Paula Becker Alexander, "Affirmative Action and Reverse Discrimination: Does Taxman v. the Township of Piscataway Board of Education Define the Permissible Outer Limits of Voluntary Race Conscious Affirmative Action," *Seton Hall Constitutional Law Journal* 8, no. 1 (1997): 13–46.

31  539 U.S. 306. See also Paula Alexander Becker, Susan A. O'Sullivan, and Karen A. Prelich Passaro, "Recent Supreme Court Decisions Affecting the Employer-Employee Relationship: Arbitration of Employment Disputes, The Scope and Remedies of The Americans With Disabilities Act and Affirmative Action," *Hofstra Labor & Employment Law Journal* 21, no. 1 (Fall 2003): 209–31.

32  539 U.S. 244 (2003).

33  *Schuette v. Coalition to Defend Affirmative Action*, 572 US __ (2014). See Adam Liptak, "Court Backs Michigan on Affirmative Action," *New York Times*, April 22, 2014. See also Joan Biskupic, "Voice of First U.S. Hispanic Justice Heard in Major Race Case," *Reuters/ Chicago Tribune,* April 22, 2014.

34  For text of California Proposition 209 see http://vote96.sos.ca.gov/Vote96/html/BP/209text.htm.

35  Richard D. Kahlenberg, "No Longer Black and White: Why liberals should let California's affirmative-action ban stand," *Slate.com*, last modified March 12, 2014, http://www.slate.com/articles/news_and_politics/jurisprudence/2014/03/california_affirmative_action_ban_why_liberals_should_let_it_stand.html.

36  29 USC 621 et. seq. See *U.S. Equal Opportunity Employment Commission*, last modified 2014, http://www.eeoc.gov/laws/types/age.cfm.

37   See *Mandatory Retirement Age Rules: Is It Time To Re-evaluate?* (September 9, 2004) (testimony of Jadadeesh Gokhale of the Cato Institute to the Special Committee on Aging), http://www.cato.org/publications/congressional-testimony/ mandatory-retirement-age-rules-is-it-time-reevaluate.

38   42 USC 12101 et seq. See also Linda Greenhouse, "A Supreme Court Victory for Older Workers," *New York Times,* June 20, 2008.

39   See also Becker, O'Sullivan, and Passaro, "Recent Supreme Court Decisions."

40   The closest that the Civil Rights Act of 1964 comes to a reasonable accommodation standard is the requirement of accommodation to religious practice under Title VII.

41   See "Wage and Hour Division (WHD)," *United States Department of Labor,* last modified 2013, http://www.dol.gov/whd/fmla/.

42   Jeremy Rifkin, *The End of Work: The Decline of the Global Labor Force and the Dawn of the Post-Market Era* (New York: Putnam Publishing Group, 1994).

43   The proposed law called for unfettered layoffs of young workers who have worked for a company less than two years. See Molly Moore, "France Prepares For a General Strike: Standoff Persists Over Law on Youth Job Rights," *Washington Post,* March 28, 2006.

44   See, for example, William Ouchi, *Theory Z: How American Business Can Meet the Japanese Challenge* (New York: Avon Books, 1981).

45   See Paula Alexander Becker and Dawn Jaeckel, "Wal-Mart: Always Low Price, But at What Cost?" (LERA Annual Meeting, Portland, Oregon, May 29, 2014).

46   Democratic Staff of the U.S. House Committee on Education and the Workforce, *The Low-Wage Drag on Our Economy: Wal-Mart's low wages and their effect on taxpayers and economic growth,* May 2013, http://democrats.edworkforce.house.gov/ sites/democrats.edworkforce.house.gov/files/documents/WalMartReport-May2013. pdf. This is not a new phenomenon. See also Democratic Staff of the U.S. House Committee on Education and the Workforce, *Everyday Low Wages: The Hidden Price We All Pay for Wal-Mart,* February 16, 2004, http://www.amiba.net/assets/files/studies/everyday-low-wages-georgemiller-walmartreport.pdf.

47   U.S. General Manager of C Itoh Co., interview by Paula Becker Alexander and Samuel Estreicher, Oct. 9, 1992.

48   Ouchi, *Theory Z.*

## End of Chapter Case: Wal-Mart Employment Practices and Corporate Sustainability

### Wal-Mart: EDLP at What Cost?

*Elven Riley*

Seton Hall University

### Introduction

First, I was excited to see the clear way the paper, Wal-Mart: The High Cost of Low Price by Alexander and Jaeckel,[1] provided a multi-dimensional view of Wal-Mart labor relationship throughout the supply chain, indeed spotlighting labor cost as a fundamental economic support for the business model. The paper quickly leads to sustainability questions of the Wal-Mart business model.

Second, the Alexander Jaeckel paper clearly connected the dots on how economic gain is extracted from both employee labor and supplier labor pricing advantages compared to a smaller competitor. To my way of thinking, WM has created efficiency through performance and being able to negotiate labor price boundaries.

Third, if the WM model is DEPENDENT on labor pricing inefficiencies across geographic boundaries, a form of "labor arbitrage" where work is moved to take advantage of low cost labor, then it is only a question of time before the advantage is exhausted and no longer a source of 'competitive advantage.' Programming outsourcing to India took a few years to normalize programmer pay to a global scale, but it did.

Fourth, then if the profits are being transferred out of the company, and the business model continues to weaken, how big a hole will WM create upon failure? Are they, like General Motors and the international banks, "too big to fail"?

## Wal-Mart Is Big

- Wal-Mart is big
- 2005 undervalued work force
- Pays low wages, workers utilize public assistance, WM committed hour violations, foe of unions, discriminated against women, used illegal immigrants
- 2009 undervalued supply chain
- Unpaid overtime, unsafe work sites
- 2013 a new leaf or a tipping point?

WM is, as the Alexander Jaeckel paper and others note, very big. But I have traditionally focused on the financial reporting of labor on the balance sheet not the labor reporting as an operational component. That misses a lot of the story that their paper brings forward identifying labor as the critical ingredient that a massive company must get right and keep right to survive. And labor comes both to the store operation functions staffed by employees as well as the global supply chain staffed by production labor. At this massive size the labor availability becomes a constraining resource, especially as the demographics continue to shift in the US by 2017 from unemployment to vacant jobs. The paper's closing thought of the 'new leaf' in WM labor policy could also be recognition of the approaching tipping point as revenue increased at an annual rate of only 3% since 2008.

## Wal-Mart Is Big Globally

| | | |
|---|---|---|
| • | sales: | $444B = approximately #26 country GDP |
| • | employer: | 2.2M global; 1.4 U.S. (#2 to government) |
| • | intermediary: | supplier (China) to consumer (US) |
| • | market cap: | # 1 consumer services, # 6 over all |

BIG is not the word, MASSIVE is the word. WM is a massive point of sale distributer, a massive employer, a massive global trader, a massive company as viewed by the balance sheet. But we humans have a hard time getting our mind to comprehend without comparisons. So just like a baseball is about the size of an apple, WM is about half the market cap of Apple Corp and about the same market cap as Google, but Apple has only 3% of WM employees and Google only 2%.

## Wal-Mart Is a Disintermediary

| |
|---|
| • Between supplier labor costs (world supply) |
| • Between worker labor costs (old/young) |
| • Between communities (local/area big box) |
| |
| Increase gross margin dollars and convert to dividend payments |

WM, like other BIG BOX companies, created some efficiencies by focusing on disintermediation of local retail outlets and multiple distribution systems by binding POS to an integrated distribution warehouse. That is a fancy way of saying make somebody's role in a process unnecessary and eliminate it or significantly reduce it, like your local retail store front.

Meanwhile, the U.S. export of manufacturing jobs and knowhow created an available labor pool and simultaneously created multiple large global suppliers that enable the massive purchasing volume of WM to be presented with significant advantage. Indeed, WM appears to be courting an active strategy for achieving competitive advantage by competing on Every Day Low Price at the expense of labor. Revenue increased from 1998 through 2008 at an annual rate of 11%.

But the world is not infinite, so what remains today to disintermediate other than WM itself? If you are seen as only a supplier of cheap products then how loyal will your customer base be when price differences become insignificant? Agility is required in a dynamic market and a stable "monopsony" business strategy will fall behind.

## Wal-Mart Is Under Performing

- EPS -4%, sector average +2%
- Year/Year Net Income drop to $16B from 17B
- Interest Expense increasing
- Market saturation 90% US pop within 15mi
- International markets less open

AND STILL dividends continue to RISE

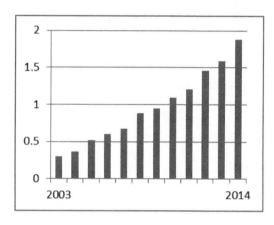

But markets are efficient and eventually according to the 'efficient market theory' only small temporary differences will remain. Meaning that if you don't, or can't, change your 'EDLP' business model and a major competitive advantage is bleeding away then what happens? Note also, that while we all know that American corporations are sitting on cash reserves of $1.45 T, up a remarkable 50 per cent since 2010, WM has transferred wealth in the form of dividend payments from the corporation to shareholders, permanently.

## Wal-Mart End-of-Life Model

- Exhausted labor cost differentials
- Exhausted government support
- Rising cost of capital
- Model requires revenue and margin dollar increases (no shareholder loyalty expected without increasing dividend)
- Rising tide of litigation by communities/states

Where is WM today? Heading for a stormy future.

1. The global labor cost differences are rapidly disappearing.
2. The government is having difficulty continuing to convince citizens to shoulder the cost of subsidizing the working poor.
3. The Fed is talking about 2015 for the rise in the cost of capital and WM cost of capital is already moving up.
4. The shareholder, including 'the family', will not hold risky equity without an ever increasing dividend payment. The sell-off could be sharp and painful.
5. The WM municipalities are becoming aware of their risk as other smaller BIG BOX models leave multi-year craters in the local economy and municipal budgets. The municipal bond rating downgrade will be quick and the litigation endless.

## Is Wal-Mart Too-Big-to-Fail?

- GM, AIG, American Airlines, Enron, Global Crossing, Lehman, Pacific Gas & Electric, Tyco, WorldCom were all very large companies that went into bankruptcy
- Risk of failure transferred to communities/Government
  - Unemployment of employees
  - Unemployment of suppliers
  - International trade
  - Multi-year micro/macro-economic disruptions
- Old style strategy on maintaining 'competitive advantage' by squeezing costs and suppliers

Maybe, the developed world has never seen a global corporation with as much risk exposure as WM in the consumer services sector. Everyone was caught off guard with the financial crisis and we have had many practice crises over the decades. If the General Motors ecosystem was too significant to let fail then there clearly is an argument for saving the #1 employer in the US. Is failure inevitable? No. But what is most troubling is that the WM 2.0 model is based on economic theory developed decades ago by strategists like Michael Porter and enhanced by Hamel & Prahalad. These 'competitive advantage' models tend to under fund investments in long-term strategic advantage and fail to respond to change. So what would the Fed do if a WM failure left many Detroit economies in its capsized wake?

## There Are Very Few Companies with a 20 Year History

**Today:** "fast strategy" is a balance of stability and agility
**Goal:** long term sustainability
**Requires:** long term relationship with labor

WM 1.0 was about labor arbitration, WM 2.0 is about global services, WM 3.0 is yet to appear (the continuous reconfiguration business model achieving balance between stability and agility). The new 'fast strategies' can provide social good for the hosting community by connecting long term sustainability to incentives. Not all of our troubled societal challenges can be addressed by corporate social responsibility, but if the Democratic staff of the U.S. House Committee on Education and the Workforce's May 2013 report is correct and there is a $5,000/year government subsidy per WM employee then we can find corporate incentives to prioritize sustainability or withdraw access to the subsidy. The Affordable Care Act (ACA) is expected to provide the S&P 500 corporations with a $700B potential savings through 2025 (first decade of implementation) and again is seen as support for the working poor struggling to attain a living wage. The Becker-Jaeckel paper spotlights WM antiquated strategy but on the larger stage of 'consumer services' we hopefully will not require a global crisis to reform and coordinate regulating these massive companies.

See also: Documentary "Wal-Mart: The High Cost of Low Price." Robert Greenwald and Brave New Films. 2005.

## Note

1  Paula Alexander Becker and Dawn J. Jaeckel, Wal-Mart: The High Cost of Low Price, 2014 Annual Meeting of the Labor and Employment Relations Association.

## References and Additional Reading

"The End of Competitive Advantage: How to keep your strategy moving as fast as your business" by Rita Gunther McGrath 2013 Harvard Business Review Press.
"Market Intellect from Global Markets Intelligence: The Affordable Care Act Could Shift Health Care Benefit Responsibility Away From Employers, Potentially Saving S&P 500 Companies $700 Billion" by Thompson, Keiser, and Albanese, May 1, 2014, S&P Capital IQ McGraw Hill Financial.
Price Waterhouse 2013 ranking 100 top global http://www.pwc.com/gx/en/audit-services/capital-market/publications/top100-market-capitalisation.jhtml
"Do Minimum Wages Reduce Employment? A Case Study of California, 1987–89" by D. Card; *Industrial and Labor Relations Review*, Vol. 46, No. 1. (Oct., 1992), pp. 38–54.
"Minimum Wages and Employment: A Case Study of the Fast-Food Industry in New Jersey and Pennsylvania" by D. Card and A. Kruger; *The American Economic Review* Sept. 1994.
Wal-Mart published financial reports.
"Among Equals" by The Equality Trust Spring 2014.
"Making Ends Meet at Walmart," by Gretchen Morgenson, *The New York Times*, May 10, 2014.

## Case Discussion Questions

1. The thesis in the end of chapter case is that Wal-Mart uses a corporate model that is not sustainable. Do you agree or disagree? Substantiate your argument with evidence.
2. What measures would be required for Wal-Mart to develop a sustainable business model?
3. Contrast Wal-Mart's employment policies with those of Costco and Target. What factors make the difference?

# 11 Global Labor Markets

## Chapter Outline

Global Labor Markets
    Globalization
What Makes a Sweatshop?
Impact of Globalization on the Economies of Less Economically
    Developed Countries
Conclusion
End of Chapter Case: Rana Plaza Collapse, Bangladesh

## Chapter Introduction

With the globalization of labor markets, the issues of international labor standards and abusive labor conditions arise. Global sourcing and outsourcing first of manufacturing, then of white collar and professional jobs, are emergent trends in the early twenty-first century, impacting both countries with developed economies and less economically developed countries.

## Chapter Goal and Learning Objectives

*Chapter Goal:* To understand the implications of, and ethical challenges posed by, the globalization of labor markets and to fashion employment policies that are both competitive in a global environment and fair.

*Learning Objectives:*

1. Understand the mechanisms by which labor markets have become globalized.
2. Explain what makes a sweatshop.
3. Debate the impact of globalization of labor markets on less economically developed countries and the related ethical challenges.

4. Develop proposals to mitigate the most egregious practices victimizing workers in low labor cost countries, including child labor and de facto slavery.

5. Recommend a supplier code of conduct and an inspection system for the Children's Place in Bangladesh.

## Global Labor Markets

Global standards of living are on the rise. Even LEDCs are experiencing dramatic rise in the standard of living in the early twenty-first century, spurred by the invention and spread of *microenterprise*[1] and by global sourcing.[2] Although microenterprise is typically discussed in terms of the benefits to the entrepreneur, bringing increased income to poor mothers and their families, production by the microenterprise also increases access to consumer goods and raises the standard of living among predominantly rural, poor people living in LEDCs, such as Bangladesh.

Furthermore *global sourcing*, such as the development of call centers in India, the manufacture of products for Wal-Mart in China, and the growth of textile production in Bangladesh, leads to an increase in worker income enabling a rise in the standard of living for the workers in their role as consumers in less-developed countries. China, for example, has been a consumer goods shortage society, so that a benefit of direct foreign investment in China and global sourcing by multinational enterprise, as well as the growth of local enterprise, has been that consumer goods have become both affordable and abundant. With the globalization of labor markets, the issues of international labor standards and abusive labor conditions arise.

### *Globalization*

While global product markets were developed as early as the Age of Exploration, the post-Industrial Revolution has given rise to global labor markets as well. The creation of global rapid shipping routes, air travel and the information "highway," created by the synergy of computer technology and the invention of the Internet, has made the integration of global product and labor markets possible. Thomas L. Freidman calls this phenomenon the "flattening" of the world.[3]

Friedman attributes the flattening of the world to the end of the Cold War, the development of the computer and the linking of computers via the Internet, as well the application of computer software to project management. Additional forces that serve to integrate, or "flatten," the world include outsourcing and offshoring. Actually, outsourcing and offshoring are consequences of the more fundamental facilitators, and they further integrate global enterprise and relationships among enterprises, including the creation of supply chains.[4]

True globalization makes possible "the global web." Robert Reich uses the term "the global web" to point out the rise of an international division of labor between countries.[5] The shift of routine, mass production operations to LEDCs occurred in the 1970s. Initially, the destination countries were cheap labor market countries such as South Korea and Mexico. US workers displaced by the move of manufacturing operations offshore were retrained under special legislation, including the Job Training Partnership Act.[6] However, more recently, Mexico and South Korea have been displaced as low-labor cost countries by such countries as mainland China, Sri Lanka, Vietnam and Indonesia. Because communications, including shipping, have become low cost and rapid, products can be "produced" among a web or network of companies. The final product may be produced among several companies. For example, Friedman uses Dell Computer as an example of production using the global web.

The consequence of the global web, or production networks among countries that compete with each other for the location of operations, is that countries may become specialized among each other for particular types of operations. Initially, low-skill, low-wage manufacturing jobs were located in LEDCs. More recently, however, service jobs such as customer service call centers, have moved offshore, particularly to India, which is an English-speaking country. Most recently, high-end, high-technology jobs are being located in developing countries. Taiwan, for example, is specializing in computer chip manufacturing. India, with its good technical education systems and English-speaking population, may be becoming a center for high technology. For example, Microsoft located a research and development facility in Bangalore, India.[7] Ironically, South Asian Indian engineers, who emigrated to the United States for employment opportunities, are being displaced by the move of engineering work to India.[8]

The global network is facilitated by the creation of transnational trading organizations. For example the General Agreement on Tariffs and Trade (GATT) was established after World War II, in 1947. Then the European Common Market was created in 1958, with internal tariffs among member countries removed in 1968. The Common Market laid the groundwork for the present day European Union. In the Americas, the North American Free Trade Association, executed in 1994, created a trading partnership among the United States, Canada and Mexico. In 2005, the Central America Free Trading Association was approved by the United States Congress. The South East Asian Nations created a regional trading association among Indonesia, Singapore, Malaysia, Thailand, the Philippines and Brunei in 1967. The World Trade Organization was created in 1995, as an outgrowth of GATT to promote tariff free trading among its member states.[9] See Table 11.1.

## What Makes a Sweatshop?

The location of manufacturing operations in LEDCs raises concerns about possible exploitation of workers in the less economically developed countries. The concerns include child labor, abusive working conditions, hazardous and unsafe working conditions, environmental hazards and fair wages. Some

*Table 11.1* Transnational Trading Organizations

| Transnational Trading Organizations | Year Created | Member Countries |
|---|---|---|
| GATT,General Agreement on Tariffs and Trade | 1947 | 159 countries |
| Common Market | 1958 | France |
| European Economic Community | 1967 | West Germany, Italy, Netherlands, Belgium, Luxembourg original members |
| ASEAN, Association of South East Asian Nations | 1967 | Indonesia, Singapore, Malaysia, Thailand, Philippines, Brunei |
| NAFTA, North American Free Trade Organization | 1994 | Canada, United States, Mexico |
| WTO, World Trade Organization | 1995 | 2005, 145 nations |
| CAFTA, Central American Free Trade Organization | 2005 | Costa Rica, El Salvador, Guatemala, Honduras, Nicaragua, Dominican Republic |
| SAFTA, South Asian Free Trade Organization | 2006 | Bangladesh, Bhutan, India, Maldivia, Nepal, Pakistan, Sri Lanka |

companies, such as Nike, locate their production facilities in LEDCs as a matter of corporate strategy. Levi Strauss also locates its manufacturing plants for its jeans in LEDCs , and in fact, closed all its North American facilities during 2003 and 2004.[10] Apple produces its iPad and iPhones in China, with an important subcontractor at FoxConn.[11] The question arises: would companies such as Nike, Levi Strauss, and Apple choose to produce in developing countries if there were no labor cost and regulatory cost differentials?[12] Do these strategies amount to using sweatshops?

The International Labor Organization (ILO), based in Geneva, Switzerland, has developed model international labor standards for fair employment practices by international organizations.[13] In the years since the 1990s, when the subcontractor sweatshop conditions became known, the ILO, as well as multinational corporations including Nike, Levi Strauss, and Kathy Lee Gifford enterprises, have developed supplier codes of conduct and learned to how to enforce them. Apple joined the Fair Labor Association (FLA) after its problems with overtime were publicized in January 2012.[14] It is the only technology company to have joined the FLA. Apple is working on resolving the criticisms of the employment conditions but it finds the issue of overtime to be relatively intractable; Apple anticipates that it will take several years to bring overtime to conformity with the requirements of Chinese law.[15] Sweatshops are not exclusively a problem of LEDCs. The US Congress requested the General Accounting Office (GAO) to issue a report about the prevalence of sweatshops in the garment industry. The GAO defines a sweatshop as "an employer that violates more than one federal or state labor law governing minimum wage and overtime, child labor, industrial homework, occupational safety and health, workers' compensation, or industry registration."[16]

When Nike Corporation became embroiled in its "sweatshop" controversy, it defended its corporate reputation by asserting that it did not operate sweatshops and that any adverse conditions among the subcontractors in its supply chain had been corrected. A consumer activist in California brought suit against Nike for "false and deceptive" advertising.[17] Nike defended the charges against it on the basis that it was engaged in political speech, for which there is wide latitude in opinion-giving. Kasky argued that Nike was engaged in commercial speech and that Nike's claims must be verifiable. Although Nike contested the characterization of its advertising that it did not operate sweatshops as commercial speech, and although the ACLU defended Nike's position, marketers generally conclude that Nike was using its statements that it did not operate sweatshops to induce consumers to purchase its products and, therefore, Nike's statements constitute commercial speech. However, the case settled without the issue in controversy being determined: whether Nike was engaged in political or commercial speech and whether corporations would be held to a "truth in advertising" standard when they assert to their customers that they do not operate sweatshops.[18]

Can Nike shift the ethical burden of sweatshop or exploitive labor conditions to subcontractors who actually produce the product? Or should Nike be held responsible for the working conditions of its subcontractors? The monitoring of working conditions in its subcontractors involves supply chain management, as discussed in Chapter 7. Nike, in its evolution of its monitoring and compliance process, has acted as a learning organization, following the model developed by Peter Senge.[19]

A related issue is: what is an appropriate wage for workers in developing countries who work for Nike, Levi Strauss, or other multinational corporations? Is it sufficient to meet the local minimum wage of the host country or is there an obligation to pay a "living wage?" Is there an obligation on the part of the multinational corporation to ensure that real wages keep up with inflation or other monetary problems in the country where the goods are manufactured? Would such an obligation be fair to the enterprise, since monetary issues such as inflation or currency devaluation are beyond the control of the enterprise?

## Impact of Globalization on the Economies of Less Economically Developed Countries

The benefits of global sourcing of work on LEDCs are significant. Global sourcing is a significant means of poverty alleviation. Moreover, the premise of "wealth at the bottom of the pyramid" is that it is in the self-interest of corporations to market to citizens of LEDCs.[20] Prahalad and Hart urge multinational, global corporations to see the enormous opportunities that derive from marketing to the poorest people in the world, those at the bottom of the pyramid. The market at the bottom of the pyramid are people who live on less than US1\$

per day or US2$ per day. Their thesis is that an orientation of global corporations to people at the bottom of the pyramid will bring prosperity to the poorest people of the world, as well as serve as an effective business proposition for private enterprise. Other strategists have joined the effort to eradicate global poverty through business solutions. Jeffrey Sachs's *The End of Poverty* was linked to the United Nations Millennium Development Goal of halving global poverty by 2015.[21] Banerjee and Duflo's *Poor Economics: A Radical Rethinking of The Way To Fight Global Poverty*, which won the *Financial Times*/Goldman Sachs best business book of the year in 2011[22] proposed anti-poverty interventions based on how the poor live and chose within their life parameters. Paul Polak and Mal Warwick in 2013 proposed *The Business Solution to Poverty: Designing Products and Services for Three Billion New Consumers*, which advocates "designing for the market"[23] of those at the bottom of the pyramid.

Concerns for employees working in outsourced firms must involve their physical conditions of work. For example, soccer ball are typically produced in LECDs. There are toxic hazards in the production of soccer balls. The Global Forum for Sports and Environment convened a forum that negotiated standards for the production of soccer balls in LEDCs, the Lahore/Sialkot Declaration on Corporate Responsibility. See Box 11.1.

---

### Box 11.1   The Lahore/Sialkot Declaration on Corporate Responsibility

Lahore/Sialkot, 26 November 2004—Following two days of discussions in Lahore and Sialkot, Pakistan, during the Third Global Forum for Sports and Environment (G-ForSE), organized by UNEP and the Global Sports Alliance (GSA), the leaders of the sporting goods industry in Sialkot, who produce 60 per cent of the soccer balls used around the world, unanimously endorsed a declaration calling for environmental concerns to be fully taken into account in their industry…

Leaders have courageously tackled the issue of child labour in recent years and have committed to continue to improve working and environmental standards in line with the UN Global Compact initiated by the UN Secretary-General, Kofi Annan.

---

The Lahore/Sialkot Declaration on Corporate Environmental Responsibility
Recognizing the value of involving the private sector in achieving the United Nations Millennium Goals;
Recognizing the role of the environment in the Global Compact of the United Nations Secretary General;
Recognizing the importance that an increasing number of companies are placing on the Global Reporting Initiative of the United Nations Environment Programme;
Noting the importance of the participation of the corporate sector in the implementation of the United Nations Decade on Education for Sustainable Development and the celebration of the United Nations Year of Sport and Physical Education—2005;

Further recognizing that considerable progress has already been accomplished in incorporating environmental concerns in the work of sporting goods companies;

Further inspired by the social progress achieved in many parts of the world, including Lahore and Sialkot where child labour has been eliminated for the soccer ball industry;

Determined to contribute to the efforts for human progress and the reduction of poverty;

1. We sport related industries therefore agree: to raise the importance of sustainable development and the environment in our work principles;
2. to include the environment as a key factor in our non-financial reporting;
3. to reduce and improve the use of water and energy during the production of sporting goods;
4. to introduce cleaner technology, reduce the amount of toxic and chemical waste produced and other pollutants in our production facilities;
5. to raise environmental awareness and action among company workers;
6. to promote and sponsor children and youth activities linking good health, sport and environment;
7. to participate in and support initiatives that seek to promote the linkages between sport and the environment including with athletes.

Source: http://www.unep.org/Documents.Multilingual/Default.asp?DocumentID=412&ArticleID=4673&1

The working conditions that have come to light in Bangladesh were worse than imagined by the contractors. A fire at Tazreen Plaza killed 117 workers and burned at least 200 others.[24] The violations at Tazreen Plaza harkened back to the Triangle Shirtwaist Fire of 1911.[25] Then in April 2013 Rana Plaza collapsed, killing more than 1,100 workers.[26] Rana Plaza was inspected the day before the collapse and the building had been condemned. However, workers, mostly women, were visited at their homes and instructed to return to work and threatened with pay being docked. The scope of codes for subcontracts must be expanded to include building integrity, fire codes and other matters that might have been taken for granted by outsourcing firms. Building integrity and fire codes are subjects of both the Bangladesh Accord on Fire and Building Safety[27] and the Alliance for Bangladesh Worker Safety.[28] Issues of global sourcing and supply chain management after Rana Plaza are the subject of the end of chapter case.

## Conclusion

The technological forces that have "flattened" the world and created the "global web" lead to ethical challenges in the management of the global labor market. Is the motivation for locating operations in LEDCs purely opportunistic, exploiting wage and cost of living differentials, as well as a more lax, lower cost regulatory environment? Or is the globalization of operations done with an appreciation for the economic development that global sourcing brings creating "wealth at the bottom of the pyramid"? Are global companies developing best practice standards for operations, both environmental and labor standards, avoiding the creation of double standards for operations? Are global companies sensitive to, and managing with compassion, the unintended negative consequences of global sourcing on the displaced workers of more economically developed countries?

## Chapter Discussion Questions

1. Nike uses subcontractors in developing countries to manufacture its products, as a matter of corporate strategy. Does this strategy amount to using sweatshops?
2. What makes a sweatshop?
3. Would companies such as Nike, Levi Strauss, Wal-Mart, Apple, and apparel companies such as Kathy Lee Gifford choose to produce in developing countries if there were no labor cost and regulatory cost differentials?
4. What is an appropriate wage for workers in developing countries who work for multinational corporations? Is there an obligation on the part of the multinational corporation to ensure that real wages keep up with inflation or other monetary problems in the country where the goods are manufactured?
5. How can the most egregious human rights abuses be prevented in production facilities of outsourcing companies?

## Notes

1  See Muhammad Yunus, *Banker to the Poor: Micro-Lending and the Battle Against World Poverty* (London: Aurum Press, 1999). See also David Bornstein, *The Price of a Dream: The Story of the Grameen Bank* (Champaign, IL: University of Chicago Press, 1996).
2  See Thomas L. Friedman, *The World is Flat: A Brief History of the Twenty-First Century* (New York: Farrar, Straus and Giroux, 2005).
3  Friedman, *The World is Flat.*
4  The infrastructure enabling *outsourcing* lay in fiber optic cables, making possible web based communications worldwide as well as satellites for communications. The problems associated with Y2K were resolved by the programming skills of Asian Indian programmers using the global communications network. The coupling of the ability to communicate globally and the urgent need for programming power to resolve the Y2K programming code issues spurred the outsourcing initiatives to India. *Offshoring* was spurred by China's open door policy initiated by Premier Deng Xiaoping in 1977 and then China's accession to the World Trade Organization in 2001. Offshoring involves moving operations from one location to another location, one that has "cheaper labor, lower taxes, subsidized energy, and lower health-care costs." *Supply chaining* involves the integration of retailers with their task environment: suppliers and customers. Wal-Mart is a master of inventory management.

Supply-chaining depends on the ability to interface across organizational boundaries among interdependent, linked systems. See Friedman, *The World is Flat.*

5 Robert Reich, *The Work of Nations: Preparing Ourselves for 21st Century Capitalism* (New York: Alfred A. Knopf, 1992). The title is a play on the words and title of Adam Smith's *The Wealth of Nations.*

6 Robert Guttman, "Job Training Partnership Act," *Monthly Labor Review,* March 1983, 3–10.

7 "Microsoft opens R&D facility in Bangalore", *The Times of India,* July 26, 2011.

8 Saritha Rai, "Is the Next Silicon Valley Taking Root in Bangalore (India)?," *New York Times,* March 20, 2006.

9 "Welcome to the Regional Trade Agreements Information System (RTA-IS)," *World Trade Organization,* last modified June 27, 2014, http://rtais.wto.org/UI/PublicAllR-TAList.aspx.

10 Jenny Strasburg, "Levi's to Close Last U.S. Plants: Much of the Work Once Done in This Country Has Moved Instead to Cheaper Contract Factories in Asia and Latin America," *San Francisco Chronicle,* Sept. 26, 2003.

11 Charles Duhigg and Keith Bradsher, "How the U.S. Lost Out on iPhone Work," *The i Economy part 1: An Empire Built Abroad, New York Times,* Jan. 21, 2012 http://www.nytimes.com/2012/01/22/business/apple-america-and-a-squeezed-middle-class.html?pagewanted=all&_r=0, and Charles Duhigg and David Barboza, "In China, Human Costs Are Built Into an iPad," *The i Economy part 2: A Punishing System, New York Times,* Jan. 25, 2012.

12 As discussed in Chapter 4, is it ethical for companies to rely on the local environmental regulatory framework if best practices indicate other standards?

13 International Labour Office
   Bureau for Workers' Activities
   CH-1211 Geneva 22
   Fax: +41 22 799 6570
   ACTRAV Homepage: http://www.ilo.org/actrav/

14 Duhigg and Bradsher, "How the U.S. Lost Out"; Duhigg and Barboza, "In China, Human Costs."

15 "Final Foxconn Verification Status Report," December 2013, *Fair Labor Association,* http://www.fairlabor.org/sites/default/files/documents/reports/final_foxconn_verification_report_0.pdf.

16 "GAO/HEHS-95-29 Prevalence of Sweatshops," Nov. 1994, *U.S. Government Accountability Office,* http://www.gao.gov/archive/1995/he95029.pdf.

17 *Kasky v. Nike,* 539 U.S. 654 (2003).

18 *Kasky v. Nike* proceeded through the California state trial court, to the appellate court as well as to the California Supreme court. The verdict of the California Supreme Court was appealed to the U.S. Supreme court, which granted certiorari in the case. The U.S. Supreme Court determined that Kasky had standing under California law to bring the suit on behalf of consumers but that the writ of certiorari had been improvidently granted, with the result that the United States Supreme Court would not decide the issues in the case. The case then settled.

19 Peter Senge, *The Fifth Discipline: The Art and Practice of the Learning Organization* (New York: Doubleday/Currency, 1990).

20 See C.K. Prahalad and Stuart Hart, "The Fortune at the Bottom of the Pyramid," *Strategy+Business* 26 (2004): 54–67. See also C.K. Prahalad, *The Fortune at the Bottom of the Pyramid: Eradicating Poverty Through Profits* (Upper Saddle River, NJ: Prentice Hall/FT Press, 2004) and Stuart L. Hart, *Capitalism at the Crossroads: The Unlimited Business*

*Opportunities in Solving the World's Most Difficult Problems* (Upper Saddle River, NJ: Prentice Hall /FT Press, 2005). An early approach is given by Joshua D. Margolis and James P. Walsh, "Misery Loves Companies: Rethinking Social Initiatives by Business," *Administrative Science Quarterly*, Vol. 48, No. 2 (Jun 2003) 268.

21  Jeffrey Sachs, *The End of Poverty: Economics Possibilities of Our Time* (New York: Penguin Press, 2005). For a statement of the Millennium Development Goals, see "Millennium Development Goals," *UNICEF*, last modified 2014, http://www.unicef.org/mdg/index_proverty.htm.

22  Abhijit Banerjee and Esther Duflo, *Poor Economics: A Radical Rethinking of the Way to Fight Global Poverty* (New York: Public Affairs, 2011).

23  Paul Polak and Mal Warwick, *The Business Solution to Poverty: Designing Products and Services for Three Billion New Consumers* (San Francisco: Berrett-Koehler, 2013).

24  Steven Greenhouse, "Documents Reveal New Details About Walmart's Connection to Tazreen Factory Fire," *New York Times*, Dec. 10, 2012, http://www.nytimes.com/2012/12/11/world/asia/tazreen-factory-used-by-2nd-walmart-supplier-at-time-of-fire.html. See also Julfikar Ali Manik and Ellen Barry, "Months After Deadly Fire, Owners of Bangladesh Factory Surrender to Court," *New York Times*, Feb. 9, 2014, http://www.nytimes.com/2014/02/10/world/asia/owners-of-bangladesh-factory-surrender-in-deadly-fire.html?_r=0.

25  See "Triangle Fire," *PBS American Experience*, last modified 2014, http://www.pbs.org/wgbh/americanexperience/films/triangle/player/.

26  Jim Yardley, "Report on Deadly Factory Collapse in Bangladesh Finds Widespread Blame," *New York Times*, May 22, 2013, http://www.nytimes.com/2013/05/23/world/asia/report-on-bangladesh-building-collapse-finds-widespread-blame.html.

27  *The Accord on Building Fire and Safety in Bangladesh*, last modified 2014, http://www.bangladeshaccord.org/.

28  *Alliance for Bangladesh Worker Safety*, last modified 2014, http://www.bangladesh-workersafety.org/.

## End of Chapter Case: Rana Plaza Collapse, Bangladesh

### Business as usual is not an option : Supply chains and sourcing after Rana Plaza

*by Sarah Labowitz and Dorothee Baumann-Pauly*
Center for Business and Human Rights, Stern School of Business, New York University, April 2014.

One year ago, the collapse of a factory complex at Rana Plaza in the industrial outskirts of Dhaka, Bangladesh, killed almost 1,200 garment workers. It was the world's worst industrial accident in 30 years, and came in the aftermath of the Tazreen factory fire in Dhaka only five months earlier that killed more than 120 workers. The images of grief-stricken families combing through the rubble is now seared in our consciousnesses. The size and scope of these disasters have captured public attention, focused on gaps in factory safety in Bangladesh. But a closer look reveals the uncomfortable truth that these tragedies are the almost inevitable result of a highly disaggregated sourcing model which has become the basis of global supply chains.

This report looks behind the headlines to reveal the way business operates at different levels of the supply chain in Bangladesh, the seventh most populous country in the world. We focus on global business relationships and especially what we call "indirect sourcing." Indirect sourcing relies on the routine practice of subcontracting, often through purchasing agents and in a manner that is not transparent to buyers, to increase margins and boost production capacity while keeping costs low. As orders are subcontracted and in some cases re-subcontracted, production moves into facilities that are outside the scope of current regulation and often are "noncompliant" with minimum standards for safety and workers' rights.

Indirect sourcing is an essential, though poorly understood, feature of the business models of global buyers and national-level suppliers in Bangladesh. Acknowledging these relationships is key to understanding the real scope of the factory safety challenges in Bangladesh. It also is essential for developing comprehensive policy responses that both will protect workers throughout the sector and ensure the sustained growth of Bangladesh's export economy.

Indirect sourcing increases risk by reducing control and transparency in the supply chain. While this is the most prevalent sourcing model in Bangladesh, an alternative model is beginning to emerge. A small group of leading buyers and suppliers are starting to practice a more direct, transparent sourcing model in which the buyer works with partner suppliers on a long-term basis. We discuss the elements of this more direct and transparent sourcing strategy as an important alternative to indirect sourcing.

Second, the report examines public and private and governance of the garment sector. The government of Bangladesh should be the principal regulator of the garment sector. The country is deeply reliant on garments in its export economy and as a driver of employment and social development. The government also should be centrally involved in ensuring safety and high standards for working conditions, in addition to implementing public policies that encourage continued business growth in a way that benefits the whole society.

But today the government of Bangladesh lacks the political will, the technical capacity, and the resources necessary to protect the basic rights of its workers. Bangladesh ranks at or near the bottom across all measures of good governance, including civil justice, regulatory enforcement, and absence of corruption. In these areas, it is on the same level as Sierra Leone, Venezuela, Zimbabwe, Ethiopia, and Pakistan.

After years of halting progress, the government launched a National Action Plan to upgrade the garment sector in 2013. This plan is ambitious in scope, but unrealistic in terms of the government's ability to implement it. The United States' suspension of Bangladesh's participation in a preferential trade program, coupled with the threat of suspension from the European Union's program, has been a key motivator for the government's commitments in this area.

We examine the status of public governance in the garment sector, including the legal framework for labor law and compensation for victims of industrial accidents, as well as the government's own National Action Plan.

We also explore the prospects for successful implementation of the International Labour Organization (ILO) and the International Finance Corporation (IFC)'s Better Work Bangladesh program. Governments, companies, civil society, and unions have all looked to this program as an important means of enhancing governance in the garment sector.

In the absence of strong government oversight, global companies have stepped in to provide some measure of private governance. Two major private initiatives were created in 2013 by global brands and retailers—the Bangladesh Accord on Fire and Building Safety ('Accord') and the Alliance for Bangladesh Worker Safety ('Alliance'). These represent an unprecedented collaboration among most of the biggest clothing companies in the world to collectively address structural weaknesses in the garment sector.

Much attention has been devoted to parsing differences between these two initiatives. Our analysis concludes that the Accord and the Alliance are fundamentally similar and that in key aspects, both are insufficient. Neither the Accord nor the Alliance addresses the role of indirect sourcing practices in their members' supply chains. Both are prioritizing rapid inspection of those factories that maintain direct relationships with their member brands, but neither initiative has yet developed a coordinated and clear system for financing remediation efforts based on the results of their inspections.

It is impossible to consider the long-term viability of Bangladesh as a major garment production center without addressing significant gaps in the country's infrastructure. Despite the extraordinary growth of the garment sector over the last 30 years, Bangladesh's infrastructure is among the most underdeveloped in the world.

In some respects, the demands of the garment sector have actually exacerbated the problem, placing even greater demands on an already overtaxed system. Erratic electrical supply and poor transport networks aggravate production delays and raise production costs. Ultimately, it is workers who pay the price for the country's poor infrastructure, in the form of long hours in unsafe facilities, where an electrical spark can lead to a deadly fire in a cramped building.

Many experts argue that moving garment production into export zones should be a key feature of a forward-looking strategy for the sector. We discuss the positive infrastructure attributes of the export processing zones, as well as longstanding governance challenges and weak labor law protections in the zones.

Foreign funding—from donor governments and international financial institutions like the World Bank and IFC—should be part of a response to the infrastructure challenges that underlie many safety risks in the garment sector. But our analysis reveals that while significant funding is being directed at training, inspection, and empowerment programs in the garment sector, relatively little funding is directed at infrastructure development. Corruption remains a significant obstacle to funding large-scale projects such as power plants and bridges, but these are essential for the sector's sustained growth and safety.

Filling the governance gap will require a network of interconnected actors—national and international companies, governments, civil society, unions, and international organizations—to enhance governance in the garment sector through a mix of public and private mechanisms.

This means fostering greater transparency in business relationships, investing in enhanced regulatory oversight, coordinating financing systems for making factories safer, and prioritizing infrastructure development.

This report delves into the nuances of the garment business in Bangladesh, but the lessons of the garment sector there apply broadly to all companies that rely on global manufacturing supply chains. Subcontracting and indirect sourcing relationships are increasingly prevalent in global business models everywhere. We hope this report sparks a discussion about increasing transparency, control, and oversight in the supply chain and what this would mean for the workers who are the heart of the system.

In the aftermath of Rana Plaza, "business as usual is not an option" was a popular refrain among people in the garment sector in Dhaka. We believe business has been and will continue to be a force for good in Bangladesh. Achieving better working conditions and a sustainable garment sector will require that business operate differently. We present this report as a reflection of a year of listening, research, and close observation of the way business operates in the supply chain. Our goal is to make it possible to discuss publicly what many people in the sector already know. This report attempts to connect the pieces of a complex business landscape and their relationships to workplace safety and workers' rights. This represents a new way of viewing human rights challenges through a business lens that we hope will make a positive contribution to the sector and the country's continued growth.

## Executive Summary

This is a report about the garment industry in Bangladesh, its supply chain, and the workers at its heart. It is written in the context of intense international attention on working conditions in the global supply chain, and a shared desire for higher standards in the factories that produce the inexpensive clothing on which consumers in the United States and Europe have come to rely. It starts from the premise that the garment sector has greatly benefited the people and the economy of Bangladesh. But for low-cost garment production to continue to create value for business and society in Bangladesh and around the world, actors across the supply chain need to acknowledge and address the risks created by an indirect sourcing model.

There are significant challenges to achieving the objective of a sustainable garment sector in Bangladesh. To date, too little attention has been paid to connecting the dots to provide an overall assessment of where things stand and what really needs to be done to ensure safer factories and better working conditions. In this report, the Center for Business and Human Rights at NYU Stern provides that overview.

## Conclusions

1. Indirect sourcing is the routine practice of subcontracting, often through purchasing agents and in a manner that is not transparent to buyers or regulators. It has become an essential feature of the garment sector in Bangladesh as a means of increasing margins and boosting production capacity while keeping costs low. In the absence of an effective regulatory

framework, the prevalence of indirect sourcing strategies has resulted in a supply chain driven by the pursuit of lowest nominal costs. This has increased risks for business and workers by undermining wages and working conditions, as well as investment in technology and training, and improvements in productivity and quality.

2.  The two major remedial plans launched in the last year, the Bangladesh Accord on Fire and Building Safety and the Alliance for Bangladesh Worker Safety, fail to address the greatest risks of this system. The two initiatives have established parallel, and in some cases overlapping, systems of factory monitoring and worker training. But the universe of factories encompassed by their programs is less than 2,000, while the total base of factories and facilities producing for the export garment sector is likely between 5,000 and 6,000. The worst conditions are largely in the factories and faculties that fall outside the scope of these agreements.

3.  The government of Bangladesh lacks the resources, administrative capacity, and often the will to protect workers in garment factories. The labor law remains weak and enforcement weaker still. Local industry enjoys outsized influence in the country's politics, which impedes the establishment and enforcement of rigorous regulation. The government has launched an ambitious National Action Plan aimed at addressing factory safety gaps, but few of its provisions have been successfully implemented and the government lacks resources to make it real.

4.  The poor state of critical infrastructure, especially the weakness of the electrical supply throughout the country, exacerbates risks of factory fires and the likelihood of future tragedies. The international community has contributed significant funds to develop the garment sector in Bangladesh, but these programs are largely limited to training and for workers and management, inspections, and funds to support the International Labour Organization and International Finance Corporation's Better Work program. Especially in light of major corruption challenges, foreign governments and the World Bank are now shying away from investment in the infrastructure development that will be necessary to truly upgrade the sector.

## The Way Forward

People across the sector recognize that Bangladesh's sustained economic and social development depends on the expansion and vitality of the garment sector, including through the continued investment of global buyers. We share the goal expressed by many people of ensuring that "made in Bangladesh" is a sign of pride for workers, business, and consumers. This is the right moment to assess the current status of efforts to improve the garment sector in Bangladesh and make necessary course corrections. We divide our recommendations into three broad categories, focused on business practices, governance, and infrastructure and foreign funding.

## Recommendations to the Business Community

Global brands and their first-tier manufacturing partners need to recalibrate their business relationships to prioritize transparency and longer-term commitments. This must begin with a thorough assessment of the overall universe of garment factories and facilities—big and small, registered and unregistered—that is producing products for export. The Accord and Alliance should join forces in this effort, working closely with the trade associations and the government. Once a comprehensive factory list has been compiled that identifies which factories or facilities produce for each brand, actors around the supply need to develop an ambitious but practical plan, consistent with business realities, to address the most urgent risks. Though this will be a long-term and difficult task, global brands should not cut and run from Bangladesh.

## Recommendations to the Government of Bangladesh

The government needs to reclaim ownership of the country's regulatory system. It can not continue to outsource regulatory functions to the trade associations and others. International organizations like the ILO that a re working with the government need to focus their resources and attention on building the government's capacity and expertise to monitor factory conditions and to develop credible, well-resourced remedial systems. The government should quickly complete the work of compensating victims of Rana Plaza and should institutionalize this effort to meet the needs of victims of future industrial accidents. Ultimately the government needs to take the lead in overseeing this system, though the private sector also needs to contribute.

## Recommendations to the International Donor Community

The task of repairing and rebuilding the most hazardous factories in Bangladesh will take years to complete and cost hundreds of millions of dollars. The effort to build a functional infrastructure will require still greater resources. It is unfathomable that the government of Bangladesh and the private sector can do this alone. The international community—foreign governments, the World Bank, and other multilateral institutions—need to step up as well. As we mark the one year anniversary of the Rana Plaza tragedy, this is a propitious time for the international community to convene a major donors conference on factory safety and critical infrastructure in Bangladesh. Absent an infusion of significant international support, we a re destined to see recurring tragedies in Bangladesh which represent a growing threat to the long-term sustainability of its garment industry.

We believe that it is possible to see a different future, where the garment industry continues to grow and compete by producing large volumes of clothing in a timely manner at competitive prices and where workers enjoy safety in the workplace. As we mark the one year anniversary of Rana Plaza, this is the future of Bangladesh we all need to pursue.

## Appendix 1

### A Primer on Buying and Selling Garments in Bangladesh

## Making an Inquiry

Either directly or through a purchasing agent, the brand makes an inquiry about a factory's capacity and availability to produce a given garment—say 100,000 shirts—to certain quality specifications and by a specified delivery date. The factory may be subject to inspections to assess its capacity, levels of quality, and social compliance.

## Negotiating the Sales Contract

If the factory is available, it will be asked to make samples of the garment. A sales contract is then negotiated, including design and materials specifications, quantity, price per piece, protections for intellectual property, and a delivery date. (Note that design specifications often are not finalized at this stage and may be adjusted up until the time of production.) The delivery date is often several months ahead to allow time to import the necessary materials and manufacture the order. The factory owner reserves the appropriate number of lines in the factory to meet the delivery date. (A line is the number of machines it takes to complete a given garment, ranging from 10 machines up to 50 machines, depending on the complexity of the product.) To illustrate how this works, let's say we will produce 100,000 shirts at $1.00 per piece by September l, for a total order value of$100,000.

## Opening an Export Letter of Credit

The buyer sends an export letter of credit ('export LJC') to the factory or agent's bank. Under the export L/C, payment will be remitted only when the buyer has received the finished goods. This means that the factory owner must procure all of the materials, pay workers, and cover operational expenses well before receiving payment.

## Opening a Back-to-Back Letter of Credit to Procure Materials

The export letter of credit is a guarantee that the factory owner or agent will receive payment in the future if the goods are delivered as specified. On the basis of this guarantee, the factory owner or agent is able to open another letter of credit for the purpose of importing materials (hence the "back to back" LJC). In our example, we will need fabric, buttons, zippers, labels, trim, thread, and packaging materials in order to complete the jackets, in addition to the cost of utilities and labor. Most banks allow an owner or agent to borrow up to 75% of an order's total value, or $75,000. The remaining $25,000 will cover labor costs, utilities, and any goods purchased on the local market.

## Getting Permission to Import from BGMEA or BKMEA

To import materials duty free, the owner requires a 'utilization declaration 'or 'UD; which is issued by the BGMEA or the BKMEA. The UD ensures that goods imported duty free for the purpose of export production do not end up on the local market. This means that in Bangladesh, the trade associations issue import and export authorizations, rather than the government's trade or customs ministry. The UD includes authorization for a specific quantity of imported material matched to the specifications of the order. So if we need two yards of fabric for each shirt, the BGMEA will authorize the import of 200,000 yards of fabric.

## Procuring Materials

The factory owner procures materials, most likely from China. Once the fabric is shipped, the factory owner's bank pays the fabric supplier. This is called a bank guarantee and allows the factory owner to borrow against the value of the export letter of credit in order to import fabric. If the factory owner fails to deliver the goods to the buyer, he is still liable for the bank guarantee and the purchase price of the fabric. In this way, the system for financing pushes risk downward from the brand to the factory owner.

## Production

Once all materials have been procured and the design specifications are finalized, production can begin. But if the materials arrive late or the buyer delays in submitting its final design, the factory owner's system for reserving lines is thrown off, while the delivery date remains the same. Production is closely monitored by a series of people from inside and outside the factory management structure. The factory's production manager is responsible for all aspects of production quality and delivery time. Quality control specialists from the agent or the brand visit the factory sometimes two or three times per week. Social compliance auditors, either from a third party auditor or the brand itself, visit factories at intervals ranging from every few weeks to once a year. Once the garments are sewn, they are finished with labels and tags listing the retail price and even the plastic security devices that will be removed once the garment is sold. Garments are wrapped in plastic and packed in boxes for transport.

Transporting the finished goods and receiving payment.

If everything goes smoothly and the order is completed on time, the goods are transported by truck to the port in Chittagong (about three hours from Dhaka) and sent by ship to the U.S. or Europe. Once the goods are 'free on board', the factory owner submits the appropriate documentation to his bank, which requests payment from the buyer. The time buyers take to process payments is notoriously slow, and factory owners may not receive payment for six months to a year after the order is shipped.

But often, everything does not go smoothly. If the design is complicated and production takes longer than expected, or if other delays have created time pressure against the delivery date, a factory owner has several options. If he has the space, he can open up additional lines in his own factory. He can either offer workers overtime or require them to work extra hours. If he has **a** strong relationship with the buyer, he can negotiate for an extension on the delivery date. In the worst case scenario, he can pay the significantly higher costs of sending the goods by air rather than by sea.

## Or He Can Subcontract.

In our example, let's say the mother factory needed to subcontract 25,000 pieces of the original order. In the best case scenario, the mother factory would announce its need to subcontract to the buyer, which would work with the factory owner to identify a pre-approved subcontractor that meets the mother factory's level of quality and social compliance. A CSR manager for a European brand walked through the process for authorizing a subcontractor, saying, "[The factory] informs the agent they need a subcontractor, we [the CSR team] send the request to Germany and we do an assessment [of the subcontractor]. If the subcontractor meets the minimum standard, then they are in the list" and the order can proceed.

But the process of notification, inspection, and authorization can take a long time, which often does not meet the needs of a factory facing a looming delivery deadline. So in another, more common scenario, the subcontract is negotiated bilaterally between the two factories or through an agent without the knowledge of the buyer. If both factories are members of one of the trade associations, the trade association registers the subcontract through an 'interbond license'. The license is important for certifying that the materials imported duty free remain within the 'bonded area' of export production. The interbond license is a one-page, typewritten form signed by the mother factory, the subcontract factory, and two representatives from the BGMEA or BKMEA.

In addition, the two factories will draw up a short contract specifying the terms of the agreement. In one subcontract shared with the Center for Business and Human Rights, the subcontract was a simple one-page document that contained information about price, quantity, and delivery, but no provisions related to intellectual property, labor compliance, or design.

All transactions up to this point have been conducted in U.S. dollars and based on credit, with the exception of wages and any materials purchased on the local market. Subcontracting transactions are conducted in Bangladeshi Taka (Tk) through local banks on the basis of bills and receipts that are paid directly by the mother factory.

"Both parties agree to execute this agreement under the following terms and conditions: The 1st party . . . shall supply the necessary Cutting Fabric and Accessories to the 2nd party. The 2nd party . . . Only complete the Cutting, Making, packing & finishing of 8,000 pieces of Men's Shorts Pant Style # . . . against Export L/C No. . . . . The production will proceed under the full care of the 1st party. The 2nd party will also look after production and if any damage of losses, they will be liable for that. After finishing the 2nd party will be bound to return the readymade garments within (date). The agreed CM will be Tk25.00/Pc total sub-contract bill will be paid on delivery by Cash/ Cheque."

The mother factory sends the required materials to produce 25,000 pieces and a supervisor to instruct workers at the subcontracting facility in design and production specifications. Upon delivery of the 25,000 finished shirts, the mother factory pays the subcontractor in Taka, often through a bank transfer. The subcontracted order is combined with the rest of the order and all 100,000 pieces are transported to Chittagong for shipment.

In the third tier of subcontracting—the unregistered, informal system— documentation and contracting is even looser. In our example, the factory that took the subcontract for 25,000 shirts has also faced production delays. So a mid-level cutting manager at this factory phones a friend who runs a very small, unregistered facility with the capacity to produce 5,000 pieces. The manager negotiates with the unregistered factory owner and they reach a verbal agreement on a price and delivery date. The original subcontractor has now become the mother factory.

Unregistered subcontracting is a cash-based system run on bills and receipts. One set of receipts shared with the Center for Business and Human Rights illustrates how the movement of material and finished garments takes place. If, for example, the sub-subcontracting agreement is for 5,000 shirts, the now-mother factory will deliver the component materials as they a re available. The mother factory may only cut 500 pieces of the 5,000 piece order on the first day of production. The mother factory calls the subcontract factory, which is responsible for picking up the available materials, including fabric, thread, and other inputs and accessories. The unregistered subcontract factory then hires a truck or a rickshaw to go to the mother factory to get the materials. One example of a receipt for this kind of transaction follows.

The delivery 'challenge' lists the materials that have been delivered to the unregistered subcontractor, including 90 cones of golden thread, 105 cones of navy thread, 35 rolls of two kinds of elastic, and 25 rolls of twill tape. The materials are delivered "for subwork."

The transport of materials proceeds over the course of several days or a week until all of the inputs for the 5,000 pieces are delivered. At the start of the order, a line manager from the mother factory will visit the subcontractor to demonstrate the proper production process and ensure that production meets its standard. When the order is completed, the 5,000 pieces are combined with the remaining 20,000 pieces of the original subcontract, which are returned to the original mother factory and transported to the port for shipment.

## Appendix 2

### The Accord and the Alliance

The following analysis updates the comparison of the Accord and the Alliance included in the Center's February 11, 2014 submission to the U.S. Senate Committee on Foreign Relations Hearing, "Prospects for Democratic Reconciliation and Workers' Rights in Bangladesh." It is intended as a snapshot of the two initiatives at an early stage of their development, not as an exhaustive comparison. The Center's conclusion is that the similarities between the two initiatives far outweigh their differences.

## Dimension 1: Participation

Both the Accord and the Alliance are comprised primarily of multinational corporations from North America and Europe. The Accord includes two global trade unions as signatories and several Bangladeshi unions. In this respect, it reflects the European industrial relations context, which has been characterized by political involvement through labor parties, worker participation in company decision-making, and relatively high levels of union membership. The Alliance includes the participation of local industry on its board.

| | *Accord* | *Alliance* |
|---|---|---|
| Brands and retailers | Over 150 retailers. The majority of participants are based in Europe; a smaller group is from the Americas. Also includes Asia's largest retailer. | 27 retailers. All are North American companies, representing 90% of readymade garment exports to the United States from Bangladesh. |
| Worker organizations or unions | Two global union Signatories, and a minimum of four unions from Bangladesh | None |
| Local industry | None | The BGMEA President sits on the board. |
| Other participants, observers, or advisors | Four international labor rights NGOs are "witness signatories." | "Supporting associations" include several North American trade associations and the NGO BRAe. U & Fung serves in an advisory capacity. |

## Dimension 2: Decision-Making and Governance

Both initiatives have small governing boards with an independent chair. Membership in the Accord's steering committee is split between retailers and unions. The Alliance's board is split between retailers and outside experts. Both have some international staff, as well as offices and staff in Dhaka.

| | *Accord* | *Alliance* |
|---|---|---|
| Decision-making body | The steering committee is comprised of 3 representatives selected by trade union participants and 3 representatives selected by retailer participants. The ILO selects a neutral chair. | The board of directors includes 4 brand representatives, 4 outside experts, and an elected chair. The Board of advisors comprises 12 multi-stake holder industry experts. |
| Staff | Led by an Executive Director for International Operations and an Executive Director for Bangladesh Operations, with an office and staff in Dhaka. | Formerly led by a President and CEO in Washington, DC; now led by consultants in Washington, DC and Hong Kong, with an office and staff in Dhaka. |

## Dimension 3: Commitments

Each initiative is envisioned to last for five years, through 2018. The Alliance requires that members participate for two years; the Accord requires five years, with some requirements for maintaining order volumes for the first two years. if a member company leaves the Alliance, the member pays a financial penalty. If an Accord member is subject to a dispute, the issue is referred to the Steering Committee, whose decision either party can appeal to binding arbitration. Advocates of the Accord have emphasized that this constitutes a legally binding agreement, but it is not clear that the penalties associated with dispute resolution are significantly different from the more straightforward financial penalties contained in the Alliance.

| | *Accord* | *Alliance* |
|---|---|---|
| Overall program commitment | 5 years (2013–2018) | 5 years (2013–2018) |
| Individual participant commitments | 5 years of participation in the initiative. Member companies commit to maintaining order volumes for two years with Tier 1 and 2 suppliers as long as such business is commercially viable and the factory meets the member company's requirements. | Minimum commitment of 2 years participation in the initiative. |
| Penalties for leaving the initiative | Disputes between partiesare referred to the Steering Committee, whose decisions can be appealed to a binding arbitration process. | Financial penalties assessed if a member Leaves the initiative before the 2-year mark; lesser financial penalties if a member leaves after the 2-year mark. |

## Dimension 4: Program and Approach

In total, the two initiatives encompass 1,894 factories out of the approximately 5,000–6,000 factories and facilities we estimate are part of the export garment manufacturing sector in Bangladesh. The two initiatives offer similar programs, focused on factory safety and building inspections, worker training and empowerment, and making funds available for factory remediation. All program activities in both initiatives focus on building and fire safety and do not address broader issues of labor rights, freedom of association, or business relationships in the supply chain.

|  | *Accord* | *Alliance* |
| --- | --- | --- |
| Core program elements | Safety inspections, remediation, fire and building safety training, member sponsored funding for factory improvements. | Safety inspections, safety and empowerment training, voluntary loans for factory improvements. |
| Transparency | A single aggregated factory list was published on October 3, 2013 and is updated on an ongoing basis. Inspection reports will become public within a maximum of 6 weeks after the inspection. The stake holders of the factory are informed at least 2 weeks after the inspection, except in the event of immediate danger, when they are informed immediately. | Since October 2013, an up-to-date factory lists is released every month. Inspection reports will become public after a remediation plan has been agreed, or in case of imminent danger. |
| Factories covered | "All suppliers producing products for the signatory companies"; approximately 1619 suppliers across three tiers. | "100% of factories in the members' respective supply chains"; approximately 626 factories. |

## Dimension 5: Fees and Funding

In both initiatives, corporate participants make an annual contribution based on dollar volume of exports to cover the inspection and training programs and operational expenses. A heated debate is now playing out about who will pay for the necessary remediation efforts identified through inspections. Our conclusion is that for all practical purposes, both the Accord and the Alliance put the burden of funding repairs on factory owners, with the option of financing from brands to be negotiated bilaterally between Alliance and Accord members and their suppliers. Neither initiative imposes a firm obligation on brands to fund repair of safety deficiencies uncovered by their audits, but both initiatives require factories supplying their members to be in compliance in order to continue to receive orders. This means factory owners are caught in a Catch-22. They are required to be in compliance in order to maintain relationships with Accord and Alliance members, but if they cannot afford the remediation the initiatives determine is necessary, no one is obligated to assist them.

| | Accord | Alliance |
| --- | --- | --- |
| Participant fees to support core programming and operations | Company signatories make a maximum annual contribution of $500,000 ona sliding scale basis relative to volume of sourcing from Bangladesh. Fees cover safety inspections, trainings, and operational expenses. | Members contribute up to $1,000,000 per year to a Worker Safety Fund. Fees are assessed on a tiered basis, based on dollar volume of exports in the previous year. Fees underwrite fire and building safety initiatives in factories supplying member companies and operational expenses. |
| Additional costs to support factory-level remediation | Factory owners are responsible to pay for structural repairs or renovations in factories where remediation is required; brands have agreed to find funding if the owners cannot afford renovations. | Individual members may make affordable financing available to suppliers in their individual supply chains to help finance factory repairs and improvements ona voluntary basis. Terms are set by the individual member company. |
| Support for displaced workers during remediation | Factories must continue paying workers for up to 6 months during the remediation period. Signatory companies shall make reasonable efforts to ensure that displaced workers who cannot return to their original job can find employment with safe suppliers. | 10% of fees directed to the Worker Safety Fund are reserved to support temporarily displaced workers. |

The full report can be found at http://www.stern.nyu.edu/sites/default/files/assets/documents/con_047408.pdf

## Case Discussion Questions

1.  Compare the Bangladesh Accord on Fire and Building Safety and the Alliance for Bangladesh Worker Safety.
    Which approach will produce better outcomes for the workers and enterprises in Bangladesh and other less economically developed countries? How can cooperation and joint action be achieved?

2.  What can be done to surface the sub-contractors that are unknown to the sourcing companies? The NYU report states that 2,000 factories are known but that another 3,000 or 4,000 factories are producing garments for export.

3.  What can be done to end the use of purchasing agents for the placement of contracted garment production?

4.  Disney pulled out of Bangladesh after the Rana Plaza collapse. Is this the most ethical position? Is it possible for firms to stay in Bangladesh ethically? Are there lessons to be learned from the Sullivan Principles? If so, what are they?

# 12  Corporate Governance

## Chapter Outline

Corporate Governance
The Sarbanes Oxley Act
    Board Composition Modified by SOX
    Role of Accounting Firms Under SOX: Accounting Oversight Board
Shareholder Lawsuits
Alternative Models of Incorporation
End of Chapter Case: Bernard Madoff's Ponzi Scheme

## Chapter Introduction

What are the roles and responsibilities of corporate executives? Does the stakeholder model change the responsibilities of corporate executives and boards of directors compared to the model of shareholder capitalism? If so, in what respects? CEO compensation is debated in business circles and the incentives that compensation structures may create for corporate earnings management practices and even fraud in financial statements have been recognized. The Sarbanes Oxley Act makes CEOs and CFOs personally accountable for the accuracy of a corporation's financial statements and requires board audit committees to be independent and to have accounting expertise. SOX also created an Accounting Standards Oversight Board, to strengthen the practices and standards for the certification of financial statements of publicly traded firms by their auditors.

## Chapter Goal and Learning Objectives

*Chapter Goal:* To understand corporate governance and the responsibilities of executives and boards of directors in a global environment.

*Learning Objectives:*

1.    To examine the fiduciary duty of directors to shareholders in light of the stakeholder model of corporate responsibility.

2.  To understand the theory of managerial capitalism and how it sowed the seeds of the current CEO compensation debates.
3.  To evaluate whether earnings management practices may be an unintended negative effect of CEO compensation using stock options.
4.  To explain the Sarbanes Oxley Act and how it changes corporate governance.
5.  To identify and evaluate alternative models of incorporation: Benefit (B) corporations and ESOPS.

Shareholders supply equity capital to enterprise. Classic economic theory views the goal of a firm as to maximize shareholder value, while the behavioral theory of the firm takes issue with management for a single maximizing value and a single stakeholder, providers of equity capital. It is incumbent upon those who lead discussions of corporate responsibility that business ethics, corporate governance and organization effectiveness be related to each other. Specifically, the role of profits needs to be addressed: the corporate mantra, "the goal of business is to maximize shareholder value" is challenged by the stakeholder model of business and the fiduciary duty of directors to shareholders should be examined in light of the stakeholder model of corporate responsibility. The conflict between shareholder capitalism and the behavioral theory of the firm can lead to a conflict about management: is management for output, in the interests of customers, or in view of measurements of financial performance? Corporate governance puts leadership and organizational structures in place to manage enterprise. The dysfunctional management that has come to light with the Enron and WorldCom bankruptcies, among others, reveals that the interest of shareholders in fact is for long-term performance and that the interests of shareholders align with the interests of customers for high-quality product.

## Corporate Governance

Corporate governance of *publicly held companies* is vested in the *Board of Directors*, elected by shareholders.[1] The directors have a *fiduciary obligation* to shareholders to manage in their interests.[2] A fiduciary obligation is the obligation of one in a position of trust; it is a heightened level of obligation, beyond simple prudent management.[3]

The fiduciary obligations of directors, however, do not require the maximization of quarterly profits, often the measure used for assessing managerial and corporate performance.[4] Directors are subject to the *business judgment rule*.[5] Under the business judgment rule, directors are permitted to use their judgment and discretion in making decisions that affect the corporation and its shareholders. Under the business judgment rule, directors may not be obligated to accept the highest dollar offer in the sale of the company. The buyout of Unocal Oil Company illustrated this point. Unocal was being bid by a Chinese Oil Company, CNOOC. Ultimately, however, the directors of Unocal accepted the bid by Chevron Texaco Company, even though the financial terms of the offer by the CNOOC were more attractive. The exercise of prudent judgment consistent with the fiduciary obligation of directors also encompasses the expenditure of corporate resources by strategic philanthropy. Courts have recognized that the best interests of shareholders may align with the interests of the community.[6] Thus a corporation may engage in philanthropy and charitable donations, even if this means that lower dividends are distributed to shareholders.[7] Directors may also decide to invest profits in research and development or expansion and growth, rather than return profits to shareholders as dividends, under the business judgment rule.[8]

Executive management is exercised by the chairman of the board, the chief executive officer (CEO), the president, and the chief operating officer (COO). Sometimes, the chairman of the board and CEO positions are held by a single individual. Similarly, often the president and COO positions are held by a single individual. In the post-Enron /post-WorldCom bankruptcy world, the chief financial officer (CFO) may be considered part of the executive team, since the CFO must personally certify company financial statements with the CEO under the Sarbanes Oxley Act. When the chairman also acts in the role of CEO, the fiduciary representative of the shareholders manages the enterprise.

Some executive compensation packages have been criticized as excessive, notwithstanding the fact that board compensation committees must approve those packages. Although board committees need to approve executive compensation, many boards were "insider" boards, nominated by top management, and thus basically under the control of top managers.

Some think that executive compensation packages recommended by consulting firms may be grounded in conflict of interest problems.[9]

CEOs in the United States earn the largest multiple relative to rank-and-file production workers, and this differential has become even greater over time. There are some indications of push-back from boards and from regulators. The authorization of the compensation package of Dick Grasso, former chairman of the New York Stock Exchange (NYSE), by the board of the NYSE, has been criticized as involving such a conflict of interest. The directors who authorized Grasso's compensation were selected from companies that are members of the NYSE. Criticism of executive compensation at the NYSE led to the resignation of both the NYSE Chairman Dick Grasso, as well as most of its board.[10] Dick Grasso was prosecuted by Eliot Spitzer for violating New York State not-for-profit laws in his compensation package, a charge to which he was vulnerable because the NYSE is incorporated as a not-for-profit organization. However, the prosecution was dropped when NYSE reorganized itself as a for-profit organization.[11] The CEO of American Airlines' parent organization was forced to resign while he was requesting concessions from the unions so that American Airlines could avoid bankruptcy at the when time his personal compensation package was revealed.[12]

As far back as the 1930s, Berle and Means, in their *The Modern Corporation and Private Property,* articulated the theory of managerial capitalism, noting the differentiation of interests between owners/shareholders and managers of companies.[13] In order to more closely align the interests of shareholders and managers, executive compensation methods, such as stock options and bonuses linked to firm financial performance, were developed. Certain executive compensation methods, such as bonuses linked to stock price or profits, can have unintended negative consequences, including the earnings management practices and accounting fraud that were so problematic in the Enron and WorldCom debacles.[14]

## The Sarbanes Oxley Act

The Public Company Accounting Reform and Investor Protection Act of 2002, commonly known as the Sarbanes Oxley Act (SOX), was passed on July 25, 2002, as Congress's response to the corporate scandals, including Enron's collapse and bankruptcy in 2001 and WorldCom's financial restatement in May 2002 and bankruptcy filed in July. Public accounting firms had certified the financial statements of both companies but then Enron issued a revised financial statement in October 2001 and filed for bankruptcy in December 2001; WorldCom issued a restatement in May 2002 and filed for bankruptcy in July 2002. SOX targeted the fraud on the market that had been perpetrated by the accounting fraud by Enron and WorldCom and the failure of the external auditors of publicly traded companies to identify the fraud.[15] The legislative history of the Sarbanes Oxley Act is given in Box 12.1.

---

### Box 12.1  How Did The Capitalist Threaten Capitalism?

**House Report 107-414—Corporate and Auditing Accountability, Responsibility, and Transparency Act of 2002**

*Background and Need for Legislation*

The Federal securities laws are designed to ensure that public companies provide investors with full and accurate disclosure of the true financial condition of the company. Following the bankruptcies of Enron Corporation and Global Crossing LLC, and restatements of earnings by several prominent market participants, regulators, investors and others expressed concern about the adequacy of the current disclosure regime for public companies.

Additionally, they expressed concerns about the role of auditors in approving corporate financial statements. Questions regarding the independence of auditors of public companies led to calls for greater supervision of the profession. The SEC raised the need for the creation of a new oversight body to review compliance of public auditors with the profession's standards of ethics and competency; this suggestion received widespread support.

The bankruptcy of Enron Corporation also raised issues relating to the security of employee retirement accounts. When allegations arose that some Enron insiders were able to sell their company stock even as Enron employees were

prohibited from doing so because of an administrative lockdown in the company's retirement plan, new calls arose for protecting the access of employees to
their accounts to the same degree as insiders.

This legislation responds to the problems of the marketplace through a fair
and balanced approach that ensures that the Nation's capital markets continue to
be the strongest in the world.

Source: http://thomas.loc.gov/cgi-bin/cpquery/?&&sid=cp107Y3U6l&&db_id=cp107&&r_
n=hr414.107&&sel=DOC&&item=&

SOX legislated changes in executive accountability and in board composition
and accountability. The provisions of SOX are oriented toward fair disclosure
of the financial condition of publicly traded companies and competent financial oversight. Chief executive officers and chief financial officers are required
to personally certify that the financial statements materially reflect the financial
condition of the firm.[16] Personally attesting makes the CEO and CFO personally liable for fraud in the financial statements; the CEO and CFO will not be
shielded by the corporate form of organization, which ordinarily shields individuals from personal liability for corporate wrongs. SOX imposes criminal
liability for material misstatements by the CEO or the CFO of the corporation's
financial condition. SOX also prohibits personal loans to executive officers and
directors, as had been done for the CEO of WorldCom, and requires the public
reporting of CEO and CFO compensation.[17]

Although Sarbanes Oxley did not require splitting the roles of chairman and
CEO, there was an increase in the number of corporations that separated the
role of CEO from chairman of the board after the passage of SOX. For example,
Disney separated the roles held by its CEO Michael Eisner in 2004.[18] The separation of roles and responsibilities of chairman of the board from the role and
responsibilities of CEO is a more common practice in Europe and an increasing trend in the United States (see Table 12.1).

### Board Composition Modified by SOX

Board composition was modified by SOX. The requirements of SOX regarding boards of directors were passed in the context of management domination of boards of directors and the possibility of a link between management

*Table 12.1* Separation of Roles: CEO and Chairman of the Board

| Index | Split Roles 2001 | Split Roles 2005 | Rate of Change |
|---|---|---|---|
| S&P 500 | 21% | 29% | 38% |
| NASDAQ 100 | 41% | 45% | 10% |
| FTSE 100 | 92% | 93% | 1% |
| Eurotop 100 | 74% | 79% | 7% |

domination of boards and the securities fraud that provided the impetus for SOX. SOX requires that the board of directors establish an audit committee that includes independent directors and include at least one individual with accounting expertise.[19]

Board composition was further modified by the Dodd-Frank Act. Under the Dodd-Frank Act, the board compensation committee must be independent. Moreover, shareholders must vote about executive compensation and golden parachutes, although these votes are advisory. Advisors to the board compensation committees must be neutral. Executive compensation must be disclosed, including CEO "pay for performance," such as bonuses and equity-based compensation such as stock options, and the ratio of CEO compensation to the average compensation of other employees of the enterprise. Boards must develop claw-back provisions of CEO's "pay for performance" when there has been an "error" in the performance measures, such as mis-reporting of the firm earnings and material financial restatements; unless the claw-back provisions are developed, firms may not be listed on the US exchanges. Important provisions of the Dodd-Frank Act are identified in Box 12.2.

---

### Box 12.2  Corporate Governance Issues, Including Executive Compensation Disclosure and Related SRO Rules

The *Dodd-Frank Wall Street Reform and Consumer Protection Act of 2010* contains numerous provisions which affect the governance of issuers.

- Section 951 requires advisory votes of shareholders *about executive compensation and golden parachutes.* This section also requires specific disclosure of golden parachutes in merger proxies. This section further requires institutional investment managers subject to Section 13(f) of the Securities Exchange Act to report at least annually how they voted on these advisory shareholder votes.
- Section 952 requires disclosure about the role of, and potential conflicts involving, *compensation consultants.* This statute also requires the Commission to direct that the exchanges adopt listing standards that include certain *enhanced independence requirements for members of issuers' compensation committees.* The Commission is also directed to establish competitively neutral independence factors for all who are retained to advise compensation committees.
- Section 953 requires additional *disclosure* about certain *compensation* matters, including *pay-for-performance* and the *ratio between the CEO's total compensation* and the median total compensation for all other company employees.
- Section 954 requires *the Commission* to direct the exchanges to *prohibit the listing of securities* of issuers that have *not developed and implemented compensation claw-back policies.*

- Section 955 requires additional disclosure about whether directors and employees are permitted to hedge any decrease in market value of the company's stock.

**Implementation:** On October 18, 2010, the [Securities and Exchange] Commission proposed rules to implement the Section 951 provisions related to institutional investment managers. The rules would require institutional investment managers to report their votes on executive compensation and "golden parachute" arrangements at least annually, unless the votes are otherwise required to be reported publicly by SEC rules.

On January 25, 2011, the Commission adopted rules concerning shareholder approval of executive compensation and "golden parachute" compensation arrangements to implement Section 951 of the Dodd-Frank Act. (Release No. 33–9178)

On June 20, 2012, the Commission adopted rules directing the national securities exchanges to adopt certain listing standards related to the compensation committee of a company's board of directors as well as its compensation advisers, as required by Section 952 of the Dodd-Frank Act. (Release No. 33–9330)

In January, 2013, the Commission approved the listing standards.[a]

On September 18, 2013, the Commission proposed rules regarding pay ratios to implement Section 953 of the Dodd-Frank Act. (Release No. 33–9452)

[a] SEC listing standards: Release Nos. 34–68643 [BATS]; 34–68642 [CBOE]; 34–68653 [CHX]; 34–68640 [NASDAQ]; 34–68641 [BX]; 34–68662 [NSX]; 34–68635 [NYSE]; 34–68638 [NYSEARCA]; 34–68637 [NYSEMKT]

Release Nos. 34–68643 [BATS]; 34–68642 [CBOE]; 34–68653 [CHX]; 34–68640 [NASDAQ]; 34–68641 [BX]; 34–68662 [NSX]; 34–68635 [NYSE]; 34–68638 [NYSEARCA]; 34–68637 [NYSEMKT]

Source: *http://www.sec.gov/spotlight/dodd-frank/corporategovernance.shtml* (emphasis added)

---

Unusually, Citibank CEO Vikram Pandit's compensation package was rejected by shareholders after approval by the board of directors.[20] Two proxy advisory firms recommended rejection by shareholders; the vote was required but advisory under Frank-Dodd. CalPERS, the California Public Employees Retirement fund, a large institutional investor, voted against CEO Pandit's compensation package because "the bank has not anchored rewards to performance."

The claw-back requirement was enacted because of outrage when AIG and other firms that received "bailout" funds from Congress nevertheless awarded their CEOs and other employees performance bonuses.[21] AIG's claw-back provision is listed with the SEC under Edgar.[22] The board is not required to exercise the claw-back provision but "may" do so in the exercise of its discretion and judgment. Furthermore, the claw-backs do not include the recovery of "excess compensation" from the sale of stock by the executives when stock prices have been inflated by errors in the reported earnings: "Dodd-Frank's claw-back requirement does not go far enough. In particular, it does not appear to require firms to recoup excess pay arising from executives' sale of company stock at prices inflated by errors in earnings or other metrics."[23] For example, Enron executives sold their stock in August 2001, prior to the restatement of earnings in October 2001. They were, however, convicted of insider trading for the sale of their stock while they were in possession of material, non-public information about Enron's financial condition.

### *Role of Accounting Firms Under SOX: Accounting Oversight Board*

The certification of the financial statements of Enron, WorldCom, and Global Crossings by public accounting firms indicates "failed audits."[24] For example, in Enron's annual report, there were so many questions, each, however, amounting to less than 5% of revenues, and, therefore, just under a "rule of thumb" threshold of "materiality," that 50% of Enron's financial statements in its 2000 annual report, was questionable![25] The Accounting Oversight Board created by SOX creates "a new oversight body to review compliance of public auditors with the profession's standards of ethics and competency."[26] The Public Company Accounting Oversight Board (PCAOB) created by SOX is a five-member board appointed by the SEC and which is subject to oversight by the SEC.[27] It represents a change from self-regulation of the public accounting profession to a situation where auditors of public companies, as well as reports of broker-dealers, are subject to external oversight and standards. The Frank-Dodd Act amended SOX to provide funding for PCAOB through assessment on public companies and broker-dealers.[28] The PCAOB established standards for auditing; auditors are required to render an assessment of internal controls of the public firms which are being audited. The assessment of internal controls required by the Public Accounting Oversight Board implementing Dodd-Frank are explained in Box 12.3.

---

## Box 12.3  Auditing Standard No. 5

*An Audit of Internal Control Over Financial Reporting That Is Integrated with An Audit of Financial Statements*

1.  This standard establishes requirements and provides direction that applies when an auditor is engaged to perform an audit of **management's assessment**[1] of the effectiveness of **internal control over financial reporting** ("the audit of internal control over financial reporting") that is integrated with an audit of the financial statements.[2]
2.  Effective internal control over financial reporting provides reasonable assurance regarding the reliability of financial reporting and the preparation of financial statements for external purposes.[3] If one or more **material**

**weaknesses** exist, the company's internal control over financial reporting cannot be considered effective.[4]

3.  The auditor's objective in an audit of internal control over financial reporting is to express an opinion on the effectiveness of the company's internal control over financial reporting. Because a company's internal control cannot be considered effective if one or more material weaknesses exist, to form a basis for expressing an opinion, the auditor must plan and perform the audit to obtain appropriate evidence that is sufficient to obtain reasonable assurance[5] about whether material weaknesses exist as of the date specified in management's assessment. A material weakness in internal control over financial reporting may exist even when financial statements are not materially misstated.

[1] Terms defined in Appendix A, Definitions, are set in boldface type the first time they appear.

[2] This auditing standard supersedes Auditing Standard No. 2, An Audit of Internal Control Over Financial Reporting Performed in Conjunction with An Audit of Financial Statements, and is the standard on attestation engagements referred to in Section 404(b) of the Act. It also is the standard referred to in Section 103(a)(2)(A)(iii) of the Act.

[3] See Securities Exchange Act Rules 13a-15(f) and 15d-15(f), 17 C.F.R. §§ 240.13a-15(f) and 240.15d-15(f); Paragraph A5.

[4] See Item 308 of Regulation S-K, 17 C.F.R. § 229.308.

[5] See AU sec. 230, Due Professional Care in the Performance of Work, for further discussion of the concept of reasonable assurance in an audit.

Source: http://pcaobus.org/Standards/Auditing/Pages/Auditing_Standard_5.aspx

---

The requirement of an assessment of the corporation's control over internal reporting is intended to prevent situations such as occurred in Enron and WorldCom where the financial control systems were inadequate, even coopted by executives who engaged in the accounting fraud.

In the immediate aftermath of the passage of SOX in July 2002, there was a rash of financial restatements.[29] Table 12.2 lists the number of financial restatements by publicly traded companies between 2001 and 2005.

*Table 12.2* Instances of Corporate Financial Restatement

| Year | Material Restatements |
| --- | --- |
| 2001 | 439 |
| 2002 | 597 |
| 2003 | 780 |
| 2004 | 741 |
| 2005 | 154 |

## Shareholder Lawsuits

Shareholder lawsuits that ensued in the wake of the Enron and WorldCom bankruptcies, including settlements by the investment banks, indicate that shareholders want truthfulness and fair disclosure rather than earnings management and inflated stock prices. Shareholder lawsuits were also brought against the investment banks and their research analysts that continued to recommend "buy" even though their own internal analysis indicated problems had been identified. According to *The Economist*: "Institutional Shareholder Services, a research service which tracks class-action suits, says payments 'in the pipeline' [in 2005] . . . includes $7.1 billion so far in tentative settlements made by banks and other parties linked to Enron, $6.1 billion in pending settlements by WorldCom and related parties."[30]

Although shareholders have become more proactive in the wake of the corporate fraud scandals and prosecutions, the United States Supreme Court has recently acted to circumscribe shareholder lawsuits. The threshold for litigation by shareholders against managers and boards has been raised, so that managers and directors have more protection from class action lawsuits by shareholders seeking to recoup loss of stock value.

The United State Supreme Court ruled in 2006 that federal securities law, the Securities Litigation Uniform Standards Act of 1998, preempted state law and the ability of a broker to sue in a class action lawsuit on behalf of investors for securities fraud.[31] And in 2007, the United States Supreme Court raised the proof of intent required for investors to sue boards of directors from the standard customary in civil suits, preponderance of the evidence, to a higher standard, clear and convincing evidence of "scienter" or intention to defraud.[32] Box 12.4 gives a synopsis of the case that redefined the intent, or "scienter," required to hold boards responsible for securities fraud in shareholder lawsuits.

---

**Box 12.4** *Tellabs, Inc., et al., Petitioners v. Makor Issues & Rights, Ltd., et al.*

**Supreme Court of the United States**

**551 U.S. 308**

**March 28, 2007, Argued**

**June 21, 2007, Decided**

### Syllabus

As a check against abusive litigation in private securities fraud actions, the Private Securities Litigation Reform Act of 1995 (PSLRA) includes exacting pleading requirements. The PSLRA requires plaintiffs to state with particularity both the facts constituting the alleged violation, and the facts evidencing scienter, i.e., the defendant's intention "to deceive, manipulate, or defraud." Ernst & Ernst v. Hochfelder, 425 U.S. 185, 194, 96 S. Ct. 1375, 47 L. Ed. 2d 668, and n. 12 As set out in § 21D(b)(2), plaintiffs must "state with particularity facts giving rise to a strong inference that the defendant acted with the required state of mind." 15 U.S.C. § 78u-4(b)(2). Congress left the key term "strong inference" undefined.

Petitioner Tellabs, Inc. manufactures specialized equipment for fiber optic networks. Respondents (Shareholders) purchased Tellabs stock between December 11, 2000, and June 19, 2001. They filed a class action, alleging that Tellabs and petitioner Notebaert, then Tellabs' chief executive officer and president, had engaged in securities fraud in violation of § 10(b) of the Securities Exchange Act of 1934 and Securities and Exchange Commission Rule 10b-5, and that Notebaert was a "controlling person" under the 1934 Act, and therefore derivatively liable for the company's fraudulent acts. Tellabs moved to dismiss the complaint on the ground that the Shareholders had failed to plead their case with the particularity the PSLRA requires. The District Court agreed, dismissing the complaint without prejudice. The Shareholders then amended their complaint, adding references to 27 confidential sources and making further, more specific, allegations concerning Notebaert's mental state. The District Court again dismissed, this time with prejudice. The Shareholders had sufficiently pleaded that Notebaert's statements were misleading, the court determined, but they had insufficiently alleged that he acted with scienter. The Seventh Circuit reversed in relevant part. Like the District Court, it found that the Shareholders had pleaded the misleading character of Notebaert's statements with sufficient particularity. Unlike the District Court, however, it concluded that the Shareholders had sufficiently alleged that Notebaert acted with the requisite state of mind. In evaluating whether the PSLRA's pleading standard is met, the Circuit said, courts should examine all of the complaint's allegations to decide whether collectively they establish an inference of scienter; the complaint would survive, the court stated, if a reasonable person could infer from the complaint's allegations that the defendant acted with the requisite state of mind.

Held: To qualify as "strong" within the intendment of § 21D(b)(2), an inference of scienter must be more than merely plausible or reasonable—it must be cogent and at least as compelling as any opposing inference of nonfraudulent intent.

[Since] neither the District Court nor the Court of Appeals had the opportunity to consider whether the Shareholders' allegations warrant "a strong inference that [Notebaert and Tellabs] acted with the required state of mind," 15 U.S.C. § 78u-4(b)(2), in light of the prescriptions announced today. Thus, the case is remanded for a determination under this Court's construction of § 21D(b)(2).

437 F.3d 588, vacated and remanded.

---

Tellabs involved direct parties to the alleged fraud. A subsequent case, *Stoneridge Investment Partners v. Scientific-Atlanta,* presented the question of whether shareholders may sue investment banks, as aiders and abettors in securities fraud, such as the fraud for which the executives of Enron and WorldCom were convicted.[33] The standards for finding investment banks complicit as aiders and abettors in securities fraud is defined by the Stoneridge Investments case explained in Box 12.5.

# Box 12.5  *Stoneridge Investment Partners, LLC. v. Scientific-Atlanta, Inc.*

## 552 U.S. 148 (2009)

**Prior History:** In re: Charter Communications, Inc., Securities Litigation, Stoneridge Investment Partners, LLS, Plaintiff-Appellant, v. Scientific-Atlanta, Inc; Motorola, Inc., Defendants-Appellees.

United States Court Of Appeals For The Eighth Circuit 443 F.3d 987

The stock purchasers alleged that the equipment vendors entered into sham transactions with a cable television corporation concerning payments for cable boxes knowing that it intended to rely on them to inflate its cash flow. The [appellate]court held that the district court properly dismissed the purchasers' securities law claims that the vendors knowingly aided and abetted the corporation in deceiving investors because the vendors were not alleged to have engaged in any deceptive act regarding the corporation's financial results and operations or to have had a duty to disclose information about its true financial results; therefore, the vendors, who merely entered into an arm's length non-securities transaction with an entity that used the transaction to publish false statements, were not liable under the Act or any subpart of S.E.C. Rule 10b-5, 17 C.F.R. § 240.10b-5.

## Syllabus

Alleging losses after purchasing Charter Communications common stock, [Stoneridge Investment Partners] filed suit against [Scientific-Atlanta] and others under § 10(b) of the Securities Exchange Act of 1934 and Securities and Exchange Commission (SEC) Rule 10b-5. Acting as Charter's customers and suppliers, [Scientific-Atlanta] had agreed to arrangements that allowed Charter to mislead its auditor and issue a misleading financial statement affecting its stock price, but they had no role in preparing or disseminating the financial statement. Affirming the District Court's dismissal of [Scientific-Atlanta], the Eighth Circuit ruled that the allegations did not show that [Scientific-Atlanta] made misstatements relied upon by the public or violated a duty to disclose. The court observed that, at most, respondents had aided and abetted Charter's misstatement, and noted that the private cause of action this Court has found implied in § 10(b) and Rule 10b-5 (citations omitted) does not extend to aiding and abetting a § 10(b) violation, see Central Bank of Denver, N.A. v. First Interstate Bank of Denver, N.A., 511 U.S. 164.

Held: The § 10(b) private right of action does not reach [Scientific-Atlanta] because Charter investors did not rely upon respondents' statements or representations.

(a) Although Central Bank prompted calls for creation of an express cause of action for aiding and abetting, Congress did not follow this course. Instead, in § 104 of the Private Securities Litigation Reform Act of 1995 (PSLRA), it directed the SEC to prosecute aiders and abettors. Thus, the

§ 10(b) private right of action does not extend to aiders and abettors. Because the conduct of a secondary actor must therefore satisfy each of the elements or preconditions for § 10(b) liability, the plaintiff must prove, as here relevant, reliance upon a material misrepresentation or omission by the defendant.

(b) The Court has found a rebuttable presumption of reliance in two circumstances. First, if there is an omission of a material fact by one with a duty to disclose, the investor to whom the duty was owed need not provide specific proof of reliance. (citation omitted). Second, under the fraud-on-the-market doctrine, reliance is presumed when the statements at issue become public. Neither presumption applies here: [Scientific-Atlanta] had no duty to disclose; and their deceptive acts were not communicated to the investing public during the relevant times. [Stoneridge Investment Partners] as a result, cannot show reliance upon any of [Scientific-Atlanta] actions except in an indirect chain that is too remote for liability.

(c) Petitioner's reference to so-called "scheme liability" does not, absent a public statement, answer the objection that petitioner did not in fact rely upon respondents' deceptive conduct. Were the Court to adopt petitioner's concept of reliance—i.e., that in an efficient market investors rely not only upon the public statements relating to a security but also upon the transactions those statements reflect—the implied cause of action would reach the whole marketplace in which the issuing company does business. There is no authority for this rule. Reliance is tied to causation, leading to the inquiry whether respondents' deceptive acts were immediate or remote to the injury. Those acts, which were not disclosed to the investing public, are too remote to satisfy the reliance requirement.

443 F.3d 987, affirmed and remanded.

---

Although limiting the private right of action under 10b,[34] the United States Supreme Court identified the SEC as the appropriate party to prosecute for aiding and abetting violations of the Securities laws. The SEC, even prior to the Stoneridge Partners decision, prosecuted Merrill Lynch for aiding and abetting Enron's fraud. The fraud had the direct effect of increasing Enron's reported net income in 1999, earnings per share, increasing the stock price and the executive bonuses awarded based on financial performance measures. Merrill Lynch negotiated a settlement with the SEC regarding their financing of Enron.

WorldCom's financing partners were also prosecuted for aiding and abetting WorldCom's securities fraud.[35] Citigroup agreed to pay $2.65 billion to settle the WorldCom investor suit.[36] Other WorldCom defendants include Bank of America, Lehman Brothers, Deutsche Bank and JP Morgan Chase, as underwriters of bonds.[37]

*Table 12.3* GMI/CR Best Governed list

| Companies that had Governance Score of 1 for all years 2010–2014 |
| --- |
| Bristol-Myers Squibb Co. |
| Campbell Soup Co |
| Cisco Systems Inc. |
| Colgate-Palmolive Co |
| E.I. DuPont De Nemours & Co |
| Gap Inc. |
| Occidental Petroleum Corp |
| Sempra Energy |
| State Street Corp |
| Wisconsin Energy Corp |

In June 2014, the United States Supreme Court gave corporations who are being sued by shareholders for fraud an opportunity to defend prior to the certification of the class by showing that the fraud had no "price impact."[38] The defense permitted chips away at the "fraud on the market" doctrine accepted in *Basic v. Levinson*,[39] and incorporated by reference in *Stonehedge*, by permitting defendants to show "no loss causation."

Notwithstanding the fraudulent, or complicit, behavior of some companies, there are leading corporate citizens that are well governed. Table 12.3 shows the set of companies that were rated as best governed for five years running, 2010–2014, according to Corporate Responsibility (CR) and Governance Metrics International (GMI).[40]

Noteworthy is the fact that only a single large financial institution, State Street Corporation, is among GMI best-governed corporations for the five-year period 2010–2014.[41] Even more concerning is that not a single financial institution is among CR's top 50 leading corporate citizens for the five years 2010–2014 (Table 12.4).

## Alternative Models of Incorporation

There has been a recent trend to develop alternative models of incorporation, perhaps in part to avoid the conflicts that derive from managing in the interests of the community and to finesse the issue of maximizing shareholder value. Employee stock ownership plans (ESOPs) are a form of organization that frankly recognizes the interest of employees in the operation and viability of the enterprise. During the "rust belt" era of plant closings in the steel, tire and rubbers industries, some firms such as Weirton Steel reorganized as ESOPs.[42] Chrysler and United Airlines also reorganized under financial duress as ESOPs.[43]

*Table 12.4* Companies on CR's Top 50
Leading Corporate Citizens
for Five Years, 2010–2014

---

Bristol-Myers Squibb Co.

Johnson & Johnson

Gap Inc.

Microsoft Corporation

Mattel Inc.

Intel Corp.

Coca-Cola Co.

Campbell Soup Co.

Johnson Controls Inc.

Kimberly-Clark Corp.

International Business Machines Corp.

Nike Inc.

Merck & Co. Inc.

Eaton Corporation plc.

Texas Instruments Inc.

Abbott Laboratories

General Mills Inc.

---

Benefit corporations are a new form of incorporation recognized in Britain and in 27 states of the United States, including the District of Columbia; legislation has been introduced in 13 more states or territories, including Puerto Rico.[44] Benefit corporations include a public purpose or good in their charter.[45] Many social entrepreneurship firms are organized as benefit corporations.[46] Patagonia, Ben & Jerry's, and King Arthur Flour Company are benefit corporations. A key issue with benefit corporations is how to measure whether they have achieved their public purpose.[47]

Corporations also restructure for tax reasons. For example, Pfizer proposed to acquire AstraZeneca and move its corporate headquarters to the UK for the purpose of avoiding US corporate taxes. Pfizer also stated as its reason to acquire AstraZeneca's pipeline of products. Tyco provides another of example of corporate restructuring driven by tax purposes and a cautionary note. Tyco engaged in a reverse takeover of ADT, a much smaller company.[48] The Tyco reverse takeover had the effect of moving the corporate headquarters to Bermuda and had tax consequences beneficial to the firm. However, the Tyco reverse takeover yielded bad results in the long run. CEO Dennis Koslowski was prosecuted and convicted in 2005 for misappropriate of corporate funds and securities fraud.[49] He was sentenced to prison, then released on parole in early 2014.[50] Tyco settled a consolidated class action litigation by shareholders.[51] It is likely that the heightened scrutiny was occasioned by the reverse buy-out and move of corporate headquarters to Bermuda. The firm rehabilitated itself by conducting a clean sweep of the executive officers and the board and creating a chief ethics officer.[52]

It is clear from the examples discussed herein and from the Madoff Ponzi scheme case discussed in the following, that boards must not simply be passive and act as rubber stamps but be proactive and inquisitive in their oversight of enterprise.

## Chapter Discussion Questions

1. The US has the highest ratio of CEO salary compared to the salary of production workers. Is this justified? Why or why not?
2. Is it a problem that CEO compensation increases even when corporate earnings and stock price are down?
3. What constitutes due diligence by financing partners and public accounting firms? What could Merrill Lynch have done instead of obtaining financing for Enron and what could Arthur Andersen have done instead of certifying Enron's financial statements?
4. What is the impact of shareholder lawsuits on corporate management, if any?
5. Does the structure of publicly held corporations require a new form of incorporations such as benefit corporations or ESOPs to govern in the interests of stakeholders?
6. Debate the proposal of Pfizer to acquire UK AstraZeneca for US corporate tax avoidance purposes.

## Notes

1 Del. Code Ann. tit. 8, § 141(a).
2 *Smith v. Van Gorkom*, 488 A.2d 858 (Del. 1985).
3 *Stone v. Ritter*, 911 A.2d 362 (Del. 2006) See also Clair A. Hill and Brett H. McDonnell, "Stone v. Ritter and the Expanding Duty of Loyalty," *Fordham Law Review* 76, no. 3 (2007–2008): 1769–96.
4 Eric Bennett Rasmusen, "The Goals of the Corporation under Shareholder Primacy: Just Profit—Or Social Responsibility and Religious Exercise Too?," (Jan. 12, 2014), available at SSRN: http://papers.ssrn.com/sol3/papers.cfm?abstract_id=2365135.
5 *Smith v. Van Gorkom*, 488 A. 2d 858 (Del. 1985). See also *Unocal Corp. v. Mesa Petroleum Co.*, 493 A. 2d 946 (Del. Supr. 1985) and *Paramount Communications, Inc. v. Time Inc.*, 571 A. 2d 1140 (Del. Supr. 1989).
6 *Shlensky v. Wrigley*, 237 N.E. 2d. (1968).
7 *A. P. Smith Mfg. v. Barlow*, 13 NJ 145 (1953).
8 *Dodge v. Ford Motor Co.*, 170 N.W. 668 (1919).
9 "[How] Verizon Communications, decides what to reward its chief executive, Ivan Seidenberg . . . offers an illuminating look at a system gone completely haywire. The outside consultants who advise Verizon, Hewitt Associates, do loads of other business for the company . . . Hewitt operates Verizon's employee benefits Web sites and

performs actuarial work for three of the company's pension plans. . . . Hewitt has a strong incentive not to rock the boat by offending Verizon executives. The end result is predictable. Mr. Seidenberg received a package worth $19.4 million last year, as his shareholders felt the pinch of a stock that fell 26 percent." "A Cozy Arrangement" (Editorial), *New York Times*, April 13, 2006. The executive compensation consultants for Verizon have conflicts, not unlike the conflicts of interest that Arthur Andersen experienced with Enron, in both auditing Enron and providing consulting services to Enron.

10   Kate Kelly, Susanne Craig and Ianthe Jeanne Dugan, "Grasso Quits NYSE Amid Pay Furor: Behind Chief's Departure, Profit Squeeze, Governance Questions at the Big Board," *Wall Street Journal*, Sept. 18, 2003.

11   Christopher Twarowski, "New York Ends Grasso Compensation Lawsuit," *Washington Post*, July 2, 2008. See also Greg Farrell, "Court Ruling Ends Pay Case against Grasso," *USA TODAY*, available at http://abcnews.go.com/Business/story?id=5292820 and Stephen F. Diamond and Jennifer W. Kuan, *On Restructuring the NYSE: Might a Non-profit Stock Exchange Have Been Efficient?* (2006), available at: http://digitalcommons.law.scu.edu/facpubs/189.

12   James F. Peltz, "CEO at American Airlines Resigns: Carty's Departure Comes as the Carrier Tries to Get Workers to OK New Deal and Avoid Bankruptcy," *LA Times*, April 25, 2003.

13   Adolf Berle and Gardiner Means, *The Modern Corporation and Private Property*, (Piscataway, NJ: Transaction Press, 1932).

14   The particular type of stock option that is related to financial misstatements are "in-the-money" (i.e., stock price above exercise price)" stock options. See Jap Efendi, Anup Srivastava, and Edward P. Swanson, "Why Do Corporate Managers Misstate Financial Statements? The Role of In-The-Money Options and Other Incentives," (April 5, 2006), available at SSRN: http://ssrn.com/abstract=547922 or doi: 10.2139/ssrn.547922. See also Merle Erickson, Michelle Hanlon, and Edward Maydew, "Is There a Link Between Executive Compensation and Accounting Fraud?," University of North Carolina at Chapel Hill, working paper, Feb. 24, 2004. There was a rash of backdating stock options in 2007, discussed in Chapter 14.

15   Pub. L. No. 107–204, 116 Stat. 745 (July 30, 2002). Arthur Andersen was the external auditor of both Enron and WorldCom.

16   TITLE 15 > CHAPTER 98 > SUBCHAPTER III > § 7241

§ 7241. Corporate responsibility for financial reports

(a)   Regulations required

The Commission shall, by rule, require, for each company filing periodic reports under section 78m (a) or 78o (d) of this title, that the principal executive officer or officers and the principal financial officer or officers, or persons performing similar functions, certify in each annual or quarterly report filed or submitted under either such section of this title that—

(1)   the signing officer has reviewed the report;

(2)   based on the officer's knowledge, the report does not contain any untrue statement of a material fact or omit to state a material fact necessary in order to make the statements made, in light of the circumstances under which such statements were made, not misleading;

(3)   based on such officer's knowledge, the financial statements, and other financial information included in the report, fairly present in all material respects

the financial condition and results of operations of the issuer as of, and for, the periods presented in the report;

(4) the signing officers—

    (A) are responsible for establishing and maintaining internal controls;

    (B) have designed such internal controls to ensure that material information relating to the issuer and its consolidated subsidiaries is made known to such officers by others within those entities, particularly during the period in which the periodic reports are being prepared;

    (C) have evaluated the effectiveness of the issuer's internal controls as of a date within 90 days prior to the report; and

    (D) have presented in the report their conclusions about the effectiveness of their internal controls based on their evaluation as of that date;

(5) the signing officers have disclosed to the issuer's auditors and the audit committee of the board of directors (or persons fulfilling the equivalent function)—

    (A) all significant deficiencies in the design or operation of internal controls which could adversely affect the issuer's ability to record, process, summarize, and report financial data and have identified for the issuer's auditors any material weaknesses in internal controls; and

    (B) any fraud, whether or not material, that involves management or other employees who have a significant role in the issuer's internal controls; and

(6) the signing officers have indicated in the report whether or not there were significant changes in internal controls or in other factors that could significantly affect internal controls subsequent to the date of their evaluation, including any corrective actions with regard to significant deficiencies and material weaknesses.

    (b) Foreign reincorporations have no effect

Nothing in this section shall be interpreted or applied in any way to allow any issuer to lessen the legal force of the statement required under this section, by an issuer having reincorporated or having engaged in any other transaction that resulted in the transfer of the corporate domicile or offices of the issuer from inside the United States to outside of the United States.

    (c) Deadline

The rules required by subsection (a) of this section shall be effective not later than 30 days after July 30, 2002.

17 "The Sarbanes-Oxley Act of 2002 and Key Issues Relevant to Business Valuation and Litigation Services," *American Institute of CPAs*, last modified 2014, http://www.aicpa.org/interestareas/forensicandvaluation/resources/standards/pages/the%20sarbanes-oxley%20act%20of%202002%20and%20key%20issues%20relevant%20to%20business%20valuation%20and%20litigation%20services.aspx.

18 "Disney Splits Roles Top Posts; Eisner Pulled as Chair," *Associated Press*, Mar. 4, 2004, http://www.nbcnews.com/id/4437434/ns/business-us_business/t/disney-splits-top-posts-eisner-pulled-chair/#.U5jv_LdOXaE.

19 "Section 301: Public Company Audit Committees.

Each member of the audit committee shall be a member of the board of directors of the issuer, and shall otherwise be independent.

'Independent' is defined as not receiving, other than for service on the board, any consulting, advisory, or other compensatory fee from the issuer, and as not being an affiliated person of the issuer, or any subsidiary thereof.

The SEC may make exemptions for certain individuals on a case-by-case basis.

The audit committee of an issuer shall be directly responsible for the appointment, compensation, and oversight of the work of any registered public accounting firm employed by that issuer.

The audit committee shall establish procedures for the 'receipt, retention, and treatment of complaints' received by the issuer regarding accounting, internal controls, and auditing.

Each audit committee shall have the authority to engage independent counsel or other advisors, as it determines necessary to carry out its duties.

Each issuer shall provide appropriate funding to the audit committee."

20  Suzanne Kapner, Joann S. Lublin, and Robin Sidel, "Citigroup Investors Reject Pay Plan," *Wall Street Journal*, April 17, 2012.

21  Edmund L. Andrews and Peter Baker, "A.I.G. Planning Huge Bonuses After $170 Billion Bailout," *New York Times*, March 15, 2009.

22  AIG's claw-back provision is given at: "American International Group, Inc.: Claw-Back Policy," *U.S. Securities and Exchange Commission*, last modified 2014, http://www.sec.gov/Archives/edgar/data/5272/000119312513129417/d509859dex103.htm.

23  Jesse M. Fried and Nitzan Shilon, "The Dodd-Frank Clawback and the Problem of Excess Pay," *The Corporate Board*, Jan./Feb. 2012, http://www.law.harvard.edu/faculty/jfried/1201FriedShilon.pdf. .

24  See the "Powers Report," Report of Investigation by the Special Investigative Committee of the Board of Directors of Enron Corp., Feb. 1, 2002.

25  Paula Alexander Becker and Kenneth Heaslip, "Ethical Dilemmas Related to Earnings Management Practices: The Case of Sunbeam, Xerox and Lucent Technologies," International Conference Promoting Business Ethics, Chicago, Oct. 2001. See also Bala B. Dharan and William R. Bufkins, "Red Flags in Enron's Reporting of Revenues and Key Financial Measures," available at http://baladharan.com/files/dharan-bufkins_enron_red_flags.pdf.

26  Corporate and Auditing Accountability, Responsibility, and Transparency Act of 2002: Background and Need for Legislation, 107th Cong., HR Rep 107–414.

27  *Public Company Accounting Oversight Board*, last modified 2014, http://pcaobus.org/Pages/default.aspx.

28  http://pcaobus.org/About/Pages/default.aspx.

29  The SEC commissioned study undertaken by Lord & Benoit, LLC, estimates that 14% of filing firms restated their financial statements in 2005. See Robert J. Benoit to the SEC Advisory Committee on Smaller Public Companies, March 31, 2006, http://www.sec.gov/rules/other/265–23/rbenoit8977.pdf.

30  "Finance and Economics: A Blazing Summer; Shareholder Lawsuits," *The Economist* 376, no. 8439 (Aug. 13, 2005): 59.

31  *Merrill Lynch, Pierce, Fenner & Smith, Inc., Petitioner v. Shadi Dabit*, 547 U.S. 71 (2006).

32  The burden of proof for criminal liability is "beyond a reasonable doubt." See "Burden of Proof," *Wikipedia*, last modified June 28, 2013, http://en.wikipedia.org/wiki/Burden_of_proof.

33  Centerior granted by 127 S. Ct. 1873; 167 L. Ed. 2d 363; 2007 U.S. LEXIS 3582; 75 U.S.L.W. 3511.

Prior history: In re: Charter Communications, Inc., Securities Litigation, Stoneridge Investment Partners, LLS, Plaintiff-Appellant, v. Scientific-Atlanta, Inc; Motorola, Inc., Defendants-Appellees.

UNITED STATES COURT OF APPEALS FOR THE EIGHTH CIRCUIT
443 F.3d 987; 2006 U.S. App. LEXIS 8798; Fed. Sec. L. Rep. (CCH) P93,743

December 12, 2005, Submitted
April 11, 2006, Filed

34  In a 2009 case subsequent to *Stoneridge Investment Partners v. Scientific-Atlanta*, the district court for the Southern District of New York held that secondary actors are not liable for aiding and abetting violations of the federal securities statutes: In re Refco, Inc., Sec. Lit., 609 F. Supp. 2d 304 (S.D.N.Y. 2009); United States Court Of Appeals For The Second Circuit 603 F.3d 144.

35  Securities and Exchange Commission v. Worldcom, Civ No. 02-CV-4963 (JSR) (Southern District of NY 2002), http://www.sec.gov/litigation/complaints/comp 17829.htm.

36  Floyd Norris, "WorldCom Settlement Is Latest Cleanup : Citigroup Is to Pay $2.65 Billion in Suit," *New York Times*, May 11, 2004. See also Worldcom Securities Litigation, last modified December 20, 2013, http://www.worldcomlitigation.com/.

37  Jeb Horowitz, "Deutsche Bank, Two Others Settle WorldCom Bond Suit," *Wall Street Journal*, March 10, 2005, http://online.wsj.com/news/articles/SB111048506088976210. See also Mitchell Pacelle, "Citigroup Will Pay $2.65 Billion to Settle WorldCom Investor Suit," *Wall Street Journal*, May 11, 2004, http://online.wsj.com/news/articles/SB108419118926806649.

38  *Haliburton v. Erica P. John Fund*, No 13–317 US, (2013).

39  485 U.S. 224 (1988). The fraud on the market doctrine relies on "efficient markets hypothesis, that 'the market price of shares traded on well-developed markets reflects all publicly available information, and, hence, any material misrepresentations'" (246).

40  The methodology used by CRO is explained on their website: http://www.thecro.com/files/CR%20Corporate%20Citizenship%20Protocol,%202012.pdf for 2012 and http://www.thecro.com/node/616 for 2008. CRO contracts with WI Financial to develop the list of "best corporate citizens." WI Financial uses measures reported by GMI (Governance Metrics International http://www3.gmiratings.com ) to rate corporate governance.

41  "State Street Corporation," *Hoovers: A D&B Company*, last modified 2014, http://www.hoovers.com/company-information/cs/company-profile.State_Street_Corporation.4630541026b7b33b.html.

42  See Joyce Rothschild-Whitt, "Who Will Benefit from ESOPs?," *Labor Research Review, Workers as Owners* 1, no. 6 (1985). See also Paula Becker Alexander, "Plant Closings in the Tire and Rubber Industry" (*Proceedings of the Industrial Relations Research Association*, Annual Meeting, 1987).

43  See John D. Menke, "The Origin and History of the ESOP and its Future Role as a Business Succession Tool," available at http://www.menke.com/blog/the-origin-and-history-of-the-esop-and-its-future-role-as-a-business-succession-tool/. See also John D. Russell, "Lessons from the Recent Failure of Weirton Steel's ESOP," *Labor Notes*, April 30, 2004, http://labornotes.org/2004/04/lessons-recent-failure-weirton-steels-esop.

44  See "State by State Legislative Status," *Benefit Corp Information Center*, last modified 2014, http://benefitcorp.net/state-by-state-legislative-status.

45  Briana Cummings, "Benefit Corporations: How to Enforce a Mandate to Promote the Public Interest," *Columbia Law Review* 112, no. 3 (2012): 578–627, http://columbialawreview.org/wp-content/uploads/2012/07/112-3_Cummings.pdf.

46  Social Entrepreneurship and Benefit Corporations: An Interdisciplinary Conversation with Panel: Elizabeth Babson, Lyman Johnson, Haskell Murray, John McVea, Michael Naughton and Elizabeth Schiltz (St. Thomas University, April 24, 2014). See also "The Governance of Social Enterprises: Managing Your Organization for

Success," *World Economic Forum*, last modified 2012, http://www.weforum.org/pdf/schwabfound/Governance_Social_Enterprises.pdf.

47    "Maryland First State in Union to Pass Benefit Corporations Legislation," *CSR Wire*, April 14, 2014, http://www.csrwire.com/press_releases/29332-Maryland-First-State-in-Union-to-Pass-Benefit-Corporation-Legislation.

48    Charles V. Bagli, "ADT and Tyco Plan to Merge in $5.4 Billion Stock Swap," *New York Times*, March 18, 1997, http://www.nytimes.com/1997/03/18/business/adt-and-tyco-plan-to-merge-in-5.4-billion-stock-swap.html.

49    Ben White, "Ex-Tyco Executives Convicted," *Washington Post*, June 18, 2005, http://www.washingtonpost.com/wp-dyn/content/article/2005/06/17/AR2005061701003.html.

50    Alan Farnham, "Dennis Kozlowski's Life after Prison," *ABC News*, Dec. 5, 2013, http://abcnews.go.com/Business/dennis-kozlowski-ceos-life-parole/story?id=21097934&page=2.

51    Floyd Norris, "Tyco to Pay $3 Billion to Settle Investor Lawsuits," *New York Times*, May 16, 2007. See also Tyco International Ltd. Securities Class Action Settlement, last modified 2011, http://www.tycoclasssettlement.com/.

52    Rob Boostrom, under the direction of John Fraedrich, O.C. Ferrell, and Linda Ferrell, *Tyco International: Leadership Crisis*, last modified 2011, http://danielsethics.mgt.unm.edu/pdf/Tyco%20Case.pdf.

## End of Chapter Case: Bernard Madoff's Ponzi Scheme

*Report of Investigation*

*United States Securities and Exchange Commission Office of Inspector General*

### Investigation of Failure of the SEC

To Uncover Bernard Madoff's Ponzi Scheme

### Executive Summary

The OIG investigation did not find evidence that any SEC personnel who worked on an SEC examination or investigation of Bernard L. Madoff Investment Securities, LLC (BMIS) had any financial or other inappropriate connection with Bernard Madoff or the Madoff family that influenced the conduct of their examination or investigatory work. The OIG also did not find that former SEC Assistant Director Eric Swanson's romantic relationship with Bernard Madoff's niece, Shana Madoff, influenced the conduct of the SEC examinations of Madoff and his firm. We also did not find that senior officials at the SEC directly attempted to influence examinations or investigations of Madoff or the Madoff firm, nor was there evidence any senior SEC official interfered with the staffs ability to perform its work.

The OIG investigation did find, however, that the SEC received more than ample information in the form of detailed and substantive complaints over the years to warrant a thorough and comprehensive examination and/or investigation of Bernard Madoff and BMIS for operating a Ponzi scheme, and that despite three examinations and two investigations being conducted, a thorough and competent investigation or examination was never performed. The OIG found that between June 1992 and December 2008 when Madoff confessed, the SEC received six[1] substantive complaints that raised significant red flags concerning Madoff's hedge fund operations and should have led to questions about whether Madoff was actually engaged in trading. Finally, the SEC was also aware of two articles regarding Madoff' s investment operations that appeared in reputable publications in 2001 and questioned Madoff's unusually consistent returns.

The first complaint, brought to the SEC's attention in 1992, related to allegations that an unregistered investment company was offering "100%" safe investments with high and extremely consistent rates of return over significant periods of time to "special" customers. The SEC actually suspected the investment company was operating a Ponzi scheme and learned in their investigation that all of the investments were placed entirely through Madoff and consistent returns were claimed to have been achieved for numerous years without a single loss.

The second complaint was very specific and different versions were provided to the SEC in May 2000, March 2001 and October 2005. The complaint submitted in 2005 was entitled "The World's Largest Hedge Fund is a Fraud" and detailed approximately 30 red flags indicating that Madoff was operating a Ponzi scheme, a scenario it described as "highly likely." The red flags included the impossibility of Madoff's returns, particularly the consistency of those returns and the unrealistic volume of options Madoff represented to have traded.

In May 2003, the SEC received a third complaint from a respected Hedge Fund Manager identifying numerous concerns about Madoff's strategy and purported returns, questioning whether Madoff was actually trading options in the volume he claimed, noting that Madoff's strategy and purported returns were not duplicable by anyone else, and stating Madoff's strategy had no correlation to the overall equity markets in over 10 years. According to an SEC manager, the Hedge Fund Manager's complaint laid out issues that were "indicia of a Ponzi scheme."

The fourth complaint was part of a series of internal e-mails of another registrant that the SEC discovered in April 2004. The e-mails described the red flags that a registrant's employees had identified while performing due diligence on their own Madoff investment using publicly-available information. The red flags identified included Madoff's incredible and highly unusual fills for equity trades, his misrepresentation of his options trading and his unusually consistent, non-volatile returns over several years. One of the internal e-mails provided a step-by-step analysis of why Madoff must be misrepresenting his options trading. The e-mail clearly explained that Madoff could not be trading on an options exchange because of insufficient volume and could not be trading options over-the-counter because it was inconceivable that he could find a counterparty for the trading. The SEC examiners who initially discovered the e-mails viewed them as indicating "some suspicion as to whether Madoff is trading at all."

The fifth complaint was received by the SEC in October 2005 from an anonymous informant and stated, "I know that Madoff [sic] company is very secretive about their operations and they refuse to disclose anything. If my suspicions are true, then they are running a highly sophisticated scheme on a massive scale. And they have been doing it for a long time." The informant also stated, "After a short period of time, I decided to withdraw all my money (over $5 million)."

The sixth complaint was sent to the SEC by a "concerned citizen" in December 2006, advising the SEC to look into Madoff and his firm as follows:

> Your attention is directed to a scandal of major proportion which was executed by the investment firm Bernard L. Madoff. . . . Assets well in excess of $10 Billion owned by the late [investor], an ultra-wealthy long time client of the Madoff firm have been "co-mingled" with funds controlled by the Madoff company with gains thereon retained by Madoff.

In March 2008, the SEC Chairman's office received a second copy of the previous complaint, with additional information from the same source regarding Madoff's involvement with the investor's money, as follows:

> It may be of interest to you to that Mr. Bernard Madoff keeps two (2) sets of records. The most interesting of which is on his computer which is always on his person.

The two 2001 journal articles also raised significant questions about Madoff's unusually consistent returns. One of the articles noted his "astonishing ability to time the market and move to cash in the underlying securities before market conditions turn negative and the related ability to buy and sell the underlying stocks without noticeably affecting the market." This article also described that "experts ask why no one has been able to duplicate similar returns using [Madoff's] strategy." The second article quoted a former Madoff investor as saying, "Anybody who's a seasoned hedge-fund investor knows the split-strike conversion is not the whole story. To take it at face value is a bit naïve."

[Just one month after the SEC's Northeast Regional Office decided not to pursue Markopolos' second submission to the SEC, in May 2001, *MARHedge* and *Barron's* both published articles questioning Madoff's unusually consistent returns and secretive operations. The *MARHedge* article, written by Michael Ocrant and entitled "Madoff tops charts; skeptics ask how," stated how many were "baffled by the way [Madoff's] firm has obtained such consistent, nonvolatile returns month after month and year after year," describing the fact Madoff "reported losses of no more than 55 basis points in just four of the past 139 consecutive months, while generating highly consistent gross returns of slightly more than 1.5% a month and net annual returns roughly in the range of 15.0%." The *MARHedge* article further discussed how industry professionals "marvel at [Madoff's] seemingly astonishing ability to time the market and move to cash in the underlying securities before market conditions turn negative and the related ability to buy and sell the underlying stocks without noticeably affecting the market." It further described how "experts ask why no one has been able to duplicate similar returns using [Madoff's] strategy."

The *Barron's* article, written by Erin Arvedlund and entitled "Don't Ask, Don't Tell: Bernie Madoff is so secretive, he even asks his investors to keep mum," discussed how Madoff's operation was among the three largest hedge funds, and has "produced compound average annual returns of 15% for more than a decade" with the largest fund "never [having] had a down year." The *Barron's* article further questioned whether " Madoff's trading strategy could "have been achieving those remarkably consistent returns.

The OIG found that the SEC was aware of the *Barron's* article when it was published in May 2001. On May 7, 2001, an Enforcement Branch Chief in the BDO followed up with NERO regarding Markopolos' 2001 complaint and the *Barron's* article, and asked the Director of NERO if he wanted a copy of the article. However, the decision not to commence an investigation was not reconsidered and there is no evidence the *Barron's* article was ever even reviewed. In addition, we found that former OCIE Director Lori Richards reviewed the *Barron's* article in May 2001 and sent a copy to an Associate Director in OCIE shortly thereafter, with a note on the top stating that Arvedlund is "very good" and that "This is a great exam for us!" However, OCIE did not open an examination, and there is no record of anyone else in OCIE reviewing the *Barron's* article until several years later.]

The complaints all contained specific information and could not have been fully and adequately resolved without thoroughly examining and investigating Madoff for operating a Ponzi scheme. The journal articles should have reinforced the concerns about how Madoff could have been achieving his returns.

The OIG retained an expert in accordance with its investigation in order to both analyze the information the SEC received regarding Madoff and the examination work conducted. According to the OIG's expert, the most critical step in examining or investigating a potential Ponzi scheme is to verify the subject's trading through an independent third party.

The OIG investigation found the SEC conducted two investigations and three examinations related to Madoff s investment advisory business based upon the detailed and credible complaints that raised the possibility that Madoff was misrepresenting his trading and could have been operating a Ponzi scheme. Yet, at no time did the SEC ever verify Madoff's trading through an independent third-party, and in fact, never actually conducted a Ponzi scheme examination or investigation of Madoff.

The first examination and first Enforcement investigation were conducted in 1992 after the SEC received information that led it to suspect that a Madoff associate had been conducting a Ponzi scheme. Yet, the SEC focused its efforts on Madoff's associate and never thoroughly scrutinized Madoff's operations even after learning that the investment decisions were made by Madoff and being apprised of the remarkably consistent returns over a period of numerous years that Madoff had achieved with a basic trading strategy.

While the SEC ensured that all of Madoff's associate's customers received their money back, they took no steps to investigate Madoff. The SEC focused its investigation too narrowly and seemed not to have considered the possibility that Madoff could have taken the money that was used to pay back his associate's customers from other clients for which Madoff may have had held discretionary brokerage accounts. In the examination of Madoff, the SEC did seek records from the Depository Trust Company (DTC) (an independent third-party), but sought copies of such records from Madoff himself. Had they sought records from DTC, there is an excellent chance that they would have uncovered Madoff's Ponzi scheme in 1992.[2]

In 2004 and 2005, the SEC's examination unit, OCIE, conducted two parallel cause examinations of Madoff based upon the Hedge Fund Manager's complaint and the series of internal e-mails that the SEC discovered. The examinations were remarkably similar. There were initial significant delays in the commencement of the examinations, notwithstanding the urgency of the complaints. The teams assembled were relatively inexperienced, and there was insufficient planning for the examinations. The scopes of the examination were in both cases too narrowly focused on the possibility of front-running, with no significant attempts made to analyze the numerous red flags about Madoff's trading and returns.

During the course of both these examinations, the examination teams discovered suspicious information and evidence and caught Madoff in contradictions and inconsistencies. However, they either disregarded these concerns or simply asked Madoff about them. Even when Madoff's answers were seemingly implausible, the SEC examiners accepted them at face value.

In both examinations, the examiners made the surprising discovery that Madoff's mysterious hedge fund business was making significantly more money than his well-known market-making operation. However, no one identified this revelation as a cause for concern.

Astoundingly, both examinations were open at the same time in different offices without either knowing the other one was conducting an identical examination. In fact, it was Madoff himself who informed one of the examination teams that the other examination team had already received the information they were seeking from him.

In the first of the two OCIE examinations, the examiners drafted a letter to the National Association of Securities Dealers (NASD) (another independent third-party) seeking independent trade data, but they never sent the letter, claiming that it would have been too time-consuming to review the data they would have obtained. The OIG's expert opined that had the letter to the NASD been sent, the data would have provided the information necessary to reveal the Ponzi scheme. In the second examination, the OCIE Assistant Director sent a document request to a financial institution that Madoff claimed he used to clear his trades, requesting trading done by or on behalf of particular Madoff feeder funds during a specific time period, and received a response that there was no transaction activity in Madoff's account for that period. However, the Assistant Director did not determine that the response required any follow-up and the examiners testified that the response was not shared with them.

Both examinations concluded with numerous unresolved questions and without any significant attempt to examine the possibility that Madoff was misrepresenting his trading and operating a Ponzi scheme.

The investigation that arose from the most detailed complaint provided to the SEC, which explicitly stated it was "highly likely" that Madoff was operating a Ponzi scheme," never really investigated the possibility of a Ponzi scheme. The relatively inexperienced Enforcement staff failed to appreciate the significance of the analysis in the complaint, and almost immediately expressed skepticism and disbelief. Most of their investigation was directed at determining whether Madoff should register as an investment adviser or whether Madoff's hedge fund investors' disclosures were adequate.

As with the examinations, the Enforcement staff almost immediately caught Madoff in lies and misrepresentations, but failed to follow up on inconsistencies. They rebuffed offers of additional evidence from the complainant, and were confused about certain critical and fundamental aspects of Madoff's operations. When Madoff provided evasive or contradictory answers to important questions in testimony, they simply accepted as plausible his explanations.

Although the Enforcement staff made attempts to seek information from independent third-parties, they failed to follow up on these requests. They reached out to the NASD and asked for information on whether Madoff had options positions on a certain date, but when they received a report that there were in fact no options positions on that date, they did not take any further steps. An Enforcement staff attorney made several attempts to obtain documentation from European counterparties (another independent third-party), and although a letter was drafted, the Enforcement staff decided not to send it. Had any of these efforts been fully executed, they would have led to Madoff's Ponzi scheme being uncovered.

The OIG also found that numerous private entities conducted basic due diligence of Madoff's operations and, without regulatory authority to compel information, came to the conclusion that an investment with Madoff was unwise. Specifically, Madoff's description of both his equity and options trading practices immediately led to suspicions about Madoff's operations. With respect to his purported trading strategy, many simply did not believe that it was possible for Madoff to achieve his returns using a strategy described by some industry leaders as common and unsophisticated. In addition, there was a great deal of suspicion about Madoff's purported options trading, with several entities not believing that Madoff could be trading options in such high volumes where there was no evidence that any counterparties had been trading options with Madoff.

The private entities' conclusions were drawn from the same "red flags" in Madoff's operations that the SEC considered in its examinations and investigations, but ultimately dismissed.

We also found that investors who may have been uncertain about whether to invest with Madoff were reassured by the fact that the SEC had investigated and/or examined Madoff, or entities that did business with Madoff, and found no evidence of fraud. Moreover, we found that Madoff proactively informed potential investors that the SEC had examined his operations. When potential investors expressed hesitation about investing with Madoff, he cited the prior SEC examinations to establish credibility and allay suspicions or investor doubts that may have arisen while due diligence was being conducted. Thus, the fact the SEC had conducted examinations and investigations and did not detect the fraud, lent credibility to Madoff's operations and had the effect of encouraging additional individuals and entities to invest with him.

***

A more detailed description of the circumstances surrounding the five major investigations and examinations that the SEC conducted of Madoff and his firm is provided below.

As the foregoing demonstrates, despite numerous credible and detailed complaints, the SEC never properly examined or investigated Madoff's trading and never took the necessary, but basic, steps to determine if Madoff was operating a Ponzi scheme. Had these efforts been made with appropriate follow-up at any time beginning in June of 1992 until December 2008, the SEC could have uncovered the Ponzi scheme well before Madoff confessed.

H. David Kotz, Inspector General

**Follow up**: In March 2014, five Madoff employees were convicted of knowingly engaging in securities fraud, and conspiracy. They were also convicted of tax evasion, for failing to report their true compensation by Madoff.[1] The individuals convicted of criminal conspiracy were the operations people who supported the Ponzi scheme, including two portfolio managers, the operations director and two computer programmers who created the fake records presented to auditors and the SEC. Others employee who made guilty pleas or were convicted, include Bernard L. Madoff Investment Securities CFO Frank DiPascali Jr., who testified at the trial of the operations employees; Bernard Madoff's brother, Peter Madoff, who served as Madoff Investments Chief Compliance Officer; Peter Konigsberg, a former accountant for Madoff; accountant David Friehling.

## Notes

1   There were arguably eight complaints, since as described in greater detail below, three versions of one of these six complaints were actually brought to the SEC's attention, with the first two versions being dismissed entirely, and an investigation not opened until the third version was submitted.

2   As discussed in the body of the Report of Investigation this is premised upon the assumption that Madoff had been operating his Ponzi scheme in 1992, which most of the evidence seems to support.

3   Rachel Abrams and Diana B. Henriques, "Jury Says 5 Madoff Employees Knowingly Aided Swindle of Clients' Billions," *Dealbook*, *New York Times*, March 24, 2014, http://dealbook.nytimes.com/2014/03/24/5-former-madoff-employees-found-guilty-of-fraud. See also Jim Zarroli, "Madoff Aides Found Guilty for Role in Massive Ponzi Scheme," *NPR*, March 24, 2014, http://www.npr.org/2014/03/24/293897804/madoff-aides-found-guilty-for-role-in-massive-ponzi-scheme.

## Case Discussion Questions

1.  Was the failure of SEC investigators to follow up on red flags in the complaints regarding Bernard Madoff's alleged Ponzi scheme a failure of critical thinking?

2.  Are the SEC findings that the conflicts of interests by SEC investigators were unrelated to the SEC failure to investigate worthy of credence?

3.  Make a decision tree mapping each of the complaints and the SEC investigation. Recommend alternative actions that might have been done at each choice point and justify your suggested alternatives.

4.  The massive Ponzi scheme was managed by a very few individuals, as revealed by the subsequent prosecution of Madoff's co-conspirators. How can future fraudulent schemes be averted, or at least caught early?

# Unit III

Unit III consists of two concluding chapters, Chapter 13 "Corporate Responsibility—What Went Wrong? Lessons from the Dark Side" and Chapter 14 "Corporate Governance, Social Responsibility and Organizational Effectiveness: The Bottom Line." It addresses the questions of what can be learned from corporate social irresponsibility, whether socially responsible enterprises are effective from managerial and financial points of view, and how socially responsible management can be incentivized.

# 13 Corporate Social Responsibility—What Went Wrong? Lessons from the Dark Side

## Chapter Outline

## Chapter Introduction

In the 1990s there were many initiatives to develop corporate social responsibility. The 1991 Sentencing Guidelines were passed in the US, and corporations were encouraged to develop codes of ethics. Business for Social Responsibility was founded in 1992. Why, therefore, did the 1990s close with such a spate of corporate debacles and scandals? Conflicts of interest, the failure to disclose material information to business stakeholders and fraud in financial statements resulting in fraud on the market are troubling aspects of the spate of corporate debacles of the 1990s and early twenty-first century. What lessons can be learned from corporate wrongdoing? How can a company with ethical lapses be rehabilitated?

The Sarbanes Oxley Act and other measures were undertaken to avoid similar corporate debacles such as Enron and WorldCom and other fraudulent schemes. However, Sarbanes Oxley did not prevent the meltdown of the financial markets and institutions of 2008. The Dodd-Frank "Wall Street Reform and Consumer Protection Act of 2010" and the Volcker Rule were enacted after the 2008 global financial crisis with the intention of managing risk in the financial services sector. The meltdown of financial markets and institutions has affected the global economy, and sovereign debt poses challenges to international stability. Can future ethical crises be prevented? If so, how?

## Chapter Goal and Learning Objectives

*Chapter Goal:* Describe the lessons that can be learned from corporate wrongdoing and whether regulation is or can be effective to prevent ethical wrongdoing and its consequences.

*Learning Objectives:*

1. Recall early initiatives to develop corporate social responsibility, including the 1991 Sentencing Guidelines in the US and corporate code of conduct initiatives.
2. Explain externalization of risk and "moral hazard."
3. Discuss regulatory failure as a possible cause or contributing factor to enterprise and industry failures.
4. Explain the factors underlying the 2008 meltdown of financial markets and institutions.
5. Explain the Dodd-Frank "Consumer Protection and Wall Street Reform Act," including the Volcker Rule.
6. Debate whether Basel III regulation of systemically important financial institutions (SIFIs) will avert new financial crises.

Troubling questions are raised about the spate of corporate debacles the occurred in the late 1990s and the early twenty-first century. There were many initiatives to develop corporate social responsibility in the 1990s. The Sentencing Guidelines, passed in 1991, were an important initiative. The Sentencing Guidelines encouraged corporations to develop codes of conduct for their employees, and many companies did so, including Enron Corporation. Business for Social Responsibility was founded by leading corporate citizens in 1992. In general, corporate responsibility, business ethics and corporate citizenship were celebrated in the 1990s; however, the decade ended and the twenty-first century began with a spate of corporate debacles. Why did the twentieth century close, and the twenty-first century open, with such a round of corporate debacles and scandals?

## Long History of Fraud in Financial Markets

There is a long history of fraud in financial markets. For example, Charles Ponzi defrauded investors using a "pyramid" marketing scheme during the period 1907–1921.[1] Ponzi marketed an investment opportunity to exploit the differentials in US and foreign currencies by selling international postage stamps. He attracted many investors, giving high returns to a few early investors, which gave the appearance of legitimacy before the scheme collapsed. His scheme was fraudulent, insofar as he did not actually purchase the international postage stamps at the rate required by the investments he attracted. Such fraudulent pyramid marketing plans have been dubbed "Ponzi schemes."

High leveraging and fraud were also factors in the collapse of the US stock market in 1929 and its further erosion between 1929 and 1932, during which time the stock market lost 90% of its value.[2] The Securities Act of 1933 and the Securities Exchange Act of 1934, which established the SEC, were passed in response to collapse of stock market in 1929.

However, there were several major frauds even after the enactment of the Securities and Exchange Act. In 1963, Tino DeAngelis, a commodity trader who founded the Allied Crude Vegetable Oil Refining Co., used water-filled vats with oil floating on top to secure loans, constituting "phantom inventory." The fraud caused major losses for American Express, which had issued financing for the phantom inventory. The Allied Crude Vegetable Oil Refining Co. fraud led to changes in auditing procedures.[3] The collapse of Lincoln Federal Savings and Loan in 1987 presaged a wider collapse within the savings and loan (S&L) industry. Deregulation,[4] failed investments in real estate, and fraud were major factors in the collapse of Lincoln Federal Savings.[5] The Depository Institutions Deregulation and Monetary Control Act of 1980 was intended to make S&Ls more competitive by removing Regulation Q, which had imposed caps on savings accounts and prohibited interest on "on demand" accounts, and raising the insured limit from $40,000 to $100,000.[6] The Garn-St. Germain Depository Institutions Act of 1982, titled "An Act to revitalize the housing industry by strengthening the financial stability of home mortgage lending institutions and ensuring the availability of home mortgage loans," permitted banks to offer adjustable-rate mortgages and authorized S&Ls to make commercial loans.[7] The legislative intent of the regulatory reform was to eliminate "asset-liability mismatch," which resulted from the regulatory limits on interest that could be paid on deposits to the S&Ls in the context of the double-digit inflation rates of the 1970s and early 1980s and the long-term mortgages loaned by the S&Ls.[8] Within nine years of the passage of the Depository Institutions Deregulation and Monetary Control Act of 1980 and the Garn-St. Germain Depository Institutions Act of 1982, the Financial Institutions Reform, Recovery and Enforcement Act of 1989 (FIRREA) was enacted. During this interval almost half of S&L institutions closed. FIRREA established the Resolution Trust Company and granted regulatory authority to the Office of Thrift Supervision, transferring it from the Federal Home Loan Bank Board.[9] FIREEA was used to resolve and close distressed S&Ls. The bailout of the savings and loan industry by Congress may have created the "moral hazard" that laid the groundwork for the mortgage crisis of 2007 and 2008.[10] In the aftermath of the S&L failures, controls were proposed but were not passed until the Sarbanes Oxley Act in 2002.[11]

Even though there has been a history of fraud and ensuing financial collapse, the question arises: what were the factors related to the alarming rate of corporate wrong-doing characterized by the discovery of fraud, ensuing financial collapse and bankruptcies, as well as prosecution of corporate executives, that characterized the turn of the twenty-first century and the years since? Conflicts of interest; earnings management practices; failure to disclose material information; fraud in financial statements, leading to fraud on the market; individual greed and a corporate culture of greed and unintended negative consequences of executive compensation plans are factors related to recent failures of corporate business ethics and social responsibility. Just as deregulation was a factor in the widespread collapse of the S&L institutions rampant in the 1980s, deregulation was a factor as well in the collapse of the investment banks in 2008. Moreover, regulatory failure, such as the SEC failure to investigate Bernard Madoff's Ponzi scheme, was a contributing factor to enterprise and industry failures.

## Earnings Management Practices

Earnings management practices involve issues of revenue recognition. New rules about revenue recognition were issued by the SEC in December 1999, as Staff Accounting Bulletin (SAB) 101.[12] Until the issuance of SAB 101, companies recognized revenue based on pronouncements made by the Financial Accounting Standards Board and its predecessors, which generally stated that revenue should not be recognized until it is realized or realizable and earned: "an entity's revenue-earning activities involve delivering or producing goods, rendering services, or other activities that constitute its ongoing major or central operations, and revenues are considered to have been earned when the entity has substantially accomplished what it must do to be entitled to the benefits represented by the revenues."[13] In many cases, companies presented financial statements using an aggressive interpretation of the standards. In other cases, they misapplied accounting rules in order to reach financial statement goals.[14] "Bill and hold and channel stuffing abuses" were identified by the SEC as particularly problematic issues in revenue recognition.[15] Sunbeam, Xerox and Lucent Technologies engaged in, and were investigated for, earnings management practices prior to the securities fraud prosecutions and bankruptcies of Enron and WorldCom.[16] The SEC prosecuted Sunbeam Corporation, and its former chief executive Albert Dunlap, for fraudulent earnings management practices.[17] Xerox Corporation was investigated by the SEC, for improper revenue recognition, including recognizing revenue of leased equipment in Mexico, after which Xerox restated its financial reports for the years 1998 and 1999.[18] A complaint was also issued by the SEC against six Xerox executives, who settled the charges. Xerox ceased the practice of financing customer sales, as part of its turnaround program.[19] Lucent Technologies restated its financial statements in December 2000 and took back $200 million of inventory "sold" to Anixter International.[20] Thereafter, Lucent Technologies stock crashed and never recovered. Lucent was subsequently purchased by Alcatel, SA.[21]

*Harvard Business Review* tracked reported earnings compared to predicted earnings over the year 2001. They observed that there were very few deviations from predicted earnings. The author of the study concluded that earnings were managed, since more deviation of actual earnings from expected earnings would be expected.[22] The incentive for earnings management practices is that the market rewards exceeding earnings even by one penny but punishes missing earnings targets even by a penny with a decline in stock price. Investor expectations for growth may drive earnings management practices.[23]

## Failure to Disclose Material Information, Fraud in Financial Statements and Fraud on the Market

The fundamental problem with earnings management practices and the failure to disclose material financial information is that the reasonable investor wants and needs to use financial information about firm performance in his or her decision about whether to invest in a firm. Fraud in financial statements deprives investors of the information necessary to make a prudent investment decision and perpetrates a fraud on the market. With fraud in a financial statement, only insiders have accurate information as to the financial status of the firm. Insiders in possession of material non-public information are prohibited from trading on that information.[24] The top executives at Enron sold their stock starting in August 2001; Enron restated earnings in October 2001, then filed for bankruptcy in December. One mechanism by which Enron hid its true financial status was special purpose entities (SPEs).[25] The SPEs were designed specifically to hide material information about Enron's true financial status from investors and indeed other financiers. In so doing, Enron perpetuated a fraud on the market. The research conducted by this author on ethical management and firm financial performance revealed that Enron was at risk of bankruptcy as early as 1998.[26] Enron managers likely had early "inside" knowledge that their firm was under financial duress. Enron's unethical conduct may have been a dysfunctional way of coping with the firm's real financial duress. Enron executives CEO Kenneth Lay and CFO Andrew Fastow and Jeffrey Skilling, among others, were convicted of insider trading and securities fraud.[27] The manipulation of corporate financials by corporate executives generally identified as "earnings management practices" have been the mechanism for much corporate fraud.

Arthur Andersen's fate was tied to the bankruptcy and subsequent prosecution of Enron Corporation. Arthur Andersen was charged with obstruction of justice in Enron's financial fraud for shredding documents related to Enron's financial audits. Arthur Andersen's conviction for obstruction of justice was overturned by the United States Supreme Court in June 2005, based on invalid jury instructions by the judge trying the case.[28] But the charges, and the trial itself, along with prior failed audits, resulted in the effective demise of accounting firm Arthur Andersen.[29]

## Conflicts of Interest

The identification of and ability to resolve conflicts of interest may be among the key management skills required of executive management if they are to successfully negotiate ethical challenges. Conflicts of interest underlie many, if not most, of the ethical and legal violations discussed herein. The ability to recognize and resolve conflicts of interests is the touchstone of a manager's personal ethics, as suggested in Chapter 3, Business Ethics. Yet, even the Accounting Oversight Board created by the Sarbanes Oxley Act contained an appearance of impropriety and conflicts of interest in its initial appointments.[30] Harvey Pitt, chairman of SEC, appointed William Webster to be chair of the Public Company Accounting Oversight Board.[31] However, Pitt failed to inform the four other commissioners of the SEC that Webster served as the chair of the audit committee of a company that was under investigation for accounting fraud, U.S. Technologies. The controversies surrounding both William Webster and Harvey Pitt could have been averted if the disclosure rule and the smell test had been invoked.

More serious conflicts of interest were involved in the financial services industry, whereby research analysts reached private conclusions about the financial health of a firm that they were evaluating but failed to disclose to investors the risks associated with providing financing to such firms.[32] Important examples of such conflicts of interest involve Merrill Lynch and Henry Blodgett, who was the senior Internet/e-commerce analyst for Merrill Lynch,[33] and Citibank's Salomon Smith Barney's Jack Grubman, a research analyst for the telecommunications industry.

Citigroup/Salomon Smith Barney and Grubman settled conflict of interest charges with the SEC, National Association of Securities Dealers, New York Stock Exchange, and New York Attorney General.[34] In fact, there was an industry-wide settlement for conflicts of interest between research analysts and their employing investment banks.[35] The firms participating in the industry-wide settlement were Bear Stearns; Credit Suisse First Boston; Goldman Sachs; Lehman Brothers; J.P. Morgan Securities Inc.; Merrill Lynch, Pierce, Fenner & Smith; Morgan Stanley & Co.; Citigroup Global Markets Inc., f/k/a Salomon Smith Barney Inc.; UBS Warburg; and U.S. Bancorp Piper Jaffray.[36]

Unfortunately, conflicts of interest are not a thing of the past. The SEC charged Goldman Sachs with fraud in the structuring of its collateralized-debt obligation Abacus; Goldman Sachs settled the charges with the SEC in 2010, within months of the SEC charges.[37]

### *The Role of Greed?*

Conflicts of interest can be career wrecking, if not worse. Martha Stewart and Sanford Weill both were nominated to the board of the New York Stock Exchange but were forced to withdraw their nominations. Weill withdrew his name from nomination to the board of the New York Stock Exchange because he was CEO of Citigroup when its investment wing, Solomon Smith Barney, settled conflict of interest charges with New York Attorney General Eliot Spitzer.[38] Martha Stewart was charged, and later convicted of, lying to prosecutors about the sale of her ImClone stock; Stewart sold her ImClone stock one day before the FDA denied ImClone's application for an anti-cancer drug, Erbitux.[39] Martha Stewart settled an inside trading claim with the SEC.[40] However, Samuel Waksal, former CEO of Imclone, pled guilty to a charge of insider trading and was sentenced to seven years in jail and a fine of $4.3 million.[41] Ironically, Erbitux was later approved for cancer treatment by the FDA.[42]

Chief executive officers convicted and sentenced to jail include Dennis Koslowski, CEO of Tyco, Bernard Ebbers, CEO of WorldCom, John Rigas, founder and CEO of Adelphia Communications and his sons,[43] as well as Kenneth Lay, Jeffrey Skilling, Andrew Fastow and others at Enron Corporation. Rigas, Ebbers, Lay and Skilling led their companies into bankruptcy.

The conviction and jailing of high-profile executives provides a "lesson" to other CEOs. The Sarbanes Oxley Act imposition of personal liability for material misstatements of a firm's financial condition and the Section 404 requirement that a company establish internal controls over financial reporting are geared toward rectifying misrepresentation in financial reporting.[44]

## The Meltdown of Financial Markets and Institutions of 2008

Like the War to End All Wars, which was followed by World War II in less than a generation, so too the Sarbanes Oxley Act was thought to prevent future corporate ethical and legal debacles. Disappointingly, SOX was followed by a meltdown in financial markets and institutions arising from the development and use of mortgage-backed securities and other collateralized debt obligations within six years of the passage of SOX!

It is the nature of the financial services industry to search for new financial instruments and high rates of return. However, risk is embodied in financial instruments and markets. The management of that risk is essential to the sound operation of financial markets.

### Regulatory Focus and the Recognition of Systemic Risk

An alarm about risks to the financial system from high/excessive leverage was raised in the late 1990s by the failure of Long Term Capital Management.[45] Long Term Capital Management was a hedge fund founded by the former head of bond trading at Salomon Smith Barney and was advised by Myron S. Scholes and Robert C. Merton. Scholes and Merton won the Nobel Prize in Economics in 1997 for developing the Black-Scholes "options pricing model."[46] In 1998, Long Term Capital Management failed after the collapse of the Asian and the Russian currencies in 1997 and 1998, respectively. The Federal Reserve Bank of New York bailed out Long Term Capital Management to prevent a worldwide collapse of the financial markets.[47]

After the collapse of Long Term Capital Management and the exponential growth of hedge funds after 2000,[48] the question of whether hedge funds should be regulated was under debate in financial circles. Chairman of the Federal Reserve Ben Bernanke weighed in against imposing federal regulation on hedge funds (see Box 13.1).

---

**Box 13.1   Remarks by Chairman Ben S. Bernanke at the Federal Reserve Bank of Atlanta's 2006 Financial Markets Conference**

May 16, 2006: Hedge Funds and Systemic Risk

Thank you for inviting me to speak today. In keeping with the theme of this conference, I will offer some thoughts on the systemic risk implications of the rapid growth of the hedge fund industry and on ways that policymakers might respond to those risks.

The collapse of Long-Term Capital Management (LTCM) in 1998 precipitated the first in-depth assessment by policymakers of the potential systemic risks posed by the burgeoning hedge fund industry. The President's Working Group on Financial Markets, which includes the Federal Reserve, considered the policy issues raised by that event and, in 1999, issued its report, Hedge Funds, Leverage, and the Lessons of Long-Term Capital Management. The years since then have offered an opportunity to consider whether the Working Group's recommendations for addressing those issues have been effective and whether new concerns have arisen that warrant an alternative approach.

As the title of the report indicated, the Working Group focused on the potential for leverage to create systemic risk in financial markets. The concern arises because, all else being equal, highly leveraged investors are more vulnerable to market shocks. If leveraged investors default while holding positions that are large relative to the markets in which they have invested, the forced liquidation of those positions, possibly at fire-sale prices, could cause heavy losses to counterparties. These direct losses are of concern, of course, particularly if they lead to further defaults or threaten systemically important institutions; but, in addition, market participants that were not creditors or counterparties of the defaulting firm might be affected indirectly through asset price adjustments, liquidity strains, and increased market uncertainty.

The primary mechanism for regulating excessive leverage and other aspects of risk-taking in a market economy is the discipline provided by creditors, counterparties, and investors. In the LTCM episode, unfortunately, market discipline broke down. LTCM received generous terms from the banks and broker-dealers that provided credit and served as counterparties, even though LTCM took exceptional risks. Investors, perhaps awed by the reputations of LTCM's principals, did not ask sufficiently tough questions about the risks that were being taken to generate the high returns. Together with the admittedly extraordinary market conditions of August 1998, these risk-management lapses were an important source of the LTCM crisis.

The Working Group's central policy recommendation was that regulators and supervisors should foster an environment in which market discipline—in particular, counterparty risk management—constrains excessive leverage and risk-taking. Effective market discipline requires that counterparties and creditors obtain sufficient information to reliably assess clients' risk profiles and that they have systems to monitor and limit exposures to levels commensurate with each client's riskiness and creditworthiness. Placing the onus on market participants to provide discipline makes good economic sense; private agents generally have strong incentives to monitor counterparties as well as the best access to the information needed to do so effectively.

*For various reasons, however, creditors may not fully internalize the costs of systemic financial problems; and time and competition may dull memory and undermine risk-management discipline* (emphasis added). The Working Group concluded, accordingly, that supervisors and regulators should ensure that banks and broker-dealers implement the systems and policies necessary to strengthen and maintain market discipline, making several specific recommendations to that effect. The Working Group's recommendations on this point have largely been followed. Domestically, regulatory authorities issued guidance on risk-management practices, and bank supervisors now actively monitor and conduct targeted reviews of banks' dealings with hedge funds. The Securities and Exchange Commission (SEC) intensified its risk-management inspections of the larger broker-dealers after LTCM. Internationally, both the Basel Committee on Banking Supervision and the International Organization of Securities Commissions produced papers on sound practices in dealings with highly leveraged institutions, and the Basel Committee conducted a series of follow-up studies.

An alternative policy response that the Working Group considered, but did not recommend, was direct regulation of hedge funds. Direct regulation may be justified when market discipline is ineffective at constraining excessive leverage and risk-taking but, in the case of hedge funds, the reasonable presumption is that market discipline can work. Investors, creditors, and counterparties have significant incentives to rein in hedge funds' risk-taking. Moreover, direct regulation would impose costs in the form of moral hazard, the likely loss of private market discipline, and possible limits on funds' ability to provide market liquidity.

. . .[S]ome concerns about counterparty risk management remain and may have become even more pronounced given the increasing complexity of financial products. . .[S]upervisors are concerned that the assessment of counterparty risks should be better tied to the amount of transparency offered by hedge funds. In particular, good risk management should link the availability and the terms of credit granted to a hedge fund to the fund's willingness to provide information on its strategies and risk profile. Our supervisors are pushing banks to clearly link transparency with credit terms and conditions.

. . . The continuing challenge for supervisors, counterparties, and hedge funds is to ensure that rigorous and appropriate methods of risk management are brought to bear even as institutions, instruments, and markets change. Two recent challenges of note are the spread of prime brokerage services and the emergence of operational issues in the settling of trades in newer types of over-the-counter (OTC) derivatives, particularly credit derivatives.

The proliferation of new financial products also poses risk-management challenges, including challenges on the operational side. For example, trading in credit derivatives has grown dramatically in recent years, and firms have had difficulties in processing and settling these and other OTC derivative trades in a timely way. These problems are not limited to hedge funds but affect all participants in the

OTC derivatives market and all dealers in credit derivatives. Recently, supervisors in several jurisdictions, working with the Federal Reserve Bank of New York, have pushed firms to improve their processes for confirming and assigning trades. So far, good progress has been made, with private-sector participants meeting most of their objectives for reducing backlogs. Commitments are in place to effect still further improvement.

A noteworthy feature of these efforts is the cooperation among authorities. The Federal Reserve has devoted more effort in recent years to maintaining a dialogue with international supervisors, such as the U.K. Financial Services Authority, and we will continue to do so. Domestically, the Federal Reserve is coordinating with the SEC, which is the primary regulator of several large firms that deal in OTC derivatives or engage in prime brokerage activities.

Following the LTCM crisis and the publication of the Working Group's recommendations, the debate about hedge funds and the broader effects of their activities on financial markets abated for a time. That debate, however, has now resumed with vigor—spurred, no doubt, by the creation of many new funds, large reported inflows to funds, and a broadening investor base. Renewed discussion of hedge funds and of their benefits and risks has in turn led to calls for authorities to implement new policies, many of which will be topics of this conference. I will briefly discuss one of these proposals: the development of a database that would contain information on hedge-fund positions and portfolios.

*It is commonly observed that hedge funds are "opaque"—that is, information about their portfolios is typically limited and infrequently provided. It would be more accurate to say that the opacity of hedge funds is in the eye of the beholder; the information a fund provides may vary considerably depending on whether the recipient of the information is an investor, a counterparty, a regulatory authority, or a general market participant. From a policy perspective, transparency to investors is largely an issue of investor protection* (emphasis added). The need for counterparties to have adequate information is a risk-management issue, as I have already discussed. Much of the recent debate, however, has focused on the opacity of hedge funds to regulatory authorities and to the markets generally, which is viewed by some as an important source of liquidity risk. Liquidity in a particular market segment might well decline sharply and unexpectedly if hedge funds chose or were forced to reduce a large exposure in that segment.

Concerns about hedge fund opacity and possible liquidity risk have motivated a range of proposals for regulatory authorities to create and maintain a database of hedge fund positions. Such a database, it is argued, would allow authorities to monitor this possible source of systemic risk and to address the buildup of risk as it occurs. Various alternatives that have been discussed include a database maintained by regulators on a confidential basis, a system in which hedge funds submit position information to an authority that aggregates that information and reveals it to the market, and a public database with non-confidential information on hedge funds.

I understand the concerns that motivate these proposals but, at this point, remain skeptical about their utility in practice. To measure liquidity risks accurately, the authorities would need data from all major financial market participants, not just hedge funds. As a practical matter, could the authorities collect such an enormous quantity of highly sensitive information in sufficient detail and with sufficient frequency (daily, at least) to be effectively informed about liquidity risk in particular market segments? How would the authorities use the information? Would they have the authority to direct hedge funds or other large financial institutions to reduce positions? If several funds had similar positions, how would authorities avoid giving a competitive advantage to one fund over another in using the information from the database? Perhaps most important, would counterparties relax their vigilance if they thought the authorities were monitoring and constraining hedge funds' risk-taking? A risk of any prescriptive regulatory regime is that, by creating moral hazard in the marketplace, it leaves the system less rather than more stable.

Source: http://www.federalreserve.gov/Boarddocs/speeches/2006/200605162/default.htm

Federal Reserve Chairman Bernanke identified the "opaqueness" of the hedge fund investment strategies and risks. "Opaqueness" instead of transparency and the lack of disclosure on the grounds that the information is proprietary raises a red flag. The ethical risks, related to characteristics of hedge funds, are: 1) creditors do not internalize all costs, and 2) opaque, asymmetric information. These characteristics of hedge funds are alarming with respect to the risks of ethical and perhaps legal infractions. Investors and markets depend on complete information. Additionally, while the Coase Theorem, discussed in Chapter 8, concludes regulation is not necessary to affect firm behavior and that the market may be sufficient to lead firms to minimize costs, a fundamental assumption underlying the effective operation of the Coase Theorem is that enterprise absorbs its costs. If a firm can externalize costs, then the constraints on firm behavior under the Coase Theorem would fail to operate. Ultimately, regulators determined not to regulate hedge funds until the passage of the Dodd-Frank Act in the aftermath of the great recession of 2008.[49]

### High-Return, High-Risk Products: CMOs/MBSs, CDOs and CDSs

*Business Week* raised a red flag about risk management strategies of investment banks in 2006.[50] These concerns were "prophetic" insofar as the collapse of Bear Stearns and Lehman Brothers was caused by high leveraging, permitted by the SEC for the big five investment banks,[51] and the collapse of AIG in 2008 related to its insuring credit derivative swaps.

### Micro-Origins and Unintended Negative Consequences

The analysis of Elven Riley on the micro-origins of the 2008 financial crisis points to high leverage, opacity, and lack of regulation as factors in the meltdown of financial markets and institutions of 2008.[52] This hearkens back to Bernanke's discussion of the merits of regulation of hedge funds. The underlying risks were correctly identified, but regulatory action awaited the Dodd-Frank Act enacted following the Great Recession of 2008.

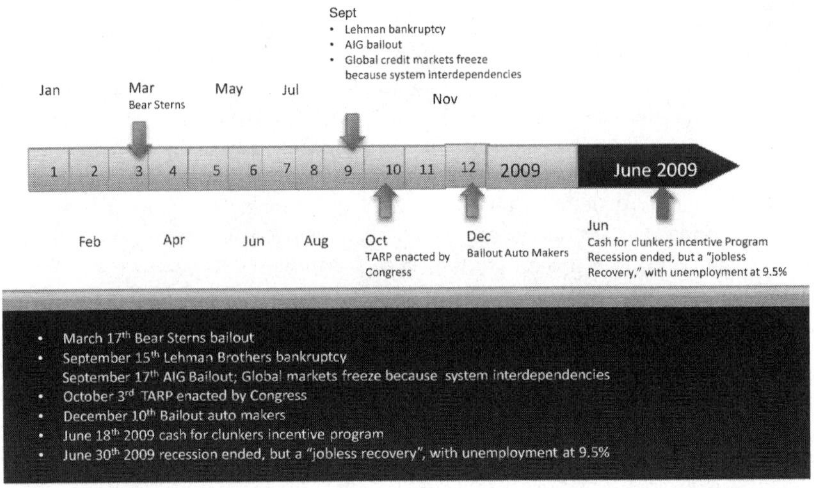

*Figure 13.1* Great Recession of 2008–2009

### Financial Meltdown 2008

The collapse of Bear Stearns in March 2008 marked the beginning of the Great Recession of 2008.[53] It did not precipitate, however, the freeze of the global credit markets. Lehman filed for bankruptcy on September 15, 2008[54] and AIG was bailed out September 16, 2008.[55] The global credit markets froze because of system interdependencies. The regulatory response to the 2008 meltdown included the enactment of the Troubled Asset Relief Program (TARP), enacted by the U.S. Congress on October 3, 2008, followed by the bailout of automakers on December 10, 2008. The "cash for clunkers" incentive program was enacted on June 18, 2009. The Great Recession officially ended June 30, 2009, but it was a "jobless recovery," with unemployment at 9.5%.

## Dodd-Frank Wall Street Reform and Consumer Protection Act of 2010

### *Volcker Rule: Section 619 of Dodd-Frank Wall Street Reform and Consumer Protection Act*

A key provision of the Dodd-Frank Act is the Volcker Rule, which prohibits proprietary trading by commercial banks.[56] That is, banks cannot use customer deposits to leverage/borrow money for the bank's own accounts to increase its revenues. Trades must be to the benefit of customers, except that commercial banks can hedge their positions and engage in "market making" for their securities and "under writing."[57] The Volcker Rule went into effect April 14, 2014, with full compliance by July 21, 2015. JPMorgan Chase's losses by the London-based "Whale" were losses arising from proprietary trading (see Box 13.2).

# Box 13.2  JPMorgan Chase and Derivatives: The Whale

The financial crisis of 2008 had little impact on JPMorgan Chase. The company seemed to anticipate the US housing crisis and carefully avoided holding the toxic assets that hurt so many individuals and companies. This strategy was followed under the leadership of Jamie Dimon, who had become the CEO of the bank a few years earlier. After the crisis, JPMorgan grew in size to more than $2 trillion in assets in 2013.

Just prior to the 2008 crisis, Mr. Dimon changed the bank's investment strategy. Previously, the bank always sought relatively safe investments that protected its capital and the funds of customers. The new set of objectives pursued profits from trading in complex financial instruments such as derivatives. The investment side of the bank endorsed the policy fully and trading became a large and profitable business.

The bank gave increasing authority to Bruno Iksil, a JPMorgan derivatives trader nicknamed "the London Whale," a recognition of the size of his trades. In 2011, he risked $1 billion on a single gamble that worked. It earned JPMorgan half a billion dollars. After this success, the sky seemed to be the limit. By early 2012, he held exposed positions on more than $150 billion in assets.

Boaz Weinstein was a derivative trader who managed a hedge fund with $6 billion of assets under management in 2012. His financial community nickname was "the Monster." Weinstein spotted a flaw in the trading strategy being followed by Iksil. Weinstein bought the JPMorgan derivatives and steadily increased his position.

The men dueled with each other for more than half a year in 2011 and 2012. Iksil sold more. Weinstein bought more. At first, Iksil held a profitable position on the dealings. Then, everything collapsed for JPMorgan when the market recognized the weakness in its strategy. The "Monster" had beaten the "Whale." In the process, JPMorgan experienced a total loss of more than $6 billion. Subsequently, the bank fired Iksil.

Epilogue. Iksil, the "Whale" in the JPMorgan story, testified in a US Senate subcommittee hearing investigating the activities of derivative traders. Iksil explained that he lost the $6 billion while engaged in "trades that make sense." His risk management strategy:

> *"Sell the forward spread and buy protection on the tightening move.*
> *Use indices and add to existing position.*
> *Go long risk on some belly tranches, especially where defaults may realize.*
> *Buy protection on HY and Xover in rallies and turn the position to monetize volatility."*

It is hard to believe that many of the senators understood how the trades "made sense" with this testimony. The committee did recommend and the Senate did approve a plan to regulate future derivative trades.

Source: John J. Hampton, PhD

### Resolution Plans ("Living Wills")

The Frank-Dodd Act, Section 165, also requires systemically important financial institution (SIFIs) to adopt "resolution plans." The resolution plans, also known as "living wills," set out a plan for their orderly dissolution.[58] This provision aligns with the asserted policy that "too big to fail" bailouts are a thing of the past.

The causes of the Great Recession, the Dodd-Frank Act and Basel III regulation of global SIFIs (G-SIFIs) are discussed in the following in an interview with Professor John Hampton, PhD. We conclude with a consideration of whether a global financial crisis can be prevented in the future (see Box 13.3).

---

**Box 13.3  P. Alexander Interview with John J. Hampton**

Paula Alexander (PA):

PA    Good Afternoon, Dr. Hampton. Thank you for granting this interview. Let me introduce you. You are a professor of business and teach MBA courses at Saint Peter's University.

John J. Hampton (JJH):

JJH   Yes. My book on financial risk management, published by the American Management Association, was selected as a top business reference book of 2012 by the American Library Association.

PA    You have been observing the financial scene for many years and reflecting on it.

JJH   In 2008, at the height of the financial crisis, Lehman Brothers had a major risk exposure. It held some $50 billion of toxic assets, mostly secured by mortgages on homes that were in danger of foreclosure. As it neared the closure of its accounting books and recognition of its annual profit or loss in 2007, the company recognized a disaster would result from exposing the situation.

As a protective step, Lehman transferred toxic assets to an offshore banking firm under an agreement to repurchase them a few days later after the close of the accounting period. The agreement temporarily removed the securities from the company's balance sheet. This was legal under US accounting practices. Thus, the Lehman auditors did not report the temporary transfer.

PA    So I think we all know the outcome.

JJH   Yes. In 2008 the decline of home values forced the firm into bankruptcy. Then, Lehman was accused of using cosmetic accounting techniques to improve the appearance of its finances. Lawyers said this created a "materially misleading picture" of the firm's financial condition in 2007 and 2008. It is a lesson in risk management gone wrong to recognize how the deception was achieved.

PA    Do you see the Lehman crisis as one of insolvency, not a crisis of liquidity?

JJH   Insolvency or liquidity? Actually it was both. Even a full guarantee of its obligations by the US government might not have saved the company.

JJH The regulatory response to the 2008 financial crisis was to enact the Frank Dodd Act of 2010.

JJH The act created a Financial Stability Oversight Council (FSOC) to:
- Identify threats to financial stability.
- Promote market discipline.
- Respond to emerging risks.

JJH FSOC voting members are:
- Secretary of the Treasury (Council Chair)
- Chair of the Federal Reserve
- Comptroller of the Currency
- Securities and Exchange Chair
- Federal Deposit Insurance Chair
- Experts on consumer protection, insurance, commodities, housing, and lending

JJH Non-voting members of the FSOC are:
- Director of the Office of Financial Research (newly established)
- Director of the Federal Insurance Office (newly established)
- A State Insurance Commissioner
- A State Banking Supervisor
- A State Securities Commissioner

PA The Dodd Frank Act increases bureaucracy!

JJH It sure does.
- It increases the number of agencies that regulate the banking system.
- Creates 243 rules to be followed by financial institutions.
- Requires regulators to conduct 67 studies and issue 22 periodic reports.

PA You and my colleague Elven Riley, a finance executive in residence, both say: "No more 'too big to fail.'" But look what happened when Lehman was allowed to fail. It crashed the world economy. What is different now?

JJH Lehman does not get credit for the crash. It was the result of systemic risk, a rather new concept that describes exposure when all financial markets are linked together. Even the survivors, AIG for example, were devastated. Its stock dropped from $70 a share to less than one dollar.

To answer the second part of the question, nothing has been done to change too big to fail. The capital requirements of Dodd-Frank and Basel III are not the problem. Size makes many current financial institution simply too big to fail.

$50 trillion in the capital markets but $550 trillion in derivatives is the problem. Everybody has obligations to everyone else.

JPMorgan Chase alone has more than $2 trillion in assets and operations spanning commodities, consumer and corporate banking, credit cards, finance and insurance, and foreign currency exchange. Not to mention global banking, mortgage loans, risk management, treasury services, and underwriting.

No matter what happens with Chase, Bank of America, AIG, and other institutions, we cannot let them fail. They must be smaller and there must be more of them. Plus, we must separate commercial banks, insurance companies, and speculative capital.

Many aspects of our financial system occur at the intersection of corporate irresponsibility and regulatory ineptitude.

PA   What is required for long-term stability in financial markets?

JJH   We must recognize three institutional roles.

  • **Commercial Banks.** Money to finance economic activity.
  • **Investment Banks.** Capital to encourage investment.
  • **Insurance Companies.** Funds to cover unexpected losses.

PA   Should these institutions be separate?

JJH   Absolutely. Just consider the goals of each. A commercial bank should protect depositors, not encourage investment returns by accepting high levels of risk. Insurance companies must be ready to pay for unexpected losses. Liquidity, not profitability, is the primary goal.

PA   What about Basel III? It recognizes systemically important financial institutions (SIFIs), including insurance companies.

JJH   Basel III offers an improvement. It recognizes weaknesses in Basel II after the 2008 financial crisis:

  • Require banks to hold risk-weighted assets (RWA)
  • Adds additional capital requirements
  • Requires minimum leverage and liquidity ratios

PA   Will it work?

JJH   Only if we eliminate financial institutions protected by "too big to fail."

PA   My own thought is that Basel III makes the SIFIs harder to fail. That getting rid of "too big to fail" is an elusive goal.

JJH   It may make it harder for an SIFI to fail. If we reduce the size of the financial institutions, it would make it harder for the whole system to collapse.

PA   One question before we finish. What are you working on now?

JJH   I am moving into managing risk using what I call high-tech electronic platforms (HTEPs). All the information we need real-time can be carried with us at all times on smart phones and portable devices connected to the cloud. Pretty exciting stuff for risk management.

## Chapter Discussion Questions

1. Are financial crises such as the 2008 meltdown of financial markets and institutions systemic failures, or are they caused by specific human actions?

2. To what extent was regulatory failure a cause or contributing factor to enterprise and industry failures?

3. The financial system survived after the collapse of Bear Stearns. Why then did it collapse after the bankruptcy of Lehman?

4. Debate whether the bailout of AIG was worth it.
5. Will Basel III's regulation of SIFIs prevent a systemic failure in the global financial system?

**View:**
*Too Big to Fail*
*Inside Job*
*Margin Call*
*Wall Street 2: Money Never Sleeps*

## Notes

1 See "Ponzi Schemes," U.S. Securities and Exchange Commission, last modified 2014, http://www.sec.gov/answers/ponzi.htm. See also "Pyramid Schemes," U.S. Securities and Exchange Commission, last modified 2014, http://www.sec.gov/answers/pyramid.htm and "Consumer Information," Federal Trade Commission, last modified 2014, http://www.ftc.gov/bcp/conline/pubs/invest/mlm.htm.
2 The Hatry Affair in England caused a constriction in international liquidity. See "The Hatry Crash," *Western Argus* (Karlgoorlie, WA), Feb. 11, 1930, last modified 2014, http://trove.nla.gov.au/ndp/del/article/34492861. The Federal Reserve raised interest rates, as did the Bank of England, aggravating the liquidity crisis.
3 Statement on Auditing Standards no. 82, Consideration of Fraud in a Financial Statement Audit. See Association of Certified Fraud Examiners, last modified 2014, http://www.acfe.com/.
4 "Depository Institutions Deregulation and Money Control Act of 1980," Wikipedia, last modified Dec. 31, 2013, http://en.wikipedia.org/wiki/Depository_Institutions_Deregulation_and_Monetary_Control_Act, and "Garn-St. Germain Depository Institutions Act of 1982," *Wikipedia*, last modified May 8, 2014, http://en.wikipedia.org/wiki/Garn%E2%80%93St._Germain_Depository_Institutions_Act.
5 See also Glenn Yago and James Barth, *The Savings and Loan Crisis: Lessons from a Regulatory Failure* (Dordrecht, the Netherlands: Kluwer Academic Publishers, 2004).
6 See "Depository Institutions Deregulation and Monetary Control Act of 1980," *Federal Reserve Bank of Boston*, last modified 2014, https://www.bostonfed.org/about/pubs/deposito.pdf.
7 See Matthew Sherman, "A Short History of Financial Deregulation in the United States," *Center for Economic Policy and Research*, last modified July 2009, available at http://www.cepr.net/documents/publications/dereg-timeline-2009–07.pdf. See also "Reagan's Economic Legacy," *PBS Newshour*, June 10, 2004, available at http://www.pbs.org/newshour/bb/business-jan-june04-reagan_06–10/.
8 Bodie, Zvi. "On Asset-Liability Matching and Federal Deposit and Pension Insurance," *Federal Reserve Bank of St. Louis Review* 88, no. 4 (July/Aug. 2006): 323–29.
9 Financial Institutions Reform, Recovery & Enforcement Act of 1989, H.R.1278.ENR, 101st Cong., http://thomas.loc.gov/cgi-bin/query/z?c101:H.R.1278.ENR:.
10 Yeomin Yoon and Robert McGee, "A Plan to Help Paulson Socialise Gains and Privatise Losses," *Financial Times*, Sept. 30, 2008.
11 Remarks of James Doty, General Counsel, Securities and Exchange Commission to the American Bar Association, Federal Regulation of Securities Committee Annual Fall Meeting, Washington, DC, Nov. 9, 1990, available at http://www.sec.gov/news/speech/1990/110990doty.pdf.

12　SAB 101 issued, in example format, more detailed guidelines on the four factors that the SEC believes are necessary before revenue can be recognized on the income statement. These factors are: 1) persuasive evidence of an arrangement exists; 2) delivery has occurred or services have been rendered; 3) the seller's price to the buyer is fixed or determinable; and 4) collectability is reasonably assured.

13　Statement of Financial Accounting Concept (SFAC) No 5, issued by FASB.

14　For example, Xerox admitted that they misapplied accounting rules, Xerox 10-K SEC, June 7, 2001.

15　Lynn Turner, "Revenue Recognition," speech by SEC Staff member, May 31, 2001 at section, "Transparent Disclosure of Relevant Trends," http://www.sec.gov/news/speech/spch495.htm.

16　Paula Alexander Becker and Kenneth Heaslip, "Ethical Dilemmas Related to Earnings Management Practices: The Case of Sunbeam, Xerox and Lucent Technologies," International Conference Promoting Business Ethics, Chicago, Oct. 2001.

17　Floyd Norris, "SEC Accuses Former Sunbeam Official of Fraud," *New York Times*, May 16, 2001. "SEC Sues Former CEO, CFO, Other Top Former Officers of Sunbeam Corporation in Massive Financial Fraud," May 15, 2001, SEC Press Release 2001–49, http://www.sec.gov/news/press/2001–49.txt. "Order Instituting Public Administrative Proceedings, Pursuant to Section 8A of the Securities Act of 1933 and Section 21C of the Securities Exchange Act of 1934, Making Findings and Imposing A Cease-and—Desist Order" (AAER No. 1393), May 15, 2001.

18　Xerox 2000 Annual Report to Shareholders; see also "Xerox Denies Fraudulent Accounting," *Associated Press*, May 31, 2001, home-news.excite.com.

19　Xerox 2000 Annual Report to Shareholders, Restructuring Charges. See also, "Concession by Xerox May not Satisfy the SEC," *Wall Street Journal*, June 1, 2001.

20　"Anixter International Comments on Inventory Returns to Lucent Technologies," PR Newswire, Jan. 26, 2001. "Behind Lucent's Woes: All-Out Revenue Goal and Pressure to Meet It," *Wall Street Journal*, March 29, 2001.

21　Arshad Mohammed, "Alcatel Agrees to Buy Lucent," *Washington Post*, Apr. 3, 2006, http://www.washingtonpost.com/wp-dyn/content/article/2006/04/02/AR2006040200867.html.

22　See Harris Collingwood, "The Earnings Game: Everyone Plays, Nobody Wins," *Harvard Business Review* 79, no. 6 (June 2001).

23　See Karl Schoenberger, "When the Numbers Just Don't Add Up: Regulators Check the New Economy's Books," *New York Times*, Aug. 19, 2001. Schoenberger specifically references Wall Street's expectations for growth as driving improper earnings management practices.

24　Insider trading prohibited by Sections 16(b) and 10(b) of the Securities and Exchange Act of 1934.

25　Enron's executives, authorized by the Board of Directors, violated the conflict of interest provisions of Enron code of conduct in establishing the special purpose entities, which were managed by CFO Andrew Fastow. See "Justice Department Expands Charges Against Former Enron CFO Andrew Fastow, Broadband Executives," Department of Justice, last modified May 1, 2003, http://www.usdoj.gov/opa/pr/2003/May/03_crm_268.htm.

26　The risk of bankruptcy can be predicted by the "Z score," a statistic developed by Edward Altman. See "Summary of Altman's Z-Score, Abstract," *ValueBasedManagement. net*, last modified Apr. 11, 2014, http://www.valuebasedmanagement.net/methods_altman_z-score.html.

27 See "Guilty Verdicts Reached at Enron Trial," *NPR*, last modified 2014, http://www.npr.org/series/5181660/guilty-verdicts-reached-at-enron-trial. Kenneth Lay's conviction was over-turned by courts because he died before he could appeal the jury conviction. See also Kurt Eichenwald, *A Conspiracy of Fools: A True Story* (New York: Broadway Books, 2005).

28 544 U.S. 696 (2005).

29 The SEC prosecuted Arthur Andersen for its audits of Waste Management, and Sunbeam Corporation. Arthur Andersen was censured by the SEC and paid a fine in settlement of the charges. Arthur Andersen also served as the auditor of Global Crossings, which declared bankruptcy in January 2002, as well as WorldCom, which declared bankruptcy in July 2002, after restating earnings in May. See 544 U.S. 696, at footnote 2. See also "Order Instituting Public Administrative Proceedings, Making Findings and Imposing Remedial Sanctions Pursuant to Rule 102 (e) of the Commission's Rules of Practice," United States of America Before the Securities and Exchange Commission, June 19, 2001, http://www.sec.gov/litigation/admin/34–44444.htm.

30 *Public Company Accounting Oversight Board*, last modified 2014, http://www.pcaobus.org/.

31 Jeanne Cummings, Yochi Dreazen, and Michael Schroeder, "SEC Chairman Pitt Resigns Amid Webster Controversy: The Embattled Chief's Missteps Left Him With Few Allies; Fury Inside White House," *Wall Street Journal*, Nov. 6, 2002, http://online.wsj.com/news/articles/SB1036548136249093108.

32 See "The Wall Street Fix," *PBS Frontline*, last modified 2014, http://www.pbs.org/wgbh/pages/frontline/shows/wallstreet/.

33 See Patrick McGeehan, "Henry Blodget to Leave Merrill Lynch," *New York Times*, Nov. 15, 2001. See also "NOW: Politics," *PBS*, last modified 2002, http://www.pbs.org/now/politics/wallstreet.html.

34 "Litigation Release No. 18111 / April 28, 2003: Securities and Exchange Commission v. Citigroup Global Markets Inc., f/k/a Salomon Smith Barney Inc., 03 CV 2945 (WHP) (S.D.N.Y.); Securities and Exchange Commission v. Jack Benjamin Grubman, 03 CV 2938 (WHP)(S.D.N.Y.)," *U.S. Securities and Exchange Commission*, last modified April 28, 2003, http://www.sec.gov/litigation/litreleases/lr18111.htm.

35 "Litigation Release No. 18438 / October 31, 2003: Federal Court Approves Global Research Analyst Settlement," U.S. Securities and Exchange Commission, last modified Oct. 31, 2013, http://www.sec.gov/litigation/litreleases/lr18438.htm.

36 "SEC Fact Sheet on Global Analyst Research Settlements," U.S. Securities and Exchange Commission, last modified Apr. 28, 2003, http://www.sec.gov/news/speech/factsheet.htm.

37 "Goldman Sachs to Pay Record $550 Million to Settle SEC Charges Related to Subprime Mortgage CDO: Firm Acknowledges CDO Marketing Materials Were Incomplete and Should Have Revealed Paulson's Role," SEC press release 2010–123, July 15, 2010.

38 Ari Weinberg, "The NYSE Follows Its Own Rules," *Forbes*, March 24, 2003, http://www.forbes.com/2003/03/24/cx_aw_0324nyse.html.

39 Kara Scannell and Matthew Rose, "Martha Stewart Is Found Guilty of All Charges," *Wall Street Journal*, March 7, 2004.

40 "Martha Stewart and Peter Bacanovic Settle SEC's Insider Trading Charges," Aug. 7, 2006 press release, *U.S. Securities and Exchange Commission*, last modified Aug. 7, 2006, http://www.sec.gov/news/press/2006/2006–134.htm.

41 "Timeline: The Rise and Fall of Samuel Waksal," *FOXNews*, last modified June 10, 2003, http://www.foxnews.com/story/2003/06/10/timeline-rise-and-fall-samuel-waksal/.

42 "FDA Approves First Head & Neck Cancer Treatment in 45 Years; Data Shows Treatment with Erbitux Extends Survival," U.S. Food and Drug Administration, March 1, 2006, http://www.fda.gov/NewsEvents/Newsroom/PressAnnouncements/2006/ucm108609.htm.

43 "SEC Charges Adelphia and Rigas Family With Massive Financial Fraud," U.S. Securities and Exchange Commission, July 24, 2002, http://www.sec.gov/news/press/2002-110.htm. See also Roger Lowenstein, "The Company They Kept," *New York Times Magazine*, Feb. 1, 2004, http://www.nytimes.com/2004/02/01/magazine/the-company-they-kept.html.

44 "Section 404: Management Assessment of Internal Controls.

Requires each annual report of an issuer to contain an 'internal control report,' which shall:

(1) state the responsibility of management for establishing and maintaining an adequate internal control structure and procedures for financial reporting; and

(2) contain an assessment, as of the end of the issuer's fiscal year, of the effectiveness of the internal control structure and procedures of the issuer for financial reporting.

Each issuer's auditor shall attest to, and report on, the assessment made by the management of the issuer. An attestation made under this section shall be in accordance with standards for attestation engagements issued or adopted by the Board. An attestation engagement shall not be the subject of a separate engagement.

The language in the report of the Committee which accompanies the bill to explain the legislative intent states, '—the Committee does not intend that the auditor's evaluation be the subject of a separate engagement or the basis for increased charges or fees.'

Directs the SEC to require each issuer to disclose whether it has adopted a code of ethics for its senior financial officers and the contents of that code.

Directs the SEC to revise its regulations concerning prompt disclosure on Form 8-K to require immediate disclosure 'of any change in, or waiver of,' an issuer's code of ethics."

Summary of SOX by AICPA, http://www.aicpa.org/info/sarbanes_oxley_summary.htm.

45 See Roger Lowenstein, *When Genius Failed* (New York: Random House, 2000).

46 "In a modern market economy it is essential that firms and households are able to select an appropriate level of risk in their transactions. This takes place on financial markets which redistribute risks towards those agents who are willing and able to assume them. Markets for options and other so-called derivatives are important in the sense that agents who anticipate future revenues or payments can ensure a profit above a certain level or insure themselves against a loss above a certain level. (Due to their design, options allow for hedging against one-sided risk—options give the right, but not the obligation, to buy or sell a certain security in the future at a pre-specified price.) A prerequisite for efficient management of risk, however, is that such instruments are correctly valued, or priced. A new method to determine the value of derivatives stands out among the foremost contributions to economic sciences over the last 25 years." "The Prize in Economic Sciences 1997—Press Release," *Nobelprize.org*, last modified 2014.

http://www.nobelprize.org/nobel_prizes/economic-sciences/laureates/1997/press.html.

47 "Hedge Funds, Leverage, and the Lessons of Long-Term Capital Management," Report of the President's Working Group on Financial Markets, April 15, 1999 Report-3097.

The Honorable J. Dennis Hastert

The Speaker

United States House of Representatives Washington, D C. 20515

Dear Mr. Speaker:

We are pleased to transmit the report of the President's Working Group on Financial Markets on Hedge Funds, Leverage, and the Lessons of Long-Term Capital Management (LTCM).

The principal policy issue arising out of the events surrounding the near collapse of LTCM is how to constrain excessive leverage. By increasing the chance that problems at one financial institution could be transmitted to other institutions, excessive leverage can increase the likelihood of a general breakdown in the functioning of financial markets. This issue is not limited to hedge funds; other financial institutions are often larger and more highly leveraged than most hedge funds.

In view of our findings, the Working Group recommends a number of measures designed to constrain excessive leverage. These measures are designed to improve transparency in the system, enhance private sector risk management practices, develop more risk-sensitive approaches to capital adequacy, support financial contract netting in the event of bankruptcy, and encourage offshore financial centers to comply with international standards.

The LTCM incident highlights a number of tax issues with respect to hedge funds, including the tax treatment of total return equity swaps and the use of offshore financial centers. These issues, however, are beyond the scope of this report and are being addressed separately by Treasury.

A number of other federal agencies were full participants in this study and support its conclusions and recommendations: the Council of Economic Advisers, the Federal Deposit Insurance Corporation, the National Economic Council, the Federal Reserve Bank of New York, the Office of the Comptroller of the Currency, and the Office of Thrift Supervision. We are grateful for their extensive assistance.

We appreciate the opportunity to convey this report to you. and we look forward to continuing to work with you on these important issues.


Sincerely,

|  |  |
|---|---|
| (signed) | (signed) |
| Robert E. Rubin | Alan Greenspan |
| Secretary | Chairman |
| Department of Treasury | Board of Governors of the Federal Reserve |
| | |
| (signed) | (signed) |
| Arthur Levitt | Brooksley Born |
| Chairman | Chairperson |
| Securities and Exchange Commission | Commodity F |

Source: http://www.treasury.gov/press/releases/report3097.htm.

48   Joseph Nocera, "The Quantitative, Data-Based, Risk-Massaging Road to Riches," *New York Times Magazine*, June 5, 2005.

49   "Hedge Funds and Dodd-Frank Reform," *Managed Funds Association*, last modified 2014, http://www.managedfunds.org/issues-policy/issues/hedge-funds-and-dodd-frank-reform/.

50   "Inside Wall Street's Culture of Risk: Investment Banks Are Placing Bigger Bets Than Ever and Beating the Odds—at Least for Now," *Bloomberg Businessweek Magazine*, June 11, 2006, http://www.businessweek.com/magazine/content/06_24/b3988004.htm.

51   "Net Capital Requirements for Brokers or Dealers: SEA Rule 15c3-1," *Financial Industry Regulatory Advisory*, last modified 2014, http://www.finra.org/web/groups/industry/@ip/@reg/@rules/documents/interpretationsfor/p037763.pdf.

52   See Elven Riley, "Origins of the Great Recession," Presentation to Financial Economics and Accounting Conference, Sept. 18, 2009. See also Elven Riley, "The Place from Whence We Came: Micro Origins of the Financial Crisis, the Investment Professional," *Journal of the New York Society of Security Analysts* (2009).

53   William D. Conan, *House of Cards: A Tale of Hubris and Wretched Excess on Wall Street* (New York: Random House: 2009).

54   "Statement by Anton R. Valukas, Examiner, Lehman Brothers Bankruptcy before the Committee on Financial Services United States House of Representative Regarding 'Public Policy Issues Raised by the Report of the Lehman Bankruptcy Examiner,'" The Committee on Financial Services, April 20, 2010, http://archives.financialservices.house.gov/media/file/hearings/111/valuks_4.20.10.pdf.

55   James Kwak, "The Profitable Bailout? Inside the Real Costs of the Saving AIG and Wall Street," *The Atlantic*, Sept. 12, 2012, http://www.theatlantic.com/business/archive/2012/09/the-profitable-bailout-inside-the-real-costs-of-the-saving-aig-and-wall-st/262281/.

56   Kevin Drum, "Prop Trading and the Volcker Rule," *Mother Jones*, April 30, 2010, http://www.motherjones.com/kevin-drum/2010/04/prop-trading-and-volcker-rule. See also Neil Irwin, "Everything You Need to Know About the Volcker Rule" *Washington Post*, Dec., 10, 2013, http://www.washingtonpost.com/blogs/wonkblog/wp/2013/12/10/everything-you-need-to-know-about-the-volcker-rule/.

57   Floyd Norris, "Bank Rules That Serve Two Masters," *New York Times*, Oct. 13, 2011.

58   "Living Wills Overview," *Federal Deposit and Insurance Corporation*, Jan. 25. 2012, http://www.fdic.gov/about/srac/2012/2012-01-25_living-wills.pdf.

## End of Chapter Case: Origins of the Financial Crisis of 2008

by Elven Riley

THE JOURNAL OF The New York Society of Security Analysts

# THE INVESTMENT PROFESSIONAL.

## The Place from Whence We Came

Micro Origins of the Financial Crisis
by Elven Riley

The current global financial crisis and the US government's response to it—bailouts of too- big-to-fail banks, tax-financed props for an ailing auto industry, mortgage-rescue plans for overextended households—have upset the public's sense of fair play. Citizens have also had to struggle with their attempts to link the fragile, ethereal, economic construct revealed by recent events to the concrete realities of food on their tables and roofs over their heads. And they don't want to have to study the intricacies of monetary policy, public debt management, and international capital flows to maintain their faith in capitalism.

Unfortunately, everywhere they look, they find cause for concern. During the first quarter of 2009, investors had more money in money market fund accounts than in equity market fund accounts, the leading US investment banks and several international banks had vanished, and $50 trillion worldwide—a year's global economic output—was devalued to $0. People can't help but ask how this happened. And some of the answers are fairly simple—who's to blame (O'Hara 2009; Schmudde 2009; Star 2009), solutions we might try (Persand 2008; Sachs 2009; Schmudde 2009; Star 2009), or what caused the crisis at a macro level (Nanto 2009).

A thorough investigation of the actual dynamics of the securities industry is not one of those simple answers, but it's an essential component of any meaningful response. Nevertheless, partly out of exhaustion and partly out of fear, little has been written, at a detailed micro level, about the way legislation such as the Glass–Steagall Act forged, more than 70 years ago, fundamental aspects of our markets; about the basic credit products and the markets that have supported their growth; about the evolution of financial products over the past 30 years; about the combined devolution of regulation over the past eight presidential terms; or about the lead-ups to the individual corporate failures at the cusp of the "Great Recession."

The broad historical attributes of the securities industry—the industry's formational event, differences in transaction types, or participant responsibilities, for example—are cornerstones of the crisis. So is the evolution of the CMO (collateralized mortgage obligation) and of the CDS (credit default swap). And so is the massive expansion of leverage and the implosion that followed.

## The STO

"STO" (security trading organization) can be used in place of "investment bank" or the more common term "brokerage firm" to identify corporations licensed for and focused on making a profit with investment products (Simmons 2002). An STO has two roles for transacting trades in markets: it trades for clients with their money as an "agent," and it trades for itself with its own money as a "principal." Keeping the capital sources segregated has been a hallmark of the industry; keeping the risk separate has not.

Agent trades earn modest fees and are riskless to the STO, with the exception of operational risk. Principal trades put the firm's capital at risk, incur fees, and may realize either a profit or a loss when converted back into capital. Traditional commercial banks prefer and historically have been restricted to the predictability of the agency business. Agency fees are the same as any other bank transaction fees: small profits and small risks. They can be explained and correlated to conventional metrics, such as volume of transactions or transactions per customer, in the annual earnings report, with a simple graph.

That's not the case with business transacted as principal, which represents investments made with the firm's capital and which is actively hidden from competitors. STOs prefer principal business, for which the potential profit is dramatically higher. However, the outcomes of principal transactions are difficult to predict, uncorrelated to metrics, and entail a large risk of losing the firm's capital. All transaction types are either agent or principal, and all STOs are classified by degrees of intensity and the extent of the blend of agent and principal business activity.

STOs trade two categories of products: regulated (for which government rule-making bodies permit market participants specific practices) and unregulated. STOs will insist those product categories should really be money, debt, and equity, as on all retail account statements. But the division of money, debt, and equity is not as useful as the dichotomy of regulated and unregulated products when it comes to breaking down marketplace dynamics. Indeed, it is rare for STOs to identify which of their products are subjected to regulation except in the fine print of the opening contract of a new client's account. Across STOs, product names are distinguished by subtle differences that only add confusion to an already complex discussion.

Congressional records and SEC committee reports spanning the past eight presidential terms, or 32 years, show Glass–Steagall being effectively revoked in order to enhance market efficiencies through increased competition and to mitigate government regulatory burdens on the free market system. It was never updated for today's world. It was simply eliminated, and an alternative was not sought by any administration or offered by any Congress.

One misconception, for example, is that a money market fund contains cash. Actually, a money market fund's valuation of $1,000 is the STO's estimation of the real cash the owner may receive when the owner requests liquidation of the shares in the money market fund. When an account owner of a bank checking account sees a statement with $1,000, the owner knows there is really $1,000 of cash in the account that can be used in exchange for goods and services. The checking bank account reports the amount of legal tender held for the depositor while the money market fund account reports the estimated liquidation value if converted to legal tender.

## Regulated and Unregulated Products

Those two different types of accounts—checking and money market fund—are offered by two different types of licensed banks. Those two types of banks were created, 76 years ago, by a grouping of regulations commonly referred to as Glass–Steagall. Glass–Steagall was born when the Great Depression allowed then-President Franklin Roosevelt to segregate savings banks, which transacted loans and took deposits, from STOs, which bought and sold securities, in order to separate the risk of loss of "savings" capital from the risk of loss of "investment" capital. In 1933, the FDIC (Federal Deposit Insurance Corporation) emerged as a vehicle allowing the government to insure savings depositors without insuring the greater risk associated with investment depositors. This, in turn, boosted people's confidence that a savings bank's investment activity could not result in the loss of the savings capital deposited with the bank.

Congressional records and SEC (Securities and Exchange Commission) committee reports spanning the past eight presidential terms, or 32 years, show Glass–Steagall being effectively revoked in order to enhance market efficiencies through increased competition and to mitigate government regulatory burdens on the free market system. It was never updated for today's world. It was simply eliminated, and an alternative was not sought by any administration or offered by any Congress.

What kind of update would have been required? What new demands were these regulations facing? To answer this, it's important to understand first that, on a basic level, regulated investment products represent an ownership interest (equity shares, for example) in a corporation. Their valuation is related to the corporation's solvency as defined by laws, accounting standards, and governmental rules. The valuation of the regulated product is defined by the underlying components of the corporation issuing the shares.

Unregulated investment products, on the other hand, represent speculation on events expected to occur. They are written legal "contracts" and may be unsecured, or secured by assets representing a debt interest (that is, by bonds and loans). All unregulated investment products trade in the OTC (over the counter) markets, which means that they trade informally: over the phone or through systems of convenience. The valuation of an unregulated product is defined by the historical experience of similar products and the probability of realizing an expected return.

Although conventional GAAP (Generally Accepted Accounting Principles) accounting equates savings and investing, they're unequal in this context. Savings are fixed-interest payments over a defined period with only counterparty risk and little or no risk of loss of principal. Investments are speculative agreements contractually linking payments with the acceptance of counterparty risks and principal risks for a defined period. Cash in a tin can, in comparison, is a neutral reference point, neither a savings product nor an investment product, exposed only to a serious operational loss like theft or fire.

Clear, detailed regulations pertain to what lies to the left of the tin can. For example, some basic regulations are specific to the securities industry and apply generally to all activity. One such basic regulatory grouping includes the KYC (know your customer) regulations. Originally created to address STOs' responsibilities in accepting drug money from terrorists and sanitizing its entry into the monetary system, KYC regulations were expanded by best practices guidelines to include the concept of professional behavior. They make the seller liable for client losses resulting from selling high-risk products to very clearly risk-averse and trusting clients, such as retirees and orphans. As part of the licensing process, the seller's expertise is made responsible for discerning and maintaining an internal level of best practices for appropriately matching the product-risk and client-risk profiles. Sellers are not allowed to invoke "buyer beware" if the buyer is obviously incapable of recognizing the exposure to capital loss.

But these low-risk savings products were not the catalyst of the current financial crisis. For that, look to the tin can's extreme right: the CDS zone, where almost no regulation intrudes. Even financial professionals have difficulty understanding CDS products. How are these derivatives created? What are their markets?

### The CMO And CDO

The financial debt vehicle called the CMO was first created in June 1983 by Salomon Brothers (as well as, independently, by First Boston for use by the Federal Home Loan Mortgage Corporation, aka Freddie Mac). In the early 1980s, disintermediation and collateralization were innovations. Disintermediation was used to gain access to new capital and collateralization was used to move assets into products. The result was capital exchanged for new high-yield collateralized products. Freddie Mac owned a huge inventory of home loans and needed additional capital to issue more loans to pursue its Congressionally mandated mission of providing liquidity, stability, and affordability to the housing market. The concept was to move assets off Freddie Mac's balance sheet and move working capital onto it. The CMO allowed for the creation of securitized high-yield products by repackaging mortgage pools.

A CMO is a contract between a special-purpose entity (created and incorporated as the owner of the mortgage payments) and the CMO buyer to share a defined portion of the mortgage payment stream. An STO sells investors a CMO contract, sometimes whole, sometimes in parts, as a high-yield investment product. In reality, though, the contract is an investment in the special-purpose entity. The CMO is like shares in a company established to process mortgages and distribute the mortgage payments to the shareholders. The original cash the investors provide for these shares is given to the STO, creating the special-purpose entity as payment for the mortgages and services, always at a mark-up (spread) from the cost of acquiring the assets, or mortgages.

Unique marketing terms still make differentiation between regulated and unregulated products needlessly inconsistent and opaque. Disclosure regarding the relationships between regulations and products are still minimal. And, as of September 2008, we now have financial superstores active in all aspects of transactions, as agent or principal, in an echo of the days before Glass–Steagall.

In the early days of the CMO market, the spreads for the CMO creator were outstanding. It was such a profitable process that it was applied to other types of assets that fit the pattern, including credit cards, student loans, and car loans. The industry products grew and became asset-backed securities. All together, they became collectively known as CDOs (collateralized debt obligations) and constituted a huge unregulated market of structured credit products, some associated with hard assets and some not. Once such a structured credit product was created, it was traded OTC between STOs: in agency transactions, on behalf of the STOs' clients, using the clients' capital; or in principal transactions, using the STOs' own capital.

## The CDS

Some STOs retained parts of the original assets or underlying products during the CDO creation process, first as a way to earn greater profits by holding onto higher-quality segments, and later as a way to contain quality problems that would prevent sales. In the latter instance, a retained segment was kept on the STO's books as a principal transaction. Eventually, as its quality continued to decrease, it became known as "toxic waste." One approach to improving and possibly selling these lower-quality CDOs was to contract for a CDS: that is, for a guarantee in the event the CDO failed. These insurance-like contracts—credit derivative contracts between two counterparties—were written to protect capital invested from risk of loss and were often developed by other participants (AIG being a noteworthy example).

The ability to improve the risk rating of low-quality CDO contracts with the addition of insurance-like CDS products meant that the contracts could be sold to even those investors affected by federal regulations constraining their capital's exposure to risk—an investor such as a pension fund. The ability to sell the toxic waste with an attached insurance policy allowed for increased sources of capital to enter the market. In exchange for the capital, STOs were able to remove sizable quantities of the toxic waste from their books. This had an incentivizing effect on everyone. As new working capital poured in, more products with effectively greater leverage were created on an increasingly grand scale, for an ever-swelling crowd.

Productized risk is a product, just like a lottery ticket, and for 30 years the CDS market and CDO industry have been complicated, opaque, unregulated, broad markets. The buyer makes periodic payments to the seller, and in return receives a payoff if an underlying financial instrument defaults. CDS contracts have been compared to insurance because the buyer pays a premium and in return receives a sum of money if a specified event occurs. For example, Goldman Sachs may sell Citibank a CDS for $100,000 per year that pays $10 million if Lehman defaults on its obligations. Citibank would find this CDS very useful if Citibank also owned $10 million of the Lehman CDO and the existence of the CDS allowed for a lower risk rating on the Citibank position.

The ISDA (International Swaps and Derivatives Association), an industry trade group, announced on October 31, 2008, that $25 trillion in notional value had been eliminated from the CDS market since the beginning of 2008, reducing the total to $47 trillion. It wasn't until November 2008 that the DTCC (Depository Trust and Clearing Corporation), the private electronic vault of record, first began reporting metrics on CDS transactions (DTCC 2008).

In the first weekly report there were a total of $33.6 trillion in CDSs outstanding on corporate, government, and asset-backed securities. The concept of a trillion of anything is difficult to comprehend. For comparison, in June 2009 the US national debt was estimated at $11.3 trillion, the US housing market at about $18 trillion, and the market value of all US listed equities at $18 trillion.

This derivatives market segment is huge and was, until November 2008, completely hidden. And there's another interesting wrinkle—the fact that CDSs no longer entail any requirement that either party have any exposure to the counterparty at risk. That's why, for example, Goldman Sachs could have bought a CDS from AIG that would have paid out if Lehman were to have failed, without Goldman owning any Lehman product exposure. The CDS would have been a leveraged bet between Goldman Sachs and AIG on the likelihood that Lehman would remain creditworthy and solvent.

## Market Dynamics

In 2000, the Commodity Futures Modernization Act largely exempted OTC from regulation by the Commodity Futures Trading Commission and seriously limited SEC authority. The bulk of these CDS contracts are directly transacted between two companies OTC, with no structured defined exchange or regulated marketplace. The aggregate market for all these products is the equivalent of a mind exercise. It exists in the same sense that there is a global used car market. There is, however, now the bare beginning of a central view of the size and only a hint at the ownership of the marketplace, with the DTCC providing a limited two- week view to the public, although the only information available is what each participant is willing to share. Still, on June 17, 2009, the US Department of the Treasury issued an encouraging report, "Financial Regulatory Reform": "Investors and credit rating agencies should have access to the information necessary to assess the credit quality of the assets underlying a securitization transaction at inception and over the life of the transaction, as well as the information necessary to assess the credit, market, liquidity, and other risks of [asset- backed securities]."

Operational support for the CDS market has snarled, turning into the same kind of traffic jam that necessitated restructuring the listed equities markets. Regulators therefore continue to push for a central clearinghouse that would, for a small uniform fee, stand between counterparties, provide guarantees in the event of a counterparty's default on a contract, and establish standard contracts.

While a CDS does not send a corporate stock price up or down, the movement in the stock price, and certainly any change in the corporate debt rating, will directly affect a CDS's valuation. Lehman is, of course, the defining example. At the time of its bankruptcy filing, it was involved heavily and globally in every possible CDS combination. The DTCC took weeks to unwind all Lehman's positions, even in the face of the bankruptcy court's directive to liquidate with haste. This one insolvency prompted a mass stampede to safety and a dramatic reduction in liquidity, precipitating a downward spiral in valuations as products were reduced for sale again and again, spreading insolvency through contamination.

The issues are now twofold: how to unwind the transactions, and where to begin. The ISDA insists that the total notional amount of the CDS market, about \$45 trillion, is not the amount that is in fact at risk (2008), and most people agree. Many contracts between the same counterparties can be "netted" to a smaller net amount. But because of the lack of standard documentation, the lack of a central depository or clearinghouse, and the lack of any regulatory reporting requirements (as the Treasury Department points out in the white paper quoted above) it might take a very long time for the ISDA to actually back up that claim.

Meanwhile, the insolvency has spread globally. This complicates our response to the crisis because it makes it necessary for us to identify the beneficiary of any relief effort. If a loan from the Troubled Asset Relief Program is aimed at a CDS asset, it's not necessarily any more likely to benefit the US economy than to aid participants elsewhere on the globe. At the time the US Treasury was asked to help Lehman Brothers, Lehman derived less profit from the US than from its activity in the European and Asian–Pacific zones. A rescue of Lehman, then, would have been a rescue of many international counterparties as well. The political optics of the use of US taxpayer funds to pay non-US counterparties would undoubtedly have been negative. Recently, AIG disclosed foreign banks as the largest receivers of the AIG bailout monies.

## Can't Drive 55?

Individual STOs are still not motivated to consider the market's collapse in any terms other than the immediate loss of their own principal. They continue to view their clients' principal risks as riskless agency trades. Unique marketing terms still make differentiation between regulated and unregulated products needlessly inconsistent and opaque. Disclosure regarding the relationships between regulations and products are still minimal. And, as of September 2008, we now have financial superstores active in all aspects of transactions, as agent or principal, in an echo of the days before Glass–Steagall.

For decades, various administrations and Congresses have actively dismantled industry regulations. The regulations that remain are national, while the

OTC market for derivative products is multinational and disdains the standardized reporting a central clearinghouse provides. Each one of these structural deficiencies works to the advantage of the STO and the disadvantage of the individual investor.

An increased individual savings rate must be coupled with increased transparency of the differences between savings and investing. Glass–Steagall is gone, and the separation of banking from investment is gone with it. That separation was not perfect, and it was at odds with the rest of the developed banking world. But new regulation is required to provide greater transparency for an aggregate market view. Adam Smith believed government involvement in the market economy was justified. In his *Inquiry into the Nature and Causes of the Wealth of Nations* (1776), he encouraged a pragmatic, conservative bifurcation of capitalism and government, like travelers in opposite directions who share a roadway. The point is not to usurp the steering wheels of other drivers, but to enforce speed limits and build guardrails.

## References

DTCC. October 31, 2008. "DTCC to Provide CDS Data from Trade Information Warehouse."

ISDA. October 31, 2008. "ISDA Applauds $25 Trn Reductions in CDS Notionals, Industry Efforts to Improve CDS Operations."

Nanto, Dick. April 3, 2009. "The Global Financial Crisis: Analysis and Policy Implications." Congressional Research Service. 1–105.

O'Hara, Neil A. Spring 2009. "Don't Shoot the Messenger: The Unfair Attack on Fair Value Accounting." Investment Professional, vol. 2, no. 2. 47–53.

Persand, Avinash. 2009. "Ratings War?" *Public Policy Research*, vol. 15, no. 4. 187–191.

Sachs, Jeffrey. 2009. "The Geithner–Summers Plan Is Even Worse Than We Thought." Huffington Post.

Schmudde, David. 2009. "Responding to the Subprime Mess: The New Regulatory Landscape." *Fordham Journal of Corporate and Finance Law*, vol. 14, no. 4. 708–770.

Simmons, Michael. 2002. *Securities Operations: A Guide to Trade and Position Management*. New York, NY. John Wiley & Sons. 9–31.

Star, Marlene Givant. Spring 2009. "Hive Mind: Organizational Psychology and the Origins of the Financial Crisis." Investment Professional, vol. 2, no. 2.

US Department of the Treasury. June 17, 2009. "Financial Regulatory Reform: A New Foundation, Rebuilding Financial Supervision and Regulation." 45. [PDF available via http://www.bespacific.com/mt/archives/021616.html.]

*Elven Riley, who has over 30 years of Wall Street experience, is the director of the Center for Securities Trading and Analysis at Seton Hall University. He wishes to thank Paula Alexander, Kurt Rotthoff, Eleanor Xu, Glenna Riley, Michael Majewski, Reverend Deacon Diane Riley, and Tony Loviscek.*

## Case Discussion Questions

1. The risks of credit derivative obligations (CDOs) traded by hedge funds were recognized by financial regulators, articulated for example, in Bernanke's remarks to the Federal Reserve in 2006. What were the failures in risk management?

2. Is it "too big to fail" or "too interconnected" to fail?

3. The problems described by Elven Riley resonate in the problem of the tragedy of the commons. "Individual STOs [security trading organizations] are still not motivated to consider the market's collapse in any terms other than the immediate loss of their own principal." What can be done to get individual STOs to act in terms of the system effects of their actions?

# 14 Corporate Governance, Social Responsibility and Organizational Effectiveness
## The Bottom Line

### Chapter Outline

Ethical Business Practice, Corporate Social Responsibility
  and Firm Financial Performance
    Unethical Management Practices May Be a Dysfunctional Way
      of Managing Organizational Duress
Executive Compensation Systems Differentiate Ethically Managed from
  Ethically Challenged Firms
How Can Ethical Management for the Long Term Be Incentivized?
End of Chapter Case: Emmanuel Levinas' Ethics of Responsibility

### Chapter Introduction

Are corporate governance best practices and corporate social responsibility related to a better bottom line than corporate conflicts of interest, poor corporate governance structures and unethical or socially irresponsible business practice?

### Chapter Goal and Learning Objectives

*Chapter Goal:* Describe the relationship between corporate governance, social responsibility and firm financial performance.

*Learning Objectives:*

1. Identify risk factors for unethical management and factors associated with affirmative ethical management.
2. Discuss how unethical management practices may be a dysfunctional way of managing organizational duress.
3. Develop strategies to rehabilitate firms that have engaged in unethical or socially irresponsible management practices.
4. Debate the relationship between ethical business practice, corporate social responsibility and firm financial performance.
5. Develop executive compensation systems that reward executives for effective and ethical management in the long term.

## Ethical Business Practice, Corporate Social Responsibility and Firm Financial Performance

Are ethically managed firms better performers than "ethically challenged" firms?[1] This author tested this question by conducting research that compared the financial performance of "ethically managed" firms to "ethically challenged" firms.[2] The ethically managed group was constructed from *Business Ethics* magazine's top ethically managed firms that made *Business Ethics'* list for the entire period of five years, 2000–2004 (see Table 14.1). The "ethically challenged" group consisted of firms that were prosecuted by the SEC, the New

*Table 14.1* Ethically Managed Companies, Business Ethics magazine

| | |
|---|---|
| FNM | Fannie Mae |
| PG | Procter and Gamble |
| INTC | Intel |
| SPC | St. Paul Companies |
| DE | Deere and Company |
| AVP | Avon Products |
| HPQ | Hewlett Packard |
| ECL | Ecolab Inc. |
| IBM | IBM |
| MLHR | Herman Miller |
| TBL | Timberland Co |
| CSCO | Cisco systems |
| LUV | Southwest Airlines |
| MOT | Motorola |
| CMI | Cummins Inc. |
| RKY | Adolph Coors |
| MOD | Modine Manufacturing |
| CLX | Clorox |
| T | AT&T |
| PBI | Pitney Bowes |
| SBUX | Starbucks Coffee |
| MRK | Merck & Co. |
| GGG | GracoGrady Corporation |
| MDT | Medtronic |
| NYT | New York Times |
| GDW | Golden West Financial |
| SON | Sonoco Products |
| WHR | Whirlpool |

York Attorney General, or the US Department of Justice and that were convicted or that settled during the same time period. There were approximately 30 firms in each group (see Table 14.2). Each firm was publicly traded.

*Table 14.2* Ethically Challenged Companies

| | |
|---|---|
| ENE | Enron |
| HLSH.PK | Healthsouth |
| C | Citigroup |
| | Salomon Smith Barney |
| TYC | Tyco |
| MER | Merrill Lynch |
| MO | Philip Morris / Altria |
| WCOM later MCIP | WorldCom bought by MCI |
| ADLAC | Adelphia Communications |
| RAI then RJR | R J Reynolds |
| XRX | Xerox |
| LU | Lucent Technologies |
| BMY | Bristol Myers Squibb |
| GS | Goldman Sachs |
| JPT | JP Morgan Chase |
| | JPM Securities |
| MWD | Morgan Stanley |
| Q | Qwest Communications |
| SGP | Schering Plough |
| CD | Cendant Corporation |
| COL later HCA | Columbia HCA |
| LH | Lehman Brothers |
| USB | US Bancorp Piper Jaffray later US Bancorp |
| MMC | Marsh & McLennan |
| | Putnam Mutual Fund |
| AC | Alliance Capital Management |
| PRU | Prudential |
| | Prudential Securities |
| AIG | AIG |
| JNS | Janus Capital Group |
| FBF | FleetBoston Financial Corp (merged with Bank of America) |
| BOA | Bank of America |

(*Continued*)

*Table 14.2* (*Continued*)

| | |
|---|---|
| ONE | Banc One |
| BSC | Bear Stearns |
| | Credit Suisse First Boston |
| UBS | UBS Warburg |
| VGR | Liggett Group |
| BAT | British American Tobacco |
| CG | Carolina Group |
| WMI | Waste Management |
| GLBC | Global Crossings |
| RFXCQ.PK | REFCO |
| UCL | Unocal |
| CVX | Texaco merged with Chevron |

***Financial Performance Measured.*** The financial performance measures included rate of return, beta, and Edward Altman's Z score. The time period for measurement of financial performance was 1998–2004. Rate of return was defined as stock price plus dividends compared year to year; 1998 was defined as the base year; 1999–2004 were the comparison years. Financial data were obtained from Standard & Poor's Compustat database.

***Results.*** There were no differences in rates of return between ethically challenged and ethically managed firms (see Table 14.3).

However, when rate of return is compared with financial services and cigarette firms eliminated from the ethically challenged comparison groups, ethically managed firms outperform ethically challenged groups (see Table 14.4).

### Unethical Management Practices May Be a Dysfunctional Way of Managing Organizational Duress

***Z Score.*** Z score predicts bankruptcy using a model developed by Edward Altman at New York University. Z score measures are interpreted as follows:

> If a Z score value of less than 1.81 is returned, then there is a high probability of bankruptcy.
> If a Z score value greater than 3.0 is returned, then there is a low probability of bankruptcy.

Ethically challenged firms had Z scores that were significantly different than ethically managed firms. Ethically challenged firms were at high risk of bankruptcy, whereas ethically managed firms, except for ATT, were predicted to be "safe" from bankruptcy (see Figure 14.1).

*Table 14.3* Rates of Return, Comparing Ethically Managed and Ethically Challenged Companies, 1998–2004

|  | Challenged/ Ethically Managed | N | Mean | Std. Deviation | Std. Error Mean |
|---|---|---|---|---|---|
| IRR1999 | C | 32 | .123 | .4812 | .0851 |
|  | E | 26 | .238 | .4737 | .0929 |
| IRR2000 | C | 34 | .259 | .6535 | .1121 |
|  | E | 25 | .109 | .5603 | .1121 |
| IRR2001 | C | 36 | −.059 | .4200 | .0700 |
|  | E | 25 | −.012 | .2686 | .0537 |
| IRR2002 | C | 37 | −.325 | .3260 | .0536 |
|  | E | 25 | −.105 | .2409 | .0482 |
| IRR2003 | C | 37 | .498 | 1.1640 | .1914 |
|  | E | 26 | .343 | .2881 | .0565 |
| IRR2004 | C | 34 | .124 | .2057 | .0353 |
|  | E | 26 | .164 | .2562 | .0503 |

*Table 14.4* T-Test Comparing Rates of Return of Ethically Managed to Ethically Challenged Companies, with Financial Services and Cigarette Companies Removed

| | Group Statistics | | | | |
|---|---|---|---|---|---|
|  | C/E | N | Mean | Std. Deviation | Std Error Mean |
| ONE99 | C | 20 | .097 | .4637 | .1037 |
|  | E | 26 | .221 | .4822 | .0946 |
| TWO00 | C | 20 | −.007 | .3497 | .0782 |
|  | E | 26 | .078 | .3234 | .0634 |
| THREE01 | C | 20 | −.123 | .2853 | .0638 |
|  | E | 26 | .019 | .1470 | .0288 |
| FOUR02 | C | 20 | −.271 | .3235 | .0723 |
|  | E | 26 | −.018 | .1440 | .0282 |
| FIVE03 | C | 20 | −.162 | .2844 | .0636 |
|  | E | 26 | .035 | .1325 | .0260 |
| SIX04 | C | 17 | −.093 | .1880 | .0456 |
|  | E | 26 | .049 | .1338 | .0262 |

Ethically challenged firms had Z scores that were predictive of bankruptcy for all years 1998–2004. Ethically challenged firms had Z scores that predicted bankruptcy for the years 1998–2000, years before the corporate fraud scandals became known. The managers of the ethically challenged firms likely had early

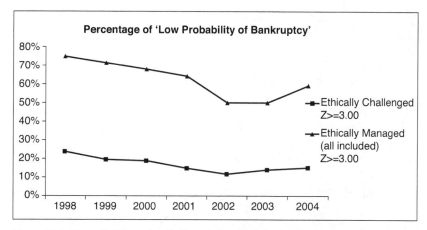

*Figure 14.1* Altman's Z Score Predicting Bankruptcy of Ethically Managed and Ethically Challenged Companies

"inside" knowledge that their firms were under financial duress. Unethical conduct may be a dysfunctional way of coping with a firm's financial duress.

Confirmation of these findings are given by research studies conducted by Governance Metrics International (GMI) and Audit Integrity. GMI and Sung Je Byun investigated the association between corporate governance ratings and financial performance and found that companies rated in the top 10% of GMI's global database achieved a higher return on equity (ROE), return on assets (ROA) and return on capital (ROC) than companies in the bottom 10%.[3] The Byun study was published in 2006. A later study, focusing on stock returns in 2008, confirmed that ethically challenged companies have weaker financial performance.[4] One explanation is that socially responsible and ethical firm behavior serves as "insurance" against firm financial performance.[5] Studies conducted after the financial crisis of 2008 also confirm the positive relationship between socially responsible management and firm financial performance.[6]

## Executive Compensation Systems Differentiate Ethically Managed from Ethically Challenged Firms

This author also investigated the question of whether executive compensation differentiates ethically managed from ethically challenged firms. This study was conducted using the Compustat database reporting executive compensation. The ethically challenged firms in my database, using data of Audit Integrity, pay their CEOs more in the money stock options and higher overall compensation than ethically managed firms.[7] There is also a difference in compensation of other executives, not only the CEO, between ethically challenged and ethically managed firms. My findings are consistent with the findings of Efendi, Srivastava and Swanson, "Why Do Corporate Managers Misstate Financial Statements?"[8]

The role of stock options was so problematic in 2007 that *Business Ethics* accommodated the issue in developing its list of leading corporate citizens:

> Another issue that snared companies on the list this year was the back-dating of stock options. The practice largely occurred in the stock market boom of the late 1990s and early 2000s so executives could gain from a dip in their company's stock price. Aside from the inflated payoff to the option holders, backdating presents problems because a company's annual revenues may appear higher. According to KLD, more than 100 cases of improper backdating are under investigation by the SEC and others.
>
> The options backdating scandal demonstrates how far off perfection is among all corporations. SEC investigations, labor violations and disputes over cleanup of toxic pollutants pepper the records of even the best corporate citizens.[9]

Furthermore, the backdating of stock options required the attention of the New York Society of CPAs in 2007.[10]

## How Can Ethical Management for the Long Term Be Incentivized?

Compensation plans need to be developed that evaluate CEO performance over time and with respect to multiple indicants of performance.

> A multifaceted measurement of the stakeholder engagement is required, including measurement of engagement with and effect on shareholders, bondholders, supply chain, employees, communities where the firm operates, and the environment. For each of the dimensions of stakeholder engagement, a behaviorally anchored rating system (BARS) should be developed. The rating system should include both harms and goods to the particular stakeholder. Executive compensation should be tied to the rating system. A compensation system should be developed that includes reduction of compensation and claw backs for longer term consequences that come to light. For example, a stakeholder lawsuit would be counted negatively, with consequential reduction of executive compensation. Furthermore, prosecution and settlement with the SEC would be indicative of negative long-term relations with some stakeholders, including shareholders, bondholders, and insurers. Goldman Sachs settled its prosecution by the SEC for both selling and short-selling its CDOs. Under this methodology, the executives of Goldman Sachs would return compensation as a consequence of the settlement with the SEC. Instead, the reality was that the CEO of Goldman Sachs, Lloyd Blankfein, received an increase in compensation in 2010, the same year as the settlement with the SEC.[11]

Claw-back provisions provide a giant step in the direction of incentivizing executives for managing over the long term. An earlier implementation of claw-backs occurred after the bankruptcy of Drexel Burnham Lambert. Drexel Burnham Lambert declared bankruptcy after Michael Milken was prosecuted; however, six weeks before the bankruptcy, the board voted end- of-year bonuses.[12] The bonuses voted by the board to themselves were recovered in a claw-back proceeding, alleging fraud.[13] The Dodd-Frank Act requires boards to develop claw-back provisions, although they are not required to implement them.[14]

## Chapter Discussion Questions

1. What are the risk factors for unethical management?
2. Is there evidence of a positive relationship between ethical business practice, corporate social responsibility and firm financial performance?
3. What about the finding that big money banks make so much money that their return on investment (ROI) obfuscate the relationship between ethical business practice and firm financial relationship?
4. How can firms that have engaged in unethical management be rehabilitated?
5. Develop an executive compensation system that rewards executives for effective and ethical management in the long term.

## Notes

1  The question of whether ethically managed firms have better financial performance than ethically challenged firms has been the subject of significant inquiry and research. See P. Cochran and R. Wood, "Corporate Social Responsibility and Financial Performance," *Academy of Management Journal* 27, no. 1 (1984): 42–56; S.A. Waddock, and S.B. Graves, "The Corporate Social Performance—Financial Performance Link," *Strategic Management Journal*, 18 (1997): 303–19; Lee E. Preston and Douglas P. O'Bannon, "The Corporate Social-Financial Performance Relationship," *Business and Society* 36, no. 4 (Dec. 1997): 419–29; Curtis Verschoor, "A Study of the Link Between a Corporation's Financial Performance and Its Commitment to Ethics," *Journal of Business Ethics* 17, no. 13 (October 1998): 1509–16; Samuel B. Graves and Sandra A. Waddock, "A Look at the Financial-Social Performance Nexus When Quality of Management Is Held Constant," *International Journal of Value-Based Management* 12, no. 1 (1999): 87–99; Shawn L. Berman, Andrew C. Wicks, Suresh Kotha, and Thomas M. Jones, "Does Stakeholder Orientation Matter? The Relationship Between Stakeholder Management Models and Firm Financial Performance," *The Academy of Management Journal* 42, no. 5 (Oct. 1999): 488–506; Marc Orlitzky and John D. Benjamin, "Corporate Social Performance and Firm Risk: A Meta-Analytic Review," *Business Society* 40, no. 4 (December 1, 2001): 369–96; Marc Orlitzky, Frank L. Schmidt, and Sara L. Rynes, "Corporate Social and Financial Performance: A Meta-Analysis," *Organization Studies* 24 (March 2003): 403–41; P. Gompers, J. Ishii, and A. Metrick, "Corporate Governance and Equity Prices," *The Quarterly Journal of Economics* 118, no. 1 (2003): 107–56.

2   Paula Becker, "Corporate Governance, Business Ethics and Firm Financial Performance: Can Unethical Conduct Be Predicted?," Labor and Employment Relations Association Meeting, 2007.

3   Sung Je Byun, Governance and Performance Studies, Sept. 2006, available from GovernanceMetrics International, http://www.gmiratings.com/Performance.aspx.

   See also Jay W. Eisenhofer, "Does Corporate Governance Matter to Investment Returns?," 2010, Grant & Eisenhofer, http://www.gelaw.com/wp-content/uploads/2011/05/ART_004A_corp_governance_colorchart.pdf and G. Kevin Spellman and Robert Watson, "Corporate Governance Ratings and Corporate Performance: An Analysis of Governance Metrics International (GMI) ratings of US Firms, 2003 to 2008," Jan. 1, 2009, Social Science Research Network, http://papers.ssrn.com/sol3/papers.cfm?abstract_id=1392313.

4   Audit Integrity Analysis Shows Significant Impact of Corporate Integrity on 2008 Stock Returns: As Markets Grew Bleak for Investors, Lowest Rated Companies Fared the Worst," Business Wire, Feb. 2, 2009, http://www.businesswire.com/news/home/20090202005277/en/Audit-Integrity-Analysis-Shows-Significant-Impact-Corporate#.U58_X7dOXaE.

5   Peloza, John. "Using Corporate Social Responsibility as Insurance for Financial Performance." *California Management Review* 48, no. 2 (2006): 52.

6   M. D. Statman and D. Glushkov, "The Wages of Social Responsibility," *Financial Analysts Journal* 65 (2009): 33–46; M. I. Azim, "Corporate Governance Mechanisms and Their Impact on Company Performance: A Structural Equation Model Analysis," *Australian Journal of Management* 37, no. 3 (2012); Omid Sabbaghi and Min Xu, "ROE and Corporate Social Responsibility: Is There a Return On Ethics?," *Journal of Accounting & Finance* 13, no. 4 (2013): 82–95; Priyanka Aggarwall, "Impact of Corporate Governance on Corporate Financial Performance," *IOSR Journal of Business and Management* 13, no. 3 (Sept.-Oct. 2013): 1–5.

7   Derived from factor analysis, six variables explain 85% of the variance between firms. Social scientists are accustomed to explaining a much lower percentage of variance, so that the identification of a few variables that together explain so much variance is both statistically and conceptually important.

8   Efendi, Jap, Anup Srivastava, and Edward P. Swanson. "Why Do Corporate Managers Misstate Financial Statements? The Role of Option Compensation and Other Factors." *Journal of Financial Economics* 85, no. 3 (2007): 667–708.

9   Abby Schultz, "100 Best Corporate Citizens 2007: Highlights of the List," *Corporate Responsibility Magazine*, 2007, http://www.thecro.com/node/304.

10  Raquel Meyer Alexander, Mark Hirschey, and Susan Scholz, "Backdating Employee Stock Options: Accounting and Legal Implications," *The CPA Journal, New York State Society of CPAs*, October 2007, http://www.nysscpa.org/cpajournal/2007/1007/infocus/p18.htm.

11  Paula Alexander Becker, "The Contribution of Emmanuel Levinas to Corporate Social Responsibility and Business Ethics in the Post-Modern Era," *Journal of International Business Ethics* 6, no. 1–2 (2013): 19–26. With permission.

12  See Douglas Frantz, "Fraud Is Possible in Drexel Bonuses," *Los Angeles Times*, Oct. 4, 1991, http://articles.latimes.com/1991–10–04/business/fi-3362_1_drexel-bonuses. See also Kurt Eichenwald, "Drexel Suit to Recover Bonus Pay," *New York Times*, Feb. 12, 1992, http://www.nytimes.com/1992/02/12/business/drexel-suit-to-recover-bonus-pay.html.

13  Dealbook, "Will Creditors Look to Lehman's Bonuses?" *New York Times*, September 16, 2008.
14  Jesse M. Fried and Nitzan Shilon, "The Dodd-Frank Clawback and the Problem of Excess Pay," *The Corporate Board*, Jan.–Feb. 2012, http://www.law.harvard.edu/faculty/jfried/1201FriedShilon.pdf.

## End of Chapter Case: Emmanuel Levinas' Ethics of Responsibility

*The Contribution of Emmanuel Levinas to Corporate Social Responsibility and Business Ethics in the Post-Modern Era*

*Paula Alexander Becker*

*International Journal of Business Ethics, Vol. 6, No. 1–2 (2013)*

**Abstract:** Emmanuel Levinas developed an ethics of inter-subjectivity and responsibility. According to the phenomenology of Levinas, moral impulse and intuition are elicited by the encounter with the Other. Encounter with the Other, particularly the face and the voice of the Other, gives rise to a sense of responsibility for that Other. Business leaders are challenged by Levinas' approach, to move from a way of doing business that insulates the corporations and its constituent members from customers and other stakeholders to engagement with the other(s) in ways that enhance their wellbeing, by creating positive social effects from the work of the corporation and engagement with corporate stakeholders.

**Keywords:** alterity, business ethics, corporate social responsibility, ethics of responsibility, inter-subjectivity, Emmanuel Levinas, Levinas, the Other (Autrie), phenomenology, stakeholder, stakeholders

## Introduction

We live in the Post-Modern era.[1] Post-Modernism is a philosophy developed in reaction to the experience of World War II. Those who reflect on the human condition, namely philosophers, were disillusioned by the experience of World War II. Immanuel Kant's reliance on human reason and rationality became distrusted. Rule-based imperatives were discredited with the rise of Phenomenology and Existentialism.[2] Most of these intellectual developments occurred in Europe, the grounds of World War II. Phenomenologists and Existentialists were profoundly affected by the fact that Germany, one of the most intellectually and industrially developed nations, a home of the industrial revolution and of the development of bureaucracy, committed the human atrocities of the Holocaust. Emmanuel Levinas emerged in that context. Levinas was a Jewish

Philosopher who was born in Russia (now Lithuania) and who migrated to France. Levinas was a student of Martin Heidegger, a leading philosopher of Phenomenology. Although Levinas was fully engaged intellectually with the philosophy of Heidegger, Levinas became disillusioned with Heidegger because of the latter's affiliation with the Nazis: Heidegger served as chancellor of Freiburg University under Hitler's ruling National Socialist German Worker's Party, the Nazis. In Levinas' view, Heidegger's cooperation with the Nazis demonstrated his lack of authenticity and the failure of metaphysics, an intellectual concern for Being (Dasein) divorced from ethics. [3] Levinas developed an approach based on encounter with the Other (Autrie) and responsibility for the Other.

## Levinas' Ethics of Inter-Subjectivity and Responsibility

Emmanuel Levinas developed an approach wherein he rejected a Heideggerian analysis of being, or a subject-object analysis as "first philosophy." In "Is Ontology Fundamental?" Levinas understands that he breaks with "the theoretical structure of Western thought" when he articulates that "[t]o think is no longer to contemplate, but to be engaged. Launched—the dramatic event of being-in-the-world . . ." [4] Levinas considered ethics to be " first philosophy". Ethics is concerned with the relationship of the self ("moi") to the other (autrui), but ethics is other than knowledge. The Other ("autrui") is not an object of one's comprehension, and the fundamental being-ness of the Other is not reducible to one's comprehension. [5] Levinas was particularly concerned that the otherness (alterity) of the other (autrui) would be diminished through intellectual comprehension of the universal human condition. [6] Levinas understands that categorization and generalization, an inquiry of ontology and epistemology, whereby being and objects are classified as "the same," contains the risk that the ego seeks to reduce all alterity/ otherness to itself. [7]

Furthermore, and a reason that Levinas argues that ethics is "first philosophy" is that moral impulse and intuition are pre-rational and are elicited by the encounter with the Other. [8] The encounter with the Face of the other elicits a sense of responsibility of the self for the Other. [9] The encounter with the Other is alternatively cast as an encounter with the Other's voice, or touch/ caress, and is based on proximity to the other. The meaning of being is presented in a face to face relationship. However the relationship to the other is fundamentally a "speaking" relationship. [10] "I" means "here I am," present to the Other in vulnerability. [11] To Levinas, language is proximity to or contact with the other, not communication of information. The response to the alterity of the Other is responsibility and "putting oneself in the place of the other." "Putting oneself in the place of the other" is called "substitution" by Levinas. [12] The responsibility for the Other is not based on transactional symmetry or reciprocity.

Although Levinas' language is abstract, his approach appeals to and is verified in experience, particularly the experience of parenthood, as in the encounter of a mother with her newborn child. Some language of the ethics of responsibility is also couched in erotic love, but the imagery of silent appeal and asymmetry of relationship resonates more in the parental relationship. Although an intuitive understanding of the asymmetrical responsibility for the other can be grasped through the experience of parenthood or erotic love, Levinas extends the responsibility for the other beyond these relationships into an infinite responsibility for all others, although the content and specifics of the responsibility of the self for the Other(s) depends on the proximity to the other(s).[13]

Fulfillment of the self's responsibility to the other must acquire content to be meaningful. To do that, one must listen to the voice of the other, to determine his or her specific needs. However, there is a risk in identifying the other's needs, because the responsible self may seek to dominate the other in a well-intentioned effort to best serve the needs of the other. The voice of the other must be heard, but the issue of "whose judgment should prevail" arises in the effort to meet the needs of the other, according to the ethic of responsibility. Rooted in the conviction that I understand the needs of the other better than he or she does, I might over-ride the other's voice. The ethics of inter-subjectivity thereby swings between duty- based norms about how to meet the needs of the other and spontaneously responding to the face and the voice of the other and the expression the other's needs in this encounter.

The relationship of the self to the other becomes complicated or, at least, modified by the recognition of The Third (other): that there are other Others, to whom responsibility is owed by the self, and which are Others to the Other, to whom the Other is himself or herself also responsible. The introduction or recognition of the presence of the Third must weigh in the self's actions relative to the Other, who is the Neighbor. The alterity of the Other commands my response to the fact that I am not alone in the world as justice.[14] The concern with justice becomes intensified as the self realizes that there are other Others, " the Third," and that the Other is also a self who relates to the other Others or the Third in responsibility. For example, what are the ethics of a mother devoting so much attention to a single, disabled child that the other children in the family and her spouse are neglected? Or, is it ethical for a hospital to expend so many resources on the care of a single patient or a few patients that the hospital goes from "running in the black" to "running in the red" with the result that the hospital is unable to serve others in the neighborhood?[15] Questions of justice thus arise from the presence of the Third to the self and the Neighbor.

The question arises, "Can Levinas' ethics of inter-subjectivity and responsibility enrich Corporate Social Responsibility and Business ethics in the Post-Modern Era?"[16] Emmanuel Levinas' approach is that a genuine encounter with the other would avert the injuries to others perpetrated by corporations and the managers who are their agents under the guise of shareholder capitalism, economic development, and the costs of doing business.[17]

### Application of Emmanuel Levinas to Corporate Social Responsibility and Business Ethics Using a Stakeholder Approach

The phenomena of corporate wrong-doing, corporate culture grounded in individualism and greed,[18] and corporate criminal conduct weigh in favor of the notion, or at least the need for, of a business ethics based on the phenomenology of Emmanuel Levinas. The Other: The first Other for corporate managers is the Shareholder, according to Berle and Means's "Theory of Managerial Capitalism." The encounter of a corporate manager with the Other, who is a shareholder, gives rise to a fiduciary obligation of the managers to the shareholder(s) and duty of prudence. Managers must recognize the opportunity costs and expectation of reasonable return on part of shareholders in the management of corporate affairs. Equity capital is that resource most at risk, since returns to the other factors of production are guaranteed if a firm is to remain a going concern or protected if a firm declares bankruptcy. It is easy to lose a sense of proximity to the shareholder. The scandals of Robert Brennan with the securities fraud by First Jersey Securities led to the loss of lifetime savings of his investors.[19] Enron's collapse led to loss of savings for employees who had vested their 401K investments in Enron stock. Enron Officers fraudulently engaged in sham transactions blocking employee shareholders from selling stock in the Fall of 2001 while the Officers were selling off shares.[20] Kenneth Lay and Jeffrey Skilling were later convicted of insider trading and securities fraud.[21]

However I would argue that the first "others," the others most proximate to the corporation are the customers. Customers are the purpose of the corporation, the others who are the recipients or beneficiaries of the product of the producing organization. Acts like Ford Motor Company, and Lee Iacocca's cost benefit analysis about whether to recall Ford Pintos or to pay damages to the burn victims would never be done if Levinas' encounter with the face and voice of the other, and his approach of Responsibility to the Other were used by managers. More recently, some company officials of Sanlu Dairy Company knowingly included toxic additives, which enhanced the perceived protein content of the infant formula but which led to kidney damage and even death among infants drinking the tainted formula.[22]

The Third: other stakeholders. Employees, suppliers, the environment, and communities where the firms operate constitute the Third. Levinas' approach profoundly challenges corporations to lose the anonymity of their encounters with their customers, in particular, and to regard the situation of the others, including their employees, their suppliers, and the communities in which the corporate plants are located. For example, the decision in Russia to construct Chernobyl and other nuclear power plants without a concrete dome to contain possible radioactive products of a nuclear accident, thereby shifting the risks and costs onto the surrounding community, would not be made. Total and Unocal in a joint venture constructed a gas pipeline in Burma (Myanmar) under conditions in which the human rights of villagers were violated.

Interestingly enough, the films of the extraordinary producer director, Milena Kaneva, bring face to the villagers affected by Total and Unocal in Burma[23] and to the Ecuador villagers in the Amazon rain forest whose land and waters were polluted by the oil mining and disposal procedures of Texaco. Texaco and Chevron, which purchased Texaco, defended its actions on the basis that it conformed to the environmental law in Ecuador of the time. Corporate executive should re-consider the approach of hiding behind legalities when they know that the production standards in use in less economically developed countries are not permitted in more economically developed countries; prudence requires a re-examination of that approach, particularly as the courts in Ecuador rejected Texaco/Chevron's defense and held the company liable for eight billion dollars, in clean-up costs and other penalties.[24]

**Implications for organizations: insularity of wealth and power.** Disturbingly, face-to-face encounters of prison guards in the Nazi concentration camps with the Jewish and other prisoners did not always lead to the encounter giving rise to responsibility for the other. The guards insulated themselves from the human face and voice of the other, the prisoners in the concentration camps. Insulating mechanisms, such as referencing the prisoners by number rather than name, were at work in the case of the guards in the Nazi concentration camps.[25]Likewise, mechanisms are at work to insulate corporate executives from their lower-level employees and their customers. Corporations blunt the sensitivity of the self to proximate others; particularly accounting can reduce the other to impersonal terms. Corporate executives tend toward egotistic/narcissistic pre-occupation with themselves and concentrate on how they appear to powerful others.[26] In identifying such narcissism, Roberts warns of a risk of a "terminal moment for ethics" because bosses within corporations "encrust" themselves in the notion that they are independent of others, thereby cutting themselves off from the fundamental premise of Levinas' ethics, openness to the Other.[27] Roberts points out the distancing effect of accounting systems on corporate life.

The so-called "neutral mirror" of business activity embodied in the accounting statements disembodies the work of the corporation, causing abstraction, loss of proximity with the actual work done in the corporation, and, particularly, contact with the corporation's customers.[28] Even though there has been a surge in the development of corporate codes of ethics starting in the 1990s, these reflect an ethics of narcissus rather than a genuine concern for the Other; codes of ethics were a shield in cases of wrong-doing by employees of the corporation under the U.S. Federal Sentencing Guidelines.[29] Corporations should re-focus their efforts from being seen as ethical to activating real issues of sensibility to the Other, particularly concern for their customers, their employees, and environmental sustainability. Measures of CSR need to be developed to counteract purely financial performance embodied in accounting systems. The triple bottom line is a step in that direction. Moreover, actions of CEOs, such as Southwest Airlines former CEO Herb Kelleher, who took pride in spending one day a month at the airports working alongside SWA gate crews, establish a culture of responsibility to employees and customers.[30] In addition to measures of CSR, performance measures must be developed to incentivize executives to personal engagement of the corporation and its executives with its stakeholders, including, of course, shareholders/ investors.

## Conclusion: Beyond Philosophy to Action

In terms of the implications of the phenomenology of Emmanuel Levinas for business organizations and their actions, business leaders are challenged to move from a way of doing business that insulates the corporations and its constituent members from customers and other stakeholders to engagement with the other(s) in ways that enhance their wellbeing by creating positive social effects from the work of the corporation and engagement with corporate stakeholders.

### *Appendix: Managerial Incentives for Stakeholder Engagement*

A multifaceted measurement of the stakeholder engagement is required, including measurement of engagement with and effect on shareholders, bondholders, supply chain, employees, communities where the firm operates, and the environment. For each of the dimensions of stakeholder engagement, a behaviorally anchored rating system (BARS)[31] should be developed. The rating system should include both harms and goods to the particular stakeholder. Executive compensation should be tied to the rating system. A compensation system should be developed that includes diminishment of compensation and claw backs for longer term consequences that come to light. For example, a stakeholder lawsuit would be counted negatively, with consequential reduction of executive compensation. Furthermore, prosecution and settlement with the SEC would be indicative of negative long-term relations with some stakeholders, including shareholders, bondholders, and insurers. Goldman Sachs settled its prosecution by the SEC for both selling and short-selling its CDOs.[32] Under this methodology, the executives of Goldman Sachs would return compensation as a consequence of the settlement with the SEC. Instead, the reality was that the CEO of Goldman Sachs, Lloyd Blankfein, received an increase in compensation in 2010, the same year as the settlement with the SEC.[33]

Compensation plans need to be developed that evaluate CEO performance over time and with respect to multiple indicants of performance, as suggested herein.

## Notes

1 Jean-Francois Leotard, *La Condition postmoderne: rapport sur le savoir* (Paris: Minuit, 1979). Translated by Geoff Bennington and Brian Massumi in The Postmodern Condition: A Report on Knowledge (Manchester: Manchester University Press, 1984).

2 Although Levinas' doctoral dissertation was on Husserl's Phenomenology and his theory of intuition, Levinas's development of the ethics of responsibility is based on and develops phenomenology, as interaction between abstract and concrete. Levinas came to consider Ethics rather than Ontology as First Philosophy, based on his life experience and his reflections on those experiences.

3 Martin Heidegger, Sein und Zeit, (Tubingen: Max Neimeyer Verlag 1927. See also, Martin Heidegger, Being and Time, trans. by John Macquarrie and Edward Robinson (London: SCM Press, 1962) Martin Heidegger was the successor at the University of Freiburg to Husserl, who founded the philosophical school of Phenomenology. Heidegger was elected Rector of the University of Freiburg by the faculty in April 1933, when Adolf Hitler had been elected Chancellor of Germany; Heidegger joined the Nazi Party within a month of his becoming Rector of Freiburg. Heidegger gave several addresses which indicated his support of Nazism in Germany. See for example. "German Men and Women!", a speech delivered on 10 November 1933 at Freiburg university; printed in the *Freiburger Studentenzeitung*, November 10, 1933. English translation in R. Wolin, ed., The Heidegger *Controversy* (MIT Press, 1993), chapter 2.

4 "Is Ontology Fundamental?" is an essay written in 1951, and serves as chapter 1 in *Entre Nous*, a collection of essays published by Levinas, translated by Michael B. Smith and Barbara Horshav (New York: Columbia University Press, 1998). Citation to p. 3.

5 Emmanuel Levinas in *Entre Nous*, Alterity and Diachrony, at p. 166.

6 See Emmanuel Levinas in *Otherwise than Being*, at pp. 131–132.

7 Emmanuel Levinas in *Totality and Infinity*, at pp. 47–48: "For the philosophical tradition the *conflicts* between the same and the other are resolved by theory whereby the other is reduced to the same ..."

8 Emmanuel Levinas, *Autrement qu'etre ou au-delà de l'essence*, 1974. Published in translation as *Otherwise than Being or Beyond Essence* (Pittsburgh: Duquesne University Press, 1998).

9 See also Zygmunt Bauman, Postmodern Ethics (Malden, MA, Blackwell Publishing: 1993).

10 Some other philosophers understand the relationship of the self to the other as a "Speaking relationship." See for example, Martin Buber, I and Thou. See also Harold Stahmer, "Speak that I may see Thee," and John M. Oesterreicher, "The Unfinished Dialogue." For Levinas on Buber, see *The Philosophy of Martin Buber: Library of Living Philosophers Vol. 12* (Open Court Publishing: 1991).

11 Emmanuel Levinas, "Substitution" in The Levinas Reader at p. 104.

12 In substitution the self (moi) puts itself "in place of the other by taking responsibility for the other's responsibilities." Critchley and Bernasconi at p. 239. Levinas frames substitution as the passage of the "identical" subject to the other in sacrifice. This act of the subject is prior to consciousness and fundamental to the being of the self. See Levinas, *Otherwise than Being, or Beyond Essence* at p. 114: "The word *I means here I am,* answering for everything and for everyone" and at footnote 22: "Substitution is the communication of the one to the other and the other to the one ..."

13 See Levinas, *Otherwise than Being, or Beyond Essence* at footnote 22: "It is the proximity of the third party that introduces ... justice ... Being will be non-indifferent.... because ... space belongs to the sense of my responsibility for the other. The everywhere of space is from the everywhere of faces that concern me ..." The extension of

the responsibility for the Other is reminiscent of "Six Degrees of Separation," wherein the hypothesis is that everyone in the world is connected to every other via a network of six persons, hence six degrees of separation.

14  See *The Levinas Reader,* on Substitution at pp. 117–118.

15  This is a real life example, conveyed to the author in a private communication. It is likely, moreover, that such a dilemma is encountered by many other hospitals.

16  See Jean-Frangois Leotard, in La Condition postmoderne: rapport sur le savoir (Paris: Minuit, 1979). Translated by Geoff Bennington and Brian Massumi in The Postmodern Condition: A Report on Knowledge (Manchester: Manchester University Press, 1984) distinguished post-modern as philosophy and as economic production. Thus, the Post-Modern Era is the Post-Industrial Era, a phrase coined by Daniel Bell, in economic history. The post-industrial revolution is also called the Third Wave by Alvin Toffler.

17  In the business context, the "other" or others are stakeholders. The primary or most proximate stakeholder is the customer, not as finance would have it, shareholders of a corporation.

18  http://www.nytimes.com/2012/03/14/opinion/why-i-am-leaving-goldman-sachs.html?pagewanted=all

19  http://en.wikipedia.org/wiki/Robert_E._Brennan

20  Tittle v. Enron, 463 F.3d 410 (5th Cir., 2006). See also, Ruling Lets Enron Workers Sue Lay, Northern Trust Over Lost Savings, Wall Street Journal, October 2, 2003.

21  http://www.usdoj.gov/opa/pr/2006/October/06_crm_723.html

22  See   http://www.nytimes.com/2009/01/22/world/asia/22iht-milk.2.19593612.html?r=0

23  Milena Kaneva's documentary about the pipeline in Burma, Total Denial, received international recognition. See http://www.totaldenialfilm.com/

24  http://www.businessweek.com/articles/2012–10–09/chevron-fails-to-squelch-19-billion-ecuador-verdict

25  See Luna Kaufman, *Luna's Life: A Journey of Forgiveness and Triumph* (ComteQ Publishing:2009).

26  John Roberts, "Corporate Governance and the Ethics of Narcissus," in Business Ethics Quarterly (2001), Vol. 11, Issue 1, pp 109–127.

27  Ibid. at p. 110.

28  Ibid. at p. 117.

29  See Henry Amoroso, *The Federal Sentencing Guidelines Endorsement of Corporate-Level Restitution: Furtherance of Public Policy or Discrimination on the Basis of Entity Capitalization?,* 18 Campbell L. Rev. 225 (1996).

30  See *Flying High with Herb Kelleher: A Profile in Charismatic Leadership,* in the Journal of Leadership Studies, June 22, 1999, by Jane Whitney Gibson.

31  Schwab, D. P., Henemen, H. G. and DeCotiis, T. A. (1975), *Behaviorally Anchore Rating Scales: A Review of the Literature.* Personnel Psychology, 28: 549–562.

32  http://www.sec.gov/news/press/2010/2010–123.htm

33  http://www.guardian.co.uk/business/2011/apr/02/lloyd-blankfein-executive-pay-bonuses

# Bibliography

Bauman, Z. (1989). *Modernity and the Holocaust.* Ithaca, NY: Cornell University Press.
Bauman, Z. (1993). *Postmodern ethics.* Malden, MA: Blackwell Publishing.

Bevan, D., & Corvellec, H. (2007). The Impossibility of a corporate ethics: For a Levinasian approach to managerial ethics. *Business Ethics: A European Review, 16(3),* 208–219.

Buber, M. (1937). *I and Thou.* Originally published in 1923 as Ich und Du.

Critchley, S., & Bernasconi, R. (editors (2002). *The Cambridge companion to Levinas.* New York: Cambridge University Press.

Desmond, J. (2007). Levinas: beyond egoism in marketing and management. *Business Ethics: A European Review, 16(3),* 227–238.

Hand, S. (Ed.) (1989). *The Levinas Reader: Emmanuel Levinas.* Cambridge, MA: Blackwell.

Heidegger, Martin. (1927). Sein und Zeit. Tubingen: Max Neimeyer Verlag. See also, Martin Heidegger, Being and Time, trans. by John Macquarrie & Edward Robinson. London: SCM Press, 1962.

Jones, C. (2003). As if business ethics were possible, "within such limits." *Organization, 10(3),* 223–248. Karamali, E. (2007). Has the guest arrived yet? Emmanuel Levinas, a stranger in business ethics. *Business Ethics: A European Review, 16(3),* 313–321.

Knights, D., & O'Leary, M. (2006). Leadership, ethics and responsibility to the other. *Journal of Business Ethics, 67,* 115–137.

Levinas, E. (1961). *Totalite et Infiniti.* Published in translation as *Totality and Infinity.* Pittsburgh: Duquesne University Press, 1998.

Levinas, E. (1974). *Autrement qu'etre ou au-delà de l'essence.* Published in translation as *Otherwise* than *Being or Beyond Essence,* Pittsburgh: Duquesne University Press, 1998.

Levinas, E. (1991). *Entre-Nous: Thinking-of-the Other.* Translated from the French by Michael B. Smith and Barbara Harshav. New York: Columbia University Press, 1998.

Léotard, Jean-Frangois. (1979). *La Conditionpostmodeme: rapport sur le savoir.* Paris: Minuit. Translated by Geoff Bennington and Brian Massumi in The Postmodern Condition: A Report on Knowledge. Manchester: Manchester University Press, 1984.

Moyn, S. (2005). *Origins of the other: Emmanuel Levinas between revelation and ethics.* Ithaca, NY: Cornell University Press.

Roberts, J. (2001). Corporate governance and the ethics of Narcissus. *Business Ethics Quarterly, 11(1),*109–127.

Schlipp, P., & Friedman, M. (Eds). (1967). *The philosophy of Martin Buber.* Library of Living Philosophers Volume XII. Chicago: Open Court Publishing Company.

Van de Ven, B. (2005). Human rights as a normative basis for stakeholder legitimacy. *Corporate Governance, 5(2),* 48–57.

## Case Discussion Questions

1. Explain Levinas' ethics of responsibility.
2. How can executives stay in touch with their employees and customers?
3. How can accounting systems be used to measure firm performance without losing the human perspective on the enterprise employees and customers?

# Index

DATE DUE